S0-EGN-152

WITHDRAWN
UTSA LIBRARIES

RENEWALS 458-4574

MA.

The Political Economy of Environmental Regulation

The International Library of Critical Writings in Economics

Series Editor: Mark Blaug

Professor Emeritus, University of London, UK
Professor Emeritus, University of Buckingham, UK
Visiting Professor, University of Amsterdam, The Netherlands

This series is an essential reference source for students, researchers and lecturers in economics. It presents by theme a selection of the most important articles across the entire spectrum of economics. Each volume has been prepared by a leading specialist who has written an authoritative introduction to the literature included.

A full list of published and future titles in this series is printed at the end of this volume.

Wherever possible, the articles in these volumes have been reproduced as originally published using facsimile reproduction, inclusive of footnotes and pagination to facilitate ease of reference.

For a list of all Edward Elgar published titles visit our site on the World Wide Web at
www.e-elgar.com

The Political Economy of Environmental Regulation

Edited by

Robert N. Stavins

Albert Pratt Professor of Business and Government
John F. Kennedy School of Government
and Director, Environmental Economics Program
Harvard University, USA

THE INTERNATIONAL LIBRARY OF CRITICAL WRITINGS IN ECONOMICS

An Elgar Reference Collection
Cheltenham, UK • Northampton, MA, USA

© Robert N. Stavins 2004. For copyright of individual articles, please refer to the Acknowledgements.

All rights reserved. No part of this publication may be reproduced, stored in a retrieval system, or transmitted in any form or by any means, electronic, mechanical, photocopying, recording, or otherwise without the prior permission of the publisher.

Published by
Edward Elgar Publishing Limited
Glensanda House
Montpellier Parade
Cheltenham
Glos GL50 1UA
UK

Edward Elgar Publishing, Inc.
136 West Street
Suite 202
Northampton
Massachusetts 01060
USA

A catalogue record for this book is available from the British Library.

ISBN   1 84376 447 4

Printed and bound in Great Britain by MPG Books Ltd, Bodmin, Cornwall

Library
University of Texas
at San Antonio

Contents

Acknowledgements

The editor and publishers wish to thank the authors and the following publishers who have kindly given permission for the use of copyright material.

American Economic Association for articles: James M. Buchanan and Gordon Tullock (1975), 'Polluters' Profits and Political Response: Direct Controls Versus Taxes', *American Economic Review*, **65** (1), March, 139–47; Joseph P. Kalt and Mark A. Zupan (1984), 'Capture and Ideology in the Economic Theory of Politics', *American Economic Review*, **74** (3), June, 279–300; Robert W. Hahn (1989), 'Economic Prescriptions for Environmental Problems: How the Patient Followed the Doctor's Orders', *Journal of Economic Perspectives*, **3** (2), Spring, 95–114.

Blackwell Publishing Ltd for article: John A. List and Shelby Gerking (2000), 'Regulatory Federalism and Environmental Protection in the United States', *Journal of Regional Science*, **40** (3), 453–71.

Elsevier for articles: James C. Murdoch and Todd Sandler (1997), 'The Voluntary Provision of a Pure Public Good: The Case of Reduced CFC Emissions and the Montreal Protocol', *Journal of Public Economics*, **63**, 331–49; Toke S. Aidt (1998), 'Political Internalization of Economic Externalities and Environmental Policy', *Journal of Public Economics*, **69**, 1–16; Friedrich Schneider and Juergen Volkert (1999), 'No Chance for Incentive-oriented Environmental Policies in Representative Democracies? A Public Choice Analysis', *Ecological Economics*, **31** (1), October, 123–38; Robert W. Hahn (2000), 'The Impact of Economics on Environmental Policy', *Journal of Environmental Economics and Management*, **39** (3), May, 375–99; Per G. Fredriksson and Daniel L. Millimet (2002), 'Strategic Interaction and the Determination of Environmental Policy across U.S. States', *Journal of Urban Economics*, **51**, 101–22.

Harvard Environmental Law Review and the President and Fellows of Harvard College for articles: Nathaniel O. Keohane, Richard L. Revesz and Robert N. Stavins (1998), 'The Choice of Regulatory Instruments in Environmental Policy', *Harvard Environmental Law Review*, **22**, 313–67; Robert W. Hahn, Sheila M. Olmstead and Robert N. Stavins (2003), 'Environmental Regulation in the 1990s: A Retrospective Analysis', *Harvard Environmental Law Review*, **27** (2), 377–415.

Harvard Law Review Association for article: Richard L. Revesz (2001), 'Federalism and Environmental Regulation: A Public Choice Analysis', *Harvard Law Review*, **115** (2), December, 553–641.

Journal of Law and Economics, University of Chicago for articles: Michael T. Maloney and Robert E. McCormick (1982), 'A Positive Theory of Environmental Quality Regulation',

Journal of Law and Economics, **XXV** (1), April, 99–123; Paul L. Joskow and Richard Schmalensee (1998), 'The Political Economy of Market-Based Environmental Policy: The U.S. Acid Rain Program', *Journal of Law and Economics*, **XLI**, April, 37–83.

MIT Press Journals and the President and Fellows of Harvard College for article: Roger D. Congleton (1992), 'Political Institutions and Pollution Control', *Review of Economics and Statistics*, **74** (3), August, 412–21.

Oxford University Press for articles: Donald N. Dewees (1983), 'Instrument Choice in Environmental Policy', *Economic Inquiry*, **XXI** (1), January, 53–71; James T. Hamilton (1997), 'Taxes, Torts, and the Toxics Release Inventory: Congressional Voting on Instruments to Control Pollution', *Economic Inquiry*, **XXXV** (4), October, 745–62; Per G. Fredriksson and Noel Gaston (2000), 'Environmental Governance in Federal Systems: The Effects of Capital Competition and Lobby Groups', *Economic Inquiry*, **38** (3), July, 501–14.

RAND for article: Marcel Boyer and Jean-Jacques Laffont (1999), 'Toward a Political Theory of the Emergence of Environmental Incentive Regulation', *RAND Journal of Economics*, **30** (1), Spring, 137–57.

University of Chicago Press for article: Maureen L. Cropper, William N. Evans, Stephen J. Berardi, Maria M. Ducla-Soares and Paul R. Portney (1992), 'The Determinants of Pesticide Regulation: A Statistical Analysis of EPA Decision Making', *Journal of Political Economy*, **100** (1), February, 175–97.

University of Illinois Law Review and the Board of Trustees of the University of Illinois for article: Wallace E. Oates (2000), 'From Research to Policy: The Case of Environmental Economics', *University of Illinois Law Review*, **2000** (1), 135–53.

University of Wisconsin Press for article: Andrew Metrick and Martin L. Weitzman (1996), 'Patterns of Behavior in Endangered Species Preservation', *Land Economics*, **72** (1), February, 1–16.

Every effort has been made to trace all the copyright holders but if any have been inadvertently overlooked the publishers will be pleased to make the necessary arrangement at the first opportunity.

In addition the publishers wish to thank the Library of the University of Warwick and the Library of Indiana University at Bloomington, USA for their assistance in obtaining these articles.

Introduction

*Robert N. Stavins**

The first task in assembling a collection of papers is to specify the scope of the volume. Although readers will agree about what is meant by 'environmental regulation', the meaning of 'political economy' may be less clear. Indeed, the meaning of this phrase has changed considerably over time (Oates and Portney 2003). At one time, it denoted the entire realm of the study of economics, but since early in the last century it has come to refer to a sub-field, namely the study – from the perspective of economics – of the processes through which political decisions are made. That provides a fair statement of the scope of this volume – economic analyses of the processes through which political decisions regarding environmental regulation are made, principally in the institutional context found in the United States. Despite this geographic focus, however, many of the papers contain analytical models that are methodologically of interest and/or have lessons that are relevant in other parts of the world.

In the environmental realm, questions of political economy emerge along three fundamental dimensions, which are closely interrelated but conceptually distinct: (1) the *degree* of government activity; (2) the *form* of government activity; and (3) the *level* of government that has responsibility. The first three parts of the book deal respectively with these three fundamental dimensions of inquiry. Part I features a set of six articles that examine – from a political economy perspective – how the targets and goals of individual environmental policies are established. Part II brings together nine articles that employ the analytical apparatus of positive political economy to address questions related to the choice of policy instruments for environmental regulation. Part III features four articles that examine – both positively and normatively – the level of government that is delegated responsibility for environmental protection. Finally, in Part IV, three articles are featured that assess the use of economic analysis in contemporary environmental policy.

Setting the Targets and Goals of Environmental Policies

The fundamental theoretical argument for government activity in the environmental realm is that pollution is a classic example of an externality. Because firm-level decisions systematically fail to take into account full social costs, pollutant emissions tend to be greater than socially efficient levels. As environmental quality is naturally under-provided by competitive markets, a possible role arises for government regulation. Private negotiation will not internalize such externalities adequately without government intervention, and exclusive reliance on judicial remedies is demonstrably insufficient to the task.[1] Since the time of the first Earth Day in 1970, which we may take as the beginning of the modern era of environmental policy, industrialized countries throughout the world have relied mainly upon a combination of legislative and administrative procedures to foster improvements in their natural environments.

If it is appropriate for government to be involved in environmental protection, how intensive should that activity be? In real-world environmental policy, this question becomes, 'How stringent should our environmental goals and standards be?' For example, in the United States, should sulfur dioxide (SO_2) emissions be reduced by 10 million tons, or would a 12 million ton reduction be better? In general, how clean is clean enough? How safe is safe enough?

Most economists would argue that economic efficiency – measured as the difference between benefits and costs – ought to be one of the major criteria for evaluating proposed environmental, health and safety regulations.[2] From an efficiency standpoint, the answer to the question of how much regulation is enough is quite simple – regulate until the incremental benefits from regulation are just offset by the incremental costs. In practice, of course, the problem is much more difficult, in large part because of inherent challenges in measuring marginal benefits and costs.

Over the years, policy makers have sent mixed signals regarding the use of benefit–cost analysis, which assesses policies on the basis of the efficiency criterion. Congress has passed several statutes to protect health, safety and the environment that effectively preclude the consideration of benefits and costs in the development of certain regulations, even though other statutes actually require the use of benefit–cost analysis.[3] But this has not prevented regulatory agencies from considering the benefits and costs of their regulatory proposals.

At the same time as Congress has sent mixed signals regarding the use of economic analysis in environmental policy assessment, Presidents Carter, Reagan, Bush, Clinton and Bush all introduced formal processes for reviewing economic implications of major environmental, health and safety regulations (using so-called Regulatory Impact Analysis). Apparently the Executive Branch, charged with designing and implementing regulations, has seen a greater need than Congress to develop a yardstick against which the efficiency of regulatory proposals can be assessed; benefit–cost analysis has been the yardstick of choice.

Despite such arguments, formal benefit–cost analysis has only infrequently been used to help set the stringency of environmental standards. The politics of environmental policy have favored a very different set of approaches to setting standards, such as that embraced by the Clean Air Act: set the standard to 'protect the public health with an adequate margin of safety'.

Part I of this volume features six articles that develop and apply the tools of positive political economy to provide insights into how the targets and goals of environmental policies have been established, with particular attention to the US institutional context over the period since the 1970s.[4]

In the first article in Part I, Joseph Kalt and Mark Zupan (1984) provide an empirical analysis of 'Capture and Ideology in the Economic Theory of Politics'. By the early 1980s, public interest theories of regulation, in which politicians were assumed to make decisions simply and exclusively to benefit the public, were already out of favor, having been replaced by 'interest group' or 'capture' theories whereby politicians were modeled as making decisions to maximize their own political support, typically as provided by interest groups within their constituencies (Downs 1957; Buchanan and Tullock 1965; Stigler 1971; Peltzman 1976). In the context of the latter literature, Kalt and Zupan argue that the ideological preferences of policy makers, not just their constituents' economic or other self-interests, may also play a significant role in determining legislative and regulatory outcomes.

Following Stigler (1972), Kalt and Zupan distinguish two types of utility that an elected official may be expected to seek: utility derived from increased wealth or likelihood of re-election (the 'investment motive') and utility from acting according to moral or 'ideological' beliefs (the 'consumption motive'). Stigler believed that the investment motive, satisfied by maximizing constituent support, would be vastly more important in understanding and modeling political behavior. Kalt and Zupan challenge this, hypothesizing that imperfect 'policing' of political representatives (agents) by their constituents (principals) might leave politicians room to indulge their own ideological preferences.[5] Through a carefully constructed econometric analysis of US Senate votes on the Surface Mining Control and Reclamation Act of 1977, the authors find that although the capture model explains a considerable amount of the variation in voting patterns, Senators' ideological preferences are also highly significant.

The second paper turns from Congressional voting behavior to agency rule making, and examines the factors – both those associated with special interests and those associated with perceptions of general welfare – that can explain public decision making in the environmental realm. In 'The Determinants of Pesticide Regulation: A Statistical Analysis of EPA Decision Making', Maureen Cropper, William Evans, Stephen Berardi, Maria Ducla-Soares and Paul Portney (1992) find empirical support for the proposition that regulators take into account both special interests and general welfare when setting environmental standards.

Although economic efficiency would require that standards be set at the level that maximizes the difference between benefits and costs, this is rarely the approach taken in actual public policy, and there has been considerable scholarly debate over how environmental standards are actually set. Do agencies weigh benefits and costs, or are they driven by the demands of politically influential interest groups? Do agencies take action when risks exceed certain statistical thresholds, regardless of costs (Milvy 1986; Travis *et al.* 1987; Travis and Hattemer-Frey 1988)?[6] Cropper *et al.* (1992) analyze EPA's decision making in an effort to test these alternative theories of standard setting.[7]

In their econometric analysis of EPA's decisions between 1975 and 1989 regarding the registration of pesticides, Cropper *et al.* (1992) test two main hypotheses: (1) that EPA takes into account benefits and costs when setting standards, and so the probability that EPA will cancel the use of a pesticide is influenced by relative benefits and costs; and (2) that special interest groups representing business and the environment also affect the likelihood of cancellation decisions. They find that EPA does appear to balance the risks of pesticide use against the benefits of continuation, but they also find that EPA places much greater weight on risks to pesticide applicators (farm-workers) than risks to consumers: the implicit value of a statistical life is $35 million per cancer case for pesticide applicators, but only $60 thousand for consumers! The authors do not find evidence supporting the 'bright lines' hypothesis, but do find that political intervention by environmental groups and growers affects policy outcomes.

The third paper in Part I stands back and considers the role of broader political institutions in setting environmental goals by comparing how the presence of authoritarian versus democratic government affects choices of environmental targets. In 'Political Institutions and Pollution Control', Roger Congleton (1992) posits a model of national decision making related to environmental standards, and with it demonstrates that anticipated differences in parameters between authoritarian and democratic regimes affect national choices of pollution control. Under plausible assumptions about regime preferences, Congleton demonstrates that autocrats place a higher relative cost on pollution abatement than democratic (median voter) regimes. Hence authoritarian regimes tend to choose more lax environmental standards. Congleton carries out an empirical test using data on signatories to the Montreal Protocol, and finds general support for his theory.

In the fourth paper in Part I, 'Patterns of Behavior in Endangered Species Preservation', Andrew Metrick and Martin Weitzman (1996) carry out an empirical analysis of factors that affect US government decisions regarding the protection of endangered species. The authors do not specify a formal political economy model but provide a reduced-form analysis of factors that affect government decision making.[8] Metrick and Weitzman posit two sets of explanatory variables: 'scientific' characteristics and 'visceral' characteristics, the former including degree of endangerment and taxonomic uniqueness, and the latter including size of species and phylogenic class, intended to proxy for species' status as higher forms of life.

In their econometric analysis, the authors examine the effects of these characteristics on two major types of decisions: (1) whether a species is listed by the Federal government as threatened or endangered; and (2) the amount the government directly spends on the recovery or preservation of the species. The authors examine differences between observed patterns and the stated goals of the US Fish and Wildlife Service's own priority system, which is intended to guide listing and spending decisions. Metrick and Weitzman find that visceral characteristics play a significant role in government decisions, with considerable favoritism being shown to the preservation of 'charismatic mega-fauna' (essentially species that are cute and large). Although scientific characteristics are found to play a role at the listing stage, they are overwhelmed in importance by the visceral characteristics in decisions about spending. In addition, the authors find that political factors (proxied by whether efforts to protect species have been in direct conflict with development projects) have had more influence on listing and spending decisions than is proscribed by the government's priority system.

The fifth paper in Part I – 'The Voluntary Provision of a Pure Public Good: The Case of Reduced CFC Emissions and the Montreal Protocol', by James Murdoch and Todd Sandler (1997) – provides a game-theoretic analysis of worldwide reductions in CFC emissions in the late 1980s. At its core, the paper develops a model of the voluntary provision of public goods and provides an empirical test of this hypothesis using data on CFC emissions prior to the beginning of official limits linked with the Montreal Protocol.[9]

In Murdoch and Sandler's model, nations' preferences vary according to their tastes, which are a function of factors such as income, geophysical characteristics, population size and political regime. The quantity of the public good (the ozone layer) is jointly determined by the decisions of each nation, and nations with higher incomes are assumed to contribute more to the provision of the public good. The authors find that the variation in voluntary CFC reductions is explained largely by GNP, political and civil rights, and geographical latitude, and that emissions reduction patterns support their hypothesized model. They conclude that the Montreal Protocol codified emissions reductions that countries would have provided voluntarily.

The sixth and final paper in Part I is by Toke Aidt (1998), 'Political Internalization of Economic Externalities and Environmental Policy'. Aidt develops a theoretic model of the political economy of environmental regulation, based on the interactions of competing interest groups.[10] The government maximizes its political support, which is modeled as a weighted average of interest group contributions and constituent social welfare. The analysis features a two-stage game, where interest groups first present a menu of political contributions (taking as fixed the contributions of other groups) contingent on policy choices. In the second stage, the government chooses its policy (setting both the target and the instrument) to maximize its objective function. Aidt's contribution is to demonstrate that competition among interest groups results in policies that internalize environmental externalities but that this political solution generally is sub-optimal.

Choosing the Instruments of Environmental Regulation

Once the goals or standards of any given environmental policy are established (whether on political, scientific, economic, ethical or any other grounds), policy makers are left to ask what *form* should government involvement take. In other words, what means – what policy instruments – should be used to achieve the established ends? Economists consistently have urged the use of 'market-based' instruments – principally pollution taxes and tradeable permits – rather than so-called 'command-and-control' instruments, such as design standards, which require the use of particular technologies, or performance standards, which prescribe the maximum amount of pollution that individual sources can emit. At least in theory, market-based instruments are cost-effective; that is, they can minimize the aggregate cost of achieving a given level of environmental protection, and provide dynamic incentives for the adoption and diffusion of cheaper and better control technologies. Despite these advantages, however, market-based instruments have been used far less frequently than command-and-control standards.

Part II of this volume features nine articles that apply positive political economy analysis to the question of how governments select particular policy instruments for environmental protection. The first paper is a seminal one in the field, 'Polluters' Profits and Political Response: Direct Controls Versus Taxes', by James Buchanan and Gordon Tullock (1975). The authors follow the public choice framework in assuming that policy outcomes are determined by industry influence, rather than by pure social welfare considerations. The major contribution of the paper is to demonstrate that firms will prefer direct regulation (emissions quotas) over taxes, offering a plausible explanation for the prevalence of command-and-control instruments, despite the known cost-effectiveness of market-based instruments.[11] Quotas that restrict entry create scarcity rents, which firms may appropriate, while taxes reduce the value of a firm.[12]

The second paper in Part II is a direct extension of the Buchanan and Tullock (1975) model. In 'A Positive Theory of Environmental Quality Regulation', Michael Maloney and Robert McCormick (1982) extend the earlier work by specifying the conditions under which firms benefit from quantity regulations. Like Buchanan and Tullock (1975), they demonstrate how quantity restrictions create cartel-like situations, allowing scarcity rents to be captured by firms. In particular, Maloney and McCormick derive conditions on the cost structures of firms and on the degree of regulation under which quantity regulations will lead to an increase in aggregate industry profits.[13]

To explore the empirical validity of their theories, the authors test whether specific regulations did in fact enhance the profitability of regulated firms. They employ data on firms affected by the US Occupational, Safety and Health Administration (OSHA) cotton-dust standards and by court-mandated rule changes in air quality regulation. Their examination of the rates of return in the stock market on a portfolio of firms in the relevant industries indicates support for their explanation of environmental regulation.

The third paper in Part II is also an extension of Buchanan and Tullock's (1975) seminal work. In 'Instrument Choice in Environmental Policy', Donald Dewees (1983) analyzes how instrument choice affects certain groups ('concentrated interests') who are expected to experience significant impacts as a result of a proposed policy. He considers the effects on shareholders and employees of three alternative instruments: an effluent standard (set as a rate of pollution per unit of output); an effluent charge; and effluent rights (essentially a system of tradeable permits).

Dewees finds that both capital and labor suffer more from effluent rights or effluent charges than from uniform effluent standards. Furthermore, charges and permits look even worse when compared with regulatory regimes that impose more stringent standards on new plants than on existing plants (so-called vintage-differentiated regulations). This result – which is consistent with Buchanan and Tullock (1975) – does not hold under all conditions, and Dewees' major contribution is to show for which conditions (with respect to factor specificity, initial allocations of permits, and differential treatment of old and new firms) the result holds.

The fourth paper in Part II represents a departure from the first three in its empirical focus and informal approach. In 'Economic Prescriptions for Environmental Problems: How the Patient Followed the Doctor's Orders', Robert Hahn (1989) provides one of the earliest and still one of the most frequently cited reviews of experience with market-based instruments for environmental protection (with specific focus on tradeable permit systems and pollution charges).[14] Hahn finds that actual practice has diverged considerably from the textbook instruments envisioned by theorists. Further, he concludes that for this reason, the cost savings have not lived up to expectations.

Hahn provides a variety of explanations for these departures, including political economy factors that produce less than optimal design of instruments. For example, he notes that the cost-effectiveness of tradeable permit systems is reduced by the presence of any barrier to trading activity, and many such barriers (linked with location, trading ratios and property rights definitions) are best understood as a result of interest group pressure. Hahn argues for a richer conceptualization of the political economy factors affecting instrument choice.[15]

In the fifth paper in Part II, 'Taxes, Torts, and the Toxics Release Inventory: Congressional Voting on Instruments to Control Pollution', James Hamilton (1997) raises an additional factor to consider in the political economy of instrument choice: the degree of public scrutiny given to a particular legislative decision. Earlier theories of the positive political economy of Congressional voting decisions held that the economic interests of members' constituencies and the ideology of constituents or members could have significant explanatory power (Ackerman and Hassler 1981; Crandall 1983; Kalt and Zupan 1984; Pashigian 1985; Yandle 1989). Hamilton moves beyond this by noting that it is not just the final vote on a bill that is important. Rather, earlier rounds of voting on amendments, which typically include choices regarding instruments, may be important but are unlikely to be highly visible to the public. Hence, the Congressional votes on amendments are more likely to be influenced by concentrated interests with significant lobbying power, rather than broad constituent interests.[16]

Hamilton's empirical test examines voting on amendments to the reauthorization of the Superfund law in 1985. These amendments called for specific instruments in separate votes: information provision; a targeted tax on chemical and petroleum producers to fund the program; and liability rules. Through his empirical analysis, Hamilton finds broad support for the notion that votes on these instruments were more affected by concentrated special interests than the overall vote on the Superfund bill, in which broad constituent interests and ideology had greater effects. He concludes that it is important to consider the type of vote and level of public scrutiny when examining Congressional decisions on environmental policy, including the choice of instruments.

In the sixth paper in Part II, 'The Political Economy of Market-Based Environmental Policy: The U.S. Acid Rain Program', Paul Joskow and Richard Schmalensee (1998) examine the factors affecting the allocation of permits in a marketable rights scheme. In particular, they analyze the allocations for Phase I (1995–1999) and Phase II (2000–2009) of the SO_2 allowance trading program under the Clean Air Act amendments of 1990. They examine how the actual allocation differed from a number of allocations under hypothetical rules, and seek to explain the difference, drawing upon theories from positive political economy.

Overall, Joskow and Schmalensee find that the allocation of allowances in the acid rain program suggests 'both a more complex and more idiosyncratic pattern of political forces than one might expect from previous work on the political economy of clean air'. While interest group politics, Congressional influence and electoral politics all appear to have played important roles in the allocation process, the final distribution of allowances suggests that the legislative process is simply more complex than has been captured by available models.

The seventh paper in Part II, 'The Choice of Regulatory Instruments in Environmental Policy', by Nathaniel Keohane, Richard Revesz and Robert Stavins (1998), provides a survey and synthesis of the positive political economy of environmental policy instrument choice. The authors begin by noting the great divergence in this realm between the recommendations of normative economic theory and positive political reality. In particular, they highlight four anomalies. First, despite the advantages of cost-effectiveness and dynamic efficiency associated with market-based policy instruments, these approaches to environmental protection have been used to a minor degree, compared with conventional command-and-control instruments. Second, pollution-control standards have typically been much more stringent for new than for existing sources (vintage-differentiated regulation), despite the well-known inefficiency of this approach. Third, in the few instances in which market-based instruments have been adopted, they have nearly always taken the form of tradeable permits allocated without charge, rather than auctioned permits or pollution taxes, despite the advantages in some situations of these other instruments. Fourth, the political attention given to market-based environmental policy instruments has increased dramatically in recent years.

In their search for explanations for these four apparent anomalies, Keohane, Revesz and Stavins draw upon intellectual traditions from economics, political science and law. They find that all fit quite well within an equilibrium framework, based upon the metaphor of a political market. The authors develop their 'market model' of the supply and demand of environmental policy instruments. In general, explanations from economics tend to refer to the demand for environmental policy instruments, while explanations from political science refer to the supply side. Overall, the authors find that there are compelling theoretical explanations for the four apparent anomalies, although these theories have not been empirically verified.

In the eighth paper in Part II, 'Toward a Political Theory of the Emergence of Environmental Incentive Regulation', Marcel Boyer and Jean-Jacques Laffont (1999) provide an analysis of instrument choice that emphasizes the principal–agent problems inherent in the design of regulatory mechanisms.[17] In a world of perfect information, instruments are equivalent, but the realities of incomplete information necessitate consideration of contracting problems between the public and regulators. Boyer and Laffont develop a formal political economy model that compares two stylized instruments: a uniform standard and a more flexible instrument that varies the standard among firms. In contrast to standard theory, they identify conditions under which the uniform standard is more efficient than the flexible policy.

The ninth and final paper in Part II, 'No Chance for Incentive-oriented Environmental Policies in Representative Democracies? A Public Choice Analysis', is authored by Friedrich Schneider and Juergen Volkert (1999). This paper examines political economy explanations for the relative prevalence of command-and-control and market-based instruments, relying on the public choice approach. The authors find that it is difficult to implement market-based environmental regulations for a variety of reasons, including the following. First, firms – which prefer command-and-control instruments, for the reasons put forward by Buchanan and Tulloch (1975) – have relatively great lobbying power because they can overcome collective action problems more easily than environmental interests. Second, voters may not favor an environmental program unless they are well informed about it, and incentive-based policies are more difficult to understand. Third, politicians favor policies that get immediate results and postpone the costs (or make them less visible to voters), and command-and-control policies lead to more immediate results that voters can see easily while making their costs less transparent. Fourth, bureaucrats responsible for implementing environmental policies prefer command-and-control approaches because they give them a more important role and allow them to maximize their own budgets and staff.

Setting the Level of Government to be Delegated Responsibility

Inseparable from the first two questions is this third aspect of the overall inquiry into the role of government in environmental protection. What *level* of government should be delegated responsibility and authority: local, state, regional, Federal, multinational or global? There is no single, correct answer. Even from a relatively narrow economic perspective, the answer depends upon specific characteristics of individual environmental policy issues.

What I have defined as the beginning of the modern era of environmental policy, the time of the first Earth Day in 1970, is also the beginning of major involvement by the Federal government in the United States in environmental protection. At that time and since, three sets of arguments have been made in favor of a strong Federal role: (1) that in the absence of national controls, states would compete economically by lowering their environmental standards in a so-called 'race to the bottom';[18] (2) that many environmental problems are inter-state externalities, and as such cannot be efficiently regulated by individual states; and (3) that a set of other factors, many linked with public choice arguments, also indicate the necessity of strong, national supervision.

Part III of this volume features four articles that examine the level of government at which environmental policies are developed and implemented. The first paper in Part III, 'Environmental Governance in Federal Systems: The Effects of Capital Competition and Lobby Groups', by Per Fredriksson and Noel Gaston (2000), examines the optimal level of government at which to make decisions regarding environmental regulation. The striking claim of the Fredriksson and Gaston paper is that environmental regulation is independent of the level at which it is set.[19] In their model,[20] centralized and decentralized governance lead to equivalent environmental regulations.

At the same time, the authors recognize that there are important distributional differences. In the decentralized case, the full costs of regulation are borne by workers, whereas in the centralized case the costs are shared by workers and the owners of capital. The authors present empirical evidence that is consistent with their theory, including an analysis of voting behavior on environmental policies in state legislatures, the US House of Representatives and the US Senate. They find no significant differences in the level of support for environmental policies at the different levels of government.

The second paper in Part III, 'Regulatory Federalism and Environmental Protection in the United States', by John List and Shelby Gerking (2000), refutes the hypothesis that letting regions (states) determine environmental policies will necessarily result in a 'race to the bottom'. The authors carry out an empirical analysis that leads to two conclusions. First, greater environmental quality in a state responds positively to increases in income. Second, while it has frequently been argued that granting more power to states will result in a 'race to the bottom' in environmental quality, List and Gerking do not find compelling evidence that environmental quality declined when states had more control over setting rules for environmental protection. Specifically, they examine the results of the Reagan era's federalism policies.

The third paper, 'Federalism and Environmental Regulation: A Public Choice Analysis', by Richard Revesz (2001), challenges the claim that environmental regulation should be carried out at the Federal (national) level because environmental interests are systematically under-represented at the state level. Revesz develops his argument both theoretically and empirically. Like List and Gerking (2000), he challenges the view that states are ineffective as environmental regulators. He demonstrates that there were significant accomplishments at the state level prior to the initiation of Federal activity in 1970, and that the states have continued to undertake significant environmental protection measures, including ones that go beyond Federal requirements. Revesz asks why some states are more aggressive in this regard than others, and argues that the most plausible explanation is that states differ in their preferences for environmental protection.

Revesz is careful to point out that his conclusions regarding state-level environmental regulation do not imply that the states enact socially optimal (efficient) environmental regulations; that state environmental regulation is likely to lead to higher levels of national welfare than Federal regulation; or that state governments are subject to less serious public choice constraints than the Federal government. Rather, his major point is that the arguments that are typically put forward in support of primary reliance on the Federal government for environmental regulation – such as those that claim under-representation of environmental interests at the state level – are themselves theoretically flawed and empirically incorrect.

The fourth and final paper in Part III, 'Strategic Interaction and the Determination of Environmental Policy across U.S. States', by Per Fredriksson and Daniel Millimet (2002), takes a different approach from previous researchers to examine the 'race to the bottom' hypothesis. The authors note two reasons why state-level environmental policies have been claimed to be inefficient: the presence of transboundary pollution problems and competition for capital. But, as the authors note, such arguments assume implicitly the existence of strategic policy making at the state level. Thus, Fredriksson and Millimet set out to test the empirical validity of this assumption.

The authors' empirical strategy employs two measures of state-level stringency of standards in econometric analyses that seek to examine whether one state's environmental standards are dependent upon the standards in other states. Their finding, in brief, is that there are strategic interactions – that is, states are influenced by the actions of their neighbors – but the weight of the evidence suggests a 'race to the top' not a 'race to the bottom'.

Assessing the Use of Economic Analysis in Environmental Policy

Part IV of this volume brings together three papers that assess the use of economic analysis in the development and implementation of environmental policy. In the first of these, 'The Impact of Economics on Environmental Policy', Robert Hahn (2000) examines the historical impact of economic thinking on environmental policy in the United States. He observes that over two decades, interest has grown in market-based environmental policy instruments and benefit–cost analysis of proposed and enacted policies. Hahn finds that economists have influenced environmental policy in three ways: by advocating the use of particular policy instruments; by developing improved methods to analyze benefits and costs; and by analyzing the political economy of environmental policies.

Hahn's overall assessment is that 'despite a few notable successes, the influence of economists on environmental policy to date has been modest'. While the economic approach has gained significant traction in the policy community, this has not translated directly into better public policies. The reason is that real-world policy formulation faces severe political economy constraints, which affect both design and implementation of instruments and the process of economic analysis. Because of this, Hahn argues that it is critical for economists to improve their understanding of the political constraints, so that they can help design public policies that are both feasible and more efficient.

The second paper in Part IV, 'From Research to Policy: The Case of Environmental Economics', by Wallace Oates (2000), is a retrospective analysis of the influence of economics on thirty years of US environmental policy. Oates notes that in the early years of environmental policy, economists already had well-developed theories of externalities but these had little influence in the policy world. Oates maintains that the economic perspective on environmental management had little influence on the major legislation of the early 1970s because: first, there was no interest group for which economic prescriptions had much appeal; second, environmental economics was itself a new field and had not yet focused on the complexities of design and implementation of market-based instruments; and third, there was a general lack of understanding in the policy community of the economic approach to environmental protection. Subsequently, however, there was what the author characterizes as a 'remarkable transformation', both with regard to targets and with regard to instruments. The system evolved from one which ignored costs and relied exclusively on direct controls to one which explicitly considers benefits and costs and gives considerable attention to market-based instruments.[21]

The third and final paper in Part III, 'Environmental Regulation in the 1990s: A Retrospective Analysis', by Robert Hahn, Sheila Olmstead and Robert Stavins, examines environmental policy making during that decade from the perspective of economics. The paper focuses on the Clinton Administration and highlights important trends and changes in the impacts of economic thinking. The authors begin with a review of environmental quality changes during the 1990s and then focus their discussion around three themes: efficiency, cost-effectiveness and distributional equity.

First, they highlight the ways in which the role of efficiency as a criterion for assessing environmental and natural resource regulations was very controversial in the Clinton Administration, while efficiency emerged as a central goal of the regulatory reform movement in Congress. Second, they examine how cost-effectiveness was embraced by both the Administration and Congress in the 1990s as a criterion for adopting specific policy instruments. Third, they analyze how and why the decade witnessed an increasing role for equity concerns as a consideration in environmental policy making. They contend that both the efficiency and the cost-effectiveness criteria may be hard to swallow when the distributional impacts of regulation are highly skewed, and that the focus on equity in environmental policy debates is likely to intensify as the costs and benefits of regulation continue to rise.

Thus, this volume brings together twenty-two papers that have contributed to the scholarly literature on the political economy of environmental regulation. The publication dates of these twenty-two diverse papers range from 1975 to 2003, and the topics are spread across four areas: setting targets and goals; choosing instruments; setting the level of government; and assessing economic analysis. But all the papers in this volume have in common their focus on economic analyses of the processes through which political decisions regarding environmental protection are made.

Notes

* Albert Pratt Professor of Business and Government, John F. Kennedy School of Government, and Director, Environmental Economics Program at Harvard University; and University Fellow, Resources for the Future. Valuable research assistance was provided by Katharine Emans. The author is responsible for any remaining errors.

1. Externalities in the environmental realm are *not* bilateral but involve public goods with multi-party impacts. Transaction costs and third-party impacts preclude the possibility of private negotiation consistently leading to simple, efficient solutions (Coase 1960). For largely the same reasons, private tort litigation – with its considerable transaction costs – cannot solve the bulk of environmental problems.

2. See Arrow *et al.* (1996).

3. Statutes that have been interpreted (in part, at least) to restrict the ability of regulators to consider benefits and costs include: the Federal Food, Drug and Cosmetic Act; health standards under the Occupational Safety and Health Act; safety regulations from the National Highway and Transportation Safety Agency; the Clean Air Act; the Clean Water Act; the Resource Conservation and Recovery Act; and the Comprehensive Environmental Response, Compensation and Liability Act. On the other hand, parts of the Clean Water Act, the Consumer Product Safety Act, the Toxic Substances Control Act, the Federal Insecticide, Fungicide and Rodenticide Act, and the Safe Drinking Water Act explicitly allow or require regulators to consider benefits and costs.

4. The six articles included in Part I of this volume are not intended to represent a comprehensive review of the literature in this area. Among other works that are important are the following: Stigler (1971) provided the original exposition of capture theory, which was subsequently formalized and extended by Peltzman (1976). Becker (1983) followed by explaining political outcomes as the consequence of competition among interest groups, adding the wrinkle that such political competition could be efficiency enhancing. In early empirical analyses, Crandall (1983), Pashigian (1985), and Elliott, Ackerman and Millian (1985) found evidence that self-interest could explain patterns of regulation, a view that received further empirical support from Hird (1990). Hahn (1990) stepped back from empirical analysis to develop further the theoretical framework within which the political economy of environmental regulation could be considered. More recent works have included Fredriksson's (1997) model of how pollution tax rates are determined, building upon earlier work

by Bernheim and Whinston (1986) and Grossman and Helpman (1994), and a related empirical analysis by Ekins and Speck (1999) of implementation of environmental taxes in Europe.

5. Kalt and Zupan refer to a then-current debate about the empirical importance of public interest or ideological motives, citing Kau and Rubin (1979), Kalt (1981), Peltzman (1982), and Mitchell (1979).

6. Such thresholds have been termed 'bright lines'.

7. At the time of their writing, there had been only one other such *ex post* analysis of EPA decision making (Magat, Krupnick and Harrington 1986).

8. This work can be seen as an extension of earlier research by McFadden (1975), Weingast and Moran (1983), Thomas (1988) and Cropper *et al.* (1992).

9. Previous literature on the voluntary provision of public goods includes: Bergstrom, Blume and Varian (1986) and Cornes and Sandler (1984, 1996). Previous applications of the 'subscription model' of public good contributions include Andreoni (1988) and Andreoni and McGuire (1993).

10. The common agency model employed by Aidt follows the approaches of Bernheim and Whinston (1986) and Grossman and Helpman (1994).

11. In a widely cited application of the approach taken by Buchanan and Tullock (1975), Ackerman and Hassler (1981) document the emergence of regulations that required power plants to install scrubbers.

12. Hahn (1990) notes that Buchanan and Tullock's (1975) analysis is more narrow than the authors claim. They do not actually demonstrate why industry prefers standards over taxes in general, but why industry will prefer a specific type of standard over a specific type of tax.

13. In addition, the authors note that some firms may lobby for regulation even if it does not benefit the industry as a whole. Essentially, firms who can comply most cheaply with the regulation stand to gain a competitive advantage over higher-cost firms.

14. For a more recent review, see Stavins (2003).

15. He notes, for example, that whether standards will be preferred to taxes depends upon the precise nature of each set of instruments (Coelho 1976; Yohe 1976; Dewees 1983).

16. The notion of 'rational political ignorance' has been attributed to Downs (1957). See also Arnold (1990).

17. Previous work in this vein on the regulation of natural monopolies was by Loeb and Magat (1979).

18. The view of inter-jurisdictional competition as beneficial received early support from Tiebout's (1956) analysis demonstrating that people's ability to choose their locations could result in the efficient provision of public goods. Brennan and Buchanan (1980) suggest that competition among regions may constrain the taxing power of public agents, forcing them to be more fiscally responsible. On the negative side of the decentralization (or federalism) issue, important early arguments for the so-called 'race to the bottom' are found in Break (1967), Cumberland (1979) and Cumberland (1981). Other important analyses include Crandall (1983), Pashigian (1985) and Oates and Schwab (1988). A recent overview of the literature is provided by Oates (2002).

19. The conclusion that the level of government authority makes no difference contrasts both with normative arguments for the need for Federal standards, such as to avoid a 'race to the bottom' (Cumberland 1981), and with counter arguments that Federal regulations tend to be inefficient because of their inability to take into account regional differences (Burtraw and Portney 1991). The conclusions also contrast with those of Oates and Schwab (1988).

20. Their political model is similar to that developed by Aidt (1998) and follows Grossman and Helpman (1994). Politicians maximize a weighted average of contributions and general welfare.

21. Oates (2000) highlights the research contributions of Dales (1968) and Weitzman (1974) to increased knowledge of the potential advantages of tradeable permits, as well as Tietenberg (1985) for demonstrating the cost-effectiveness of market-based instruments.

References

Ackerman, B.A. and W.T. Hassler (1981), *Clean Coal/Dirty Air*, New Haven, CT: Yale University Press.

Aidt, T.S. (1998), 'Political Internalization of Economic Externalities and Environmental Policy', *Journal of Public Economics*, **69**, 1–16.

Andreoni, J. (1988), 'Privately Provided Public Goods in a Large Economy: The Limits of Altruism', *Journal of Public Economics*, **35**, 57–73.

Andreoni, J. and M.C. McGuire (1993), 'Identifying the Free Riders: A Simple Algorithm for Determining Who Will Contribute to a Public Good', *Journal of Public Economics*, **51**, 447–54.

Arnold, R.D. (1990), *The Logic of Congressional Action*, New Haven, CT: Yale University Press.

Arrow, K., M. Cropper, G. Eads, R. Hahn, L. Lave, R. Noll, P. Portney, M. Russell, R. Schmalensee, K. Smith and R. Stavins (1996), 'Is There a Role for Benefit–Cost Analysis in Environmental, Health, and Safety Regulation?', *Science*, **272**, 221–2.

Becker, G. (1983), 'A Theory of Competition Among Pressure Groups for Political Influence', *Quarterly Journal of Economics*, **98**, 371–400.

Bergstrom, T.C., L. Blume and H.R. Varian (1986), 'On the Private Provision of Public Goods', *Journal of Public Economics*, **29**, 25–49.

Bernheim, B.D. and M. Whinston (1986), 'Menu Auctions, Resource Allocation, and Economic Influence', *Quarterly Journal of Economics*, **101**, 1–31.

Boyer, M. and J.-J. Laffont (1999), 'Toward a Political Theory of the Emergence of Environmental Incentive Regulation', *Rand Journal of Economics*, **30**, 137–57.

Break, G.F. (1967), *Intergovernmental Fiscal Relations in the United States*, Washington, DC: The Brookings Institution.

Brennan, G. and J. Buchanan (1980), *The Power to Tax: Analytical Foundations of a Fiscal Constitution*, Cambridge, UK and New York, US: Cambridge University Press.

Buchanan, J.M. and G. Tullock (1965), *The Calculus of Consent*, Ann Arbor: University of Michigan Press.

Buchanan, J.M. and G. Tullock (1975), 'Polluters' Profits and Political Response: Direct Controls Versus Taxes', *American Economic Review*, **65**, 139–47.

Burtraw, D. and P.R. Portney (1991), 'Environmental Policy in the United States', in D. Helm (ed.), *Economic Policy Towards the Environment*, Cambridge, MA: Blackwell.

Coase, R. (1960), 'The Problem of Social Cost', *Journal of Law and Economics*, **3** (1), 1–44.

Coelho, P. (1976), 'Polluters' Profits and Political Response: Direct Control Versus Taxes: Comment', *American Economic Review*, **66**, 976–8.

Congleton, R.D. (1992), 'Political Institutions and Pollution Control', *Review of Economics and Statistics*, **74**, 412–21.

Cornes, R. and T. Sandler (1984), 'Easy Riders, Joint Production, and Public Goods', *Economic Journal*, **94**, 580–98.

Cornes, R. and T. Sandler (1996), *The Theory of Externalities, Public Goods, and Club Goods*, 2nd edn, Cambridge: Cambridge University Press.

Crandall, R.W. (1983), *Controlling Industrial Pollution: The Economics and Politics of Clean Air*, Washington, DC: Brookings Institution.

Cropper, M.L., W.N. Evans, S.J. Berardi, M.M. Ducla-Soares and P.R. Portney (1992), 'The Determinants of Pesticide Regulation: A Statistical Analysis of EPA Decision Making', *Journal of Political Economy*, **100**, 175–97.

Cumberland, J.H. (1979), 'Interregional Pollution Spillovers and Consistency of Environmental Policy', in H. Siebert, I. Walter and K. Zimmerman (eds), *Regional Environmental Policy: The Economic Issue*, New York: New York University Press, 255–83.

Cumberland, J.H. (1981), 'Efficiency and Equity in Interregional Environmental Management', *Review of Regional Studies*, **10** (2), 1–9.

Dales, J. (1968), *Pollution, Property and Prices*, Toronto: Toronto University Press.

Dewees, D. (1983), 'Instrument Choice in Environmental Policy', *Economic Inquiry*, **21**, 53–71.

Downs, A. (1957), *An Economic Theory of Democracy*, New York: Harper and Row.

Ekins, P. and S. Speck (1999), 'Competitiveness and Exemptions from Environmental Taxes in Europe', *Environmental and Resource Economics*, **13**, 369–96.

Elliott, E.D., B.A. Ackerman and J.C. Millian (1985), 'Toward a Theory of Statutory Evolution: The Federalization of Environmental Law', *Journal of Law, Economics, and Organization*, **1**, 313–40.

Fredriksson, P. (1997), 'The Political Economy of Pollution Taxes in a Small Open Economy', *Journal of Environmental Economics and Management*, **33**, 44–58.

Fredriksson, P. and N. Gaston (2000), 'Environmental Governance in Federal Systems: The Effects of Capital Competition and Lobby Groups', *Economic Inquiry*, **38**, 501–14.

Fredriksson, P. and D. Millimet (2002), 'Strategic Interaction and the Determination of Environmental Policy Across U.S. States', *Journal of Urban Economics*, **51**, 101–22.

Grossman, G.M. and E. Helpman (1994), 'Protection for Sale', *American Economic Review*, **84**, 833–50.

Hahn, R.W. (1989), 'Economic Prescriptions for Environmental Problems: How the Patient Followed the Doctor's Orders', *Journal of Economic Perspectives*, **3**, 95–114.

Hahn, R.W. (1990), 'The Political Economy of Environmental Regulation: Towards a Unifying Framework', *Public Choice*, **65**, 21–47.

Hahn, R.W. (2000), 'The Impact of Economics on Environmental Policy', *Journal of Environmental Economics and Management*, **39**, 375–99.

Hahn, R.W., S.M. Olmstead and R.N. Stavins (2003), 'Environmental Regulation in the 1990s: A Retrospective Analysis', *Harvard Environmental Law Review*, **27**, 377–415.

Hamilton, J. (1997), 'Taxes, Torts, and the Toxics Release Inventory: Congressional Voting on Instruments to Control Pollution', *Economic Inquiry*, **35**, 745–62.

Hird, J. (1990), 'Superfund Expenditures and Cleanup Priorities: Distributive Politics or the Public Interest?', *Journal of Policy Analysis and Management*, **9**, 455–83.

Joskow, P.L. and R. Schmalensee (1998), 'The Political Economy of Market-Based Environmental Policy: The U.S. Acid Rain Program', *Journal of Law and Economics*, **41**, 37–83.

Kalt, J.P. (1981), *The Economics and Politics of Oil Price Regulation*, Cambridge, MA: MIT Press.

Kalt, J.P. and M.A. Zupan (1984), 'Capture and Ideology in the Economic Theory of Politics', *American Economic Review*, **74**, 279–300.

Kau, J.B. and P.H. Rubin (1979), 'Self-Interest, Ideology and Logrolling in Congressional Voting', *Journal of Law and Economics*, **22**, 365–84.

Keohane, N.O., R.L. Revesz and R.N. Stavins (1998), 'The Choice of Regulatory Instruments in Environmental Policy', *Harvard Environmental Law Review*, **22**, 313–67.

List, J.A. and S. Gerking (2000), 'Regulatory Federalism and Environmental Protection in the United States', *Journal of Regional Science*, **40**, 453–71.

Loeb, M. and W.A. Magat (1979), 'A Decentralized Method for Utility Regulation', *Journal of Law and Economics*, **22**, 399–404.

Magat, W.A., A.J. Krupnick and W. Harrington (1986), *Rules in the Making: A Statistical Analysis of Regulatory Agency Behavior*, Baltimore: Johns Hopkins University Press.

Maloney, M.T. and R.E. McCormick (1982), 'A Positive Theory of Environmental Quality Regulation', *Journal of Law and Economics*, **25**, 99–123.

McFadden, D. (1975), 'The Revealed Preference of a Public Bureaucracy: Theory', *Bell Journal of Economics*, **6**, 401–16.

Metrick, A. and M.L. Weitzman (1996), 'Patterns of Behavior in Endangered Species Preservation', *Land Economics*, **72**, 1–16.

Milvy, P. (1986), 'A General Guideline for Management of Risk from Carcinogens', *Risk Analysis*, **6**, 69–79.

Mitchell, E.J. (1979), 'The Basis of Congressional Energy Policy', *Texas Law Review*, **57**, 591–613.

Murdoch, J.C. and T. Sandler (1997), 'The Voluntary Provision of a Pure Public Good: The Case of Reduced CFC Emissions and the Montreal Protocol', *Journal of Public Economics*, **63**, 331–49.

Oates, W.E. (2000), 'From Research to Policy: The Case of Environmental Economics', *University of Illinois Law Review*, **2000**, 135–53.

Oates, W.E. (2002), 'A Reconsideration of Environmental Federalism', in J.A. List and A. de Zeeuw (eds), *Recent Advances in Environmental Economics*, Cheltenham, UK: Edward Elgar.

Oates, W.E. and P.R. Portney (2003), 'The Political Economy of Environmental Policy', in K.G. Mäler and J. Vincent (eds), *Handbook of Environmental Economics*, Amsterdam: North-Holland/Elsevier Science.

Oates, W.E. and R.M. Schwab (1988), 'Economic Competition Among Jurisdictions: Efficiency Enhancing or Distortion Inducing?', *Journal of Public Economics*, **35**, 333–54.

Pashigian, B.P. (1985), 'Environmental Regulations: Whose Self Interests are Being Protected?', *Economic Inquiry*, **23**, 551–84.

Peltzman, S. (1976), 'Toward a More General Theory of Regulation', *Journal of Law and Economics*, **19** (2), 211–40.

Peltzman, S. (1982), 'Constituent Interest and Congressional Voting', unpublished, University of Chicago Economic and Legal Organization Workshop, February.

Revesz, R.L. (2001), 'Federalism and Environmental Regulation: A Public Choice Analysis', *Harvard Law Review*, **115**, 553–641.

Schneider, F. and J. Volkert (1999), 'No Chance for Incentive-oriented Environmental Policies in Representative Democracies? A Public Choice Analysis', *Ecological Economics*, **31**, 123–38.

Stavins, R.N. (2003), 'Experience with Market-Based Environmental Policy Instruments', in K.G. Mäler and J. Vincent (eds), *Handbook of Environmental Economics*, Amsterdam: North-Holland/Elsevier Science.

Stigler, G.J. (1971), 'The Theory of Economic Regulation', *Bell Journal of Economics and Management Science*, **2** (1), 3–21.

Stigler, G.J. (1972), 'Economic Competition and Political Competition', *Public Choice*, **13**, 91–106.

Thomas, L.G. (1988), 'Revealed Bureaucratic Preference: Priorities of the Consumer Product Safety Commission', *Rand Journal of Economics*, **19**, 102–13.

Tiebout, C.M. (1956), 'A Pure Theory of Local Expenditures', *Journal of Political Economy*, **64**, 416–24.

Tietenberg, T.H. (1985), *Emissions Trading: An Exercise in Reforming Pollution Policy*, Washington, DC: Resources for the Future.

Travis, C.C. and H.A. Hattemer-Frey (1988), 'Determining an Acceptable Level of Risk', *Environmental Science and Technology*, **22**, 873–6.

Travis, C.C., S.A. Richter, E.A.C. Crouch, R. Wilson and E.D. Klema (1987), 'Cancer Risk Management', *Environmental Science and Technology*, **21** (5), 415–20.

Weingast, B.R. and M.J. Moran (1983), 'Bureaucratic Discretion or Congressional Control? Regulatory Policymaking by the Federal Trade Commission', *Journal of Political Economy*, **91** (5), 765–800.

Weitzman, M.L. (1974), 'Prices vs. Quantities', *Review of Economic Studies*, **41** (4), 477–91.

Yandle, B. (1989), *The Political Limits of Environmental Regulation: Tracking the Unicorn*, New York: Quorum Books.

Yohe, G. (1976), 'Polluters' Profits and Political Response: Direct Control Versus Taxes: Comment', *American Economic Review*, **66**, 981–2.

Part I
Setting the Targets and Goals of Environmental Policies

[1]

Capture and Ideology in the Economic Theory of Politics

By Joseph P. Kalt and Mark A. Zupan*

The economic theory of regulation long ago put public interest theories of politics to rest. These theories have correctly been viewed as normative wishings, rather than explanations of real world phenomena. They have been replaced by models of political behavior that are consistent with the rest of microeconomics (Anthony Downs, 1957; James Buchanan and Gordon Tullock, 1965; George Stigler, 1971; Sam Peltzman, 1976). Recently, however, debate has arisen over whether some version of a public interest theory of regulation will have to be readmitted to our thinking about actions and results in the political arena. What is at issue is the empirical importance of the altruistic, publicly interested goals of rational actors in determining legislative and regulatory outcomes (James Kau and Paul Rubin, 1979; Kalt, 1981; Peltzman, 1982).

This study assesses the nature and significance of publicly interested objectives in a particular instance of economic policymaking: U.S. Senate voting on coal strip-mining regulations. The existence of such objectives is, of course, no contradiction of the economic view of human behavior (Kenneth Arrow, 1972; Gary Becker, 1974); and may well be rooted in genetic-biological history (Becker, 1976; Jack Hirshleifer, 1978). Generally, however, individuals' altruistic, publicly interested goals have been given little attention. This reflects the judgment that such goals are so empirically unimportant as to

*Departments of Economics, Harvard University, Cambridge, MA 02138, and Massachusetts Institute of Technology, Cambridge, MA 02139, respectively. We thank Harold Demsetz, Allen Jacobs, Paul Joskow, Thomas Romer, Richard Schmalensee, Harry Watson, Mark Watson, and workshop participants at Harvard, MIT, and the University of Chicago for helpful comments and suggestions. Peter Martin, Kevin Mohan, and Margaret Walls provided valuable research assistance. The support of the Sloan Foundation and the Energy and Environmental Policy Center at the Kennedy School of Government has been greatly appreciated.

allow the use of Occam's razor in positive models, or well-founded apprehensions that these goals are unusually difficult to identify, measure, and analyze. Notwithstanding the latter problem, we find that approaches which confine themselves to a view of political actors as narrowly egocentric maximizers explain and predict legislative outcomes poorly. The tracking and dissecting of the determinants of voting on coal strip-mining policy suggest that the economic theory of politics has been prematurely closed to a broader conception of political behavior.

I. Interests and Ideology in the Economics of Politics

A. *The Setting: Coal Strip-Mining Regulation*

The Surface Mining Control and Reclamation Act (SMCRA) was the product of a protracted political struggle. Congress twice passed versions of SMCRA—in 1974 and 1975—only to have them vetoed by President Ford. SMCRA was finally signed into law by President Carter on August 3, 1977. The Act requires the restoration of strip-mined land to its premining state. In addition, the Act established an Abandoned Mine Reclamation Fund and clarified previously indefinite property rights to water and land in areas underlain by strippable coal.

The Act reduces the use of environmental inputs and raises the costs of strip mining. This tends to raise the price of coal and generates income transfers *from* surface coal producers and coal consumers *to* underground producers and the consumers of environmental amenities. The combined losses of surface producers and coal consumers appear to be on the order of $1.4 billion per year (split approximately 70/30, respectively; Kalt, 1983). After accounting for a small deadweight loss, the annual gains of noncoal environmental users and underground producers are in the range of $1.3 billion (split roughly 90/10).

While incidence analysis can produce more or less precise estimates of particular market participants' gains or losses from SMCRA, there is clearly no reason to expect these economic stakes to translate one-for-one into political clout (Mancur Olson, 1971; Stigler, 1971). Indeed, one of the tasks of the economic theory of regulation and the research below is to describe how economic stakes map into political influence. For our purposes, incidence analysis indicates the *direction* of relevant parties' interests in SMCRA: the regulation of the environmental damage attendant to strip mining should be expected to be opposed by surface coal producers and coal consumers; underground coal producers and consumers of affected environmental amenities should support SMCRA.

B. *Related Research*

The tenor of economic ("capture") theories of regulation, when applied to a specific case such as SMCRA, might suggest that the incidence of the legislation summarizes not only the economics, but also the politics of the issue: narrowly self-interested underground coal producers and environmental consumers captured policymakers at the expense of narrowly self-interested coal consumers and surface coal producers. This line of reasoning, however, cannot be disproved. Since every economic policy decision produces transfers of wealth, it is always possible to infallibly relate political outcomes to distributional impacts. This approach, in fact, leaves open the question of whether the behavior and results we observe in the political arena are the product of something more than the parochial pecuniary interests of affected parties.

Probably the most basic proposition of economic, capture models of regulation is the (sometimes implicit) assertion that the altruistic, publicly interested goals of individuals are such insignificant factors in political processes that they are empirically uninteresting and dispensable. Stigler (1972) has noted the possibility of altruistic motives in political action. These might take the form of a sense of "civic duty," that is, a duty to serve the interests of the public. Pursuit of such a duty is a consumption activity that yields utility in the form of the warm glow of moral rectitude. Classifying this type of argument in the utility function as a "consumption motive" (as distinguished from the self-interested "investment motive" of increasing one's own wealth), Stigler asserts with respect to economic theories of politics: "The investment motive is rich in empirical implications, and the consumption motive is less well-endowed, so we should see how far we can carry the former analysis before we add the latter" (p. 104).

The sentiment of this assertion may yet prove to be supportable. A number of recent investigations, however, have suggested that policymakers' self-defined notions of the "public interest" are dominant explanatory factors in congressional voting behavior (Edward Mitchell, 1979; Kau and Rubin; Kalt, 1981). These studies have attempted to explain voting records on specific issues (for example, oil price controls) as functions of relevant economic interest variables *plus* some measure of the "ideological" orientation of congressmen. The latter is typically based on rating scales provided by ideological watchdog organizations such as the Americans for Democratic Action (ADA) or the Americans for Constitutional Action (ACA). The consistent findings are that economic interest variables play surprisingly weak roles in legislative outcomes, while the hypothesis of no ideological effect is quite easily rejected.

Peltzman (1982) has taken a critical look at these findings. The interests of constituents and the ideological "preferences" of their representatives are plausibly interrelated—perhaps with causation running from the former to the latter. The apparent importance of ideology may, therefore, be due to left-out economic interest variables. By examining Senate voting across a broad sample of issues, Peltzman is able to "explain away" most of the importance of ideological preferences with an extended array of constituent interest measures (for example, demographic characteristics). The research strategy behind these results, however, differs in a fundamental way from the approach taken in the research it critiques. Specifically, Peltzman examines a sample covering essentially the entire package of votes offered by senators to their constituents, rather than voting on a specific issue. The query remains whether conclusions reached at such a high level of bundling can safely be applied to the specific case. The economic theory of regulation has generally been put forth and applied as an issue-specific theory (Stigler, 1971; Peltzman, 1976; Burton Abrams and Russell Settle, 1978).

C. Possible Sources of Ideological Voting

In the jargon of recent research, the purported social objectives of political actors have been termed "ideology." Political ideologies are more or less consistent sets of normative statements as to best or preferred states of the world. Such statements are moralistic and altruistic in the sense that they are held as applicable to everyone, rather than merely to the actor making the statements. Accordingly, political ideologies are taken here to be statements about how government can best serve their proponents' conceptions of the public interest. Behavior in accord with such statements has two possible sources: 1) the direct appearance of altruism in actors' preference functions (termed "pure" ideology); and 2) a convenient signalling mechanism when information on political decisions is otherwise costly.[1]

1. *Pure Ideology in Voters and their Representatives.* Pure ideology, if it exists at all, is the manifestation of altruism in the political sector. The returns from the furtherance of an ideology appear to come in at least two forms. First, the successful promotion of an

ideology may give individuals the satisfaction of knowing that they have concretely improved the lot of others. Second, even if the pursuit of ideology has no effect on others, individuals may derive satisfaction from "having done the right thing" (Stigler's consumption motive).[2] Do individuals really get utility from these sources? It is not our intention here to dispute tastes. We take the presence of ideological tastes 'as given by introspection and observation. Following Becker (1974), we also take the pursuit of such tastes to be rational—to be responsive, that is, to opportunity costs. This contrasts with the unfortunate terminology which characterizes altruistic-ideological behavior as "non-economic" (Peltzman, 1982) and/or "irrational" (Yoram Barzel and Eugene Silberberg, 1973). The rationality of ideological behavior is tested below.

Political behavior based on pure ideology may arise from either the publicly interested objectives of constituents or the independent publicly interested objectives of their representatives.

Constituents: Voters' ideological goals might include, for example, anticommunism, communism, Jeffersonian agrarianism, Rawlsian egalitarianism, and so on.[3] The presence of such goals poses no problems for the economic theory of politics. Publicly interested ideologues are just another special interest capable of capturing the political process, subject to the comparative statics of organizational costs and benefits as modeled by Peltzman (1976). We suspect, however, that most economists would conclude that the pursuit of ideological objectives is not an important phenomenon. At least on the basis of behavior observed in the market sector, this would appear to be well-founded. Is there any reason to expect pure ideological actions to be relatively more common in the

---

[1] These two sources of ideology have often been noted. Downs' exposition is particularly clear. Jerome Rothenberg (1965), Bruno Frey and Lawrence Lau (1968), and Albert Breton (1974) provide systematic theoretical treatments of pure ideology; and empirical implementation of the concept has been pushed furthest by the literature on the "paradox of voting" (William Riker and Peter Ordeshook, 1968; Robert Tollison and Thomas Willett, 1975; and Orley Ashenfelter and Stanley Kelley, 1975).

[2] Of course, in either case, individuals may also receive returns in the form of the esteem of, or even reciprocal favors from, other individuals (Becker, 1976).

[3] The notion of "public interest" embodied in any particular ideology need not include the promotion of economic efficiency (Tullock, 1982). Indeed, ideologies appear to typically center around the "equity" (i.e., rights and distributional assignments) side of the economists' equity-efficiency dichotomy.

282   *THE AMERICAN ECONOMIC REVIEW*   *JUNE 1984*

political arena? Several factors suggest the answer may be affirmative.

First, altruistic ideological interests that depend upon actually improving the welfare of others have clear collective good attributes. The apparatus of government provides the classic Samuelsonian (1954) means (i.e., coercive power) for overcoming the free-rider problems that can plague a marketplace. Indeed, this apparatus may be made comparatively inexpensive for the representative altruist to the extent it can be hijacked and used to require outsiders to finance the benefits delivered to the altruist's targeted group.

Second, in much political activity, the individual has no meaningful prospect of influencing outcomes. In the case of large-number majoritarian elections, for example, the individual voter is generally incapable of promoting his or her investment interests. This observation has led to the recognition that altruistic-ideological preferences play central roles in motivating the act of voting. Nevertheless, it has typically been assumed that, once the decision to vote has been made, we can explain the ballot cast by reference to the voter's economic interests. As Geoffrey Brennan and Buchanan (1982) have pointed out, however, this is a *non sequitur*: if the decision to vote is based on consumption motives, it does not follow that these motives are set aside upon entering the voting booth. Comparing the consumption choices made in voting with investment decisions in the marketplace (emphasis in original):

> ...we may presume that the individual *cares* as to which outcome emerges from the voting process. But this does not permit us to presume that his choice in the polling booth *reflects* or corresponds with his preferences over outcomes. For the voter is not *choosing* between outcomes.... When the voter pulls a particular lever, the opportunity cost of doing so is not a particular policy forgone....   [pp. 14–15]

[Thus]...the choice of candidate...depends overwhelmingly on tastes for showing "preferences" as such—and hardly at all on the evaluation of outcomes. Voting behavior is then to be understood perhaps as "symbolic" or

"liturgical"...and [is] hardly at all like the choice among alternative investments.   [p. 18]

Third, even when political participation is motivated by the prospect of pecuniary gains, such gains are often subject to substantial public goods problems. Pecuniary political gains commonly must be shared with large numbers of congruent parties (for example, all coal consumers or all environmental users). While private sector investments can be accompanied by free-rider problems, such problems are virtually the rule at the legislative level in U.S.-style democracy (the Chrysler and Lockheed cases notwithstanding). In contrast, at least that part of ideology based on individuals' tastes for the warm glow of moral rectitude is a strict private good in both the public and private sectors. Thus the opportunity cost (i.e., forgone pecuniary return) of ideology might be expected to be generally lower in the political arena than in the marketplace. Accordingly, the rational actor in the political sector would be expected to reveal behavior tilted relatively more toward altruistic-ideological objectives.

Representatives: Institutional attributes of the political sector may allow pure ideological action by representatives themselves. This opportunity could arise because, analogous to the case of management in the private corporation, there may be some separation of "ownership" by constituents and "control" by policymakers. Any such slack in the principal-agent relationship can be expected to result in policymaker independence or "shirking"—as Armen Alchian and Harold Demsetz (1972) call it.

Models of the specific-issue legislative process that have grown out of the economic theory of regulation (Peltzman, 1976) seldom leave room for policymaker shirking.[4] By

---

[4]Notable exceptions in which ideological shirking appears are the formal models of Rothenberg and Frey and Lau, although the focus of these models is primarily on policymakers' electoral success. In a model motivated by institutional attributes similar to those considered here and below, Robert Barro (1973) allows slack in the principal-agent relationship and (albeit, nonideological) utility maximization by elected officials.

endowing legislators with goals such as vote maximization, rather than own-utility maximization, such models preclude behavior that is not directly controlled by constituents. This conception of the strength of the principal-agent bond in the legislative process, however, does not seem to be in line with the conception of this bond that comes out of the property rights theory of institutions (Alchian and Demsetz; Michael Jensen and William Meckling, 1976) and the bulk of associated empirical evidence (see the summary by Louis De Alessi, 1982). Conditions under which the market system's invisible hand is likely to encounter difficulty in narrowing the separation of ownership and control would appear to be especially prevalent in the legislative context.[5]

First, the "market for control" (Henry Manne, 1965) is characterized by significant indivisibilities that impair adjustment at the margin by constituents. The typical constituent is presented with all-or-nothing choices between a small number of large bundles of issues to be addressed by policymakers over their tenure; *and* the market meets only infrequently—every six years in the case of the U.S. Senate. Second, as "hirers" of political representation, voter-owners have poor incentives to be well-informed. As Olson has stressed, collective decisions are subject to classic free-rider problems that affect participants' willingness to invest in the acquisition of information. Third, these free-rider problems are exacerbated by the fact that "ownership" by constituents is held under attenuated property titles. Political ownership is nontransferable, and, as residual claimants to the net benefits of correct decisions, constituent-owners promoting such decisions cannot easily capture resulting gains (see Alchian and Demsetz). Fourth, the political market is apparently subject to less than perfect competition (John Ferejohn, 1977). The provision of representation services in the U.S. political system takes place under conditions of effective duopoly; barriers to entry are significant (Abrams and Settle);

[5] Ideological shirking does not require that separation of ownership and control be *more* prevalent in the legislative setting than in the marketplace. It is sufficient that there be *some* principal-agent slack.

elements of natural monopoly are present (Stigler, 1971); and collusion to prevent Tiebout-type (1956) competition is officially sanctioned. Finally, these attributes of the market for legislative seats create conditions conducive to "opportunism" in Oliver Williamson's (1975) sense; and the range of enforceable contractual agreements of the type examined by Benjamin Klein, Robert Crawford, and Alchian (1978) that might be struck to minimize opportunism is notably limited (for example, to the verbal agreement that "I will keep my campaign promises").

It must be stressed that none of this implies that shirking is costless to legislative representatives. Analogous to the position of shirking private sector managers vis-à-vis shareholders, representatives face some control through the voting booth, as well as more continuous pressure from constituents who have some ability to affect the pleasantness of the policymaker's working day, future employment opportunities, and other aspects of the returns to positions of policy responsibility. Nevertheless, legislative institutions such as the U.S. Senate would appear to be archetypical Alchian-Demsetz organizations in which agents are imperfectly policed by their principals—where "imperfectly" is defined relative to a nirvana world of zero policing costs. The implied result is some amount of own-welfare maximization by representatives at the expense of their constituents—an amount that may be optimal for constituents given the real world policing costs they face.

Any shirking by imperfectly policed representatives can be expected to center around those activities that have low opportunity costs (for example, in terms of reelection prospects) and/or poor substitutes off the job. Paralleling Becker's (1957) analysis of private managers' on-the-job consumption and Alchian and Reuben Kessel's (1962) examination of nonprofit institutions, shirking by legislators may focus on nonpecuniary perquisites of office holding—although opportunities for personal pecuniary gain are certainly available. The perquisites of political office range from "fact finding" junkets and postservice employment connections with rent-seeking interest groups to public notoriety, prestige, and the ability to use the

284   *THE AMERICAN ECONOMIC REVIEW*   *JUNE 1984*

power of government to impose one's own pet theories of the "good" society. The last of these emoluments is almost uniquely available in the political sector and is what we have termed ideological consumption.

For a number of reasons, shirking in an activity such as Senate voting might be expected to have an ideological component. Morris Fiorina and Roger Noll (1978) have noted, for instance, that legislators' fates depend heavily on the provision to constituents of so-called "facilitation services" (for example, supportive intervention at other levels of government), as distinguished from their provision of floor votes. This is complemented by the fact that nonideological shirking on floor votes (for example, taking bribes, failing to be informed, or missing roll calls in favor of office parties) is comparatively costly as a result of institutional penalties, while a legislator does not face expulsion or censure for voting his or her "conscience" (i.e., ideology).[6] Furthermore, to the extent the individual legislator can rationally take the fate on the floor of any particular piece of legislation as given, that legislator's vote becomes valueless to any constituent—that vote, that is, has no impact on the economic well-being of constituents since it does not affect outcomes.[7] The only remaining value of the vote to the legislator, then, would be its consumption value—no constituent would be willing to pay anything for it. This is, of course, the legislative-floor analogue to Brennan and Buchanan's analysis (noted above) of voting booth behavior by citizens, although it would be inappropriate to conclude that the investment value of a vote in a place like the U.S. Senate is typically nil as it is in the very-large-number majoritarian voting booth. Lastly, the governmental apparatus is the preeminent mechanism for affecting broad

---

[6] Note, also, that shirking in the pecuniary form of taking bribes (at the expense of support maximization) is service to some constituent's interest and would show up accordingly in the empirical analysis of voting below, unless bribery is uncorrelated with measures of constituent influence. In the latter situation, bribery and other forms of nonideological shirking (say, failing to be informed on issues) should show up as white noise.

[7] This point is also noted, in the context of a parliamentary system, by Frey and Lau (p. 358).

social change. The opportunities this creates, if coupled with comparatively low costs to ideological shirking, would imply a self-selection process that attracts individuals with relatively intense demands for ideology to the political sector.

2. Impure Ideology and Costly Information. It is certainly possible that policymakers base their decisions on consultation with the precepts of an ideology when nothing more than narrow self-interest is being served. In a world in which information on the concordance between constituent interests and the consequences of policy proposals is scarce, political representatives may serve their investment motives (for example, the desire to get reelected) by relying on the dictates of an ideology as a shortcut to the service of their constituents' goals (Downs; Buchanan and Tullock). In this view, ideology plays the same role in the economic theory of the political process that managerial rules of thumb play in the theory of the profit-maximizing firm. The implication that the apparent ideologies of representatives are in fact proxies for constituents' interests suggests collinearity between measures of ideology and those interests. This implication has not received support in studies of voting on individual issues, but has been borne out in Peltzman's (1982) examination of voting on the aggregated bundle of issues addressed by senators. These apparently conflicting results are analyzed below within the context of a Downsian view of representative democracy.

Downs' seminal look at representative democracy suggests an important implication of ideology as a device for economizing on information: if legislators are not perfectly policed on every vote, the rational constituent could be expected to support representatives whose demands for pure ideology are intense relative to other motives for shirking. To be sure, as each specific issue arises between elections, the constituent prefers that representatives vote the constituent's interests on that issue, not their own ideologies. But the constituent faced with 1) an uncertain bundle of issues to be decided by representatives over their terms of office, 2) uncertainty about the effects of policy decisions, and 3) positive policing costs and hence shirking, can attempt to wind up on net on the winning sides of issues (in a pecuniary or nonpecuniary sense) by supporting candidates with appropriate ideologies. Upon election, such candidates will engage in pure ideological shirking on particular issues rather than permit themselves to be captured by the issue-specific interests that organize and present themselves at any particular moment; an economic incidence approach to issue-specific political economy will be inadequate. Over the full slate of issues, however, representatives' voting should fall in line with general indicators of their constituents' ideological and investment interests—as Peltzman (1982) finds. We now examine these Downsian implications in the context of the specific issue of SMCRA.

II. Senate Voting on SMCRA

A. *Study Design*

Our objective is to untangle the causal forces behind Senate voting on strip-mining controls. We seek to separate the effects of constituents' interests (economic and ideological) and senators' ideology. In addition, we would like to be able to uncover that part, if any, of senators' ideology which is purely publicly interested shirking and that part of ideology which merely stands in for otherwise difficult to identify constituent interests.

Voting on strip-mining legislation is observed as either a "yea" or a "nay." To measure senators' positions, a variable AN-TISTRIP is constructed to reflect the frequency, f_i, with which the ith senator casts a vote unfavorable to strip mining. A senator voting an anti-strip position on r_i out of n_i opportunities has $f_i = r_i/n_i$. This frequency is bounded by zero and unity. Adjusting for $r_i = 0$, $r_i = n_i$, and heteroskedasticity (John Gart and James Zweifel, 1967), the weighted logit technique of Arnold Zellner and Tong Lee (1965) is employed in our econometric analysis. Thus

(1)

$$ANTISTRIP_i = \ln[(r_i + .5)/(n_i - r_i + .5)];$$

and has variance estimator:

(2) $Var_i = 1/(r_i + .5) + 1/(n_i - r_i + .5);$

The variable ANTISTRIP is based on the voting of the 100 senators that served in the 95th Congress (1977–78); and is derived from 21 roll call votes in which the interests of surface coal producers, underground producers, coal consumers, and the consumers of environmental amenities were clearly delineated. These votes deal with either SMCRA or its vetoed predecessors.[8] Measures that would have raised the costs of surface mining were taken to be detrimental to surface mining—and conversely. Selected votes and their economic implications are not identical; and Charles Phelps (1982) suggests the possibility of aggregation problems in ANTISTRIP. In this case, however, results are unaffected when individual votes are used as dependent variables (see our earlier paper).

B. *Interests and their Influence*

The economic theory of regulation provides the basis for measures of constituents' interests and influence. Specifically, the *interests* constituents have in capturing the political process are their prospective gains or losses from any policy proposal. The *ability* constituents have to capture the political process depends critically on their ability to overcome the free-rider effects inherent in collective decisions. Any group's influence will depend positively on members' per capita stakes and the concentration of their interests; and negatively on the heterogeneity of members' objectives and group size. Where data permit, we employ variables reflecting determinants of group effectiveness, as well as the magnitude of groups' interests in SMCRA.

Turning first to the magnitude of groups' interests, we introduce variables reflecting the stakes of surface coal producers, underground coal producers, coal consumers, and

---

[8]Votes are taken from Congressional Quarterly, Inc., *Congressional Quarterly Almanac* (1973, 1975, 1977). A descriptive list is available in our 1983 paper.

consumers of affected environmental amenities.

Coal Producers: The variables *SURFRES* and *UNDERRES* measure each state's reserves (in Btus) in 1977 of surface and underground coal, respectively; and are expressed as fractions of state personal income to scale for the relative importance of coal production to states' economies. Reserve-based measures are used to proxy for the present value of SMCRA's impacts on coal resources. Particularly in many western states where strip mining was in its infancy in 1977, current production figures inadequately capture the present-valued importance of the industry to states' economies. Results of most interest, namely the relative roles of economic and ideological variables, are not affected by switching to production- or employment-based measures (see our earlier paper).[9]

There are significant differences across states in SMCRA's impact on strip mining costs. The variable *MC* measures the regulation-induced increase in the long-run average cost of surface mining in each state, as derived by ICF, Inc. (1977). Because surface mining interests were adversely affected by SMCRA, *MC* as well as *SURFRES* are expected to be negatively related to *ANTISTRIP*. The variable *UNDERRES* is expected to have a positive impact on *ANTISTRIP*.

Coal Consumers: The variable *CONSUME* is employed to represent the importance of coal consumption in each state. Electric power generation accounts for 78 percent of U.S. coal demand and *CONSUME* is the share of state electricity generated from coal in 1977.[10] It is preferred to other measures such as total coal Btus consumed per capita if it is primarily electric utilities, small in number and large in size, who overcome the

free-rider problems that plague political lobbying.[11] The organizational effectiveness of the electric power industry is examined below. Reflecting the effect of SMCRA on coal prices, *CONSUME* is expected to be negatively related to *ANTISTRIP*.

Environmental Consumers: Environmental interests may be classed into two broad types: environmental users in the literal sense; and those for whom environmental protection represents an ideological cause. Empirical evidence on the existence of the latter is provided by William Schulze et al. (1981). They find that, based on willingness to pay, the most significant value of an undeveloped environment is derived from individuals' demands for just knowing that an area is used "properly," independent of whether such individuals ever visit or even plan to visit the area themselves. These values are notably altruistic-ideological. They arise from prescriptive opinions about what environmental uses are consistent with self-defined standards of ethical propriety and the public interest. These standards include the view of wilderness as an antidote for purported psychological costs of urbanization; the conception of the American West as a peculiar cultural and natural history lesson; the quasi-religious question of the propriety of appropriating of environmental resources for human ends; the social desirability of rapid economic growth; and the appropriate beneficiaries of public lands. Moreover, the results of Schulze et al. suggest that people's willingness to pay to uphold these precepts has standard comparative static properties—ideological environmentalism is just another economic good.

To capture the ideological interests that constituents have in SMCRA, we employ a variable *ENVIROS*. This is defined as state membership in the six largest environmental groups (as a fraction of voting-age population). Interestingly, the correlation between *ENVIROS* and measures of actual recreational use of the environment (for example, hunting and fishing, budgets for parks

---

[9]Reserves are from National Coal Association, *Coal Data 1978* (1979). These are highly correlated with the projections of new mine development over 1978–87 reported in McGraw-Hill, Inc., *Keystone Coal Industry Manual* (1977).

[10]*CONSUME* is from *Coal Data 1978*. The correlation between *CONSUME* and an alternative measure, total coal Btus consumed per capita, is 0.72. Results reported below are essentially unchanged when the alternative measure is utilized (see our earlier paper).

[11]Of the over 50 coal consumers who appeared before congressional hearings on SMCRA, only one was not a utility.

and recreation, visits to parklands) is quite low.[12] If senators' voting has been captured by ideological environmentalists, *ENVIROS* should have a positive effect on *ANTI-STRIP*.

The interests of actual nonmining consumers of the environment threatened by strip mining are represented by three variables: *HUNTFISH, SPLITRIGHTS,* and *UNRECLAIMED.* The variable *HUNT-FISH* is defined as the number of hunting and fishing licenses as a percentage of state population. It is highly correlated with other measures of outdoor recreational activity. The analysis in Kalt (1983) indicates that outdoor recreation is little threatened by strip mining; and *HUNTFISH* is consistently insignificant in the econometric analysis. Since results of interest are invariant with respect to the inclusion of *HUNTFISH*, the variable is excluded here (see our earlier paper). The variable *SPLITRIGHTS* captures the support of ranchers, farmers, lumberers, and other noncoal business interests for legislation that preserved their preferential rights to the large land areas underlaid by federally controlled strippable coal. The economic values at stake are measured by the agriculture/timber revenue yield of the disputed surface acres, expressed as a percentage of state personal income. Similarly, *UNRECLAIMED* measures the prospective value of already stripped but unrestored acres to noncoal interests who stood to benefit from the Abandoned Mine Reclamation Funds' subsidies. The variables *SPLITRIGHTS* and *UNRE-CLAIMED* should be positively related to *ANTISTRIP*.[13]

Group Influence: The magnitude of a group's interests, even when scaled by state size, does not account fully for that group's ability to overcome the free-rider problems associated with political lobbying. These sorts of problems have been incorporated into empirical research on nonpolitical collective action, most notably in dealing with joint maximization in oligopolistic markets. Available data permit us to address this issue in the political context. To reflect the likelihood that a group can surmount free-rider difficulties, we introduce Herfindahl indices by state for surface coal producers, underground coal producers, coal consumers, and environmental organizations (*HSURF, HUNDER, HCONSUME,* and *HENVIROS*).[14] Data do not permit similar measures for *SPLIT-RIGHTS* and *UNRECLAIMED*.[15] Herfindahl indices are negatively related to group size and positively related to the concentration of interests within a group. Accordingly, *HSURF* and *HCONSUME* are expected to have negative effects on *ANTISTRIP*, while *HUNDER* and *HENVIROS* should have positive impacts.

C. Senator Ideology

The final variable to be introduced into the examination of *ANTISTRIP* voting is some (arguably impure) measure of senators' own ideologies. Following the lines of previous research, we rely on the independent (but not disinterested) "pro-environment" rating scale of the League of Conservation Voters (LCV). This rating scale is based on 27 not-surface-mining-related Senate votes taken in the 95th Congress and deemed to be ideologically revealing by the LCV.[16] The

---

[12] The groups are Sierra Club, National Audubon Society, Environmental Defense Fund, Friends of the Earth, National Wildlife Federation, and Wilderness Society (data provided by Resources for the Future, Inc.,). The correlation between *ENVIROS* and total hunting and fishing licenses in a state (U.S. Department of Commerce, *Statistical Abstract*, 1979) is 0.37. The correlation with state budgets for parks and recreation (*Statistical Abstract*, 1977) is −0.13; and is 0.003 with visits to state and federal forests and parklands (data from Charles Goeldner and Karen Dicke, 1981).

[13] Data for *SPLITRIGHTS* and *UNRECLAIMED* are from ICF, Inc. and the *Survey of Current Business*.

[14] The *Keystone Coal Industry Manual* provides state mine-by-mine data; *HCONSUME* is based on coal-fired electric generating capacity as reported in National Coal Association, *Steam Electric Plant Factors* (1978), *HENVIROS* is based on the six environmental groups mentioned in fn. 12 above.

[15] The omission does not appear to be consequential; the memberships of *SPLITRIGHTS* and *UNRE-CLAIMED* are relatively small and easily self-identified. Our earlier paper examined free-rider problems affecting these groups by introducing squared values of *SPLITRIGHTS* and *UNRECLAIMED*. Results are insignificant and do not alter any conclusions of interest.

[16] Votes are from LCV, *How Senators Voted on Critical Environmental Issues* (1978) and are listed in our earlier paper.

288   THE AMERICAN ECONOMIC REVIEW   JUNE 1984

LCV notion of environmentalism conforms well with the aforementioned moralistic values of an undeveloped environment.[17] Analogous to *ANTISTRIP*, the frequency of pro-environmental votes is transformed according to (1) and is denoted *PROLCV*. Reflecting the LCV's own stance, *PROLCV* is expected to be positively related to *ANTISTRIP*. The extremes of *PROLCV* are occupied by senators with reputations as ideologues—for example, Kennedy (D-MA), Culver (D-IA), Zorinsky (R-NE), and Hatch (R-UT). Of course, this observation begs the question of the purity of ideology.

To the extent, if any, *PROLCV* reflects pure ideology, a move from a lower to a higher *PROLCV* represents a move from a less to a more intense demand for ideological support of an undeveloped environment. The variable *PROLCV* is built up from dichotomous, pro- or anti-environment choices by senators. Holding other things constant, including the opportunity cost of shirking, senators with relatively more intense demands for ideological environmentalism will choose the "pro" position more frequently and, hence, will have higher *PROLCV* values.

To the extent *PROLCV* reflects apparent ideology that is in fact proxying for constituents' interests in SMCRA, *PROLCV* should exhibit significant collinearity with the other factors that explain *ANTISTRIP* voting. Of course, as in any econometric

analysis, there may be left-out variables. If these are correlated with the (apparent) ideologies of senators, the hypothesis that pure ideology matters in specific-issue politics may be inappropriately accepted. Consequently, a major part of the effort undertaken in Section III is aimed at uncovering such a correlation. At this stage, it can only be noted that each of the interests appearing in the record of SMCRA lobbying efforts and suggested by theory has been identified to the extent allowed by the data: all voters at least have "homes" in the selected variables and account is taken of the nature of political organization. To be sure, the groupings of voters according to their interests in coal strip mining most likely do not correspond to the groupings ("constituencies") that originally got a senator elected—as a result of the "bundling" discussed in Section I. But, the capture models of regulation do not suggest that the search for left-out variables should begin with these original groupings. Insofar as these models are specific-issue models, the search for left-out variables should be guided by analysis of SMCRA's impacts on consumers' and producers' surplus.

D. *Interstate Lobbying and Logrolling*

Two aspects of the legislative process not included in our empirical model are worth noting here. First, the conception of senators' voting choices embodied in our analysis portrays "captured" senators as casting their ballots based on the likely impact of SMCRA on their own states' constituents—with better organized constituents getting more attention. This obscures the ability of voters to apply pressure across state lines. Data inadequacies do not permit us to formally incorporate this phenomenon. Nevertheless, to the extent that cross-state lobbyers must appeal to within-state impacts in order to be effective, the problem recedes. Moreover, there is no obvious reason why SMCRA-*specific* out-of-state interests should cluster around *PROLCV* or any other measure of ideology based on a bundle of a senator's *non*-SMCRA votes. Still, this possibility becomes a central object of investigation below.

---

[17]Joseph Sax (1980) provides the archetypical statement of ideological environmentalism:

> The preservationist is not an elitist who wants to exclude others, notwithstanding popular opinion to the contrary; he is a moralist who wants to convert them. He is concerned about what other people do in the parks not because he is unaware of the diversity of taste in the society but because he views certain kinds of activity as calculated to undermine the attitudes he believes the parks can, and should encourage.   [p. 14]

> ...Engagement with nature provides an opportunity for detachment from the submissiveness, conformity, and mass behavior that dog us in our daily lives; it offers a chance to express distinctiveness and to explore our deeper longings. At the same time, the setting—by exposing us to the awesomeness of the natural world in the context of "ethical" recreation—moderates the urge to prevail without destroying the vitality that gives rise to it: to face what is wild in us and yet not revert to savagery.   [p. 42]

A second aspect of the legislative process not covered explicitly by our model is logrolling. This in part reflects the paucity of help provided by theory and data that would allow measurement of the extent and direction of any logrolling and coalition-forming on the specific issue of SMCRA—of the hundreds of issues to choose from, which issue(s) would a logrolling senator trade his SMCRA vote for? Note, however, there are no apparent a priori reasons why logrolling would make ideology appear any more or any less important relative to constituent interests in explaining SMCRA voting. That is, the willingness of a senator to trade away *either* his constituents' interests *or* his own ideology should be negatively related to the political strength of those interests and the intensity of his ideological preferences, respectively. Furthermore, in the absence of pure ideology, the hypothesis that ideology matters will incorrectly be accepted only if two conditions hold:

1) The non-SMCRA interests that are in fact served when a senator votes against his constituents' SMCRA-specific interests are systematically related to the interests that were served (either indirectly through logrolling or directly) by the senator's voting on the issues from which *PROLCV* is constructed.

2) At the same time, for the senator buying SMCRA votes by giving up his constituents' interests on other issues, SMCRA-specific constituent interests must be systematically related to the interests that are being served (either indirectly or directly) by his *PROLCV* voting.

With *PROLCV* issues ranging from the regulation of nitrogen oxide emissions from automobiles and the elimination of phosphates in dishwashing detergent to expansion of Redwood National Park and charging congressional staffers for parking privileges, satisfaction of these two requirements seems somewhat implausible. Nevertheless, we address this important question empirically in Section III—for the cases of both *PROLCV* and measures of ideology that are completely unrelated to the environment.

Finally, for the second condition above to hold without introducing collinearity between *PROLCV* and the included interest variables used to explain *ANTISTRIP*, the SMCRA-specific constituent interests being served by "buying" senators must be unrelated to the interests we have been able to identify. Again, a reading of the history of SMCRA provides little help in identifying such potent left-out variables. Still, this implication suggests a further object for empirical investigation.

E. Initial Results

It is clear that the task of isolating the determinants of legislative voting on an economic issue such as SMCRA is extraordinarily complex. As a first cut, we present the "standard" analysis that has been applied in previous research. Table 1 compares the Capture Model argued for by the economic theory of regulation (i.e., *PROLCV* is excluded) and a Capture-plus-Ideology Model that includes a variable (*PROLCV*) intended to account for senators' ideological preferences. Both models lend support to a multigroup (for example, see Peltzman, 1976) capture theory of politics—perhaps amended to include capture by ideologues. Noncoal beneficiaries of the environment, coal consumers, underground coal producers, and surface coal producers all appear to have appreciably influenced senators' voting on SMCRA; and interest groups' organizational capacities appear to have generally pushed senators in expected directions, although without especially strong statistical significance.

The most striking result of Table 1 is the sharp increase in explanatory power that results from the introduction of *PROLCV*. Indeed, it is this type of result that led Kau and Rubin, and Kalt (1981) to conclude that pure ideology was at work in legislative politics. The foregoing discussion, however, argues that such a conclusion is premature. Section III proceeds with a dissection that accounts for the extent to which an extended array of constituent characteristics (including *ENVIROS*) can explain *PROLCV*. At this stage, we can only note that, while the behavior of selected coefficients indicates that *PROLCV* is not completely orthogonal to

TABLE 1—THE DETERMINANTS OF ANTI-STRIP-MINING VOTING IN THE U.S. SENATE[a]

Explanatory Variable	Capture Model	Capture-plus-Ideology Model[b]
PROLCV	–	0.466
		(10.05)
		[0.65]
MC	– 0.513	– 0.375
	(– 4.78)	(– 3.47)
		[– 0.22]
SURFRES	– 16.765	– 17.198
	(– 1.66)	(– 1.71)
		[– 0.57]
UNDERRES	12.512	14.132
	(2.09)	(2.37)
		[0.73]
SPLITRIGHTS	– 26.546	68.488
	(– 0.55)	(1.40)
		[0.12]
ENVIROS	83.375	0.501
	(4.48)	(0.02)
		[0.00 +]
UNRECLAIMED	0.019	0.015
	(3.77)	(3.03)
		[0.22]
CONSUME	– 0.350	– 0.440
	(– 1.46)	(– 1.83)
		[– 0.13]
HSURF	– 0.294	0.017
	(– 1.24)	(0.07)
		[0.00 +]
HUNDER	0.305	0.150
	(1.10)	(0.54)
		[0.03]
HENVIROS	1.935	– 1.286
	(1.78)	(– 1.14)
		[– 0.07]
HCONSUME	– 0.486	– 0.261
	(– 2.42)	(– 1.29)
		[– 0.08]
Constant	– 0.154	1.414
	(– 0.33)	(2.86)
$\bar{R}^2$	0.45	0.74
Condition-Stat.	25.99	27.47

[a]Dependent variable is *ANTISTRIP*; *t*-statistics are shown in parentheses.

[b]*Beta* coefficients are shown in brackets.

the set of other explanatory factors, the variable's statistical significance and the condition statistics (David Belsley et al., 1980) indicate there is insufficient collinearity to justify the conclusion that *PROLCV* is merely a proxy for the constituent interests identified by the capture theory.

III. Separating Interests and Ideology

Even if *PROLCV*'s sources—indiscernible constituent interests or the elusive notion of senatorial concerns for the public interest—are unclear, its explanatory power is striking. In the following analysis, we attempt to pry open the black box of ideology from a number of different angles. We first look for a purer measure of senators' own demands for altruistic, publicly interested behavior. Second, after isolating that portion which is most clearly pure, we examine the relative importance of the pure and remaining, arguably interest-proxy, parts of ideology. We then investigate the apparent interest-proxy part of ideology more closely. Finally, to assay whether ideological consumption is economically rational, we subject it to a revealing comparative statics test.

A. SMCRA *Voting and Social Issue Ideology*

Among the many issues senators vote on are certain moral and ethical matters around which economic-interest lobbying is infrequent. Examples include such issues as child pornography, the neutron bomb, and capital punishment. While Peltzman (1982) rejects ideology as an explanation for voting on economic issues such as SMCRA, he suggests that voting on noneconomic socio-ethical questions is especially likely to be based on individuals' preferences for moral rectitude, that is, pure ideology. Indeed, he finds evidence that voting on such issues reflects senators' own preferences more than does voting on "pocketbook" issues. Following this line of reasoning, we throw *PROLCV* out of the analysis of *ANTISTRIP* and replace it with measures of senators' social issue ideology. These measures are based on senators' voting on, for example, increased penalties for trafficking in child pornography, expanding the applicability of the death penalty, allowing the immigration of avowed communists, and "giving away" the Panama Canal. (Subsequent sections assess whether these measures actually reflect left-out interests and/or capture by ideological constituents.)

Two types of social issue ideology variables are examined. First, *PROLCV* is replaced by (dichotomous) voting on individual issues. Second, two indexes are created (according to (1)) from the sample of individual votes. The sample includes all votes taken in the 95th Congress that could be identified as general socio-ethical questions, uncontaminated by pocketbook concerns.[18] The issues thus identified are the column headings in Table 2. Selection was based on a priori judgment; that is, there was no econometric "fishing."

One of the indexes, the "SI (Social Issue) Index," is based on 34 votes dealing with the 12 non-Panama Canal issues indicated in Table 3. The second index, the "Panama Canal Index," is based on a sample of 25 procedural votes taken during the ratification process for President Carter's Panama Canal Treaty. The ceding of the Panama Canal was selected because a reading of the legislative history indicates that first, it was probably the most striking recent case in which conservatives "stonewalled it" against liberals; and second, no identifiable economic interest groups were coalesced by the issue.

The ideological content of the social issue votes cuts along modern liberal/conservative lines. To provide consistency to expected signs, senators are assigned a value of unity when voting the liberal position (as defined by, for example, the ADA) and a value of zero otherwise. It turns out that politicians consistently package liberalism and environmentalism together—the correlation between the LCV's and the ADA's rating scales is 0.94. Accordingly, if the apparent ideology embodied in *PROLCV* is, in fact, as pure as the ideology expressed in voting on socio-ethical matters, the social issue measures should have strongly positive effects on *ANTISTRIP*. Moreover, overall estimation results should closely resemble those found when using *PROLCV*.

Table 2 reports representative results when social issue ideology replaces *PROLCV* in

the explanation of *ANTISTRIP*. Table 3 shows results of interest when an *individual* vote on one of the socio-ethical issues covered by the SI Index replaces *PROLCV*. The striking finding is how well voting on an issue with as much pocketbook content as SMCRA can be explained by senators' positions on the death penalty, sex education, the neutron bomb, the ceding of the Panama Canal, the immigration of avowed communists, and so on. In every case, the social issue variable has a strongly positive impact on *ANTISTRIP*.[19] Furthermore, the explanatory power of the Capture-plus-Ideology Model is remarkably similar when social issue voting replaces *PROLCV*. As might be expected, this is most evident when indexes are used. The thrust of these first results tilts toward the interpretation of *PROLCV* as reflecting relatively pure ideology.

B. *Isolating the Purest Part of Senator Ideology*

In an analysis of voting on the aggregate bundle of issues senators faced in the 96th Congress, Peltzman (1982) demonstrates that, at least on economic issues, measures of senatorial ideology (for example, ADA rating scales and senators' choices of party affiliation) stand in for a detailed list of constituent characteristics that plausibly correspond to their underlying economic interests. In the following analysis, we assume that this finding applies in the particular case of SMCRA. We further allow capture by ideological constituents. We then split measured ideology into that part that can be explained by constituent characteristics and the remaining senator-specific component. Our primary object is to examine whether the latter has any explanatory power.

We first estimate *PROLCV* and the SI Index as functions of the types of factors suggested by Kau and Rubin, and by Peltzman (1982)—factor such as general constituent characteristics and each senator's *PARTY* (Democrat = 1). Included constitu-

---

[18]Votes are from *Congressional Quarterly Almanac* (1977, 1978) and are described in our earlier paper.

[19]The *beta* coefficient for the SI Index (0.57) is the second largest in the model.

292   *THE AMERICAN ECONOMIC REVIEW*   *JUNE 1984*

TABLE 2—IDEOLOGY, SOCIAL POLICIES, AND SMCRA VOTING: REPRESENTATIVE RESULTS[a]

Explanatory Variable	Communist Immigration	Death Penalty	SI Index	Panama Canal Index	PROLCV[b]
IDEOLOGY	0.842	1.013	0.296	0.193	0.466
	(5.92)	(7.19)	(9.62)	(8.93)	(10.05)
MC	−0.503	−0.464	−0.372	−0.434	−0.375
	(−4.22)	(−4.23)	(−3.44)	(−4.02)	(−3.47)
SURFRES	−21.157	−15.152	−16.204	−16.845	−17.198
	(−2.07)	(−1.46)	(−1.61)	(−1.67)	(−1.71)
UNDERRES	15.519	11.025	12.201	13.079	14.132
	(3.43)	(1.77)	(2.04)	(2.17)	(2.37)
SPLITRIGHTS	−1.077	−16.656	19.663	45.120	68.488
	(−0.02)	(−0.29)	(0.41)	(0.93)	(1.40)
ENVIROS	41.602	61.048	21.450	44.194	0.501
	(2.02)	(3.13)	(1.09)	(2.29)	(0.02)
UNRECLAIMED	0.014	0.022	0.011	0.013	0.015
	(2.75)	(3.86)	(2.10)	(2.46)	(3.03)
CONSUME	−0.223	−0.301	−0.280	−0.293	−0.440
	(−0.88)	(−1.14)	(−1.16)	(−1.18)	(−1.83)
HSURF	−0.048	−0.556	−0.380	−0.428	0.017
	(−0.19)	(−2.19)	(−1.60)	(−1.77)	(0.07)
HUNDER	0.159	0.435	0.416	0.407	0.150
	(0.53)	(1.43)	(1.50)	(1.39)	(0.54)
HENVIROS	0.164	1.370	0.192	0.962	−1.286
	(0.13)	(1.18)	(0.17)	(0.87)	(−1.14)
HCONSUME	−0.466	−0.138	−0.138	−0.197	−0.261
	(−2.21)	(−0.64)	(−0.67)	(−0.96)	(−1.29)
Constant	0.343	−0.614	0.730	0.111	1.414
	(0.69)	(−1.23)	(1.53)	(0.24)	(2.86)
$\bar{R}^2$	0.54	0.66	0.71	0.67	0.74

[a] See fn a, Table 1.
[b] From Table 1, Capture-plus-Ideology Model.

ent characteristics consist of demographic variables *and* measures intended to reflect constituents' independent ideological interests. By employing demographic variables, we are accepting the methodology of those who have found that senators' pure ideological goals play no role in legislative politics (Peltzman, 1982) and that demographic variables provide suitable proxies for constituents' underlying economic interests.[20]

[20] Becker (1983) also argues that demographics provide natural groupings for constituents' interests. However, Arrow's 1963 General Possibility Theorem and the associated literature on coalitions, cycling, and electoral equilibria (see Dennis Mueller, 1979, for an excellent survey) suggest less confidence in the implicit econometric assumption (embodied in this work and elsewhere) that states' constituent characteristics can be mapped uniquely into their choices of elected representatives. Such concerns over uniqueness and existence, however, do not provide guidance as to why we find below that the explanatory power of constituent interests improves

The variables *ENVIROS* and *HENVIROS* are included to reflect constituents' (environmental) ideological interests. More generally, constituent ideology may be reflected by a measure such as the percentage of the state's vote going to McGovern (*MCGOV*) in the 1972 presidential election. The recognized hopelessness of McGovern's candidacy at election time probably made voting on the basis of investment motives unusually fruitless, and, by Stigler's (1972) argument, votes cast would uncommonly reflect ideological consumption motives.[21] Thus, *MCGOV* is

as a senator approaches his next electoral test (if that senator is not retiring!). This is consistent, however, with the interpretation of at least the part of the ideology measures which is *not* related to constituent characteristics as ideological shirking (see Section III, Part D, below).

[21] George McGovern was president of the ADA in 1976–78.

TABLE 3—IDEOLOGY, SOCIAL POLICIES, AND
SMCRA VOTING: SOCIAL ISSUE VOTES[a]

Issue:	Coefficient	$\bar{R}^2$
Communist Immigration	0.842 (5.92)	0.54
Death Penalty	1.013 (7.19)	0.66
Pardon Draft Resisters	0.902 (6.53)	0.57
Sex Education	1.177 (7.70)	0.64
Neutron Bomb	0.893 (5.90)	0.54
School Desegregation	0.945 (6.67)	0.62
Abortion	0.591 (4.73)	0.53
Child Pornography	0.623 (3.52)	0.44
Pregnancy Disability	1.209 (6.07)	0.56
Pregnancy Discrimination	1.319 (7.11)	0.61
Cuba in Africa	0.882 (5.54)	0.62
Loans to Communists	0.888 (6.45)	0.55
Panama Canal Treaty	1.185 (8.64)	0.65

[a]Capture-plus-ideology specification, Table 2; *t*-statistics are shown in parentheses.

included in the explanation of *PROLCV* and the SI Index. Arguably, it is correlated with left-out constituent characteristics; but the exact source of *MCGOV* is irrelevant to our purpose of isolating that portion of *senators'* voting which is not related to some constituent (economic *or* ideological) interest. The source of *PARTY*, on the other hand, is a matter of concern.

If the list of included constituent characteristics is complete, *PARTY* reflects senator-specific "non-economic factors" (Peltzman, 1982) such as a senator's world view (liberal or conservative) at the time of the party affiliation choice. In the absence of a guarantee that our set of constituent characteristics is complete, we perform our analysis from both perspectives: party as ideology and party as proxy for unidentified constituent interests. The latter interpretation is rendered less plausible by the inclusion of *MCGOV*.

The estimated models of *PROLCV* and the SI Index (see our earlier paper) closely resemble the patterns of correlation reported by Kau and Rubin, Kalt (1981), and Peltzman (1982).[22] Their primary role here is to allow the breaking down of ideology. Specifically, *PROLCV* and the SI Index are split into that part predicted by constituent (economic and ideological) interests and a residual component. The fitted component (denoted the constituent part) of *PROLCV* and the SI Index is obtained both with *PARTY* included as a possible left-out interest proxy and with *PARTY* excluded. Correspondingly, the residual, senator-specific component consists of either each model's prediction errors alone or these errors plus the fitted *PARTY* effect. If there is any senator ideology at work in *PROLCV* or SI voting, this senator-specific component is the purest part that might be isolated.

The constituent part and the senator-specific component of *PROLCV* and, alternatively, the SI Index are entered as separate explanatory variables in the model of *ANTISTRIP*. Clearly, given previous results, the constituent part of the ideology measures should have a significant effect on *ANTISTRIP*. Of central interest, however, is the effect of the senator-specific part of the ideology measures. If senators are well policed on strip mining issues or if, when shirking, they do so nonideologically and independent of constituent interests, this variable should not be systematically related to *ANTISTRIP* voting. The alternative hypothesis that the senator-specific variable has a significantly positive impact on *ANTISTRIP* depends on two conditions. First, the variable must be isolating senators' pursuit of their own altruistic, publicly interested goals on general environmental issues (*PROLCV*) or socio-ethical matters (the SI Index).

[22]Variables included are *PARTY, MCGOV, ENVIROS,* per capita income, voter educational attainment, the fraction of state personal income generated by manufacturing, voter age, the urban-rural distribution of voters, the rate of growth of the state economy, and a southern dummy. Results of interest here are insensitive to lengthening the list of variables to include, for example, racial characteristics, unionization, and the blue-collar/white-collar split.

TABLE 4—LCV IDEOLOGY AND CONSTITUENT INTERESTS IN SMCRA VOTING[a]

Explanatory Variable	Excluding Party & Error Part of PROLCV		Party & Error Part of PROLCV		Excluding Error Part of PROLCV		Error Part of PROLCV	
	Coefficient	Beta	Coefficient	Beta	Coefficient	Beta	Coefficient	Beta
Senator-Specific Part of PROLCV								
Party & Error	–	–	0.442	0.45	–	–	–	–
			(7.73)					
Error Only	–	–	–	–	–	–	0.401	0.30
							(4.89)	
Constituent Part of PROLCV	0.615	0.48	0.527	0.41	0.570	0.56	0.511	0.50
	(6.45)		(5.49)		(8.83)		(7.78)	
MC	−0.422	−0.24	−0.370	−0.21	−0.483	−0.28	−0.389	−0.22
	(−3.91)		(−3.42)		(−4.50)		(−3.57)	
SURFRES	−25.826	−0.86	−18.427	−0.61	−24.446	−0.81	−18.615	−0.62
	(−2.54)		(−1.80)		(−2.42)		(−1.83)	
UNDERRES	18.634	0.96	14.894	0.77	17.467	0.90	14.860	0.77
	(3.08)		(2.46)		(2.91)		(2.47)	
SPLITRIGHTS	66.982	0.12	76.481	0.13	80.400	0.14	75.804	0.13
	(1.33)		(1.52)		(1.62)		(1.53)	
ENVIROS	−8.770	−0.03	−7.932	−0.03	6.150	0.02	−2.794	−0.01
	(−0.37)		(−0.34)		(0.30)		(−0.14)	
UNRECLAIMED	0.016	0.24	0.015	0.22	0.017	0.25	0.015	0.22
	(3.15)		(2.97)		(3.49)		(3.06)	
CONSUME	−0.493	−0.15	−0.455	−0.14	−0.544	−0.16	−0.465	−0.14
	(−2.04)		(−1.89)		(−2.26)		(−1.92)	
HSURF	0.009	0.00+	0.043	0.01	−0.115	−0.03	0.009	0.00+
	(0.04)		(0.18)		(−0.48)		(0.04)	
HUNDER	0.373	0.08	0.168	0.04	0.571	0.12	0.223	0.05
	(1.35)		(0.60)		(2.05)		(0.78)	
HENVIROS	−0.630	−0.04	−1.474	−0.08	−0.883	−0.05	−1.379	−0.08
	(−0.54)		(−1.27)		(−0.78)		(−1.21)	
HCONSUME	−0.139	−0.04	−0.225	−0.07	−0.032	−0.01	−0.205	−0.06
	(−0.67)		(−1.08)		(−0.16)		(−0.98)	
Constant	1.706	–	1.590	–	1.190	–	1.454	–
	(3.10)		(2.89)		(2.42)		(2.93)	
$\bar{R}^2$	0.57		0.74		0.67		0.74	

[a] See fn. a, Table 1.

Second, senators must have pursued these goals in their voting on the specific issue of coal strip mining policy.

Table 4 reports estimated *ANTISTRIP* models under the fitting and splitting of *PROLCV*. Table 5 reports the analogous case for SI ideology. As anticipated, the constituent parts of both *PROLCV* and the SI Index have a strongly positive influence on *ANTISTRIP*. Independent of the interpretation of *PARTY* (i.e., ideology or interest proxy), the senator-specific measure also has a highly significant and positive effect on

ANTISTRIP voting. In fact, in every case, its inclusion appreciably improves the explanatory power of the model.[23] Further, it seems noteworthy that these conclusions are not obviously weaker when looking at the senator-specific part of *social issue* voting.

The results of Tables 4 and 5 may, of course, be due to the exclusion of some

[23] In every case, the hypothesis that the senator-specific variable has no effect on the model's explanatory power is rejected at above the 99 percent confidence level.

VOL. 74 NO. 3   KALT AND ZUPAN: CAPTURE AND IDEOLOGY OF POLITICS   295

TABLE 5—SOCIAL ISSUE IDEOLOGY AND CONSTITUENT INTERESTS IN SMCRA VOTING[a]

Explanatory Variable	Excluding Party & Error Part of Index		Party & Error Part of Index		Excluding Error Part of Index		Error Part of Index	
	Coefficient	Beta	Coefficient	Beta	Coefficient	Beta	Coefficient	Beta
Senator-Specific Part of Index								
Party & Error	–	–	0.288 (7.86)	0.44	–	–	–	–
Error Only	–	–	–	–	–	–	0.233 (4.93)	0.29
Constituent Part of Index	0.452 (5.55)	0.38	0.326 (3.94)	0.27	0.501 (8.44)	0.52	0.393 (6.20)	0.41
MC	−0.432 (−4.00)	−0.25	−0.369 (−3.40)	−0.21	−0.473 (−4.41)	−0.27	−0.389 (−3.58)	−0.22
SURFRES	−20.969 (−2.08)	−0.70	−16.575 (−1.64)	−0.55	−20.761 (−2.06)	−0.69	−17.593 (−1.74)	−0.58
UNDERRES	15.148 (2.53)	0.78	12.433 (2.07)	0.64	14.765 (2.47)	0.76	12.984 (2.17)	0.67
SPLITRIGHTS	16.589 (0.34)	0.03	22.087 (0.45)	0.04	40.386 (0.83)	0.07	31.148 (0.64)	0.05
ENVIROS	18.950 (0.86)	0.06	17.641 (0.80)	0.06	19.517 (0.97)	0.06	14.273 (0.71)	0.05
UNRECLAIMED	0.016 (3.10)	0.24	0.011 (2.08)	0.16	0.016 (3.23)	0.24	0.012 (2.27)	0.18
CONSUME	−0.355 (−1.48)	−0.11	−0.282 (−1.17)	−0.09	−0.413 (−1.72)	−0.12	−0.315 (−1.31)	−0.10
HSURF	−0.186 (−0.78)	−0.04	−0.369 (−1.54)	−0.09	−0.270 (−1.14)	−0.06	−0.354 (−1.49)	−0.08
HUNDER	0.457 (1.64)	0.10	0.426 (1.53)	0.09	0.665 (2.38)	0.14	0.507 (1.80)	0.11
HENVIROS	−0.105 (−0.09)	−0.01	0.066 (0.06)	0.01	−0.744 (−0.66)	−0.04	−0.290 (−0.26)	−0.02
HCONSUME	−0.178 (−0.86)	−0.05	−0.121 (−0.58)	−0.04	−0.020 (−0.10)	−0.01	−0.063 (−0.30)	−0.02
Constant	1.227 (2.31)	–	0.823 (1.55)	–	1.022 (2.09)	–	0.916 (1.87)	–
$\bar{R}^2$	0.54		0.71		0.65		0.72	

[a]See fn. a, Table 1.

as-of-yet-unidentified SMCRA-specific constituent interest—perhaps even an out-of-state interest, or a non-SMCRA interest served indirectly by logrolling. Tables 4 and 5, however, reduce the likelihood that such a variable exists. That is, if such a variable were to exist, it would have to be relatively orthogonal to not only states' identified SMCRA-specific interests, but also to the constituent interest variables used in the explanation of *PROLCV* and the SI Index. Moreover, it would have to be *simultaneously* and causally (in the capture sense) related to voting on coal strip-mining regulation, gen-

eral environmental issues, sex education, the neutron bomb, child pornography, etc. Pending further search for such a variable, Tables 4 and 5 further suggest that ideology probably should not be excluded from analyses of particular-issue politics.

C. The Role of Left-Out Constituent Characteristics

The preceding analysis has assumed that a large part of senators' apparent ideology is correlated with causal constituent (economic or ideological) interests left out of the basic capture-plus-ideology explanation of *ANTI-STRIP*. As noted in Section I, however, such correlations could arise for two very different reasons. On the one hand, it may be happenstance: what looks like senator ideology is the reflection of left-out constituent economic or ideological interests that actually have direct effects on SMCRA voting. On the other hand, *PROLCV* and the SI Index may be entirely pure senator ideology, unrelated to the interests constituents have in the *specific* issue of SMCRA, but related to broad constituent characteristics via Senate elections and voters' interests in putting the "right" ideologies into office—a la Downs.

The problem of inferring causation from correlation is notably difficult. In the case at hand, we approach this problem by focusing on whether there are different implications: 1) when the variables that are correlated with measures of ideology are operating directly on *ANTISTRIP*, as opposed to 2) when policing is imperfect and they operate indirectly through their impact on the types of senators elected (and, hence, the ideologies manifested by shirking senators).

One such difference in implications concerns the way the constituent characteristics (i.e., demographics, ideology, and perhaps *PARTY*) that explain *PROLCV* and the SI Index enter the explanation of *ANTISTRIP*. The same set of characteristics may play a causal role in all three types of voting. The obvious differences in the economic content

of SMCRA, general environmental issues, and socio-ethical matters, however, suggest that the roles played by the individual variables in this set will not be identical across the three cases in terms of their size, signs, and significance. Consequently, if the variables that make up the constituent part of ideology play direct causal roles in SMCRA voting, their explanatory power will be higher if they are not constrained to enter the *ANTISTRIP* model in the same linear combinations they have in the explanation of *PROLCV* or the SI Index. On the other hand, the constituent part of ideology may in fact be pure senator ideology in the particular case of SMCRA *and* the route of influence by the set of general constituent characteristics may thus be the indirect Downsian route. If so, constraining these characteristics to enter the *ANTISTRIP* model in the same way they enter the explanation of the ideology measures should not affect their explanatory power.

Results when the general constituent characteristics are constrained to enter the *ANTISTRIP* model as the fitted constituent parts of *PROLCV* and the SI Index are what is reported in Tables 4 and 5. Table 6 compares the explanatory power of the constrained characteristics with that obtained in the unconstrained case (see our earlier paper for full results). Table 6 indicates that, of course, the R^2 is higher when the general constituent characteristics are not con-

TABLE 6—IDEOLOGY AND THE PATH OF GENERAL CONSTITUENT
CHARACTERISTICS IN ANTISTRIP VOTING

Model	LCV Ideology: Constituent Characteristics		SI Ideology: Constituent Characteristics	
	Unconstrained	Constrained[a]	Unconstrained	Constrained[b]
Party as Ideology:				
R^2	0.78	0.77	0.79	0.75
$\bar{R}^2$	0.73	0.74	0.73	0.71
F-Test[c]		84%		14%
Party as Interest Proxy:				
R^2	0.79	0.77	0.79	0.76
$\bar{R}^2$	0.73	0.74	0.74	0.72
F-Test[c]		89%		21%

[a]From Table 4.
[b]From Table 5.
[c]The level of significance at which equality of the two regressions may be rejected. Lower values signify increased confidence in rejection of equality.

strained. In the SI Index case, the adjusted R^2 also improves when the characteristics are unconstrained—although only slightly. In the *PROLCV* case, however, the adjusted R^2 actually falls when constituent characteristics are unconstrained. In each case, classical tests of the equality of the constrained and unconstrained models provide little confidence that equality can be rejected.

The general constituent characteristics that might have been supposed to be directly affecting SMCRA voting appear to be operating indirectly through the pure ideology of elected and shirking senators. That is, *PROLCV* and the SI Index do not appear to be standing in for otherwise unidentified economic or ideological interests that might have captured senators in their voting on the particular issue of SMCRA. The suggested conclusion is that a senator's overall bundle of votes reflects the constituent preferences that were expressed on election day. The interests of those same constituents, when those interests are subsequently reshuffled by the prospective effects of a particular decision on the Senate floor, however, do not fully control the senator on that decision. The capture theory may work well as a theory of elections, but not so well as a theory of issue-specific politics.

D. *Electoral Policing and Ideological Shirking*

If the evident roles of *PROLCV* and the SI Index in SMCRA voting largely reflect senators' own ideological preferences, they do so because of imperfect issue-specific policing. Accordingly, the extent to which shirking senators' notions of the public interest enter their voting behavior should be systematically related to the opportunity costs of shirking. The investigation of this cost is a promising source of comparative statics tests for the presence, importance, and rationality of ideology in representative politics. In general terms, the opportunity cost of shirking should vary directly with constituents' incentives to police (i.e., the producers' and consumers' surplus stakes); and vary inversely with organization-information costs and institutional impediments

to monitoring. The cost of shirking should also be inversely related to the security, somehow measured, with which a senator intending to remain in office holds his or her seat. This security is plausibly related to such factors as the senator's margin of last victory, tenure, committee power (a major source of facilitation services), and personal wealth. These relationships obviously involve substantial simultaneity—tenure, for example, affords senators security, but they get tenure by serving their constituents.

The development of a full simultaneous model of shirking is considerably beyond the scope of this study. Nevertheless, one component of the cost of shirking that is clearly determined exogenously can be examined— the proximity of a senator's next electoral test (Robert Barro, 1973). In a world in which voters have positive discount rates and/or memories that decay, a senator can, in a sense, run down his or her security capital in midterm and build it back up again as the next election approaches. Ideological shirking should, therefore, be directly related to the time remaining in a senator's term.

Table 7 reports one test of this hypothesis. In our sample, 33 senators were up for reelection in 1978. If present, ideological shirking should have been less prevalent (*ceteris paribus*) among these senators than in the sample as a whole during the strip-mining voting of 1977. To examine this, we look for errors in the predictions of the Capture-plus-Ideology Model of *ANTISTRIP*. On any particular vote, the expected outcome, yea or nay, is given by the sign of the senator's predicted *ANTISTRIP* value. The absolute magnitude of this value suggests the confidence to be placed in the expected outcome. An error is inferred when an actual outcome on a vote differs from the expected outcome. An error is interpreted as running against a senator's ideology when its sign is opposite to the sign of the senator's LCV rating.

Twelve errors are made in predicting SMCRA voting in 1977. Of these, approximately 50 percent were made by the 33 percent of the senators who were up for reelection. Moreover, of the 6 up-for-reelection

TABLE 7—THE EFFECT OF ELECTORAL POLICING ON IDEOLOGICAL VOTING

Senator's Electoral Status	Incorrect Predictions in 1977[a]		of which:	Voted Against LCV Ideology	
	Number	Percent of Total		Number	Percent of Col. 1
Up for Reelection	6	50		5	83.3
Not Up for Reelection	6	50		3	50
Total	12			8	

[a] Predictions based on Table 1, Capture-plus-Ideology Model. "Incorrect" signifies sign of predicted *ANTISTRIP* differed from sign of actual *ANTISTRIP* voting in 1977.

senators predicted incorrectly, 5 were voting against their ideologies; and the remaining senator voting with his ideology was retiring. Of the 6 not-up-for-reelection errors, only 3 were represented by senators voting against their ideologies. The probability that this pattern was generated by chance is very low.[24] Thus, it appears that the proximity of the next election inhibits ideological shirking: senators shirk less as the policemen approach.

IV. Summary and Conclusions

The evidence thus far suggests the need for some broadening in the economic theory of politics. This theory has effectively precluded from its list of determining factors anything other than the parochial, narrowly self-interested objectives of policymakers' constituents. This reflects the fact that economic, capture models of regulation are largely institution-free. Our analysis has attempted to bring certain aspects of the property rights theory of institutions—policing costs, opportunism, appropriability—to bear on the legislative process. Specifically, we have asked whether slack in control of legislators is empirically important enough to warrant incorporation into positive models of politics. At the level of specific-issue policymaking, the answer appears to be yes. Our results also

suggest that the discretionary consumption afforded policymakers by institutional slack is taken, to a substantial degree, in the form of rational altruistic-ideological promotion of self-defined notions of the public interest. At least in the case of federal coal strip-mining policy, this ideological shirking appears to have significantly affected the course of public policy.

If the concept of ideological shirking does prove to be significant, its usefulness will depend on the development of models that can predict the conditions (for example, types of issues, institutional settings, economic contexts) under which ideological shirking is likely to be an important phenomenon. Of course, it still may be that the phenomenon does not even exist. There may yet be constituent interests missing from this and previous analyses that will explain away ideology's importance in specific-issue politics. The search for these interests should continue. For now, it appears that the economic theory of regulation will have to keep the door open to ideological behavior.

REFERENCES

Abrams, Burton A. and Settle, Russell F., "The Economic Theory of Regulation and Public Financing of Presidential Elections," *Journal of Political Economy*, April 1978, *86*, 245–57.

Alchian, Armen and Kessel, Reuben, "Competition, Monopoly, and the Pursuit of Pecuniary Gain," in H. G. Lewis, ed., *Aspects of Labor Economics*, Princeton:

[24] Bearing in mind the small sample, a *Chi*-squared test indicates that the hypothesis that the contingencies in Table 7 were generated by chance can be rejected at above the 99 percent confidence level.

National Bureau of Economic Research, 1962, 156–83.

_____ and Demsetz, Harold, "Production, Information Costs, and Economic Organization," *American Economic Review*, December 1972, *62*, 777–95.

Arrow, Kenneth J., "Gifts and Exchanges," *Philosophy and Public Affairs*, Summer 1972, *1*, 343–62.

Ashenfelter, Orley and Kelley, Stanley, Jr., "Determinants of Participation in Presidential Elections," *Journal of Law and Economics*, December 1975, *18*, 162–70.

Barro, Robert J., "The Control of Politicians: An Economic Model," *Public Choice*, Spring 1973, *14*, 19–42.

Barzel, Yoram and Silberberg, Eugene, "Is the Act of Voting Rational?," *Public Choice*, Fall 1973, *16*, 51–58.

Becker, Gary S., *The Economics of Discrimination*, Chicago: University of Chicago Press, 1957.

_____, "A Theory of Social Interactions," *Journal of Political Economy*, December 1974, *82*, 1063–93.

_____, "Altruism, Egoism, and Genetic Fitness," *Journal of Economic Literature*, September 1976, *14*, 817–26.

_____, "Competition Among Pressure Groups for Political Influence," *Quarterly Journal of Economics*, August 1983, *98*, 371–98.

Belsley, David A., Kuh, Edwin and Welsch, Roy E., *Regression Diagnostics: Identifying Influential Data and Sources of Collinearity*, New York: Wiley & Sons, 1980.

Brennan, Geoffrey and Buchanan, James M., "Voter Choice and the Evaluation of Political Alternatives: A Critique of Public Choice," unpublished, Center for the Study of Public Choice, Virginia Polytechnic Institute and State University, 1982.

Breton, Albert, *The Economic Theory of Representative Government*, Chicago: Aldine Publishing, 1974.

Buchanan, James M. and Tullock, Gordon, *The Calculus of Consent*, Ann Arbor: University of Michigan Press, 1965.

De Alessi, Louis, "On the Nature and Consequences of Private and Public Enterprises," *Minnesota Law Review*, October 1982, *67*, 191–209.

Downs, Anthony, *An Economic Theory of Democracy*, New York: Harper and Row, 1957.

Ferejohn, John A., "On the Decline of Competition in Congressional Elections," *American Political Science Review*, March 1977, *71*, 166–76.

Fiorina, Morris and Noll, Roger G., "Voters, Legislators, and Bureaucracy: Institutional Design in the Public Sector," *American Economic Review Proceedings*, May 1978, *68*, 256–60.

Frey, Bruno S. and Lau, Lawrence J., "Towards a Mathematical Model of Government Behavior," *Zeitschrift fur Nationalokonomie*, December 1968, *28*, 355–80.

Gart, John J. and Zweifel, James, "On the Bias of Various Estimators of the Logit and its Variance with Application to Quantal Bioassay," *Biometrika*, June 1967, *54*, 181–87.

Goeldner, Charles R. and Dicke, Karen P., *Travel Trends in the United States and Canada*, Boulder: GSBA, University of Colorado, 1981.

Hirshleifer, Jack, "Competition, Cooperation and Conflict in Economics and Biology," *American Economic Review Proceedings*, May 1978, *68*, 238–43.

Jensen, Michael C. and Meckling, William H., "Theory of the Firm: Managerial Behavior, Agency Costs and Ownership Structure," *Journal of Financial Economics*, October 1976, *3*, 305–60.

Kalt, Joseph P., *The Economics and Politics of Oil Price Regulation*, Cambridge: MIT Press, 1981.

_____, "The Costs and Benefits of Federal Regulation of Coal Strip Mining," *Natural Resources Journal*, October 1983, *23*, 893–915.

_____ and Zupan, Mark A., "Further Evidence on Capture and Ideology in the Economic Theory of Politics," unpublished, Harvard Institute of Economic Research, April 1983.

Kau, James B. and Rubin, Paul H., "Self-Interest, Ideology and Logrolling in Congressional Voting," *Journal of Law and Economics*, October 1979, *22*, 365–84.

Klein, Benjamin, Crawford, Robert G. and Alchian, Armen, "Vertical Integration, Appropriable Rents, and the Competitive

Contracting Process," *Journal of Law and Economics*, October 1978, *21*, 297–326.

Manne, Henry G., "Mergers and the Market for Corporate Control," *Journal of Political Economy*, April 1965, *73*, 110–20.

Mitchell, Edward J., "The Basis of Congressional Energy Policy," *Texas Law Review*, March 1979, *57*, 591–613.

Mueller, Dennis C., *Public Choice*, Cambridge: Cambridge University Press, 1979.

Olson, Mancur, *The Logic of Collective Action*, New York: Shocken Books, 1971.

Peltzman, Sam, "Toward a More General Theory of Regulation," *Journal of Law and Economics*, August 1976, *19*, 211–40.

_____, "Constituent Interest and Congressional Voting," unpublished, University of Chicago Economic and Legal Organization Workshop, February 1982.

Phelps, Charles E., Book Review: "Kalt's *The Economics and Politics of Oil Price Regulation...*," *Bell Journal of Economics*, Spring 1982, *13*, 289–95.

Riker, William H. and Ordeshook, Peter C., "A Theory of the Calculus of Voting," *American Political Science Review*, March 1968, *62*, 25–42.

Rothenberg, Jerome, "A Model of Economic and Political Decision Making," in J. Margolis, ed., *The Public Economy of Urban Communities*, Washington: Resources for the Future, Inc., 1965.

Samuelson, Paul, "The Pure Theory of Public Expenditure," *Review of Economics and Statistics*, November 1954, *36*, 387–89.

Sax, Joseph L., *Mountains Without Handrails, Reflections on the National Parks*, Ann Arbor: University of Michigan Press, 1980.

Schulze, William D. et al., *The Benefits of Preserving Visibility in the National Parklands of the Southwest*, Washington: U.S. Environmental Protection Agency, 1981.

Stigler, George J., "The Economic Theory of Regulation," *Bell Journal of Economics*,

Spring 1971, *2*, 3–21.

_____, "Economic Competition and Political Competition," *Public Choice*, Fall 1972, *13*, 91–106.

Tiebout, Charles M., "A Pure Theory of Local Expenditures," *Journal of Political Economy*, October 1956, *64*, 416–24.

Tollison, Robert D. and Willett, Thomas D., "Some Simple Economics of Voting and Not Voting," *Public Choice*, Winter 1975, *24*, 43–49.

Tullock, Gordon, "A (Partial) Rehabilitation of the Public Interest Theory," unpublished, Center for the Study of Public Choice, Virginia Polytechnic Institute and State University, 1982.

Williamson, Oliver E., *Markets and Hierarchies: Analysis and Antitrust Implications*, New York: Free Press, 1975.

Zellner, Arnold and Lee, Tong H., "Joint Estimation of Relationships Involving Discrete Random Variables," *Econometrica*, April 1965, *33*, 382–94.

Congressional Quarterly, Inc., *Congressional Quarterly Almanac*, Washington, various years.

ICF, Inc., *Final Report: Energy and Economic Impacts of H.R. 13950 (Surface Mining Control and Reclamation Act of 1976)*, Washington, 1977.

League of Conservation Voters, *How Senators Voted on Critical Environmental Issues*, Washington, 1978.

McGraw-Hill, Inc., *Keystone Coal Industry Manual*, New York, various years.

National Coal Association, *Coal Data 1978*, Washington, 1979.

_____, *Steam Electric Plant Factors*, Washington, 1978.

U.S. Department of Commerce, *Statistical Abstract of the United States*, Washington: USGPO, various years.

_____, *Survey of Current Business*, Washington: USGPO, various months.

[2]

The Determinants of Pesticide Regulation: A Statistical Analysis of EPA Decision Making

Maureen L. Cropper

University of Maryland and Resources for the Future

William N. Evans

University of Maryland

Stephen J. Berardi

U.S. Department of Energy

Maria M. Ducla-Soares

New University of Lisbon

Paul R. Portney

Resources for the Future

This paper examines the EPA's decision to cancel or continue the registrations of cancer-causing pesticides that went through the special review process between 1975 and 1989. Despite claims to the contrary, our analysis indicates that the EPA indeed balanced risks against benefits in regulating pesticides: Risks to human health or

We would like to thank Scott Farrow, Bill Gormley, Darrell Hueth, John Mullahy, John Quiggin, and an anonymous reviewer for their comments on an earlier version of this paper, as well as participants at seminars at Resources for the Future, Stanford University, Duke University, George Mason University, the University of Chicago, the University of California, Berkeley, and the University of California, Santa Barbara. We would especially like to thank Roger Holtorf and Leonard Gianessi for their help during the project.

[*Journal of Political Economy*, 1992, vol. 100, no. 1]
© 1992 by The University of Chicago. All rights reserved. 0022-3808/92/0001-0005$01.50

the environment increased the likelihood that a particular pesticide use was canceled by the EPA; at the same time, the larger the benefits associated with a particular use, the lower was the likelihood of cancellation. Intervention by special-interest groups was also important in the regulatory process. Comments by grower organizations significantly reduced the probability of cancellation, whereas comments by environmental advocacy groups increased the probability of cancellation. Our analysis suggests that the EPA is fully capable of weighing benefits and costs when regulating environmental hazards; however, the implicit value placed on health risks—$35 million per applicator cancer case avoided—may be considered high by some persons.

When asked how standards should be set in environmental, safety, and health regulation, virtually all economists would urge that at least some account be taken of economic factors. Most would probably support the view that such standards should be set at levels that equate marginal social benefits and costs. This approach does not command overwhelming support when legislation is written, however. In fact, U.S. environmental policy could be termed schizophrenic with respect to the balancing of benefits and costs in standard setting: Most major statutes appear to *prohibit* such balancing, with the Clean Air and Clean Water acts perhaps being the most prominent examples; however, other important environmental laws *require* that benefits and costs be balanced when decisions are made. This is the case with the Toxic Substances Control Act and also the Federal Insecticide, Fungicide, and Rodenticide Act (FIFRA), the latter being the statute under which most U.S. pesticide regulation is conducted.

What laws require is one thing; what agencies do is another. In environmental regulation, for example, White (1981) has argued that although the Clean Air Act has been construed by courts to prohibit consideration of costs in setting ambient air quality standards (*Lead Industries Assoc., Inc. v. EPA* [1980]), the Environmental Protection Agency has in fact taken economics into account in setting such standards for common pollutants. Similarly, for a time the EPA explicitly balanced health risks against economic costs in regulating certain carcinogenic air pollutants. Others have argued, however, that even when the relevant statutes require the balancing of economic and health considerations, agencies will always take action against cancer risks that exceed certain statistical thresholds, often referred to as "bright lines" (Milvy 1986; Travis et al. 1987; Travis and Hattemer-Frey 1988), regardless of costs.

Finally, still others maintain that no matter what "objective" factors the statutes direct regulatory agencies to consider, the agencies are sure to be influenced in their rule making in important and predictable ways by political considerations (Stigler 1971; Peltzman 1976). This view is of particular interest to us in light of the history of pesticide regulation, the focus of our attention here. Prior to the creation of the EPA in 1970, all pesticides were regulated by the Department of Agriculture. One of the reasons for transferring regulatory responsibility to the EPA was to lessen the influence of farmers and pesticide manufacturers in the regulatory process and increase the influence of environmental and consumer groups (Bosso 1987).

Although there is a substantial literature on the determinants of legislative voting on environmental issues (see Crandall 1983; Pashigian 1985; Yandle 1989; Hird 1990), there exists but one published analysis of EPA decision making to ascertain, ex post facto, the factors that explain the regulatory actions taken (see Magat, Krupnick, and Harrington 1986).[1] This paper presents such an analysis for a particular class of environmental regulations, namely, the EPA's decisions to allow or prohibit the continued use of certain pesticides on food crops. We are interested in whether the economic benefits that pesticides confer are, in fact, balanced against the risks these substances may pose to human health and the environment. We also examine the extent to which these decisions are affected by the active involvement of special-interest groups: on the one hand, the companies that manufacture pesticides and the farmers that use them and, on the other, the environmental advocacy organizations that often oppose the widespread application of pesticides.

We focus on three specific hypotheses. First, is the probability that the EPA will disallow continued use of a pesticide on a particular crop positively related to the risks that pesticide poses to human health and the environment and negatively related to the economic benefits associated with the use of the pesticide? In other words, does the EPA follow its congressional mandate under FIFRA? If both factors are taken into account by the EPA, what is the implicit "price" of the resulting risk reductions? This question is important because of concern that the cost per life saved as revealed in health and safety regulation differs markedly, both within and across agencies (Morrall 1986); this *may* signal an inefficient allocation of resources among lifesaving programs.[2]

Second, do special-interest groups—both business and environmental—affect the likelihood that certain pesticide uses will be

---

[1] For analyses of decision making at other government agencies, see McFadden (1975, 1976), Weingast and Moran (1983), and Thomas (1988).

[2] If individuals attach higher values to the reduction of certain kinds of risks (e.g., involuntary vs. voluntary) or if certain regulations save more life-years than others, variations in cost per life saved may be perfectly rational.

banned? If so, when opposite sides both intervene, do their efforts merely offset one another?

Third, can particular political appointees influence the likelihood of regulatory action? During the period covered by our study, the EPA was headed by five different administrators including Anne Burford, a Reagan appointee widely regarded as unsympathetic to environmentalists' concerns. We test the hypothesis that she had a significant impact on pesticide regulation during her tenure.

We have investigated these questions by assembling data on all cancer-causing pesticides that underwent special review by the EPA between 1975 and 1989. Under FIFRA, the special review process is initiated whenever a pesticide is thought to pose a danger to human health (e.g., cancer or adverse reproductive effects) or to wildlife; this review entails a risk-benefit analysis of the pesticide for every crop on which it is used. Following this analysis, the EPA issues a proposed decision and invites all interested parties to submit comments, which are compiled in a public docket. A final decision (or notice of final determination) is issued after the agency has reconsidered its proposed action in light of these comments and any new information it has developed. We have assembled data on the risks and benefits associated with each pesticide from official data published by the EPA, as well as information on which special-interest groups entered comments in the public docket.

These data are used to estimate a model that explains the probability that a pesticide was canceled for use on a particular crop, as a function of the risks and benefits associated with its use and as a function of political variables. Our findings provide both comfort and concern to those interested in improving the efficiency of environmental regulation.

I. An Overview of the EPA's Pesticide Registration Process

In its 1972 amendments to FIFRA, Congress required the EPA to reregister the approximately 40,000 pesticides previously approved for sale in the United States. In the 1978 amendments to FIFRA, this task was simplified by requiring reregistration of the 600 active ingredients used in these pesticides rather than the pesticides themselves.

Reregistration of each active ingredient requires assembling the data necessary to evaluate whether it causes "unreasonable adverse effects on the environment" for each use for which it is registered. By "use" is meant the application of a pesticide to a specific crop (e.g., alachlor on soybeans). If, in the process of data collection, it is determined that the active ingredient poses sufficient risks to humans or animals, it is put through the special review process. The purpose of the process is to determine whether the risks posed by the active ingredient are outweighed by the benefits of its use.

The results of these risk-benefit analyses are published along with the EPA's proposed regulatory decision. The following regulatory outcomes are considered for each use of the active ingredient: (1) cancellation of registration; (2) suspension of registration; (3) continuation of registration, subject to certain restrictions; or (4) unrestricted continuation of registration.

Publication of the proposed decision is followed by a comment period, during which members of the public, including growers, public-interest groups, and registrants, can respond. If cancellation or restrictions on use are contemplated, the U.S. Department of Agriculture and the EPA's Scientific Advisory Panel are asked to review the risk-benefit analyses. Final regulatory decisions, together with the names of all those who commented on the proposed decision, are then issued, and these decisions become law unless a hearing is requested by interested parties.

Between 1975, when the special review process was initiated, and 1989, a total of 68 special reviews were begun (U.S. Environmental Protection Agency 1989). Of these, 18 ended at a pre–special review stage, 37 had been completed by December 1989, and 13 were ongoing, as of that date. Our study focuses on a subset of the 37 substances for which reviews were completed, namely, those that both involve pesticides used on food crops and have been found to cause cancer in laboratory animals. We focus on this subset because health risks other than the risk of cancer are seldom quantified, which makes a statistical analysis of regulatory decisions difficult.

The set of food-use pesticides causing cancer in laboratory animals that have gone through special review is listed in table 1. Note that although there are only 19 such pesticides, there were 245 separate pesticide/crop combinations or uses. What we shall try to explain is the decision to cancel or not cancel each of these uses.[3]

---

[3] Of the 245 final decisions in our data base, 39 percent represent cancellations, 4 percent suspensions of registration for failure to provide data, 5 percent unrestricted continuations, and 52 percent continuations with restrictions. The types of restrictions typically imposed consist of measures to protect pesticide mixers and applicators, such as requiring that protective clothing be worn. These decisions are to be made by comparing the risks and benefits of the restrictions; however, the documents the EPA develops typically do not contain enough data to permit an analysis of each restriction. For this reason we consider only two regulatory outcomes: continuation of registration (with or without restrictions) and cancellation. Suspensions for failure to provide data are grouped with continuations since registrations are continued as soon as the data are provided.

180   JOURNAL OF POLITICAL ECONOMY

TABLE 1

ACTIVE INGREDIENTS IN THE PESTICIDE DATA BASE

Active Ingredient	Year of Decision	Number of Food-Use Registrations	Number of Proposed Cancellations	Number of Final Cancellations
DBCP	1978	12	1	12
Amitraz	1979	2	1	1
Chlorobenzilate	1979	3	2	2
Endrin	1979	8	4	4
Pronamide	1979	4	0	0
Dimethoate	1980	25	0	0
Benomyl	1982	26	0	0
Diallate	1982	10	10	0
Oxyfluorfen	1982	3	0	0
Toxaphene	1982	11	7	7
Trifluralin	1982	25	0	0
EDB	1983	18	4	18
Ethalfluralin	1983	3	0	0
Lindane	1983	8	7	0
Silvex	1985	6	6	6
2, 4, 5-T	1985	2	2	2
Dicofol	1986	4	4	0
Alachlor	1987	10	3	0
Captan	1989	65	65	44
Totals		245	116	96

II. Factors Influencing the Cancellation Decision

Risks of Pesticide Use

In deciding whether a pesticide should be canceled for use on a crop, the EPA is required to prevent any unreasonable risk to humans or the environment, taking into account the economic, social, and environmental costs and benefits of the use of the pesticide. Paramount among these risks is the risk of cancer to persons who mix and apply pesticides and to consumers who ingest pesticide residues on food.[4] Evidence that a chemical is carcinogenic usually comes from animal bioassays, which produce a relationship between pesticide dose and lifetime risk of cancer. This estimate is extrapolated to humans and multiplied by an estimate of human dosage (exposure) to estimate lifetime risk of cancer to a farm worker or consumer.[5]

---

[4] In its official documents, the EPA lists cancer risks to pesticide applicators and to persons who mix and load pesticides (mixer/loaders), but not to farm workers who harvest crops. Risks to farm workers are controlled by adjusting the time between pesticide application and harvest (the preharvest interval).

[5] It is well known that the methods used to calculate the slope of the dose-response

Lifetime cancer risks are typically much higher for pesticide applicators than for consumers of food products; for example, in our
sample the median estimated incremental lifetime cancer risk for pesticide applicators (as a result of applying a particular pesticide to a
particular crop) is one in 100,000 (1.0×10^{-5}), but it is only 2.3 in
100 million (2.3×10^{-8}) for consumers of food products.[6] The number of persons assumed to be exposed to dietary risks—usually the
entire U.S. population—is, however, much greater than the number
of applicators exposed to pesticides. The latter may range from a few
dozen to a few thousand, depending on the particular crop and the
number of acres treated, and the number of persons mixing pesticides is typically a few hundred.

This raises a very difficult regulatory issue: Should the EPA's decisions be driven by very high risks to certain individuals (the so-called
maximally exposed individuals) or by the overall risk to the entire
exposed population (i.e., the expected number of deaths)? Although
economists have typically emphasized the latter, regulatory officials
at the EPA and other agencies are often more preoccupied with reducing very high individual risks to acceptable levels.

In addition to cancer risks, pesticides may have adverse reproductive effects, causing fetal deformities or miscarriages or lowering the
sperm counts of applicators. While there is human evidence for the
latter effects, information on the mutagenic or teratogenic effects of
a chemical usually comes from animal experiments, and the extent
of such effects is generally difficult to quantify. Finally, the EPA is
required to consider the possibly adverse ecological effects of pesticides: Is the pesticide toxic to fish, birds, or wildlife or is it likely to
contaminate ecologically fragile environments such as wetlands?

Benefits of Pesticide Use

Against these risks, the EPA must weigh the benefits of use, that is,
the costs to consumers and producers of banning the pesticide on the
crop in question. Losses accrue if producers must switch to a more
costly substitute for the pesticide in question or if the substitute is an
imperfect one and yield losses will occur on cancellation. Decreases
in supply may, in turn, lead to price increases to consumers.

---

function, and those used to estimate human exposure to the pesticide, generally err
on the side of conservatism (Nichols and Zeckhauser 1986). The slope of the dose-
response function is the upper bound of a 95 percent confidence interval rather than
the midpoint.

[6] To put this in perspective, we note that the average lifetime cancer risk from all
causes is one-third.

Losses to producers from cancellation vary widely for the pesticides and crops studied here. The highest loss expected during the first year following cancellation is $227 million (1986 dollars) for alachlor on corn. Mean first-year losses, however, are considerably lower: only $9.1 million. In 35 percent of all cases, losses are negligible because of the availability of substitute pesticides. What is likely to be as important as the magnitude of losses is their distribution among growers. A 0.1 percent reduction in corn revenues will greatly exceed that associated with a 50 percent decrease in mango production; however, since there are relatively few mango growers, the distribution of losses is far more concentrated in the latter case than in the former.

The Role of Political Factors

This raises directly the question of the importance of interest groups in the regulatory process. Pesticide manufacturers are, of course, involved throughout: they are informed when the EPA contemplates a special review and are given an opportunity to rebut the presumption that the pesticide causes adverse effects to humans or to the environment. In addition to negotiating with the EPA, manufacturers are responsible for providing data on the risks of pesticide usage.

Farmers also bear the costs of cancellation and thus have an interest in dissuading the EPA from banning pesticides. One would expect farmers to become involved when the cost of switching to substitute pesticides is high and when the losses that would result constitute a large percentage of profits. An interesting question is at what stage in the regulatory process farmers become involved. While anecdotal evidence suggests communication between the EPA and grower organizations throughout the regulatory process, farmers have no need to exert leverage unless they feel that a pesticide is threatened with cancellation. Thus one would expect grower organizations or their representatives to comment more often when the EPA proposes to cancel rather than to allow continued use of the pesticide(s) in question.

Environmental groups, which attempt to identify and fight for the cancellation of pesticides hazardous to humans or wildlife, can be expected to behave differently. They may, moreover, exert an influence earlier in the regulatory process by bringing pesticide risks to the EPA's attention before the official comment period. Finally, one would expect the views of the EPA administrator to affect the outcome of the special review process since it is the job of the administrator to review the evidence on health and environmental risks and the economic effects associated with the cancellation decision and to issue a final decision.

III. Statistical Analysis of the EPA's Pesticide Decisions

If the EPA follows its mandate under FIFRA to take into account the economic, social, and environmental costs and benefits of the use of any pesticide, one would expect that pesticide i would be canceled for use on crop j if the value of the vector of risks associated with use, $\mathbf{R}_{ij}$, exceeded the weighted sum of benefits of use, $\mathbf{B}_{ij}$. When unmeasured components of risks and benefits, u_{ij}, are treated as random, the probability that pesticide i is canceled for use on crop j is

$$P(\text{cancel}_{ij}) = P(\alpha_1 \mathbf{R}_{ij} + \alpha_2 \mathbf{B}_{ij} + u_{ij} \geq 0), \tag{1}$$

where α_1 and α_2 are the vectors of policy weights attached to risks and benefits, respectively.

Special-interest groups enter the model by augmenting the vectors of risks and benefits considered by the EPA, or by altering the policy weights attached to risks and benefits. Suppose, for example, that $\mathbf{X}$ is a vector of variables indicating intervention in the policy-making process by each of several special-interest groups. Then the general model becomes

$$P(\text{cancel}_{ij}) = P(\alpha_1 \mathbf{R}_{ij} + \alpha_2 \mathbf{B}_{ij} + \delta_1 \mathbf{X}_{ij} + u_{ij} \geq 0). \tag{2}$$

An alternative to equation (2) frequently proposed by researchers in the risk assessment area is that risks and benefits are balanced only for intermediate risk levels but not when risks are very high or very low. This so-called bright-line theory of risk regulation hypothesizes that a health or safety regulation will always be undertaken if the risk to the maximally exposed individual, R, exceeds some risk threshold, R_{max}, and will never be adopted if the risk to the maximally exposed individual falls below some critical level, R_{min}. Between these thresholds, the theory holds, the regulation will be adopted if the risks outweigh the benefits. Formally,

$$
\begin{aligned}
P(\text{cancel}) &= 1 && \text{if } R \geq R_{max}, \\
P(\text{cancel}) &= \text{eq. (2)} && \text{if } R_{max} > R > R_{min}, \\
P(\text{cancel}) &= 0 && \text{if } R \leq R_{min}.
\end{aligned}
\tag{3}
$$

In adapting this theory to the case of pesticide cancellations, we note that there are three groups of individuals whose health the EPA is supposed to protect: consumers of food products, pesticide applicators, and those who mix and load the pesticides. Because of differences in the magnitude and degree of voluntariness of the risks facing these three groups, it is plausible that the EPA, if it follows (3), sets different risk thresholds for each of the three groups and will cancel a registered use if the risk to the maximally exposed individual in any of the three groups exceeds the relevant threshold. On the other hand, for the substance to be judged "safe," it must fall below the R_{min} for each group. Because equation (2) is nested in (3), we can statistically test one hypothesis against another.

If sufficient information were available, the models in equations (2) and (3) could be estimated both for the proposed decision to cancel a pesticide registration and for the final decision. Unfortunately, lack of information about the role of intervenors prior to the public comment period makes estimation of either model impossible for the proposed decision. Although it is well known that the EPA meets with interested parties throughout the special review process, it is only since 1985 that information about such meetings was required to be made public. Since we know only about interventions that occurred after the preliminary decision was made, our analysis is confined to explaining whether or not a pesticide was canceled in the EPA's notice of final determination.

Variable Selection and Treatment of Missing Values

To explain the EPA's final decision, we have gathered data on the cancer and other health risks, and the benefits, associated with each food crop for which the 19 pesticides listed in table 1 were registered before entering special review. We have also attempted to measure the participation of interest groups. The variables for which sufficient observations are available are listed in table 2 and are described below.

Risk Variables

The (individual) risk associated with use of pesticide i on crop j is correctly computed as the difference between the lifetime cancer risk associated with pesticide i and the risk associated with the pesticide that will replace it if it is canceled. The EPA's published risk estimates, however, measure the risk of pesticide i as the incremental lifetime cancer risk associated with that pesticide, as though the alternative to using pesticide i were riskless. In this and in other instances cited below, we used the EPA's published figures even if they do not measure the theoretically correct construct, because it is these figures that were available to decision makers.

In addition to measuring the maximum individual risk to applicators, mixer/loaders, and consumers of food products, we would like to measure the number of expected deaths associated with pesticide i on crop j. For cancer risks, however, data on the size of the exposed population are seldom reported. This poses little problem for mea-

TABLE 2

MEANS AND STANDARD DEVIATIONS OF VARIABLES USED IN MODEL

VARIABLE NAME	USES THAT WERE BANNED			USES THAT WERE NOT BANNED		
	Number of Observations	Mean	Standard Deviation	Number of Observations	Mean	Standard Deviation
Whether canceled	96	1.0	.0	149	.0	.0
Dietary risk*	78	9.6E-4	3.5E-3	94	4.2E-6	1.4E-5
Applicator risk	63	1.2E-2	2.1E-2	66	1.5E-4	7.3E-4
Mixer risk	42	2.2E-4	8.8E-4	35	1.2E-5	9.9E-6
Producer benefits[†]	86	2.873	7.637	81	15.685	41.453
Whether yield loss	96	.240	.429	149	.530	.501
Reproductive effects	96	.458	.501	149	.376	.486
Danger to marine life	96	.583	.495	149	.470	.501
Environmental groups comment	96	.729	.447	146	.329	.471
Academics comment	96	.104	.307	146	.390	.490
Growers comment	96	.042	.201	146	.144	.352

* All risks are risks of cancer based on a lifetime of exposure to the pesticide.
† Millions of 1986 dollars.

suring dietary risks, which are usually based on total U.S. food consumption and, hence, the total U.S. population, but it is problematic for occupational exposures. Because the size of the exposed population is unavailable, the risk variables in our model represent risks to the maximally exposed individual, which, in practice, is the average applicator or mixer/loader. These can be scaled to represent the expected number of deaths caused by the pesticide annually, as long as it is assumed that the size of the exposed population is constant across all observations.[7]

Noncancer health risks and ecological risks are inherently difficult to measure. Noncancer health effects are measured by a dummy variable indicating that the pesticide exhibits adverse reproductive effects. Ecological risks are measured using a dummy variable that indicates whether a substance is harmful to marine life.

Benefit Data

The only measure of benefits to consumers and producers that is consistently provided in the risk-benefit studies the EPA conducts is the losses that producers would sustain in the first year after cancellation of the pesticide. These are measured as the increased control costs from switching to a substitute pesticide and the value of any yield losses. If yield losses are large enough to raise the price of the product, losses to producers are reduced by the resulting increase in revenues. Because losses to consumers are seldom quantified in the background documents, we rely exclusively on first-year losses to producers.

Even the latter, however, are not available for all pesticides and all crops. It should be emphasized that, although pesticide manufacturers are responsible for data on health risks, the EPA must bear the cost of calculating the benefits of pesticide use. If information on the number of acres treated and on input and output prices is not available from other sources (e.g., the Department of Agriculture), budgetary limitations make it unlikely that benefits will be calculated. Even when such data are available, uncertainty about yield losses makes the cost of pesticide cancellation hard to quantify. When producer benefits are not measured in dollars, we use a dummy variable to indicate whether cancellation of the pesticide would result in yield losses to producers.

---

[7] We cannot, however, distinguish the individual contributions of size of exposed population and individual risk to the regulatory decision.

Political Variables

Quantifying the participation of special-interest groups is a difficult task. Because the only information publicly available is whether comments were entered following the proposed decision, we use dummy variables that indicate whether such comments were made by at least one member of each interest group. The interest groups we distinguish include environmental groups, which commented on 49 percent of all decisions; grower organizations, which commented on 10 percent of all decisions; and academics, who commented on 28 percent of all decisions. The results below suggest that academics most often commented on behalf of growers or manufacturers.

One group whose influence we are unable to measure is pesticide manufacturers. Because these manufacturers comment on virtually every decision, the use of a registrant dummy is unproductive. Ideally, one would like to measure the financial stake that manufacturers have in individual pesticides, but such information is proprietary.

To capture the effect of one particularly controversial political administration, a dummy variable is included for the years in which Anne Burford was administrator of the EPA.[8]

Treatment of Missing Values

One problem with the data is the large number of missing values, especially for cancer risks and producer benefits (see table 2). In the case of cancer risks, data may be missing either because an estimate of dietary or occupational exposure is unavailable for a particular crop or because toxicological data are not deemed sufficiently reliable to estimate a dose-response relationship. Although both situations occur in the data, it is the latter that accounts for the majority of missing observations.

A similar problem occurs with producer benefits from pesticide use. Because the EPA does not have the budget to launch a primary data collection effort, lack of information from secondary sources about acres of the crop treated or about input and output prices makes it likely that benefit data will not be quantified.

We handle missing data problems by defining an indicator variable M_{ij} ($= 1$ if data are missing) and multiplying the variable of interest

---

[8] The fact that we have only 19 active ingredients prevents more extensive use of political dummy variables in the probit model. If, for example, a dummy variable were added for each political administration, the Carter administration dummy would explain perfectly all decisions on DBCP, the only pesticide to complete the special review process during that administration.

TABLE 3

PROBABILITY OF CANCELLATION EQUATIONS

	CONTINUOUS MODEL			BRIGHT-LINE MODEL		
	(1)	(2)	(3)	(4)	(5)	(6)
Intercept	-.050 (.344)	-.822 (1.091)	-1.824 (.785)	.589 (.451)	-.852 (1.167)	-1.391 (1.035)
Diet risk per million persons	.003 (.006)	.009 (.006)	.012 (.006)*	-.018 (.030)	-.027 (.039)	-.030 (.036)
Diet risk missing	-.864 (.386)*	-.626 (.565)	-.775 (.540)	-1.020 (.404)*	-.718 (.575)	-.821 (.556)
Applicator risk per million persons	4.4E-4 (2.2E-4)*	8.2E-4 (3.0E-4)*	6.7E-4 (2.7E-4)*	4.2E-4 (2.3E-4)	7.8E-4 (3.2E-4)*	6.2E-4 (2.8E-4)*
Applicator risk missing	.554 (.361)	-.836 (.672)	-.529 (.630)	.471 (.364)	-1.09 (.690)	-.869 (.667)
Mixer risk per million persons	.005 (.008)	8.2E-4 (2.5E-2)	1.5E-4 (1.3E-2)	-.053 (.027)	-.007 (.042)	-.022 (.037)
Mixer risk missing	-.860 (.414)*	.681 (.726)	.540 (.683)	-1.374 (.482)*	.881 (.823)	.644 (.785)
Producer benefits[†]	-.048 (.018)*	-.074 (.028)*	-.066 (.025)*	-.050 (.019)*	-.075 (.0282)*	-.069 (.025)*
Producer benefits missing × yield loss	-1.984 (.361)*	-2.420 (.454)*	-2.413 (.446)*	-2.043 (.379)*	-2.46 (.460)*	-2.47 (.458)*

Producer benefits missing × no yield loss	-1.797 (.446)*	-.296 (.889)	-.934 (.789)	-1.794 (.447)*	-.273 (1.00)	-.943 (.862)
Reproductive effects	.530 (.324)	.908 (.532)	1.026 (.518)*	.843 (.360)*	1.03 (.552)	1.13 (.537)*
Danger to marine life	.782 (.281)*	-.893 (.861)	-.283 (.701)	.617 (.293)*	-.990 (.869)	-.593 (.769)
Burford years	⋯	-1.621 (1.112)	⋯	⋯	-1.38 (1.22)	⋯
Academics comment	⋯	-1.807 (.902)*	-1.333 (.753)	⋯	-1.91 (.914)*	-1.58 (.819)
Growers comment	⋯	-2.017 (.874)*	-1.829 (.762)*	⋯	-2.42 (1.02)*	-2.21 (.871)*
Environmental groups comment	⋯	3.070 (.617)*	3.398 (.604)*	⋯	3.27 (.67)*	3.48 (.667)*
R_{max} diet	⋯	⋯	⋯	1.7E-4	1.7E-4	1.7E-4
R_{max} applicator	⋯	⋯	⋯	1.1E-2	1.1E-2	1.1E-2
R_{max} mixer/loader	⋯	⋯	⋯	3.1E-5	3.1E-5	3.1E-5
Log likelihood	-87.0	-44.9	-46.0	-83.4	-42.8	-43.4
Percentage of decisions correctly predicted	86.0	95.0	95.0	84.0	94.0	94.0

NOTE.—Standard errors appear in parentheses below coefficients.
* Significant at the .05 level, two-tailed test.
† Millions of dollars.

(e.g., dietary cancer risk) by $1 - M_{ij}$. The missing data indicator also appears as an independent variable. The coefficient of the risk variable thus represents the effects of dietary cancer risk conditional on the availability of such information.

IV. The Determinants of Pesticide Decisions, 1975–89

Estimates of equations (2) and (3) appear in table 3 for three different sets of variables: (i) risk and benefit variables only, (ii) risk and benefit variables augmented by commenter dummies, and (iii) all the preceding variables augmented by a dummy variable indicating the Burford administration at the EPA.[9]

Are Risks and Benefits Balanced?

Table 3 indicates that the EPA does balance risks and benefits in deciding whether or not to ban a pesticide. Indeed, for each set of variables, the bright-line theory of risk regulation, which asserts that risks and benefits are not balanced for very low or very high risk levels, can be rejected in favor of a simple probit model. In examining the so-called bright-line theory (cols. 4–6), we note that there are no risk levels below which all pesticide uses were allowed. For example, some uses of captan were banned even though incremental risks to applicators were 10^{-9} and incremental dietary risks were 10^{-12}, presumably because benefits from captan usage were very small.[10] The maximum acceptable risk levels in our data (levels above which all uses were banned) differ somewhat from the 10^{-4} cutoff often emphasized in the risk management literature (Travis and Hattemer-Frey 1988). For instance, the maximum acceptable risk level is highest for applicators (1.1×10^{-2}) but somewhat closer to conventional levels for mixers (3.1×10^{-5}) and for dietary risks (1.7×10^{-4}).

Because the bright-line models were estimated by maximum likelihood techniques (see the Appendix), likelihood ratio tests were performed to test the null hypothesis that bright lines do not exist (i.e.,

---

[9] Equations (2) and (3) were estimated by maximum likelihood methods, assuming that $u_{ij} \sim IN(0, \sigma^2)$ for all i and j. Details on the estimation of the switch points in eq. (3) appear in the Appendix. The three observations on ethalfluralin were dropped from the analysis since no information on public comments was available for these decisions.

[10] The EPA banned the use of captan on 44 fruits and vegetables. In each case, the benefits of captan use were estimated to be negligible. Average dietary risk was less than or equal to 10^{-6} in all cases and less than or equal to 10^{-9} in 28 cases. Risks to mixer/loaders and applicators were 10^{-6} in about half the cases and 10^{-5} in the other half.

that [2] is the correct model) against the alternative that they do. In all three cases the null hypothesis cannot be rejected at conventional levels. We therefore focus our discussion on the simple probit results (cols. 1–3 of table 3).

Given that the EPA does weigh risks and benefits, what weight does it place on risks to different populations? In considering cancer risks, the EPA clearly places most weight on risks to applicators. This variable is significant in all probit equations, and the ratio of its coefficient (suitably scaled) to that of producer benefits implies a value per statistical cancer case avoided of roughly $35 million (1986 dollars).[11] By contrast, risks to mixers are insignificant in determining the probability of cancellation, and dietary risks are significant at conventional levels only in column 3. The value per cancer case avoided implied by this coefficient, however, is only $60,000.

It is interesting to speculate on the reasons for these results. One reason for placing so much weight on reducing risks to applicators is that applicators constitute an identifiable population who face large risks. It is certainly plausible that equivalent risk reductions (in terms of numbers of cancer cases) are valued more highly when the level of individual risk is high (as it is for applicators) than when it is low (as it is for consumers). It may also be the case that decision makers discount risk estimates based on dietary exposure, which are widely known to be upward biased, relative to risk estimates for applicators, which are based on more accurate estimates of exposure.[12]

As far as other risks are concerned, the presence of adverse reproductive effects increases the probability of cancellation, although this effect is only marginally significant in columns 1 and 2. Danger to marine life, however, raises the probability of cancellation only in column 1. One reason for this may be the presence of comments by environmental groups in columns 2 and 3. As will be shown below, environmental groups are more likely to comment when a pesticide poses danger to marine life; hence, the environmental group dummy in equations (2) and (3) may be capturing some of the effects of this risk variable.

Producer benefits significantly lower the probability of cancellation. A $1 million increase in producer benefits lowers the probability of cancellation (with all variables at median values) between 0.7 and 1.1

[11] The exact figures for cols. 1, 2, and 3 of table 3 are, respectively, $32.1 (14.2), $38.8 (21.2), and $35.5 (19.5) million (standard errors in parentheses). (These calculations are explained in detail in the Appendix.) It is interesting to note that intervenors do not significantly change the value per cancer case avoided.

[12] Estimates of dietary cancer risk are usually based on the assumptions that pesticide residues are present at the maximum levels allowed by law and that the pesticide is used on all acres of the crop in question.

percentage points. Even when producer benefits are not quantified, merely knowing that yield losses would occur if the pesticide were banned significantly reduces the probability of cancellation.

How Important Are Political Interests in the Regulatory Process?

The dramatic increase in the log of the likelihood function when interest group variables are added to the model attests to the importance of intervenors in the regulatory process. Participation by environmental groups dramatically increases the probability of cancellation, whereas participation by grower organizations and academics reduces the probability of cancellation. From this we infer that most academics are commenting on behalf of growers or registrants.

While having the expected sign, the dummy variable indicating the Burford period at the EPA is not significant at conventional levels, although it alters somewhat the magnitude of the coefficients on the interest group variables. This fact prompts us to examine whether Burford may have exerted influence indirectly by discouraging comments from environmental groups and encouraging comments from growers. To investigate this issue we estimated separate probit models to explain the participation of environmental groups and grower organizations (see table 4). The Burford regime appears to have influenced environmental groups since none of them bothered to enter comments in the public docket during her administration. (The Burford dummy does not appear in the environmental group equation because it would have a coefficient of minus infinity.) By contrast, she appears to have increased the probability that grower organizations would comment. This may reflect the fact that environmental groups felt it futile to intervene during Burford's tenure, whereas grower organizations expected a more sympathetic hearing.

The results of table 4 also shed light on an issue raised earlier. To some extent, participation by interest groups in the regulatory process is motivated by the risks and benefits of pesticide use that an unbiased "social planner" would consider. Environmental groups, for example, are more likely to comment on pesticides that pose a danger to marine life, and grower organizations are more likely to comment the larger are benefits to them from pesticide use. Because some of the factors that the EPA is required to consider under FIFRA may be captured by intervenor dummies, one should not be surprised if, as in columns 2 and 3, variables such as danger to marine life and producer benefits become less significant than they appear in column 1.

Finally, something should be said about the effect of the proposed decision to cancel a pesticide on the likelihood that interest groups

TABLE 4

PROBABILITY OF COMMENTING EQUATIONS

	Environmental Groups (1)	Grower Organizations (2)
Intercept	−1.073 (.211)	−2.634 (.381)
Reproductive effects	.077 (.218)	
Danger to marine life	.471 (.201)*	
Proposed decision = cancel	1.615 (.222)*	1.550 (.365)*
Burford years		.973 (.296)*
Producer benefits[†]		.011 (.004)*
Producer benefits missing × yield loss		−.196 (.345)
Producer benefits missing × no yield loss		−.334 (.547)
Log likelihood	−115.0	−62.3
Percentage of decisions correctly predicted	93.0	90.0

NOTE.—Standard errors appear in parentheses below coefficients.
* Significant at the .05 level, two-tailed test.
† Millions of dollars.

comment. While it is certainly plausible that a proposed decision to cancel a pesticide increases the chances that growers will comment, it is puzzling that a proposed decision to cancel increases the chances that environmental groups comment. It is, after all, environmental groups that usually oppose pesticide use. The positive sign here may, however, reflect reverse causality: by exerting influence before as well as during the public comment period, environmental groups may actually increase the chances of a proposed cancellation.

V. Conclusions

We suggested in the Introduction that our findings would both comfort and concern those interested in environmental regulation. With respect to comfort, it appears that the EPA is indeed capable of making the kind of balancing decisions that economists presumably support and that FIFRA clearly requires. Our results convincingly demonstrate that the existence of risks to human health or the environment increases the likelihood that a particular pesticide use will be canceled by the EPA; at the same time, the larger the economic beliefs associated with a particular use, the lower the likelihood of cancellation.

On the other hand, our results also provide some cause for concern. For instance, we find that the value of a statistical life implicit in the 242 regulatory decisions we consider is $35 million for applicators but only $60,000 for consumers of pesticide residues on food. Why is the EPA apparently willing to spend nearly 600 times as much to protect those who apply pesticides as those whose exposures come through food residues? Two explanations seem likely. First, although they are much fewer in number, each applicator faces a much larger individual risk than a typical consumer—on average about 15 times larger. The EPA may be especially concerned about allowing larger individual risks. Second, because they are fewer in number, applicators are more identifiable than the more than 200 million consumers of food in the United States. As with the proverbial baby in the well, society stands willing to spend much more to save the lives of identifiable victims than mere "statistical lives," and this may be reflected in our findings.

There are other aspects of the pesticide regulatory process that provide some cause for concern. First, although hardly unique to pesticide regulation, the procedures used to assess risks to all parties are almost sure to lead to upwardly biased estimates. To take but one example from the decisions analyzed here, risks to applicators and consumers are predicated on the assumption that no other active ingredient will be substituted for one banned in a particular use. Since such substitutions are the rule rather than the exception, however, a more accurate measure of risk reductions would reflect the *differential* riskiness of the two substances. (It is conceivable, in fact, that a more hazardous—yet to date untested—ingredient could be substituted for one whose use was discontinued by the EPA.) This suggests, incidentally, that groups of active ingredients be considered together in the regulatory process. This would encourage more accurate estimation of both risks and benefits since it would make clear those situations in which simple substitutions are no longer possible. Finally, the EPA should be given the resources to make more accurate estimates of the benefits of pesticide usage. It is simply not sufficient to calculate losses to growers and call this the "cost" of restricting a particular pesticide use. More sophisticated measures, which include forgone consumers' surpluses, must become a standard part of FIFRA regulation.

It is less clear how one should view our findings concerning the political variables we examined. Clearly, intervention in the regulatory process—by both business and environmental groups—affects the likelihood of pesticide use restrictions. All other things being equal, interventions by environmental groups have about twice the impact on the likelihood of cancellation as those by growers (although the combined effect of growers and academic commenters, who weigh in against cancellations, outweighs that of environmentalists). Moreover, Anne Burford's short and controversial tenure at the EPA is seen to have had a negative effect on the likelihood of pesticide cancellations. To those who view pesticide or other similar regulation as the proper province of scientists, engineers, and economists alone, these findings may be discouraging. On the other hand, those taking the view that regulation—like government taxation or spending—is inherently a political act may find it encouraging that affected parties not only participate actively in the regulatory process but do so quite effectively.

Appendix

Maximum Likelihood Estimation of Bright Lines

Our risk levels R_{max} have been chosen by ordering observations from most to least risky and finding the lowest risk level in each category (diet risk, applicator risk, or mixer risk) above which all uses were canceled.

It can be argued that this is equivalent to picking R_{max} to maximize a likelihood function for which the individual terms are

$$P(\text{cancel}) = 1 \qquad\qquad \text{if } R \geq R_{max},$$
$$P(\text{cancel}) = \Phi(\alpha_1 R + \alpha_2 B) \qquad \text{if } R < R_{max}, \qquad \text{(A1)}$$
$$P(\text{don't cancel}) = 0 \qquad\qquad \text{if } R \geq R_{max},$$
$$P(\text{don't cancel}) = 1 - \Phi(\alpha_1 R + \alpha_2 B) \quad \text{if } R < R_{max},$$

where Φ is the standard normal distribution function.

The argument that our procedure maximizes the likelihood function is as follows: If one were to raise R_{max}, this would take observations that were canceled and now contribute a "1" to the likelihood function and reduce their contribution to $\Phi(\alpha_1 R + \alpha_2 B) \leq 1$, thus lowering the value of the likelihood function. If one were to lower R_{max}, observations that were not canceled would now be above R_{max}. From equation (A1), the contribution of these observations to the likelihood function would fall to zero from $1 - \Phi(\alpha_1 R + \alpha_2 B) \geq 0$, thus lowering the value of the likelihood function. Our procedure thus maximizes the likelihood function.

We can, therefore, view the threshold model as consisting of 242 observations and $k + 3$ parameters, where k is the number of parameters estimated in the continuous model. A test of the threshold model can be conducted by comparing $2[\ln L(\text{threshold}) - \ln L(\text{continuous})]$ with the critical value of the χ^2 distribution with three degrees of freedom.

Calculation of Implied Value per Cancer Case Avoided

Equation (1) in the text indicates that pesticide i will be canceled for use on crop j if the risks associated with the pesticide, R_{ij}, plus other considerations, u_{ij}, outweigh the benefits of use, B_{ij}:

$$\alpha_1 R_{ij} + \alpha_2 B_{ij} + u_{ij} > 0.$$

Equivalently, the pesticide will be banned if the value of the risks outweighs the dollar value of the benefits:

$$-\frac{\alpha_1}{\alpha_2} R_{ij} - \frac{u_{ij}}{\alpha_2} \geq B_{ij}. \tag{A2}$$

If R_{ij} is the number of cancer cases avoided by banning the pesticide for a year and B_{ij} is the annual value of benefits, then $-\alpha_1/\alpha_2$ is the value per cancer case avoided.

In the estimation of α_1 and α_2, R_{ij} has been replaced by N_{ij}, the number of cancer cases avoided per million exposed persons, based on a lifetime (T years) of exposure. The relationship between R_{ij} and N_{ij} is thus given by

$$R_{ij} = \frac{N_{ij}}{T \times 10^6} \times \text{number of persons exposed}, \tag{A3}$$

where the first term on the right-hand side of (A3) is the risk to a single person from a year of exposure to the pesticide. Equation (A3) implies that the coefficient of N_{ij} must be multiplied by $T \times 10^6$ and divided by the number of persons exposed to equal α_1.

To calculate the value per applicator cancer case avoided, the coefficient of applicator risk (N_{ij}) must be divided by the number of applicators exposed and multiplied by 35×10^6. (A lifetime of exposure for an applicator is assumed to be 35 years.) The resulting estimate of α_1 must then be divided by minus the coefficient of producer benefits. To illustrate the calculation, we use the coefficients in the third column of table 3 and assume an exposed applicator population of 10,000. This implies a value per applicator cancer case avoided of \$35.53 million (1986 dollars):

$$-\frac{\alpha_1}{\alpha_2} = \frac{6.7 \times 10^{-4}}{.066} \frac{35 \times 10^6}{10,000} = 35.53.$$

In calculating the value per cancer case avoided associated with dietary risks, $T = 70$ and $N = 2.1 \times 10^8$, that is, the U.S. population during the period of study.

References

Bosso, Christopher J. *Pesticides and Politics: The Life Cycle of a Public Issue.* Pittsburgh: Univ. Pittsburgh Press, 1987.

Crandall, Robert W. *Controlling Industrial Pollution: The Economics and Politics of Clean Air.* Washington: Brookings Inst., 1983.

Hird, John A. "Superfund Expenditures and Cleanup Priorities: Distributive Politics or the Public Interest?" *J. Policy Analysis and Management* 9 (Fall 1990): 455–83.

McFadden, Daniel. "The Revealed Preferences of a Government Bureaucracy: Theory." *Bell J. Econ. and Management Sci.* 6 (Autumn 1975): 401–16.

———. "The Revealed Preferences of a Government Bureaucracy: Empirical Evidence." *Bell J. Econ.* 7 (Spring 1976): 55–72.

Magat, Wesley; Krupnick, Alan J.; and Harrington, Winston. *Rules in the Making: A Statistical Analysis of Regulatory Agency Behavior.* Baltimore: Johns Hopkins Univ. Press, 1986.

Milvy, Paul. "A General Guideline for Management of Risk from Carcinogens." *Risk Analysis* 6 (March 1986): 69–79.

Morrall, John F., III. "A Review of the Record." *Regulation* 10 (November/ December 1986): 25–44.

Nichols, Albert L., and Zeckhauser, Richard J. "The Perils of Prudence: How Conservative Risk Assessment Distorts Regulation." *Regulation* 10 (November/December 1986): 13–24.

Pashigian, Peter. "Environmental Regulation: Whose Self-Interests Are Being Protected?" *Econ. Inquiry* 23 (October 1985): 551–84.

Peltzman, Sam. "Toward a More General Theory of Regulation." *J. Law and Econ.* 19 (August 1976): 211–40.

Stigler, George J. "The Theory of Economic Regulation." *Bell J. Econ. and Management Sci.* 2 (Spring 1971): 3–21.

Thomas, Lacy Glenn. "Revealed Bureaucratic Preference: Priorities of the Consumer Product Safety Commission." *Rand J. Econ.* 19 (Spring 1988): 102–13.

Travis, Curtis C., and Hattemer-Frey, Holly A. "Determining an Acceptable Level of Risk." *Environmental Sci. and Tech.* 22 (August 1988): 873–76.

Travis, Curtis C., et al. "Cancer Risk Management." *Environmental Sci. and Tech.* 21 (May 1987): 415–20.

U.S. Environmental Protection Agency. "Report on the Status of Chemicals in the Special Review Program and Registration Standards in the Reregistration Program." Washington: Office Pesticide Programs, 1989.

Weingast, Barry R., and Moran, Mark J. "Bureaucratic Discretion or Congressional Control? Regulatory Policymaking by the Federal Trade Commission." *J.P.E.* 91 (October 1983): 765–800.

White, Lawrence J. *Reforming Regulation: Process and Problems.* Englewood Cliffs, N.J.: Prentice-Hall, 1981.

Yandle, Bruce. *The Political Limits of Environmental Regulation: Tracking the Unicorn.* Westport, Conn.: Quorum, 1989.

[3]

POLITICAL INSTITUTIONS AND POLLUTION CONTROL

Roger D. Congleton*

Abstract—This paper models the selection of environmental policies under authoritarian and democratic regimes, and tests the hypothesis that political institutions systematically affect the enactment of environmental regulations. The results support the contention that political institutional arrangements, rather than resource endowments, largely determine policies concerning environmental regulation.

I. Introduction

THE essential economics of pollution are fairly straightforward. Pollution is largely an undesired byproduct of production and transport. Consequently, countries that engage in more production and/or more transport will, *ceteris paribus*, generate more pollution. A country's output of pollution, thus, is evidence of its material prosperity, and is to a large extent a consequence of purely economic considerations: the pool and distribution of natural resources available to it, the productivity of its people, the nature of available production technologies and market structure.[1]

However, clearly *more* than economic considerations are involved. Political institutions affect the extent of a nation's output of effluents insofar as they directly affect environmental policies, or indirectly encourage or discourage economic development. Grier and Tullock (1989) demonstrate that economic growth rates in nations with liberal democratic institutions are higher than those with less liberal political arrangements, other things being equal. Ignoring direct regulation, democratic regimes would tend to exhibit higher growth

rates of pollutants than less liberal regimes. Democratic political institutions will moderate these economic tendencies if they are systematically more likely to adopt policies that encourage firms and/or consumers to use less polluting technologies.

Domestic political institutions also affect attempts to negotiate international environmental standards insofar as decisions to sign and abide by multilateral agreements are ultimately decisions of distinct policies. In most cases, states that find a particular proposed regulation or convention to be against "their interests" can opt out of the negotiations and ignore any conventions signed by those that remain at little cost; as there are, at best, only weak international legislative and enforcement institutions. Inasmuch as domestic political institutions effectively determine the range of interests that are accounted for in policy decisions, regimes that enact stringent domestic environmental standards are likely to find international agreements along similar lines to be in their interest.[2]

The purpose of this paper is to explore the effect of political institutions on the willingness of governments to control outputs of domestic effluents. To this end, models of democratic and authoritarian environmental policy making are developed in section II. The analysis demonstrates that an authoritarian confronts a higher relative price for pollution abatement than a median voter does. In cases where this relative price effect dominates, authoritarian regimes will adopt less stringent domestic environmental standards than democratic regimes, and by extension, be less willing to sign international conventions on environmental matters.

Empirical evidence on the latter proposition is developed in section III of the paper. Generally,

Received for publication October 16, 1990. Revision accepted for publication August 5, 1991.

* George Mason University.

Financial support from the International Institute is gratefully acknowledged. The paper has benefited from discussions with John Moore, the data assistance of Nicole Verrier, and the comments of three anonymous referees.

[1] See Baumol and Oates (1975) for an overview of economic aspects of pollution. Tobey (1990) and Leonard (1988) discuss trade aspects of environmental policies. However, Tobey was unable to find a relationship between domestic environmental policies and patterns of international trade. For recent overviews of the economics of air pollution, see Firor (1990). Drysek (1987) discusses the effects of political institutions on environmental policy. The analysis developed here supports Drysek's contention that liberal democracies are more responsive to environmental concerns than authoritarian or bureaucratic regimes.

[2] Economic aspects of domestic and international environmental protection differ somewhat for import and export industries. For example, export industries restricted by environmental domestic standards would be inclined to oppose cost increasing domestic standards. However, once domestic standards are enacted, affected domestic industries would tend to support similar strictures for their international competitors.

Copyright © 1992

the results support the contention that liberal democracies are both relatively high sources of air pollution (because of their higher income) and more likely to sign international conventions on the environment. Section IV summarizes the results and suggests possible extensions.

II. Environmental Politics

The essential difference between authoritarian regimes and democracies is their decision-making procedure. Democracies make policy by counting the votes of ordinary citizens or their elected representatives. Authoritarian regimes only take account of the "votes" of an unelected elite, in the limit the "vote" of a single ruler. While many secondary features of authoritarian and democratic regimes indirectly influence public policies insofar as they affect public debate or planning horizon, they are initially neglected to focus attention on similarities in decision-making procedures. With this in mind, global markets in technology and capital are assumed to be sufficiently competitive that technological aspects of environmental policy are the same for authoritarian and democratic regimes.[3] Voters and dictators are assumed to face the same technological tradeoff between environmental quality and non-environmental income.

At this level of abstraction, both authoritarian and democratic decision-making procedures are fundamentally similar in that they yield environmental policies that maximize the welfare of a single individual given various political and economic constraints. Under a democratic regime,

the pivotal voter is the mean or median voter.[4] Under an authoritarian regime, the pivotal decision maker is the dictator (or the pivotal member of the ruling group). Any systematic difference between policies adopted by these regimes must be ascribed to differences in the parameters of their decision problems.

A. Utility Maximizing Pollution Standards

For purposes of analysis, individuals are assumed to maximize a two-dimensional utility function defined over measured real income (or consumption) as per GNP accounting practices and environmental quality. Measured real income is a pure private good measured as an index of goods purchased in markets. Environmental quality is a public good measured as an index of the average density of undesired (often toxic) chemicals in the voter's environment. These two areas of choice, while technologically linked, are disjoint since environmental quality is not normally included in measured real income.

The relationship between measured (real) national income and the measured (real) income of a typical individual is assumed to be a monotone increasing function of national income. This is a fairly severe assumption since environmental regulations often have quite different effects on different industries or regions within a country. However, the voter of most interest for the purposes of this paper is the median voter, who, because of his position at the midpoint of the distribution of voter ideal pollution standards, is unlikely to be one of the most (or least) affected individuals. Authoritarians also have incomes that

---

[3] Nations will face different costs for capital in perfectly competitive markets if they are more or less stable and/or have different regulatory environments. However, such differences are fundamentally political in nature inasmuch as they reflect political uncertainties, and/or import-export restrictions. Kormendi and Meguire (1985) report that political regimes provide the strongest explanation of international investment flows. Costs will also vary if there are important non-transportable natural resources that affect local relative prices of alternative production techniques. Cost differences due to differences in tax policies, infrastructure, land use restrictions and so forth can be modelled in a manner similar to that used for economic standards developed above.

The paper models the enactment of environmental standards rather than pollution taxes or land use regulations to simplify analysis. Buchanan and Tullock (1975) argue that political considerations tend to make standards more attractive than appropriate Pigovian taxes.

[4] Stochastic models of voter choice generally imply an equilibrium at the average voter's ideal point. See Enelow and Hinich (1984) or Coughlin (1990) for an overview of such models. In the case where voter ideal points are symmetrically distributed, the mean and median voter positions are the same and the policy predictions of both models are identical. The median voter model is used in this paper because of its more conventional representation of voter decision making and because median voter models are more widely used in the public policy literature. Sufficient conditions are met in the model for the existence of a median voter equilibrium. The policy domain is single dimensioned and the concavity of equation (2) implies that objective functions are single peaked in this domain.

The political effects of economic interest groups are ignored in this paper. As a first approximation, the efforts of economic interest groups are assumed to offset each other as in the symmetric case characterized by Congleton (1989), leaving the median voter or authoritarian decisive.

are linked to the national economy insofar as their income is based on tax revenues and gratuities. Initially, each individual is assumed to receive a constant share of GNP. Given national income Y and an individual's income share v, personal income is $C = vY$.

National income is a function of environmental regulations, E^*, market institutions, M, and resource base, R, in the country of interest. National income increases as economic resources increase, and as market arrangements become less centrally managed. National income initially rises as environmental standards become more stringent, peaks at standard E^y, and falls thereafter. Over the initial range, more stringent environmental standards increase national output by improving the health and productivity of labor and/or by freeing resources previously devoted by individuals to reduce exposure to the local environment, air conditioners and the like, for more valuable uses. Over the latter range, more stringent environmental standards reduce ordinary national output as less productive technologies are mandated and inputs are diverted from ordinary economic production to environmental improvement without offsetting productivity increases.[5] In this range, more stringent regulations improve average environmental quality but increase the cost of consumer goods relative to income, reducing measured national income and thereby the measured income of individuals.

Economic regulations affect the size of a voter's opportunity set through relative and absolute price effects that affect the size of national GNP. In this respect, environmental standards (and other regulations) are unlike ordinary public ex-

penditure programs for which tax revenues are raised to finance provision of a publicly produced service. The cost of environmental quality is not reflected by changes in ordinary tax burden, but rather by indirect effects that environmental standards have on personal income.

The link between environmental standard E^* and environmental quality is assumed to be probabilistic. This reflects stochastic elements of the underlying natural processes and scientific uncertainty about the physical and social mechanisms involved. An individual's assessment of the probability of environmental deterioration, $P = p(E|E^*, Y)$, falls as the environmental standard, E^*, becomes more stringent and increases as national output, Y, increases. Environmental standards are a form of social insurance which reduce downside environmental risk.

Each individual prefers the environmental standard that maximizes life-time expected utility given various personal constraints. Given our characterization of the choice at issue and a finite time horizon, T,[6] an individual's preferred standard can be modelled as that which maximizes:

$$U^e = \int_0^T \left[U^o P^o \right.$$

$$\left. + \int u(C, E, t) P(E|E^*, Y, t)\, dE \right] dt$$

(1a)

where

$$U^o \equiv U(Y, E^o, t)$$

and

$$P^o \equiv 1 - \int P(E|E^*, Y, t)\, dE$$

with

$$U_C > 0,\ U_E > 0,\ U_t < 0,$$

$$U_{CC} < 0,\ U_{CE} > 0,\ U_{EE} < 0$$

$$U_{tC} < 0,\ U_{tE} < 0,\ U_{tt} > 0,$$

$$P \geq 0,\ P_{E^*} < 0,\ P_{Y/A} > 0$$

---

[5] For those skeptical of the initial range where GNP increases with increases in environmental controls, recall that resources have been invested in waste management (dumps, latrines and so forth) by even prehistoric human communities. These investments tend to improve the health and longevity of community members with a consequent increase in the effective labor supply of the community. This suggests that over some range environmental standards increase productivity and thereby personal income. Ridgeway (1970) reports that such arguments played an important role in promoting sanitation efforts by western democracies during the last century.

To see that a similar upward sloping range exists for air quality, imagine the problem faced by a mine owner. If he fails to maintain some minimal level of environmental controls within the mine, his labor force will be less productive as air quality and temperature take their toll. A suitable investment in ventilation and cooling equipment can increase productivity.

[6] Congleton and Shughart (1990) provide evidence that median years to retirement and expected longevity affect policy decisions regarding social security benefit streams. Their results suggest that the median voter has a finite planning horizon in excess of thirty years.

subject to

$$C = vY \qquad (1b)$$
$$Y = y(E^*, M, R, t) \qquad (1c)$$

with

$$Y_R > 0,\ Y_{E^*} > 0$$

and

$$Y_{E^*E^*} > 0 \text{ for } E^* < E^{y'},$$
$$Y_{E^*} = 0 \quad \text{for } E^* = E^y,$$

and

$$Y_{E^*} < 0 \text{ for } E^* > E^y.$$

Subscripted variables represent partial derivatives with respect to the variable subscripted. U^o is utility generated by the original (or maximum) level of environmental quality with a measured income determined by the implied public policy. Conditional probability function P represents the probability distribution of environmental qualities below E^o in period t. Thus, the integral of P represents the probability that environmental quality falls below E^o. Utility increases as measured income, C, and/or environmental quality, E, increase and declines with postponement, t.

Substituting the constraints into the objective function, in order to specify the choice in terms of the environmental standard, E^*, yields:

$$U^e = \int_0^T \left[U(vY, E^o, t) P^o \right.$$
$$\left. + \left[\int u(vY, E, t) P(E|E^*, y(E^*), t) \right] dE \right] dt. \qquad (2)$$

Differentiating with respect to environmental standard E^*, and setting the result equal to zero yields a single first order condition for a typical individual's ideal environmental standard:

$$\int_0^T vU_C^o Y_{E^*} P^o + U^o(P_{E^*} + P_Y^o Y_{E^*})$$
$$+ \left[\int vU_C Y_{E^*} P \right.$$
$$\left. + U(P_{E^*} + P_Y Y_{E^*}) \, dE \right] dt = 0 \qquad (3a)$$

or

$$\int_0^T vU_C^o Y_{E^*} P^o - \left[\int vU_C Y_{E^*} P \, dE \right] dt$$
$$= \int_0^T - U^o(P_{E^*}^o + P_Y^o Y_{E^*})$$
$$+ \int U(P_{E^*} + P_Y Y_{E^*}) \, dE \right] dt. \qquad (3b)$$

FIGURE 1.—UTILITY MAXIMIZING ENVIRONMENTAL REGULATIONS

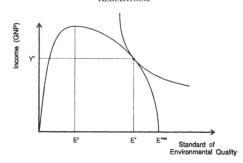

Equation (3b) demonstrates that the effect of environmental regulation on utility occurs through its effects on personal income and the probability distribution of environmental quality. Each individual prefers the environmental standard that sets the expected present value of his subjective marginal cost for the standard in terms of reduced measured income (consumption) equal to the present discounted value of the time stream of marginal utility from greater environmental quality.

Such environmental standards have the geometry of the curves in figure 1. The tradeoff between economic output and environmental quality is the envelope of the opportunity set. It represents the steady-state tradeoff between measured (or pecuniary) income and environmental quality. The indifference curves represent constant levels of expected lifetime utility over the time horizon of interest. Note that the relevant part of the constraint is from E^y to E^{max}. A rational decision maker who regards neither economic income nor environmental quality as "bads" would never intentionally adopt a standard below E^y. An individual who values income but cares nothing for the environment, per se, prefers the standard which maximizes measured income, E^y. The median voter is by definition in the middle of the distribution voter ideal points, and therefore opts for an intermediate solution similar to that depicted. The situation of a dictator is not similarly constrained, and thus more extreme environmental policies are possible. Yet the general shape of the opportunity set implies that both sorts of regimes tend to have some environmental regulation.

The implicit function theorem implies the existence of an equation, based on (3a), which represents an individual's preferred environmental standard as a function of variables beyond his control.

$$E^{**} = e(v, T, R, M). \tag{4}$$

Ultimately, the level of environmental regulation preferred depends upon the individual's share of national income, v, his time horizon, T, the resource base of the country, R, and its market institutions, M. The implicit function differentiation rule allows the effect of changes in these parametric variables on environmental standards to be calculated.

Define the left-hand side of equation (3a) to be H, then

$$E_v^{**} = H_v/ - H_E \tag{5a}$$

$$E_T^{**} = H_T/ - H_E \tag{5b}$$

$$E_R^{**} = H_R/ - H_E \tag{5c}$$

$$E_M^{**} = H_M/ - H_E. \tag{5d}$$

H_E is the second derivative of equation (2) with respect to environmental quality, which must be negative at the expected utility maximum. Consequently, the signs of equations (5a) through (5d) are determined by the numerators. Somewhat surprisingly, given the simplicity of the model used, none of these are unambiguously determined. An increase in the share of national income going to the individual, an increase in his time horizon, or an increase in national resources or geographical area can lead to stronger or weaker environmental standards according to the relative sizes of various interaction terms.

An increase in the fraction of national income going to the individual of interest increases the marginal cost of environmental standards faced by him, since he will now bear a larger fraction of associated reductions in national income. On the other hand, his income is higher for any given standard and thus would, except for the relative price effect, opt for greater expected environmental quality. In the case where the relative price effect dominates, $E_v^{**} < 0$, the utility maximizing environmental standard becomes less stringent as the individual's share of national income increases.

The effect of an increased planning horizon depends on the incremental costs and benefits from higher environmental standards at the end of the period evaluated. It is often argued that the time stream of benefits from environmental standards is such that the costs of environmental standards are concentrated in the early periods while the benefits are concentrated in later time periods. See, for example, Nordhaus (1989). Consequently, it is likely that at the end of the planning horizon the marginal benefits of environmental standards exceed their marginal costs, which implies that $E_T^{**} > 0$. In this case, the longer the time horizon used, the more stringent an individual's ideal environmental standards tend to be.

The effect of changes in a nation's resource base or market institutions is more complex. A larger resource base or more efficient collection of market institutions implies a larger national income for any environmental standard, which increases the probability of environmental deterioration and makes more stringent environmental standards more attractive. However, greater national income also implies that each voter is wealthier and inclined to "purchase" both more measured income and more environmental quality. On the other hand, greater personal wealth may increase the marginal cost of environmental regulation to the voter. In the case where increased environmental downside risk and income effects more than offset any increase in the marginal cost of environmental standards, equations (5c) and (5d) will exceed zero. Here, the stringency of environmental standards would increase as the resource base and/or quality of market institutions increase, $E_R^{**} > 0$ and $E_M^{**} > 0$.

B. *Differences Among Utility Maximizing Political Regimes*

The above analysis implies that utility maximizing decision makers will disagree about the optimal environmental standard, even if their utility functions are fundamentally similar, if their position in the national economy, planning horizon, or national endowments differ. To demonstrate that political regimes affect environmental policies, it is sufficient to show that the circumstances of policy makers under these two systems tend to be systematically different.

FIGURE 2.—UTILITY MAXIMIZING ENVIRONMENTAL
REGULATIONS FOR DICTATOR AND MEDIAN VOTER

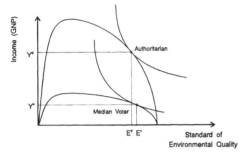

FIGURE 2.—UTILITY MAXIMIZING ENVIRONMENTAL
REGULATIONS FOR DICTATOR AND MEDIAN VOTER

The effect of a change in regime on environmental policy can be analyzed with reference to equations (5a) and (5b). Recall that the median voter is approximately the voter with the median income share and time horizon. Authoritarians have greater than the median income share, and probably tend to have a shorter than average time horizon given the high turnover of authoritarian regimes.[7] Under the restricted circumstances previously discussed, a larger national income *share* and shorter time horizon tends to reduce the stringency of the desired environmental standard. Consequently, authoritarians tend to prefer a lower environmental standard than a median voter does.

The essential geometry of such median voter and authoritarian choices is depicted in figure 2. The effect of a change from authoritarian regimes to democratic regimes in a given economy is analogous to a rise in the price of environmental quality. The higher marginal cost faced by a dictator is evidenced by the more steeply downward sloping portion of his income/environmental-standard constraint. In the case depicted, the marginal rate of substitution between income and environmental quality is independent of measured income, and consequently differences in marginal cost are decisive. Here, the authoritarian opts for more pecuniary income and less

[7] The median term of office for African authoritarians reported by Bienen and van de Walle (1989) is about 4 years. Differences in utility functions are also very likely. The highly uncertain career path to the top of an authoritarian regime, and the relatively low typical term of office suggest that authoritarians tend to be relatively less risk averse than median voters tend to be. The relatively risky nature of the ascent to power suggests that authoritarians will be less inclined to purchase insurance of any kind, including environmental insurance.

stringent environmental standards than the median voter does.

III. Empirical Evidence

The above analysis makes a fairly good case for democratic regimes to be inclined to adopt more stringent environmental regulations than authoritarian regimes, although the results are not completely general. The model provides a framework for testing this and other hypotheses generated in the course of analysis. Equation (4) is the reduced form equation for environmental policy formulation. Under both authoritarian and democratic regimes, pollution standards are functions of national endowments and characteristics of the decisive voter. If democratic regimes are more inclined to enact strict environmental standards than authoritarian regimes, then estimates of equation (4) should have positive coefficients for democratic variables. Reduced form equations for other endogenous variables are similarly functions of policy-maker characteristics, national resources and market institutions. The model also characterizes several structural equations. The estimates reported below are broadly consistent with the model, although a variety of data problems had to be circumvented in order to generate the estimates.

(1) Data on domestic environmental regulations tend to be sparse and the regulations themselves different enough to make a cross section analysis problematic. On the other hand, there have been several recent international agreements on environmental concerns. So while it is not possible to test hypotheses with respect to domestic policies, it is possible to test whether a country's political regime affects its international environmental policies. To the extent that domestic considerations dictate whether a nation signs on to a particular covenant or protocol, these international agreements also indirectly cast light on domestic policies.

In 1985, a global convention was negotiated under United Nations auspices at Vienna which committed signatories to coordinate research efforts and to enact domestic legislation for reducing emissions of ozone depleting substances, chiefly chlorofluorocarbons (CFCs). In 1987, a protocol was developed in Montreal which obliged developed countries to reduce their CFC production and consumption levels to half their 1986 levels by June 1999 and developing nations to limit their future consumption of CFCs.[8] In both agreements, countries could exempt themselves from the negotiated targets by not signing the final document. As of 1989, 27 countries had signed the 1985 conventions or enacted national legislation which accomplished the same end. Twenty-nine countries signed or enacted national legislation supporting the Montreal protocol, *World Resources 1989–90*, table 24.1. Nineteen countries supported both agreements. To the extent that domestic politics determine whether a particular country agrees to sign a particular covenant or protocol, the above analysis suggests that democratic regimes will be more likely to participate in these international agreements than other regimes, other things being equal.

(2) Data on the personal characteristics of median voters and dictators are largely unavailable. However, if these characteristics vary systematically with the type of regime, one can use regime-type as a proxy for the personal characteristics of decision makers under the two regimes. Unfortunately, (3) classification of countries into democratic and authoritarian regimes is also somewhat problematic. Many authoritarian regimes have formal institutional structures that superficially parallel those of democratic regimes. For example, according to the *CIA Fact Book*, 1988, both Zaire and Syria have political parties and elections, although most would consider these governments to be authoritarian. Gastil (1987, p.

40–41) classifies countries into seven categories according to their political liberties. Although Gastil's classification scheme yields a plausible ranking of countries, only the extremal values are used here to distinguish democratic from non-democratic government types. Countries that receive the highest values for political liberties (categories 1 and 2, table 3) are essentially well-functioning democracies whose citizens have broad political rights of participation. Differences in time horizon and share of national income relevant for policy makers are proxied by the resulting 0-1 dichotomous variable labeled "Democratic Country" in the tables below. Gastil also constructed a nine-fold classification of countries according to market structure (p. 74, table 8). The two most market-oriented categories are countries with relatively unregulated open markets. A 0-1 dichotomous variable constructed from these two categories, denoted capitalist country in the tables below, is used as a proxy for the efficacy of a country's market institutions.

(4) The model implies that a country's resource base plays a role in determining national standards insofar as resources affect personal income and the marginal cost of environmental regulation. However, reliable data on a nation's mineral reserves and labor force are available for relatively few countries. For example, complete data on recoverable fossil fuel reserves are available for only 46 countries from the World Petroleum Institute. However, resource endowments are largely the result of geological accidents more or less uniformly distributed about resource base. Consequently, resource endowment is proxied using area. (Area is highly correlated with proven fossil fuel reserves.) Labor force numbers are similarly problematic, and are proxied by national population. Data for population and area are from the *World Fact Book* (CIA, 1988). Data on real gross national product in U.S. dollars (1987) are from the World Petroleum Institute (1990/91).

Linear estimates of equation (4) are reported in the first 4 columns of table 1. Columns 1 and 2 report logit estimates of the probability that a particular country would have agreed to the 1985 Vienna Convention or the 1987 Montreal Protocol, using proven reserves of fossil fuels as a proxy for national resource endowment. Columns 3 and 4 report similar estimates based on the full

---

[8] Paragraph 4 of Article 2 of the Protocol specifies that "each party shall ensure that for the period 1 July 1998 to 30 June 1999, and in each twelve month period thereafter, its calculated level of consumption on the controlled substances in Group I of Annex A (chiefly CFCs) does not exceed, annually, fifty percent of its calculated level of consumption in 1986." Paragraph 1 of Article 5 exempts developing countries with "consumption of controlled substances... less than 0.3 kilograms per capita" from reductions in their current consumption levels, but restricts them to "either the average of its annual calculated level of consumption for the period 1995 to 1997 inclusive or a calculated level of consumption of 0.3 kilograms per capita, which ever is lower." CFC levels ranged from 0 to 0.91 kilogram per capita in 1986 within the 118 countries used above. A typical western democracy had levels of 0.75 kilograms per capita.

Signatories or contracting parties to the Montreal Protocol, as of 1989, include: Egypt, Ghana, Kenya, Morocco, Senegal, Togo, Canada, Mexico, Panama, United States, Venezuela, Israel, Japan, Belgium, Denmark, Finland, France, W. Germany, Greece, Italy, Luxembourg, Netherlands, Norway, Portugal, Sweden, Switzerland, United Kingdom, USSR, and New Zealand (*World Resources* 1988–90, table 24.1).

POLITICAL INSTITUTIONS AND POLLUTION CONTROL   419

TABLE 1.—SIGNATORIES OF INTERNATIONAL CFC AGREEMENTS

Variable Name	CFC85$_{89}$ Logit	CFC87$_{89}$ Logit	CFC85$_{89}$ Logit	CFC87$_{89}$ Logit	CFC85$_{89}$ Logit	CFC87$_{89}$ Logit
C	−0.437 (0.642)	−1.869 (2.330)[a]	−2.254 (5.516)[c]	−2.114 (5.37)[c]	−2.448 (5.586)[c]	−2.286 (5.474)[c]
Democratic Country	2.228 (2.863)[b]	3.033 (3.422)[c]	2.596 (4.836)[c]	2.836 (5.151)[c]	2.227 (3.832)[c]	2.506 (4.261)[c]
Capitalist Country	−0.896 (1.049)	−0.755 (0.836)	−0.267 (0.458)	−0.726 (1.194)	−0.251 (0.415)	−0.748 (1.193)
GNP per capita					0.064 (1.817)[a]	0.058 (1.675)[a]
Oil Reserves	−6.05 E-7 (0.050)	−1.040 E-5 (0.556)				
Coal Reserves	2.252 E-5 (1.706)[a]	1.403 E-6 (0.157)				
Gas Reserves	1.490 E-8 (0.628)	2.423 E-6 (0.963)				
Area			2.356 E-4 (1.857)[a]	1.102 E-4 (1.266)	2.356 E-4 (1.672)[a]	9.672 E-5 (1.097)
Population	−0.017 (1.868)[a]	−0.00202 (0.355)	−3.624 E-3 (0.784)	−8.270 E-4 (0.324)	−0.004 (0.671)	−0.0007 (0.251)
Sample Size	46	46	118	118	118	118
Log Likelihood	−22.671	−20.830	−46.377	−47.264	−44.632	−45.814

[a]Significant at the 10% level.
[b]Significant at the 1% level.
[c]Significant at the 0.1% level.

118 country sample using national area as a proxy for national resources. Columns 5 and 6 augment the model by adding real per capita gross national product to the list of dependent variables. This creates some risk of simultaneous equation bias, but demonstrates that the results of the reduced form estimates of the model are not an artifact of the higher income levels of democratic governments. (The simple correlation coefficient for democracy and real per capita gross national product is 0.46 which is well outside the range where multicollinearity is considered to be a problem.)

Note that, consistent with the main thesis of this paper, the coefficient for the democratic country variable is significantly different from zero at the one thousandth level of significance for each of the six estimates of international environmental policy although the economic endowment and market structure variables are not. This suggests that environmental policy decisions are largely determined by a nation's political institutions rather than by its economic resource endowments. Moreover, these results are robust in the sense that small changes in data set or specification do not change the signs or significance of the coefficient estimates.

Table 2 reports estimates of other structural and reduced form equations from the model. Columns 1–4 focus on two pollutants of current interest because of their roles as greenhouse gases: net methane and CFC output as reported in World Resources 1989–1990. Column 5 reports a reduced form estimate of real gross national product. Column 1 reports a two stage estimate of methane output. This is an estimate of the probability function of environmental quality characterized used in equation (1) of the model. Recall that observed environmental quality is a probabilistic function of RGNP and environmental standards. A country's participation in the Montreal Protocol is used as a proxy for its

The Political Economy of Environmental Regulation

TABLE 2.—NATIONAL EFFLUENT OUTPUT AND ECONOMIC PRODUCTION

Variable Name	Methane 2-Stage LS	Methane/GNP OLS	Methane OLS	CFC OLS	GNP OLS
C	235.204 (2.079)[a]	12.363 (6.553)[c]	−86.239 (1.367)	−2.105 (0.849)	−73.640 (1.421)
GNP$_{1987}$ (in US dollars)	2.481 (8.145)[c]				
Montreal Signatory or Contracting Party	−1011.481 (2.506)[b]				
Democratic Country		−9.501 (2.980)[b]	236.868 (2.904)[b]	12.285 (2.934)[b]	254.147 (2.904)[b]
Capitalist Country		0.128 (0.042)	122.570 (1.483)	4.103 (1.038)	122.570 (1.483)
Area		−0.0028 (0.478)	0.1004 (6.234)[c]	0.0043 (5.601)[c]	0.1004 (6.234)[c]
Population		0.00885 (0.720)	0.161 (0.478)	0.008 (0.499)	0.1612 (0.477)
Sample Size	118	118	118	118	118
R^2	0.219	0.082	0.748	0.321	0.386
Log Likelihood	−964.424	−483.430	−897.538	−515.596	−874.302
F-Statistic	16.092	2.522	84.087	14.829	17.747

[a]Significant at the 10% level.
[b]Significant at the 1% level.
[c]Significant at the 0.1% level.

regulatory environment. Both coefficient estimates are statistically distinguishable from zero. An increase in a country's GNP increases its Methane output while the domestic propensity to regulate reduces it. Column 2 provides indirect evidence of the effects of domestic regulation on national outputs of methane per unit of GNP. Democratic regimes produce more methane in total but significantly less per unit of national output. Together with the other results, this suggests that liberal democracies are more inclined to regulate environmental outputs than other regimes are.

Columns 3 and 4 are reduced form estimates of net outputs of methane and CFCs. A country's area again serves as a proxy for its natural resource base. The coefficients all have positive signs consistent with our previous discussion. However, again, only the coefficient estimates for the effects of liberal democratic regimes and national area are statistically significant. Democratic regimes produce more methane and more CFCs than their less liberal and/or authoritarian counterparts. This apparently reflects the higher national incomes associated with liberal democracies and the consequent production of more refuse of all sorts.

Both series of estimates are broadly similar. They suggest that liberal democracies are significantly more likely than other regimes to have supported global efforts at environmental regulation. While the signs of other coefficients are plausible, for example, capitalist countries are less inclined to regulate than other regimes, the estimates cannot rule out the possibility that the other variables had no effect on the probability of supporting the Vienna Convention or the Montreal Protocol. In contrast, the coefficients for democratic regime are statistically significant in every case.[9]

[9] Similar results for domestic policies can be obtained using indexes from Gastil (1987), and Walter and Ugelow (1979). Walter and Ugelow constructed a seven value index of the severity of environmental regulations for 25 countries. Regressing this environmental index (E) on the seven value Gastil index (adjusted to make higher numbers imply greater political liberty) of the liberalness of a country's political institutions (D) yields:

$$E = 2.135 + 0.390D \qquad F = 4.391$$
$$\quad (1.86)^a \quad (2.07)^a$$

[a] Significant at the 10% level.

IV. Conclusion

This paper has argued that environmental policies are affected by political institutions. Analysis of incentives faced by authoritarian regimes and democratic policy makers implies that relevant decision makers in democracies have a smaller marginal cost for pollution control than authoritarians do. Moreover, the highly uncertain career path to the top of an authoritarian regime, and their relatively short term of office suggest that authoritarians tend to have a relatively shorter time horizon and be relatively less risk averse than median voters tend to be. Together these differences imply that authoritarian regimes are inclined to enact less stringent environmental standards than democratic regimes.

Empirical evidence supports the contention that political institutions affect domestic and international environmental policies. Cross-sectional analysis of both pollution outputs and willingness to take part in international conventions on the environment strongly suggests that liberal democracies are more willing to regulate environmental effluents than less liberal regimes. The empirical results support the contention that political institutions largely determine environmental regulation, rather than technological aspects of pollution control or market structure.

The results also suggest that international agreements on environmental matters of global concern will attract more signatories as the number of democratic regimes increases. Seen in this light, the recent increase in the number of countries with democratic political institutions implies

that global environmental agreements will be more broadly supported in the future.

REFERENCES

Baumol, W., and W. Oates, *The Theory of Environmental Policy*, second edition (New York: Cambridge University Press, 1975).

Bienen, H., and N. van de Walle, "Time and Power in Africa," *American Political Science Review* 83 (1989), 19–34.

Buchanan, J. M., and G. Tullock, "Polluters' Profits and Political Response: Direct Controls Versus Taxes," *American Economic Review* 65 (1975), 139–147.

Congleton, R. D., "Campaign Finances and Political Platforms: The Economics of Political Controversy," *Public Choice* 62 (1989), 101–118.

Congleton, R. D., and W. F. Shughart, "The Growth of Social Security: Electoral Push or Political Pull?," *Economic Inquiry* 28 (1990), 109–132.

Coughlin, P., "Majority Rule and Elections Models," *Journal of Economic Surveys* (1990).

Dryzek, J. S., *Rational Ecology: Environment and Political Economy* (New York: Basil Blackwell, 1987).

Enelow, J. M., and M. J. Hinich, *The Spatial Theory of Voting* (New York: Cambridge University Press, 1984).

Firor, J., "The Straight Story about the Green House Effect," *Contemporary Policy Issues* 8 (1990), 3–15.

Gastil, R. D., *Freedom in the World: Political Rights and Liberties 1986–1987* (New York: Greenwood Press, 1987).

Grier, K. B., and G. Tullock, "An Empirical Analysis of Cross-National Economic Growth, 1951–80," *Journal of Monetary Economics* 24 (1989), 259–276.

Kormendi, R. C., and Meguire, "Macroeconomic Determinants of Growth: Cross Country Evidence," *Journal of Monetary Economics* 16 (1985), 141–163.

Leonard, H. J., *Pollution and the Struggle for World Product* (New York: Cambridge University Press, 1988).

Nordhaus, W. D., "The Economics of the Green House Effect," mimeograph Yale University (1989).

Ridgeway, J., *The Politics of Pollution* (New York: Dutton, 1970).

Tobey, J. A., "The Effects of Domestic Environmental Policies on Patterns of World Trade," *Kyklos* 43 (1990), 191–208.

Walter, I., and J. Ugelow, "Environmental Policies in Developing Countries," *Ambio* 8 (1979), 102–109.

World Resources Institute, *World Resources 1989–90* (New York: Oxford University Press, 1989).

_____, *World Resources 1990–91* (New York: Oxford University Press, 1990).

In this quite restricted sample, the more liberal (democratic) a political regime is, the more severe its environmental regulations tend to be.

[4]

Patterns of Behavior in Endangered Species Preservation

Andrew Metrick and Martin L. Weitzman

ABSTRACT. *This paper analyzes statistically the main determinants of government decisions about the preservation of endangered species. As explanatory variables, we use proxies that include 'scientific' species characteristics, such as "degree of endangerment" and "taxonomic uniqueness," as well as 'visceral' characteristics, such as "physical size" and the degree to which a species is considered a "higher form of life." These proxies are used to study the government's protection and spending decisions on individual species. Overall, we find that the role of visceral characteristics is much greater than the role of scientific characteristics.* (JEL Q28)

I. INTRODUCTION

As a society, we seem to have made a generalized commitment to conserving biodiversity; but how do we spend our limited resources on this commitment? Our goal is to answer this question by studying actual decisions made by the U.S. government about which species to protect and how much to spend on them.

Narrowly, this paper is about explaining the species-by-species protection and spending decisions of certain relevant U.S. federal and state government organizations.[1] To perform this analysis, we have combined several distinct datasets from different government and scientific sources. We think that the resulting combination offers a rare opportunity for empirically based insights into preferences about biodiversity conservation. Decisions about endangered species reflect the values, perceptions, and contradictions of the society that makes them. Thus, more broadly, this paper addresses some very general issues about humankind's relation to nature and about our choices when confronted by competing and often unquantifiable objectives. Nevertheless, we should stress that our paper is strictly a positive study of government choices—no normative claims are made. This is not an attempt to value species, but rather an analysis of preferences revealed through actual decisions.

The Endangered Species Act of 1973 (U.S. Fish and Wildlife Service 1992b) gave the federal government the power to protect U.S. species from extinction. Simply by listing a species as endangered, the government opens a legal avenue for development projects to be delayed or canceled, and for millions of dollars in opportunity costs to be incurred. Indeed, once a species is placed on the endangered species list, cost-benefit analysis is practically precluded. Additionally, all listed species are eligible to have funds spent directly on their recovery, with the eventual goal of having their endangerment reduced to levels that would allow them to be removed from the list. Overall, the relevant government agencies face difficult problems of, first, deciding which species to place on the endangered species list and, second, deciding how much to spend on the recovery of each listed species. In the sections that follow, we examine these two decisions in detail. We believe this subject deserves serious attention from economists because the direct and indirect costs of this type of environmental protection are already substantial, and such expenditures are growing more rapidly than almost any other item of comparable size in the national economy.[2]

Department of Economics, Harvard University.

We thank Shara Howie and Melissa Morrison at the Nature Conservancy and Judy Jacobs, Gloria Parham, and Jay Shepard at the Fish and Wildlife Service for generously providing us with data and background information. We also thank Mark L. Plummer and two anonymous referees for detailed, helpful comments. We alone retain responsibility for the contents, including errors and omissions.

[1] Readers interested in other studies of revealed preference of government decision making are referred to McFadden (1975, 1976), Weingast and Moran (1983), Thomas (1988), and Cropper et al. (1992). The most closely related work to our own is Mann and Plummer (1993).

[2] One illustration of this growth is the dramatic rise in direct expenditures on species-by-species preservation. These figures are studied in Section IV.

Land Economics • February 1996 • 72 (1): 1–16

Copyright © 2001. All Rights Reserved.

TABLE 1
THE TOP TEN SPECIES BY TOTAL SPENDING

Common Name	Spending ($Millions)	Cumulative Spending (%)
1. Bald Eagle	31.3	9.9
2. Northern Spotted Owl	26.4	18.3
3. Florida Scrub Jay	19.9	24.5
4. West Indian Manatee	17.3	30.0
5. Red-Cockaded Woodpecker	15.1	34.8
6. Florida Panther	13.6	39.1
7. Grizzly (or Brown) Bear	12.6	43.1
8. Least Bell's Vireo	12.5	47.1
9. American Peregrine Falcon	11.6	50.7
10. Whooping Crane	10.8	54.2

Table 1 lists every species on which over $10 million has been reported spent by all U.S. federal and state agencies from 1989 to 1991.[3] The species are listed in descending order of total reported expenditures. Also shown is cumulative spending as a percentage of all expenditures on endangered species. What follows now are some speculations, intended to be suggestive, on some possible spending patterns.

First, the spending appears to be extremely concentrated. Just 10 species account for over half of all expenditures, out of a total of 554 species that were officially listed as endangered or threatened as of November 1990. Next, notice that all of the species listed in Table 1 are animals. More precisely, they are all mammals or birds; in fact, most are relatively *large* mammals and birds. Furthermore, there might even be some doubt about whether these species are truly endangered, or even threatened, in any objective absolute sense. The Bald Eagle, Northern Spotted Owl, Florida Scrub Jay, and Grizzly Bear, for example, have relatively large viable breeding populations that, while being pressed upon by habitat destruction in some regions, do not appear to be even remotely exposed to any overall danger of going extinct. The same cannot be said, for example, of the Texas Blind Salamander, Monitor Gecko, Choctawahatchee

Beach Mouse, or Waccamaw Silverside, which are objectively much closer to extinction, but nonetheless each claim less than $10,000 in total expenditures.

A quick reading of Table 1 would also appear to suggest that the degree of biological uniqueness plays no role, or even a perverse role, in expenditure decisions. Of the 10 listings, constituting over 54 percent of total spending, only 4 are full species (Bald Eagle, West Indian Manatee, Whooping Crane, Red-Cockaded Woodpecker). The other 6 are of a lower taxonomic rank. The Northern Spotted Owl, Florida Scrub Jay, Grizzly Bear, and so forth are *subspecies*. They each have very closely related near-twin subspecies, genetically very similar, that are in little danger of going extinct. At the opposite extreme are such creatures as the Sand Skink, Red Hills Salamander, and Alabama Cave Fish. Total spending on any one is less than $10,000, yet each of these three endangered species forms a monotypic genus—meaning that they are the genetically distinct unique representatives of an entire genus, having no sister-species and being only very distantly related to their nearest safe cousin-species in other genera.

The observations note above seem provocative. But are the perceived patterns real? And what do they mean? This paper is an attempt to answer these questions using a careful statistical analysis.

The remainder of the paper is organized as follows: Section II contains a discussion of various normative justifications for the preservation of biodiversity and of the difficulties of constructing a single objective function that the government might be expected to follow. We then identify a subset of these normative justifications that can be defined operationally and quantified, and we describe the data that we use for them. This subset includes 'scientific' characteristics such as "degree of endangerment" and "taxonomic uniqueness" as well as more 'visceral' characteristics such as "physical

---

[3] The exact source of the data, and other details, will be explained in the next section.

Copyright © 2001. All Rights Reserved.

size" and the degree to which a species is perceived as a "higher form of life." In Section III, we describe the Endangered Species Act and the listing process in more detail, and then estimate a regression to determine the relative importance of these species characteristics in the listing decision. We find that both scientific and visceral elements play an important role in determining whether a species becomes listed. In Section IV, we focus on the government's direct spending to improve the condition of listed species. First, we describe the available spending data and the method by which it was collected. Then, using the same independent variables as in Section III, we estimate a regression with "species-by-species" spending as the dependent variable. We find that the visceral characteristics play a highly significant role in explaining the observed spending patterns, while the more scientific characteristics appear to have little influence. Next, in Section V, we extend the analysis to include explanatory variables of a more openly bureaucratic nature. The goal here is to determine how closely the government is following its own system for prioritization of spending. Results are mixed; while the formal priority system is followed to some degree, there is evidence that its least important component plays a disproportionate role. Finally, Section VI concludes with a summary of the results and a discussion of some broader themes which we believe are suggested by the analysis.

II. OBJECTIVES IN BIODIVERSITY PRESERVATION

A. Overview

In this section we attempt to identify all relevant variables which might influence endangered species policy. This exercise is not intended to have normative implications, but rather to frame the empirical analysis of the following sections. In an ideal study of this subject, we would have a well-defined objective function for society as a whole, and the observed government behavior could be judged on the basis of how well it satisfied such a standard. In the case of biodiversity

preservation, however, the most striking feature is the almost complete lack of any such anchor. Even in fields as contentious as health policy or environmental risk management, there is some 'currency' around which the analysis can be framed. In biodiversity preservation, however, no such measure has yet been agreed upon, and decision-making bodies are left with a shopping list of objectives that are not easily comparable. In our opinion, it is essential to recognize this "lack of an anchor" as a central feature of biodiversity preservation, and we do not propose any solution to such a difficult problem. Instead, we study only the elements that are both *relevant* and *measurable*: relevant because they usually show up in the "shopping list of objectives," and measurable because it is possible to identify quantifiable proxies. Then, we attempt to determine which of these elements is actually important for explaining the patterns of behavior in the data.

Throughout our discussion, we use the conservation of *species* as the main vehicle for biodiversity preservation.[4] In this species-oriented approach, we find it useful to divide arguments for the preservation of biodiversity into three broad classes.[5] First, species may have *commercial* value in uses such as food, medicine, clothing, or tourism. Second, *existence* value represents the pleasure people derive from simply knowing that a species exists in the wild, even if representatives are never actually observed directly. Such existence values can also encompass

---

[4] We recognize that some conservation professionals would argue that the proper unit of measurement is not species, but ecosystems. At an extreme, researchers who hold this view might question the entire foundation of a species-oriented approach. We take no position in this debate. Since the relevant governmental organizations use a species approach, it is logical for us to use this same approach when studying their behavior.

[5] As we pointed out earlier, this discussion in no way attempts to claim that these categories are the normatively "correct" ones to be using. There is a huge literature on this topic, spanning many disciplines, and we could not do it full justice here. Rather, our choices of these categories is done purely out of convenience; we want to find out what actually influences government choices, and to do this we need some simple and efficient categorization.

Copyright © 2001. All Rights Reserved.

moral arguments, originating ultimately from religious and philosophical convictions, that humankind has an ethical obligation to preserve species, notwithstanding any direct benefits. Third, it is sometimes argued that if we allow biodiversity to deteriorate below (currently unknown) critical levels, then ecosystems may collapse, thus causing significant repercussions in other spheres. We refer to this as a *contributory* value.[6] If we believe that this value is important, then we should act to preserve species that may be important "keystones" for their respective ecosystems. Note that "option values" can occur in any of these three categories, and cannot be thought of separately from the underlying value (commercial, existence, or contributory).

Within each of these three types of arguments, there may be several components that provide motivation for current government policy; in the next subsection we attempt to isolate those which seem to be both relevant and measurable. These "relevant and measurable" components fall exclusively within the category we have labeled existence value. This is not to say that the other two categories are not valid motivations; rather, it is that we cannot find measurable components of these other categories that can be used to understand current policy. The reasons are different in each case. First, although there are some exceptions, most endangered species have little or no commercial value, so this category can be effectively ignored as a significant motivation in government spending.[7] Next, the contributory value is not understood well enough to be useful for making decisions about individual species and, therefore, is not likely to explain any of the patterns in our data.[8]

B. Relevant and Measurable Objectives in Biodiversity Preservation

As stated previously, there are many components which might on principle be included in society's objective function for biodiversity, but only a subset are both relevant and measurable at this time. Below, we describe the three components of this subset that we have been able to identify, all of which fall into the class of existence values. Because it is not possible to obtain reliable measures of any component for all species of plants and animals, we confine our analysis to cover only vertebrate species, which in effect constitute a single phylum of the animal kingdom.

1. People often speak of the large amount of attention paid to "charismatic megafauna." Just knowing that elephants and pandas exist in the wild has value to some people, even if they never actually witness the wild elephants and pandas firsthand; such an effect is likely to be less pronounced for species of wild toads or eels. Since existence value of a species may indeed be a function of its charisma and physical size, we would ideally like some good measure of both. We capture the "megafauna" part by using the physical length of an average representative of the species.[9] At this stage, we have not obtained a satisfactory measure of "charisma," although we have received many creative suggestions.[10]

---

[6] This usage is introduced in Norton (1988).

[7] Some fisheries fall into the class of exceptions, with whale species perhaps the most obvious examples. Since, as is explained later, our analysis does not include marine species, the importance of commercial value in our sample seems minimal.

[8] In rejecting inclusion of an "ecological significance" variable in the government's priority system, Fay and Thomas (1983, 43101) state that "this kind of information is seldom available at the time a species is considered for listing."

[9] Lowe, Matthews, and Mosely (1990) and Mosely (1992) give fairly precise length ranges for all species on the U.S. endangered species list. For non-listed species, we consulted several standard biological references to obtain length estimates (Allen 1983; Grzimek 1984; Lee et al. 1980; Nowak 1991). In some cases, we were not able to obtain a published length for a species and it was necessary to form an estimate by using data from closely related species.

[10] Among the suggestions are: eye-size or eye-body ratio, number of times the animal's name appears in children's books or in articles in *The New York Times*, space devoted to the animal in zoos, and subjective charisma ratings from an as yet unperformed psychology experiment. Our judgment at this time is that none of these measures would be useful enough to justify their inclusion, even if they were readily available.

Copyright © 2001. All Rights Reserved.

2. Another possible component of existence value is the degree to which a species is considered to be a higher form of life. In many contexts, it seems obvious that human beings care about other people in proportion to the degree to which they are related to them or can 'identify' with them. We might believe that this feeling extends to higher forms of life as well. We are not suggesting that this is an ideal ethical criterion to use; in fact, we are making no normative judgment at all. Instead, we want to recognize that if people do actually make distinctions among species in this way, then it will necessarily be a component of existence value. To test for the possible role of such a component, we have divided the dataset into the five broad classes of vertebrates: mammal, bird, reptile, amphibian, and fish. In the regressions of the following sections, we include dummy variables for each of these classes to see if current policy discriminates among them.

3. Since we also may have existence value for "biodiversity" as a whole, some measure of the amount that a species adds to this diversity may play a role in deciding how much to spend on it. As a measure of such added diversity, we might use a species' taxonomic distinctiveness, or difference, from other species.[11] Other things equal, the more unique a species is, as measured by distance from its closest living relative, the more attention we would pay to its preservation. As a measure of taxonomic uniqueness, we use dummy variables to discriminate among three possibilities. First, a "Full Species" is our term for a genuine species in the generally accepted biological sense.[12] Next, a "Monotypic Genus" is a full species that constitutes the sole representative of its genus.[13] Finally, we use the term "Subspecies" to mean any taxonomic unit below the level of a full species. Of these three types, Monotypic Genus is the most taxonomically distinct, while Subspecies is the least.

Finally, a fourth factor to be considered does not relate directly to species value, but rather to the probability of preventing extinction.

4. Any preservation decision is likely to pay some attention to the actual level of endangerment of the species in question. Other things equal, we expect that preservation dollars would go to recover the more endangered species.[14] Our data for endangerment comes from the Nature Conservancy (NC), which tracks an exhaustive subset of all vertebrate "full species" in the U.S. and provides "global endangerment" ranks on a scale of 1 (most endangered) to 5 (least endangered). Overall, the NC ranking system is by far the most comprehensive and objective measure of species endangerment that we could find. Each of the interval rankings of 1 through 5 has a well-defined meaning, and a serious effort is made by the NC to apply the rankings consistently.[15]

---

[11] This theme is developed more fully in Weitzman (1992, 1993).

[12] The "generally accepted" biological-species definition is typically ascribed to Ernst Mayr: "Species are groups of actually or potentially interbreeding natural populations reproductively isolated from other such groups."

[13] The Genus is the taxonomic level just above species.

[14] In a formal model of biodiversity preservation, such as Weitzman (1993), a more appropriate statement is something like the following: other things equal, we should spend more money on species with higher marginal decreases in extinction probability per dollar spent. In practice, there probably is a high correlation between a species' "absolute" and "marginal" level of endangerment, so the two concepts may actually turn out to be similar. Due to our data constraints, we are forced to finesse the possible distinction between marginal and absolute levels of endangerment.

[15] The Nature Conservancy distinguishes between global ranks, called "G-ranks," which are given to full species, and "T-ranks," which are given to subspecies or populations. In our dataset, we use the ranking relevant to the taxonomic unit being studied, i.e. G-ranks for full species and T-ranks for subspecies. The definitions of G-ranks given by the NC are: G1—critically imperiled throughout their range and typically have fewer than 6 occurrences in the world, or fewer than 1,000 individuals; G2—imperiled throughout their range and typically have between 6 and 20 occurrences, or fewer than 3,000 individuals; G3—vulnerable throughout their range and typically have fewer than 100 occurrences, or fewer than 10,000 individuals; G4—apparently secure throughout its range (but possibly rare in parts of its range); G5—demonstrably secure throughout its range (however, it may be rare in certain areas). See National Heritage Data Center (1992, 1993a, 1993b).

Copyright © 2001. All Rights Reserved.

These four factors make up the subset that we feel is both relevant and measurable. In an attempt to adjust for the importance of any relevant but *unmeasurable* factors, we later define a "residual" component of existence value and attempt to estimate the effect of its omission from the regressions. This artificial construction will be explained in Section IV, where it plays an important role in interpreting the pattern of spending decisions.

III. THE LISTING DECISION

A. Background: The Endangered Species Act of 1973

The Endangered Species Act of 1973 ("the Act") created a framework for the preservation of endangered plants and animals in the United States. This framework is administered primarily by the U.S. Fish and Wildlife Service (FWS), an agency of the Department of the Interior, which oversees the recovery of all terrestrial and freshwater species of plants and animals.[16] The term "species," although having a fairly precise technical meaning to taxonomists, is defined in the Act to include subspecies, varieties (for plants), and populations (for vertebrates), in addition to 'true' species in the technical biological sense.[17] Where not otherwise specified, we follow this biologically imprecise terminology and use the word species to refer to any taxonomic unit eligible for protection under the Act.

The process of listing a species for protection begins when the species is proposed by FWS as a "candidate." During its period of candidacy, FWS gathers data from internal and external scientific sources in order to determine whether the species warrants listing and protection. The process stalls here for most candidates; of more than 3,600 candidates for listing in 1993, there was insufficient scientific data to make a decision on about 3,000.[18] If sufficient scientific data exist and the data are judged to warrant listing, then FWS can place a formal proposal in the Federal Register. After a public comment period, FWS makes a final decision. A species may be listed as "en-dangered" or "threatened." An endangered species is "in danger of extinction through-out all or a significant portion of its range." A threatened species is "likely to become endangered in the foreseeable future."[19] Both types are considered to be "listed" and, while there are some legal distinctions, in practice they are given the same protection under the Act. For the remainder of the paper, we ignore the distinction between endangered and threatened species and we refer to all listed species as endangered.

For good reasons, the decision to list a species is given considerable attention by the FWS. Once protected, endangered species can cause large disruptions and force developers to delay or even cancel projects that might harm the species. For expositional purposes, we can effectively divide the stipulations of the Endangered Species Act into 'protective' and 'recovery' measures. Protective measures are restrictions on activities which harm listed species. These restrictions are more stringent for public, especially federal, activities than for private activities. On federal land or in projects requiring federal permits, species are protected from any adverse effect of an activity, including habitat alteration. The most prominent examples of such activities are dam or other construction, and mining or logging on federal land. On private land, it is primarily forms of direct harm that are

---

[16] The National Marine Fisheries Service is responsible for the administration of the Act for most marine species. In this paper, we focus our attention exclusively on the species monitored by the FWS. We focus on the FWS because the National Marine Fishery Service does not publish data comparable to our FWS sources. Since the vast majority of recovery programs are managed by the FWS, this restriction does not play a role in our results.

[17] A vertebrate "population" is a taxonomic group below the subspecies level. Our analysis combines subspecies and populations in the same category.

[18] This total includes invertebrates and plants as well as the vertebrates studied in this paper.

[19] The background and definitions are drawn from the Endangered Species Act of 1973 and from the FWS publication, "Placing Animals and Plants on the List of Endangered and Threatened Species," U.S. Fish and Wildlife Service (1993). This publication also includes a detailed description of the listing process.

Copyright © 2001. All Rights Reserved.

restricted. Direct harm is defined specifically in the Act and includes such obvious examples as shooting, trapping, and selling.

Recovery measures give the government the power to improve the condition of listed species. The Act provides FWS with the authorization to develop and implement plans to preserve and improve the condition of listed species. More importantly, the Act gives FWS and other federal agencies the authority to purchase significant habitat sites and to aid state agencies that have agreements with FWS.

B. Regression #1: Factors in the Listing Decision

Since listing a species is the crucial first step in its protection, it would be helpful to gain a better understanding of the determinants of the government's decision. What role, if any, is played by the relevant and measurable objectives discussed in the previous section? To answer this question, we constructed a sample of all vertebrate full species which might possibly be considered for listing. This sample excludes all taxonomic units below the full species level; that is, we do not include any subspecies or populations. Such a sample is possible because the Nature Conservancy database contains an exhaustive list of *all* U.S. vertebrate (full) species.[20] We restrict our sample to all full species, listed and unlisted, that meet a minimum threshold of endangerment—the NC endangerment rank of 3 or lower. This leaves us with a sample of 511 full species, of which almost half are fish. Using this sample, we estimate a logit regression with a dependent dummy variable, *LISTED*, which is set to 1 if the (full) species was listed as of March 1993 and to 0 otherwise. The independent variables are Nature Conservancy degree of endangerment rank (*NCRANK*), log of physical length (*LNLENGTH*), dummies for the taxonomic class (*MAMMAL, BIRD, REPTILE,* and *AMPHIBIAN*—fish is the benchmark), and a dummy for monotypic genus (*MONOTYPIC*).

The results of Regression #1 indicate

REGRESSION #1
THE LISTING DECISION

LISTED	Coef.	Std. Err.	t	P > |t|
MAMMAL	1.11	.42	2.679	0.008
BIRD	1.21	.38	3.224	0.001
REPTILE	.92	.44	2.102	0.036
AMPHIBIAN	−1.51	.45	−3.339	0.001
NCRANK	−1.47	.16	−9.238	0.000
LNLENGTH	.25	.14	1.713	0.087
MONOTYPIC	.84	.39	2.177	0.030
CONSTANT	1.07	.42	2.550	0.011

Notes: Dependent variable is *LISTED*; method of estimation is logit; 511 observations.

that many forces play a role in the listing process.

1. The coefficient on *LNLENGTH* is positive and significant at the 10 percent level; other things equal, a 1 percent increase in physical length translates into approximately a .05 percentage point increase in the likelihood of listing.[21]

2. Similar translations yield statistically significant estimates for mammals, birds, reptiles, and amphibians (relative to fish) of 20, 22, 17, and −27 percentage points, respectively. All of these results are significant at the 5 percent level.[22]

---

[20] We exclude subspecies from this analysis because the NC does not track a complete list of U.S. subspecies. We do not even know how many non-listed subspecies exist, much less what they are.

[21] As a first approximation, logit coefficients can be translated into probability terms by multiplying by $p(1 - p)$, where p is the mean of the dependent variable. In this case, $p \approx .24$ and $p(1 - p) \approx .18$.

[22] Readers may notice that the order of listing preference suggested by this regression places fish ahead of amphibians, while an evolutionary tree would place humans closer to amphibians than to fish. We are not sure that an evolutionary tree is the correct measure of what constitutes a higher form of life, and the main reason we ran the regression with dummies rather than a single ordered "evolutionary" variable was to remain agonistic on this issue. Nevertheless, the overall pattern of the coefficient estimates is roughly consistent with a loose evolutionary interpretation of "higher" as being "more closely related to humans."

Copyright © 2001. All Rights Reserved.

3. Monotypic genera show a statistically significant increased listing likelihood of 15 percentage points.[23]

4. *NCRANK* has the expected influence on listing. The negative coefficient implies that a low *NCRANK*—which implies high endangerment—results in a higher likelihood of listing. A translation of the coefficient into probability terms implies that a one unit increase in *NCRANK* results in an approximate 26 percentage point rise in the likelihood of listing.

Most of these coefficient values are not surprising. As mentioned in Section II, a species become listed only after there is significant scientific evidence on its endangerment. Thus, we would expect that well-studied species would have a greater chance of meeting the necessary scientific standard and passing from being a candidate for listing to becoming listed. Since humans allocate their scarce scholarly resources for many of the same reasons cited for preservation, our results may indicate which species we like to study as much as they indicate which species we want to preserve. This complication is unavoidable. Nevertheless, the results of this regression certainly show that species are listed for more than just scientific characteristics such as uniqueness and endangerment; visceral components of existence value, like size and the degree to which a species is considered a higher form of life, seem to affect the listing decision as well.

IV. THE SPENDING DECISION

A. Background: Spending Data and the 1988 Amendment

Once a species has been listed under the Act, FWS is charged with the creation of a "recovery plan," which sets out the steps to be taken to improve the condition of the species. Internal audits by the U.S. Department of the Interior estimate that the potential direct costs implied by the recovery plans of all listed species are about $4.6 billion (U.S. Fish and Wildlife Service 1990b, 7).[24] Since the total available budget falls

far short of this figure, all agencies with spending programs must make choices among projects.[25] During the 1980s, some members of Congress seemingly became concerned that a disproportionate share of these limited conservation dollars were being used to preserve a small number of species. Apparently, there was sufficient interest in this issue to pass an Amendment to the Act in 1988 requiring FWS to prepare annual reports on the amount of federal and state spending, broken down by species. The data collected by FWS were first published for fiscal year 1989, and have subsequently been published for fiscal year (FY) 1990 and FY 1991.[26] Spending from these three years is the main object of study in this section. In the following paragraphs, we explain the nature of these data, how they were collected, and what types of spending are and are not included.

The 1988 Amendment specifically charged FWS with making a "good faith" effort to calculate all expenditures that were

---

[23] Although we are only able to study the *MONOTYPIC* dummy in this regression, we would ideally like to know if subspecies are treated differently from full species in the listing process. Since an exhaustive list of all vertebrate subspecies does not exist, it is impossible to answer this question formally. We can, however, make an educated guess by using some simple ratios. Tear et al. (1993) estimate that the ratio of subspecies to full species in North America is 6.9:1 for mammals and 4.9:1 for birds; in the sample of listed species, the ratio of subspecies to full species is 2.4:1 for mammals and 1.1:1 for birds. Although these ratios consider only one factor and cannot be calculated for all vertebrate classes, the disparity is at least suggestive that full species are given preference to subspecies at the listing stage.

[24] This figure includes only the costs that would be paid by the government to carry out its recovery plans. It does not include any estimate of private or other opportunity costs.

[25] Calculating the total budget available for recovery projects is not straightforward. There are several sources of discretionary funds that can be used for many purposes in any year, with biodiversity preservation only one possibility. Any way that it is calculated, however, the budget is much less than $4.6 billion.

[26] The relevant sources are U.S. Fish and Wildlife Service (1990a, 1991, and 1992a). We plan to update this dataset to include FY 1992 spending when FWS releases this information, but we do not anticipate major changes in our results.

Copyright © 2001. All Rights Reserved.

"reasonably identifiable" to an individual species. If spending cannot be broken down by species, then it is not included in the final total. Although the term "reasonably identifiable" may seem somewhat imprecise, in practice it seems to cover fairly broad classes of expenditures that are more or less operationally defined. Examples of expenditures usually included are habitat acquisitions designed primarily for a single species, captive breeding programs, operating expenses of wildlife preserves mostly dedicated to a single species, population censuses, and scientific study. Examples of expenditures that are typically not identifiable to a single species are salaries of FWS personnel, operating expenses of general wildlife preserves, multi-species habitat purchases, and the opportunity costs of legal restrictions on development.

Since the published expenditure figures exclude some public as well as all private expenditures, they do not completely account for the overall cost of wildlife preservation. As a result of this incomplete data, and for other reasons, we do not envision ourselves here as doing any kind of formal, comprehensive, society-wide cost-effectiveness analyis of current policies. Basically, we think of the reported spending figures as a noisy reflection of some underlying measure of concern for the various species. In studying reported species-by-species spending, we seek only the modest goal of finding patterns in the data which may reflect underlying preferences of the relevant decision-making organizations.

As for mechanics of the spending decision, the first thing to note is that the aggregate government spending figures we use come from many different agencies, at both the federal and state levels. Some of the spending is on items specifically mandated in the budget of a relevant agency. In essence, the legislative branch controls this mandated expenditure directly. Another part of spending is discretionary and comes from funds managed by FWS or appropriated by FWS from other government sources. To guide these discretionary spending decisions, FWS has developed a system for prioritizing species; we discuss this prioritiza-

tion system in Section V. In our opinion, it would be an oversimplification to ascribe some fraction of spending to Congress and the remainder to other relevant agencies, because many of the decisions are made with input from both sides. Therefore, we treat all of the spending as if it comes from "the government" in general, although this clearly leaves many subtle political factors beyond the scope of our analysis.

The spending figures published in the annual expenditure report are collected from three sources. First, FWS calculates its own spending. Second, expenditures by the states are reported to a central conservation organization, which then passes the totals along to FWS. Third, each federal agency reports its expenditures individually to FWS. Since its inception in the 1989 fiscal year, the process has become more efficient and agencies have become more adept at identifying conservation expenditures from within their budgets. (In the early years, for example, the state numbers were somewhat incomplete.) Some of the remarkable growth in total reported expenditures, which have risen from \$43 million in 1989 to \$102 million in 1990 to \$177 million in 1991, is attributable to this improvement in data gathering. The bulk of the spending is done by the federal government, with FWS itself comprising about half of the federal total. For all three years, the federal total of conservation expenditures is \$248 million, while the state total is \$74 million. Expenditure data is collected on all listed plant and animal species. However, as already noted, we confine our attention here to the vertebrates. Since approximately 95 percent of the identifiable conservation budget is spent on vertebrates, we are confident that any patterns uncovered here would be robust in the complete sample of listed species.

B. Regression #2: Determinants of Spending

Regression #2 uses the log of total spending from 1989 to 1991 (*LNTOTAL*) as the dependent variable. Since we only observe spending on a species when it is greater than \$100, the dependent variable is censored at ln(100) and the appropriate esti-

Copyright © 2001. All Rights Reserved.

REGRESSION #2
THE SPENDING DECISION

LNTOTAL	Coef.	Std. Err.	t	P > |t|
MAMMAL	.75	.44	1.717	0.087
BIRD	.27	.37	0.721	0.472
REPTILE	-1.72	.50	-3.443	0.000
AMPHIBIAN	-.94	.66	-1.422	0.156
NCRANK	.65	.19	3.423	0.000
LNLENGTH	1.03	.15	6.747	0.000
MONOTYPIC	-.37	.50	-0.736	0.462
SUBSPECIES	-.35	.30	-1.177	0.240
CONSTANT	7.69	.45	16.959	0.000

Notes: Dependent variable is *LNTOTAL*; method of estimation is Tobit; 237 observations.

mating procedure is a Tobit regression.[27] The independent variables are the same as those in Regression #1, with the addition of a *SUBSPECIES* dummy for listed taxonomic units below the full species level.

Before discussing the regression results, it is helpful for the exposition to introduce a hypothetical variable which we call *CHARISMA*. We think of this variable as the unmeasurable part of existence value, and we *mechanically define it to be orthogonal to all of the independent variables used in Regression #1*.[28] Although it may seem to be an unorthodox construction, *CHARISMA* is just a statistically harmless fiction that enables us to discuss a possible bias in our estimates. In writing about this hypothetical variable as if it actually exists in the real world, we seek only to simplify the exposition. For this purpose, we treat *CHARISMA* as a 'real' variable omitted from the right-hand-side of Regressions #1 and #2, and we assume that its coefficient would have been positive in both regressions. We then discuss how the estimated coefficients on the other regressors would be biased by this omission.

In Regression #1, we could think of the sample as being randomly selected from the population of all vertebrate full species. By construction, *CHARISMA* is uncorrelated in this population with the right-hand-side variables: *LNLENGTH, NCRANK, MONOTYPIC*, and the taxonomic class dummies. Hence, in principle, there is no omitted variable bias introduced in Regression #1. The sample used in Regression #2, however, consists only of *listed* species, and thus is specially selected by the listing process. If *CHARISMA* has a positive influence on listing likelihood, then within this sample it may well be correlated with other variables found to affect the listing decision. For example, since the estimated coefficient on *LNLENGTH* is positive in Regression #1, then, other things equal, a species with high *CHARISMA* would require *lower LNLENGTH* to achieve the same listing likelihood. Therefore, in a sample of only listed species, *CHARISMA* and *LNLENGTH* are likely to be inversely correlated. Analogous reasoning can be used on each of the other regressors—in general, each variable's correlation with *CHARISMA* will be opposite to the sign of its respective coefficient in Regression #1. Thus, if we make the natural assumption that *CHARISMA* also has a positive influence on the spending decision, then the direction of the omitted variable bias on each coefficient in Regression #2 will also be opposite to the sign of the respective coefficient in Regression #1. The likely effect of this bias is discussed below on a case-by-case basis.

The results of Regression #2 suggest several patterns in spending behavior.[29]

---

[27] Because there are only two censored observations, the results of the Tobit estimation are practically identical to those of an OLS regression using the same variables.

[28] We can do a thought experiment to envision what the *CHARISMA* variable represents. First, imagine that we could create a perfect measure for the existence value of each species. Next, regress this perfect measure on the set of independent variables used in Regression #1. Define the residuals from this regression to be the *CHARISMA* variable. This variable should *not* be thought of as exactly the same thing as the common usage of the word, "charisma." Although the two meanings have some overlap, our *CHARISMA* is a statistical construct which will, by definition, have the specific properties that we need to use for our analysis.

[29] We note here that the patterns discussed below are not driven by a small subset of the sample. For example, if we exclude the 10 species with the highest spending, which together comprise more than half of all spending, then the same qualitative results are found.

Copyright © 2001. All Rights Reserved.

1. The coefficient on *LNLENGTH* is highly significant, statistically and quantitatively. This coefficient may be interpreted here in the usual fashion as an elasticity; it implies an approximate 1 percent increase in spending for a 1 percent increase in length. Since our analysis suggests that *LNLENGTH* and *CHARISMA* are negatively correlated in the sample of listed species, the omission of *CHARISMA* from Regression #2 should bias the coefficient on *LNLENGTH* downward. This further strengthens our finding of a highly significant positive effect.[30]

2. The taxonomic class dummies, as a group, seem to have a significant effect on spending. Since the fish dummy is left out, all of the other taxonomic class coefficients measure spending on that class relative to fish. The results show that the *MAMMAL* dummy enters positively and the *REPTILE* dummy enters negatively. The coefficients on *BIRD* and *AMPHIBIAN* are of the expected sign, but the magnitudes are not significantly different from zero. The overall pattern to the coefficients is fairly consistent with the onetime official policy of FWS to give spending preference to the "higher" animals in the following order: mammal–bird–fish–reptile–amphibian. This policy was officially abandoned in 1983, when Congress explicitly directed the FWS to implement a priority system that *ignored* the distinction between "higher" and "lower" life forms. However, as the regression results suggest, such a policy may actually reflect underlying preferences.[31] The effect of omitted variable bias would mostly support this interpretation. Since *MAMMAL* and *BIRD* are probably negatively correlated with *CHARISMA* in this sample, their estimated coefficients should be biased downward. Conversely, the coefficient on *AMPHIBIAN* should be biased upward. Adjusting for this bias would tend to reinforce the pattern already found. Only for the coefficient on *REPTILE* would the omitted variable bias possibly change the coefficient sign, since it is likely to be biased downward in this estimate.

3. Since the Full Species dummy is left out, the other two taxonomy dummies measure spending relative to this class. Our qualitative prediction from the discussion in Section II is that taxonomic uniqueness should have a positive influence on spending, so that we should find a positive coefficient on *MONOTYPIC* and a negative coefficient on *SUBSPECIES*. Actually, we find estimated coefficients on both to be negative but statistically insignificant. Adjusting for bias due to the omission of *CHARISMA* yields inconclusive results. It is likely that the *MONOTYPIC* coefficient is biased downward and the *SUBSPECIES* coefficient is biased upward. This bias could conceivably be sufficient to mask a small role for taxonomic uniqueness.

4. A surprising and counterintuitive result is the highly statistically significant positive coefficient on *NCRANK*. At face value, this means that a *decreased* level of endangerment—thus, a higher *NCRANK*—implies *more* spending. The appropriate interpretation of this result depends on the size of the bias from the omission of *CHARISMA*. Suppose, at one extreme, that the omitted variable bias is small or negligible. Then, we would conclude that *NCRANK* actually plays a perverse role in spending decisions. We consider it to be an implausible conclusion that, controlling for all other observable factors, a more truly endangered species actually gets less money spent on it; nevertheless, such an interpretation cannot be excluded by our results.

---

[30] To support a reproductively viable population, physically large species typically require more habitat than do physically small species. Hence, it is conceivable that the significant positive coefficient on *LNLENGTH* is capturing different species' "needs." We think the explanatory power of this argument is small. Nevertheless, as with all other plausible explanations, we would gladly return to this question if relevant data on species' needs become available.

[31] There is an issue here, and throughout the paper, about taking the spending on species at face value. For example, spending on fish living in rivers might be a proxy for our desire to preserve rivers, and have little to do with a desire to preserve fish per se. This kind of problem occurs often in empirical work and, at some level, it is impossible to eliminate completely. We have no reason to believe that the problem is particularly acute in this case.

Copyright © 2001. All Rights Reserved.

At the other extreme, suppose that the omitted variable bias is large. Under this scenario, the 'true' *NCRANK* coefficient could be negative, but the omitted variable bias would be large enough to turn a significant negative coefficient into a significant positive coefficient. If this is indeed the explanation for the positive coefficient on *NCRANK*, then it is a powerful illustration of the role *CHARISMA* is playing in the spending decision. In this case, we would conclude that any influence of *NCRANK* in its "expected" direction is more than outweighed by the role of *CHARISMA*. We believe that this conclusion is probably correct. Since *NCRANK* plays a very significant role in the listing process, it is likely that *CHARISMA* and *NCRANK* are highly correlated in the population of listed species and that the omission of *CHARISMA* from Regression #2 severely biases the *NCRANK* coefficient upwards. There is also considerable casual evidence to support this conclusion. Species with the highest spending include many "charismatic" species with very low actual endangerment—the Bald Eagle, Florida Scrub Jay, and Grizzly Bear among the most prominent examples. Adjustments for other characteristics fail to explain why these species receive high spending, as each also has large positive residuals in Regression #2.

It seems fair to conclude that spending choices are determined much more by visceral than by scientific characteristics: *LNLENGTH* and taxonomic class play significant roles, while the effect of taxonomic uniqueness and *NCRANK* are, at best, overshadowed by bias due to the omission of *CHARISMA*. Indeed, the results are even more striking when we realize that the inclusion of taxonomic class dummies essentially restricts *LNLENGTH* to the role of explaining "within" class variation of spending; absent taxonomic class dummies on the right-hand-side, the coefficient on *LNLENGTH* would be even greater, as length explains some of the "between" class variation as well. Overall, the one-line message to take away from our study of spend-

ing behavior is "size matters a lot." Again, we should note that this is not necessarily 'wrong', since "size" might justifiably be included in a society's objective function. However, it should also be noted that such heavy weighting of visceral elements seemingly goes against the language and spirit of current FWS policy, which strongly stresses scientific characteristics. For example, the FWS numerical priority system is based entirely on scientific elements. In the next section, we study this priority system in more detail and test for its relative importance in the spending decision.

V. THE FWS PRIORITY SYSTEM

A. Background and Discussion

In 1983, FWS created a formal "priority system" to serve as a guide in its listing and spending decisions.[32] In this section, we describe the official system adopted for spending decisions and we discuss several aspects that can yield insights into underlying preferences towards conservation. Then, we test for the priority system's role in explaining the observed pattern of spending. Overall, the system is intended to be used as a guide rather than a strict set of rules; nevertheless, if the government were using the system as it was designed, we would expect the data to show some evidence of successful implementation.

To study this issue, Regression #3 includes a regressor called *PRIORITY*, a variable which is equal to FWS's published priority rank. *PRIORITY* ranges from 1 (FWS's highest rank) to 18 (FWS's lowest rank). There are three components of this number. In strictly decreasing lexicographic order of importance, these components are "degree of threat" (most important: 3 grades), "recovery potential" (middle importance: 2 grades), and "taxonomy" (least important: 3 grades), making a total of 18 combinations. In principle, "degree of threat" is a similar concept to *NCRANK*, as both attempt to

---

[32] The official FWS description and defense of its priority system is contained in Fay and Thomas (1983).

Copyright © 2001. All Rights Reserved.

measure the absolute endangerment level of the species. Also, each is on a three-point scale in our sample. Despite this conceptual similarity, the two measures are not highly correlated—an issue we return to later. "Recovery potential" is a measure of the ease or difficulty of improving a species' condition. Species with a "high" recovery potential are perceived to have well-understood threats which do not require intensive management to be alleviated. The three "taxonomy" grades are the same as we used in Regression #2: monotypic genus, full species, and subspecies. In addition, the priority system recognizes species seen to be in "conflict with construction or other development projects or other forms of economic activity" (Fay and Thomas 1983, 43104). Species in conflict do not receive a higher priority number than those not in conflict, but they are given a tiebreaking preference between species with the same (#1–18) ranking. We include a dummy variable, *CONFLICT* (1 if species is in conflict, 0 if not), to recognize this additional distinction.

It is not part of our purpose here to have a complete discussion about the merits and faults of the priority system described above. Nevertheless, there are several observations about this system which may yield insight into the attitudes and preferences of its creators. First, it is notable that a lexicographic ordering is used in creating the ranking. This ordering means, for example, that any species with the highest grade of "degree of threat" will always be assigned a higher priority than any other species with the middle grade of "degree of threat," even if the latter species has higher grades of "recovery potential" and "taxonomy." Such a method effectively precludes any possibility of trade-offs among the three criteria. This rigidity suggests a very extreme objective function. Second, the inclusion of "recovery potential" could be viewed as an attempt to quantify the cost-effectiveness of recovery. But, by placing "degree of threat" prior to "recovery potential" in the ordering, FWS is essentially making the statement that "cost issues are dominated by endangerment issues." Our final observation concerns the use of conflict as a posi-

REGRESSION #3
THE SPENDING DECISION WITH FWS PRIORITIES

LNTOTAL	Coef.	Std. Err.	*t*	$P > |t|$
MAMMAL	.54	.40	1.354	0.177
BIRD	.46	.34	1.342	0.181
REPTILE	−1.62	.47	−3.470	0.000
AMPHIBIAN	−1.19	.62	−1.917	0.057
NCRANK	.80	.18	4.398	0.000
LNLENGTH	.85	.14	5.944	0.000
PRIORITY	−.10	.04	−2.716	0.007
CONFLICT	1.20	.29	4.177	0.000
CONSTANT	7.99	.47	17.126	0.000

Notes: Dependent variable is *LNTOTAL*; method of estimation is Tobit; 237 observations.

tive tiebreaker for species priority. It seems more reasonable to suppose that, other things equal, it is more cost-effective to spend money on species that are *not* in conflict with development, since species in conflict are already imposing opportunity costs on society. The stated preference for preserving species in conflict may reflect some underlying desire to pay attention to species that are in the public spotlight.

B. Regression #3: The FWS Priority System

Regression #3 is identical to Regression #2 except for the addition of *PRIORITY* and *CONFLICT* and the subtraction of *MONOTYPIC* and *SUBSPECIES* from the list of regressors. *MONOTYPIC* and *SUBSPECIES* are dropped for statistical reasons because they are included as components of *PRIORITY*.

The coefficient on *PRIORITY* is negative and statistically significant. Other things equal, high priority species, i.e., those with a low numerical *PRIORITY*, receive more spending than do low priority species. At first glance, this suggests successful implementation of the priority system. Such a conclusion is mitigated, however, by the size of the estimated coefficient on *CONFLICT*. Recall that *CONFLICT* is intended to be the least important component of the priority system, as it acts only to break ties between species with the same priority num-

Copyright © 2001. All Rights Reserved.

REGRESSION #4
DETERMINATION OF DEGREE OF THREAT

DEGREE	Coef.	Std. Err.	t	P > |t|
NCRANK	.20	.05	4.333	0.000
CONFLICT	− .41	.07	− 5.637	0.000
CONSTANT	1.28	.47	15.394	0.000

Notes: Adjusted $R^2 = .17$; dependent variable is DE-GREE; method of estimation is OLS; 237 observations.

ber. In spite of this ostensibly small role, the estimated coefficient on CONFLICT is more than 10 times the estimated coefficient on PRIORITY, and its t-statistic is greater than 4. Since 10 units of PRIORITY—moving up from 14 to 4 on the 1–18 scale, is intended to play a far greater role than the existence of conflict, such a result seems difficult to explain within the framework of the FWS system.[33] It is possible, however, that the CONFLICT variable is capturing other influences which are playing a major role in the spending decision. Specifically, species in conflict may generate extra political attention. If so, then through a variety of mechanisms, such political attention might translate into increased spending.

There are also indications that species in conflict receive higher priority numbers than they objectively deserve. As mentioned earlier, the NC endangerment rank (NCRANK) and FWS's "degree of threat" component of PRIORITY attempt to measure the same thing. Nevertheless, the correlation between the two measures is far from perfect, and some of the deviation can be explained by the existence of conflict. To illustrate this point, we estimate an OLS regression of the FWS degree of threat (DEGREE) on independent variables NCRANK and CON-FLICT.[34] (See Regression #4.) The coefficient on NCRANK is positive and significant, but considering that a coefficient of 1 would indicate a perfect correlation, the size of the coefficient seems low. The coefficient on CONFLICT is negative and significant; this implies that species in conflict are considered to be more endangered by the FWS than they are by the NC. Since the NCRANK measure is designed to take into account

any conflict that threatens the global survival of a species, the results of Regression #4 suggest that FWS may be inappropriately factoring individual findings of local conflict into its supposedly objective endangerment ratings. Thus, not only does CON-FLICT have a disproportionate influence on the spending decision, but it may also subtly influence the rest of the priority system as well.[35]

VI. CONCLUSIONS

How do we spend our limited resources on preserving endangered species? We analyzed this question by examining the actual listing and spending decisions of the relevant government agencies. The overall pattern to these results is clear: visceral characteristics of species, such as their physical size and the degree to which they are considered to be higher forms of life, explain a

[33] Mann and Plummer (1993) were the first to indicate the importance of the CONFLICT variable. Their results motivated us to include CONFLICT in our analysis.

[34] An OLS regression implies that we take the actual numerical DEGREE rankings seriously. If we believe that DEGREE rankings are only ordered classes, then the proper estimation procedure would be ordered logit. Since, in this case, the results of an ordered logit estimation are very similar to OLS, we only report the latter. In either case, the indicated choices of independent and dependent variables are natural because DEGREE is a somewhat subjective measure created by the FWS, while NCRANK and CONFLICT are more objectively determined. No specific standards have been published by the FWS to explain why species receive different DEGREE ranks. NCRANK, by contrast, has fairly specific guidelines summarized in National Heritage Data Center (1992). Also, CONFLICT is the most objective of the FWS ranks; the published guidelines state that "Any species identified . . . as having generated a negative biological opinion which concluded that a given proposed project would violate Section 7(a)(2) of the Endangered Species Act or resulted in the recommendation of reasonable and prudent alternatives to avoid a negative biological opinion would be assigned to the conflict category" (Fay and Thomas 1983).

[35] It is also possible to explain the results of Regressions #4 by positing that CONFLICT contains some superior information on the part of FWS. Because NCRANK is continually updated while DEGREE is not, we feel that this explanation is unlikely to be correct.

Copyright © 2001. All Rights Reserved.

large part of both listing and spending decisions. More scientific characteristics, such as endangerment or uniqueness, play a role at the listing stage but are overpowered by strong visceral elements at the spending stage. The evidence indicates that we pay more attention to species in the degree to which they are perceived to resemble us in size or characteristics. A provocative interpretation is to summarize current preservation policy as an expansion of rights and obligations towards species that remind us of ourselves. Although it remains highly speculative, this interpretation of our results may indeed be the best single explanation.

We also analyzed the implementation of the government's current system for setting spending priorities. The analysis finds that, while the priority system is being implemented to some degree, the least important component of the system had an influence which far exceeded its prescribed role. This component, a fairly 'objective' measure of whether a species is in conflict with development, is also found to influence the priority system itself. Such influence suggests that it might be useful to have a more formal separation between an agency making policy and an agency gathering the scientific information necessary for the setting of priorities. Without such a separation, even a well-intentioned government is prone to mixing these two distinct activities.

References

Allen, Thomas B. 1983. *Field Guide to the Birds of North America*. Washington, DC: National Geographic Society.

Cropper, Maureen L., William N. Evans, Stephan J. Berardi, Maria M. Ducla-Soares, and Paul Portney. 1992. "The Determinants of Pesticide Regulation: A Statistical Analysis of EPA Decision Making." *Journal of Political Economy* 100 (Feb.):175–97.

Fay, John J., and W. L. Thomas. 1983. "Endangered Species Listing and Recovery Priority Guidelines." *Federal Register* 48 (184): 43098–105. Washington, DC: U.S. Government Printing Office.

Grzimek, Bernhard. 1984. *Grzimek's Animal Life Encyclopedia*, 13 vols. New York: Van Nostrand Reinhold Co.

Lee, David S., Carter R. Gilbert, Charles H. Hocutt, Robert E. Jenkins, Don E. McAllister, and Jay R. Stauffer, Jr. 1980. *Atlas of North America Freshwater Fishes*. North Carolina: North Carolina State Museum of Natural History.

Lowe, David W., John R. Matthews, and Charles J. Mosely, eds. 1990. *The Official World Wildlife Fund Guide to Endangered Species of North America*. Vol. 2. Washington: Beacham Publishing Inc.

Mann, Charles J., and Mark L. Plummer. 1993. "Federal Expenditures on Endangered Species Recovery." Discovery Institute, Seattle.

McFadden, Daniel. 1975. "The Revealed Preference of a Public Bureaucracy: Theory." *The Bell Journal of Economics* 6 (Aut.):401–16.

Mosely, Charles J., ed. 1992. *The Official World Wildlife Fund Guide to Endangered Species of North America*. Vol. 3. Washington: Beacham Publishing Inc.

National Heritage Data Center Network. 1992. *Heritage Program Element Ranks*. Arlington: The Nature Conservancy.

———. 1993a. *Perspectives on Species Imperilment* (revised version). Arlington: The Nature Conservancy.

———. 1993b. Conservation Data Base. Arlington: The Nature Conservancy.

Norton, Bryan. 1988. "Commodity, Amenity, and Morality: The Limits of Quantification in Valuing Biodiversity." In *Biodiversity*, ed. E. O. Wilson, 200–205. Washington, DC: National Academy Press.

Nowak, Ronald M. 1991. *Walker's Mammals of the World*. Baltimore: Johns Hopkins University Press.

Tear, Timothy H., J. Michael Scott, Patricia H. Hayward, and Brad Griffith. 1993. "Status and Prospects for Success of the Endangered Species Act: A Look at Recovery Plans." *Science* 262 (5136):976–77.

Thomas, Lacy Glenn. 1988. "Revealed Bureaucratic Preference: Priorities of the Consumer Product Safety Commission." *Rand Journal of Economics* 19 (Spr.): 102–13.

U.S. Fish and Wildlife Service. 1990a. *Federal and State Endangered Species Expenditures—Fiscal Year 1989*. Washington, DC: U.S. Department of the Interior, Fish and Wildlife Service.

———. 1990b. *Report to Congress: Endangered and Threatened Species Recovery Program*. Washington, DC: U.S. Department of the Interior, Fish and Wildlife Service.

Copyright © 2001. All Rights Reseved.

————. 1991. *Federal and State Endangered Species Expenditures—Fiscal Year 1990.* Washington, DC: U.S. Department of the Interior, Fish and Wildlife Service.

————. 1992a. *Federal and State Endangered Species Expenditures—Fiscal Year 1991.* Washington, DC: U.S. Department of the Interior, Fish and Wildlife Service.

————. 1992b. *The Endangered Species Act of 1973 as Amended by the 100th Congress.* Washington, DC: U.S. Department of the Interior, Fish and Wildlife Service.

————. 1993. *Placing Animals and Plants on the List of Endangered and Threatened Species.* Washington, DC: U.S. Department of the Interior, Fish and Wildlife Service.

Weingast, Barry R., and Mark J. Moran. 1983. "Bureaucratic Discretion or Congressional Control? Regulatory Policymaking by the Federal Trade Commission." *Journal of Political Economy* 91 (Oct.): 765–800.

Weitzman, Martin L. 1992. "On Diversity." *Quarterly Journal of Economics* 107 (May): 363–405.

————. 1993. "What to Preserve? An Application of Diversity Theory to Crane Conservation." *Quarterly Journal of Economics* 108 (1):157–83.

Copyright © 2001. All Rights Reseved.

[5]

ELSEVIER Journal of Public Economics 63 (1997) 331–349

JOURNAL OF PUBLIC ECONOMICS

The voluntary provision of a pure public good: The case of reduced CFC emissions and the Montreal Protocol*

James C. Murdoch[a], Todd Sandler[b,†]

[a]*School of Social Sciences, University of Texas-Dallas, Richardson, TX 75083, USA*
[b]*Department of Economics, Iowa State University, Ames, IA 50011-1070, USA*

Received June 1995; final version received January 1996

Abstract

This paper applies the theory of the voluntary provision of a pure public good to the behavior of nations to curb chlorofluorocarbon (CFC) emissions during the late 1980s. By devising an empirical test, we determine that these cutbacks in emissions are consistent with Nash behavior. When taste parameters are controlled, the relationship between emission cutbacks and national income is nearly linear as implied by the theory. If the sample is purged of potential outliers, then the linear relationship results. A significant taste parameter is the extent of political and civil freedoms, while a marginally significant parameter is geophysical position in terms of latitude.

Keywords: Public good; Montreal Protocol; Ozone shield; CFCs; Nash equilibrium

JEL classification: H41; D62; Q20

1. Introduction

In recent years, there has grown an increased awareness of transboundary pollution that places environmental assets at risk both globally and

* This paper was prepared under a cooperative agreement between the Institute for Policy Reform and the Agency for International Development (AID), Cooperative Agreement No. PDC-0095-A-00-1126-00. Our research was also funded by the National Science Foundation, grant SBR-9222953. Comments from two anonymous referees are gratefully acknowledged.

† Corresponding author. Tel. 515-294-5783, Fax: 515-294-0221, E-mail: tsandler@iastate.edu

0047-2727/97/$17.00 © 1997 Elsevier Science S.A. All rights reserved
PII S0047-2727(96)01598-8

332   J.C. Murdoch, T. Sandler / Journal of Public Economics 63 (1997) 331–349

regionally. Traditional nation-state jurisdictions need not coincide with the economic domain over which the economic impacts of consumption and production activities extend. Globally, manmade pollutants have degraded the stratospheric ozone shield, the oceans, the atmosphere, and the biodiversity of the planet; regionally, these pollutants have harmed aquifers, rivers, lakes, soils, and forests.[1] Many transboundary pollution problems share two common features: strategic interactions among nations and public good properties. Strategic interactions occur when the choices or the beliefs for these choices of two or more nations are mutually dependent in a significant fashion. To account for these interactions, a game theory formulation is often presented (see Barrett, 1994; and Sandler, 1993). Public good properties arise when the benefits (costs), derived from limiting (not limiting) the pollutant, provide consequences that are nonrival and nonexcludable to a set of nations. In the case of the stratospheric ozone, the release of chlorofluorocarbons (CFCs) and other halocarbons thins the shield that protects plants and animals from harmful ultraviolet radiation. This thinning has consequences for countries worldwide and is, thus, nonexcludable. Furthermore, one nation's increased exposure to enhanced ultraviolet radiation does not lessen the risks to any other nation; hence, nonrivalry is clearly present.

The purpose of this paper is to analyze *cutbacks* in CFC emissions *that, in large part, preceded* the ratification and institution of the Montreal Protocol on Substances that Deplete the Ozone Layer. It is our contention that the Montreal Protocol was initially enacted because it codified reductions in CFC emissions that polluters were voluntarily prepared to accomplish as the scientific case against CFCs grew. We investigate empirical predictions derived from the theory of the voluntary provision of public goods,[2] and find that the data are remarkably consistent with these predictions. That is, when tastes are controlled, the relationship between emission cutbacks and national income is nearly linear. A linear relationship is statistically significant if three outlier nations are removed from the sample. Our analysis is noteworthy because it provides the first statistical application of the group self-selection process as derived from the modern theory of the voluntary provision of pure public goods. If this latter theory is to prove useful, then empirical applications, such as the one here, need to be put forward.

Our findings suggest that the Montreal Protocol may be more symbolic than a true instance of a cooperative equilibrium, since nations' CFC

---

[1] See Helm (1991) and Sandler (1992) for analyses of a host of global and regional transboundary problems.

[2] On the private provision of public goods, see Andreoni (1988), Bergstrom, Blume, and Varian (1986), and Cornes and Sandler (1984, 1996).

J.C. Murdoch, T. Sandler / Journal of Public Economics 63 (1997) 331–349   333

reductions prior to the treaty taking effect appear to fit the predictions of a single-shot Nash equilibrium. By examining the data qualitatively, we provide further evidence that CFC cutbacks were voluntary, because these reductions characterized both ratifiers and nonratifiers, were at levels greater than the initial mandate, and displayed a large standard deviation.

This study differs from an important analysis by Congleton (1992), who related the ratification of the Vienna Convention of 1985 and the Montreal Protocol to political and market institutions. As such, Congleton did not explicitly account for public good attributes and did not include gross national product (GNP) levels of the participating nations.[3]

2. Background

2.1. The Stratospheric Ozone Shield

Despite its small concentration in the earth's atmosphere, representing less than one part per million, ozone absorbs much of the ultraviolet radiation (UV) of the sun and, thus, protects all living organisms and their DNA from UV's harmful effects. Any dissolution of the stratospheric ozone shield would not only increase the risk of skin cancer to humans, but would also threaten food supplies by adversely affecting phytoplankton at the base of the marine food chain. Disastrous consequences could result. The Environmental Protection Agency (EPA) estimated that the implementation of the Montreal Protocol of 1987 could save the United States $6.4 trillion by 2075 in reduced costs associated with skin cancers (EPA, 1987a, 1987b). In the absence of the Protocol, skin cancer incidence was based on an annual growth of CFC use at 2.5 percent through 2050. The long-run cost from cutting CFC use, as mandated by the Protocol, was estimated to be between $20 and $40 billion during the 1989-2075 period, given these projected growth rates (Morrisette et al., 1990, p. 16). For the United States, net gains would come from cutbacks in CFC emissions.

In 1985, the British Antarctic Survey presented evidence that an alarming 40 percent drop (from 1964 levels) in the springtime atmospheric concentration of ozone took place over Halley Bay, Antarctica, between 1977 and 1984. This so-called "hole" in the ozone layer of the stratosphere then drifts northward during the summer and mixes with other air masses, thus allowing the depletion to be shared worldwide on a more or less equal basis.

---

[3] Congleton (1992, p. 419) included GNP *per capita* in two of the six empirical models, but later dropped the variable, because of concerns that CFC regulations could affect GNP. Given the small percentage of GNP that is related to CFC production and consumption, we chose to ignore any such simultaneity.

334   J.C. Murdoch, T. Sandler / Journal of Public Economics 63 (1997) 331–349

The uniform mixing during the summertime reinforces the pure publicness of ozone depletion on a global basis. As the scientific case against CFCs mounted and the depletion process became understood, the main producer nations were motivated to curb emissions even if they had to act alone. The rapid development of CFC substitutes (e.g., hydrofluorocarbon) meant that there was little opposition to limiting CFC production by the CFC producers (Morrisette et al., 1990).

2.2. Montreal Protocol of 1987

Just prior to the discovery of the Antarctic ozone hole, nations negotiated the Convention for the Protection of the Ozone Layer in Vienna on 22 March 1985. This precursor to the Montreal Protocol mandated the ratifiers to study the harmful effects of CFC emissions on the ozone layer. Nations were committed to monitor the ozone layer, to exchange scientific findings, and to develop domestic programs for limiting ozone-depleting substances (see the U.N. Environment Programme (UNEP), 1991 for treaty texts).

On 16 September 1987, the Montreal Protocol extended the Vienna Convention by setting explicit limits to the emission of ozone-depleting substances, particularly CFC-11 and CFC-12. The Montreal Protocol entered into force on 1 January 1989, and included the following features: By 1 July 1993, ratifiers must reduce their annual consumption and production of CFCs to 1986 levels. For subsequent years until 1 July 1998, this annual production and consumption cannot exceed 80% of 1986 levels. Thereafter, it could not exceed 50% of 1986 levels. Beginning in 1990, the ratifiers must ban the import of ozone-depleting substances from nonratifiers; starting in 1993, a similar ban would apply to the export of these substances.

Ratifiers of the Montreal Protocol were automatically considered to be parties to the Vienna Convention. During 1989, the ratifiers were only obligated to return to 1986 emission levels; this fact becomes important for interpreting the empirical findings. Developing nations had a great inducement to ratify the Protocol, because they could delay compliance by ten years, gain technical and financial assistance, and be exempted from trade sanctions. If a developing nation qualified for these special treatments, it is referred to as an "Article 5" country.

During 1990, scientific evidence indicated that the thinning of the ozone layer had worsened and that a large hole had opened over the North Pole. On 29 June 1990, the Montreal Protocol was strengthened with a set of amendments (UNEP, 1991).

3. Theoretical Considerations

The theoretical model draws from the work of Andreoni (1988), Andreoni and McGuire (1993), and others, who used a subscription model of public

J.C. Murdoch, T. Sandler / Journal of Public Economics 63 (1997) 331–349   335

good contributions to identify contributors. This model is extended by allowing for a non-normalized price of the public good. We assume that a nation's preferences for a global public good, G, is represented by a quasi-concave, strictly increasing utility function,

$$U_i = U_i(y_i, G), \tag{1}$$

where y_i is the ith nation's consumption of a composite private good and G is the total amount of the public good available for consumption, so that

$$G = \sum_{i \in C} g_i. \tag{2}$$

In Eq. (2), g_i is the ith nation's contribution to the public good and C denotes the set of contributors ($g_i > 0$). Total contributions can also be written as $g_i + G_{-i}$, where G_{-i} is the sum of contributions from contributors other than nation i, so that

$$G_{-i} = \sum_{j \neq i} g_j. \tag{3}$$

We normalize just the price of the private good and write the ith nation's linear income constraint as

$$w_i = y_i + pg_i, \tag{4}$$

where w_i denotes national income and p is the per-unit price of the public good. A full-income budget constraint follows from adding pG_{-i} to both sides of Eq. (4) to give

$$w_F^i = w_i + pG_{-i} = y_i + pG, \tag{5}$$

where w_F^i denotes the ith nation's full income – income plus spillins of public good benefits. To derive the nation's demand for the total amount of the public good, we depict the nation as solving the following problem:

$$\max_{y_i, G} \{ U_i(y_i, G) | w_i + pG_{-i} = y_i + pG; G \geq G_{-i} \}. \tag{6}$$

In Eq. (6), the inequality constraint indicates that the ith nation is a contributor and, hence, a member of C only when $G > G_{-i}$, so that $g_i > 0$. Noncontributors choose a G that equals G_{-i} and contribute nothing. The Kuhn-Tucker first-order conditions imply the following continuous demand function,

$$G = \max\{f_i(w_i + pG_{-i}; p), G_{-i}\}, \tag{7}$$

for the pubic good. When contributions are positive, the nation's demand for G is $f_i(\cdot)$; otherwise it is G_{-i}. A Nash equilibrium results when we have a vector of individual contributions, g_i, that maximize utility in (1) subject to (4) and to the best-response level for spillins, G_{-i}^*. This equilibrium is unique

336   J.C. Murdoch, T. Sandler / Journal of Public Economics 63 (1997) 331–349

provided that all goods have positive income elasticities, which we, hence-forth, assume.

When the stratospheric ozone shield is considered, g_i denotes the reduction in ozone-depleting CFC emissions and y_i represents all other goods. To maintain tractability and facilitate analogy with the public goods literature, we analyze only the nation's behavior with respect to current emission policy. Although this approach ignores dynamic stock adjustments, it is consistent with the language and articles of the Montreal Protocol.

To distinguish contributors and allow for heterogeneous tastes, we must put some structure on the taste pattern. Following Andreoni (1988, pp. 64–66), we allow nations' tastes to differ according to a taste parameter, Θ, so that

$$U_i = U_i(y_i, G; \Theta),\tag{8}$$

where Θ is used to *index* the various (finite) types of nations and may be a vector of exogenous parameters. For a given Θ, nations' demand for the public good can be rank ordered by income so that $g_i > g_j$ when $w_i(\Theta) > w_j(\Theta)$ owing to the assumption of income normality (Andreoni, 1988). The taste parameter, Θ, orders contributors among different taste classes. For a given income, this parameter is greater when the nation's taste for the public good is greater. We can utilize the result in Bergstrom, Blume, and Varian (1986, Fact 4) to identify the critical income level, w^*, conditional on p and Θ, below which no nation contributes. Specifically, a nation's equilibrium contribution, g_i^*, is[4]

$$g_i^* = \begin{cases} w_i/p - w^*(p, \Theta)/p & \text{if } w_i > w^*(p, \Theta), \\ 0 & \text{if } w_i \leq w^*(p, \Theta), \end{cases}\tag{9}$$

where critical income $w^*(p, \Theta)$ equals $f^{-1}(G^*; p, \Theta) - pG^*$ and $f^{-1}(\cdot)$ is the inverse of $f(\cdot)$. Eq. (9) indicates that pollution cutbacks are a linear function of income with a slope of $1/p$. It also follows that all contributors within the same taste category consume the same amount of the private good, which equals $w^*(p, \Theta)/p$, and allocate their remaining income to the public good. This last result is not as unrealistic as it might seem, since, for a given Θ, $w^*(\cdot)$ might be quite high. By including taste parameters based on geophysical location, freedom indices, and other considerations, we have a

---

[4] This follows from examining total equilibrium contributions, which implies

$$G^* \geq f(w_i + pG_{-i}^*; p, \Theta) \quad i = 1,\ldots,n,$$

with equality for $g_i^* > 0$. To derive Eq. (9), we invert both sides of the above equation, add pg_i^* to both sides, and rearrange terms.

J.C. Murdoch, T. Sandler / Journal of Public Economics 63 (1997) 331–349   337

fair number of classes. When population is included in Θ, each nation is a class unto itself; when it is not included in Θ, there are still numerous classes. By (9), there is a critical income level for *each* class of nations. Type Θ nations will contribute whenever their income exceeds $w^*(p, \Theta)$.

Eq. (9) indicates that a nation's demand for a global public good depends on national income and taste attributes. For instance, the Θ parameter could relate to the country's geographical position in terms of latitude. Temperate and arctic countries may have a greater preference for curbing CFCs emissions than tropical nations owing to generally fairer-skinned populations and to greater springtime exposure at higher latitudes to ultraviolet radiation.[5] Population size is another taste parameter, since countries with larger populations are exposed to greater potential damage from the incidence of skin cancers. The number of such cancers is expected to be proportional to population size.

Tastes may also differ between autocratic and democratic regimes. Congleton (1992) theorized that autocratic regimes will do less to protect the ozone shield, insofar as these autocracies confront a higher relative price for pollution abatement than their democratic median-voter counterpart. Congleton also argued that autocracies are less risk averse and, hence, less interested than democracies in insurance-type actions that protect against contingencies such as ozone depletion. Given the relatively short-term nature of most autocracies,[6] he also hypothesized that autocratic governments would not be as concerned about the long-run consequences of ozone depletion. Olson (1993) characterized autocracies as maximizing tax revenues and maintaining their monopoly rights over these taxes. As such, autocracies should be suspicious of protocols that could impose taxes or else could mandate contributions to a Multilateral Fund used to provide technology transfer and financial assistance to others. Olson indicated that autocracies would provide public goods when their provision *augments* taxable income sufficiently to finance the goods and leave some net gain. No short-run augmentation in taxable income can be expected to arise from cutting CFC emissions.[7] Autocracies may, therefore, be less willing than democracies to support ozone protection. Within the group of autocracies or

---

[5] This exposure difference could be taken into account by using a technology function, $k_i(G)$, so that $U_i = U_i(y_i, k_i(G), \Theta)$. This extension means that cut-off income is now $wi^*(p, \Theta)$, which differs even within the same taste class. We avoid this complication by assuming $k_i(G) = G$ and letting the taste parameter adjust for different risk perceptions. There is no empirical data that would allow us to calibrate the $k_i(G)$ functions, especially since ozone concentrations vary greatly even over the same country (de Gruijl, 1995).

[6] Bienen and van der Walle (1989) provided evidence that African autocracies lasted only four years on average.

[7] Reduced CFC emissions will improve health and productivity in the long run, but since we are concerned with only a four-year span, income augmentation is ignored.

338   *J.C. Murdoch, T. Sandler / Journal of Public Economics 63 (1997) 331–349*

democracies, the theory predicts that the cutback in CFCs emissions will be related to income.

4. Empirical Results

4.1. Empirical Model

Eq. (9) provides the theoretical predictions that can be tested with observed data. When tastes differences are ignored, Eq. (9) suggests that if we measure the voluntary contributions (g_i) and the income (w_i) of countries and then plot these data with income on the horizontal axis and contributions on the vertical axis, the data *should* lie on either the horizontal axis $(g_i = 0)$ or on a line beginning at w^*/p with slope $1/p$. If we limit our investigation to countries with positive voluntary contributions, then the data should lie on the straight line. This prediction is, in principle, testable, but a major obstacle is to measure g_i and w_i precisely. If we assume random errors in measuring g_i and w_i, then

$$g_i = \beta_0 + \beta_1 w_i + \epsilon_i \tag{10}$$

is a reasonable empirical model for the data-generating process described in Eq. (9) for Θ constant. β_0 and β_1 can be estimated with ordinary least squares (OLS). We can test how well the model adheres to the straight line by assuming that the ϵ_i is normally distributed with mean zero and standard deviation σ.

Although the regression model described in Eq. (10) provides a simple method for testing whether the slope, β_1, of the hypothesized line is $1/p$, it does not facilitate a test of linearity. One means to test linearity is to estimate the transformation parameter of the Box-Cox transformation (Box and Cox, 1964; Spitzer, 1982). With λ denoting this parameter, the model becomes:

$$g_i = \beta_0 + \beta_1 \left[(w_i^\lambda - 1)/\lambda \right] + \epsilon_i \,, \tag{11}$$

requiring a nonlinear least squares estimator. A test for linearity is based on λ. If λ is equal to one, then the model is linear with respect to w_i.

According to Eq. (9), the linearity of the relationship between w_i and g_i only holds within each group of nations as defined by the Θ parameter. To implement an empirical test of this prediction, we need to measure the taste differences of nations. Let Θ_i denote a 1 by k vector of observable taste measures and γ denote a k by 1 vector of unknown parameters. Then a statistical model based on Eq. (9) is

$$g_i = \beta_0 + \beta_1 \left[(w_i^\lambda - 1)/\lambda \right] + \Theta_i \gamma + \epsilon_i \,. \tag{12}$$

J.C. Murdoch, T. Sandler / Journal of Public Economics 63 (1997) 331–349   339

If the Andreoni (1988) model is more appropriate, then we should see significance in the estimates for the γ parameters and more linearity in the relationship between g_i and w_i when we compare estimates of Eq. (12) to (11).

4.2. Data and Variable Definitions

Our primary measure of g_i is DEMIT$_i$, which is the change in the CFC emissions for country i from 1986 to 1989 (EMIT86 — EMIT89). In total, 61 nations had positive values for DEMIT$_i$, thus making a positive contribution to the protection of the ozone layer. To test for voluntary behavior, we include only these countries, whether they ratified the Montreal Protocol or not,[8] in the regression estimates. The data for EMIT86 and EMIT89 are reported in World Resources Institute (WRI)(1990, 1992). Since 1986 is the benchmark year for the Montreal Protocol and 1989 is before any emission reductions (contributions) are mandated under the treaty, DEMIT$_i$ is a satisfactory measure of *voluntary* contributions.[9]

To measure income (w_i), we use gross national product in 1985 (GNP85). For the majority of the countries, GNP85 is obtained from the *World Tables* produced by the World Bank (1990). For some nations, in particular those with nonmarket economies, GNP data are taken from the *World Fact Book: 1989* (Central Intelligence Agency, 1989).

We use three measures for the components of the vector (Θ) of taste variables. The first is GASTIL, which is the sum of Gastil's (1986) index of civil liberties and index of political rights. These indices are integers, with 1 representing the most liberties and rights and 7 representing the least. Thus, GASTIL takes on integer values from 2 to 14. A country with a value of 2 would be considered the most "free." Because it is not clear that freedom can be measured on a nominal scale, as assumed in the GASTIL measure, we define three dummy variables to measure freedom: FREE equals 1 when GASTIL is 4 or smaller, and 0 otherwise; PFREE (partly free) equals 1 when GASTIL is greater than 4 but less than or equal to 9, and 0 otherwise; and NFREE (not free) equals 1 when GASTIL is greater than 9, and 0 otherwise. The second empirical measure of tastes is based on geographical location, in which LAT is defined to equal: 1 for all countries located above the Tropic of Cancer; 2 for all countries between the Tropic of Cancer and

---

[8] The status of countries with respect to the Montreal Protocol is obtained from UNEP (1993).

[9] WRI (1990, 1992) do not report any nations with zero emissions in both 1986 and 1989 or with the same emissions in both 1986 and 1989. Thus, we do not have data on the countries with zero contributions and the only testable hypothesis is that the relationship between positive contributions and income is linear.

340   *J.C. Murdoch, T. Sandler / Journal of Public Economics 63 (1997) 331–349*

the Tropic of Capricorn; and 3 for the countries below the Tropic of Capricorn.[10] Dummy variables corresponding to LAT were also defined. Thus, L1 is 1 when LAT is 1, and 0 otherwise; L2 is 1 when LAT is 2, and 0 otherwise; and L3 is 1 when LAT is 3, and 0 otherwise. Because of the risks that a thinning ozone layer poses for human health, we include POP85, the population in 1985, as the third taste shift variable.

A summary of the empirical variables and their definitions is displayed in Table 1, while the raw data are presented in Table A1. Included are two additional variables: RAT equals 1 for the nations that ratified the Montreal Protocol before 1 January 1990, and 0 otherwise; while ART5 equals 1 for nations designated as Article 5 developing nations, and 0 otherwise. These variables allow us to *qualitatively* assess a cooperative model of emission reductions, which is the most likely alternative to the subscription model. There are four grounds for rejecting a cooperative model. First, only 38 of these 61 nations (some 54%) ratified the Montreal Protocol during the time period covered by our data. If emission reductions are simply a reflection of the treaty mandate and, therefore, assumed to be generated by a model of

Table 1
Variable Descriptions

Variable	Description
GNP85	Gross National Product in 1985, expressed in hundred billions of dollars.
EMIT86	CFC emissions in 1986, expressed in thousand metric tons.
EMIT89	CFC emissions in 1989, expressed in thousand metric tons.
DEMIT	EMIT86 — EMIT89.
GASTIL	The sum of the Gastil's indices of civil liberties and political freedom.
FREE	A dummy variable equal to 1 for GASTIL $\leq$ 4, and 0 otherwise.
PFREE	A dummy variable equal to 1 for $4 <$ GASTIL ≤ 9, and 0 otherwise.
NFREE	A dummy variable equal to 1 for GASTIL ≥ 10.
L1	A dummy variable equal to 1 if a country is located above the Tropic of Cancer, and 0 otherwise.
L2	A dummy variable equal to 1 if a country is located between the Tropics of Cancer and Capricorn, and 0 otherwise.
L3	A dummy variable equal to 1 if a country is located below the Tropic of Capricorn, and 0 otherwise.
LAT	Equal to 1 for L1 = 1; equal to 2 for L2 = 1; and equal to 3 for L3 = 1.
POP85	Population in 1985, expressed in millions.
RAT	A dummy variable equal to 1 if a country ratified the Montreal Protocol before 1 January 1990, and 0 otherwise.
ART5	A dummy variable equal to 1 if a country is an Article 5 country, and 0 otherwise.

[10] In cases where the latitude cut through a country's border, we coded the country based on where the largest area is located.

J.C. Murdoch, T. Sandler / Journal of Public Economics 63 (1997) 331–349   341

cooperative behavior,[11] we would expect a much larger percentage to have ratified. In fact, nonratifiers would have no institutionalized reason for reducing their emission levels as they were not party to the Protocol. If, however, emission reductions reflect a nation's voluntary subscription level, then the fact that a CFC-reducing nation is almost equally likely to be a ratifier or nonratifier is not unexpected. Second, recall that the Montreal

Table A1
Raw Data

Country	GNP85	POP85	DEMIT	GASTIL	LAT	RAT	ART5
United States	40.128	239.283	67.400	2	1	1	0
USSR	23.540	276.946	34.398	14	1	1	0
Germany, FR	6.708	61.035	15.991	3	1	1	0
France	5.379	55.170	14.922	3	1	1	0
United Kingdom	4.796	56.618	15.455	2	1	1	0
Italy	4.411	57.141	15.433	2	1	1	0
Canada	3.589	25.379	9.405	2	1	1	0
China	3.432	1040.04	6.066	12	1	0	1
Brazil	2.264	135.564	2.616	5	2	0	1
Germany, DR	2.081	16.644	4.404	13	1	1	0
Australia	1.831	15.758	4.276	2	3	1	0
Mexico	1.712	78.524	0.218	8	2	1	1
Iran	1.680	44.212	2.245	11	1	0	1
Spain	1.649	38.523	10.653	3	1	1	0
Netherlands	1.355	14.491	3.861	2	1	1	0
Switzerland	1.053	6.472	3.443	2	1	1	0
Saudi Arabia	0.991	11.595	0.475	13	2	0	0
Sweden	0.989	8.350	0.796	2	1	1	0
Nigeria	0.947	99.669	9.883	12	1	1	1
Indonesia	0.856	164.630	4.447	11	2	0	1
Belgium	0.836	9.858	2.671	2	1	1	0
Poland	0.774	37.203	2.025	11	1	0	0
Austria	0.684	7.555	1.852	2	1	1	0
Argentina	0.649	30.331	0.285	4	3	0	1
Denmark	0.578	5.114	1.372	2	1	1	0
Turkey	0.543	50.310	3.832	8	1	0	1
Finland	0.541	4.908	2.119	4	1	1	0
Yugoslavia	0.476	23.123	0.752	11	1	0	0
Colombia	0.384	28.418	1.272	5	2	0	0
Greece	0.358	9.919	2.746	4	1	1	0
Iraq	0.310	15.898	0.721	14	1	0	0
Egypt	0.309	47.578	0.168	8	1	1	1

[11] By cooperative behavior, we mean cutbacks beyond those that a nation was prepared to make on their own. As information about ozone depletion was revealed, some nations made voluntary CFC cutbacks.

342   J.C. Murdoch, T. Sandler / Journal of Public Economics 63 (1997) 331-349

Table A1 cont.

Country	GNP85	POP85	DEMIT	GASTIL	LAT	RAT	ART5
U. Arab Emirates	0.284	1.350	0.323	10	2	1	0
Israel	0.278	4.233	0.298	4	1	0	0
Kuwait	0.256	1.712	0.404	8	1	0	1
New Zealand	0.219	3.247	1.169	2	3	1	0
Portugal	0.200	10.157	2.716	3	1	1	0
Singapore	0.195	2.558	1.433	9	2	1	0
Chile	0.176	12.121	0.888	11	3	0	1
Ireland	0.171	3.521	1.074	2	1	1	0
Ecuador	0.109	9.378	0.669	5	2	0	1
Tunisia	0.085	7.261	0.359	10	1	1	1
Trinidad & Tob.	0.072	1.185	0.197	3	2	1	1
Cote d'Ivoire	0.065	10.252	0.471	11	2	0	0
Zimbabwe	0.053	8.406	0.389	10	2	0	1
Luxembourg	0.052	0.366	0.137	2	1	1	0
Uruguay	0.051	2.940	0.119	4	3	0	1
Dominican R.	0.049	6.416	0.325	4	2	0	0
Ghana	0.047	12.620	0.637	13	2	1	1
Panama	0.046	2.180	0.023	9	2	1	1
Afghanistan	0.040	18.087	0.993	14	1	0	0
El Salvador	0.040	4.768	0.225	6	2	0	1
Costa Rica	0.035	2.489	0.153	2	2	0	1
Honduras	0.032	4.383	0.089	5	2	0	0
Bahrain	0.032	0.425	0.038	10	1	0	0
Iceland	0.028	0.241	0.046	2	1	1	0
Nicaragua	0.025	3.272	0.220	10	2	0	0
Senegal	0.024	6.567	0.353	7	2	0	0
Barbados	0.012	0.253	0.061	3	2	0	1
Fiji	0.011	0.700	0.060	4	2	1	1
Liberia	0.010	2.178	0.067	10	2	0	0

Note: See Table 1 for the definitions of variables.

Protocol mandated that ratifiers achieve 1986 levels by 1 July 1993. However, for the sample nations, *the average percent reduction from 1986 to 1989 is greater than* 41% implying voluntary behavior. Third, there is the variation in the DEMIT data. The Protocol called for equal percentage reductions in CFCs; however, the standard deviation of DEMIT is greater than 17%. If a cooperative solution were responsible for the observed behavior, we would expect the standard deviation to be close to zero. Finally, there is the behavior of the Article 5 countries. Because the Protocol excuses them for ten years from complying with the mandates, it would not be unexpected if none of the Article 5 nations appeared in our data set. Surprisingly, 22 of these Article 5 nations are among the contributors. Moreover, their average percentage reduction in emissions is greater than 45%, which is somewhat greater than the overall average! We find it difficult to conceive that these figures correspond to a cooperative

J.C. Murdoch, T. Sandler / Journal of Public Economics 63 (1997) 331–349   343

model, the outcome of which is the Montreal Protocol. We, thus, concentrate on using the subscription model as the basis for our empirical estimations.

4.3. Regression Results

Nonlinear least squares estimates of the parameters in Eqs. (11) and (12) are presented in Table 2. The estimates on GNP85 and LAMBDA are significant at conventional levels in all seven specifications. The coefficient on the GASTIL index is negative and significant in models 2, 4 and 6, indicating that nations with fewer political and civil freedoms voluntarily contributed less when the other influences are held constant. Designating NFREE as the left-out dummy variable, the estimates on FREE and PFREE re-enforce the GASTIL estimates. In particular, we find that the primary distinction is between the nations categorized as FREE and all other nations. The positive sign on FREE indicates that the conditional expected value of $DEMIT_i$ is greater relative to NFREE, while the essentially zero coefficient on PFREE means that the conditional expected

Table 2
Nonlinear Least Squares Estimates of the Box—Cox Model. (n = 61)

Variable	Models						
	(1)	(2)	(3)	(4)	(5)	(6)	(7)
INTERCEPT	3.160	4.022	2.631	4.366	2.904	4.372	3.137
	(9.95)	(7.72)	(5.25)	(7.83)	(5.21)	(7.82)	(5.12)
GNP85	2.535	2.493	2.446	2.327	2.326	2.423	2.429
	(10.39)	(10.46)	(10.11)	(8.98)	(8.89)	(8.63)	(8.57)
GASTIL		−0.137		−0.134		−0.116	
		(−2.05)		(−1.98)		(−1.64)	
FREE			1.129		1.134		0.957
			(1.81)		(1.77)		(1.43)
PFREE			−0.212		−0.094		−0.176
			(−0.27)		(−0.12)		(−0.22)
L2				−0.904	−0.651	−0.898	−0.656
				(−1.40)	(−0.93)	(−1.38)	(−1.28)
L3				−1.283	−1.343	−1.284	-1.341
				(−1.24)	(−1.29)	(−1.24)	(−1.28)
POP85						−0.002	−0.002
						(−0.88)	(−0.93)
LAMBDA	0.822	0.828	0.835	0.853	0.852	0.840	0.838
	(20.05)	(20.44)	(20.07)	(18.76)	(18.55)	(18.16)	(18.00)
R^2	0.95	0.96	0.96	0.96	0.96	0.96	0.96

Note: The dependent variable is $DEMIT_i$. Asymptotic t-ratios are in parentheses.

value of DEMIT$_i$ is the same for PFREE and NFREE nations. The effect of FREE is marginally significant, since the critical values for the t-statistics are 1.678 and 1.282 (0.10 level of significance) for a two-tailed and one-tailed test, respectively. Regardless of whether we use GASTIL or the freedom dummy variables, the findings with respect to these rights and freedom measures are consistent with the predictions of Congleton (1992) and Olson (1993).

The latitude dummy variables are included in models 4, 5, 6, and 7. At a 0.10 level of significance, the latitude effects are technically insignificant in these models. The northern latitudes are the left-out category; hence, the estimates on L2 and L3 are relative to L1. The negative signs mean that the expected value of DEMIT$_i$, conditional on income, freedoms, and population, is less for the middle and lower (southern) latitude countries when compared to the expected value of the northern latitude group. Somewhat surprisingly, POP85 is insignificant and negative in both models 6 and 7. The R-squares are very high for cross-sectional data, which may indicate an "outlier" problem that we investigate below.

We are particularly interested in the estimates for the Box-Cox transformation parameter, LAMBDA, whose estimate from Model 1 is significantly different than one. The asymptotic standard error is .04, thus yielding a 95% confidence interval of .822 ± .08. Andreoni's (1988) analysis indicates that linearity between income and contributions may not hold over all nations, but should hold within subclasses defined by taste parameters. By examining the remaining six estimates for LAMBDA, we see some empirical support for this hypothesis. As the tastes of the nations are controlled, the point estimate for LAMBDA moves closer to one; but, the 95% confidence interval estimates never include one.

From a purely statistical point-of-view, the results concerning the Box-Cox transformation parameter provide sufficient evidence to reject the pure subscription model. At the practical level, we cannot ignore the fact that the point estimates of LAMBDA are very close to one. To better understand this finding, we estimated the linear models using ordinary least squares (OLS) and give the results in Table 3. The qualitative conclusions are essentially the same, when comparing the nonlinear estimates in Table 2 to the OLS estimates in Table 3. Notable differences are that the estimates on L2 are more precise and the POP85 point estimates are positive for OLS estimates.

How do the estimates of $\partial g_i / \partial w_i$ vary between the Box-Cox and linear specifications? For the Box-Cox model, the estimated derivative depends on the value of w_i. Based on Box-Cox model 7, the largest estimated derivative is approximately 5.07 for Liberia whose 1985 GNP equals approximately $1 billion, while the lowest estimated derivative is approximately 1.35 for the

J.C. Murdoch, T. Sandler / Journal of Public Economics 63 (1997) 331–349   345

Table 3
Ordinary Least Squares Estimates of the Linear Model. (n = 61)

Variable	Models						
	(1)	(2)	(3)	(4)	(5)	(6)	(7)
INTERCEPT	1.061	2.050	0.559	2.712	1.213	2.714	1.203
	(3.28)	(3.61)	(1.06)	(4.50)	(2.03)	(4.46)	(1.87)
GNP85	1.649	1.643	1.633	1.612	1.609	1.611	1.608
	(31.60)	(32.34)	(32.06)	(32.19)	(31.79)	(30.17)	(29.77)
GASTIL		−0.152		−0.136		−0.138	
		(−2.09)		(−1.91)		(−1.85)	
FREE			1.296		1.170		1.179
			(1.92)		(1.73)		(1.67)
PFREE			−0.422		−0.080		−0.076
			(−0.50)		(−0.09)		(−0.09)
L2				−1.568	−1.312	−1.560	−1.308
				(−2.47)	(−1.89)	(−2.42)	(−1.85)
L3				−1.680	−1.744	−1.675	−1.742
				(−1.55)	(−1.59)	(−1.53)	(−1.57)
POP85						0.0002	0.0001
						(0.09)	(0.05)
R^2	0.94	0.95	0.95	0.95	0.95	0.95	0.95

Note: The dependent variable is $DEMIT_i$. t-ratios are in parentheses.

United States whose 1985 GNP equals approximately \$4 trillion. Using the linear model 7, we see that the estimated derivative is constant at 1.608, which lies within the range of estimates from the Box-Cox model.

From linear model 7, our estimate of p, the implied price of g_i, is \$62.19 per gram. EPA (1987b) estimated that the social opportunity cost of reducing CFC emissions in the United States starting in 1989 ranged between \$0.30 and \$1.00 per gram in 1985 dollars. Our estimate should be interpreted as an estimate of the world *average* price for the 1986–89 period. One explanation for the size of this estimate is the fact that the cheap substitute compounds for CFCs were unavailable before 1989. As these substitutes were made available, the *marginal* cost of emission reduction fell substantially as is evidenced by the EPA estimates.

Heteroskedasticity is always a possibility with cross-sectional data. With White's (1980) general test for heteroskedasticity on models 2-7, we fail to reject the null hypothesis of homoskedastic errors. The hypothesis is rejected for model 1, indicating a specification error in the model that has no taste parameters. This result provides additional support for Andreoni's characterization of the theory, since the data appear to fit the statistical model when the taste parameters are included.

Because the ordinary least squares and the nonlinear least squares (NLS) estimators minimize the sum of squared deviations, they are sensitive to "outliers." To check the robustness of our primary conclusion (linearity between $GNP85_i$ and $DEMIT_i$), we analyze the coefficient sensitivity for model 7 of the OLS estimates using the diagnostic measures proposed by Belsley, Kuh, and Welsch (1980, ch. 2). A particularly relevant diagnostic measure is $DFBETA_i$, which shows the impact on the estimated regression parameter from dropping the ith observation. Focusing on the relationship between DEMIT and GNP85, we find two observations, China and the USSR, with $DFBETA_i$s that fall outside the acceptable bounds established by Belsley, Kuh and Welsch. Moreover, both of these observations and that of the United States are identified as influential by the diagonal elements of the "hat matrix" (referred to as leverage points). When the model is re-estimated with just the United States *or* the USSR *or* China removed, there is little effect on the estimates for LAMBDA. If, however, all three countries are dropped, the NLS estimate for LAMBDA increases to 1.192 with a standard error of 0.20 (t-ratio equal to 6.1). In this case, the 95% confidence interval contains one, and we cannot statistically rule out the linear model. This finding indicates additional support for our hypothesis of linearity; *the influential observations appear to be the cause of the slight nonlinearity identified by the Box-Cox model.* The primary problem is that the model overpredicts the actual value of DEMIT for the United States, the USSR, and China, when these countries are left out of the sample. Because they are three of the largest nations (ranked first, second, and eighth, respectively, in terms of GNP), their inclusion makes the functional form slightly concave in order to provide a better fit between the observed and predicted DEMIT values.

The Belsley, Kuh, and Welsch (1980) procedures provide tools for checking the role of individual observations in regression. They do not give guidelines for dropping data points. We argue that the 61 country data set is still the most appropriate for our tests. However, we feel some confidence in stating that the "true relationship" between income and voluntary contributions is nicely approximated by the linear specification.[12]

---

[12] We also tested the model with other shift parameters. In particular, we added the percent of GNP from agriculture *and* the percent of land area in cropland. Both measures are available from WRI (1990) and measure potential physical damage from UV radiation. Like POP85, the measures were insignificant in the OLS models. In the Box-Cox models, these additional variables reduced the significance of the GNP85 parameter, but left our overall conclusions unchanged. These additional results are available upon request from the authors.

J.C. Murdoch, T. Sandler / Journal of Public Economics 63 (1997) 331–349   347

5. Conclusions

Based on the theory of the voluntary provision of pure public goods, we have hypothesized linear relationship between CFC emission reduction and GNP within each taste class of nations in the absence of a cooperative agreement or treaty. Our regressions indicated that the variation in CFC emission reductions between 1986 and 1989 is, in large part, explained by GNP and two taste parameters – political and civil rights, and geographical latitude. A Box-Cox transformation test comes close to verifying that a linear relationship between CFC emission reduction and GNP is the appropriate relationship for the 61 sample nations. When three outliers are dropped from the sample, linearity is verified. Nations are seen as reducing emissions beyond treaty-mandated levels even prior to the Montreal Protocol taking effect. On average, 61 nations in our sample set reduced CFC emissions by 41.6% from 1986 to 1989, which is well in excess of the 20% cutback mandated by the Protocol from the year commencing on 1 July 1993. This finding suggests that the initial provisions of the Montreal Protocol are largely consistent with voluntary subscription cutbacks in CFC emissions. Additional support for the subscription model is gleaned from the raw data.

Researchers before us have distinguished the ozone depletion problem from other global commons problems, such as global warming. For example, Barrett (1992, p. 17) argued that "The Montreal Protocol may not have increased global net benefits substantially compared with the noncooperative outcome." Although our research results concur with this view, we have taken a different tack and applied an explicit voluntary theory of emission reduction to test empirically whether the Montreal Protocol, as initially formulated, may have been largely symbolic. Our conclusions are only with respect to the initial Montreal Protocol, and not its subsequent amendments.

A number of policy conclusions follow. First, the Montreal Protocol may be a poor blueprint for other global agreements. Each global commons problem has its own pattern of payoffs based on publicness. Currently, ozone depletion is associated with more-certain and more-costly consequences than problems like global warming. Second, the wealthiest CFC emitters may be expected to adhere to the Montreal Protocol without the need of an enforcement mechanism, because the net benefits from doing so are apparently positive. Self-interests motivate compliance. Third, an increase in the number of democratic countries is apt to increase the number of nations that will take steps to curb transboundary emissions (also see Congleton, 1992). Thus, increases in the Gastil indices, achieved after 1989 by the transitional countries of Central and Eastern Europe, may serve to

348   *J.C. Murdoch, T. Sandler / Journal of Public Economics 63 (1997) 331–349*

increase compliance with the Protocol's provision. Fourth, foreign aid, which expands the set of CFC reducers or increases the GNP level of developing and transitional economies by more than the donation, should accelerate the adherence to the mandated reductions in CFC emissions. An environmental dividend can stem from foreign aid, because the preservation of environmental assets is a normal good.

References

Andreoni, J., 1988, Privately provided public goods in a large economy: The limits of altruism, Journal of Public Economics 35, 57–73.

Andreoni, J. and M. C. McGuire, 1993, Identifying the free riders: A simple algorithm for determining who will contribute to a public good, Journal of Public Economics 51, 447–454.

Barrett, S., 1994, Self-enforcing international environmental agreements, Oxford Economic Papers 46, 878–894.

Belsley, D. A., E. Kuh, and R. E. Welsch, 1980, Regression diagnostics: Identifying influential data and sources of collinearity (Wiley, New York).

Bergstrom, T. C., L. Blume and H. R. Varian, 1986, On the private provision of public goods, Journal of Public Economics 29, 25–49.

Bienen, H. and N. van der Walle, 1989, Time and power in Africa, American Political Science Review 83, 19–34.

Box, G. E. P. and D. R. Cox, 1964, An analysis of transformations, Journal of the Royal Statistical Society, Series B, 26, 211–264.

Central Intelligence Agency (CIA), 1989, The world factbook: 1989 (CIA, Washington, DC).

Congleton, R. D., 1992, Political institutions and pollution control, Review of Economics and Statistics 74, 412–421.

Cornes, R. and T. Sandler, 1984, Easy riders, joint production, and public goods, Economic Journal 94, 580–598.

Cornes, R. and T. Sandler, 1996, The theory of externalities, public goods, and club goods, 2nd Ed. (Cambridge University Press, Cambridge).

de Gruijl, F. R., 1995, Impacts of a projected depletion in the ozone layer, Consequences 1, 13–21.

Environmental Protection Agency (EPA), 1987a, Assessing the risks of trace gases that can modify the stratosphere, 7 vols. (EPA, Washington, DC).

EPA, 1987b, Regulatory impact analysis: Protection of stratospheric ozone, 3 vols. (EPA, Washington, DC).

Gastil, R. D., 1986, Freedom in the world: Political rights and civil liberties 1985 (Greenwood Press, Westport, CT).

Helm, D. (ed.), 1991, Economic policy towards the environment (Blackwell, Oxford).

Morrisette, P. M., J. Darmstadter, A. J. Plantinga, and M. A. Toman, 1990, Lessons from other international agreements for a global CO_2 accord, Resources for the Future, Washington, DC, Discussion Paper ENR91-02.

Olson, M., 1993, Dictatorship, democracy, and development, American Political Science Review 87, 567–576.

Sandler, T., 1992, Collective action: Theory and applications (University of Michigan Press, Ann Arbor).

Sandler, T., 1996, A Game-theoretic analysis of carbon emissions, in: R. Congleton, ed., The political economy of environmental protection (University of Michigan Press, Ann Arbor), 9, 251–272.

Spitzer, J. J., 1982, A primer on Box-Cox estimator, Review of Economics and Statistics 64, 645–652.

United Nations Environment Programme (UNEP), 1991, Selected multilateral treaties in the field of the environment, Volume 2 (Grotius Publications Ltd., Cambridge).

UNEP, 1993, Status of ratification of the Montreal Protocol: June 1993 (UNEP, Nairobi).

White, H., 1980, A heteroskedasticity-consistent covariance matrix estimator and a direct test for heteroskedasticity, Econometrica, 48, 817–838.

World Bank, 1992, World Tables: 1991 (Johns Hopkins University Press, Baltimore).

World Resources Institute, 1990, World Resources 1990-91 (Oxford University Press, New York).

World Resources Institute, 1992, World Resources 1992-93 (Oxford University Press, New York).

[6]

ELSEVIER   Journal of Public Economics 69 (1998) 1–16

JOURNAL OF
PUBLIC
ECONOMICS

Political internalization of economic externalities and environmental policy

Toke S. Aidt[*]

University of Aarhus, Department of Economics, Building 350, Dk-8000 Aarhus C, Denmark

Received 31 January 1997; received in revised form 30 October 1997; accepted 20 November 1997

Abstract

This paper derives the characteristics of endogenous environmental policy in a common agency model of politics, and proceeds to show that competition between lobby groups is an important source of internalization of economic externalities. Our analysis generalizes Bhagwati's principle of targeting to the case of distorted political markets. Moreover, we show that the politically optimal structure of environmental taxes incorporates a Pigouvian adjustment. However, since lobby groups care about the distribution of income as well as about efficiency, the equilibrium structure of taxes differs considerably from the Pigouvian rule. © 1998 Elsevier Science S.A.

Keywords: Environmental policy; Lobby groups; Positive environmental economics

JEL classification: D78; H23; Q28

1. Introduction

As stressed by the traditional public-choice approach to economics, economic policy, including environmental policy, is determined by political and economic self-interest. In a pioneering paper, Buchanan and Tullock (1975) point out that economic agents (e.g. firms) are motivated to influence environmental policy because the choice of instrument has income distributional consequences. Another

[*]Corresponding author. Tel.: +45 8942 1496; fax: +45 8613 6334; e-mail: taidt@eco.aau.dk

0047-2727/98/$19.00 © 1998 Elsevier Science S.A. All rights reserved.
PII: S0047-2727(98)00006-1

2   *T.S. Aidt / Journal of Public Economics 69 (1998) 1–16*

reason why lobby groups seek influence on environmental policy is that pollution reduces welfare directly.

This paper is based on the notion that environmental policy is a product of political self-interest, and proceeds to show that political competition is an important source of internalization of economic externalities. The underlying idea is simple: lobby groups give voice to different aspects of environmental policy making sure that all aspects are considered in the political trade off and reflected in the implemented policy. We distinguish between lobby groups that are functionally specialized and lobby groups that have multiple goals. A functionally specialized lobby group acts as an advocate for only one aspect of environmental policy. Accordingly, the government protects the environment to the extent that the political compromise favours environmental interests over other, say, profit interests. An example in point is the CO_2 duty discussed in many European countries and implemented in some. Here, environmentalists seek a high common duty on CO_2 emission, whereas producer interests seek as low a duty as possible. Some lobby groups, like trade unions and employers' associations, advocate multiple goals reflecting the variety of interests that their membership has. Environmental concerns, accordingly, enter the agenda to the extent that environmental protection is of concern to the members. As a consequence, lobby groups modify their demands to reflect environmental concerns before they enter the competitive political process, and, opposite to the case of functionally specialized lobby groups, political internalization is not only a product of political competition. An example in point is the Danish Aquatic Environmental Plan (AEP) from 1987 (see, e.g. ATV, 1990). The AEP is a blueprint that specifies how to protect the aquatic environment in Denmark by means of reductions in the emission of nitrogen and phosphor from agriculture, industry and households. In the political game surrounding the design of the plan, the behaviour of at least industry and household lobby groups provide evidence of multiple goals. That is, besides wanting to reduce their share of the total cost of reduction (the beggar-thy-neighbour element of lobbying), these lobby groups voluntarily accepted to reduce emission.

The idea of political internalization of externalities brings together elements of the Coasian (see Coase, 1960) and Pigouvian (see, e.g. Baumol and Oates, 1989) approach to environmental policy. In line with the Coasian tradition, affected parties mobilize to protect their interests. However, instead of working out a private transfer scheme, they further their goals via political markets, presumably because doing so minimizes transaction costs. A self-interested policymaker with coercive power to implement environmental policy (the Pigouvian element) then trades off the demands of the various lobby groups against the general interest of the voters. In a sense, we may say that the public-choice axiom of political self-interest bridges the Coasian and Pigouvian approach to environmental policy.

To formalize our ideas, we implement the structure of a common agency of politics in a small open economy with n productive sectors as in Grossman and

T.S. Aidt / Journal of Public Economics 69 (1998) 1–16 3

Helpman (1994).[1] A political distortion arises from the fact that lobby groups offer campaign contributions to an electorally motivated government in exchange for particular political favours. The issue of environmental policy arises because of a production externality. We assume that firms in each industry use an input (raw materials, clean water etc.) that has an external effect on the well-being of consumers (smoke, toxic waste water etc.). Furthermore, we assume that the government has access to two environmental policy instruments. Production taxes-cum-subsidies can be used to affect activity in the various sectors, and, by that, presumably the use of the externality generating input. Input taxes-cum-subsidies, which in our specification are equivalent to pollution taxes-cum-subsidies, can be aimed directly at the source of the externality, and by that presumably give firms an incentive to use a cleaner production technology.

Independently of whether lobby groups have multiple goals or are functionally specialized, only the tax-cum-subsidy on the externality generating activity (called raw materials) includes an environmental adjustment. Accordingly, we have a political economy version of Bhagwati's principle of targeting: the competitive political process internalizes the externality by means of the most efficient instrument, i.e., the one that aims directly at the source. Moreover, the environmental adjustment of the raw material tax reproduces the Pigouvian adjustment. In particular, if environmental damage and the distortionary cost of raw material taxation receive equal weight in the political trade off, then the price structure reflects the full Pigouvian adjustment. Due to the various income distributional considerations that enter the political trade off, the political equilibrium does, of course, not replicate the social optimum. In particular, under plausible conditions, sectors that have a lobby group to further their profit interests get a production subsidy and pay a reduced raw material tax (compared to the Pigouvian level). Moreover, if lobby groups have multiple goals, including a desire for monetary transfers from the government, then the government taxes unorganized sectors at an inefficiently high rate to produce extra tax revenue, part of which the government distributes among organized citizens.

Our analysis is part of a growing literature on positive environmental economics. In one branch of this literature, the interaction between trade and environmental policy is brought into focus. Bommer (1996); Bommer and Schulze (1997) consider the effect of trade liberalization on endogenous environmental policy, while Hillman and Ursprung (1992, 1994) introduce environmental lobby groups in a model of endogenous trade policy. While not at the forefront of the analysis, these papers, implicitly, rely on a notion of political internalization of externalities. In another, more recent branch of the literature, which has developed independently of our paper, Schleich (1997) and Fredriksson (1997) consider

---

[1] The basic common agency model is due to Bernheim and Whinston (1986). It has previously been applied to trade policy (see Grossman and Helpman, 1994, 1995a,b) and commodity taxation (see Dixit, 1996; Dixit et al., 1997).

4   *T.S. Aidt / Journal of Public Economics 69 (1998) 1–16*

environmental policy within the framework of a common agency model of politics similar to ours. Both papers consider externalities related directly to output or to consumption, and, so, the structure of their political equilibrium differs considerably from ours. In particular, the generalization of the principle of targeting is a specific feature of our model. Likewise, neither of the papers focuses on the issue of political internalization. Schleich (1997) analyses the choice between domestic price instruments and trade policy in the presence of a consumption and production externality. Two interesting results emerge. First, if the externality is related to consumption, then the political equilibrium fully internalizes the externality by means of a consumption tax. Second, if the externality is related to output, then it is uncertain in terms of the effect on environmental quality whether a production tax-cum-subsidy or trade intervention is the most effective. Fredriksson (1997) considers a pollution tax in a model with functionally specialized lobby groups. A special feature of his model is that firms can, at a cost, invest in pollution control that reduces emission per unit of output. It is shown that a subsidy to pollution control may, due to the endogenous response of lobby groups, lead to an increase in total pollution.

The common agency model of politics, as developed by Grossman and Helpman (1994), is a promising workhorse model of special-interest group politics. It is well-suited to analyse the structure of economic policy across a set of industries and to analyse the choice between various policy instruments.[2] However, applying this model is not without problems. First, at the heart of a common agency model with perfect information is a coordination problem among the principals. Bernheim and Whinston (1986) show existence of an efficient equilibrium, i.e., an equilibrium that is efficient for the group of active players (here, the lobby groups and the government). It is this equilibrium, we, as do Grossman and Helpman (1994) and others, focus on. This has an important implication. If all agents have their interests represented by a lobby group, then the political equilibrium is socially efficient, leading to a complete political internalization of the externality. Accordingly, the internalization is incomplete because some citizens do not organize lobby groups. Unfortunately, it is hard, within the model, to justify why some people can overcome the free rider problem of collective action and coordinate perfectly, while others cannot. Accordingly, we must resort to an implicit assumption that some groups face much lower organizational cost or are much more effective in providing "selective" benefits (see Olson, 1965) than others. Second, embodied in the underlying structure of the model is an (implicit) assumption that the lobby groups can commit to a particular contribution strategy. In the context of a one shot game, seeing why these promises is kept is hard, but, of course, in a dynamic context, reputational considerations may enforce them.

---

[2]For surveys of other models of endogenous policy formation, see, e.g. Hillman (1989); Rodrik (1995); Potters and van Winden (1996).

T.S. Aidt / Journal of Public Economics 69 (1998) 1–16   5

Third, the underlying electoral process is unspecified, and, accordingly, it is unclear why the incumbent government cares about campaign contributions.[3]

We organize the rest of the paper as follows. In Section 2, we describe the formal model. In Section 3, we analyse the political equilibrium and illustrate the principle of political internalization when lobby groups have multiple goals. In Section 4, we consider the case of functionally specialized lobby groups. In Section 5, we provide some concluding remarks.

2. The model

2.1. The economy

Consider a small open economy with $n + 1$ competitive sectors of production, $k = 0, 1, \ldots, n$. Good 0 is numeraire. The international prices of the n non-numeraire goods are p_k^*. The domestic consumer and producer prices are given by q_k and p_k, respectively. Production in the numeraire section takes place by means of a CRS technology using only labour as input. Consequently, profit maximization and mobility of labour across sectors pin down the wage rate of the economy at $w = 1$. Moreover, in the numeraire sector, firms do not pollute.

In the remaining n sectors, firms use three inputs: Labour, l_k, industry specific capital in fixed supply, K_k, and raw materials, r_k. A standard neoclassical production function with CRS describes technology. Raw materials can be thought of as either energy inputs, such as crude oil or coal, traded at a world market with a (common) world market price, z^*, or it can be thought of as environmental goods such as clean water. In the latter case $z^* > 0$ refers to an exogenously given duty on water[4] or to the cost of extracting water from the subsoil. The use of raw materials has an external effect that does harm to the consumers of the economy. We refer to this as emission. We denote emission from sector k as e_k, and assume that $e_k = h_k(r_k)$, $h_r^k > 0$, $h_{r,r}^k \geq 0$.[5] That is, emission is increasing in the use of raw materials at a non-decreasing rate. If r_k is energy inputs, we can think of e_k as emission of smoke (e.g. SO_2), and if r_k is clean water, we can think of e_k as waste water. Each firm is a price taker and supplies its output to a competitive market. With no spillover between prices in different sectors, profit maximization leads to the following restricted profit functions: $\pi^k(p_k, w, z_k)$, where z_k is the domestic

[3]See Grossman and Helpman (1996) for a recent model that is explicit about the relationship between electoral competition and lobby groups that provide campaign money.
[4]Our specification cannot accommodate environmental goods that are free ($z^* = 0$) due to discontinuities in the profit function. Accordingly, to avoid difficulties, we restrict attention to inputs that have a positive market price ($z^* > 0$), and assume that p_k^* and z^* are sufficiently large to avoid non-positive prices in equilibrium.
[5]We use f_j^i as generic notation for the partial derivative of function f^i with respect to argument j.

6   *T.S. Aidt / Journal of Public Economics 69 (1998) 1–16*

price of raw materials in sector k. π^k is strictly convex and has the derivative property, i.e., $\partial\pi^k/\partial p_k = x^k(p_k, w, z_k)$ and $\partial\pi^k/\partial z_k = -r^k(p_k, w, z_k)$, where x^k is firm k's supply function, and r^k is firm k's demand for raw materials. We notice that each firm can respond to environmental policy either by holding output constant while changing the input mix, i.e., by substituting to a cleaner technology, or by fixing the input mix while scaling production down.

The economy has N identical consumers. Each consumer derives utility from consumption of the $n + 1$ goods and disutility from the total level of emission, $E = \Sigma^n_{k=1} e_k$. Hence, emission is assumed to be perfectly mixed in the sense that each consumer does not care about the distribution of emission across firms; only the total level of emission matters. Utility is quasi-linear and additively separable: $U^h = c_0 + \Sigma^n_{k=1} u(c_k) - g(E)$, $u' > 0$, $u'' < 0$, $g' > 0$, $g'' \geq 0$. Each consumer receives income from three sources. First, she supplies, inelastically, her endowment of labour, l_h, to the competitive labour market, and receives the wage income wl_h. Second, she owns a share, $s_{k,h}$, of specific capital in sector k. To simplify, we assume that each individual holds capital claims in at most one sector, i.e., for each h, the share, $s_{k,h}$, is at most positive for one k and zero for all other k. One can think of capital as human capital, e.g. entrepreneurial skills, which is only usable in a particular sector. Third, each consumer receives $1/N$ of any government revenue, $R(\mathbf{p,q,z})$, as a lump sum transfer. From utility maximization subject to income, I, domestic consumer prices, $\mathbf{q}$, and emission, E, we derive the demand, $d^k(q_k)$, for the n non-numeraire goods. The residual determines the demand for the numeraire good: $d^0(\mathbf{q}) = I - \Sigma^n_{k=1} q_k d^k(q_k)$. We assume that $d^0(\mathbf{q}) > 0$ $\forall q_k$ such that the wage rate is well-defined. Now, we can write the indirect utility of consumer h as:

$$V^h(\mathbf{p,q,z}) = l_h + \sum_{k=1}^n s_{k,h} \pi^k(p_k,z_k) + \tfrac{1}{N}R(\mathbf{p,q,z}) + \sum_{k=1}^n u(d^k(q_k)) - \sum_{k=1}^n q_k d^k(q_k)$$
$$- g\left(\sum_{k=1}^n h^k(r^k(p_k,z_k))\right). \tag{1}$$

Add the indirect utilities up to get the following social welfare function:

$$W(\mathbf{p,q,z}) = l + \sum_{k=1}^n \pi^k(p_k,z_k) + R(\mathbf{p,q,z}) + N\left[\sum_{k=1}^n u(d^k(q_k)) - \sum_{k=1}^n q_k d^k(q_k)\right]$$
$$- Ng\left(\sum_{k=1}^n h^k(r^k(p_k,z_k))\right). \tag{2}$$

2.2. The political process

The incumbent government chooses environmental policy. To this end, it has access to two environmental policy instruments: output and input taxes-cum-subsidies. The idea is that the government can decide to tax either production, and,

T.S. Aidt / Journal of Public Economics 69 (1998) 1–16   7

thereby, presumably, via the resulting contraction of output, reduce emission, or it can tax the source of the externality (raw materials) directly. Notice that, due to the functional relationship between e_k and r_k, taxation of emission and raw materials amounts to the same thing. Accordingly, we can, if emission is measurable, think of a raw material tax as a pollution tax. The net revenue from production and raw material taxes-cum-subsidies is given as:

$$R(\mathbf{p,z}) = \sum_{k=1}^{n}(p_k^* - p_k)x^k(p_k,z_k) + \sum_{k=1}^{n}(z_k - z^*)r^k(p_k,z_k). \tag{3}$$

We assume that the government pursues its own goals. It cares about a mixture of political contributions and social welfare. What we have in mind is a democratically elected government that during a term in office collects campaign contributions that will become handy in a later, un-modelled election. The objective function of the government is given as:

$$G(\mathbf{p,z}) = \theta W(\mathbf{p,z}) + \sum_{j=1}^{m} C^j(\mathbf{p,z}),$$

where $C^j(.)$ is the contribution from lobby group j, m is the total number of lobby groups and $\theta \geq 0$ is the weight that the government attributes to social welfare.

It is well-known that the internal organization of lobby groups is a complex matter (see, e.g. Olson, 1965). We assume that some agents for unspecified reasons overcome the free rider problem and organize lobby groups that offer campaign contributions to the government in exchange for environmental policy, while others do not. This is a crucial assumption because it is the presence of unorganized citizens that introduce an inefficiency in an otherwise socially efficient equilibrium. In Section 3, we assume that the owners of specific capital in a subset of the n industries organize lobby groups. Let $j=1$ to m be the organized sectors, while sectors with index $j=m+1$ to n remain unorganized. The key point is that each lobby group represents the preferences of its membership (e.g. the median member) sincerely, and, accordingly, has multiple goals. In particular, each lobby group cares about industry profit (to the extent that members hold stocks), environmental damage (to the extent that members are harmed by emission) and transfers from the government. Let the number of members of lobby group j be N_j. Then, from Eq. (1), we derive the gross welfare function of lobby group j:

$$W^j(\mathbf{p,z}) = l_j + \pi^j(p_j,z_j) + s_j R(\mathbf{p,z}) + s_j N\left[\sum_{k=1}^{n} u(d^k(q_k)) - \sum_{k=1}^{n} q_k d^k(q_k)\right]$$
$$- s_j N g\left(\sum_{k=1}^{n} h^k(r^k(p_k,z_k))\right), \tag{5}$$

where s_j is the share of the total population organized in lobby group j (N_j/N). The fact that each lobby group cares about the harm that emission does to its own constituency has important implications for the political internalization of the

8   *T.S. Aidt / Journal of Public Economics 69 (1998) 1–16*

externality. In particular, it implies that each lobby group trades off the achievement of high profits with environmental protection before it enters the competitive political process. In Section 4, we consider the case of functionally specialized lobby groups in which the internalization solely arises from competition between ideologically motivated lobby groups. To be specific, we assume that a subset of the n industries organizes a producer lobby group that only cares about industry profit, and that a subset of the citizens, the environmentalists, organizes a green lobby group that only cares about the environment.

3. Environmental policy and lobby groups with multiple goals

3.1. The Pigouvian solution

As a benchmark, suppose that the government is benevolent in the sense that it does not care about campaign contributions. The government then chooses its environmental policy to maximize social welfare. Showing that the benevolent government would never use production taxes to correct the externality is straight forward. Instead as predicted by Bhagwati (1971), the socially optimal policy is to go directly to the source of the externality. The Pigouvian tax imposed on sector k is implicitly defined by $\bar{t}_k^r = N g_E h_r^k$, and, hence, reflects the social marginal damage of emission from sector k. We notice that using a uniform raw material tax is not socially optimal.

3.2. Environmental policy in a political equilibrium

The relationship between the government (agent) and the m lobby groups (principals) is modelled as a common agency of politics. At a political equilibrium, environmental policy, $\{\mathbf{p}, \mathbf{z}\}$, and campaign contributions, $\{C^j(p_j, z_j)\}$, are determined as a subgame perfect Nash Equilibrium (see Bernheim and Whinston, 1986) of the following two stage game. In stage one, each lobby group determines its political contribution as a function of policy, taking the contribution schedules of the other lobby groups and the anticipated political optimization of the government in stage two as given. The result is a menu of optimal political contributions that is contingent on $\mathbf{p}$ and $\mathbf{z}$: $C^j(\mathbf{p}, \mathbf{z})$. In the second stage, the government, taking the contribution schedules as given, chooses the optimal policy, and collects the contributions from the lobby groups.

The derivation of the equilibrium in differentiable strategies follows Grossman and Helpman (1994); Dixit (1996) and Fredriksson (1997) closely and is left out. Instead, we, for ease of exposition, assume that the contribution schedules are globally truthful, i.e., the political contribution schedule of a lobby group everywhere reflects the true preference of the lobby group. So, $C^j(\mathbf{p}, \mathbf{z})$ is equal to the gross welfare function, W^j, less a constant. The constant distributes the rent

T.S. Aidt / Journal of Public Economics 69 (1998) 1–16   9

between the government and lobby group j.[6] The assumption of global truthfulness implies that the (politically) optimal policy vector can be derived as the solution to the following problem: $\max_{p,z \in \mathbb{R}_+} \theta W(\mathbf{p}, \mathbf{z}) + \Sigma_{j=1}^{m} W^j(\mathbf{p}, \mathbf{z})$. Let I_k be a dummy variable that takes on the value of one if industry j is organized and zero if not, and let $s_L = \Sigma_{j=1}^{m} s_j$. Then, we can write the first order conditions as follows:

$$p_k: (\theta + s_L)(p_k^* - p_k)\pi_{p,p}^k - (\theta + s_L)\pi_{z,p}^k((z_k - z^*) - Ng_E h_r^k)$$

$$+ (I_k - s_L)x^k(p_k, z_k) = 0,$$

$$z_k: (\theta + s_L)(p_k^* - p_k)\pi_{z,p}^k - (\theta + s_L)\pi_{z,z}^k((z_k - z^*) - Ng_E h_z^k)$$

$$- (I_k - s_L)r^k(p_k, z_k) = 0. \tag{6}$$

Solve the first order conditions to get an implicit solution for the politically optimal production and raw material tax-cum-subsidy scheme:

$$t_k^x = (p_k^* - p_k) = \frac{\pi_{z,z}^k(I_k - s_L)x^k(p_k, z_k)}{(\theta + s_L)\Delta_k} + \frac{\pi_{p,z}^k(I_k - s_L)r^k(p_k, z_k)}{(\theta + s_L)\Delta_k}, \tag{7}$$

$$t_k^r = (z_k - z^*)$$

$$= Ng_E h_r^k(p_k, z_k) + \frac{\pi_{p,p}^k(I_k - s_L)r^k(p_k, z_k)}{(\theta + s_L)\Delta_k} + \frac{\pi_{z,p}^k(I_k - s_L)x^k(p_k, z_k)}{(\theta + s_L)\Delta_k}, \tag{8}$$

where $\Delta_k = (\pi_{z,p}^k)^2 - \pi_{z,z}^k \pi_{p,p}^k < 0$, $\pi_{p,p}^k > 0$ and $\pi_{z,z}^k > 0$ because the profit function is strictly convex. The sign of $\pi_{p,z}^k = \pi_{z,p}^k$ is determined by the profit spillover between the two environmental instruments, and is related to the underlying technology. Recall that $\pi_{p,z}^k = -r_p^k = x_z^k$. Therefore, $\pi_{p,z}^k > 0$ implies that an increase in the price of good k, which leads to an expansion of the production of that good, decreases the demand for raw materials from firms in sector k. While standard assumptions about technology do not rule this scenario out, we do find it reasonable to focus on the more intuitive case in which an expansion of production leads to an increase in the demand of all input factors, including raw materials. Hence, we assume that $\pi_{p,z}^k \leq 0$ for the rest of the paper.

From Eq. (7) and Eq. (8), we observe immediately that only the tax on the externality generating activity is used to correct for the external effect. Hence, we have a *political economy version of Bhagwati's principle of targeting*: the competitive political process internalizes the externality by means of the most efficient instrument, i.e., the one that aims directly at the source. This is because the equilibrium is efficient from the point of view of the lobby groups and the

---

[6]Since the lobby groups' and the government's objective functions are linear in the political contributions, equilibrium policy can be characterized independently of the distribution of equilibrium contributions.

10   *T.S. Aidt / Journal of Public Economics 69 (1998) 1–16*

government. That is, each lobby group and the government have a common interest in maximizing the surplus of the bilateral agency relationship in which they enter. So, since raw material taxation is the most efficient mean to internalize the externality, no lobby group would, based on environmental concerns alone, lobby in favour of other distortions. We refer to the first term of Eq. (8) as the environmental adjustment. We notice that the environmental adjustment depends on the Pigouvian adjustment $\bar{t}_k^r(p_k, z_k) = Ng_E h_r^k(p_k, z_k)$.[7]

Proposition 1. *(Political Internalization of Externalities).*
  The price of the externality generating activity reflects the full Pigouvian adjustment.

  The extent to which the political process internalizes the externality depends on a trade off between the environmental gain and the distortionary cost of taxation. On the one hand, the total concern about the environment, arising from the government's concern about the social damage of emission (θ) and the lobby groups' concern about the environmental damage incurred by organized citizens (s_L), tends to push t_k^r up above $\bar{t}_k^r$. On the other hand, taxing the externality generating activity distorts the demand for raw materials. This concern enters the political trade off to the extent that the government (θ) *and* the lobby groups (s_L) care about government revenue, and tends to push t_k^r down below $\bar{t}_k^r$. Since we assume that $R(z_k, p_k)$ is distributed proportionally across all citizens, the two concerns are given equal weight in the balancing consideration, and, consequently, the environmental adjustment corresponds to the full Pigouvian adjustment. Moreover, the adjustment is independent of whether or not the government cares about social welfare per se. That is, political internalization takes place even if $\theta = 0$, and, accordingly, solely arises from the Coasian element of mobilization of the affected parties.

  It is, however, obvious that proposition 1 is sensitive to the exogenously given transfer rule that the government employs to return revenue to the citizens. In particular, if the government gives the lobby groups more (less) than their population share, then the environmental adjustment is smaller (greater) than the Pigouvian adjustment. This is because the concern for the distortionary cost of taxation is given more (less) weight than the environmental concern. However, it is generally true that the environmental adjustment depends on the Pigouvian adjustment no matter how we specify the transfer rule.

  The political equilibrium does not replicate the social optimum unless all sectors are organized. This is because the lobby groups have income distributional as well as environmental objectives, and are successful in distributing income from unorganized citizens towards themselves. It is of interest to consider in more detail how the politically optimal tax-cum-subsidy structure deviates from the social

---

[7]Notice that $\bar{t}_k'(p_k, z_k)$ is written as a function of p_k and z_k. Only if $\bar{t}_k'(p_k, z_k)$ is evaluated at the appropriate tax vector, it corresponds to the socially optimal Pigouvian tax.

optimum. First, we see immediately from Eq. (7) that the domestic producer price in each sector deviates from the world market price. If $\pi^k_{p,z}=0,$[8] this corresponds closely to the results of Grossman and Helpman (1994); Dixit (1996). Organized industries $(I_k=1)$ receive a production subsidy to boost profits. Unorganized sectors $(I_k=0)$ are taxed because each lobby group bids for taxes in all other industries to generate more tax revenue, part of which the government transfers to organized citizens. If $\pi^k_{p,z}<0$, an additional effect arises from the spillover between the two policy instruments. The spillover effect dampens the profit/ revenue effect. The intuition is straight forward. If sector k' is organized, then the lobby group bids for a lower subsidy $(p_{k'}\downarrow)$ because doing so decrease the marginal cost of raw material taxation. If section k' is unorganized, lobby groups from organized sectors bid for a lower production tax $(p_{k'}\uparrow)$ because it induces firms from industry k' to increase their use of raw materials $(r^{k'}_p>0)$, and, thereby, it generates more tax revenue to be distributed (partly) among organized citizens. Of course, since the spillover effect works against the profit/revenue effect, it could, in principle, be dominating. A necessary and sufficient condition under which the government subsidises (taxes) production from an organized (unorganized) sector is (C1) $|\epsilon(r^k, z)|>|\epsilon(x^k, z)|$, where $\epsilon(\gamma, \beta)$ is the elasticity of γ with respect to β.

Second, we notice that the income distributional considerations also distort the politically optimal tax on the externality generating activity (raw materials). To be specific, we have:

Proposition 2. Let $g_{E,E}=h^k_{r,r}=0$. If and only if (C2) $\gamma(x^k,p)>\epsilon(r^k,p)$, then t^r_k is below (above) the Pigouvian tax if k is an organized (unorganized) sector.

Proof. The assumption that $g_{E,E}=h^k_{r,r}=0$ implies that $\bar{t}^r_k=Ng_Eh^k_r$ is independent of z_k and p_k. So, the proposition follows from a simple manipulation of Eq. (8) $\square$

First, consider an organized industry, i.e., $I_k=1$. If C2 is satisfied, then each lobby group asks for an environmental discount to its own industry. Two effects are involved. The first effect is the "cost saving" effect (the second term of Eq. (8)), arising from the fact that a tax on raw materials (or emission) increases the cost of production. Although the government gives back part of the revenue to the membership of the lobby group, each lobby group asks the government for a discount to its own industry. The second effect is the spillover effect (the third term of Eq. (8)). As $\pi^k_{p,z}$ is non-positive, the spillover effect dampens the cost saving effect. That is, the lobby groups, *ceteris paribus*, ask for a higher tax in their own industry because doing so decreases the marginal cost of production

---

[8]In discussing the sign and size of the various derivatives of the profit function, it is understood that they are evaluated at the equilibrium price vector.

taxation. If the spillover effect is small relative to the cost saving effect, *the government might subsidise the externality generating activity*, even though taxation is warranted from a social point of view. On the other hand, if the spillover effect is sufficiently large so that C2 fails to hold true, then the income distributional motive adds to the environmentally motivated tax.

Next, consider an unorganized industry, i.e., $I_k = 0$. For revenue reasons, the lobby groups bid for a high tax on the use of raw materials (see the second term of Eq. (8)) in unorganized. Again, the spillover effect dampens the revenue effect. This is because a decrease in the domestic price of raw materials in sector k induces (unorganized) firms to produce more ($x_z^k < 0$), thereby generating more revenue from production taxation. However, unless C2 fails to hold, we see that the competitive political process transfers a disproportionate share of the abatement cost to unorganized sectors. So, due to revenue seeking, a substantial beggar-thy-neighbour element is involved in environmental lobbying.

How likely are conditions C1 and C2 to hold? Under the assumption that $\pi_{z,p}^k \leq 0$ in all sectors, the two conditions, basically, state that own price effects are greater than cross effects. For instance, C2 holds true if supply is more responsive to changes in the domestic price of output than the demand for raw materials. Overall, we find conditions C1 and C2 plausible, and conclude that the spillover effect is likely to dampen the various direct income distributional effects, but unlikely to dominate them.

From an environmental point of view, it is of interest to consider if political distortions lead to inefficiently high emission. The distribution of emission across industries, of course, depends on the equilibrium tax-cum-subsidy structure via the relationship $e_k = h_k(r^k(p_k, z_k))$, but also, directly, on $\pi_{p,z}^k = r_p^k \leq 0$. Hence, in general, making any predictions is difficult. However, suppose that C1 and C2 hold true. If sector k is organized (unorganized), then emission is greater (lower) than the Pigouvian level. That is, due to the environmental discount, organized sectors discharge too much, while unorganized sectors because of the "extra" tax bill discharge too little. Of course, the overall level of emission is, most likely, inefficient. However, the direction of the inefficiency depends (among many other features of the model) on the distribution of organized and unorganized sectors, and is, accordingly, ambiguous.

3.3. A uniform tax on the externality generating activity

In the previous analysis, we allowed the government to use a differentiated tax-cum-subsidy scheme, and, in the resulting political equilibrium, the government would, indeed, use this option. Thinking of t_k^r as a pollution tax, the use of differentiated taxes-cum-subsidies seems natural only if the environmental authorities can measure emission from the various sources. However, in many circumstances, the use of differentiated taxes-cum-subsidies is difficult because of measurement problems. Suppose, for instance, that raw materials are easily traded

T.S. Aidt / Journal of Public Economics 69 (1998) 1–16   13

among industries (oil, coal etc.), and it is impossible to measure (and tax) emission. An arbitrage argument suggests that the sector with the lowest domestic price buys raw materials from the market with the purpose of reselling them to other sectors, thereby circumventing the differentiated structure of taxation. Accordingly, it is of interest to analyse the political equilibrium under the restriction that only a uniform raw material tax-cum-subsidy can be used. To simplify the discussion, we assume that $\pi^k_{p,z}=0$. The politically optimal uniform raw material tax-cum-subsidy scheme is implicitly given as:

$$t^r = (\mathbf{z} - \mathbf{z}*)$$

$$= \frac{Ng_E \sum_{k=1}^{n} h^k_r \pi^k_{z,z}}{\sum_{k=1}^{n} \pi^k_{z,z}} + \frac{s_L \sum_{k=m+1}^{n} r^k(p_k, z_k) - (1 - s_L)\sum_{k=1}^{m} r^k(p_k, z_k)}{(\theta + s_L)\sum_{k=1}^{n} \pi^k_{z,z}}.$$

$$(9)$$

First, the environmental adjustment cannot be targeted at each sector, and, so, it cannot reproduce the Pigouvian adjustment. Accordingly, the environmental adjustment is a weighted average of the social marginal damage of emission from the n sectors. Next, the last term reflects a trade off between the net cost savings on the raw material bill in organized sectors and the extra tax revenue extracted from unorganized sectors. Whether the environmental adjustment is reinforced or not depends on the proportion of organized citizens, s_L, and the total demand for raw materials from organized and unorganized sectors, respectively. To summarize, since the lobby groups cannot contingent their political contributions on a sector-specific policy, redistributing income across industries becomes harder. This reduces the beggar-thy-neighbour element of environmental lobbying. On the other hand, with a uniform raw material tax-cum-subsidy, the government cannot target the environmental adjustment to correct for the sector-specific marginal social damage of emission.

4. Environmental policy and functionally specialized lobby groups

The driving force behind the political internalization analysed in the previous sections is competition between lobby groups with multiple goals. As discussed in the introduction, political internalization can also arise from competition between functionally specialized lobby groups. To see this, suppose that capital owners in a subset of the n industries, $j=1$ to m, organize a producer lobby group that is only concerned with profit, $\pi_j(p_j, z_j)$, $j=1,\ldots,m$. Moreover, a group of environmentalists organizes a (green) lobby group to advocate environmental protection. The objective function of the green lobby group is given as $W_E = K - s_E g(\sum_{k=1}^{n} h^k(r^k(p_k, z_k)))$, where s_E is the proportion of environmentalists in the population

14   *T.S. Aidt / Journal of Public Economics 69 (1998) 1–16*

and K is a constant. For $\theta > 0$, the politically optimal tax structure is implicitly given by:

$$t_k^x = (p_k^* - p_k) = -\frac{I_k x^k(p_k, z_k)}{\theta \pi_{p,p}^k},$$

$$t_k^r = (z_k - z^*) = \frac{(\theta + s_E)}{\theta} t_k^r(p_k, z_k) - \frac{I_k r^k(p_k, z_k)}{\theta \pi_{z,z}^k}. \tag{10}$$

We have, to simplify the discussion and without loss of any essential insights, imposed the restriction that $\pi_{p,z}^k = 0$. With functionally specialized lobby groups, the political internalization solely arises from competition between the various groups who get their voice represented in the political process. We notice that the environmental adjustment of the price of the externality generating activity is always larger than the corresponding Pigouvian adjustment. This is because both the government and the green lobby group care about environmental damage, while only the government, via its concern for social welfare, cares about the distortionary effect of the pollution tax.

Functional specialization also has implications for the income distributional motive for environmental lobbying. The producer lobby groups accept the environmental adjustment supported by the environmentalists in exchange for a production subsidy and an environmental discount. In unorganized sectors, the only intervention is the environmental adjustment. This is because firms in these industries have no producer lobby group to ask for subsidies, and because producer lobby groups do not care about generating government revenue. The principal difference between the case in which lobby groups have multiple goals and the case in which they are functionally specialized is the transfer motive. Functionally specialized groups have no such motive, which, in turn, reduces the beggar-thy-neighbour element of environmental lobbying, and leads to an environmental adjustment that is always larger than the Pigouvian adjustment.

5. Concluding remarks

This paper points out that competition between lobby groups is an important source of internalization of externalities. Both the competitive political process itself and the fact that some lobby groups adjust their economic objectives to reflect environmental concerns contribute to the political internalization. We show, in a common agency of politics, that the Pigouvian adjustment is reflected in the price structure despite the various political distortions. However, since not everybody is organized in a lobby group and lobby groups advance income distributional goals at the expense of efficiency considerations, the politically optimal environmental policy does not replicate the set of Pigouvian taxes needed to achieve social optimum. In particular, under plausible assumptions about the spillover between the two policy instruments, organized sectors get a discount at the expense of unorganized sectors, which are taxed at inefficiently high rates.

An important discussion in environmental economics concerns the choice of policy instrument. Our analysis generalizes the principle of targeting to distorted political markets: the environmental adjustment is targeted at the source of the externality. This is because the lobby groups and the government agree to pick the more efficient instrument to correct for the externality, or in general, as pointed out by Dixit et al. (1997), favour more efficient instruments to less efficient ones.[9] This is, in turn, driven by the fact that the focus of the common agency model of politics is on the efficient equilibrium of Bernheim and Whinston (1986) menu auction. In contrast, Buchanan and Tullock (1975) base their discussion of pollution taxation versus direct regulation on a disagreement between the government and producer-interests. The government prefers the tax because enforcing direct control requires a high enforcement cost. The lobby group prefers direct regulation because it serves as a coordination device that creates short-run monopoly rents. The disagreement is resolved by arguing that the small, concentrated group of producers is much more efficient in influencing policymaking than the large group of ordinary citizens (who, presumably, supports a pollution tax because of the revenue), and, so, in the political equilibrium, direct controls are chosen despite the fact that the pollution tax is more efficient.

Acknowledgements

This paper is based on a chapter of my dissertation at University of Aarhus. I am grateful to Jan Rose Soerensen, Per Baltzer Overgaard, H. Ursprung, two anonymous referees and, in particular, Arye Hillman for helpful comments and suggestions. Also comments and suggests from the participants of the 1996 Silvaplana workshop on political economy, the 1997 meeting of European Public Choice Society in Prague and the theory workshop at University of Aarhus are appreciated. The usual disclaimer applies.

References

ATV, 1990. Vandmiljøplanens tilblivelse og iværksættelse (The birth of the aquatic environmental plan and its implementation, my translation). Akademiet for de Tekniske Videnskaber, Vedbæk.

[9]Becker (1983, 1985) also argues that competition among lobby groups leads to efficient methods of taxation. In his model lobby groups unanimously prefer more efficient methods because of a lower dead weight loss.

16   *T.S. Aidt / Journal of Public Economics 69 (1998) 1–16*

Baumol, W.J., Oates, W.E., 1989. The Theory of Environmental Policy. Cambridge University Press, UK.

Becker, G.S., 1983. A theory of competition among pressure groups for political influence. Quarterly Journal of Economics 98, 371–400.

Becker, G.S., 1985. Public policies, pressure groups, and dead weight costs. Journal of Public Economics 28, 329–347.

Bernheim, B.D., Whinston, M., 1986. Menu auctions, resource allocation, and economic influence. Quarterly Journal of Economics 101, 1–31.

Bhagwati, J.N., 1971. The generalized theory of distortions and welfare. In: Bhagwati, J.N. et al., Trade, Balance of Payments, and Growth. North-Holland, Amsterdam.

Bommer, R., 1996. Environmental regulation of production processes in the European Union: a political-economy approach. Aussenwirtschaft 51, 559–582.

Bommer, R., Schulze, G., 1997. Trade liberalization and environmental policy as distributional substitutes: or why NAFTA improves the environment. Working paper, University of Konstanz.

Buchanan, M., Tullock, G., 1975. Polluters' profit and political response: direct controls versus taxes. American Economic Review 65, 139–147.

Coase, R.H., 1960. The problem of social cost. Journal of Law and Economics 3, 1–44.

Dixit, A., 1996. Special-interest lobbying and endogenous commodity taxation. Eastern Economic Journal 22, 375–388.

Dixit, A., Grossman, G.M., Helpman, E., 1997. Common agency and coordination: general theory and application to government policy making. Journal of Political Economy 105, 752–769.

Fredriksson, P., 1997. The political economy of pollution taxes in a small open economy. Journal of Environmental Economics and Management 33, 44–58.

Grossman, G.M., Helpman, E., 1994. Protection for sale. American Economic Review 84, 833–850.

Grossman, G.M., Helpman, E., 1995a. Trade wars and trade talks. Journal of Political Economy 103, 675–708.

Grossman, G.M., Helpman, E., 1995b. The politics of free trade agreements. American Economic Review 85, 667–690.

Grossman, G.M., Helpman, E., 1996. Electoral competition and special interest politics. Review of Economic Studies 63, 265–285.

Hillman, A., 1989. The Political Economy of Protection. Harwood Academic Publishers, Chur, Switzerland.

Hillman, A., Ursprung, H., 1992. The influence of environmental concerns on the political determination of international trade policy. In: Blackhurst, R., Anderson, K. (Eds.), The Greening of World Trade Issues. Harvester Wheatcheaf, New York, pp. 195–220.

Hillman, A., Ursprung, H., 1994. Environmental protection and international trade policy. In: Carraro, C. (Ed.), The International Dimension of Environmental Policy. Kluwer, Boston.

Olson, M., 1965. The Logic of Collective Action. Harvard University Press, Cambridge.

Potters, J., van Winden, F., 1996. Models of interest groups: four different approaches. In: Schofield, N. (Ed.), Collective Decision-Making: Social Choice and Political Economy. Kluwer, Boston.

Rodrik, D., 1995. Political economy of trade policy. In: Grossman, G.M., Rogoff, K. (Eds.), Handbook of International Economics, vol. 3. Elsevier, New York, pp. 1458–1490.

Schleich, J., 1997. Environmental protection with policies for sale. Working paper 97-2, University of Minnesota.

Part II
Choosing the Instruments of Environmental Regulation

[7]

Polluters' Profits and Political Response: Direct Controls Versus Taxes

By James M. Buchanan and Gordon Tullock*

Economists of divergent political persuasions agree on the superior efficacy of penalty taxes as instruments for controlling significant external diseconomies which involve the interaction of many parties. However, political leaders and bureaucratic administrators, charged with doing something about these problems, appear to favor direct controls. Our purpose in this paper is to present a positive theory of externality control that explains the observed frequency of direct regulation as opposed to penalty taxes or charges. In the public-choice theory of policy,[1] the interests of those who are subjected to the control instruments must be taken into account as well as the interests of those affected by the external diseconomies. As we develop this theory of policy, we shall also emphasize an elementary efficiency basis for preferring taxes and charges which heretofore has been neglected by economists.

I

Consider a competitive industry in long-run equilibrium, one that is composed of a large number of n identical producing firms. There are no productive inputs specific to this industry, which itself is sufficiently small relative to the economy to insure that the long-run supply curve is horizontal. Expansions and contractions in demand for the product invoke changes in the number of firms, each one of which returns to the same least-cost position after adjustment. Assume that, from this initial position, knowledge is discovered which indicates that the industry's product creates an undesirable environmental side effect. This external diseconomy is directly related to output, and we assume there is no technology available that will allow alternative means of producing the private good without the accompanying public bad. We further assume that the external damage function is linear with respect to industry output; the same quantity of public bad per unit of private good is generated regardless of quantity.[2] We assume that this damage can be measured and monitored with accuracy.

This setting has been deliberately idealized for the application of a penalty tax or surcharge. By assessing a tax (which can be computed with accuracy) per unit of output on all firms in the industry, the government can insure that profit-maximizing decisions lead to a new and lower industry output that is Pareto optimal. In the short run, firms will undergo losses. In the long run, firms will leave the industry and a new equilibrium will be reached when remaining firms are again making normal returns on investment. The price of the product to consumers will have gone up by the full amount of the penalty tax.

* Center for Study of Public Choice, Virginia Polytechnic Institute and State University. We wish to thank the National Science Foundation for research support. Needless to say, the opinions expressed are our own.

[1] Charles Goetz imposes a public-choice framework on externality control, but his analysis is limited to the determination of quantity under the penalty-tax alternative.

[2] This assumption simplifies the means of imposing a corrective tax. For some of the complexities, see Otto Davis and Andrew Whinston and Stanislaw Wellisz.

No one could dispute the efficacy of the tax in attaining the efficient solution, but we should note that in this setting, the same result would seem to be equally well insured by direct regulation. Policy makers with knowledge of individual demand functions, the production functions for firms and for the industry, and external damage functions, could readily compute and specify the Pareto-efficient quantity of industry output.[3] Since all firms are identical in the extreme model considered here, the policy makers could simply assign to each firm a determinate share in the targeted industry output. This would then require that each firm reduce its own rate of output by X percent, that indicated by the difference between its initial equilibrium output and that output which is allocated under the socially efficient industry regulation.[4]

Few of the standard arguments for the penalty tax apply in this setting. These arguments have been concentrated on the difficulties in defining an efficient industry output in addition to measuring external damages and on the difficulty in securing data about firm and industry production and cost functions. With accurately measured damage, an appropriate tax will insure an efficient solution without requiring that this solution itself be independently computed. Or, under a target or standards approach, a total quantity may be computed, and a tax may be chosen as the device to achieve this in the absence of knowledge about the production functions of firms.[5]

In the full information model, none of these arguments is applicable. There is, however, an important economic basis for favoring the penalty tax over the direct control instrument, one that has been neglected by economists. The penalty tax remains the preferred instrument on strict efficiency grounds, but, perhaps more significantly, it will also facilitate the enforcement of results once they are computed.[6] Under the appropriately chosen penalty tax, firms attain equilibrium only at the efficient quantity of industry output. Each firm that remains in the industry after the imposition of the tax attains long-run adjustment at the lowest point on its average cost curve only after a sufficient number of firms have left the industry. At this equilibrium, there is no incentive for any firm to modify its rate of output in the short run by varying the rate of use of plant or to vary output in the long run by changing firm size. There is no incentive for resources to enter or to exit from the industry. So long as the tax is collected, there is relatively little policing required.

This orthodox price theory paradigm enables the differences between the penalty-tax instrument and direct regulation to be seen clearly. Suppose that, instead of levying the ideal penalty tax, the fully informed policy makers choose to direct all firms in the initial competitive equilibrium to reduce output to the assigned levels required to attain the targeted efficiency goal for the industry. No tax is levied. Consider Figure 1, which depicts the situation for the individual firm. The initial competitive equilibrium is attained when each firm produces an output, q_i. Under regulation it is directed to produce only q_0, but no tax is levied. At output q_0, with an unchanged number of firms, price is above

---

[3] See Allen Kneese and Blair Bower, p. 135.

[4] No problems are created by dropping the assumption that firms are identical so long as we retain the assumption that production functions are known to the regulator.

[5] This is the approach taken by William Baumol, who proposes that a target level of output be selected and a tax used to insure the attainment of this target in an efficient manner.

[6] See George Hay. His discussion of the comparison of import quotas and tariffs on oil raises several issues that are closely related to those treated in this paper.

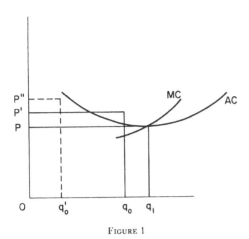

FIGURE 1

marginal cost (for example price is at P'). Therefore, the firm is not in short-run equilibrium, and would if it could expand output within the confines of its existing plant. More importantly, although each firm will be producing the output quota assigned to it at a somewhat higher cost than required for efficiency reasons, there may still be an incentive for resources to enter the industry. The administrator faces a policing task that is dimensionally different from that under the tax. He must insure that individual firms do not violate the quotas assigned, and he must somehow prevent new entrants. To the extent that the administrator fails in either of these tasks, the results aimed for will not be obtained. Output quotas will be exceeded, and the targeted level of industry production overreached.

If the administrator assigns enforceable quotas to existing firms and successfully prevents entrants, the targeted industry results may be attained, but there may remain efficiency loss since the industry output will be produced at higher average cost than necessary if firms face U-shaped long-run average cost curves. Ideally, regulation may have to be accompanied by the

assignment of full production quotas to a selected number of the initial firms in the industry. This policy will keep these favored firms in marginal adjustment with no incentives for in-firm adjustments that might defeat the purpose of the regulation. But even more than under general quota assignment there will be strong incentives for firms to enter the industry and to secure at least some share of the rents that the restriction of industry output generates. If the response to this pressure should be that of reassigning quota shares within the unchanging and targeted industry output so as to allow all potential entrants some share, while keeping all firms, actual and potential, on an equal quota basis, the final result may be equivalent to the familiar cartel equilibrium. No firm will be earning more than normal returns, but the industry will be characterized by too many firms, each of which produces its assigned output inefficiently.

II

When we examine the behavioral adjustments to the policy instruments in the manner sketched out above, a theory of policy emerges. Regulation is less desirable on efficiency grounds even in the presence of full information, but this instrument will be preferred by those whose behavior is to be subjected to either one or the other of the two policy instruments. Consider the position of the single firm in the fully competitive industry, depicted in Figure 1. Under the imposition of the tax, short-run losses are necessarily incurred, and the firm reattains normal returns only after a sufficient number of its competitors have shifted resources to other industries. The tax reduces the present value of the firm's potential earnings stream, whether the particular firm remains in the industry after adjustment or withdraws its investment and shifts to alternative employment. In terms of their own private interests, owners of firms in the industry along with employees will oppose the tax. By contrast, under regulation firms may well secure pecuniary gains from the imposition of direct controls that reduce total industry output. To the extent that the restriction is achieved by the assignment of production quotas to existing firms, net profits may be present even for the short term and are more likely to arise after adjustments in plant. In effect, regulation in this sense is the directional equivalent of cartel formation provided that the individual firm's assigned quota falls within the limited range over which average cost falls below price. Such a range must, of course, exist, but regulatory constraints may possibly be severe enough to shift firms into positions where short-term, and even possibly long-term, losses are present, despite increased output price. Such a result is depicted by a restriction to q_0' in Figure 1, with price at P''.

Despite the motivation which each firm has to violate assigned quotas under regulation, it remains in the interest of firms to seek regulatory policy that will enforce the quotas. If existing firms foresee the difficulty of restricting entry, and if they predict that governmental policy makers will be required to accommodate all entrants, the incentive to support restriction by regulation remains even if its force is somewhat lower. In final cartel equilibrium, all the firms will be making no more than normal returns. But during the adjustment to this equilibrium, above-normal returns may well be available to all firms that hold production quotas. Even if severe restriction forces short-term losses on firms, these losses will be less than those under the tax. Rents over this period may well be positive, and even if negative, they will be less negative than those suffered under the tax alternative. Therefore, producing firms will always oppose any impo-

sition of a penalty tax. However, they may well favor direct regulation restricting industry output, even if no consideration at all is given to the imposition of a tax. And, when faced with an either/or choice, they will always prefer regulation to the tax.

III

There is a difference between the two idealized solutions that has not yet been discussed, and when this is recognized, the basis of a positive hypothesis about policy choice may appear to vanish. Allocationally, direct regulation can produce results equivalent to the penalty tax, providing that we neglect enforcement cost differentials. *Distributionally*, however, the results differ. The imposition of tax means that government collects revenues (save in the case where tax rates are prohibitive) and these must be spent. Those who anticipate benefits from the utilization of tax revenues, whether from the provision of publicly supplied goods or from the reduction in other tax levies, should prefer the tax alternative and they should make this preference known in the political process. To the extent that the beneficiaries include all ███████████████████ the con█████████████████arry the█████████████████ to citi█████████████████rger nur█████████████████ dis- gru█████████████████dus- try█████████████████ow- eve█████████████████nall, con█████████████████isely inte█████████████████nore infl█████████████████than the█████████████████each of v█████████████████ts in the second order of smalls.

There is an additional reason for predicting this result with respect to an innovatory policy of externality control. The penalty tax amounts to a legislated change in property rights, and as such it will be viewed as confiscatory by owners and employees in the affected industry. Legislative bodies, even if they operate formally on majoritarian principles, may be reluctant to impose what seems to be punitive taxation. When, therefore, the regulation alternative to the penalty tax is known to exist, and when representatives of the affected industry are observed strongly to prefer this alternative, the temptation placed on the legislator to choose the direct control policy may be overwhelming, even if he is an economic theorist and a good one. Widely accepted ethical norms may support this stance; imposed destruction of property values may suggest the justice of compensation.[7]

If policy alternatives should be conceived in a genuine Wicksellian framework, the political economist might still expect that the superior penalty tax should command support. If the economist ties his recommendation for the penalty tax to an accompanying return of tax revenues to those in the industry who suffer potential capital losses, he might be more successful than he has been in proposing unilateral or one-sided application of policy norms. If revenues are used to subsidize those in the industry subjected to capital losses from the tax, and if these subsidies are unrelated to rates of output, a two-sided tax subsidy arrangement can remove the industry source of opposition while still insuring efficient results. In this respect, however, economists themselves have failed to pass muster. Relatively few modern economists who have engaged in policy advocacy have been willing to accept the Wicksellian methodological framework which does, of course, require that some putative legitimacy be assigned to rights existent in the status quo.[8]

[7] For a comprehensive discussion of just compensation, see Frank Michelman.

[8] For a specific discussion of the Wicksellian approach, see Buchanan (1959).

IV

To this point we have developed a theory of policy for product-generated external diseconomies, the setting which potentially counterposes the interest of members of a single producing industry against substantially all persons in the community. External diseconomies may, however, arise in consumption rather than in production, and these may be general. For purposes of analysis, we may assume that all persons find themselves in a situation of reciprocal external diseconomies. Traffic congestion may be a familiar case in point.

The question is one of determining whether or not persons in this sort of interaction, acting through the political processes of the community, will impose on *themselves* either a penalty tax or direct regulation. We retain the full information assumption introduced in the production externality model. For simplicity here, consider a two-person model in which each person consumes the same quantity of good or carries out the same quantity of activity in the precontrol equilibrium, but in which demand elasticities differ. Figure 2 depicts the initial equilibrium at E with each person consuming quantity Q. The

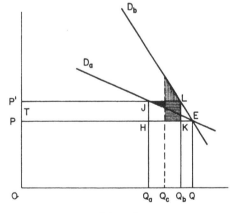

FIGURE 2

existence of the reciprocal external diseconomy is discovered. The community may impose an accurately measured penalty tax in the amount T, in which case A will reduce consumption to Q_a and B will reduce consumption to Q_b. Total consumption is reduced from $2Q$ to (Q_a+Q_b), but both A and B remain in equilibrium. At the new price P', which includes tax, neither person desires to consume more or less than the indicated quantities. The government collects tax revenues in the amount $[2(PP'JH)+HJLK]$. Alternatively, the community may simply assign a restricted quantity quota to each person. If the government possesses full information about demand functions it can reduce A's quota to Q_a, and B's quota to Q_b, securing results that are allocatively identical to those secured by the tax. However, under the quota, both A and B will find themselves out of equilibrium; both will, if allowed quantity adjustment, prefer to expand their rate of consumption.

It will be useful to examine the ideal tax against the quota scheme outlined above, which we may call the idealized quota scheme. If individuals expect no returns at all from tax revenues in the form of cash subsidies, public goods benefits, or reductions in other taxes, both A and B will clearly prefer the direct regulation. The loss in consumers' surplus under this alternative is small relative to that which would be lost under the penalty tax. Each person willingly trades off marginal quantity adjustment for the more favorable inframarginal terms offered under direct regulation, given our assumptions that both instruments achieve the same overall externality control objective.

Under extreme fiscal illusion, individuals may ignore benefits from tax revenues, but consistent methodological precept requires that we allow persons to recognize the benefit side of the fiscal account, at least to some degree. Let us allow all revenues

under the penalty tax to be returned in equal shares to all taxpayers. Under this arrangement, each person expects to get back one-half of the amount measured as indicated above for Figure 2. Simplifying, each expects to get back the amount $PP'JH$, which he personally pays in, plus one-half of the amount measured by the rectangle $JHKL$, all of which is paid in by B. From an examination of Figure 2, it is clear that individual A will favor the penalty tax under these assumptions. The situation for individual B is different; he will prefer direct regulation. He will secure a differential gain measured by the horizontally shaded area in Figure 2, which is equal to the differential loss that individual A will suffer under this alternative. The policy result, insofar as it is influenced by the two parties, is a standoff under this idealized tax and idealized quota system comparison.

For constitutional and other reasons, control institutions operating within a democratic order could scarcely embody disproportionate quota assignments. A more plausible regulation alternative would assign quotas proportionate to initial rates of consumption, designed to reduce overall consumption to the level indicated by target criteria. The comparison of this alternative with the ideal tax arrangement is facilitated by the construction of Figure 2 where the initial rates of consumption are equal. In this new scheme, each person is assigned a quota Q_c, which he is allowed to purchase at the initial price P. We want to compare this arrangement with the ideal tax, again under the assumption that revenues are fully returned in equal per head subsidies. As in the first scheme, both persons are in disequilibrium at quantity Q_c and price P. The difference between this model and the idealized quota scheme lies in the fact that at Q_c, the marginal evaluations differ as between the two persons. There are unexploited gains from trade, even under the determined overall quantity restriction.

It will be mutually advantageous for the two persons to exchange quotas and money, but, at this point, we assume that such exchanges do not take place, either because they are prohibited or because transactions costs are too high. Individual *A* will continue to favor the tax alternative but his differential gains will be smaller than under the idealized quota scheme. In the model now considered, *A*'s differential gains under the ideal tax are measured by the blacked-in triangle in Figure 2. Individual *B* may or may not favor the quota, as in the earlier model. His choice as between the two alternatives, the ideal tax on the one hand and the restriction to Q_c at price *P* on the other, will depend on the comparative sizes of the two areas shown as horizontally and vertically shaded in Figure 2. As drawn, he will tend to favor the quota scheme, but it is clearly possible that the triangular area could exceed the rectangular one if *B*'s demand curve is sufficiently steep in slope. In any case, the choice alternatives for both persons are less different in the net than those represented by the ideal tax and the idealized quota.

While holding all of the remaining assumptions of the model, we now drop the assumption that no exchange of quotas takes place between *A* and *B*. To facilitate the geometrical illustration, Figure 3 essentially blows up the relevant part of Figure 2. With each party initially assigned a consumption quota of Q_c, individual *A* will be willing to sell units to individual *B* for any price above his marginal evaluation. Hence, the lowest possible supply price schedule that individual *B* confronts is that shown by the line *RL* in Figure 3. The maximum price that individual *B* is willing to pay for additional units of quota is his marginal evaluation, shown by *SL*. The gains-from-trade are measured by the triangular area *RLS*. The distribution of

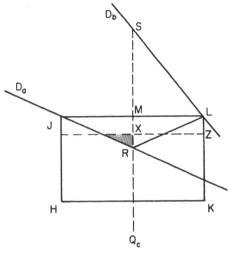

FIGURE 3

these gains will, of course, be settled in the strict two-man setting by relative bargaining skills, but let us assume that individual *B*, the buyer, wants to purchase consumption quota units from *A*, but also to do so in such a way that individual *A* will come to prefer this system over the tax. To accomplish this, he must insure that *A* gets a share of the net gains at least equal to the area *RML* on Figure 3. Individual *B*, the buyer, retains gains of *MSL* under this division of the spoils. But in this arrangement, both persons are indifferent as between the policy alternatives. The system is on the Pareto frontier, and the quota scheme plus the exchange process produces allocative and distributive results identical to those generated under the ideal tax. This becomes the analogue of the Coase theorem in the context that we are examining.[9]

V

These somewhat inconclusive results may seem to provide anything but a posi-

[9] See Ronald Coase. For a related extension of the Coase theorem, see Buchanan (1973).

tive theory of policy akin to that presented with respect to production externalities. The comparisons are, however, a necessary stage in developing such a theory. Recall that we have made these comparisons under the most favorable possible assumption concerning anticipated return of revenues under the penalty tax. In the real world, individuals will not anticipate that these will be returned dollar-for-dollar, and they will tend to place at least some discount on the value of benefits that they expect.

Let us say that each person expects an aggregate benefit value of only 80 cents on the dollar from tax revenues collected under the penalty tax. Consider what this single change does to the results of the last comparison made, that which involves proportionate quota assignments along with a free market in quotas. In this case, individual B, the buyer, can offer individual A, the seller, more than the amount required to make him prefer the quota alternative, while himself continuing to secure differential benefit under this alternative. Individual A's differential gains from the ideal penalty tax are reduced to the shaded area in Figure 3. By paying individual A the amount measured by RML, he has improved A's position relative to the penalty tax. And, in the process, he has retained for himself a differential gain measured by the area $MXZL$. Both persons in full knowledge of the alternatives will prefer the quota system, and political leaders will presumably respond by opting for regulation.

The same reasoning can readily be extended to apply to any quota system. In the idealized quota assignment first considered, we demonstrated that one person would favor the penalty tax and the other the quota. Individual A, who favors the penalty tax, loses no consumer's surplus, and he does expect to secure an income

transfer through the return of tax revenues. When we modify the assumptions concerning expectations of the value of returned revenues or benefits, however, this conclusion need not hold. Individual A will, of course, expect to get back in benefits some part of the tax revenues paid in by B that is in excess of that contributed by A himself. If, however, individual A applies the same discount factor to all revenues collected, the deadweight loss may more than offset the income transfer effect. Examination of Figure 2 indicates that under the 80 percent assumption, one-fifth of the area measured by $PP'JH$ will represent deadweight loss to A from the revenues that he pays in. This deadweight loss may well be larger than the measure of the income transfer that he expects, which amounts to 80 percent of the horizontally shaded area in Figure 2. Once we introduce any plausible discount factor into the expectation of individuals concerning the return of tax revenues, it is relatively easy to demonstrate situations under which both persons may be led by private self-interest to favor the direct regulation alternative.

VI

We have developed a positive theory of externality control policy for both the production and consumption interactions under highly abstract and simplified models which allow us to isolate influences on policy formation which have been neglected. Decisions on the alternative policy instruments in democratic governments are surely influenced by the preferences of those who are subjected to them. The public-choice approach, which concentrates attention on the individual's choice as between policy instruments, allows us to construct hypotheses that explain the prevalence of direct regulation.[10] For economists who continue to support the penalty tax alternative, the analysis suggests that they had best become good Wicksellians and begin to search out and invent institutional arrangements that will make the penalty tax acceptable to those who are primarily affected.

[10] Much of the analysis developed in this paper can be applied more or less directly to policy alternatives proposed in the energy crisis of late 1973 and early 1974. For such application, see Buchanan and Nicolaus Tideman.

REFERENCES

W. J. Baumol, "On Taxation and the Control of Externalities," *Amer. Econ. Rev.*, June 1972, *62*, 307–22.

J. M. Buchanan, "Positive Economics, Welfare Economics, and Political Economy," *J. Law Econ.*, Oct. 1959, *2*, 124–38.

———, "The Coase Theorem and the Theory of the State," *Natur. Resources J.*, Oct. 1973, *13*, 579–94.

——— and N. Tideman, "Gasoline Rationing and Market Pricing: Public Choice in Political Democracy," research pap. no. 808231-1-12, Center for Study of Public Choice, Virginia Polytechnic Inst. and State Univ., Jan. 1974.

R. H. Coase, "The Problem of Social Cost," *J. Law Econ.*, Oct. 1960, *3*, 1–44.

O. A. Davis and A. Whinston, "Externalities, Welfare, and the Theory of Games," *J. Polit. Econ.*, June 1962, *70*, 241–62.

C. J. Goetz, "Political Equilibrium vs. Economic Efficiency in Effluent Pricing," in J. R. Conner and E. Loehman, eds., *Economic Decisionmaking for Environmental Control*, Gainesville 1973.

G. A. Hay, "Import Controls on Foreign Oil: Tariff or Quota?," *Amer. Econ. Rev.*, Sept. 1971, *61*, 688–91.

A. V. Kneese and B. T. Bower, *Managing Water Quality: Economics, Technology, Institutions*, Baltimore 1968.

F. J. Michelman, "Property Utility, and Fairness: Comments on the Ethical Foundations of 'Just Compensation' Law," *Harvard Law Rev.*, Apr. 1967, *80*, 1165–1257.

S. Wellisz, "On External Diseconomies and the Government-Assisted Invisible Hand," *Economica*, Nov. 1964, *31*, 345–62.

[8]

A POSITIVE THEORY OF ENVIRONMENTAL QUALITY REGULATION*

MICHAEL T. MALONEY   and   *ROBERT E. McCORMICK*
Emory University   *University of Rochester*

On May 3, 1973, the *Wall Street Journal* carried a story about the struggle by Phelps Dodge Corporation to meet environmental quality standards. The *Journal* reported that "the most economical way to [meet the standards] at the Douglas smelter, Phelps Dodge has decided, is to *cut production* whenever the pollution levels get too high" (emphasis added). These output reductions fashioned by environmental quality standards are like the emperor's clothes. We can see the cleaner air, but the higher prices and profits occasioned by the output reductions have not received equal billing.

I. INTRODUCTION

THE purpose of this paper is to demonstrate that environmental quality regulation may enhance producer wealth while it simultaneously reduces an externality problem by restricting access to common property. Regulation not only corrects a resource misallocation, but it creates a scarcity rent as well. In the recent history of environmental quality, the common access problem has been addressed by federal and state agencies through a standards-based approach, rather than through the enforcement of tradable property rights. As a consequence, rents from the right to use these assets have accrued to producers.

Considerable attention has been paid in welfare theory to the conflict between producers of externalities and the victims. However, the interests of environmentalists and producers may coincide against the welfare

* A number of people have helped us with their comments and criticisms: Dennis Carlton; Michael Jensen; John Long; William Schwert; Bruce Yandle; participants at the Applied Economics Workshop, University of Rochester; the Industrial Organization Workshop, University of Chicago; and, especially, Sam Peltzman, Robert Tollison, and a referee of this journal. Research support was provided by the Center for Research in Government Policy and Business, University of Rochester, and the Water Resources Research Institute, Clemson University. We alone are responsible for the final product.

[*Journal of Law & Economics*, vol. XXV (April 1982)]
© 1982 by The University of Chicago. All rights reserved. 0022-2186/82/2501-0007$01.50

of consumers, because both may profit from output reductions. In the context of the economic theory of regulation (Stigler-Peltzman), environmental regulation, that is, regulation of a competitive industry in a negative externality setting, carries with it the implication that producers and the victims of pollution may find it in their self-interest to form a like-minded coalition to lobby for input restrictions and/or output reductions.[1] The difference in this case of regulation and the standard producer-consumer conflict is clear—there is extra political support from environmentalists on the side of the producers.

The maze of environmental quality regulation is overwhelming and bears little resemblance to the efficiency criteria proposed in the economics literature. Many regulatory techniques—such as technology-specific regulations, differential standards for old versus new firms, uniform percentage reductions across pollution sources, and the inalienability of pollution permits—are hard to understand on the surface. Some of the confusion is the result of only focusing on the externality effects of air and water pollution and ignoring the effects of price changes on the regulated industry.[2] It is the purpose of this paper to resolve part of this confusion by focusing attention on the cartel-like gains and losses that may accompany improved environmental quality and the self-interest motivations of agents to acquire the gains from property rights assignments to environmental assets.

In Section II we detail the conditions under which regulation can improve the value of regulated firms. Sections III and IV discuss environmental quality regulation as a means of wealth redistribution within an industry with particular emphasis on two anomalies in the actual practice of regulation—technology-specific regulation and the inalienability of pollution permits. In Section V, empirical evidence using financial market analysis of two different regulations, the OSHA cotton-dust standards and the EPA prevention of significant deterioration, are presented in support of the theory.

II. INPUT RESTRICTIONS AND PROFITS

There are several mechanisms by which the state might improve environmental quality. Effluent fees can be imposed; limitations on the production of final output can be enforced; standards or restrictions on the

---

[1] See George J. Stigler, The Theory of Economic Regulation, 2 Bell J. Econ. 3 (1971); and Sam Peltzman, Toward a More General Theory of Regulation, 19 J. Law & Econ. 211 (1976).

[2] See Buchanan & Tullock, Polluter's Profits and Political Response: Direct Controls versus Taxes, 65 Am. Econ. Rev. 139 (1975).

output of pollutants can be put in place; or technology-specific production functions can be imposed on the producers within an industry. Although economists usually focus on taxes and emission fees, regulators typically restrict pollution emissions or impose technological requirements.

As Buchanan and Tullock point out, in the fixed-proportions case taxation will always be detrimental to producer interests as the tax amounts to a charge for a resource which was previously free to the industry, and, moreover, a tax is an assignment of environmental quality rights to all society.[3] Juxtaposed to taxes, direct-output regulation can be equivalent to cartelization, with its well-known benefits (to producers), and amounts to giving the environmental assets to the producing firms. To be successful, regulation must not only restrict output, but must restrict entry as well, and the output restriction must not be so severe that average cost is raised above price.

In actual practice, environmental quality regulation usually dictates a certain input use or mandates a specific technology that firms would otherwise not have chosen. Like a shadow-price increase, regulation induces the firm to substitute out of the environmental input into other factors of production. The basic purpose of this section is to derive the conditions under which these technology-imposed regulations, combined with entry limitations, will lead to enhanced industry profitability.

Entry limitations must be enforced if the entire industry is to experience increased profits. This is frequently achieved by imposing differential pollution-control requirements on new firms—the environmental quality analogue to grandfather clauses. For example, the 1970 Clean Air Act and its amendments imposed standards on existing pollution sources as a function of the ambient air quality, while new firms had to meet the strictest standards regardless of local air quality. Moreover, the ambient air standards have been the tightest in the cleanest air regions, further restricting the entry of rivals. Entry restrictions seem to pervade every aspect of this regulatory process.[4]

---

[3] *Id.*

[4] In the early 1970s, the differential treatment of old versus new sources is obvious. Old sources were placed on a schedule of pollution control under which the economic cost of control could be considered in the enforcement determination. New sources were forced to meet the new source-performance standards without regard to cost. By 1975 the ambient standards established in the 1970 act had not been met. Two rules were changed: (1) Those areas which had not met the ambient standards (nonattainment regions) could allow no new entry under any circumstances. (This rule was modified slightly with development of the offset policy; note 13 *infra*.) (2) Those areas which were cleaner than the standard (PSD areas) had the ambient standard tightened. In addition, the 1977 amendments (1) imposed even higher performance standards, lowest achievable emission reduction (LAER), on new sources in nonattainment areas; (2) allowed old sources to meet plant-wide performance

Consider an atomistically competitive industry with the number of firms fixed. The market demand for output, D, can be divided by the number of firms already in the industry. Each firm will price along its marginal cost curve, and output is determined by the intersection of marginal cost and per firm demand, D/n.

Figure 1 shows the long-run cost curves and the per-firm demand curve of a representative firm. Prior to regulation, each firm produces q_0 output and markets it at price P_0. When an input restriction is imposed by regulation, average cost will increase. If the minimum point on the new average cost curve (point A on AC' in Figure 1) lies to the left of the per-firm demand curve, then profits for each firm will increase. The increase in profits is $(P_1 - AC_1)q_1$, and the industry is in equilibrium so long as entry is prevented. The profits in this case are actually rents accruing to the permit to use the environmental asset. Restricting the use of the input by hard and fast regulation simultaneously raises its value and assigns the claim to the existing firms in the industry.

The preregulation industry equilibrium can be characterized by the following equations:

$$P = D(nq), \tag{1}$$
$$P = MC(q, \alpha), \tag{2}$$

and

$$\Pi = [P - AC(q, \alpha)]nq, \tag{3}$$

where $P \equiv$ industry price; $q \equiv$ firm output; $n \equiv$ number of firms; $MC(\cdot)$, $AC(\cdot) \equiv$ firm marginal and average cost functions; $\Pi \equiv$ industry profits; $D(\cdot) \equiv$ industry demand; and $\alpha \equiv$ shift parameter. Equation (1) is the demand-side market-equilibrium condition; (2) is the maximizing behavior postulated for the firms; and (3) is an accounting identity for profits. The regulatory mandate shifts the cost functions of the firms as denoted by MC_α and AC_α.[5]

Displacing the equilibrium characterized in equations (1)–(3) (assuming that profits are originally zero at the margin and each firm initially oper-

---

standards (bubble concept), but did not allow this for new facilities; (3) formalized the tighter ambient standards in the cleaner areas. After the 1977 amendments new sources continued to face higher source standards than existing firms. Old sources were allowed to bubble (make in-house trade-offs), but new firms could not enjoy this cost-saving exchange. For a more detailed discussion, see Michael Maloney & Bruce Yandle, Rent Seeking and the Evolution of Property Rights in Air Quality (1980) (unpublished manuscript, Clemson Univ.).

[5] The notation $f_x = \partial f(\cdot)/\partial x$ is used.

ates at the minimum average cost) and solving for the effect on profits, we
have

$$d\Pi/d\alpha = nq \left[MC_\alpha \left(\frac{nD'}{nD' - MC_q} \right) - AC_\alpha \right]. \tag{4}$$

For (4) to be greater than zero, it is necessary that

$$\frac{1}{MC_q} \left[\frac{MC_\alpha}{AC_\alpha} - 1 \right] > -\frac{1}{nD'}. \tag{5}$$

Equation (5) represents the condition represented in Figure 1. The left
hand side of (5) measures the movement in minimum average cost.
Minimum AC must shift left within a boundary determined by the slope of
the prorated market demand curve (the right-hand side of [5]) in order for
industry profits to increase.[6]

It is possible to identify some cost conditions that will satisfy equation
(5). Consider a cost function $C(w,q)$, which maps a vector of input prices
and output into minimized cost. Average cost is

$$AC(w,q) = C(w,q)/q = \sum_i w_i \cdot x_i(w,q)/q,$$

where $x_i(w,q)$ is the ith input-demand function.

Suppose regulation increases cost to $C^*(w,q)$ by mandating a specific
amount, $\bar{x}_j$, of the environmental input. The new average-cost function is
$AC^*(w,q)$. Clearly, if there was an output level prior to restriction where
the firm would have chosen to use $\bar{x}_j$, then total and average cost are
unaffected at that output level by the regulation. In other words, if there is
a $\bar{q}$ such that $x_j(w,\bar{q}) = \bar{x}_j$, then $AC(w,\bar{q}) = AC^*(w,\bar{q})$. If $\partial x_j/\partial q > 0$ for all
q, there is at most only one output level, $\bar{q}$, where unrestricted and re-
stricted cost are the same, that is, $AC^*(w,q_0) > AC(w,q_0)$ for all $q_0 \neq \bar{q}$.
Let $\hat{q}$ be that level of output which minimizes unrestricted average cost
and $\hat{x}_j$ the amount of the jth input used to produce at minimum average
cost. In other words, $\min AC(\cdot) = C(w,\hat{q})/\hat{q}$, and then $\hat{x}_j = x_j(w,\hat{q})$. Again,
if $\partial x_j/\partial q > 0$, then the point of tangency between $C(w,q)$ and $C^*(w,q)$ will
be to the left of the original minimum average cost (if the input restriction
is binding, that is, if $\bar{x}_j < \hat{x}_j$). Thus, if $\bar{q}$ exists, then $\bar{q} < \hat{q}$. Finally, if the
difference between pre- and postrestriction average-cost curves gets
larger as the firm moves away from $\bar{q}$, then minimum average cost must
shift to the left when the input is restricted. Formally, if $\partial[AC^*(w,q) - AC(w,q)]/\partial(|\bar{q} - q|) > 0$, then $\hat{q}^* < \hat{q}$ (where $\hat{q}^*$ is that output level which
minimizes restricted average cost). Clearly, this condition will hold in a
neighborhood of $\bar{q}$ by Le Chatelier's principle.

---

[6] Minimum AC will shift to the left if $MC_\alpha > AC_\alpha$.

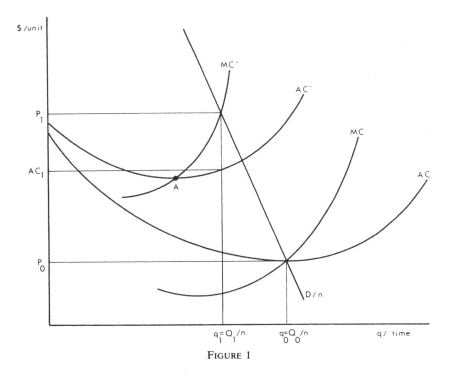

FIGURE 1

These results identify three cost conditions which guarantee the existence of profit-enhancing regulation. First, the restricted input level must have been cost minimizing at some output before the restriction. In other words, there must be an output level where the firm would voluntarily choose to emit the same level of pollution as that mandated by the law. Second, the restricted input cannot be inferior—pollution must increase with output. Finally, the input restriction must drive a wedge between the pre- and postregulation average-cost curves that are increasing in size. Average cost subject to the regulation must be more inelastic than average cost where there is no restriction on technology or inputs. If these three conditions hold, then there will always be at least one input restriction that will lead to increased industry profits, so long as industry demand is downward sloping and entry of new firms is prohibited.

Keep in mind that these are sufficient conditions for potential profit enhancement. When these conditions exist, there is always a regulation which can aid the existing firms. However, a tangency may not exist between the cost curves, and even if one does, the regulatory authority may impose an input restriction so severe as to overwhelm the price increase.[7] The necessary and sufficient condition for actual profit enhancement is that point A in Figure 1 must lie to the left of D/n. Whether the regulatory authorities will choose such a regulation is, of course, an empirical issue.

III. Intraindustry Transfers Via Regulation

It does not necessarily follow that, even if some firms suffer a decline in value as a result of regulation, all firms will be worse off. Suppose the industry has an upward-sloping supply curve because firms in the industry have different costs of production, for example, entrepreneurial rents. In this case, costs imposed on all firms by regulation may cause the low-cost firms to increase in value, while at the same time the high-cost firms suffer a decline in value. Moreover, entry does not have to be prevented for the value of these low-cost firms to increase.

Depending on the age and location of capital, managerial expertise, and many other factors, regulation via standards will not normally impose costs uniformly across firms. If the most efficient firms in the industry can comply most cheaply with the law, then the industry supply curve will shift upward and become more inelastic; market price will increase more than costs for some firms. The rents of marginal firms will decline and some will exit as they face higher costs.[8] The potential for intraindustry transfers presents an amendment to the economic theory of regulation—there is also a demand for regulation to redistribute wealth among competing firms in the industry.[9] Consequently, there may be cases where all firms in an industry do not benefit from a regulation, even if sponsored by industry. Furthermore, some firms may gain, although the industry

---

[7] For instance, the regulatory authority may mandate a pollution level, a specific technology, or a production process that was not in the firm's original cost-minimizing choice set as identified by $C(w,q)$.

[8] H. P. Marvel (Factory Regulation: A Reinterpretation of Early English Experience, 20 J. Law & Econ. 379 [1977]) presents a special case of this effect in his analysis of the seventeenth-century English child labor laws. The marginal product of child labor differed between steam- and hydropowered mills. Consequently, the rules restricting the amount children could work had differential cost effects on the industry. In more recent experience, General Motors lobbied for a stricter miles-per-gallon standard than was eventually passed by Congress. See Bruce Yandle, A Cost Benefit Analysis of the 1981–1984 MPG Standard, 6 Policy Analysis 291 (1980).

[9] In a recent insightful article, Elisabeth Landes (The Effect of State Maximum-Hours Laws on the Employment of Women in 1920, 88 J. Pol. Econ. 476 [1980]) analyzes state maximum-work-hours laws as just such a device for intraindustry transfers. Male laborers and union members are the presumed beneficiaries at the expense of immigrant women and women in general.

majority opposes a law. Even when entry is not restricted, cost-imposing regulations can increase the profits of inframarginal firms.

IV. The Inalienability of Pollution Permits

One of the most interesting regulatory perplexities is the widespread inalienability of permits or rights. We offer two explanations of this condition. Nontransferability can be a response to positive monitoring costs, and it can also result in wealth transfers among producer groups.

Casual empiricism suggests that many cartel arrangements do not allow the trading of production permits.[10] In a world of costly information, monitoring is usually required to maintain the integrity of agreements. Since it is cheaper to monitor the behavior of a firm qualitatively as opposed to measuring its precise output—it is easier to tell if a machine or plant is being used than to determine the quantity of output produced—cartels will sometimes find it valuable to assign production quotas on a pro rata or percentage basis. For example, rather than allowing each firm to produce a specific output level, the cartel manager might allow each firm to produce some fraction of time or require that plants be idled a minimum proportion of each time period. Since it will be cheaper to police this run/not-run rule than to enforce specific output levels, the extra cost of not equating marginal cost to marginal revenue might be more than offset by a saving in enforcement costs. The inalienability of tobacco allotments is a good example. It is much easier for the USDA to determine if a farmer is growing tobacco on a certain acreage than to monitor the total pounds of tobacco produced by the farmer. In the same vein, technology-imposed regulation can be used to monitor output, as it will be cheaper to check for the use of a particular technology than to precisely measure output.

---

[10] In agriculture, where output restrictions have long been used to raise the price of many products (e.g., tobacco), the production permits are not legally tradable. Although land with production privileges is alienable, the permits themselves generally are not, which makes it difficult for farmers to take advantage of any economies of scale in production that might exist. Robert Ekelund & Robert Tollison (Mercantilist Origins of the Corporation [1979] [working paper, Virginia Polytechnic Inst. and State Univ., Center for the Study of Public Choice]) discuss a number of early European cartels where trading of production privileges was not allowed, and some of the regulated cartels in this country are also characterized by nontrading. For example, the U.S. airlines under Civil Aeronautics Board regulation had fixed routes with no trades among firms, especially trades of the "one firm buys another's routes" variety that we describe. The Texas Railroad Commission is an even better example. The commission sets the production levels for oil and natural gas wells in the state of Texas monthly. Production quotas are established which allow each well operator to extract a certain number of barrels from the pool at any rate he chooses, but the production privileges are inalienable. Interesting counter examples where permits are or have been tradable include New York City taxicab medallions, New York Stock Exchange seats, ICC trucking routes, and cotton allotments.

Where there are significant costs to determining individual firm output, we expect that cartels will resort to qualitative monitoring.

If a cartel polices output restriction by qualitative monitoring, then, in general, production permits cannot be exchanged. The exchange of permits means that a firm which would have been required to shut down could have purchased permission to operate/expand, and a firm that once had the right to produce may have sold its privileges. In both cases, the on-off monitoring rule is rendered essentially worthless. In order to prevent unsanctioned production by observing the operational character of the firm (input use), cartels will sometimes find it necessary to preclude the exchange of production permits.[11]

Creating inalienable pollution permits can also redistribute wealth. Suppose there are a number of industries which each use the environment. If permits cannot be legally traded, the value to the environment in use will usually vary across industries, as the cost of production and the price elasticity of demand vary across goods. The firms which possess rights to the environment that are most valuable in use have an incentive to prevent sales by holders of permits from other industries that have low value in use. Naturally, the owners of low-value permits desire the right to trade, as it will raise the value of their permits. If the holders of high-value permits have a comparative advantage in influencing collective decisions, then they may be able to "prevent entry" in this permit market.[12]

In the single-industry case, if permits are alienable, the marginal firms that exit because of regulation-induced costs would retain their rents, even though they left the industry. Through liquidation of their permits, each of the original firms in the industry gets a share of the environmental quality rents in direct proportion to the nature and size of their permits. Making the permits inalienable means that only some of the inframarginal firms which remain in the industry capture rents from regulation. This means that restrictions on the trades of permits can result in intra- and interindustry producer wealth redistributions.[13]

---

[11] One case where it is easy to see that technology-based regulation reduces monitoring costs is provided by those fisheries which restrict net size. By imposing large net sizes, the state can limit the number of fish captured without monitoring output daily. Since possession of small nets constitutes a violation of the law (or in this case overproduction), intermittent inspection, if coupled with adequate fines, will be sufficient to solve the problem, be it cartelization or elimination of common access.

[12] Ed Mitchell (U.S. Energy Policy: A Primer 35 [1974]) argues that just such a redistribution scheme characterizes the regulation of oil production in Texas: "The formula for allocating production shares among producers was extremely generous to small high cost producers and extremely stingy to low-cost producers. . . . 'stripper wells' were usually exempted from regulation entirely. . . . It is certain that numerous inefficient producers were enriched by the cartel. Tens of thousands of stripper wells owed their survival to it. . . ."

[13] As we noted before, the modern theory of regulation and public choice do not predict

V. EMPIRICAL EVIDENCE

What might be labeled the conventional view of environmental quality regulation holds that a "social" problem exists which causes government to regulate the behavior of firms. In the case where a resource is plagued by common access, efficient regulations such as taxes could generate rents accruing to the polity in general, but government chooses to dissipate these by the form of the regulation. Firms are made worse off because of rules mandated by regulatory authorities ignorant of economic principles. Furthermore, the group recognizing the "social" problem is able politically to overwhelm the opposing producer and consumer groups.

The theory developed here takes a different view. The social reformers (environmentalists) and the producer groups have compatible goals, and this coalition carries the regulation. In the case of a common-access problem, a true scarcity rent is generated by technology-based standards and assigned either to all firms in the industry or to certain specialized resource owners within the industry.

In this theory, at least some firms always benefit from regulation. We do not expect that regulation could exist without the coalition of interests between the environmentalists and the producer groups. Drawing from the work of Peltzman, we do not expect the regulation to maximize the benefits going to the producers or the environmentalists. Hence, the theory suggests that they will accept the general principle of regulation but strive to change the degree of it.[14] In the case where entry restrictions are not present, some firms will benefit at the expense of others. The losers in this type of regulation will oppose regulation altogether. In order for the regulations to be effective in generating increased profits for producer groups, they will likely be developed on an industry by industry basis.

Most of these predictions can be supported by casual empiricism and only by such. However, the major deductive consequence and distin-

---

that governmental outcomes will favor one group to the exclusion of another. We perceive that the EPA offset regulation, which is a technique that allows limited trading of pollution permits, is another manifestation of this principle. Offsets allow firms in industry B, outside capital, to enter the regulated industry, A, if they purchase some multiple, two, three, or as much as twenty times the permits necessary for production. In the fixed-proportions case, if a firm wishes to produce k output it must buy αk permits where α is the offset. Rather than locking out the firms in industry B from the gains of regulation, some trades may occur; and the value of permits in A will be less than if no trades were permitted. The economic interests of firms in B are not completely ignored. Moreover, offsets are a predictable response to consumer well-being which are doubling damaged by the price discrimination inherent in non-transferability of permits.

[14] Peltzman, *supra* note 1.

guishing difference of our theory is profit enhancement. In this part of the paper we present two tests of the basic hypothesis, one in reference to the OSHA cotton-dust standard, the other to a court mandated air-quality-control rule change. The test method employs financial market analysis to assay the extent of profit enhancement.

The regulation of permissible cotton-dust levels in textile mills provides a convenient test of our hypothesis for a number of reasons. The regulation is industry specific, not economy-wide and, hence, partial equilibrium analysis is deemed appropriate. Since the regulation applies to just one industry, we expect that profits will be increased for some or all of the firms within the industry. Instead of taxing the incidence of cotton dust or setting performance levels which could be traded within and among firms, the regulation calls for uniform technology-based standards for similar processes across all cotton textile mills. Also, there is a prominent date that marks the beginning of the regulatory period. Finally, there are a number of firms traded on the New York Stock Exchange which allows us to use firm stock-price data to measure the market's anticipation of the effect of regulation on the value of the firms in the industry.

For the second test we consider the June 1973 Supreme Court decision ordering the Environmental Protection Agency to "prevent significant deterioration" of air quality in the clean regions of the United States. The "PSD" ruling was a court reinterpretation of the EPA mandate under the 1970 Clean Air Act (CAA). While the 1970 CAA is a law with broad scope, the PSD ruling affected only a few types of pollution, primarily nonferrous metal smelting and electric generation. The PSD ruling did not affect existing plants, but made new plant construction more difficult. We tested the value-enhancing potential of this regulation by examining the stock-market rates of return for a portfolio of copper, lead, and zinc smelters.

Cotton-Dust Standards

Cotton dust was recognized as a health hazard in the textile work environment as long as two centuries ago. Byssinosis was made a compensable occupational disease in England in 1942.[15] In 1973 research conducted

---

[15] Cotton-dust standards were first imposed in the United States in 1968 by the secretary of labor under the Walsh-Healy Act, but the standards only applied to government contractors. These same regulations were subsequently adopted by the Occupational Safety and Health Administration in 1971. It appears that the standards at that time were little more than the prevailing industry practice for most firms. For a further discussion, see R. McKenzie, B. Yandle, & H. Macaulay, The Economic Dimensions of Cotton Dust Standards for the Textile Industry: Three Essays (1979) (unpublished manuscript, Clemson Univ.).

by J.A. Merchant and others[16] indicated that the work environment was not completely safe for all workers in all U.S. cotton textile plants.[17] Work was begun on a new cotton-dust standard. In January 1974 new standards were being formulated;[18] these were delivered to the secretary of labor by the director of the National Institute of Occupational Safety and Health in September of the same year. In December, the notice of proposed rule making was issued. The process of promulgating the rules continued, culminating in the issuance of the final rules on June 23, 1978, which took effect in the summer of 1980. September 1974 stands out as the most important date in this history. It marks formal announcement of intent by the Department of Labor to place severe and binding restrictions on the emission of cotton dust in the milling process.[19]

In order for regulation to have value-enhancing effects for any firms in the industry, entry must be restricted, or firms must have different costs of production. With respect to the cotton-dust standard, the entry problem is twofold. Given the standard to be met at each plant, there is no prohibition on the entry of new firms that meet the standard. However, as with the other types of environmental regulations, entry can be prevented by differential enforcement on new and old facilities.[20] Morever, short-run rents can be earned up to the time necessary to complete new plant construction. The other entry problem is due to foreign competition. In one sense, foreign entry, which would wipe out the gains from the cotton-dust cartel restriction, is thwarted by a domestic transportation-cost advantage which gives domestic producers inframarginal (Ricardian) rents. However, an alternative argument is that the domestic industry can obtain quota protection, but this begs the question of why the industry

[16] See H. R. Imbus, The Development of a Cotton Dust Standard, 16 J. Occupational Med. 547 (1974).

[17] The questions of externality involved in the cotton-dust problem are debatable. Cotton dust does spread throughout the atmosphere of the workplace. It is a public bad inasmuch as the amount received by one worker does not significantly diminish the amount available to others. Even so, the harmful effects of cotton dust threaten only a minute portion of the work force, and these individuals are medically identifiable. Again see McKenzie, Yandle, & Macaulay, *supra* note 15.

[18] Imbus was apparently on the NIOSH panel involved in formulating and writing the report. He said in a speech before the American Occupational Medical Association on 1 May 1974 that the criteria document was in the draft stages. See Imbus, *supra* note 16, at 547.

[19] From the beginning of the discussion of a new cotton-dust standard, certain industry spokesmen, for example, Louis L. Jones, chairman of the board, Canton Cotton Mills, claimed that the dust problem was most effectively controlled at the ginning stage. See Louis Jones, Cotton and OSHA Regulations, 3 American Textiles Reporter/Bulletin 48 (1974). By the time the standards were formulated, this view had lost favor in the regulatory process. See D. W. Lyons & J. D. Hatcher, Cotton Dust Is a Yarn-Maker's Problem, 124 Textile World 56 (1974).

[20] See Maloney & Yandle, *supra* note 4.

would desire to restrict output through cotton-dust regulation. The cotton-dust restriction may be a device to inhibit domestic expansion which would have occurred in response to a tariff increase. Under these conditions, environmental regulation is a necessary, but not a sufficient, condition for profit enhancement. Of course, if differential costs within the industry are driving the environmental restriction, entry is not an important issue. By raising the costs of marginal firms, the firms, which were close to or already meeting the standard, gain a cost advantage which increases their value.

Stock Market Event Analysis

One convenient technique for assaying the effects of regulation is financial market analysis. Schwert discusses this method in detail.[21] The efficient markets theory of modern finance holds that the price of any security incorporates at each instant in time all current information and expected future returns discounted to the present at a rate of interest which includes the relative risk of the security. The use of financial data must center on event analysis. At some point in time an event occurs which signals to the capital market a change in either future returns or risk. The expected effect of this event on future cash flows is discounted into the stock-price adjustment at that time. It is possible that the capital market may receive the information slowly or that the researchers may not be able exactly to identify the point in time when the information was available, so a "window" of time preceding the event is examined to see if the returns behaved abnormally.[22]

The market model

$$r_{it} = \alpha + \beta r_{mt} + \epsilon_t, \tag{6}$$
$$\epsilon_t \sim N(0, \sigma^2),$$

is used to estimate the return to stock i, at time t, r_{it}, based on the market return, r_{mt}. It is assumed that this return includes all existing information on future dividends and the risk of those dividends, all relative to the

[21] G. William Schwert, Measuring the Effects of Regulation: Evidence from the Capital Markets, 24 J. Law & Econ. 121 (1981).

[22] An example of this approach can be found in G. William Schwert (Public Regulation of National Securities Exchanges: A Test of the Capture Hypothesis, 8 Bell J. Econ. 128 [1977]), who analyzed the effect of SEC regulation on New York and American Stock Exchange seat prices. He used a time-series model to account for other effects such as stock prices and trading volume. His findings show that the seat price on both exchanges reacted in a highly statistically significant fashion during the month of March 1934, the first month of Congressional debate on the Securities and Exchange Act.

alternative market return. Abnormal returns are measured by significant deviations of the residual, $\hat{\epsilon}_t$, from zero.

A major theoretical concern is the choice of the appropriate window reflecting the capital market's realization of the effects of regulation. For our test, September 1974 was chosen as the end of the window because this was the first formal announcement of stringent industry-wide regulation of cotton dust. The event period extends back one year. There is supporting evidence in the textile trade journals that the industry was aware of the impending regulations in January 1974. During this month the American Textile Manufacturers Institute, a trade association, sent their recommendations for standards to the Department of Labor.[23]

We tested the effect of the cotton-dust standard on a portfolio of fourteen textile firms. Each of these firms was traded on the New York Stock Exchange, and they are, in general, the major firms in the textile-mill products industry.[24] The equally weighted rate of return on this portfolio was regressed on an equally weighted portfolio of all New York Stock Exchange firms and a dummy variable representing a window preceding the first formal indication of incipient OSHA action on new standards, September 1974. Equation (6) was estimated in modified form using monthly returns from January 1965 to September 1974:

$$r_{it} = \alpha + \beta\, r_{mt} + \delta D_t + \gamma(D_t r_{mt}). \tag{7}$$

Dummy variable values, D_t, of one for September 1974 and the eleven preceding months directly tests the hypothesis that regulation made the firms more valuable. The regression coefficients are reported in Table 1. The results are not sensitive to our selection of 1965 as the beginning year or twelve months as the event period. Comparable results were obtained by beginning in 1950, any year 1960–69, or using a six-year moving estimation. Altering the event period anywhere from six to fourteen months yields estimates of the dummy which are roughly the same as the twelve-month estimate.[25]

The t-statistic on the dummy indicates that new information available to the market was associated with an increase in the value of these textile firms significantly different from zero at the 5 percent confidence level using a one-tailed test. Additional insight can be obtained by examining the residuals of the simple market-returns model, excluding the dummy,

[23] See Labor Department Considering ATMI Anti-Byssinosis Job Standard, 124 Textile World 25 (1974).

[24] The firms are Burlington Industries, Celanese, Collins & Aikman, Cone Mills, Dan River, Fieldcrest Mills, Graniteville Mills, M. Lowenstein, Reeves Bros., Riegel Textile, Springs Mills, J. P. Stevens, Texfi, and West Point–Pepperell.

[25] We will supply these tables on request.

TABLE 1
ESTIMATES OF THE COTTON-DUST STANDARD EFFECT
ON THE TEXTILE PORTFOLIO
$[r_{it} = \alpha + \beta r_{mt} + \delta D_t + \gamma(D_t r_{mt})]$

Variable	Coefficient/(t-statistic)		
Intercept	−.0004	−.0025	−.0023
	(−.13)	(−.720)	(−.669)
Market return	.9286	.9566	.9354
	(15.577)**	(15.622)**	(14.130)**
Event dummy	...	.0195	.0245
		(1.745)*	(1.939)*
Event slope shift	...	...	.1492
			(.850)
F	242.63**	125.00**	83.37**
R^2	.678	.687	.689

SOURCE.—Center for Research in Securities Prices, monthly returns tape 1965–74 (University of Chicago).
* Significant at the 5 percent level for a one-tailed test.
** Significant at the 1 percent level for a one-tailed test.

that are shown in Table 2. These residuals are based on the regression estimates for the market model, without the dummy, that are reported in Table 1.[26]

The Scholes abnormal performance index (API) is a measure of the compounded abnormal returns over the event period October 1973–September 1974: API = $\Pi_{i=1}^{12} (1 + r_i) - 1 = 0.24$.[27] As such it measures the compounded supramarket returns from investing in this portfolio at the beginning of the period and holding it until the end. This means that people who bought and held the fourteen-firm textile portfolio over the period October 1973–September 1974 earned a rate of return that was twenty-four percentage points higher than predicted by the market model. Based on the September 1973 value of these firms, the compounded abnormal return was $573 million.

There are a number of statistical concerns that arise in a regression analysis of this type. First, it is possible that the riskiness of the asset

[26] To determine if information about pending cotton-dust regulation was received continuously or in a few instances, a small sample-runs test was performed. From the residuals in Table 2 we observe three negative and nine positive returns. There are five runs in this period, which is not significantly different from randomness at the 5 percent confidence level. See S. Siegel, Nonparametric Statistics for the Behavioral Sciences (1956), for a description of this test. If information had been received constantly and the portfolio return was continuously being revised upward in value, the residuals would have exhibited nonrandomness. Since this does not appear to be the case, the reaction by the financial community probably occurred in one or two discrete jumps.

[27] M. Scholes, The Market for Securities: Substitution versus Price Pressure and the Effects of Information on Share Prices, 45 J. Bus. 179 (1972).

TABLE 2

ABNORMAL RETURNS OF THE TEXTILE PORTFOLIO

Time	Residuals of Market Model without the Dummy	Prediction Errors*
October 1973	.041	.043
November 1973	−.028	−.025
December 1973	−.024	−.022
January 1974	.055	.057
February 1974	−.025	−.023
March 1974	.057	.059
April 1974	.041	.043
May 1974	.010	.012
June 1974	.011	.013
July 1974	.019	.021
August 1974	.028	.030
September 1974	.012	.014
n	117	105
s_ϵ	.037	.037

* Deviations of actual from predicted returns where the predictions of the market model are based on data up to, but not including, the event period.

might have changed over the sample period. A change in risk causes a change in the true value of β in equation (7), which then biases the estimate of β. This change in the true model specification would also bias the estimate of the effect of the event. Moreover, the change in risk could be caused by the regulatory effect for which we are testing.[28] In order to check for changes in β not associated with the regulatory effect, we estimated a five-year, monthly moving β for 1965–74, excluding the dummy variable.[29] These coefficients were then tested for stationarity and autocorrelation, using time-series analysis. The first difference of these β coefficients is stationary and white noise. In table 1 we also report estimation of the market model with a slope-shift term. If β did in fact change during the event period, then γ, the slope-shift coefficient, will be different from zero. Since the t-statistic is 0.85, we reject the hypothesis that β changed over the event period.[30] Including the slope-shift variable marginally increases the dummy coefficient and its significance level.

The magnitude of this slope-shift coefficient is somewhat misleading. Our data source does not list returns for Texfi prior to 1972, hence the number of firms in our portfolio increases from thirteen to fourteen at the

[28] See Peltzman, *supra* note 1, at 230.

[29] Autocorrelation of the residuals of the market-returns equation is not expected based on the efficient market hypothesis; this expectation was supported in the data.

[30] We also checked for changes in β by estimating eq. (7) through 1978. Again we found no difference.

end of 1971. Changing the number of firms in the portfolio may create a specification error which biases the coefficient estimates. For example, the *t*-statistic on the slope-shift coefficient falls to 0.25 when we exclude Texfi from our sample. The *t*-statistic on δ, the regulation dummy coefficient, increases slightly to 1.95, and the magnitude of the coefficient is not substantially altered.

The significance and robustness of the dummy coefficient supports our theoretical position that impending regulation of cotton dust had a positive effect on the value of some textile firms. However, there may have been other contemporaneous events which contributed to or caused these abnormal returns. The most notable of these is the oil embargo and associated, dramatic energy price changes.[31] While the market return might capture this effect, in that the embargo effect was economy wide, the textile industry may be a less intensive energy user than the economy as a whole, or we may have a biased sample of low energy users within the industry. Consequently, the abnormal returns might be due to the favorable energy position. Additionally, cotton price changes over this period may also have impacted the value of these firms, and the abnormal returns might simply be inventory profits.

To investigate these possibilities we estimated the market model using the end of month to month percentage change in both oil and cotton prices.[32] These results are reported in Table 3 with and without Texfi. In no case do either cotton or oil prices have an effect on the portfolio returns.

Since there are a number of textile firms not traded on the NYSE, we cannot say that the entire industry benefited. In fact, based on the intraindustry transfers hypothesis, one might wonder if the large (perhaps politically powerful) firms which are traded on the NYSE benefited at the expense of the small (not traded) firms. This conjecture is reinforced by the fact that the regulations do not appear to restrict entry, which further suggests that their effect is to impose costs, drive the marginal firms out of business, and redistribute wealth within the industry.

Even though we cannot use financial analysis to test this large versus small hypothesis, we can investigate some other distributional conjectures. Specifically, we wondered if the regulation caused synthetic millers

[31] After obtaining the results of Tables 1 and 2 we checked the Wall Street Journal index and New York Times index for information concerning other events over this time period that might have been responsible for the abnormal returns, for example, changes in the textile tariffs or quotas, technological breakthroughs in the industry, or other changes in the law that might impact textile firms differently than the market. We found nothing extraordinary.

[32] Specifically we used the cotton cash price and the number two fuel oil cash price obtained from the Wall Street Journal.

TABLE 3

ESTIMATES OF COTTON-DUST STANDARD EFFECT, COTTON AND OIL PRICES ON THE
TEXTILE-PORTFOLIO RETURN

VARIABLE	COEFFICIENT (*t*-statistic)			
	Portfolio Including Texfi		Portfolio Excluding Texfi	
Intercept	−.0030	−.0029	−.0028	−.0027
	(−.854)	(−.818)	(−.797)	(−.773)
Market return	.9458	.9238	.9449	.9326
	(15.212)**	(13.867)**	(15.343)**	(14.046)**
Event dummy	.0186	.0270	.0245	.0292
	(1.419)*	(1.693)*	(1.887)**	(1.844)**
Event slope shift	· · ·	.1761	· · ·	.0986
		(.927)		(.523)
Percentage change	−.0014	.0093	.0258	.0318
in cotton price	(−.029)	(.196)	(.564)	(.672)
Percentage change	.0160	−.0174	−.0256	−.0443
in oil price	(.166)	(−.169)	(−.268)	(−.433)
F	60.70**	48.67**	61.08**	48.60**
R^2	.686	.689	.688	.688

SOURCES.—Center for Research in Securities Prices, monthly returns tape 1965–74 (University of Chicago); and the Wall Street Journal.

*Significant at the 10 percent level for a one-tailed test.

**Significant at the 5 percent level for a one-tailed test.

to be differentially affected. For example, it could be that the regulation hurt the cotton firms and thereby helped the synthetic firms, just as the English child labor laws hurt the water-powered millers and hence helped the steam-powered producers in Marvel's analysis.[33] Alternatively, the regulation could be value enhancing for cotton producers and have either a positive or zero effect on the predominantly synthetic firms.

To investigate this possibility we regressed the individual firm cumulative average returns over the twelve-month event period on the percentage of cotton to all fibers they used in production.[34] We tried a number of different specifications because we have no theoretical expectation of the form of the relationship. Table 4 reports the results, again with and without Texfi. In all specifications the intercept term, *a,* shows the effect if the cotton percentage is zero. A positive value indicates that synthetic users were made better off by the regulation. A positive value for the slope term

[33] See Marvel, *supra* note 8.

[34] Data on the cotton percentage were obtained by telephone and written communication with company representatives as well as from the annual reports and 10-K reports of the firms. In some cases these data were requested to remain confidential. In addition, the percentage of cotton-usage estimates are not all for 1973–74. For a couple of firms we could find data only for 1977–78, but we have no reason to believe that such numbers have changed drastically over time. We will gladly release the nonproprietary data on request.

TABLE 4
RELATIONSHIP OF REGULATORY GAINS TO COTTON USAGE

	SPECIFICATIONS INCLUDING Texfi*				SPECIFICATIONS EXCLUDING Texfi			
	C_1	C_2	C_3	C_4	C_1	C_2	C_3	C_4
a	.117	.143	.154	.132	.111	.144	.156	.131
	(1.49)	(2.33)	(2.91)	(2.07)	(1.21)	(2.09)	(2.66)	(1.82)
b	.245	.292	.036	−.120	.254	.290	.036	−.120
	(1.48)	(1.63)	(1.98)	(−1.76)	(1.36)	(1.49)	(1.84)	(−1.62)
R^2	.17	.19	.26	.22	.16	.18	.25	.21
F	2.20	2.66	3.91	3.09	1.84	2.24	3.37	2.62

NOTE.—See Table 1 and note 34 for sources; t-statistics are in parentheses beneath coefficients. West Point–Pepperell was excluded from this analysis due to the unavailability of data.
*CAR $= a + bC_i$; $C_1 =$ percentage of cotton to total fiber used in production; $C_2 = (C_1)^2$; $C_3 = (C_1)/(1 - C_1)$; $C_4 = \log(1 - C_1)$; CAR = cumulative average residual over event window.

in specifications 1–3 and a negative value in specification 4 indicates increased profitability as the cotton percentage increases. While the significance level varies from one model to the next, the general result supports the hypotheses that both cotton and synthetic users were made better off by the regulation but, more important, the firms with the highest percentage of cotton use experienced the largest positive residuals or abnormal returns.[35]

We interpret the cotton-dust results as evidence in support of our theoretical position that environmental quality regulation is not simply an act of government that corrects a market failure. Consistent with our expectations, since the law is industry specific, there are firms within the industry whose value increased simultaneously with regulation. In addition, as there are no apparent entry restrictions built into the law, the main effect of the law may be intraindustry wealth redistribution. In support of this hypothesis, we observe that there are differential effects of the law based on the percentage of cotton used by the firms.

The PSD Ruling

In the initial formulation of the 1970 Clean Air Act, Congress did not provide for regulation of air quality in areas which met the National Ambient Air Quality Standards (NAAQS) as established by the Environmental Protection Agency. In 1972 the EPA was in the process of

---

[35] These results were obtained using cumulative average residuals from the simple model reported in Table 1 and are subject to the same potential sources of error described earlier. Changes in energy and cotton prices may be driving these results. However, as before, using cumulative average residuals from a model which includes cotton and oil prices does not significantly alter the results.

evaluating and approving state implementation plans as authorized by the 1970 act. These plans detailed the circumstances under which new pollution sources would be granted permits. Up to this point, the EPA had not imposed any requirement on the states to control new sources of pollution that posed no threat to ambient standards. This feature would have meant that there were no entry restrictions for firms in areas which had relatively clean air, so long as they met the technological standards imposed on all new firms in the industry.

In May of 1972 the Sierra Club and three other environmental groups brought suit against the EPA to block "significant deterioration" of air quality in those regions of the country where the ambient standards were being met.[36] On June 12, 1972, the District Court for the District of Columbia issued a preliminary injunction requiring the EPA to disapprove state plans which did not prevent deterioration. On November 2, 1972, the U.S. Court of Appeals, D.C. Circuit, affirmed the lower court's decision. In January 1973, the Supreme Court agreed to hear the case and, on June 11, 1973, they affirmed the appellate court's decision upholding the "prevention of significant deterioration."[37] Following this ruling, in late 1973, the EPA proposed rules to incorporate PSD requirements into each state plan. In December 1974, the final regulations were promulgated which dictated that each state include a PSD requirement.[38]

We interpret this court ruling as a strong, binding, entry-limiting device.[39] Firms which could otherwise have constructed facilities would now either be barred from entering or forced to meet higher standards, most especially for industries which emitted sulphur oxides and particulates. According to the court-reported history of the PSD ruling: ". . . [T]he [PSD] regulations covered 19 categories of typical large industrial . . . facilities. Each source on the list had significant process emissions of particulates or sulphur dioxide which, EPA estimated, accounted for 'essentially all of (the sulphur dioxide and particulate matter) emitted in clean areas.' *New sources and modifications of existing sources* on the list of 19 were subject to preconstruction review . . . A PSD permit was required for a *new* or modified source on the list if construction was commenced after June 1, 1975" (emphasis added; brackets in original).[40]

[36] Sierra Club et al. v. Ruchelshaus, 344 F. Supp. 258 (1972).

[37] The lower court was affirmed by an equally divided Supreme Court, sub. nom. Fri v. Sierra Club, 412 U.S. 541, 93 S. Ct. 2770, 37 L. Ed. 2d 140 (1973).

[38] For a brief, succinct discussion of the PSD legal history see Alabama Power Co. v. Costle, 636 F. 2d 323 (1979) at 346.

[39] In a Wall Street Journal interview, EPA director Ruchelshaus argued that "prohibitions . . . would be tantamount to barring all industrial and population growth in rural areas . . ." Wall Street Journal, November 3, 1972, at 18.

[40] See Alabama Power Co. v. Costle, *supra* note 38, at 348.

As we have indicated, the PSD ruling limited entry primarily into industries that were sources of sulphur dioxide and particulates. According to the *Wall Street Journal,* "The . . . [PSD] decision is aimed at areas where any of the six major pollutants, including sulphur dioxide and particulate matter, are currently below the secondary limit."[41] Further, the EPA argued that it could only regulate sulphur oxides and particulates for PSD because there were currently no analytical procedures available to assess the impact of the other four pollutants by individual sources on ambient air quality.[42] Sulphur oxide and particulate pollution sources are heavily concentrated in two industries, nonferrous ore smelting and electricity production, and hence the PSD ruling should have had a direct effect on copper, lead, and zinc smelters, in that future entry was significantly impaired.[43] Such a restriction would raise the value for the existing firms in the industry.

For a second test of the commonality of interest between environmentalists and producers, we performed an event analysis on a portfolio of nonferrous metal smelters.[44] We regressed the smelting-portfolio return on the market return using monthly data from 1965 through June 1973— the Supreme Court decision. We chose an event window of twelve months which covers the appellate court's ruling.[45] The results are shown in Table 5.

Again we find support for the claim that environmental regulation is beneficial to some of the existing firms in the industry. The dummy coefficient is 0.0316 and is significant at the 1 percent level using a one-tailed test. The residuals from the market model without the dummy are reported in Table 6.[46] The Scholes API index of compounded abnormal performance for the twelve months is 0.441, indicating that the PSD ruling

---

[41] Wall Street Journal, November 3, 1972, at 18.

[42] See 39 Fed. Reg. 42511 (1974).

[43] The Department of Commerce, .Bureau of Economic Analysis, Capital Expenditures, Total and Pollution Control (1973) reports the following air pollution capital expenditures as a fraction of total capital expenditures: nonferrous metal, 29.3 percent; steel, 11.6 percent; paper, 9.2 percent; stone and clay, 8.2 percent; petroleum, 6.5 percent; utilities, 4.8 percent; chemical, 4.7.

[44] The firms are Amax, Anaconda Co, Asarco, Cerro, Copper Range Co., Gulf Resources and Chemical, Inspiration Consolidated Copper Co., Kennecott Copper Co., Newmont Mining, N. L. Industries, Phelps Dodge, St. Joe Minerals, Tenneco, and U.S. Steel. Tenneco and U.S. Steel have only minor interests in copper smelting. Deleting these two firms does not materially alter the results.

[45] Event periods of six, seven, eight, etc., or eighteen months yield similar results to those reported in Table 5. Extending the analysis through 1978 has no significant impact on the results either.

[46] Again, based on a small sample-runs test we cannot reject the hypothesis that there are not more or fewer runs than would probably occur in a random sample.

TABLE 5

ESTIMATES OF THE PSD RULING EFFECT ON THE SMELTING PORTFOLIO

$$[r_{it} = \alpha + \beta r_{mt} + \delta D_t + \gamma (D_t r_{mt})]$$

Variable	Coefficient/(t-statistic)		
Intercept	−.0011	−.0050	−.0051
	(−.29)	(−1.32)	(−1.32)
Market return	.8966	.9373	.9400
	(12.58)*	(13.31)*	(12.84)*
Event dummy	...	.0316	.0308
		(2.83)*	(2.45)*
Event slope shift	...	...	−.0405
			(−.14)
F	158.23*	88.63*	58.51*
R^2	.613	.642	.642

SOURCE.—Center for Research in Securities Prices, monthly returns tape 1965–73 (University of Chicago).

*Significant at the 1 percent level for a one-tailed test.

was associated with a smelting-portfolio return 44 percent higher than predicted by the market model.

After obtaining these results, we investigated the possibility that events other than the PSD ruling might have accounted for the positive earnings of the smelting portfolio. Two other events are contemporaneous with the PSD court case. In early 1973 copper prices increased. The *Wall Street Journal* carried stories on 15 February and 5 March 1973 in which it was speculated that increasing demand for copper was expected to boost prices. Reasons cited included production problems in Chile, political friction between Rhodesia and Zambia, and the "monetary crisis." Of course, if the copper market was responding to future output restrictions because of the PSD ruling, then the price increases may have also been due to the future effects of reduced capacity.

Second, in March of 1973 the U.S. Treasury Department announced that it was investigating the possibility that lead was being sold in the United States by Canada and Australia at illegally low prices. In October 1973, the Treasury concluded that Canada and Australia had in fact "dumped" lead in the United States at less than fair market value. These events could have led the financial market to anticipate higher lead prices through increased tariffs on foreign lead.

Unfortunately it is not easy to disentangle the separate effects of the court ruling and the metals price changes. This is especially cumbersome since the change in environmental law may itself have contributed to the copper price change. Examination of the residuals reveals large positive errors in August of 1972 and January, February, and June of 1973. The January and February residuals are coincident with the *Wall Street Jour-*

ENVIRONMENTAL QUALITY REGULATION 121

TABLE 6
ABNORMAL RETURNS OF THE SMELTING PORTFOLIO

Time	Residuals of Market Model without the Dummy	Prediction Errors*
July 1972	.017	.022
August 1972	.095	.097
September 1972	−.024	−.019
October 1972	.002	.006
November 1972	.012	.014
December 1972	−.003	.001
January 1973	.052	.058
February 1973	.109	.116
March 1973	.027	.032
April 1973	.003	.010
May 1973	−.018	−.012
June 1973	.049	.054
n	102	90
s_ϵ	.0368	.0347

*Deviations of actual from predicted returns where the predictions of the market model are based on data up to, but not including, the event period.

nal reports of increasing copper prices. June 1973 is the month of the Supreme Court ruling. We cannot isolate any extraordinary event in August of 1972. As in the textile case, one technique to correct for the portfolio value effect changes due to metal price changes is to include them in a market-model regression. We regressed the smelting portfolio on the market return, with the dummy, and we included the percentage change in copper, lead, and zinc spot prices from the London Metals Exchange. These results are reported in Table 7, and they do not change the basic conclusion. Even taking into account the effect of metal price changes, there is a significant change in the value of the smelting portfolio contemporaneous with the Supreme Court PSD ruling.

VI. Conclusions

Environmental quality regulation is a relative newcomer to government restrictions on the right to contract. We have attempted to explain some of the regulatory peculiarities by incorporating the effects of regulation on the affected firms. Specifically, environmental use restrictions create valuable rents, some of which may accrue to the regulated firms. In effect, many of the existing laws and institutions can be explained as devices for distributing the rents created by regulation.

In this theory certain industry elements, a subset of firms, a factor or collection of inelastically supplied factors, or even the entire industry work together with environmentalists to reduce pollution and output.

THE JOURNAL OF LAW AND ECONOMICS

TABLE 7

ESTIMATES OF THE PSD RULING EFFECT, COPPER, LEAD, AND ZINC PRICES ON THE
SMELTING PORTFOLIO

Variable	Coefficient/(t-statistic)		
Intercept	−.0030	−.0061	−.0061
	(−.80)	(−1.59)	(−1.58)
Market return	.9251	.9553	.9546
	(12.98)*	(13.53)*	(13.00)*
Event dummy	. . .	.0285	.0287
		(2.43)*	(2.25)*
Event slope shift	. . .	. . .	.0104
			(.03)
Percentage of change	.0995	.0982	.0982
in copper prices	(2.34)*	(2.37)*	(2.36)*
Percentage of change	.0138	.0072	.0073
in lead prices	(.18)	(.09)	(.10)
Percentage of change	.0739	−.0003	.0004
in zinc prices	(.73)	(−.01)	(.01)
F	42.23*	36.71*	30.27*
R^2	.64	.66	.66

SOURCES.—Center for Research in Securities Prices, monthly returns tape 1965–73 (University of Chicago); and Wall Street Journal.

*Significant at the 5 percent level for a one-tailed test.

Quite naturally, there is a great deal of fighting over the distribution of rents created in the process. It should come as no surprise that there are often firms or factors within an industry that lose by these regulations. In fact, the theory is explicitly constructed to explain the intraindustry transfer of wealth occasioned by environmental quality regulation.

There are a number of situations where environmental quality regulations of an industry make some or all of the firms in that industry more valuable. Since regulation necessarily reduces output, either directly or indirectly by raising cost, market price of output increases. If entry is restricted, then these price increases can be profit enhancing. Even if entry is not impeded, the price increases may exceed the cost increases for a subset of the firms in the industry. We subjected these propositions to a test based on the regulation of cotton dust in U.S. textile mills. There we found some evidence that a number of firms experienced an increase in value, based on their stock prices, contemporaneously with OSHA plans to restrict cotton-dust levels. Moreover, these value increases were positively related to the fraction of cotton used by the firms in its production process. We also found an association between the Supreme Court ruling which would limit the entry of new smelting plants and the value of a portfolio of existing copper, lead, and zinc smelters. However, the results on these nonferrous smelters are clouded by diverse contemporaneous events. Nevertheless, having controlled for these, there is still a significant association between the portfolio return and the PSD ruling.

Other casual examples where environmental quality regulation has deterred or barred the entry of rivals are not hard to construct. The U.S. landings of the Concorde by Air France and British Airways have been severely restricted because of noise pollution. Direct-output controls of this type are necessarily price increasing and must increase the value of U.S. firms in the airline industry, since they impose no costs. Regulation of the Alaska oil pipiline is another good example. To the extent that environmental quality regulation delayed construction, competing oil producers earned rents because the price of crude oil would have been lower with the increased production from the North Slope. In both cases it seems obvious that there were intraindustry transfers. The existing firms benefited from regulation while the entrants suffered.

These data convince us that there is a strong interplay between producers, consumers, and the victims of pollution. Each party has some influence on the outcome, and one-sided analysis neglects many important aspects of regulation. Environmental quality regulation is complicated, but many of the observed perplexities are consistent with a rent-seeking, self-interest theory of government.

[9]

INSTRUMENT CHOICE IN ENVIRONMENTAL POLICY

DONALD N. DEWEES*

I. INTRODUCTION

Economists have long criticized traditional pollution control policies and suggested their replacement with effluent charges or effluent rights schemes. Baumol and Oates (1979, Chapter 16), Anderson (1977, Chapter 2), Dales (1968) and Kneese and Schultz (1975, Chapter 7) argue that market-oriented pollution control policies will be more efficient in both the short and long run than traditional regulatory policies. Despite these arguments, every jurisdiction in the United States and Canada relies almost exclusively on direct regulation with rare and modest use of market policies. The United States Congress has twice rejected serious proposals for effluent charges. In 1971 and 1972 the Nixon Administration[1] and Senator Proxmire[2] produced competing proposal to tax sulfur oxide emissions into the atmosphere. At the same time, Senator Proxmire introduced a bill into the Senate which would allow the Environmental Protection Agency to levy effluent charges on a variety of water pollutants.[3] These measures were all soundly defeated.[4]

The only market policies that have been relatively successful are the sewer surcharge which imposes a special charge on "extra strength" pollution discharged into municipal sewer systems,[5] administrative penalties used to enforce emission standards,[6] and more recently the EPA's "offsets" and "bubble" policies, which operate like limited effluent rights systems.[7]

The general failure to adopt policies of proven efficiency has been viewed with despair by economists.[8] But if we are to understand why policies are not adopted and to develop policy designs that may be both efficient *and* politically attractive, we must analyze the essence of political decisions: the distributional effects of policies. To predict the political effect of a policy, one must consider those interests that are concentrated, with a large impact on a small number of firms or persons.[9] The direct short run effects of industrial pollution control policies are concentrated on the affected firms, or more precisely the shareholders of affected firms, and their employees. This is a very different focus from that of most studies of the distribu-

*Professor of Economics, Professor of Law, University of Toronto. This research has been supported in part by a grant from the Social Sciences and Humanities Research Council and by the Law and Economics Program at the University of Toronto. I would like to thank Mel Fuss and several members of the Law and Economics Workshop for providing helpful comments on an earlier draft of this paper.

1. Anderson (1977, pp. 51-53); Kneese and Schulze (1975, pp. 99-101).

2. Congressional Record, House, 92nd Congress, 2nd Session, Vol. 118, Part 4, p. 4250.

3. Congressional Record, Senate, 92nd Congress, 2nd Session, Vol. 117, Part 30, p. 38826, Nov. 2, 1971.

4. For a brief analysis of their defeat, see Anderson (1977, pp. 154-158).

5. See Sims (1977, p. 8).

6. See Connecticut Enforcement Project (1975, p. 7).

7. See Clark (1979) and Drayton (1981).

8. See Kneese and Schultze (1975, p. 120). Note that one efficiency advantage of market policies, equating marginal control costs among sources, is only relevant for a perfectly mixed or "point" environment. For widely dispersed polluters, the marginal benefit of abatement will vary with location, so marginal costs should vary as well.

9. For some analysis of the politics of regulation and the importance of concentrated interests, see Peltzman (1976) and Stigler (1971).

tional effects of pollution control policies which focus on diffuse effects on the general public, taxpayers, the rich versus the poor, or on consumers of a given product.[10]

Buchanan and Tullock (1975) offer "a positive theory of externality control that explains the observed frequency of direct regulation as opposed to penalty taxes or charges." They compare the impact on individual firm profits of an effluent charge with a pollution emission quota for each firm. They demonstrate that if the quota is available only to existing firms, it creates a barrier to entry and may actually increase firm profits and therefore be attractive to existing industry members. In contrast, the effluent charge cannot generate excess profits, and will usually generate operating losses in the short run. They conclude that firms will resist effluent charge proposals more strongly than direct regulation because the former lead to less profit than the latter.

This paper explores in more detail the impact of alternative environmental policies on those who may be greatly affected by them. We examine the impact of alternative policies on the shareholders of firms in the industry at the time that the new policy is implemented. We also examine the impact of alternative policies on the labor market, by determining the net effect on employment of each policy, and the gross number of layoffs resulting from individual plant closings. These measures are not welfare measures, but should indicate the political pressures that may be raised by capital and by labor. These pressures arise from the costs imposed on shareholders and workers by the adjustment to a new equilibrium in which relative factor prices (the cost of pollution discharge) or property rights (the right to discharge wastes at no cost) have changed. The costs in turn arise from the immobility or non-malleability of both physical capital and of labor.

We apply a simple competitive model to three cases to show that both capital and labor suffer more from effluent rights or effluent charge policies than from uniform effluent standards that yield the same pollution per unit of product output. We show further that charges and rights look still worse when compared with the typical regulatory regime that imposes more stringent standards on new plants than on existing plants. Finally, we discuss ways in which the market policies can be designed to compensate the losers and thus lessen resistance to the policies. We identify an effluent rights scheme that will be more attractive to capital than effluent charges, and may even be more attractive than no pollution control policy at all.

II. SOME CHARACTERISTICS OF PRESENT POLICIES

Two common characteristics of pollution control policies across North American are of interest because they are not captured in most economists' descriptions of the traditional regulatory approach. Most important is the distinction between the limitations on existing sources and those on new sources. In Canada, the Pulp and Paper Effluent Regulations under the Fisheries Act specify different standards for existing mills and for new mills, allowing fifty percent more pollution from existing mills.[11]

---

10. Gianessi, Peskin and Wolff (1979) look at the costs and benefits of current U.S. regulatory policies by income class and by region, and at the portion of the cost borne of industry and government by households. Baumol and Oates (1975, Ch. 13) review distributional effects of policies generally by income class and by region. Harrison (1975) examines the distribution of auto pollution control costs and benefits by income class and by region. Griffin (1974) examines the welfare gains from an effluent charge for controlling sulfur emissions from thermal power plants.

11. S.O.R./72-92, Schedule 1.

The Refinery Regulations apply only to new refineries that began operation after November 1, 1973.[12] More important is the requirement that new potential sources of pollution receive approval from the relevant agency before commencing operation. This approval requires satisfying environmental requirements far more strict than the requirements usually imposed on existing sources. In the United States, the Clean Air Act Amendments of 1970 and 1977 require all new sources (or reconstructed or expanded sources) of air pollution to meet the relevant new source performance standards, which demand the use of the best available control technology.[13] Thus in general, the demands on new sources are much tougher than on existing sources.

Another important characteristic of current policies is the variable upon which the allowed emissions are based. Buchanan and Tullock (1975) represent direct regulation as a quota allowing equal rates of discharge to all firms. In fact, such quotas are rare, represented primarily by point of impingement concentration limits. A requirement that the best available or best practicable technology be used will in the long run tend to result in a uniform rate of emission per unit of input (coal burned) or output (steel produced). An effluent concentration limit will also allow emissions in proportion to production. Some regulations explicitly relate allowable emissions to inputs or outputs.[14] Thus it is more realistic to represent present policies as allowing emissions proportional to production than as allowing fixed total emissions per source.

III. THE MODEL AND IMPACT MEASURES

The model used in this analysis incorporates a competitive industry consisting of n firms each of which has a single plant with a U-shaped long run average cost curve. The output is produced by capital k, labor l and pollution discharge e. Labor is supplied at constant cost at wage w and capital must earn the competitive rate of return r. The capital/labor ratio is the same for pollution control as it is for output production, and is constant in long run equilibrium for all output levels at a given set of factor prices regardless of the degree of pollution control undertaken. The production function is therefore homothetic. All firms may be identical, or new firms may face lower pollution control costs than existing firms. Industry demand is exogenous, and the industry elasticity of demand is –1.

Firm production is thus

$$(1) \qquad\qquad q \; = \; q(k, l, e),$$

and industry production is

$$(2) \qquad\qquad Q \; = \; Q(K, L, E) \; = \; nq.$$

12. S.O.R./73-679, s.3.

13. Hartman, Bozdogan and Nadkarni (1979) note that new source performance standards virtually preclude traditional marginal plant capacity expansion in the copper smelting industry and thus create an effective capacity constraint in the short run, which will last 10 years. Koch and Leone (1979, pp. 93, 104) conclude that in the tissue paper industry, the effect of tough new source performance standards is that pollution control costs are higher for new plants than for old plants.

14. For example, the Canadian Chlor-Alkali Mercury Effluent Regulations (S.O.R./72-92, s.5) limit the discharge of mercury to .0025 kilograms per ton of chlorine produced.

The technology of pollution control is such that there is never any reduction in the minimum efficient scale in a plant as a result of adding pollution controls.[15]

The capital equipment used in this industry may be either rigid and immobile or malleable and mobile. In either case it is infinitely durable. Malleable capital can be costlessly converted from production to pollution control, or from production in this industry to production in some other industry. This capital is indestructable, and no change in industry structure, output or the production process can affect its value. Rigid capital cannot be transformed from production to pollution control or from production in this industry to production in any other industry. Thus if a firm's capital requirement declines unexpectedly, the value of the original capital in that firm, and therefore the value of the shareholders' investment in that firm, also declines. If a plant closes, the value of its capital stock drops to nothing. Capital in the real world may fairly be characterized as rigid in the short run in most industries, while it may be malleable in the long run, over the time when it would have to be replaced anyway, often twenty to thirty years in highly polluting heavy industry. Representing capital rigidity or flexibility explicitly in this model allows us to consider the entry and exit of firms separately from the normal rate of replacement of capital. We measure the impact of a policy on shareholders by comparing the value of the original physical capital owned by the firms before the policy with the value of the same capital afterward, assuming that in long run equilibrium product prices will allow a normal rate of return on all capital used both in production and in pollution control.

It is implicit in this model that pollution control is achieved by tail-end treatment. With rigid capital one can add pollution controls to an existing plant whose output is unchanged without destroying any of the existing capital value. This is somewhat unrealistic in that frequently the least cost means of pollution control in the long run is to modify the production process, which would render some or all of the production capital less valuable.

Labor in this model may also be either mobile and flexible or immobile and rigid. If labor were perfectly mobile and all job skills were identical, then labor should be indifferent to the effects of pollution policies, since workers could move from production to pollution control or from this industry to another at no cost. Labor may be fairly characterized as mobile in the long run in most industries, and as immobile in the short run if workers suffer costs in moving from one job or city to another. In fact, workers have some plant-related skills or knowledge, and often have seniority positions or pension rights that would be lost in moving from one plant or firm to another. Thus reducing the work force at any plant more rapidly than the normal rate of attrition of the labor force will impose some costs on labor. Reducing total employment in the industry will impose still greater costs, since workers must learn new skills before they can be re-employed. We measure the impact of a policy on labor by calculating gross layoffs in the industry, measured as the sum of all reductions in employment at any plant that contracts or closes. We also calculate net layoffs in the industry which is the difference between gross layoffs and total hiring at some plants which have to add staff for increased production or for pollution control. Both gross and net layoffs should be of interest to labor, indicating the magnitude of different adjustments.

---

15. Hanke and Gutmanis (1975, p. 247) suggest the existence of economies of scale in pollution control.

Pollution control policies are assumed to be imposed at a pace that renders each set of assumptions (flexibility or inflexibility) to be of potential relevance. Thus we will talk about "long-run" adjustment (firms can enter or exit) with flexible and with inflexible capital and labor.

IV. ANALYSIS OF ALTERNATIVE POLICIES

A. *Uniform Costs, Uniform Policies*

Suppose that a representative firm and the industry are in equilibrium producing q_0 and Q_0 respectively as shown in figure 1, and consuming inputs l_0, k_0 and e_0. A pollution control policy is adopted intended to reduce emissions per unit of output by 50 per cent. In the long run, policy i will impose costs for pollution control and in some cases for paying charges or for holding pollution rights, shifting the firm's cost curves up to AC_i and MC_i yielding an equilibrium industry price p_i. If capital is malleable, it must earn the normal rate of return in this industry or it will be moved to some other industry. Thus the new supply curve is perfectly elastic at price p_i, i.e. S_i. Industry output Q will drop from Q_0 to $Q_i = Q_0(p_0/p_i)$ because we assume a unitary industry elasticity of demand. Revenue will be unchanged.

FIGURE 1

Uniform Costs, Uniform Policies

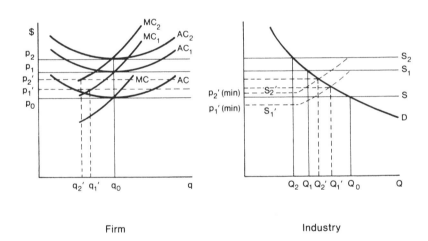

Firm	Industry

We have assumed that economies of scale in pollution control mean that the optimal firm size cannot decrease as a result of imposing controls. The number of firms that must close is thus equal to or greater than the reduction in industry output divided by the size of a single firm:

$$(3) \qquad \Delta n = (Q_0 - Q_i)/q_0 = \frac{p_i - p_0}{p_i} n_0.$$

If capital is malleable, shareholders suffer no losses from plant closings, as their capital is costlessly shifted to some other use. The number of workers laid off is all the workers in firms that close, or:

$$(4) \qquad\qquad \Delta n \; l_0 \; = \; \frac{p_i - p_0}{p_i} \; L_0 .$$

Emissions will be reduced by more than 50 per cent because output is reduced by all policies. The reduction is:

$$(5) \qquad\qquad \Delta E \; = \; 1/2 E_0 \; (1 \; + \; \frac{p_i - p_0}{p_i}).$$

If capital is non-malleable, then capital that becomes redundant becomes worthless. At output levels above Q_0, the industry supply curve is perfectly elastic at S_i. However if output declines below Q_0, firms will move down their new marginal cost curves MC_i until the price drops to AVC plus a normal return on the new capital for pollution control, or $p_i'(min)$. At and below that output level, supply is again perfectly elastic, with the quasi-rent on old capital equal to zero. This yields supply curve S_i' and price p_i', where S_i' intersects D at Q_i'. Since industry demand is unitary elastic, Q will drop to $Q_i' = Q_0(p_0/p_i')$.

Unlike the case with malleable capital, no firms need to close if D intersects the curved portion of S_i', since the entire industry output reduction can be accommodated by output reductions within existing firms as they move down their new MC curves. However, the shareholders of these firms do suffer a capital loss, since the quasi-rent on their capital is reduced. The quasi-rent is zero when $p = p_i'(min)$. At a price between $p_i'(min)$ and p_i the capital loss is at least the original capital K_0 times the proportion of the maximum price drop that has occurred, or

$$(6) \qquad\qquad \Delta K \; \geq \; K_0 \; \frac{p_i - p_i'}{p_i - p_i'(min)} .$$

This would be exact only if the MC_i curve were perfectly inelastic. All existing firms will share equally in this loss. If price drops to $p_i'(min)$ then some firms may close, and all the original capital K_0 is valueless, since there are no quasi-rents even for surviving firms. We will ignore this case by assuming that AVC is sufficiently below ATC that D intersects S_i' in its curved region.

Total employment was unchanged in the malleable capital case above. Here capital bears more of the losses, so L should increase and there are no layoffs, as long as production workers can shift to pollution control jobs.

Let policy $i = 1$ be an effluent standard limiting emissions to

$$(7) \qquad\qquad e/q \; \leq \; 1/2 E_0 / Q_0 .$$

in a world of malleable capital. This yields the results in the first column of table 1a. The layoffs in firms that close are just offset by added workers at surviving firms to operate the pollution control equipment. New capital is also added to surviving plants. Since revenues are unchanged, the labor and capital shares are unchanged although losses are imposed on some workers.

Let policy $i = 2$ be an effluent charge in an amount t per unit of discharge also designed to reduce emissions per unit of output by 50 per cent. Now firms must not only pay for pollution control, they must pay the charge for remaining emissions. Thus AC_2 and MC_2 must lie above AC_1 and MC_1 in figure 1, and p_2 must be greater than p_1 by the amount of the charge times emissions divided by output, or:

$$(8) \qquad\qquad p_2 - p_1 = \frac{te_2}{q_2} \,.$$

Since t was chosen to achieve $(e_2/q_2) = 1/2 (e_0/q_0)$, then equation (8) implies:

$$(9) \qquad\qquad p_2 = p_1 + \frac{te_2}{q_2} = p_1 + \frac{te_0}{2q_0} \,.$$

Thus the effect of the effluent charge on prices, layoffs, and emission reduction is greater than that of the effluent standard, as shown in table 1a.

Let $i = 3$ be a policy of perpetual pollution rights designed to reduce emissions per unit of output by 50 percent. For the rights to cause the same degree of abatement as the effluent charge they must impose the same opportunity cost per unit of discharge, t, as the charge. The value of a right to discharge at the rate of one unit per year will be the present value of an infinite stream of payments of t per year discounted at rate r, or t/r. The aggregate value of the rights issued is $(t/r)E_3$. But $E_3 = E_2$ since the charge and right have the same impact on emissions, and $E_2 = 1/2$ $E_0(Q_2/Q_0)$, so the value of the rights is $(t/r)(E_0/2)(Q_2/Q_0)$. Since the opportunity cost of holding the rights is the same as that of paying the charge, the effect of a rights policy on product price, output, employment and share value should be identical to the effect of the effluent charge.

If the effluent rights are sold to polluting firms, the only difference from the effluent charge is that some cash on the asset side of each firm's balance sheet will be replaced by an equivalent value of marketable rights. If the rights are given to all firms previously in the industry, then each firm is wealthier than if the rights were sold, by an amount equal to the value of the rights, $(t/r)(E_0/2)(Q_2/Q_0)$.

The results described above are summarized in table 1a. Except for the wealth of the original shareholders, the effect of an effluent charge and of either effluent rights scheme is the same. The market policies raise price more and lower quantity more than the effluent standard, and this is efficient.[16] Market policies generally will lead to more plant closings and thus more layoffs than standards because they reduce the output more. If labor is perfectly mobile over the period when the policy will take effect, then labor should be indifferent to all policies. If labor is immobile so that there are costs to being laid off, then labor should resist all pollution control policies, but resist market policies more than standards. If capital is perfectly malleable during the period when the policy will take effect, then shareholders will be indifferent to standards, charges and pollution rights sold to the existing industry.

16. Baumol and Oates (1975, Ch. 4) show that a pigovian tax yields optimal pollution levels and product output. It follows that regulation of pollution levels that yields the same environmental result will yield too much product output. The problem is that at the optimal pollution level, the marginal harm of more pollution is positive; this social cost is reflected in the effluent charge rate t, but there is no corresponding price (or expense) with regulations. Note that in the model used here, all firms have identical cost curves, so the traditional efficiency advantage of the charge, equating marginal control costs among firms, is achieved by the standards as well.

TABLE 1a

Summary of Impacts
Uniform Costs, Uniform Policies
Malleable Capital

Impact	Effluent Standard	Effluent Charge	Effluent Rights Sold	Given
Price p	p_1	$p_2 = p_1 + \dfrac{te_0}{2q_0}$	same as effluent charge	
Δ Industry Output Q	$\dfrac{-(p_1-p_0)Q_0}{p_1}$	$\dfrac{-(p_2-p_0)Q_0}{p_2}$	same as effluent charge	
Δ Firm Output q	0	0	same as effluent charge	
Firms closed Δn	$\dfrac{(p_1-p_0)n_0}{p_1}$	$\dfrac{(p_2-p_0)n_0}{p_2}$	same as effluent charge	
Δ Capital share	0	$-E_2 t K$	same as effluent charge	
Δ Share Value	0	0	0	$+ \dfrac{tE_2}{r}$
Δ Labor L	0	$\dfrac{-tE_2}{R} L_0$	same as effluent charge	
Δ Labor Share wL	0	$\dfrac{-tE_2}{R} wL_0$	same as effluent charge	
Layoffs	$\dfrac{(p_1-p_0)L_0}{p_1}$	$\dfrac{(p_2-p_0)L_0}{p_2}$	same as effluent charge	
Δ Emissions	$-\dfrac{1}{2}E_0(1 + \dfrac{p_1-p_0}{p_1})$	$-\dfrac{1}{2}E_0(1 + \dfrac{p_2-p_0}{p_2})$	same as effluent charge	
Government Revenue	0	tE_2 per year	$\dfrac{t}{r} E_2$	0

$$E_2 = \frac{1}{2} E_0 \frac{Q_2}{Q_0}$$

If capital is immobile and non-malleable, then the results are somewhat different although a similar pattern prevails, as shown in table 1b and by the dashed lines in figure 1. Any policy causes price to rise less than with malleable capital, and output to drop less. Firm output *does* decline with rigid capital, but there are no plant closings. Shareholders suffer capital losses, but there are no layoffs, assuming that production workers in a plant can be shifted to pollution control work in the same plant. All of the adjustment costs are borne by the shareholders. An effluent charge causes larger adjustment costs than does a standard, as with malleable capital.

Thus if capital is immobile and non-malleable, shareholders should resist effluent standards, and resist effluent charges and the sale of rights more vigorously. Effluent rights distributed free to the existing industry will be preferred to rights

TABLE 1b

Summary of Impacts

Uniform Costs, Uniform Policies

Rigid Capital

Impact	Effluent Standard	Effluent Charge	Effluent Rights Sold	Effluent Rights Given
Price p	p_1'	$p_2' > p_1'$	same as effluent charge	
Δ Industry Output Q	$-\dfrac{(p_1'-p_0)}{p_1'}Q_0$	$-\dfrac{(p_2'-p_0)}{p_2'}Q_0$	same as effluent charge	
Δ Firm Output q	$-(q_0-q_1')$	$-(q_0-q_2')$	same as effluent charge	
Firms Closed Δn	0	0	same as effluent charge	
Δ Share Value (approx.)	$-K_0\dfrac{p_1-p_1'}{p_1-p_1'(\text{min})}$	$-K_0\dfrac{p_2-p_2'}{p_2-p_2'(\text{min})}$	same as effluent charge	$-K_0\dfrac{p_2-p_2'}{p_2-p_2'(\text{min})}$ plus rights value
Δ Labor L	No drop	No drop	same as effluent charge	
Layoffs	0	0	same as effluent charge	
Δ Emissions	$-\dfrac{1}{2}E_0(1 + \dfrac{p_1'-p_0}{p_1'})$	$-\dfrac{1}{2}E_0(1 + \dfrac{p_2'-p_0}{p_2'})$	same as effluent charge	
Government Revenue	0	tE_2 per year	$\dfrac{t}{r}E_2$	0

$$E_2' = \frac{1}{2}E_0\frac{Q_2'}{Q_0}$$

that are sold or to charges, and might be preferred to an effluent standard. It is unlikely that the value of the rights would exceed the capital loss. Finally, environmentalists should prefer market policies because while they achieve the same reduction in emission per unit of product, they allow less total emissions because product output is reduced more than with standards.

The impact on share values of each of the policies assumes that no pollution control policy was anticipated by investors. In fact most legislation that has been effective has also been anticipated, at least for a short time. Thus one should expect to see the share values of an industry decline as regulation becomes more likely. Once it is clear which firms will not survive, their share values should collapse, while the value of the rest of the industry should recover at least in part.

What if the price elasticity of product demand is not unitary? Inelastic demand will yield a smaller reduction in output and thus reduced losses for shareholders and workers. The disadvantages of the market policies for these groups will be reduced. An elastic demand will yield greater losses to both groups, and will magnify the disadvantages of the market policies.

The effluent charge generates for the government agency annual revenues of tE_2 which has a present value equal to the revenue from the sale of effluent rights (tE_2/r). Under the effluent charge or the sale of rights, the agency could pay to the original shareholders a *pro-rata* share of either the annual stream or the present value. In either case, the shareholders would be compensated exactly as if rights were distributed free to the firms. There would be no deviation from efficient behavior of the firms so long as the compensation depended only on pre-policy emissions, output or share values.[17] Alternatively the compensation could be directed in part or in whole to the workers. Charge or rights revenues could be allocated to pre-policy workers, or the free distribution of rights could be to the workers, rather than to the firms. The three market policies do not differ in principle in their ability to compensate shareholders, workers or both.

While we have discussed equal compensation of all shareholders or workers, in fact the losses are not equal but are concentrated. Some firms close while others earn a normal rate of return. Some workers are laid off while others continue at their present jobs. One might wish to direct compensation specifically to the losers rather than to the entire group. This will tend however to have undesirable efficiency consequences. If the compensation is substantial, there may be a rush to bankruptcy, or to be laid off. It is beyond the scope of this paper to consider the politics of specific *versus* general compensation, and thus to decide whether the efficiency consequences of the former deserve to be analyzed in detail.

The above analysis suggests why business and labor have both vigorously opposed market policies. It also suggests that distributing the proceeds of the market policies, or distributing effluent rights directly, could mitigate or eliminate this opposition and perhaps generate positive demands for market-oriented pollution control policies.

Environmentalists have opposed market policies as giving a "license to pollute" or a right to pollute. These criticisms, however, apply even more forcefully to pollution standards which "grandfather" the pollution levels of existing plants. More impor-

---

17. For a discussion of the problems of paying non-distorting compensation to pollution victims, which is analogous to the problem of paying non-distorting compensation to victims of new pollution policies, see Browning (1977).

tant is the incentive problem in giving pollution rights in proportion to past emissions. Once this policy was understood, unregulated firms would try to maximize their emissions to maximize their entitlement to rights. Thus the distribution of rights might not be according to actual recent emissions, but to what emissions would have been if reasonable controls had been used.[18]

B. Uniform Costs, Strict Standard for New Plants

The preceding analysis assumed that the effluent standard would apply uniformly to all firms. It was argued in section II above that environmental policy in Canada and in the United States usually applies more strict standards to new or expanded plants than to existing plants. Let us assume an effluent standard that allows emissions per unit output of B_1 for old plants, and of B_2 for new plants, with $B_1 > B_2$, with B_2 representing a 50 per cent reduction in emissions per unit of output. Assume further that control costs are the same for new and old plants for a given degree of pollution control. We will compare this differential standard with a uniform effluent charge and identical effluent rights, since a differential market policy would be inconsistent with the efficiency gains for which market policies are admired. The market policies will achieve the same emissions per unit of output, B_2, for all plants new and old.

We have seen that imposing any form of pollution control will reduce total industry demand and in general will reduce the number of plants used. If the demand curve for the product does not shift outward over time, then with infinitely durable capital no new plants will be built. Thus the more stringent standards for new plants will be irrelevant, and the analysis will be exactly like that described in sub-section A above for a uniform standard.

Alternatively suppose that there will be a once-and-for-all increase in product demand that shifts the demand curve in figure 2 from D_0 to D_1. In the absence of any pollution control requirement the product price will in the long run remain unchanged at p_0, industry output will increase from Q_0 to Q_1, and new firms will enter to supply the increase in quantity demanded, employing more labor and more capital. The number of new entrants will be $n_1 - n_0 = (Q_1 - Q_0)/q_0$. Total emissions will increase by e_0 times the increased number of firms.

To evaluate the alternative pollution control policies, we assume that the workers and shareholders may be just as concerned with how their situation changes from the present as with how it changes from some hypothetical future possibility. The change in the value of shares in existing firms and the number of layoffs will depend upon a comparison between the pre-growth no controls case and the post-growth controls cases. Table 2 summarizes the results of the forthcoming analysis.

First consider a differential effluent standard. The pollution standards force old firms to reduce their emission rate from e_0/q_0 to $e_2/q_2^0 = B_1$, and impose more stringent standards on new firms equal to $e_2/q_2^n = B_2$, where $B_2 = 1/2 (e_0/q_0) < B_1 < (e_0/q_0)$. The effect of these emission standards will be to

---

18. See Dewees and Sims (1976) for a discussion of the problems that arise from tying policies to recent emissions levels.

64   ECONOMIC INQUIRY

TABLE 2

Strict Effluent Standard for New Plants: Demand Growth

Impact	Effluent Standard	Effluent Charge	Effluent Rights	
			Sold	Given
Price p	p_2	p_3 $(p_3 \geq p_2)$	same as effluent charge same as effluent charge	
Δ Industry Output Q	Q_2-Q_0	(Q_3-Q_0) $(Q_3 \geq Q_2)$	same as effluent charge	
Δ Firm Output q	$q_2^0-q_0$	0	same as effluent charge	
Δ Share Value Malleable	$\dfrac{+ n_0(abcd)}{r}$	0	0	$\dfrac{+ n_0 te_3}{r}$
Rigid	$\dfrac{+ n_0(abcd)}{r}$	0	0	$\dfrac{+ n_0 te_3}{r}$
Δ Labor L	Increase	Increase	same as effluent charge	
Layoffs	0	0	0	0
Emissions E	$(n_0 B_1 + (n_2-n_0)B_2)q_0$	$n_3 B_2 q_0$ $(n_3 < n_2)$	same as effluent charge	
Government Revenues	0	$\geq n_0 te_3$ per year	$\geq \dfrac{n_0 te_3}{r}$	0

Comparison of pollution policies plus growth with no pollution controls and no growth.

raise costs for old firms to AC_1 and MC_1 in figure 2 and to increase costs for new firms somewhat more to AC_2 and MC_2. The underlying cost of abatement functions for old and new firms are similar, so that the higher costs for new firms reflect only the more stringent standardss imposed upon them.

The upward shifts of the cost curves of old and new firms generate a new long run supply curve S_1 in figure 2. The supply curve is perfectly elastic at the costs of old firms, p_1, up to the capacity of old firms in the industry Q_0. Beyond this output, the long run supply curve rises along the sum of the long run marginal cost curves of the old firms until it reaches cost p_2 which is the low point on the average cost curve for a new firm. Here the supply curve once again becomes perfectly elastic in the long run as new firms may enter at this price or any price above it. Assume that D_1 intersects

FIGURE 2

Uniform Costs, Stringent Standards for New Plants

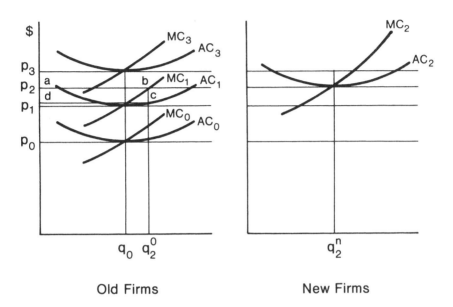

Old Firms   New Firms

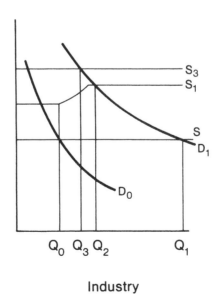

Industry

S_1 at a point which requires some entry of new firms into the industry. In this case, the industry price is p_2 so that old firms produce on their MC_1 curve at q_2^0 while new firms produce at output level q_2^n. Price p_2 will be unambiguously greater than p_1 and therefore greater than p_0. Industry output Q_2 will be less than Q_1 but by assumption greater than Q_0. In this situation there will be no plant closings, and no layoffs. Total pollution emissions will be $n_0 B_1 q_0$ from old firms plus $B_2 q_0$ times the number of new firms $(n_2 - n_0)$ that enter, since $q_2^n = q_0 = q_0^n$ given identical cost functions.

There are no plant closings and no reductions in the output of any firms because of the demand growth. Thus by our definition there is no destruction of existing capital values.

The share values of old firms will be increased as a result of the combination of demand growth and strict controls on new firms. The strict controls are a barrier to the entry of new firms, creating economic profits for existing firms. Old firms can sell at price p_2, while their costs are the point on AC_1 at output level q_2. Thus each old firm earns a profit equal to the rectangle $abcd$ in figure 2. Total profits for all old firms are therefore $n_0(abcd)$. The value of shares in the old firms will rise to reflect the present value of an infinite stream of these future profits and will thus rise by an amount equal to $n_0(abcd)/r$. While the old firms will have issued new shares to finance the expansion of their output and their pollution control investment, there is no need in competitive capital markets to share with a new shareholder the rents derived from being an old firm.

The second policy considered is a uniform effluent charge that leads all firms to the same degree of pollution control as new firms adopted under the effluent standards. Emissions become $e_3/q_3 = B_2$ for old and new firms. The cost curves for old and new firms are AC_2 and MC_2 in figure 2 plus the effluent charge payment. As before, an effluent charge of t dollars per unit of emission will increase costs by te/q to yield curves MC_3 and AC_3. We assume once again that the minimum cost output level is not reduced below q_0. The equilibrium price under the effluent charge will be p_3 yielding industry output Q_3. p_3 will be greater than p_2 by te_3/q_0. Q_3 will be less than Q_2 by an amount depending on the relationship between p_3 and p_2. There will be no plant closing and no layoffs so long as $Q_3 > Q_0$. There is no barrier to entry and thus no rent for any firm. The total emissions under the effluent charge will be much less than the emissions under the effluent standard since old firms must now clean up as much as new ones. If under the standard $E_2 = (n_0 B_1 + (n_2 - n_0) B_2) q_0$ and under the charge $E_3 = n_3 B_2 q_0$, then $E_3 = (n_0 B_2 + (n_3 - n_0) B_2) q_0$. Since $n_2 > n_3 > n_0$ then E_3 is less than E_2 by an amount greater than $n_0(B_2 - B_1) q_0$, the extra reduction in emissions by old firms under the effluent charge.

Finally, we can consider the use of effluent rights. As before, the sale of those rights to firms will yield results identical to those for the effluent charge. If, on the other hand, the effluent rights are issued free of charge to all existing firms, the existing shareholders in those firms receive an asset with a value of the stream of opportunity costs of those rights. If each firm discharges pollution at emission rate e_3, and the opportunity cost of the rights per unit of discharge is equal to t, the effluent charge rate, then each existing firm will hold an asset valued at te_3/r. The shareholders in all old firms benefit by this amount summed over all firms: $n_0 te_3/r$.

Table 2 shows that the original shareholders clearly benefit under a system of effluent rights distributed free to existing firms relative to an effluent charge system or a system of effluent rights sold to existing firms. Do they benefit with free effluent rights relative to a differential effluent standard? That depends upon whether the value of the rights is greater than the value of the rents generated by old firms. For the effluent rights scheme to benefit shareholders more, p_3 must be greater than p_2 by an amount such that the difference between production costs and the product price times output q_0 is greater than the area of the rectangle *(abcd)* for the old firm under an effluent standard.

As in the previous case, the agency revenues from an effluent charge or the sale of effluent rights could be used to compensate shareholders or workers. Of course in this case there is no loss except as compared to a differential standard, so there is little argument for compensation. Since the charge or sale of rights would apply to new firms as well, the value of the revenue would exceed the value of rights issued to old firms by an amount proportional to the number of new firms.

C. Differential Costs, Uniform Policies

Now consider a perfectly competitive industry in which the cost of pollution control is greater for old firms than for new firms. For example, pollution control is most efficiently achieved by adopting a completely different production process than that which is most efficient in the absence of environmental constraints. If new and old firms must achieve the same pollution control standards, the old firm will experience higher costs. See figure 3, in which old and new firms must both reduce emission rate e/q by 50 per cent to B_2.

If old firms install controls to achieve B_2, their average costs will rise to AC_1 while new firms experience average costs AC_2. If old firms install controls and raise their price to p_1, new firms will enter and drive the price down to p_2. Anticipating this, old firms will not install controls, but will close down. The total value of the capital of the old shareholders will be destroyed. All old workers will be laid off. New plants will be constructed to produce output Q_2 at price p_2. Employment will be unchanged, since increased costs are offset by reduced sales, with unchanged total revenues.

If new firms cannot enter the industry instantaneously, some old firms may install controls to comply with the standard, and operate until new entry forces the price low enough so they must close. In this case not all existing capital value will be lost at once.

An effluent charge or effluent rights will also leave old plants at a cost disadvantage compared to new plants. A charge or rights scheme will raise costs for old firms to AC_3 and MC_3 and for new firms to only AC_4 and MC_4 in figure 3. All old plants will close in the long run, yielding total shareholder losses of K_0 and layoffs of L_0, although a charge may allow some to continue operating in the short run if the entry of new firms is not instantaneous.

As in the previous case, a free distribution of effluent rights would tend to compensate existing shareholders for their loss. The amount of this compensation is $n_4 t e_4/r$ if new entry is instantaneous, where n_4 is the number of firms in the new equilibrium. The sale of rights would generate revenues with the same value which could be used to compensate capital or labor. The effluent charge revenues would be less than effluent rights revenues unless the adjustment was instantaneous. It is conceivable that the compensation would exceed the capital loss K_0, but this would require in effect that the right to pollute is more valuable than the productive capital of the enterprise. This suggests very high pollution control costs or very low capital investment or both. These results are summarized in table 3 for the case of instantaneous entry by new firms. The effluent charge t will be less than that necessary to

FIGURE 3

Differential Costs, Uniform Policies

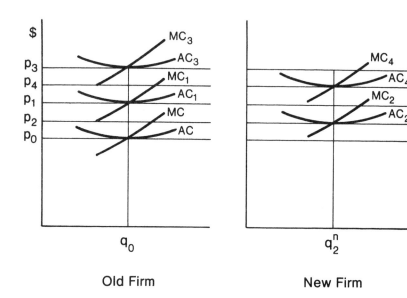

Old Firm   New Firm

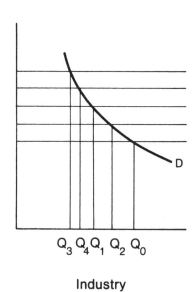

Industry

TABLE 3

Summary of Impacts

Differential Costs, Uniform Policies

Impact	Effluent Standard	Effluent Charge	Effluent Rights Sold	Effluent Rights Given
Δ Price p	$p_2 - p_0$	$p_4 - p_0$	same as effluent charge	
Δ Industry Output Q	$\dfrac{-(p_2 - p_0)Q_0}{p_2}$	$\dfrac{-(p_4 - p_0)Q_0}{p_4}$	same as effluent charge	
Δ Firm Output q	$q_2'' - q_0$	$q_4'' - q_0$	same as effluent charge	
Firms Closed	n_0	n_0	same as effluent charge	
Δ Share values Malleable	0	0	0	$+\dfrac{tE_4}{r}$
Rigid	$-K_0$	$-K_0$	$-K_0$	$-K_0 + \dfrac{tE_4}{2}$
Δ Labor L	0	$L_0\left(1 - \dfrac{tE_4}{R_0}\right)$	same as effluent charge	
Layoffs	L_0	L_0	same as effluent charge	
Δ Emissions	$\dfrac{E_0 - B_2 Q_0(1 - p_2 - p_0)}{p_2}$	$\dfrac{E_0 - B_2 Q_0(1 - p_4 - p_0)}{p_4}$	same as effluent charge	
Government Revenues	0	tE_4 per year	$\dfrac{tE_4}{r}$	0

$E_4 = n_4 e_4$

reduce emissions in *old* firms by half, since new firms can control emissions more cheaply. With a smaller t, the revenue from an effluent charge, and the value of effluent rights are less than if new firms experienced the costs of old firms. Thus compensation of existing shareholders or workers is much more difficult in this case than in the first case where new and old firms share the same control costs. Uniform policies of any kind should be vigorously resisted by both shareholders and labor. Charges and rights will be resisted more strongly than standards unless compensation is paid.

V. CONCLUSIONS

Previous studies have shown that polluting firms should prefer effluent quotas to effluent charges, and may prefer effluent quotas to no pollution control policy at all. This paper has demonstrated that shareholders of existing firms should prefer uniform effluent standards limiting pollution discharge per unit of product output to effluent charges or to the sale of effluent rights because the standards raise prices less and cause fewer plant closing than the market policies. However, these firms will prefer marketable effluent rights given to existing firms to standards, charges, or the sale of effluent rights. Firms may prefer marketable rights to no pollution control policy at all. They may also prefer effluent standards that are more strict for new plants than for old plants to no controls at all. A free distribution of marketable rights may not be preferred to an effluent standard that is more strict for new firms than for old firms.

Labor will prefer no pollution control policy, but if controls are to be applied, labor will prefer standards that are tougher for new plants than for old over any other policy. Because marketable pollution rights are given to firms and not to workers, they will have none of the appeal for labor that they hold for original shareholders.

Both effluent charges and the sale of effluent rights generate revenues that could be used to compensate those hurt by the change in property rights implicit in a new pollution control policy. In many cases the value of this revenue, and thus the ability to compensate, are equal to the value of free rights. In fact, any of the three market policies can be preferred by firms to no policy at all even with rigid capital, if the rights or revenues are distributed to the losers in proportion to their losses. While this may seem astonishing, it becomes less so when one recognizes that the harm to labor is not compensated by payments to capital. The exact compensation needed to make labor indifferent to a market policy depends on labor's mobility and its utility function, and there is no certainty that both shareholders *and* workers can be fully compensated.

If the political process responds to interest groups that are strongly affected by a policy, the effluent charge and the sale of effluent rights are in deep political trouble unless the revenues are used to compensate the losers. The failure of Canadian and U.S. jurisdictions to adopt such schemes may be seen as a reflection of the sensible self-interest of powerful groups. The policies that have been adopted are less damaging to both shareholders and workers than the more efficient market policies. The free distribution of effluent rights could lessen or eliminate the resistance of the firms themselves, yet achieve the same efficiency consequences, so politically this may be the market policy with the greatest chance of success. In any event, it seems worthwhile to examine closely mechanisms that may achieve the desirable efficiency goals of market policies yet also possess distributional characteristics that give them some hope of being adopted. The design of current policies demonstrates an ability or unwillingness of the political process to impose great losses on powerful interest groups in the cause of pollution control.

DEWEES: INSTRUMENT CHOICE IN ENVIRONMENTAL POLICY 71

REFERENCES

Ackerman, Bruce A. and Ackerman, Susan Rose, *et al.*, *The Uncertain Search for Environmental Quality,* Free Press, New York, 1974.

Anderson, Fredrich R., *et al.*, *Environmental Improvement Through Economic Incentives,* Johns Hopkins Press, Baltimore, 1977.

Baumol, William and Oates, Wallace A., *The Theory of Environmental Policy,* Prentice-Hall, Englewood Cliffs, 1975.

_____, *Economics, Environmental Policy, and the Quality of Life,* Prentice-Hall, Englewood Cliffs, 1979.

Browning, Edgar R., "External Diseconomies, Compensation and the Measure of Damage," *Southern Economic Journal,* January 1977, *43,* 1279-1287.

Buchanan, James and Tullock, Gordon, "Polluters Profits and Political Response: Direct Controls Versus Taxes," *American Economic Review,* March 1975, *65,* 139-147.

Clark, Timothy B., "A New Approach to Regulatory Reform — Letting the Market do the Job," *National Journal,* August 11, 1979, 1316-1322.

Dales, John, *Pollution, Property and Prices,* University of Toronto Press, Toronto, 1968.

Dewees, Donald N. and Sims, William A., "The Symmetry of Charges and Subsidies for Pollution Control," *Canadian Journal of Economics,* May 1976, *9,* 323-331.

Drayton, William, "Getting Smarter About Regulation," *Harvard Business Review,* July/August 1981, *59,* 38.

Gianessi, Leonard P., Peskin, Henry M. and Wolff, Edward, "The Distributional Effects of Uniform Air Pollution Policy in the United States," *Quarterly Journal of Economics,* May 1979, *93,* 281-301.

Griffin, James M., "An Econometric Evaluation of Sulfur Taxes," *Journal of Political Economy,* July/August 1974, *82,* 669-688.

Hanke, Steve H. and Gutmanis, Ivars, "Estimates of Industry Water-borne Residuals Control Costs: A Review of Concepts, Methodology and Empirical Results," in Henry M. Peskin and Eugene P. Seskin, eds., *Cost Benefit Analysis and Water Pollution Policy,* The Urban Institute, Washington, D.C., 1975.

Hartman, Raymond S., Bozdogan, Kirkor and Nadkarni, Ravindra M., "The Economic Impacts of Environmental Regulation on the U.S. Copper Industry," *Bell Journal of Economics,* Autumn 1979, *10,* 589-618.

Kneese, Allen V. and Schultze, Charles, *Pollution Prices and Public Policy,* Brookings, Washington, 1975.

Koch, James C. and Leone, R. A., "The Clean Water Act: Unexpected Impacts on Industry," *Harvard Environmental Law Review,* 1979, *3,* 84-111.

Mills, Edwin S. and White, Lawrence J., "Government Policies Toward Emissions Control," in A. F. Friedlaender, ed., *Approaches to Controlling Air Pollution,* Cambridge, MIT Press, 1978.

Peltzman, Sam, "Toward a More General Theory of Regulation," *Journal of Law and Economics,* August 1976, *49,* 211-240.

Sims, William A., *Economics of Sewer Effluent Charges,* Ph.D. Thesis, Political Economy, University of Toronto 1977; Institute for Environmental Studies, University of Toronto, Pub. No. [S.29].

Stigler, George, "The Theory of Economic Regulation," *Bell Journal of Economics and Management Science,* 1971, *2,* 3-21.

Journal of Economic Perspectives — Volume 3, Number 2 — Spring 1989 — Pages 95–114

Economic Prescriptions for Environmental Problems: How the Patient Followed the Doctor's Orders

Robert W. Hahn

O ne of the dangers with ivory tower theorizing is that it is easy to lose sight of the actual set of problems which need to be solved, and the range of potential solutions. As one who frequently engages in this exercise, I can attest to this fact. In my view, this loss of sight has become increasingly evident in the theoretical structure underlying environmental economics, which often emphasizes elegance at the expense of realism.

In this paper, I will argue that both normative and positive theorizing could greatly benefit from a careful examination of the results of recent innovative approaches to environmental management. The particular set of policies examined here involves two tools which have received widespread support from the economics community: marketable permits and emission charges (Pigou, 1932; Dales, 1968; Kneese and Schultze, 1975). Both tools represent ways to induce businesses to search for lower cost methods of achieving environmental standards. They stand in stark contrast to the predominant "command-and-control" approach in which a regulator specifies the technology a firm must use to comply with regulations. Under highly restrictive conditions, it can be shown that both of the economic approaches share the desirable feature that any gains in environmental quality will be obtained at the lowest possible cost (Baumol and Oates, 1975).

Until the 1960s, these tools only existed on blackboards and in academic journals, as products of the fertile imaginations of academics. However, some countries have recently begun to explore using these tools as part of a broader strategy for managing environmental problems.

■ *Robert W. Hahn is Senior Staff Economist, Council of Economic Advisers, Washington, D.C., and Associate Professor of Economics, Carnegie–Mellon University, Pittsburgh, Pennsylvania.*

This paper chronicles the experience with both marketable permits and emissions charges. It also provides a selective analysis of a variety of applications in Europe and the United States and shows how the actual use of these tools tends to depart from the role which economists have conceived for them.

The Selection of Environmental Instruments

In thinking about the design and implementation of policies, it is generally assumed that policy makers can choose from a variety of "instruments" for achieving specified objectives. The environmental economics literature generally focuses on the selection of instruments that minimize the overall cost of achieving prescribed environmental objectives.

One instrument which has been shown to supply the appropriate incentives, at least in theory, is marketable permits. The implementation of marketable permits involves several steps. First, a target level of environmental quality is established. Next, this level of environmental quality is defined in terms of total allowable emissions. Permits are then allocated to firms, with each permit enabling the owner to emit a specified amount of pollution. Firms are allowed to trade these permits among themselves. Assuming firms minimize their total production costs, and the market for these permits is competitive, it can be shown that the overall cost of achieving the environmental standard will be minimized (Montgomery, 1972).

Marketable permits are generally thought of as a "quantity" instrument because they ration a fixed supply of a commodity, in this case pollution. The polar opposite of a quantity instrument is a "pricing" instrument, such as emissions charges. The idea underlying emissions charges is to charge polluters a fixed price for each unit of pollution. In this way, they are provided with an incentive to economize on the amount of pollution they produce. If all firms are charged the same price for pollution, then marginal costs of abatement are equated across firms, and this result implies that the resulting level of pollution is reached in a cost-minimizing way.

Economists have attempted to estimate the effectiveness of these approaches. Work by Plott (1983) and Hahn (1983) reveals that implementation of these ideas in a laboratory setting leads to marked increases in efficiency levels over traditional forms of regulation, such as setting standards for each individual source of pollution. The work based on simulations using actual costs and environmental data reveals a similar story. For example, in a review of several studies examining the potential for marketable permits, Tietenberg (1985, pp. 43–44) found that potential control costs could be reduced by more than 90 percent in some cases. Naturally, these results are subject to the usual cautions that a competitive market actually must exist for the results to hold true. Perhaps more importantly, the results assume that it is possible to easily monitor and enforce a system of permits or taxes. The subsequent analysis will suggest that the capacity to monitor and enforce can dramatically affect the choice of instruments.

Following the development of a normative theory of instrument choice, a handful of scholars began to explore reasons why environmental regulations are actually selected. This positive environmental literature tends to emphasize the potential winners and losers from environmental policies as a way of explaining the conditions under which we will observe such policies. For example, Buchanan and Tullock (1975) argue that the widespread use of source-specific standards rather than a fee can be explained by looking at the potential profitability of the affected industry under the two regimes. After presenting the various case studies, I will review some of the insights from positive theory and see how they square with the facts.

The formal results in the positive and normative theory of environmental economics are elegant. Unfortunately, they are not immediately applicable, since virtually none of the systems examined below exhibits the purity of the instruments which are the subject of theoretical inquiry. The presentation here highlights those instruments which show a marked resemblance to marketable permits or emission fees. Together, the two approaches to pollution control span a wide array of environmental problems, including toxic substances, air pollution, water pollution and land disposal.

Marketable Permits

In comparison with charges, marketable permits have not received widespread use. Indeed, there appear to be only four existing environmental applications; three of them in the United States. One involves the trading of emissions rights of various pollutants regulated under the Clean Air Act; a second involves trading of lead used in gasoline; a third addresses the control of water pollution on a river; and a fourth involves air pollution trading in Germany and will not be addressed here because of limited information (see Sprenger, 1986). These programs exhibit dramatic differences in performance, which can be traced back to the rules used to implement these approaches.

Wisconsin Fox River Water Permits

In 1981, the state of Wisconsin implemented an innovative program aimed at controlling biological oxygen demand (BOD) on a part of the Fox River (Novotny, 1986, p. 11).[1] The program was designed to allow for the limited trading of marketable discharge permits. The primary objective was to allow firms greater flexibility in abatement options while still maintaining environmental quality. The program is administered by the state of Wisconsin in accord with the Federal Water Pollution Control Act. Firms are issued five-year permits which define their wasteload allocation. This allocation defines the initial distribution of permits for each firm.

Early studies estimated that substantial savings, on the order of $7 million per year, could result after implementing this trading system (O'Neil, 1983, p. 225).

---

[1] BOD is a measure of the demand for dissolved oxygen imposed on a water body by organic effluents.

However, actual cost savings have been minimal. In the six years that the program has been in existence, there has been only one trade. Given the initial fanfare about this system, its performance to date has been disappointing.

A closer look at the nature of the market and the rules for trading reveals that the result should not have been totally unexpected. The regulations are aimed at two types of dischargers: pulp and paper plants and municipal waste treatment plants. David and Joeres (1983) note that the pulp and paper plants have an oligopolistic structure, and thus may not behave as competitive firms in the permit market. Moreover, it is difficult to know how the municipal utilities will perform under this set of rules, since they are subject to public utility regulation (Hahn and Noll, 1983). Trading is also limited by location. There are two points on the river where pollution tends to peak, and firms are divided into "clusters" so that trading will not increase BOD at either of these points. There are only about 6 or 7 firms in each cluster (Patterson, 1987). Consequently, markets for wasteload allocations may be quite thin.

In addition, Novotny (1986) has argued that several restrictions on transfers may have had a negative impact on potential trading. Any transaction between firms requires modifying or reissuing permits. Transfers must be for at least a year; however, the life of the permit is only five years. Moreover, parties must waive any rights to the permit after it expires, and it is unclear how trading will affect the permit renewal process. These conditions create great uncertainty over the future value of the property right. Added to the problems created by these rules are the restrictions on eligibility for trades. Firms are required to justify the "need" for permits. This effectively limits transfers to new dischargers, plants which are expanding, and treatment plants that cannot meet the requirements, despite their best efforts. Trades that only reduce operating costs are not allowed. With all the uncertainty and high transactions costs, it is not surprising that trading has gotten off to a very slow start.

While the marketable permit system for the Fox River was being hailed as a success by economists, the paper mills did not enthusiastically support the idea (Novotny, 1986, p. 15). Nor have the mills chosen to explore this option once it has been implemented. Indeed, by almost any measure, this limited permit trading represents a minor part of the regulatory structure. The mechanism builds on a large regulatory infrastructure where permits specifying treatment and operating rules lie at the center. The new marketable permits approach retains many features of the existing standards-based approach. The initial allocations are based on the status quo, calling for equal percentage reductions from specified limits. This "grandfathering" approach has a great deal of political appeal for existing firms. New firms must continue to meet more stringent requirements than old firms, and firms must meet specified technological standards before trading is allowed.

Emissions Trading

By far the most significant and far-reaching marketable permit program in the United States is the emissions trading policy. Started over a decade ago, the policy attempts to provide greater flexibility to firms charged with controlling air pollutant emissions.[2] Because the program represents a radical departure in the approach to pollution regulation, it has come under close scrutiny by a variety of interest groups. Environmentalists have been particularly critical. These criticisms notwithstanding, the Environmental Protection Agency Administrator Lee Thomas (1986) character-ized the program as "one of EPA's most impressive accomplishments."

Emissions trading has four distinct elements. Netting, the first program element, was introduced in 1974. Netting allows a firm which creates a new source of emissions in a plant to avoid the stringent emission limits which would normally apply by reducing emissions from another source in the plant. Thus, net emissions from the plant do not increase significantly. A firm using netting is only allowed to obtain the necessary emission credits from its own sources. This is called *internal trading* because the transaction involves only one firm. Netting is subject to approval at the state level, not the federal.

Offsets, the second element of emissions trading, are used by new emission sources in "non-attainment areas." (A non-attainment area is a region which has not met a specified ambient standard.) The Clean Air Act specified that no new emission sources would be allowed in non-attainment areas after the original 1975 deadlines for meeting air quality standards passed. Concern that this prohibition would stifle economic growth in these areas prompted EPA to institute the offset rule. This rule specified that new sources would be allowed to locate in non-attainment areas, but only if they "offset" their new emissions by reducing emissions from existing sources by even larger amounts. The offsets could be obtained through internal trading, just as with netting. However, they could also be obtained from other firms directly, which is called *external trading*.

Bubbles, though apparently considered by EPA to be the centerpiece of emissions trading, were not allowed until 1979. The name derives from the placing of an imaginary bubble over a plant, with all emissions exiting at a single point from the bubble. A bubble allows a firm to sum the emission limits from individual sources of a pollutant in a plant, and to adjust the levels of control applied to different sources as long as this aggregate limit is not exceeded. Bubbles apply to existing sources. The policy allows for both internal and external trades. Initially, every bubble had to be approved at the federal level as an amendment to a state's implementation plan. In 1981, EPA approved a "generic rule" for bubbles in New Jersey which allowed the state to give final approval for bubbles. Since then, several other states have followed suit.

Banking, the fourth element of emissions trading, was developed in conjunction with the bubble policy. Banking allows firms to save emission reductions above and beyond permit requirements for future use in emissions trading. While EPA action was initially required to allow banking, the development of banking rules and the administration of banking programs has been left to the states.

---

[2] Pollutants covered under the policy include volatile organic compounds, carbon monoxide, sulfur dioxide, particulates, and nitrogen oxides (Hahn and Hester, 1986).

Table 1

Summary of emissions trading activity

Activity		Estimated number of internal transactions	Estimated number of external transactions	Estimated Cost savings (millions)	Environmental quality impact
Netting		5,000 to 12,000	None	$25 to $300 in Permitting costs: $500 to $12,000 in emission control costs	Insignificant in individual cases; Probably insignificant in aggregate
Offsets		1800	200	See text	Probably insignificant
Bubbles:	Federally approved	40	2	$300	Insignificant
	State approved	89	0	$135	Insignificant
Banking		< 100	< 20	Small	Insignificant

Source: Hahn and Hester (1986)

The performance of emissions trading can be measured in several ways. A summary evaluation which assesses the impact of the program on abatement costs and environmental quality is provided in Table 1. For each emissions trading activity, an estimate of cost savings, the environmental quality effect, and the number of trades is given. In each case, the estimates are for the entire life of the program. As can be seen from the table, the level of activity under various programs varies dramatically. More netting transactions have taken place than any other type, but all of these have necessarily been internal. The wide range placed on this estimate, 5000 to 12,000, reflects the uncertainty about the precise level of this activity. An estimated 2000 offset transactions have taken place, of which only 10 percent have been external. Fewer than 150 bubbles have been approved. Of these, almost twice as many have been approved by states under generic rules than have been approved at the federal level, and only two are known to have involved external trades. For banking, the figures listed are for the number of times firms have withdrawn banked emission credits for sale or use. While no estimates of the exact numbers of such transactions can be made, upper bound estimates of 100 for internal trades and 20 for external trades indicate the fact that there has been relatively little activity in this area.

Cost savings for both netting and bubbles are substantial. Netting is estimated to have resulted in the most cost savings, with a total of between $525 million to over $12 billion from both permitting and emissions control cost savings.[3] By allowing new or modified sources to locate in areas that are highly polluted, offsets confer a major

[3]The wide range of this estimate reflects the uncertainty which results from the fact that little information has been collected on netting.

economic benefit on firms which use them. While the size of this economic benefit is not easily estimated, it is probably in the hundreds of millions of dollars. Federally approved bubbles have resulted in savings estimated at $300 million, while state bubbles have resulted in an estimated $135 million in cost savings. Average savings from federally approved bubbles are higher than those for state approved bubbles. Average savings from bubbles are higher than those from netting, which reflects the fact that bubble savings may be derived from several emissions sources in a single transaction, while netting usually involves cost savings at a single source. Finally, the cost savings from the use of banking cannot be estimated, but is necessarily small given the small number of banking transactions which have occurred.

The performance evaluation of emissions trading activities reveals a mixed bag of accomplishments and disappointments. The program has clearly afforded many firms flexibility in meeting emission limits, and this flexibility has resulted in significant aggregate cost savings—in the billions of dollars. However, these cost savings have been realized almost entirely from internal trading. They fall far short of the potential savings which could be realized if there were more external trading. While cost savings have been substantial, the program has led to little or no net change in the level of emissions.

The evolution of the emissions trading can best be understood in terms of a struggle over the nature and distribution of property rights. Emissions trading can be seen as a strategy by regulators to provide industry with increased flexibility while offering environmentalists continuing progress toward environmental quality goals. Meeting these two objectives requires a careful balancing act. To provide industry with greater flexibility, EPA has attempted to define a set of property rights that places few restrictions on their use. However, at the same time, EPA has to be sensitive to the concerns of environmentalists and avoid giving businesses too clear a property right to their existing level of pollution. The conflicting interests of these two groups have led regulators to create a set of policies which are specifically designed to deemphasize the explicit nature of the property right. The high transactions costs associated with external trading have induced firms to eschew this option in favor of internal trading or no trading at all.

Like the preceding example of the Fox River, emissions trading is best viewed as an incremental departure from the existing approach. Property rights were grandfathered. Most trading has been internal, and the structure of the Clean Air Act, including its requirement that new sources be controlled more stringently, was largely left intact.

Lead Trading

Lead trading stands in stark contrast to the preceding two marketable permit approaches. It comes by far the closest to an economist's ideal of a freely functioning market. The purpose of the lead trading program was to allow gasoline refiners greater flexibility during a period when the amount of lead in gasoline was being significantly reduced. (For a more detailed analysis of the performance of the lead trading program, see Hahn and Hester, 1987.)

Unlike many other programs, the lead trading program was scheduled to have a fixed life from the outset. Interrefinery trading of lead credits was permitted in 1982. Banking of lead credits was initiated in 1985. The trading program was terminated at the end of 1987. Initially, the period for trading was defined in terms of quarters. No banking of credits was allowed. Three years after initiating the program limited banking was allowed, which allowed firms to carry over rights to subsequent quarters. Banking has been used extensively by firms since its initiation.

The program is notable for its lack of discrimination among different sources, such as new and old sources. It is also notable for its rules regarding the creation of credits. Lead credits are created on the basis of existing standards. A firm does not gain any extra credits for being a large producer of leaded gasoline in the past. Nor is it penalized for being a small producer. The creation of lead credits is based solely on current production levels and average lead content. For example if the standard were 1.1 grams per gallon, and a firm produces 100 gallons of gasoline, it would receive rights entitling it to produce or sell up to 110 (100 × 1.1) grams of lead. To the extent that current production levels are correlated with past production levels, the system acknowledges the existing distribution of property rights. However, this linkage is less explicit than those made in other trading programs.[4]

The success of the program is difficult to measure directly. It appears to have had very little impact on environmental quality. This is because the amount of lead in gasoline is routinely reported by refiners and is easily monitored. The effect the program has had on refinery costs is not readily available. In proposing the rule for banking of lead rights, EPA estimated that resulting savings to refiners would be approximately $228 million (U.S. EPA, 1985a). Since banking activity has been somewhat higher than anticipated by EPA, it is likely that actual cost savings will exceed this amount. No specific estimate of the actual cost savings resulting from lead trading have been made by EPA.

The level of trading activity has been high, far surpassing levels observed in other environmental markets. In 1985, over half of the refineries participated in trading. Approximately 15 percent of the total lead rights used were traded. Approximately 35 percent of available lead rights were banked for future use or trading (U.S. EPA, 1985b, 1986). In comparison, volumes of emissions trading have averaged well below 1 percent of the potential emissions that could have been traded.

From the standpoint of creating a workable regulatory mechanism that induces cost savings, the lead market has to be viewed as a success. Refiners, though initially lukewarm about this alternative, have made good use of this program. It stands out amidst a stream of incentive-based programs as the "noble" exception in that it conforms most closely to the economists' notion of a smoothly functioning market.

Given the success of this market in promoting cost savings over a period in which lead was being reduced, it is important to understand why the market was successful.

---

[4]One of the reasons EPA set up the allocation rule in this way was to try to transfer some of the permit rents from producers to consumers. This will not always occur, however, and depends on the structure of the permits market as well as the underlying production functions.

The lead market had two important features which distinguished it from other markets in environmental credits. The first was that the amount of lead in gasoline could be easily monitored with the existing regulatory apparatus. The second was that the program was implemented after agreement had been reached about basic environmental goals. In particular, there was already widespread agreement that lead was to be phased out of gasoline. This suggests that the success in lead trading may not be easily transferred to other applications in which monitoring is a problem, or environmental goals are poorly defined. Nonetheless, the fact that this market worked well provides ammunition for proponents of market-based incentives for environmental regulation.

New Directions for Marketable Permits

An interesting potential application for marketable permits has arisen in the area of nonpoint source pollution.[5] In 1984, Colorado implemented a program which would allow limited trading between point and nonpoint sources for controlling phosphorous loadings in Dillon Reservoir (Elmore et al., 1984). Firms receive an allocation based on their past production and the holding capacity of the lake. At this time, no trading between point and nonpoint sources has occurred.

As in the case of the Fox River program, point sources are required to make use of the latest technology before they are allowed to trade. The conventional permitting system is used as a basis for trading. Moreover, trades between point and nonpoint sources are required to take place on a 2 for 1 basis. This means for each gram of phosphorous emitted from a point source under a trade, two grams must be reduced from a nonpoint source. Annual cost savings are projected to be about $800,000 (Kashmanian et al., 1986, p. 14); however, projected savings are not always a good indicator of actual savings, as was illustrated in the case of the Fox River.

EPA is also considering using marketable permits as a way of promoting efficiency in the control of chlorofluorocarbons and halons which lead to the depletion of stratospheric ozone.[6] In its notice of proposed rulemaking, EPA suggested grandfathering permits to producers based on their 1986 production levels, and allowing them to be freely traded. This approach is similar to earlier approaches which the agency adopted for emissions trading and lead trading.

The applications covered in this section illustrate that there are a rich array of mechanisms that come under the heading of marketable permits. The common element seems to be that the primary motivation behind marketable permits is to provide increased flexibility in meeting prescribed environmental objectives. This flexibility, in turn, allows firms to take advantage of opportunities to reduce their expenditures on pollution control without sacrificing environmental quality. However, the rules of the marketable permits can sometimes be so restrictive that the flexibility they offer is more imaginary than real.

---

[5] Point sources represent sources which are well-defined, such as a factory smokestack. Nonpoint sources refer to sources whose emission points are not readily identified, such as fertilizer runoff from farms.
[6] EPA's decision to use a market-based approach to limit stratospheric ozone depletion is examined in Hahn and McGartland (1988).

Charges in Practice

Charge systems in four countries are examined. Examples are drawn from France, Germany, the Netherlands, and the United States. Particular systems were selected because they were thought to be significant either in their scope, their effect on revenues, or their impact on the cost effectiveness of environmental regulation. While the focus is on water effluent charges, a variety of systems are briefly mentioned at the end of this section which cover other applications.

Charges in France

The French have had a system of effluent charges on water pollutants in place since 1969 (Bower et al., 1981). The system is primarily designed to raise revenues which are then used to help maintain or improve water quality. Though the application of charges is widespread, they are generally set at low levels.[7] Moreover, charges are rarely based on actual performance. Rather, they are based on the expected level of discharge by various industries. There is no explicit connection between the charge paid by a given discharger and the subsidy received for reducing discharges (Bower et al., 1981, p. 126). However, charges are generally earmarked for use in promoting environmental quality in areas related to the specific charge. The basic mechanism by which these charges improve environmental quality is through judicious earmarking of the revenues for pollution abatement activities.

In evaluating the charge system, it is important to understand that it is a major, but by no means dominant, part of the French system for managing water quality. Indeed, in terms of total revenues, a sewage tax levied on households and commercial enterprises is larger in magnitude (Bower et al., 1981, p. 142). Moreover, the sewage tax is assessed on the basis of actual volumes of water used. Like most other charge systems, the charge system in France is based on a system of water quality permits, which places constraints on the type and quantity of effluent a firm may discharge. These permits are required for sources discharging more than some specified quantity (Bower et al., 1981, p. 130).

Charges now appear to be accepted as a way of doing business in France. They provide a significant source of revenues for water quality control. One of the keys to their initial success appears to have been the gradual introduction and raising of charges. Charges started at a very low level and were gradually raised to current levels (Bower et al., 1981, p. 22). Moreover, the pollutants on which charges are levied has expanded considerably since the initial inception of the charge program.[8]

Charges in Germany

The German system of effluent charges is very similar to the French system. Effluent charges cover a wide range of pollutants, and the charges are used to cover

---

[7]Charges cover a wide variety of pollutants, including suspended solids, biological oxygen demand, chemical oxygen demand, and selected toxic chemicals.

[8]For example, Brown (1984, p. 114) notes that charges for nitrogen and phosphorous were added in 1982.

administrative expenses for water quality management and to subsidize projects which improve water quality (Brown and Johnson, 1984, p. 934, 939, 945). The bills that industry and municipalities pay are generally based on expected volume and concentration (Brown and Johnson, 1984, p. 934). Charges vary by industry type as well as across municipalities. Charges to industries and municipalities depend on several variables, including size of the municipality, desired level of treatment, and age of equipment (Brown and Johnson, 1984, pp. 934, 938).

Charges have existed in selected areas of Germany for decades (Bower et al., 1981, p. 299). Management of water quality is delegated to local areas. In 1981, a system of nationwide effluent charges was introduced (Bower et al., 1981, p. 226). The federal government provided the basic framework in its 1976 Federal Water Act and Effluent Charge Law (Brown and Johnson, 1984, p. 930). Initially, industry opposed widespread use of charges. But after losing the initial battle, industry focused on how charges would be determined and their effective date of implementation (Brown and Johnson, 1984, p. 932). While hard data are lacking, there is a general perception that the current system is helping to improve water quality.

Charges in the Netherlands

The Netherlands has had a system of effluent charges in place since 1969 (Brown and Bresssers, 1986, p. 4). It is one of the oldest and best administered charge systems, and the charges placed on effluent streams are among the highest. In 1983, the effluent charge per person was $17 in the Netherlands, $6 in Germany, and about $2 in France (Brown and Bressers, 1986, p. 5). Because of the comparatively high level of charges found in the Netherlands, this is a logical place to examine whether charges are having a discernible effect on the level of pollution. Bressers (1983), using a multiple regression approach, argues that charges have made a significant difference for several pollutants. This evidence is also buttressed by surveys of industrial polluters and water board officials which indicate that charges had a significant impact on firm behavior (Brown and Bressers, 1986, pp. 12–13). This analysis is one of the few existing empirical investigations of the effect of effluent charges on resulting pollution.

The purpose of the charge system in the Netherlands is to raise revenue that will be used to finance projects that will improve water quality (Brown and Bressers, 1986, p. 4). Like its counterparts in France and Germany, the approach to managing water quality uses both permits and effluent charges for meeting ambient standards (Brown and Bressers, 1986, p. 2).[9] Permits tend to be uniform across similar discharges. The system is designed to ensure that water quality will remain the same or get better (Brown and Bressers, 1986 p. 2). Charges are administered both on volume and concentration. Actual levels of discharge are monitored for larger polluters, while small polluters often pay fixed fees unrelated to actual discharge (Bressers, 1983, p. 10).

---

[9] Emission and effluent standards apply to individual sources of pollution while ambient standards apply to regions such as a lake or an air basin.

Charges have exhibited a slow but steady increase since their inception (Brown and Bressers, 1986, p. 5). This increase in charges has been correlated with declining levels of pollutants. Effluent discharge declined from 40 population equivalents in 1969 to 15.3 population equivalents in 1980, and it was projected to decline to 4.4 population equivalents in 1985 (Brown and Bressers, 1986, p. 10). Thus, over 15 years, this measure of pollution declined on the order of 90 percent.

As in Germany, there was initial opposition from industry to the use of charges. Brown and Bressers (1986, p. 4) also note opposition from environmentalists, who tend to distrust market-like mechanisms. Nonetheless, charges have enjoyed widespread acceptance in a variety of arenas in the Netherlands.

One final interesting feature of the charge system in the Netherlands relates to the differential treatment of new and old plants. In general, newer plants face more stringent regulation than older plants (Brown and Bressers, 1986, p. 10). As we shall see, this is also a dominant theme in American regulation.

Charges in the United States

The United States has a modest system of user charges levied by utilities that process wastewater, encouraged by federal environmental regulations issued by the Environmental Protection Agency. They are based on both volume and strength, and vary across utilities. In some cases, charges are based on actual discharges, and in others, as a rule of thumb, they are related to average behavior. In all cases, charges are added to the existing regulatory system which relies heavily on permits and standards.

Both industry and consumers are required to pay the charges. The primary purpose for the charges is to raise revenues to help meet the revenue requirements of the treatment plants, which are heavily subsidized by the federal government. The direct environmental and economic impact of these charges is apparently small (Boland, 1986, p. 12). They primarily serve as a mechanism to help defray the costs of the treatment plants. Thus, the charges used in the United States are similar in spirit to the German and French systems already described. However, their size appears to be smaller, and the application of the revenues is more limited.

Other Fee-Based Systems and Lessons

There are a variety of other fee-based systems which have not been included in this discussion. Brown (1984) did an analysis of incentive-based systems to control hazardous wastes in Europe and found that a number of countries had adopted systems, some of which had a marked economic effect. The general trend was to use either a tax on waste outputs or tax on feedstocks that are usually correlated with the level of waste produced. Companies and government officials were interviewed to ascertain the effects of these approaches. In line with economic theory, charges were found to induce firms to increase expenditures on achieving waste reduction through a variety of techniques including reprocessing of materials, treatment, and input and output substitution. Firms also devoted greater attention to separating waste streams because prices for disposal often varied by the type of waste stream.

The United States has a diverse range of taxes imposed on hazardous waste streams. Several states have land disposal taxes in place. Charges exhibit a wide degree of variation across states. For example, in 1984, charges were $14/tonne in Wisconsin and $70.40/tonne in Minnesota (U.S. CBO, 1985, p. 82). Charges for disposal at landfills also vary widely. The effect of these different charges is very difficult to estimate because of the difficulty in obtaining the necessary data on the quantity and quality of waste streams, as well as the economic variables.

The preceding analysis reveals that there are a wide array of fee-based systems in place designed to promote environmental quality. In a few cases, the fees were shown to have a marked effect on firm behavior; however, in the overwhelming majority of cases studied, the direct economic effect of fees appears to have been small. Several patterns repeat themselves through these examples.

First, the major motivation for implementing emission fees is to raise revenues, which are then usually earmarked for activities which promote environmental quality.[10] Second, most charges are not large enough to have a dramatic impact on the behavior of polluters. In fact, they are not designed to have such an effect. They are relatively low and not directly related to the behavior of individual firms and consumers. Third, there is a tendency for charges to increase faster than inflation over time. Presumably, starting out with a relatively low charge is a way of testing the political waters as well as determining whether the instrument will have the desired effects.

Implementing Market-Based Environmental Programs

An examination of the charge and marketable permits schemes reveals that they are rarely, if ever, introduced in their textbook form. Virtually all environmental regulatory systems using charges and marketable permits rely on the existing permitting system. This result should not be terribly surprising. Most of these approaches were not implemented from scratch; rather, they were grafted onto regulatory systems in which permits and standards play a dominant role.

Perhaps as a result of these hybrid approaches, the level of cost savings resulting from implementing charges and marketable permits is generally far below their theoretical potential. Cost savings can be defined in terms of the savings which would result from meeting a prescribed environmental objective in a less costly manner. As noted, most of the charges to date have not had a major incentive effect. We can infer from this that polluters have not been induced to search for a lower cost mix of meeting environmental objectives as a result of the implementation of charge schemes. Thus, it seems unlikely that charges have performed terribly well on narrow efficiency grounds. The experience on marketable permits is similar. Hahn and Hester (1986)

---

[10]The actual application of fees is similar in spirit to the more familiar deposit-refund approaches that are used for collecting bottles and cans.

argue that cost savings for emissions trading fall far short of their theoretical potential. The only apparent exception to this observation is the lead trading program, which has enjoyed very high levels of trading activity.

The example of lead trading leads to another important observation; in general, different charge and marketable permit systems exhibit wide variation in their effect on economic efficiency. On the whole, there is more evidence for cost savings with marketable permits than with charges.

While the charge systems and marketable permit systems rarely perform well in terms of efficiency, it is important to recognize that their performance is broadly consistent with economic theory. This observation may appear to contradict what was said earlier about the departure of these systems from the economic ideal. However, it is really an altogether different observation. It suggests that the performance of the markets and charge systems can be understood in terms of basic economic theory. For example, where barriers to trading are low, more trading is likely to occur. Where charges are high and more directly related to individual actions, they are more likely to affect the behavior of firms or consumers.

If these instruments are to be measured by their effect on environmental quality, the results are not very impressive. In general, the direct effect of both charges and marketable permits on environmental quality appears to be neutral or slightly positive. The effect of lead trading has been neutral in the aggregate. The effect of emissions trading on environmental quality has probably been neutral or slightly positive. The direct effect of charges on polluter incentives has been modest, although the indirect environmental effect of spending the revenue raised by charges has been significant.

The evidence on charges and marketable permits points to an intriguing conclusion about the nature of these instruments. Charges and marketable permits have played fundamentally different roles in meeting environmental objectives. Charges are used primarily to improve environmental quality by redistributing revenues. Marketable permits are used primarily to promote cost savings.

The positive theory of instrument choice as it relates to pollution control has been greatly influenced by the work of Buchanan and Tullock (1975). They argue that firms will prefer emission standards to emission taxes because standards result in higher profits. Emission standards serve as a barrier to entry to new firms, thus raising firm profits. Charges, on the other hand, do not preclude entry by new firms, and also represent an additional cost to firms. Their argument is based on the view that industry is able to exert its preference for a particular instrument because it is more likely to be well-organized than consumers.

While this argument is elegant, it misses two important points. The first is that within particular classes of instruments, there is a great deal of variation in the performance of instruments. The second is that most solutions to problems involve the application of multiple instruments. Thus, while the Buchanan and Tullock theory explains why standards are chosen over an idealized form of taxes, it does little to help explain the rich array of instruments that are observed in the real world. In particular, under what situations would we be likely to observe different mixes of instruments?

Several authors have explored these different issues for instrument choice within this basic framework (Coelho, 1976; Dewees, 1983; Yohe, 1976). The basic insight of this work is that the argument that standards will be preferred to taxes depends on the precise nature of the instruments being compared.

Another weakness in the existing theory is that the instruments are not generally used in the way that is suggested by the theory. Most emissions charges, for example, are used as a revenue raising device for subsidizing abatement activity, but a few also have pronounced direct effects on polluters. Most marketable permit approaches are not really designed to create markets. Moreover, the different types of trading schemes perform with widely varying success.

The data from the examples given earlier can be used to begin to piece together some of the elements of a more coherent theory of instrument choice. For example, it is clear that distributional concerns play an important role in the acceptability of user charges. The revenue from such charges is usually earmarked for environmental activities related to those contributions. Thus, charges from a noise surcharge will be used to address noise pollution. Charges for water discharges will be used to construct treatment plants and subsidize industry in building equipment to abate water pollution. This pattern suggests that different industries want to make sure that their contributions are used to address pollution problems for which they are likely to be held accountable. Thus, industry sees it as only fair that, as a whole, they get some benefit from making these contributions.

The "recycling" of revenues from charges points up the importance of the existing distribution of property rights. This is also true in the case of marketable permits. The "grandfathering" of rights to existing firms based on the current distribution of rights is an important focal point in many applications of limited markets in pollution rights (Rolph, 1983; Welch, 1983). All the marketable permit programs in the United States place great importance on the existing distribution of rights.

In short, all of the charge and marketable permit systems described earlier place great importance on the status quo. Charges, when introduced, tend to be phased in. Marketable permits, when introduced, usually are optional in the sense that existing firms can meet standards through trading of permits or by conventional means. In contrast, new or expanding firms are not always afforded the same options. For example, new firms must still purchase emission credits if they choose to locate in a non-attainment area, even if they have purchased state-of-the-art pollution control equipment and will pollute less than existing companies. This is an example of a "bias" against new sources. While not efficient from an economic viewpoint, this pattern is consistent with the political insight that new sources don't "vote" while existing sources do.

Though the status quo is important in all applications studied here, it does not explain by itself the rich variety of instruments that are observed. For example, there has been heated controversy over emissions trading since its inception, but comparatively little controversy over the implementation of lead trading. How can economists begin to understand the difference in attitudes towards these two programs?

There are several important differences between emissions trading and lead trading. In the case of lead standards, there appears to be agreement about the distribution of property rights, and the standard that defined them. Refiners had the right to put lead in gasoline at specified levels during specified time periods. Lead in gasoline was reduced to a very low level at the end of 1987. In contrast to lead, there is great disagreement about the underlying distribution of property rights regarding emissions trading. Environmentalists continue to adhere to the symbolic goal of zero pollution. Industry believes and acts as if its current claims on the environment, without any emission reductions, represent a property right.

In the case of lead trading, output could be relatively easily monitored using the existing regulatory apparatus. This was not the case for emissions trading. A new system was set up for evaluating proposed trades. This was, in part, due to existing weaknesses in the current system of monitoring and enforcement. It was also a result of concerns that environmentalists had expressed about the validity of such trades.

The effect that emissions trading was likely to have on environmental quality was much less certain than that of the lead trading program. Some environmentalists viewed emissions trading as a loophole by which industry could forestall compliance, and Hahn and Hester (1986) found some evidence that bubbles were occasionally used for that purpose. The effects of lead trading were much more predictable. Until 1985, there was no banking, so the overall temporal pattern of lead emissions remained unchanged under the program. With the addition of banking in 1985, this pattern was changed slightly, but within well-defined limits.

To accommodate these differing concerns, different rules were developed for the two cases. In the case of lead trading, rights are traded on a one-for-one basis. In contrast, under emissions trading, rights are not generally traded on a one-for-one basis. Rather, most trades must show a net improvement in environmental quality. In the case of lead, all firms are treated equally from the standpoint of trading. In the case of emissions trading, new firms must meet stringent standards before being allowed to engage in trading.

This comparison suggests is that it is possible to gain important insights into the likely performance and choice of instruments by understanding the forces that led to their creation. Analyzing the underlying beliefs about property rights to pollution may be vital both for the political success of the measure and for how well it works in terms of pure economic efficiency.

This view of efficiency is similar to, but should not be confused with, the notion of efficiency advanced by Becker (1983). Becker argues that government will tend to choose mechanisms which are more efficient over those which are less efficient in redistributing revenues from less powerful to more powerful groups. To the extent that his argument is testable, I believe it is not consistent with the facts. For example, the U.S. currently has a policy that directs toxic waste dumps to be cleaned up in priority order. The policy makes no attempt to examine whether a greater risk reduction could be attained with a different allocation of expenditures. Given a finite budget constraint, this policy does not make sense from a purely economic viewpoint. However, it might make sense if environmentalists hoped that more stringent policies would emerge in the future. Or it might make sense if Congress wants to be perceived as doing the job "right," even if only a small part of the job gets done.

A second example can be drawn from emissions trading. It is possible to design marketable permit systems which are more efficient and ensure better environmental quality over time (Hahn and Noll, 1982; Hahn, 1987), yet these systems have not been implemented. Environmentalists may be reluctant to embrace market alternatives because they fear it may give a certain legitimacy to the act of polluting. Moreover, they may not believe in the expected results. Thus, for Becker's theory to hold in an absolute sense, it would be necessary to construct fairly complicated utility functions. The problem is that the theory does not explicitly address how choices are made by lobbyists, legislators and bureaucrats (Campos, 1987).

These choices may be made in different ways in different countries. How can it be explained, for example, that a large array of countries use fees, while only two countries use marketable permits (and the application of permits in Germany is fairly limited)? Noll (1983) has argued that the political institutions of different countries can provide important clues about regulatory strategy. In addition, the comparison of lead trading and emissions trading revealed that the very nature of the environmental problem can have an important effect on interest group attitudes.

Interest group attitudes can be expected to vary across countries. In the Netherlands, Opschoor (1986, p. 15) notes that environmental groups tend to prefer charges while employer groups prefer regulatory instruments. Barde (1986, pp. 10–11) notes that the political "acceptability" of charges is high in both France and the Netherlands. Nonetheless, some French airlines have refused to pay noise charges because the funds are not being used (Barde, 1986, p. 12). In Italy, there has been widespread opposition from industry and interest groups (Panella, 1986, pp. 6, 22). While German industry has accepted the notion of charges, some industries have criticized the differential charge rates across jurisdictions. In the United States, environmentalists have shown a marked preference for regulatory instruments, eschewing both charges and marketable permits. These preferences may help to explain the choice of instruments in various countries as well as the relative utilization of different instruments. In addition, interest groups in different countries will share different clusters of relevant experiences, which will help to determine the feasible space for alternatives.

In short, existing theories could benefit from more careful analysis of the regulatory status quo, underlying beliefs about property rights, and how political choices are actually made in different countries.

The review of marketable permits and charge systems has demonstrated that regulatory systems involving multiple instruments are the rule rather than the exception. The fundamental problem is to determine the most appropriate mix, with an eye to both economic and political realities.

In addition to selecting an appropriate mix of instruments, attention needs to be given to the effects of having different levels of government implement selected policies. It might seem, for example, that if the problem is local, then the logical choice for addressing the problem is the local regulatory body. However, this is not always true. Perhaps the problem may require a level of technical expertise that does not reside at the local level, in which case some higher level of government involvement may be required. What is clear from a review of implementing environmental policies is that the level of oversight can affect the implementation of policies. For example, Hahn and Hester (1986) note that a marked increase in bubble activity is associated with a decrease in federal oversight.

Because marketable permit approaches have been shown to have a demonstrable effect on cost savings without sacrificing environmental quality, this instrument can be expected to receive more widespread use. One factor which will stimulate the application of this mechanism is the higher marginal costs of abatement that will be faced as environmental standards are tightened. A second factor which will tend to stimulate the use of both charges and marketable permits is a "demonstration effect." Several countries have already implemented these mechanisms with some encouraging results. The experience gained in implementing these tools will stimulate their use in future applications. A third factor which will affect the use of both of these approaches is the technology of monitoring and enforcement. As monitoring costs go down, the use of mechanisms such as direct charges and marketable permits can be expected to increase. The combination of these factors leads to the prediction that greater use of these market-based environmental systems will be made in the future.

■ *This research was funded by the National Science Foundation and the Program for Technology and Society at Carnegie Mellon University. I would like to thank Gordon Hester, Dan Nagin, and the editors for helpful comments. The views expressed herein are those of the author and do not necessarily reflect the views of the Council of Economic Advisers.*

References

Barde, J., "Use of Economic Instruments for Environmental Protection: Discussion Paper," ENV/ECO/86.16, Organization for Economic Cooperation and Development, September 9, 1986.

Baumol, W. and Oates, W. *The Theory of Environmental Policy.* Englewood Cliffs, NJ: Prentice-Hall, 1985.

Becker, G., "A Theory of Competition Among Pressure Groups for Political Influence," *Quarterly Journal of Economics,* 1983, *XCVII,* 371–400.

Boland, J., "Economic Instruments for Environmental Protection in the United States," ENV/ECO/86.14, Organization for Economic Cooperation and Development, September 11, 1986.

Bower, B. et al., *Incentives in Water Quality Management: France and the Ruhr Area.* Washington, D.C.: Resources for the Future, 1981.

Bressers, J., "The Effectiveness of Dutch Water Quality Policy," Twente University of Technology, Netherlands, mimeo, 1983.

Brown, G., Jr., "Economic Instruments: Alternatives or Supplements to Regulations?" *Environment and Economics,* Issue Paper, Environment Directorate OECD, June 1984, 103–120.

Brown, G., Jr. and J. Bresser, "Evidence Supporting Effluent Charges," Twente University of Technology, The Netherlands, mimeo, September 1986.

Brown, G., Jr. and R. Johnson, "Pollution Control by Effluent Charges: It Works in the Federal Republic of Germany, Why Not in the U.S.," *Natural Resources Journal,* 1984, *24,* 929–966.

Buchanan, J. and G. Tullock, "Polluters' Profits and Political Response: Direct Controls Versus Taxes," *American Economic Review*, 1975 *65*, 139–147.

Campos, J., "Toward a Theory of Instrument Choice in the Regulation of Markets," California Institute of Technology, Pasadena, California, mimeo, January 26, 1987.

Coelho, P., "Polluters' and Political Response: Direct Control Versus Taxes: Comment," *American Economic Review*, 1976, *66*, 976–978.

Dales, J., *Pollution, Property and Prices*. Toronto: University Press, 1968.

David, M. and E. Joeres, "Is a Viable Implementation of TDPs Transferable?" In Joeres, E. and M. David, eds., *Buying a Better Environment: Cost-Effective Regulation Through Permit Trading*. Madison: University of Wisconsin Press, 1983, 233–248.

Dewees, D., "Instrument Choice in Environmental Policy," *Economic Inquiry, 1983, XXI, 53–71*.

Elmore, T. et al., "Trading Between Point and Nonpoint Sources: A Cost Effective Method for Improving Water Quality," paper presented at the 57th annual Conference/Exposition of the Water Pollution Control Federation, New Orleans, Louisiana, 1984.

Hahn, R., "Designing Markets in Transferable Property Rights: A Practitioner's Guide." In Joeres, E. and M. David, eds., *Buying a Better Environment: Cost Effective Regulation Through Permit Trading*. Madison: University of Wisconsin Press, 1983, 83–97.

Hahn, R., "Rules, Equality and Efficiency: An Evaluation of Two Regulatory Reforms," Working Paper 87-7, School of Urban and Public Affairs, Carnegie Mellon University, Pittsburgh, Pennsylvania, 1987.

Hahn, R. and G. Hester, "Where Did All the Markets Go?: An Analysis of EPA's Emission Trading Program," Working Paper 87-3, School of Urban and Public Affairs, Carnegie Mellon University, Pittsburgh, Pennsylvania, 1986. Forthcoming in the *Yale Journal on Regulation*.

Hahn, R. and G. Hester, "Marketable Permits: Lessons for Theory and Practice," *Ecology Law Quarterly*, forthcoming.

Hahn, R. and A. McGartland, "The Political Economy of Instrument Choice: An Examination of the U.S. Role in Implementing the Montreal Protocol," Working Paper 88-34, School of Urban and Public Affairs, Carnegie Mellon University, Pittsburgh, Pennsylvania, 1988.

Hahn, R. and Noll, R., "Designing a Market for Tradable Emissions Permits." In Magat, W. ed., *Reform of Environmental Regulation*. Cambridge, MA: Ballinger, 1982, 119–146.

Hahn, R. and Noll, R., "Barriers to Implementing Tradable Air Pollution Permits: Problems of Regulatory Interaction," *Yale Journal on Regulation*, 1983, *1*, 63–91.

Kashmanian, R. et al., "Beyond Categorical Limits: The Case for Pollution Reduction Through Trading," paper presented at the 59th Annual Water Pollution Control Federation Conference, Los Angeles, CA, October 6–9, 1986.

Kneese, A. and Schultze, C., *Pollution, Prices, and Public Policy*. Washington, D.C.: The Brookings Institution, 1975.

Montgomery, W. D., "Markets in Licenses and Efficient Pollution Control Programs," *Journal of Economic Theory*, 1972, *5*, 395–418.

Noll, R., "The Political Foundations of Regulatory Policy," *Zeitschrift fur die gesamte Staatswissenschaft*, 1983, *139*, 377–404.

Novotny, G., "Transferable Discharge Permits for Water Pollution Control In Wisconsin," Department of Natural Resources, Madison, Wisconsin, mimeo, December 1, 1986.

O'Neil, W., "The Regulation of Water Polllution Permit Trading under Conditions of Varying Streamflow and Temperature." In Joeres, E. and M. David, eds., *Buying a Better Environment: Cost-Effective Regulation Through Permit Trading*. Madison, Wisconsin: University of Wisconsin Press, 1983, 219–231.

Opschoor, J., "Economic Instruments for Environmental Protection in the Netherlands," ENV/ECO/86.15, Organization for Economic Cooperation and Development, August 1, 1986.

Panella, G., "Economic Instruments for Environmental Protection in Italy," ENV/ ECO/ 86.11, Organization for Economic Cooperation and Development, September 2, 1986.

Patterson, D., Bureau of Water Resources Management, Wisconsin Department of Natural Resources, Madison, Wisconsin, telephone interview, April 2, 1987.

Pigou, A., *The Economics of Welfare*, fourth edition. London: Macmillan and Co., 1932.

Plott, C., "Externalities and Corrective Policies in Experimental Markets," *Economic Journal*, 1983, *93*, 106–127.

Rolph, E., "Government Allocation of Property Rights: Who Gets What?," *Journal of Policy Analysis and Management*, 1983, *3*, 45–61.

Sprenger, R., "Economic Instruments for Environmental Protection in Germany," Organization for Economic Cooperation and Development, October 7, 1986.

Thomas, L., memorandum attached to Draft Emissions Trading Policy Statement, Environmental Protection Agency, Washington, D.C., May 19, 1986.

Tietenberg, T., *Emissions Trading: An Exercise in Reforming Pollution Policy.* Washington, D.C.: Resources for the Future, 1985.

U.S. Congressional Budget Office, *Hazardous Waste Management: Recent Changes and Policy Alternatives,* Washington, D.C.: U.S. G.P.O., May 1985.

U.S. Environmental Protection Agency, "Costs and Benefits of Reducing Lead in Gasoline, Final Regulatory Impact Analysis," Office of Policy Analysis, February 1985a.

U.S. Environmental Protection Agency, "Quarterly Reports on Lead in Gasoline," Field Operations and Support Division, Office of Air and Radiation, July 16, 1985b.

U.S. Environmental Protection Agency, "Quarterly Reports on Lead in Gasoline," Field Operations and Support Division, Office of Air and Radiation, March 21, May 23, July 15, 1986.

Welch, W., "The Political Feasibility of Full Ownership Property Rights: The Cases of Pollution and Fisheries," *Policy Sciences,* 1983, *16,* 165–180.

Yohe, G., "Polluters' Profits and Political Response: Direct Control Versus Taxes: Comment," *American Economic Review,* 1976, *66,* 981–982.

[11]

TAXES, TORTS, AND THE TOXICS RELEASE INVENTORY: CONGRESSIONAL VOTING ON INSTRUMENTS TO CONTROL POLLUTION

JAMES T. HAMILTON*

Theories of rational political ignorance and congressional voting imply that Congress members may take different interests into account when they vote on technical amendments than when they vote on a bill's final passage. This article uses votes on Superfund reauthorization to examine what factors influence politicians' support for different instruments to control pollution and how the interests Congress members take into account vary with the anticipated degree of electoral scrutiny. Controlling for a legislator's general support for environmental programs, a representative's votes on specific policy instruments in Superfund legislation depended on the district-level costs and benefits of the instruments. (JEL D72)

I. INTRODUCTION

Governments can choose from a wide variety of policy instruments to control pollution, including tax and subsidy schemes, marketable permits, information provision programs, liability systems with well-defined property rights, and command and control selection of emission standards or technologies. Economists throughout the 1980s devoted significant effort to modeling the relative merits of these instruments. The question of why politicians would prefer one manner of controlling pollution over another also attracted attention, starting with Buchanan and Tullock's [1975] positive theory of externality control in which polluters find direct regulatory controls on emissions more profitable than pollution taxes. Theories of instrument selection have been developed in which politicians choose policies based on the relative costs and benefits to shareholders, workers, and environmentalists, are affected by the constraints imposed by political institutions, and are driven to select the most efficient policy instrument to achieve a given level of redistri-

bution.[1] To date, however, there have been few empirical tests of what drives instrument selection in environmental policy.

There is a large empirical literature devoted to explaining the level of support for environmental programs in Congress. Most articles focus on the degree to which a legislator's stand on a given environmental bill can be explained by narrow district interests (generally the material interests of constituents) or by ideology (either constituents' or the member's own policy preferences). Studies of voting on environmental legislation by Ackerman and Hassler [1981], Crandall [1983], Pashigian [1985], and Yandle [1989] offer evidence that legislators' actions are in part explained by the district- or state-level impacts of proposed legislation on their constituents. Kalt and Zupan [1984] find that after controlling for constituents' material self-interest in proposed strip mining legislation, the ideology of constituents and the personal ideologies of their representatives influence voting on this aspect of environmental preservation. As Grier [1993] demonstrates, debate over the general role of the legislator's specific ideology in voting continues. In studying votes in the House and Senate on the proposed size of the Superfund during debate

* I would like to thank Miriam Jorgensen, Valeria Balfour, Steve Balla, and Robert Malme for excellent research assistance and Dennis Coates, Michael Munger, Peter Vandoren, Mark Zupan, and two anonymous referees for helpful comments.

Hamilton: Assistant Professor, Duke University
  Phone 1-919-613-7358, Fax 1-919-681-8288
  E-mail jayth@pps.duke.edu

1. See Dewees [1983], Becker [1983], Campos [1989], and Hahn [1987; 1990].

ABBREVIATIONS

NPL: National Priorities List
PRP: Potentially responsible parties
TRI: Toxics Release Inventory

745

©Western Economic Association International

over the program's renewal, Hird [1993] concludes that "congressional voting on Superfund is found to represent legislator's environmental and liberal ideologies as much as (if not more than) narrowly-defined self-interest." He links the importance of ideology to voting on Superfund in part to the bill's symbolic environmental appeal.

In environmental legislation, the final impact of a bill on industry and the environment often depends on issues resolved through technical amendments. Downs's theory of rational ignorance and Arnold's theory of the degree to which constituents will link Congressional actions with real world outcomes predict that members of Congress may be less constrained by general constituent interests on amendment votes since these votes are less likely to be covered in the media than are final legislative votes. As Denzau and Munger [1986] and Grier and Munger [1991] note, groups with specific interests such as affected industries may find it less costly to persuade a member of Congress to vote their way on a measure if the representative's constituents are supportive of or indifferent to the measure. In the case of technical amendments, affected parties may be more influential than on highly visible votes because the lack of media coverage translates into a lower probability that the vote will become a major campaign issue in future elections. This implies that voting on the instruments to control pollution will be driven in part by the specific district-level costs and benefits of these measures, while voting on the final passage of a bill will be more driven by general constituent interests.

This paper uses votes from the debate in the U.S. House of Representatives in 1985 over the reauthorization of the Superfund program to answer two related questions that emerge from theories of rational political ignorance: What factors influence politicians' support for different instruments to control pollution, and how do the interests that Congressional members take into account vary with the anticipated degree of scrutiny of their actions? Superfund voting offers a natural test of hypotheses about what drives the selection of policy instruments in environmental programs, for during the debate over reauthorization House members were presented with votes on amendments that explicitly asked them to adopt particular instruments. House

members were given the chance to vote for Coasian policies relating to the provision of information about toxic emissions by polluting facilities and the ability of facility neighbors to sue in federal courts for personal injuries arising from toxic exposure. Representatives were also given the Pigouvian option of levying a targeted tax on chemical and petroleum producers to fund the program or relying on a broader-based tax to fund the program.

Analysis of the votes on these amendments and final authorization also reveals a set of legislators who voted against the environmental position on all amendments and yet voted for the final bill. Since the amendment to provide toxic release information was voted on twice, the data also provide information on legislators who changed position after public scrutiny increased. These votes thus allow one to explore how legislator positions vary with the degree of scrutiny anticipated for a vote.

The results indicate that legislator votes on policy instruments to control pollution are affected by the district-level incidence of the costs and benefits of these particular measures. These factors are less important in passage of the final bill, a symbolic vote influenced more strongly by the broader electoral constituency of a representative. In making contributions to Congressional members, the PACs representing the affected chemical and petroleum industries appear to have contributed more on the basis of a legislator's stand on contested technical amendments than on a representative's general environmental position or vote on the final passage of the bill. This provides further evidence of the role that business interests may play in the selection of instruments to control pollution.

Section II offers a short description of the Superfund's legislative history. Section III describes hypotheses about voting on pollution instruments and section IV describes the data used to construct the empirical tests. Section V presents results and section VI provides conclusions about the lessons from Superfund voting on what drives instrument selection by legislators in environmental policy.

II. LEGISLATING SUPERFUND

The original "Superfund" legislation passed in 1980 established a $1.6 billion fund to clean up contaminated hazardous waste

The Political Economy of Environmental Regulation

sites. Debate over the program's reauthorization continued throughout 1984 and 1985 as legislators tried to address a number of questions: How large should the cleanup fund be? Who should pay for the cleanups? How many sites should be cleaned up, and how quickly? Should victims be able to sue for damages? In December 1985, the House voted on a series of Superfund amendments on whether to adopt particular instruments to control pollution. Two of the instruments, liability for toxic torts and targeted taxes on chemicals, affected both the cleanup of past waste and firm incentives for future waste handling. The third policy, information provision about pollution levels, created incentives to deter the future generation of waste.

The notion of requiring plants to report their toxic emissions to the public proved so controversial that it generated two votes. On December 5, 1985, the House passed by 183–166 an amendment by Rep. Bob Edgar (D-Pa.) that required facilities to make public their releases of substances suspected of causing cancer, birth defects, and other chronic health problems. This tightened the public reporting provision already in the bill, which required companies to report releases of acutely toxic substances. Since the vote occurred at 11 p.m. when many members were absent, the amendment's opponents hoped that the more stringent reporting requirements would be killed by another vote. In subsequent days there was significant lobbying by industry groups and the EPA against the expanded reporting provisions and activity by environmentalists who stressed the benefits of providing residents with information on polluting facilities. Edgar's right-to-know amendment survived another vote on December 10, 1985, by a margin of 212–211.

House members faced the opportunity to strengthen the incentives for firms to handle wastes properly in the future in a proposal offered by Rep. Barney Frank (D-Mass.). Frank's amendment would have given citizens the right to sue companies in federal courts for damages and injuries arising from the release of toxic substances. Though many states allowed such toxic tort suits, this amendment permitted individuals to bypass obstacles to bringing suit in state courts by explicitly allowing suits in federal courts for injuries and damages discovered after the passage of the

bill. While environmental groups supported this expansion of the liability system, insurance companies, polluters, and the Reagan administration opposed it. On December 10, the measure failed by a vote of 162–261.

The House also faced the choice of how to fund the Superfund program. The initial fund depended on a tax on oil and chemical feedstocks estimated at $1.38 billion, with the rest of the $1.6 billion fund coming from general revenues. The Ways and Means committee reported an amendment to the reauthorization bill that would have raised $4.5 billion from a new broad tax, $1.5 billion from a chemical tax, $1 billion from a petroleum tax, $1.6 billion from a tax on hazardous waste disposal, $180 million from general revenues, and money from other sources for a total of $10 billion in funding. Rep. Thomas Downey (D-N.Y.) offered an amendment that depended on raising $10 billion in funding through higher taxes targeted at polluters: $3.1 from petroleum, $2.1 billion from chemicals, $2 billion from a tax on hazardous waste disposal, $1.6 from general revenues, and the remaining funds from other sources. Votes on funding were structured so that if the Downey amendment failed the Ways and Means amendment would win by default, thereby providing House members with the opportunity to adopt a broad tax without explicitly voting for it. Downey put together a coalition for his targeted tax that included environmentalists and nonpetrochemical businesses to counter the lobbying efforts of oil and chemical firms. The Downey amendment was adopted by a vote of 220–206.

After a series of votes on these and other amendments, on December 10, 1985, the House passed the Superfund reauthorization bill by a vote of 391–33. Disagreements among House and Senate conferees kept both chambers from voting on the final version of the bill for many months. The revised conference version of the bill cleared the House by a vote of 386–27 on October 8, 1986, and was signed into law by President Reagan, despite earlier threats of a pocket veto.[2]

2. The final bill provided $8.5 billion for waste cleanups, derived its funding from taxes on petroleum and chemical feedstocks as well as a broad tax and general revenues, and contained provisions that established the Toxics Release Inventory, the EPA database containing firms' reports of their toxic emissions.

III. THE SELECTION OF POLICY INSTRUMENTS

Previous models of Congressional voting on the environment presented in Kalt and Zupan [1984; 1990], Durden, Shogren, and Silberman [1991], and Fort et al. [1993] have emphasized multiple influences on the voting decisions of legislators: the district-level incidence of benefits and costs for a representative's geographic constituents, constituent ideology, the representatives' own preferences for policy, and the particular interests of a representative's electoral constituency, both in district (e.g., voters and contributors) and outside the district (e.g., contributors). As Goff and Grier [1993] and Krehbiel [1993] stress, current controversies in this literature include the degree to which the average of district-level constituent characteristics reflects the "preferences" of a legislator's constituents given the Arrow problem and the fact that representatives may have a distinct electoral constituency. Grier [1993] questions the interpretation of ideology ratings and the accuracy with which previous researchers have been able to isolate slack in the principal-agent relationship, while Stratmann [1991] and Coates [1993] focus on the impact of interest-group influence as measured by PAC contributions. Most relevant to this article is Hird's study of House and Senate voting on Superfund reauthorization. In analyzing votes on the level of funding during the Superfund debate, Hird finds that the number of Superfund sites in a state (but not the number in the district), the amount of hazardous waste generated in the state, and a legislator's economic and environmental ideologies (as distinct from those of the member's constituents) influenced voting on the size of the Superfund program.

I focus on a different question, namely what influences preferences for policy instruments in the environmental area. Previous articles have implicitly examined legislator positions on policy instruments, since the votes on environmental policy often assume a given policy instrument will be used to implement the legislation. The amendments examined in the Superfund reauthorization debate allow one to ask what (after controlling for a legislator's support for environmental programs) influences the selection of specific policy instruments.

The factors that influence a legislator's vote on policy instruments may differ from those that determine her support for the bill overall, in part because of the rational ignorance of constituents about the details of legislation and the legislative process noted by Downs [1957] and Denzau and Munger [1986]. Votes on instrument selection generally come through amendments whose technical details are unlikely to generate much media attention in a legislator's district. As Arnold [1990] points out, a legislator may take into account the potential preferences voters in a district might have if they became informed about the details of the amendment since the possibility exists that a challenger or interest group may raise the issue in a future campaign. The relative ignorance of constituents about the details of amendment votes, however, means that the interests of those particularly affected by the amendment may be more important in determining the legislator's vote on policy instruments. A vote on final passage of a bill may be more likely to attract attention in the broader electorate, however, so that the impact of general constituent preferences will be increased relative to that of the parties who influence the legislator on the amendment votes. Nelson and Silberberg [1987] examine a similar phenomenon in voting on defense bills, where congressional voting patterns vary with the degree of anticipated scrutiny. They find evidence consistent with legislators being more likely to vote their personal ideologies on general defense bills than on narrowly focused bills dealing with particular weapons, since in the latter case there are identifiable beneficiaries who will monitor a Senator's votes.

A representative may consider at least three separate sets of parties when considering how to vote. When voting on final passage of the bill, the legislator may be most concerned with how his broad electoral constituency may view the bill. Their preferences will also be a constraint in voting on technical amendments, but the legislator here will be more likely to consider the interests of particular parties in the district that are helped or hurt by these policy instruments. The influence of particular parties affected by policy instruments may be more important on technical amendments because they are more likely to monitor behavior on these measures and because it is the technical amendments that may settle the details that have a significant impact on these groups. The preferences of the contributors inside and outside the district may also influence the representative on amendments that are not highly visible to other constituents.

The assertion that voting on final passage will involve different incentives than voting on amendments depends in part on the assumption that amendment votes receive less media coverage. For the Superfund votes, this is clearly the case. If one examines articles on Superfund that appear within ten days before or after a vote in the Lexis general interest publication file, there were 31 articles for the amendment votes on December 5, 1985, 42 articles for the passage of the full bill on December 10, 1985, and 63 articles in the days surrounding the final Superfund authorization vote on October 8, 1986.[3] In terms of the flow of information in general publications, final passage of the bill in 1986 garnered nearly twice the coverage of the amendment votes. There was a different pattern within the specialized publications read by business and environmental lobbyists. In three Bureau of National Affairs publications that track environmental policy developments for professionals, coverage of the technical amendments (30 articles in these publications in the 10 days before and after amendment votes) was nearly as large as coverage surrounding the final passage (35 articles). Thus for the general public, articles about final passage greatly outnumber those about voting on technical amendments, while in publications for the regulatory community coverage of both types of votes is about equal.[4]

According to this model of the impact of constituent information on Congressional voting, a legislator will consider the preferences of his or her broad electoral constituency

when voting on final passage of the Superfund reauthorization since the measure will be viewed as symbolic of (and even synonymous with) support for the environment. One measure of constituent ideology included in the models is the percentage of the vote for Reagan in the 1984 elections, since the more conservative the electorate in the district the more it may pay for a legislator to take an anti-environmental stand on issues. The amount of support that a legislator exhibits for environmental issues in general will also influence his or her vote on a highly publicized issue such as Superfund reauthorization. The League of Conservation Voters scorecard captures a legislator's "brand name" identification with environmentalism, though whether the member casts these votes because of constituent ideology or personal ideology is left open to interpretation here. Environmental group membership per 1,000 residents in the state is also included to reflect the ideology of voters in a district, since it measures the relative number of people who place enough of a use, existence, or bequest value on the environment to join these groups. Party is also included to control for a legislator's broader ideology.

On the final vote on passage of the bill, one would thus expect legislators to take into account the preferences of the district's broad electorate. The more conservative a member's district, the lower a member's general support for environmental programs, or the lower membership rates in environmental groups in the state, the less likely the member would be to vote for Superfund passage. Republicans would also be expected to be less likely to vote for the bill. Representatives with more sites listed or proposed for the National Priorities List of sites qualifying for cleanup funds would also be more likely to vote for

---

3. For general interest coverage the Lexis file ARCNWS was searched for articles about Superfund authorization. Specialized coverage was captured through a search of the BNAENV file, which tracks articles from *Environment Reporter, Chemical Regulation Reporter,* and *International Environment Reporter.* The full bill was voted on in the House on December 10, 1985 (the vote modeled in Table I), and again (after the conference committee) on October 8, 1986. The examination of voting on the full bill in Table I uses the vote on December 10, 1985.

4. Arnold predicts that Congressional members will also take into account general constituent interests in voting on technical amendments because these amendments may

some day become general election issues. A story from October 1986 about the North Carolina Senate campaign of Rep. James Broyhill indicates how voting on amendments and final passage may be covered in an election. The article quotes a Sierra Club lobbyist as saying that Broyhill "was a leader in opposing aggressive pollution control. He vigorously fought against Superfund in 1984 and 1985." The article then notes that "Broyhill, sensing the high political appeal of Superfund programs, voted for the measure that passed the Senate last week. Ironically, the $9 billion, five-year measure imposes new corporate taxes and a tax on crude oil, provisions that historically run against Broyhill's grain." See Moriarty [1986].

final passage, since the listing of sites would create attentive publics in the affected communities.

These forces also influence a legislator's vote on policy instruments to control pollution. In voting on amendments, however, the concentration of the costs and benefits of particular instruments to control pollution will also determine which groups directly affected by the legislation will influence voting on instrument selection.

The district-level costs and benefits of the pollution instruments varied by amendment. Consider the Edgar amendment, which required facilities to report their releases and transfers of chemicals with acute and chronic effects. Proponents argued that information provision by itself could serve as an instrument to control pollution since firms would attempt to avoid public and regulator scrutiny generated by the public reporting of their pollution figures in the Toxics Release Inventory (TRI) by reducing emissions. This amendment imposed costs on polluters in terms of gathering data, reporting information to the EPA, and reducing emissions because of the pressure generated by greater public scrutiny.[5] The more pollution in the district, the higher the expected costs for manufacturers, and hence the more likely they would be to lobby legislators. Representatives from more-polluted districts might be less likely to vote for disclosure because of the cost imposed on industry. Note that disclosure could also lead to risk reductions for residents in polluted districts since information provision could lead to reduced emissions and transfers. Since costs to polluters are concentrated (there were an average of 53 facilities per congressional district that would end up reporting under the TRI in 1987) and the benefits are dispersed

across the residents of the district, one might expect that higher toxic emissions in a district would make a representative less likely to support the creation of the Toxics Release Inventory.

Some residents of the district might be more likely to identify with the benefits of the TRI, such as neighbors around Superfund National Priorities List (NPL) sites (where uncertainty about chemical exposure often exists) or communities surrounding the facilities of companies or other entities in the district listed as potentially responsible parties at Superfund sites.[6] The greater the number of these types of neighborhoods in a district, the more likely a legislator might vote for information provision by polluters.

Likely winners and losers in a district were also identifiable for the amendment by Rep. Frank that would allow individuals injured by hazardous substances to sue in federal courts. The higher the amount of current pollution generated in a district, the less likely a representative might be to vote for provisions that would raise the costs for industry of handling hazardous waste. The higher the number of NPL sites or firms or other entities listed as potentially responsible parties (PRPs) in a district, the greater the potential that some district residents would be concerned about personal injury suits arising from hazardous waste handling. For the third instrument considered, a tax targeted at petroleum, chemical feedstocks, and hazardous waste disposal, the higher the toxic pollution generated in the district the more likely that firms in the area would be affected adversely by the proposal and hence the less likely the representative would be to vote for the targeted tax.

Hazardous waste sites with significant levels of contamination are placed by the EPA on the National Priorities List, which qualifies a site for the expenditure of federal remediation funds. While there were two sites per congressional district listed by the EPA as final or proposed NPL sites in 1986, there were 57 sites per district in the EPA's Superfund tracking database (called CERCLIS) that did not meet this criterion. The overwhelming major-

---

5. Public scrutiny of the pollution figures reported in the TRI has generated adverse publicity for companies and led many firms to reduce their reported emissions of toxic chemicals. Hamilton [1995] demonstrates that on the first day the data were released, firms reporting TRI data to the EPA experienced negative abnormal returns on the New York and American stock exchanges as investors gained information about the extent of their pollution control costs and liabilities. This information provision program has led firms to undertake significant pollution reduction programs. The U.S. EPA [1993] estimates that between 1988 and 1991, total reported TRI toxic releases and transfers dropped by one-third. For evidence on compliance with TRI reporting requirements, see Brehm and Hamilton [1996].

6. The EPA refers to the individuals, companies, small businesses, nonprofit organizations (e.g. universities), and government entities notified that they may be liable for cleanup costs at a Superfund site as "potentially responsible parties."

ity of these non-NPL sites had been investigated by the EPA, which had decided they did not merit inclusion on the list of sites qualifying for remediation funds. Some were sites still waiting evaluation, so they might eventually be added to the NPL. The number of non-NPL sites is included as a separate variable in the voting models. One might expect that the greater the number of non-NPL sites the less likely a representative would be to vote for an amendment or final passage. On amendment voting, representatives might favor polluter interests over communities threatened by pollution at non-NPL sites because those exposed to these risks might not be as energized as constituents around NPL sites. Evidence from Kohlhase [1991] indicates that actual listing on the NPL does change reactions to hazardous waste sites, as indicated by the creation of a premium for houses farther from the site once it is listed on the NPL. On voting on the full bill, representatives might be less likely to vote for the Superfund if a greater number of non-NPL sites is a measure of the relative importance of polluters to employment in the district. Since there were 57 non-NPL sites versus two NPL sites per district, non-NPL sites may thus serve as a better proxy for general polluter interests in a district while NPL sites reflect the number of communities highly attentive to risks from hazardous waste sites.

Petroleum and chemical firms faced higher costs under each of the policy instruments considered. They would be likely to generate pollution to report under the TRI, likely to be involved in suits involving personal injury from hazardous waste generation and disposal, and likely to pay significant fees under the targeted tax provisions. If one views PAC contributions from these firms as indicators that the companies believe the representative is sympathetic toward their interests, then higher PAC contributions should indicate that the legislator will be less likely to vote for policy instruments that impose higher costs on these industries. The coefficients on contributions do not capture the influence of contributions per se. Contributions are interpreted here as an indicator of the degree of the legislator's support for the interests of oil and gas firms, which may arise from a number of reasons: a legislator's desire to represent oil and gas interests in the district, willingness to trade ac-

cess or support for contributions, or agreement on policy grounds with the industry's position.[7]

Comparisons across voting on the amendments and final authorization (i.e., the December 10, 1985 authorization vote) also will yield insights into which interests legislators are responsive to in their selection of policy instruments. Although there was a core group of legislators who voted against all three amendments, nearly all of them voted in favor of the final authorization. Among those who voted against the environmentalists' position on all amendments, one would expect those representatives who came from more liberal districts or who had a general "brand name" for environmentalism to vote for the final bill and thereby demonstrate symbolic support for the environment.

Differences in voting between the first vote on the Edgar TRI amendment, which took place at 11 p.m. on December 5, 1985, when not all representatives were present, and the second vote on the Edgar amendment five days later also provide evidence on how voting may differ with additional scrutiny. In the five-day interim between votes a significant amount of lobbying took place in which parties potentially affected by the information provision legislation contacted legislators and

---

7. A large number of researchers have found that PAC contributions often flow to confirmed supporters rather than marginal legislators. See, for example, Hall and Wayman [1990]. One explanation of this pattern from Denzau and Munger [1986] may be that PACs can buy services in the legislative process more cheaply from legislators already favorably disposed toward them, perhaps because a legislator's district interests are similar to those of the PAC. Bronars and Lott [1994] present evidence consistent with the view that contributions are made to support politicians with sympathetic interests rather than to buy legislative support. Stratmann [1991; 1992] points out that a PAC may try to influence the election of friends or sway the position of marginal legislators. Stratmann [1991] and Coates [1993] both estimate simultaneous models of contributions and votes that allow one to test for which strategy a group of PACs may be pursuing and allow one to make claims about the impact of contributions on votes. Under the election of friends strategy, there should be a positive relationship between PAC contributions and general support for an industry's position. Stratmann's model indicates that under a vote-buying strategy, contributions should rise with constituency support for an industry, be highest for legislators representing the median constituency interest on an issue, and then decline for legislators representing districts with more voters sympathetic to an industry. This paper includes a squared term for PAC contributions, which may capture part of the declining contribution pattern expected under the vote-buying hypothesis. Coates includes a squared term to reflect diminishing marginal productivity of contributions.

made their concerns known. Legislators who switched positions between the first and second votes should thus be expected to base their decisions in part on the interests of the parties affected by the costs of the additional reporting requirements.

This model of policy instrument selection predicts that interest groups should be more interested in legislator votes on amendments, where significant dollar values are at stake and legislators face fewer constraints from district scrutiny, and less interested in legislator votes on the final authorization, where the outcome is a foregone conclusion and the symbolic nature of the vote is important in conveying information to constituents. This would predict that if interest group contributions for the 1986 election cycle were examined, that voting on the 1985 amendments should result in higher contributions for legislators while voting on the reauthorization should have no impact on contribution patterns. This effect should be true controlling for whether the legislator was on the Ways and Means Committee or the Energy and Commerce Committee, two committees important to the drafting of the legislation. Since committee power matters to interest groups, representatives on these committees should be expected to garner higher PAC contributions from the oil and chemical industries.[8] The model of 1986 contributions also controls for a representative's general environmental record (1986 League of Conservation Voters (LCV) scorecard). To isolate the marginal impacts of particular votes on contributions, I include 1984 PAC contributions from the relevant group of PACs (and whether the representative was an incumbent in 1984) so that one can examine, controlling for a legislator's general environmental record and past levels of industry support, how voting on particular measures influenced 1986 contributions.

The limitations of these tests should be acknowledged. Votes on both amendments and

final passage may involve strategic voting, such as log-rolling where Congressional members trade support in one area for support in another.[9] Many important issues that affected the costs of Superfund cleanups never came to a vote in amendment form, such as the requirement that the EPA give preference to permanent remedies in site cleanups and that site managers use environmental standards from state environmental programs if they were stricter than federal requirements. Many of these issues were resolved in committee rather than on the floor. Thus the absence of influence on amendment voting does not mean a particular interest did not influence a member's overall legislative effort, it simply may mean that the influence is not captured through the measure of floor votes.[10] One may also question whether these votes relate only to instrument selection, since in the liability and toxics reporting votes the decision was structured as yes/no rather than a selection among different instruments. In addition, there is not a great deal of variation to explain in the vote on the full Superfund bill since the regression sample contains 389 members voting in favor and only 33 voting against. Results will thus be interpreted with caution, although in total the votes offer a good test of theories of instrument selection and rational ignorance.

IV. DATA

The district-level incidence of the policy instruments considered during the Superfund debate is captured primarily through four variables: the total toxic releases and transfers in the district in 1987; total number of final and proposed sites in the district on the National Priorities List and the total number of non-NPL sites in the district listed in EPA's database of hazardous waste sites (CERCLIS); and a count of the companies and other entities in the district listed by the EPA as a PRP at Superfund sites. Since each of these variables may relate to the magnitude of pollution in the district, they reflect the differences across districts in both the relative costs of making waste cleanups or control more costly and the relative benefits to district

---

8. These patterns should hold whether PACs are trying to reelect friends or sway votes of particular legislators. If chemical and oil industry PACS were supporting sympathetic legislators, the votes on technical amendments and the ability to exercise influence in committee could be two ways to determine which interests were important for PACs to support. If PACs were trying to buy votes or influence, then again technical amendments and committee behavior would be two areas they might try to influence with contributions. See Grier and Munger [1991] on the importance of committee power to interest groups.

9. See Stratmann [1992] and Irwin and Kroszner [1996].

10. See Vandoren [1990].

residents of reduced risks from pollution. Thus the expected signs on these variables will vary depending on whether one believes more pollution in the district will lead a representative to be less likely to favor controls (i.e., the member is responsive to industry concerns) or more likely to favor controls (i.e., the member is responsive to environmental concerns). See the appendix for descriptive statistics for these variables.

For each congressional district total toxic releases to the air, land, and water and total offsite transfers to publicly owned treatment works and to offsite treatment and disposal facilities were calculated from the 1987 TRI data.[11] Facility zip codes were used to match the manufacturing plants reporting their pollution levels under the TRI program to congressional districts. A list of potentially responsible parties at Superfund sites was also matched through zip codes to congressional districts. The number of firms and other entities in the district listed as PRPs at Superfund sites represents a measure of potential interest by companies and other district organizations (e.g. local governments) in the liabilities arising from the program. Since PRPs also generate hazardous waste, however, their numbers can provide an additional variable measuring the risks posed by hazardous waste in the district (from residents' perspectives) and district interests in the costs of regulating future waste generation.[12] The total number of final and proposed sites on the National Priorities List, which are the sites that qualify for

large expenditures of federal cleanup funds, measures the potential number of areas in the district concerned about the cleanup of past waste contamination.[13] The number of non-NPL sites per district may reflect the importance of polluting industries in the district and (for sites that have not been evaluated yet) the potential for even greater liability under Superfund. These two site measures have different expected signs because NPL communities should be more highly attuned to the risks of Superfund sites (which would lead representatives to vote in favor of more stringent pollution control) while residents surrounding non-NPL sites may be less cognizant of the program (which would lead representatives to favor polluter interests rather than environmental concerns).

Support for environmentalism among constituents in a district is measured by statewide membership per 1,000 residents in the Sierra Club, Greenpeace, and the National Wildlife Federation. This captures people with both use values for the environment as well as existence and bequest motives. The percentage vote for Reagan in the district in 1984 is used to capture constituents' ideology, on the belief that the more conservative district residents were the higher the vote for Reagan in the 1984 election.

The 1986 League of Conservation Voters scores for legislators' environmental votes in 1985 and 1986 are also included in the analysis (though votes relating to Superfund were removed from these totals). A legislator's scorecard on votes across a wide-range of environmental issues may represent a number of influences: an attempt to represent the ideologies of constituents (who may be pro- or anti-environment); a reflection of the legislator's own ideological preferences, distinct from that of constituents; or an attempt to represent the economic interests of district constituents or "electoral constituents" such as campaign contributors.[14] I do not attempt

11. Since 1987 was the first year for reporting TRI data, the pollution figures from this year are thought to be marred by reporting flaws. The data are used because they are from the year closest to the votes and because they are meant to represent the relative magnitude (rather than absolute levels) of toxic pollutants across districts. In the matching of facilities or PRPs to congressional districts via zip codes, those plants or parties in zip codes that were shared across congressional districts were assigned to totals for both districts.

12. The number of PRPs per congressional district is positively correlated (.20, $p = .0001$) with the number of NPL sites per district and positively correlated (.11, $p = .05$) with the percentage of NPL sites in the district with cleanup costs greater than $20 million. Districts with more PRPs may have greater risks from hazardous waste because the parties may continue to generate negative externalities in their operation. Total expected liabilities under Superfund in a district may increase with the number of PRPs both because each additional party may mean more costs will be borne by entities in the district and because the nature of the sites in these districts means sites in the district will be more expensive.

13. Toxics Release Inventory data are from the U.S. EPA. A list of potentially responsible parties at Superfund sites was obtained from the EPA through the Freedom of Information Act. Superfund site information came from the EPA's CERCLIS database public extract. Environmental group data came from Hall and Kerr [1991]. Reagan voting data came from the Barone and Ujifusa [1988].

14. See Kalt and Zupan [1984; 1990], Richardson and Munger [1990], Hird [1993], and Grier [1993].

to disentangle the sources of a legislator's overall environmental voting record and the degree of slack in the principal-agent relationship between representatives and voters. Rather, the LCV scorecard is used to control for the general level of environmentalism exhibited in a representative's voting, so that one can ask, given a general level of support for environmental programs, what drives preferences over the types of instruments used to implement environmental programs. Party is also used as a measure of a legislator's general ideology, though again the question is left open as to whether a representative's party affiliation represents the member's true preferences or simply represents brand name signaling to constituents.

PAC contributions from 1984 and 1986 are also included in the analysis. The figures from 1984 are contributions reported to the Federal Election Commission by companies whose primary business was in the petroleum or chemical industry. The 1986 PAC data are broken down into three groups: contributions from the 11 companies estimated to pay 70% of the pre-1986 Superfund feedstock tax; companies whose primary business was in the petroleum or chemical industry; and companies whose primary or secondary business was in these industries.[15] In the regressions that include the 1984 PAC data, the coefficients on contributions are not meant to reflect the impact of money on voting decisions. PACs may give contributions to legislators who would support their positions without contributions in order to aid their reelection or to alter the positions of legislators. I am rather using the PAC funds to measure the extent to which a legislator is generally sympathetic toward the interests of oil and chemical firms. The "elect friendly legislators" strategy would suggest a positive relationship between PAC contributions and general support for oil and chemical interests, while the "influence legislators" strategy would suggest a nonlinear relationship where PAC contributions are highest for the median legislator in terms of support for oil and gas interests (a nonlinear relationship which is in part captured by the squared term for PAC contributions). The model of 1986 PAC contributions explores whether votes on technical amendments were rewarded more than votes on the final passage of the bill or positions on general environmental issues.

V. RESULTS

Rational voter ignorance about the details of policies implies that different factors should influence voting on technical amendments than influence final passage of a bill. Since votes on amendments are less likely to receive coverage in the press and many voters may be less likely to have preferences over some of the issues involved, representatives will be more likely to consider the particular incidence within their districts and support from contributors in deciding which instruments to use to control pollution. In the vote on the final bill, however, the ideological interests of the broader electoral constituency will be more likely to influence a representative's vote since the decision is more likely to be covered in the media and viewed as a measure of support for the environment. The results in Tables I through IV support these hypotheses.

Table I confirms that, controlling for a legislator's general level of support for environmentalism, representatives faced with the selection of different policy instruments to control pollution made their decisions in part based on the relative costs and benefits to their geographic and electoral constituencies. In the final vote on reauthorization of the Superfund, factors related to the ideology of the general electorate in a district and the interests of particular voters (as distinct from firms) in the district were the only variables that were statistically significant. The more liberal the voters in the district, and the stronger a legislator's general support for environmental programs, the more likely the representative was to vote for final passage of the bill. The vote was symbolic in the sense that constituents were likely to see it as an indicator of support for the environment. For nearly all legislators in the regression sample (389 out of 422), it paid to register suppor: for the final reauthorization. The greater the number of NPL sites the more likely a repre-

15. PAC classifications came from computer data provided to the author by the Center for Responsive Politics, Washington, D.C. The 11 companies estimated to pay 70% of the Superfund feedstock tax were Atlantic Richfield, Dow Chemical, Du Pont, Exxon, Mobil, Phillips Petroleum, Shell Oil, Standard Oil of Indiana, Texaco, Union Carbide, and Unocal.

The Political Economy of Environmental Regulation

TABLE I

Determinants of Congressional Voting on Superfund Revisions, 1985

Variable	Toxics Release Inventory (12/10/85)	Injury Liability	Targeted Tax	Superfund Reauthorization
Intercept	−.25 (1.51)	1.81 (1.44)	.16 (1.09)	9.91*** (3.09)
Toxic Releases and Transfers (lbs.)	−9.15e-9*** (3.7e-9)	−8.16e-9** (3.88e-9)	−5.65e-9* (3.15e-9)	3.87e-10 (9e-10)
NPL Final or Proposed Sites (#)	.12** (.06)	.03 (.06)	.05 (.05)	.33** (.16)
Non-NPL CERCLIS Sites (#)	.001 (.004)	−.004 (.004)	−.005 (.003)	−.01** (.006)
Potentially Responsible Parties (#)	.002 (.005)	.01*** (.005)	.003 (.004)	.002 (.01)
1984 PAC $ from Chemical and Petroleum Firms	−.0002** (.0001)	−.0003*** (.0001)	−.0002** (.00009)	−2.21e-6 (.0002)
1984 PAC $² from Chemical and Petroleum Firms	1.19e-8 (7.3e-9)	1.45e-8* (7.54e-9)	4.06e-9 (6.94e-9)	7.24e-9 (1.82e-9)
1984 Vote for Reagan (%)	−.07*** (.02)	−.09*** (.02)	−.03** (.01)	−.16*** (.04)
Environmental Group Membership (Statewide, per 1,000)	.23*** (.06)	.14*** (.05)	.21*** (.05)	.13 (.08)
1986 League of Cons. Voters Score	.03*** (.007)	.02*** (.007)	.02*** (.006)	.05*** (.02)
Democrat	1.67*** (.39)	1.11*** (.39)	−.23 (.33)	.51 (.70)
Yes/No Votes	211/210	161/260	220/204	389/33
LR Test (Chi-Square)	269.66	239.04	136.70	89.68

Note: Dependent variable in the logit = 1 if the House member voted in favor of the measure.

Standard errors are in parentheses.

***statistically significant at 1% level

**statistically significant at 5% level

*statistically significant at the 10% level.

sentative was to vote for final passage, which may indicate a response to the communities likely to be highly attuned to the program. More non-NPL sites translated into a lower probability of voting for final passage of the bill, which could indicate a greater number of constituents associated with polluting industries in a district.[16] The variables associated with the firm-level incidence of the bill's benefits and costs, such as the amount of toxic releases and number of district PRPs were not

16. NPL sites are assumed to be associated with more support for pollution control, while non-NPL sites are associated with less support. This may be because residents around NPL sites are made more attentive to the program, while residents around non-NPL sites may not be as sensitized to site risks or the Superfund program. I interpret the significance of the non-NPL sites on the final vote as relating to the interests of voters associated with polluting industries (the source of many non-NPL sites).

statistically significant. PAC contributions from chemical and petroleum firms were not statistically significant, consistent with the theory that these firms would be more likely to care about the resolution of technical amendments than symbolic positions on a final bill destined to pass.

In voting on amendments dealing with information provision, torts, and targeted taxes, representatives did take into account the ideologies of the general electorate in their districts. The vote for Reagan in the district, environmental group membership, and League of Conservation Voters scorecards were all statistically significant in explaining whether a legislator favored a particular instrument to control pollution. In voting on the instrument amendments, however, the incidence of benefits and costs in the district and among contributors became important determinants of support for particular instruments. The greater the amount of toxic releases and transfers in the district, the more likely the legislator was to oppose the provision of information about pollution. This is consistent with a representative taking into account the interests of polluters (who may be few in number and thus more easily mobilized) in the district over the interests of the many residents in the district potentially put at risk by the emissions of the firms. Most residents affected by the TRI releases may be unaware of their effects and thus unlikely to connect a vote on the amendment with toxic exposures. In districts with more Superfund NPL sites, however, residents surrounding these areas may be more likely to be concerned about information about hazards. This may explain why legislators were more likely to vote in favor of the release of the pollution data the higher the number of NPL sites in their districts.

On the Frank amendment to allow personal injury suits in federal courts for future exposure to hazardous substances, legislators again voted in part based on the amendment's district-level incidence. The more toxic pollution generated in the district, the less likely a representative was to vote in favor of the measure. The greater the number of potentially responsible parties in the district, the more likely a legislator was to favor making the tort system easier to use. Since PRPs are often firms or entities still generating hazardous waste, districts with more PRPs may be ones where there are many neighborhoods concerned about injury from exposure to waste. This concentration of the benefits of the bill into a recognizable group may help explain why legislators from these districts were more likely to support using the tort system to control future pollution.

The higher the amount of toxic waste produced in a district, the less likely the representative was to vote for a tax targeted at petroleum, chemical feedstocks, and hazardous waste disposal. The larger the contributions in the 1984 elections from PACs of firms primarily in the oil and chemical industries, the less likely a legislator was to vote for a tax targeted at these industries. Higher contributions were also associated with lower support for the toxic tort and information provision amendments. These results indicate that the

more a legislator supported the interests of oil and gas firms, the less likely he was to favor any pollution control instrument here.[17]

In the regression sample there were 133 representatives who voted against all three amendments. Yet 102 of these legislators ended up voting for final passage of the bill. Table II confirms that among those legislators who voted against the environment on all three amendments, those with more liberal constituents were more likely to vote for the environmental position on the final authorization vote. Representatives from districts with more NPL sites were more likely to vote for the final bill. This underscores the importance of using the final vote to signal support for the environment to a legislators' broad constituency if that constituency tends to be liberal and to residents surrounding toxic sites.[18] If one simply looked at legislators who voted for the final authorization as "environmentalists," however, one would miss the gradations in support evident across the votes on policy instruments. Among those who voted yes on authorization, representatives who voted against the environmental position on all three amendments were more likely to come from districts with higher pollution, more conservative constituencies, lower environmental group membership, and were more likely to be sympathetic to the interests of oil and gas contributors. Conversely, those legislators who voted for the environment on all three amendments also differed in terms of their district characteristics. They represented more liberal constituents, came from areas with more environmental group members per capita, were less likely to represent the interests of oil and gas contributors, were more likely to be Democrats, and were more likely to support general environmental measures.

Table III offers estimates of the impact of additional scrutiny on the behavior of legisla-

17. Note that the squared contribution term is statistically significant on only one of the three amendment votes in Table I and is not statistically significant in any of the votes in Tables II and III. This is consistent with the theory that PACs give to sympathetic legislators.

18. It may be the actual listing of a site on the NPL and subsequent community experience with the remediation process that generates interest in the program. Representatives with more non-NPL sites were actually less likely to vote yes on the reauthorization, suggesting that representatives side with polluter interests or the interests of employees of polluters when residents have not been made attentive through the NPL process.

TABLE II
Determinants of the Difference between Legislators' Votes on Superfund Amendments and their Votes on Reauthorization

Variable	Among those who voted no on all 3 amendments, voted yes on reauthorization?	Among those who voted yes on reauthorization, voted no on all 3 amendments?	Among those who voted yes on reauthorization, voted yes on all 3 amendments?
Intercept	7.93** (3.37)	−4.14** (1.82)	−2.58** (1.30)
Toxic Releases and Transfers (lbs.)	7.46e-10 (1.44e-9)	1.07e-8*** (3.70e-9)	−7.79e-9 (5.03e-9)
NPL Final or Proposed Sites (#)	.27* (.16)	−.11 (.08)	−.01 (.07)
Non-NPL CERCLIS Sites (#)	−.01* (.007)	.003 (.004)	−.0001 (.004)
Potentially Responsible Parties (#)	−.001 (.01)	−.0005 (.006)	.0007 (.005)
1984 PAC $ from Chemical and Petroleum Firms	.00003 (.0003)	.0003** (.0001)	−.0003** (.0001)
1984 PAC ^{2} from Chemical and Petroleum Firms	7.08e-9 (2.06e-8)	−9.72e-9 8.10e-9	9.74e-9 (1.35e-8)
1984 Vote for Reagan (%)	−.12*** (.04)	.09*** (.02)	−.05*** (.01)
Environmental Group Membership (Statewide, per 1,000)	.10 (.08)	−.16*** (.06)	.36*** (.06)
1986 League of Cons. Voters Score	.03 (.02)	−.05*** (.009)	.02*** (.007)
Democrat	.68 (.82)	.01 (.43)	1.17*** (.44)
Yes/No Votes	102/31	102/287	117/272
LR Test (Chi-Square)	32.35	174.28	189.45

Note: Dependent variable in the logit = 1 if the statement was true for the House member (i.e. yes = 1).
Standard errors are in parentheses
***statistically significant at 1% level
**statistically significant at 5% level
*statistically significant at the 10% level

tors. After the TRI amendment passed in an initial vote, opponents of the bill organized an intensive lobbying campaign against the information provision measure. Table III reveals how the additional scrutiny changed voting patterns on the bill. On the initial vote on the bill the district-level incidence variables were not statistically significant. Legislators were more likely to favor information provision the more liberal their constituents, the higher their support for environmental measures in general, the greater the environmental group membership in their area, and the lower their support for oil and gas interests (as evidenced by lower contribution levels). After the lob-

bying campaign intensified scrutiny of legislators' positions on this issue, however, Table I indicates that in the second vote on December 10, 1985, the district-level incidence of the policy instrument also became a statistically significant factor in legislators' decisions. The greater the amount of toxins released in a district, the less likely representatives were to favor the collection and release of pollution information. The more Superfund NPL sites in the district, the more likely the representative was to favor the dissemination of information about pollution. Additional lobbying by interest groups and the potentially heightened interest of affected parties in

TABLE III
The Impact of Additional Scrutiny on Congressional Voting on the Toxics Release Inventory

Variable	First Toxics Release Inventory Vote (12/5/85)	Among those who voted yes on the first TRI, voted yes on second TRI vote?	Among those who voted no on the first TRI, voted yes on second TRI vote?
Intercept	.33 (1.74)	1.66 (2.80)	4.22 (4.78)
Toxic Releases and Transfers (lbs.)	−5.42e-9 (3.50e-9)	−1.68e-8*** (6.66e-9)	−1.06e-8 (7.55e-9)
NPL Final or Proposed Sites (#)	.05 (.07)	−.02 (.18)	.36* (.20)
Non-NPL CERCLIS Sites (#)	.00009 (.005)	.01 (.01)	−.03* (.02)
Potentially Responsible Parties (#)	.006 (.006)	−.004 (.01)	.01 (.01)
1984 PAC $ from Chemical and Petroleum Firms	−.0003*** (.0001)	−.0005* (.0003)	.0003 (.0003)
1984 PAC $^{2} from Chemical and Petroleum Firms	1.13e-8 (8.28e-9)	1.28E-8 (2.51e-8)	−4.08e-9 (1.46e-8)
1984 Vote for Reagan (%)	−.07*** (.02)	−.01 (.03)	−.15** (.07)
Environmental Group Membership (Statewide, per 1,000)	.21*** (.07)	.43*** (.14)	−.18 (.15)
1986 League of Cons. Voters Score	.04*** (.008)	.009 (.02)	.03 (.03)
Democrat	1.50*** (.43)	−1.73 (1.35)	2.27* (1.34)
Yes/No Votes	183/165	164/17	12/151
LR Test (Chi-Square)	231.05	40.29	34.97

Note: Dependent variable in the logit = 1 if the House member voted in favor of the measure.

Standard errors are in parentheses

***statistically significant at 1% level

**statistically significant at 5% level

*statistically significant at the 10% level

the district caused legislators to take the district-level incidence of pollution into account.

Table III analyzes what led some legislators to change their position across the two votes. Among those who voted yes on the initial TRI vote, legislators were more likely to vote yes on the second vote on the amendment the lower the pollution level in the district and the higher the environmental group membership in the area. Representatives more sympathetic to the interests of chemical and oil firms were less likely to vote yes on the second TRI vote. Among those who voted against the TRI originally, representatives were more likely to vote yes on the second vote the greater the

number of NPL sites in the district and the more liberal their constituents. They were less likely to vote yes the greater the number of non-NPL sites in the district. These patterns are consistent with a story where additional lobbying and scrutiny led legislators from districts where residents were concerned about hazardous waste contamination or where constituents were generally liberal to find it in their interests to change their votes.

Table IV explores the contribution patterns of PACs in more depth. If the vote on the Superfund reauthorization were viewed as largely symbolic, then one would not expect PACs to penalize legislators who voted for the

TABLE IV
Tobit Models of 1986 PAC Contributions

Variable	11 Chemical and Petroleum Firm PACs	Chemical and Petroleum PACs, Primary Business	Chemical and Petroleum PACs, Primary or Secondary Business
Intercept	2760*** (568)	1060* (641)	3682*** (1090)
Voted for Toxics Release Inventory	–557* (332)	–625 (407)	–1012 (650)
Voted for Injury Liability	–332 (330)	385 (313)	283 (635)
Voted for Targeted Tax	–1104*** (315)	–954*** (288)	–2098*** (500)
Voted for Superfund Reauthorization	–35 (425)	381 (544)	530 (868)
Energy and Commerce Committee Member	914*** (364)	1621*** (471)	2415*** (754)
Ways and Means Committee Member	1051*** (400)	2936*** (501)	3876*** (798)
1986 League of Cons. Voters Score	–7 (6)	–.4 (7)	–2 (11)
Democrat	–314 (301)	169 (369)	60 (601)
Incumbent in 1984	–1343*** (356)	–686 (436)	–1397** (696)
1984 PAC $ from Relevant PACs	.7*** (.1)	.8*** (.1)	.7*** (.1)
Number of Observations	379	379	379
Log Likelihood	–2612	–3125	–3446

Note: Dependent variable is total PAC contributions ($) to a House member from a given set of PACs for the 1986 election cycle.

Standard errors are in parentheses

***statistically significant at 1% level

**statistically significant at 5% level

*statistically significant at the 10% level

bill. Votes on the policy instruments, however, would be worth more to firms since these votes involved specific amendments potentially worth billions of dollars to the industry and the detailed nature of the amendments left representatives some freedom to consider interests beyond those of the general electorate. The close votes on some of the amendments also meant that additional support by a representative would be more highly valued on these measures. If PACs in 1986 were attempting to elect legislators that had supported their interests in the past (or were rewarding legislators who had voted their way on important issues), Table IV indicates in part which votes were important in defining support for the industry. The specifications include the amount of PAC money contributed to the candidate in 1984 as a control for the general level of support by the industry for the candidate.[19] Three different aggregations of PACs are examined: PACs of the 11 chemical and petroleum firms estimated to bear 70% of the Superfund taxes (contributed in total an average of $2,040 per

19. Whether a Congressional member was an incumbent in 1984 is also included as a control, since first-term representatives may receive more from these industry PACs if the companies believe their races will be more contested and thus the contributions more appreciated. Media coverage indicates that chemical industry PACs do take into account (in addition to issue positions) whether a candidate has a "genuine need for campaign money" and a "good chance of winning." See *Chemical Week* [1984].

representative); PACs with chemical and petroleum businesses ($3,458 per representa-
tive); and PACs with primary or secondary
interests in chemical and petroleum industries
($6,406 mean). Different samples are exam-
ined since the Superfund votes may mean relatively more to the 11 companies bearing the
majority of the taxes than to companies which
only have a secondary interest in Superfund.

The vote on the reauthorization did not
have a statistically significant impact on the
amount of money received by a House member. For the 11 companies that paid 70% of
the Superfund taxes under the original financing system, the vote on the targeted tax was
central to defining support for the industry. A
legislator who voted for the targeted tax
(which entailed additional taxes of $3.1 bil-
lion on petroleum, $2.1 billion on chemicals,
and $2 billion from a tax on hazardous waste
disposal) received nearly $1100 less in contri-
butions from these firms. This is more than
half the mean contribution per representative
from these companies. These firms were also
likely targets of the TRI reporting requirements. A legislator who voted for the TRI received nearly $560 less from these firms.
Firms with primary or secondary interests in
the chemical and petroleum industries were
also likely to contribute less to a legislator
who voted for the targeted tax. Contributions
from these interests dropped by about a third
for representatives that voted for the targeted
tax.

The chemical and oil PACs gave much
more to legislators on the committees relevant
to chemical regulation and taxation, the Ways
and Means Committee and the Energy and
Commerce Committee. This is consistent with
a pattern of giving to maintain access to legislators with a greater ability to influence the
content of legislation, giving more to support
legislators whose efforts have an important
impact on industry legislation, or simply buying legislator effort in committee. For the oil
and chemical PACs as a whole, the general
environmental position of a legislator was not
important in determining the amount of PAC
money contributed. The League of Conservation Voters scorecard was not statistically significant in the contributions equations. Overall, these PACs gave support to legislators
based on their performance on votes of interest to the industry and their legislative power

on committees, not based on their general environmental stands or votes on symbolic issues.

VI. CONCLUSIONS

The results of this study indicate that the
theory of rational political ignorance can help
explain legislator preferences for policy instruments to control pollution. Controlling for
a legislator's general support for environmental programs, a representative was likely to
vote for specific policy instruments such as
targeted taxes, toxic tort reform, or the toxics
release inventory in part based on the concentration of costs and benefits from these policies in his or her district. Legislators from districts with more toxic emissions faced a di-
lemma in trading off support within their districts, for the proposed policies often would
increase the costs of polluting industries but
reduce the risks to residents from exposure to
hazardous chemicals. Perhaps because the
costs to polluters were concentrated among a
group likely to take action while the benefits
of a reduction in general toxics use would be
dispersed among constituents, legislators generally voted against environmental restrictions as toxic emissions increased in a district.
As the number of NPL sites increased in a
district, however, representatives were more
likely to vote in favor of pollution control instruments. This shift toward the interests of
those bearing pollution risks may be because
residents around NPL sites were more likely
to be attentive to legislator actions.

A comparison of legislator positions on
Superfund reauthorization versus voting on
the technical amendments also points out the
importance of allowing models of legislators'
decision processes to vary depending on the
type of vote analyzed. The vote in the House
on Superfund reauthorization was symbolic in
the sense that constituents were more likely
to see it covered in the press and could use it
as an indicator of their representative's support for environmental programs in general.
For this vote, legislator decisions were based
on the constituents' and the representative's
ideologies and the interests of attentive voters
such as those surrounding NPL sites. The variables relating to the district-level incidence of
the program, such as toxic emissions and the
number of PRPs had no explanatory power,
which could lead one to conclude that voting

on Superfund largely depended on ideology. In votes on policy instruments, however, the lower likelihood that these votes would be examined by most constituents and the significant interests at stake for polluters and some residents within the district and contributors within and outside the district meant that legislators took these interests into account. PAC contributions in 1986 confirm that legislators were rewarded for their positions on amendments rather than positions on final authorization or general environmental positions. To find the narrow interests that influence legislator behavior on a highly visible environmental program such as Superfund, one may have to look at voting on more narrow questions about policy instruments where the local incidence of costs and benefits is clear but monitoring by a representative's broader electorate is less likely.

APPENDIX
Descriptive Statistics

Variable	N	Mean	Standard Deviation	Minimum	Maximum
District Characteristics					
Toxic Releases and Transfers (lbs)	435	48,325,647	260,506,370	18,308	5.2e9
NPL Final and Proposed Sites	435	2.0	2.5	0	18
Non-NPL Sites	435	55.6	39.0	0	275
Potentially Responsible Parties (#)	435	26	31	0	201
Vote for Reagan, 1984 (%)	435	58.3	12.1	5.0	83.0
Environmental Group Membership (Statewide, per 1000)	435	8.7	3.1	2.5	20.2
Legislator Characteristics					
1984 PAC Contributions from Chemical and Petroleum Firms ($)	432	3,375	3,450	0	18,950
1986 PAC Contributions from 11 Chemical and Petroleum Firms ($)	392	2,040	2,818	0	17,250
1986 PAC Contributions from Chemical and Petroleum Firms, Primary Business ($)	392	3,458	3,376	0	22,600
1986 PAC Contributions from Chemical and Petroleum Firms, Primary or Secondary Business ($)	392	6,406	6,475	0	34,100
League of Conservation Voters Score, 1986	434	49.8	25.0	0	94
Legislator Dummies					
Democrat	435	.58	.49	0	1
Incumbent in 1984	435	.89	.32	0	1
Energy and Commerce Committee Member	435	.10	.30	0	1
Ways and Means Committee Member	435	.08	.28	0	1
Voted for Toxics Release Inventory, First Vote	349	.52	.50	0	1
Voted for Toxics Release Inventory, Second Vote	423	.50	.50	0	1
Voted for Injury Liability	423	.38	.49	0	1
Voted for Targeted Tax	426	.52	.50	0	1
Voted for Superfund Authorization	424	.92	.27	0	1

REFERENCES

Ackerman, Bruce A., and W. Hassler. *Clean Air, Dirty Coal.* New Haven: Yale University Press, 1981.

Arnold, R. Douglas. *The Logic of Congressional Action.* New Haven: Yale University Press, 1990.

Barone, Michael, and Grant Ujifusa. *Almanac of American Politics, 1988.* Washington: National Journal, 1988.

Becker, Gary. "A Theory of Competition Among Pressure Groups for Political Influence." *Quarterly Journal of Economics,* August 1983, 371–400.

Brehm, John, and James T. Hamilton. "Noncompliance in Environmental Reporting: Are Violators Ignorant, or Evasive, of the Law?" *American Journal of Political Science,* May 1996, 444–77.

Bronars, Stephen G., and John R. Lott, Jr. "Do Campaign Donations Alter How a Politician Votes?" Manuscript, University of Chicago, August 1994.

Buchanan, James, and Gordon Tullock. "Polluters' Profits and Political Responses: Direct Controls versus Taxes." *American Economics Review,* March 1975, 139–47.

Campos, Jose Edgardo L. "Legislative Institutions, Lobbying, and the Endogenous Choice of Regulatory Instruments: A Political Economy Approach to Instrument Choice." *Journal of Law, Economics, and Organization,* Fall 1989, 333–53.

Chemical Week. "Chemical PACs Pick their Candidates." August 15, 1984, 20.

Coates, Dennis. "Jobs vs. Wilderness Areas: The Role of Campaign Contributions." Manuscript, Department of Economics, University of North Carolina (Chapel Hill), 1993.

Crandall, Robert W. *Controlling Industrial Pollution: The Economics and Politics of Clean Air.* Washington, D.C.: The Brookings Institution, 1983.

Denzau, Arthur T., and Michael C. Munger. "Legislators and Interest Groups: How Unorganized Interests Get Represented." *American Political Science Review,* March 1986, 89–106.

Dewees, Donald N. "Instrument Choice in Environmental Policy." *Economic Inquiry,* January 1983, 53–71.

Downs, Anthony. *An Economic Theory of Democracy.* New York: Harper and Row, 1957.

Durden, Garey C., Jason F. Shogren, and Jonathan I. Silberman. "The Effects of Interest Group Pressure on Coal Strip-Mining Legislation." *Social Science Quarterly,* June 1991, 239–50.

Fort, Rodney, William Hallagan, Cyril Morong, and Tesa Stegner. "The Ideological Component of Senate Voting: Different Principles or Different Principals?" *Public Choice,* June 1993, 39–57.

Goff, Brian L., and Kevin B. Grier. "On the (Mis)measurement of Legislator Ideology and Shirking." *Public Choice,* June 1993, 5–20.

Grier, Kevin B., ed. "Empirical Studies of Ideology and Representation in American Politics." *Public Choice,* June 1993, 1–173.

Grier, Kevin B., and Michael C. Munger. "Committee Assignments, Constituent Preferences, and Campaign Contributions." *Economic Inquiry,* January 1991, 24–43.

Hahn, Robert W. "Jobs and Environmental Quality: Some Implications for Instrument Choice." *Policy Sciences,* 20(4), 1987, 289–306.

_____. "The Political Economy of Environmental Regulation: Towards a Unifying Framework." *Public Choice,* April 1990, 21–47.

Hall, Bob, and Mary Lee Kerr. *1991–1992 Green Index.* Washington: Island Press, 1991.

Hall, Richard L., and Frank W. Wayman. "Buying Time: Moneyed Interests and the Mobilization of Bias in Congressional Committees." *American Political Science Review,* September 1990, 797–820.

Hamilton, James T. "Pollution as News: Media and Stock Market Reactions to the Toxics Release Inventory Data." *Journal of Environmental Economics and Management,* January 1995, 98–113.

Hird, John A. "Congressional Voting on Superfund: Self-interest or Ideology?" *Public Choice,* October 1993, 333–58.

Irwin, Douglas A., and Randall S. Kroszner. "Log Rolling and Economic Interests in the Passage of the Hawley-Smoot Tariff." *NBER Working Paper No. 5510.* Cambridge, Mass.: National Bureau of Economic Research, 1996.

Kalt, Joseph, and Mark Zupan. "Capture and Ideology in the Economic Theory of Politics." *American Economic Review,* June 1984, 279–300.

_____. "The Apparent Ideological Behavior of Legislators: Testing for Principal-Agent Slack in Political Institutions." *Journal of Law and Economics,* April 1990, 103–31.

Kohlhase, Janet E. "The Impact of Toxic Waste Sites on Housing Values. *Journal of Urban Economics,* July 1991, 1–26.

Krehbiel, Keith. "Constituency Characteristics and Legislative Preferences." *Public Choice,* June 1993, 21–38.

Moriarty, Jo-Ann. "Dateline: Washington." *States News Service,* October 16, 1986.

Nelson, Douglas, and Eugene Silberberg. "Ideology and Legislator Shirking." *Economic Inquiry,* January 1987, 15–25.

Pashigian, B. Peter. "Environmental Regulation: Whose Self-interests are Being Protected?" *Economic Inquiry,* October 1985, 551–84.

Richardson, Lilliard E., Jr., and Michael C. Munger. "Shirking, Representation, and Congressional Behavior: Voting on the 1983 Amendments to the Social Security Act." *Public Choice,* October 1990, 11–33.

Stratmann, Thomas. "What Do Campaign Contributions Buy? Deciphering Causal Effects of Money and Votes." *Southern Economic Journal,* January 1991, 606–20.

_____. "The Effects of Logrolling on Congressional Voting." *American Economic Review,* December 1992, 1162–76.

U.S. Environmental Protection Agency. *1991 Toxics Release Inventory.* Washington, D.C.: 1993.

Vandoren, Peter M. "Can We Learn the Causes of Congressional Decisions from Roll-Call Data?" *Legislative Studies Quarterly,* August 1990, 311–40.

Yandle, Bruce. *The Political Limits on Environmental Regulation: Tracking the Unicorn.* New York: Quorum Books, 1989.

[12]

THE POLITICAL ECONOMY OF MARKET-BASED ENVIRONMENTAL POLICY: THE U.S. ACID RAIN PROGRAM*

PAUL L. JOSKOW and RICHARD SCHMALENSEE
Massachusetts Institute of Technology

ABSTRACT

The U.S. acid rain program enacted in 1990 gave valuable tradable sulfur dioxide emissions permits—called "allowances"—to electric utilities. We examine the political economy of this allocation. Though no Senate or House votes were ever taken, hypothetical votes suggest that the actual allocation would have beaten plausible alternatives. While rent-seeking behavior is apparent, statistical analysis of differences between actual and benchmark allocations indicates that the legislative process was more complex than simple models suggest. The coalition of states that produced and burned high-sulfur coal both failed to block acid rain legislation in 1990 and received fewer allowances than in plausible benchmark allocations. Some of these states may have received additional allowances to cover 1995–99 emissions by giving up allowances in later years, and some major coal-producing states seem to have focused on benefits for miners and on sustaining demand for high-sulfur coal.

I. INTRODUCTION AND SUMMARY

D ESPITE the attractive efficiency properties of "market-based" approaches to internalizing environmental externalities, such as emissions taxes or tradable emissions permit systems, these approaches have rarely been used.[1] United States environmental policy has relied instead on a vari-

---

* The authors are indebted to Amy Ando, Paul Ellickson, and, especially, Elizabeth Bailey for excellent research assistance and to the MIT Center for Energy and Environmental Policy Research for support. They are grateful for aid and guidance to Bruce Braine, Rob Brenner, Denny Ellerman, Dennis Epple, Robert Hahn, Karl Hausker, Brian McLean, Larry Montgomery, Richard Newell, Robert Stavins, Max Stinchcombe, and participants in seminars at Harvard University, Yale University, and the University of Texas, Austin. Despite all this help, only the authors are responsible for the views expressed in this article and any errors it may contain. Richard Schmalensee participated in the preparation of the Bush administration's acid rain proposals and in negotiations between the administration and the Senate in early 1990 on what became the Clean Air Act Amendments of 1990. Paul Joskow was a member of the EPA Acid Rain Advisory Committee, which worked with the Environmental Protection Agency to produce the regulations that implemented the acid rain program called for by that legislation.

[1] For discussions of other environmental programs employing economic instruments, see Thomas H. Tietenberg, Emissions Trading: An Exercise in Reforming Pollution Policy (1985); Robert W. Hahn & Gordon L. Hester, Marketable Permits: Lessons for Theory and

[*Journal of Law and Economics*, vol. XLI (April 1998)]
© 1998 by The University of Chicago. All rights reserved. 0022-2186/98/4101-0002$01.50

ety of source-specific "command and control" regulations that specify limits on emissions rates or mandate particular control technologies. Title IV of the 1990 Clean Air Act Amendments (1990 CAAA, Public Law 101-549) established the first large-scale, long-term U.S. environmental program to rely on tradable emissions permits (called "allowances" in the 1990 legislation) to control emissions. Its target was electric utility emissions of sulfur dioxide (SO_2), the major precursor of acid rain.

Any tradable permit scheme for controlling emissions must specify a quantity cap or emissions ceiling for each of the geographic emissions markets within which emissions permits can be traded. This emissions cap, in turn, defines the total endowment of emissions permits that will be in circulation in each emissions market. Any tradable permit scheme must also adopt a method for distributing those permits—by giving them away, by selling them at auction, or by some other means. The choice necessarily has distributional implications, and, in the presence of transactions costs or other barriers to trading, it has efficiency implications as well.[2] Because emissions permits are valuable and decisions about their distribution are made by political institutions, these decisions are likely to be highly politicized, reflecting rent-seeking behavior and interest group politics. In the U.S. acid rain program, the expectation was that allowances would be worth about $5 billion per year once the program was fully operational.

In this article, we examine how Congress, influenced by the executive branch and various special interests, distributed what was essentially (as we discuss below) a fixed endowment of SO_2 allowances among electric utilities in the process of crafting acid rain legislation. The literature contains essentially no empirical work on the distributional implications of alternative market-based control mechanisms, largely because there have been few applications of such mechanisms.[3] In particular, little attention has been devoted to how interest group politics and associated rent-seeking behavior

Practice, 16 Ecology L. Rev. 361 (1989); and National Economic Research Associates, Inc., Key Issues in the Design of NO_x Emission Trading Programs to Reduce Ground-Level Ozone, ch. 2 (1994). Roger G. Noll, Economic Perspectives on the Politics of Regulation, in 2 Handbook of Industrial Organization 1254 (R. Schmalensee & R. D. Willig eds. 1989), at 1275, discusses some of the political reasons such programs are rare.

[2] On efficiency implications in this context, see Robert N. Stavins, Transactions Costs and Tradeable Permits, 29 J. Envtl. Econ. & Mgmt. 133 (1995).

[3] For related work, see Noll, *supra* note 1; Bruce A. Ackerman & William T. Hassler, Clean Coal and Dirty Air (1981); Robert W. Crandall, An Acid Test for Congress? 8 Regulation 21 (1984); Robert W. Hahn & Roger G. Noll, Barriers to Implementing Tradeable Air Pollution Permits: Problems and Regulatory Interactions, 1 Yale J. Reg. 63 (1983); and B. Peter Pashigian, The Effects of Environmental Regulation on Optimal Plant Size and Factor Shares, 27 J. Law & Econ. 1 (1984), and Environmental Regulation: Whose Self-Interests Are Being Protected? 23 Econ. Inquiry 551 (1985).

affect the allocation of permits in a tradable permit system. This is a serious gap in the literature. The political acceptability of market-based mechanisms for internalizing environmental externalities will depend heavily on their distributional implications. Whenever valuable property rights are created by legislation,[4] the associated allocation decisions are likely to be highly politicized in much the same way as tax legislation or appropriations bills.[5] Understanding better how the political process deals with such allocational issues can help us to design environmental programs that are both economically efficient and politically acceptable.

It is difficult to apply some of the tools of modern political economic analysis to complex legislation of this sort, particularly when there are no meaningful votes.[6] However, since allowances are homogeneous and can be traded and banked, the distributive implications are easy to quantify. In this case, the allocation of allowances is similar to the allocation of government funds through the legislative appropriations process.[7] The availability of detailed data on the initial allocation of allowances permits analysis of the incidence of individual legislative provisions, as well as analysis of winners and losers under alternative allowance allocation schemes.[8]

The next section provides a brief overview of the tradable SO_2 allowance program created by the 1990 CAAA. Section III reviews important aspects

----

[4] Technically, the SO_2 allowances created by the 1990 CAAA are not property rights, since Congress can change the number of allowances issued or do away with them altogether without raising a constitutional claim for compensation (see Section 403(f) of the 1990 CAAA). In all other respects, however, allowances are treated as property rights. They are freely tradeable, a variety of market mechanisms are mediating transactions, and the EPA consciously allocated allowances to eligible parties for years beyond 2010 to provide confidence that they would be treated as durable property rights. All this would clearly make it politically difficult to alter allowance allocations in the future in response to new information about costs or benefits of reducing SO_2 emissions.

[5] Related research on congressional spending decisions has been performed by Lisa J. Kiel & Richard B. McKenzie, The Impact of Tenure on the Flow of Federal Benefits to SMSAs, 41 Pub. Choice 285 (1983); David P. Baron, Distributive Politics and the Persistence of Amtrak, 52 J. Pol. 883 (1989); and Steven D. Levitt & James M. Poterba, Congressional Distributive Politics and State Economic Performance, Pub. Choice (in press).

[6] See Noll, *supra* note 1, at 1270–72, for a general discussion of the use of empirical voting models to test interest group theories of legislative politics; see also Joseph P. Kalt & Mark Zupan, Capture and Ideology in the Economic Theory of Politics, 74 Am. Econ. Rev. 243 (1984); Pashigian, Environmental Regulation, *supra* note 3; and Sam Peltzman, How Efficient Is the Voting Market? 33 J. Law & Econ. 27 (1990).

[7] See, for example, Levitt & Poterba, *supra* note 5, and the literature they discuss.

[8] We have data on the allocation of allowances to individual *combustion units,* each of which consists of a combustion device (boiler or turbine) used to power one or more *generating units,* each of which consists of a single electric generator. Most combustion units power a single generating unit, so our use of the term *unit* for the sake of brevity in what follows should cause no confusion. A generating *plant* often houses several generating units, which may be of different scales, vintages, or types.

of earlier debates on legislation affecting SO_2 emissions. Section IV discusses the political development of the 1990 acid rain program. Section V examines the comparatively simple allocation of allowances in Phase I of that program, covering calendar years 1995 through 1999. Section VI discusses in more detail the provisions for allocating allowances in the first 10 years of Phase II, 2000–2009. Section VII compares distributional aspects and other features of the resulting allocation and of benchmark alternative allocation schemes. Section VIII presents the results of hypothetical votes by both Houses of Congress between actual and benchmark Phase II allocation patterns. Section IX employs regression analysis to relate differences between actual and benchmark patterns to a variety of variables designed to capture the influence of important interest groups, congressional leadership and committee influence, and state and national electoral politics. Section X presents a few concluding comments.

II. THE 1990 ACID RAIN PROGRAM IN BRIEF

Acid rain (or, more properly, acid deposition) occurs when sulfur dioxide (SO_2) and nitrogen oxides (NO_x) react in the atmosphere to form sulfuric and nitric acids, respectively.[9] These acids then fall to earth, sometimes hundreds of miles downwind from their source, in either wet or dry form. In North America, acid rain is a concern mainly in the northeast United States, particularly in the Adirondacks and New England, and in southeast Canada. It has been argued that in those areas acid rain damages aquatic life and harms trees in sensitive forest areas. The dominant precursor of acid rain in the United States is SO_2 from coal-fired and, to a much smaller extent, oil-fired power plants. These emissions are the focus of the tradable allowance program adopted in 1990.[10]

Title IV of the 1990 CAAA represents a fundamental change in the regu-

---

[9] U.S. General Accounting Office (GAO), Allowance Trading Offers an Opportunity to Reduce Emissions at Less Cost, at 13 (Report GAO/RCED-95-30, December 1994).

[10] Electric utilities accounted for about 70 percent of 1985 U.S. SO_2 emissions: coal-fired units accounted for 96 percent of this total, and oil-fired units accounted for the remainder; U.S. Environmental Protection Agency (EPA), National Air Pollutant Emission Trends, 1900–1993 (Report EPA-454/R-94-027, October 1994). The other 30 percent of emissions is accounted for by a wide variety of industrial, commercial, and residential boilers and process sources (including smelters and paper facilities), as well as by the use of diesel fuel for transportation. Aside from certain voluntary opt-in provisions contained in the 1990 CAAA, including these other sources in the allowance program was not given serious consideration. These sources are generally individually much smaller than utility sources and are much more diverse. Moreover, there were no systematic "baseline" emissions data available for these sources to provide a basis for allocating allowances to incumbents. On this issue, see Nancy Kete, The Politics of Markets: The Acid Rain Control Policy in the 1990 Clean Air Act Amendments, 217–21 (unpublished Ph.D. dissertation, Johns Hopkins Univ., 1992).

latory framework governing air pollution in the United States. Previous air pollution regulations focused on individual *sources,* their emission *rates,* and the application of specific *control technologies* to individual sources with certain attributes. The 1990 acid rain law, on the other hand, focuses on *aggregate* emission levels rather than individual sources, deals with the *emissions* of SO_2 rather than emission rates, places an aggregate *cap* on SO_2 emissions, and gives polluters extensive flexibility in choosing whether and how to reduce emissions at specific sources. The importance of this change of approach goes well beyond the introduction of interutility trading. In particular, the 1990 law gave utilities with multiple fossil-fired generating units enormous and unprecedented flexibility in complying with emissions limits even if they traded no allowances at all with other utilities.

Title IV of the 1990 CAAA was advertised as requiring a 10 million ton per year reduction in SO_2 emissions from 1980 levels by the year 2000. To achieve this goal, the law created a cap on SO_2 emissions from electric generating plants of roughly 9 million tons per year, effective in the year 2000 and beyond. This emissions cap was to be achieved in two phases. During Phase I (1995 through 1999), the 261 dirtiest generating units (in 110 generating plants) were required to reduce their emissions by roughly 3.5 million tons per year beginning in 1995.[11] In Phase II (2000 and beyond), virtually all fossil-fueled electric generating plants become subject to the national cap on aggregate annual SO_2 emissions. (All states had Phase II units except Idaho, which had no fossil-fueled generating units, Alaska, and Hawaii.)

The Phase I reductions and the Phase II cap were enforced through the annual issuance of tradable emissions allowances, each of which permits its holder to emit 1 ton of SO_2 in a particular year or any subsequent year.[12] Each unit has 30 days after the end of each year to deliver to EPA valid allowances sufficient to cover its emissions during the year. At that time the EPA cancels the allowances needed to cover emissions. Failure to produce the necessary allowances subjects the utility to substantial financial penalties and the need to make additional future emissions reductions. Allowances good in any particular year but not needed to cover SO_2 emissions in that year may be "banked" for future use. Owners of individual units

[11] These units are simply listed in table A of the 1990 law; they correspond to 263 *combustion* units. These units were selected because they had an emissions rate (ER) greater than 2.5 pounds of SO_2 per million Btus of heat input and a nameplate capacity of at least 100 megawatts.

[12] In fact, these allowances are like checking account deposits; they exist only as records in the EPA's computer-based allowance tracking system. This system contains accounts for all affected generating units and for any other parties that want to hold allowances. It can be used to transfer allowances from one account to another.

are free to decide what mix of emissions reductions and allowance transactions they will employ to meet each year's allowance constraint, and essentially no restrictions are placed on emissions reduction techniques. There is also no restriction on who may buy or sell allowances. Brokers have acquired some in hopes of future price increases, for instance, and environmentalists have acquired some in order to reduce emissions more than the law requires.

The units subject to Phase I reductions were issued a total of roughly 5.7 million allowances for each of the 5 years included in Phase I. The basic allocation formula for each unit in Phase I involved multiplying an emissions rate (ER) of 2.5 pounds of SO_2 per million Btus of heat input times baseline heat input (generally the unit's 1985–87 average). As we discuss in Section V, however, there were significant departures from this formula in the final bill, the most important of which was designed to favor the use of eastern high-sulfur coal. Phase I obligations cannot be met by shifting electricity production from a Phase I unit to units not affected by Phase I.

During Phase II, each utility generating unit is allocated a specific number of SO_2 allowances per year out of the roughly 9 million per year made available for the entire country. (When various bonuses are taken into account, about 9.4 million allowances are available annually from 2000 until 2009, and 8.95 million tons are available annually thereafter.) The allocation rules for the years 2000–2009, which we analyze in detail below, are specified in about 30 statutory provisions. The provisions for 2010 and subsequent years are only slightly less complex. During Phase II, utilities can cover their emissions with the allowances they were allocated, can buy allowances, sell allowances, or bank allowances for future use. Any individual or firm is free to buy and sell allowances as well.

In addition to giving allowances to each generating unit, the EPA has conducted small annual revenue-neutral allowance auctions since 1993. The auctioned allowances are acquired by the EPA by holding back 2.8 percent of the allowances issued to each unit, and each unit in turn receives a pro rata share of the proceeds of the auction. The auction provision was a response to concerns by independent power producers and rapidly growing utilities that an active market for allowances would not emerge, concerns strengthened by assertions during debates on the 1990 CAAA that utilities would hoard their initial allocations and refuse to sell at any price.[13]

---

[13] Until recently, some allowances were also held back for sale at a fixed price (which turned out to be well above market prices); any excess supply was later auctioned. Karl Hausker, The Politics and Economics of Auction Design in the Market for Sulfur Dioxide Pollution, 11 J. Pol'y Anal. & Mgmt. 553 (1992), discusses the political economy of these institutions; Paul L. Joskow, Richard Schmalensee, & Elizabeth M. Bailey, The Market for Sulfur Dioxide Emissions, Am. Econ. Rev (in press).

This type of flexible compliance mechanism requires an accurate method for measuring emissions and tracking allowances. Title IV requires utilities to install continuous emissions monitoring equipment, and the EPA's regulations contain powerful financial incentives to ensure that these monitors are operating accurately.

After the 1990 legislation was passed, EPA set up an Acid Rain Advisory Committee to assist it in developing the regulations required to implement Title IV and to provide advice on interpreting the statutory language. The EPA also created three internal teams to come to a consensus interpretation of the complex and interrelated allowance allocation provisions contained in Title IV. In order to record and defend its decisions, EPA documented the Phase II allocation methods in detail and produced the National Allowance Data Base (NADB) and Supplemental Data File (SDF).[14] The NADB and SDF are essentially large spreadsheets that display the calculations used to allocate allowances to each of 3,842 existing and planned electric units and, in order to do this, provide a good deal of unit-specific information from which allocations under alternative rules can be computed. These spreadsheets are the main source of data for the analysis that follows.

III. HISTORICAL BACKGROUND ON FEDERAL CONTROL OF SO₂ EMISSIONS

The structure of the 1990 acid rain program cannot be understood apart from the history of federal efforts to limit electric utility emissions of SO_2. The 1970 Clean Air Act Amendments, the first significant federal air pollution legislation, led to the establishment of national maximum standards for ambient concentrations of SO_2. States were largely responsible for meeting these standards in each local area. The 1970 Amendments also imposed a new source performance standard (NSPS) applicable only to emissions from *new* power plants, which took effect in 1971. According to the NSPS, the emissions rate (ER) for new coal plants could not exceed 1.2 pounds of sulfur dioxide per million Btus of fuel burned (0.8 pounds/mmBtu for oil). These regulations created a significant gap between the emissions rates of many existing plants and the rates permitted for new plants, thus providing a strong incentive to extend the lives of old, dirty plants.[15] Furthermore, in order to help meet the local ambient SO_2 standards, the states required some

---

[14] U.S. Environmental Protection Agency (EPA), Acid Rain Division, Technical Documentation for Phase II Allowance Allocations (March 1993).

[15] Pre-1970 plants were still subject to controls under State Implementation Plans (SIPs) required by the Clean Air Act to ensure that each state came into compliance with national ambient air quality standards. There was wide variation among the states in the aggressiveness of their SIPs and how they affected existing plants.

existing and new power plants to have high smokestacks to disperse emissions over a wider area. By keeping SO_2 in the atmosphere longer, however, tall stacks may increase ambient concentrations at other locations. They also generally encourage the formation of sulfates and sulfuric acid and thus increase the total amount of acid deposition, which may affect geographic areas hundreds of miles away.

Congress next amended the Clean Air Act in 1977. Ambient concentrations of SO_2 were again the focus of attention; acid rain was still not an issue. The political solution that emerged from the 1977 legislation and subsequent EPA rule making satisfied environmentalists, high-sulfur coal interests, and Midwestern utilities.[16] It required coal-fired plants built after 1978 both to meet the ER $\leq$ 1.2 constraint *and* either (*a*) to remove 90 percent of potential SO_2 emissions (as determined by the sulfur content of the fuel burned) or (*b*) to remove 70 percent of potential SO_2 emissions and to operate with ER $<$ 0.6. This "percent reduction" standard required all new coal plants to operate with flue gas desulfurization facilities—generally referred to as "scrubbers"—even if they burned low-sulfur coal.[17] This provision significantly reduced the advantage of low-sulfur coal as a means of compliance and effectively imposed a lower emissions rate on new sources in the West than in the East. As Ackerman and Hassler have stressed, this provision gave environmentalists the tighter NSPS they sought, but it raised the costs of SO_2 control and may well have dirtied the air on balance by encouraging utilities to burn high-sulfur coal and by strengthening incentives to extend the lives of old, dirty plants.[18] It is also generally viewed as a victory for high-sulfur coal producers and miners, since the scrubbing provisions reduced what would otherwise have been a very significant economic disadvantage for high-sulfur coal. Conversely, of course, Appalachian and, to a lesser extent, Western producers of low-sulfur coal lost. This legislation was viewed as a victory for most Midwestern and Northeastern coal-burning utilities and their customers, since old plants generally remained relatively lightly controlled,[19] and slow economic growth meant

[16] For more on this episode, see Ackerman & Hassler, *supra* note 3, Kete, *supra* note 10, at 158–59; Richard E. Cohen, Washington at Work: Back Rooms and Clean Air (1992), ch. 2; and Paul L. Joskow & Richard Schmalensee, The Political Economy of Market-Based Environmental Policy: The U.S. Acid Rain Program (MIT Ctr. for Energy & Environmental Policy Res., Working Paper 96-003, March 1996), Section 3.

[17] Oil-fired units built after 1978 also had to meet the 1971 ER constraint (ER $\leq$ 0.8) and to remove 90 percent of potential emissions; they faced no percent reduction requirement if ER $<$ 0.2, however. To avoid simply sending SO_2 emissions long distances downwind, the 1977 legislation sharply limited the use of tall smokestacks as a compliance strategy.

[18] Ackerman & Hassler, *supra* note 3.

[19] Controls had been imposed on some old plants by state environmental agencies in order to meet ambient SO_2 standards. The stringency of these controls varied greatly, however, and

there was little need to build new plants meeting the NSPS.[20] The big losers were those states, mainly in the West, that were using nearby low-sulfur coal and growing rapidly. Scrubbing effectively required these states to engage in costly cleanup of what was already clean coal and to bear a disproportionate share of cleanup costs because they were building a disproportionate share of new fossil-fueled capacity.

Total U.S. emissions of SO_2 peaked in the early 1970s and declined steadily during the 1980s. The focus of Clean Air Act regulation on new generating units, however, served to extend the economic lives of old, dirty plants that were not burdened with significant control costs. As a consequence of this ''new-source bias,'' by 1985 83 percent of power plant SO_2 emissions came from generating units not meeting the 1971 NSPS, and 63 percent were from units with ER $\geq$ 2.5.[21] By 1990, over two-thirds of acid rain precursors emitted by power plants were emitted by plants constructed before 1970.[22]

Table 1 shows that there were huge interstate differences in aggregate and per capita emissions in the mid-1980s. Differences in per capita emissions reflected differences in the amount of electricity generation per capita (largely reflecting differences in economic and industrial structures), in the use of coal of various types (reflecting accidents of geography and history), and in the vintages of generating plants in use. Per capita emissions tended to be highest in Midwestern states that had grown relatively little since 1970 and that are located near high-sulfur coal deposits. Emissions tended to be lowest in states that had new power plants and had made relatively little use of coal.

IV. FEDERAL ACID RAIN LEGISLATION[23]

Acid rain gradually emerged as a serious environmental and political issue only after 1977 because of pressures from environmental groups, Northeastern states, and, especially, Canadian objections to transborder pollution flows, arising from concerns about the effects of acidic deposition on prop-

---

they were rarely if ever as strict as the NSPS standard. Nonetheless, in part because of these controls, utility SO_2 emissions declined steadily after the mid-1970s, despite increased coal consumption.

[20] In the late 1970s, the technology of choice for meeting incremental generating capacity needs in the East, the South, and portions of the Midwest was nuclear power.

[21] These statistics were calculated using the National Allowance Data Base, described above. As noted above, Phase I covered only large units with ER $\geq$ 2.5.

[22] Kete, *supra* note 10, at 118.

[23] Joskow & Schmalensee, *supra* note 16, treat this history in more depth.

TABLE 1

HIGHEST AND LOWEST BASELINE SO$_2$ EMISSIONS PER CAPITA

Pounds/ Capita	Thousands of Tons	State	Pounds/ Capita	Thousands of Tons	State
1,029.5	962.5	West Virginia	53.6	42.7	Utah*
550.9	1,519.7	Indiana	53.5	82.7	Colorado*
548.4	126.7	Wyoming*	52.6	151.3	Virginia
439.3	806.6	Kentucky	44.6	396.8	New York
427.8	138.2	North Dakota	41.8	16.6	Montana*
425.6	2,303.1	Ohio	38.1	60.9	Connecticut
381.7	957.4	Missouri	32.5	68.5	Louisiana*
347.4	1,037.1	Georgia	27.9	62.8	Washington
341.0	807.2	Tennessee	25.9	97.8	New Jersey
281.0	557.5	Alabama	20.7	12.2	Maine
221.8	69.9	Delaware	6.8	3.3	Rhode Island*
197.9	1,174.7	Pennsylvania	4.3	1.3	District of Columbia
177.3	1,013.2	Illinois	.7	.9	Oregon
155.5	373.1	Wisconsin	.6	.2	Vermont*
143.0	72.6	New Hampshire	.5	6.8	California*

NOTE.—Emissions per capita are baseline sulfur dioxide emissions in pounds (from the National Allowance Data Base) divided by the average of 1980 and 1990 population. Baseline emissions for generating units operating in 1985 are generally the product of each unit's 1985 emission rate and its average 1985–87 fuel consumption. Emissions in thousands of tons are baseline generating unit sulfur dioxide emissions in thousands of tons (from the National Allowance Data Base). All states with emissions of 500,000 tons or more are shown except for Florida (635.2) and Texas (641.5). The only state with emissions of 50,000 tons or less not shown is South Dakota (25.8).

* Designated as a "Clean State" under sec. 406 of the 1990 CAAA because baseline average emissions rate (ER) from fossil fuel-fired steam generating units did not exceed 0.8 pounds per million Btu. "Clean States" not shown, with per capita emissions in parentheses, are the following: Arizona (70.50), Arkansas (63.55), Nevada (112.92), New Mexico (101.99), Oklahoma (60.66), and Texas (82.81).

erty, trees, and aquatic life.[24] Many acid rain bills were proposed by Western and Northeastern senators and representatives during the 1980s.[25] This

[24] On the early history of this issue, see Ackerman & Hassler, *supra* note 3, at 66; U.S. General Accounting Office (GAO), An Analysis of Issues concerning "Acid Rain" (Report GAO/RCED-85-13, December 1984); and Joseph A. Davis, Acid Rain to Get Attention as Reagan Changes Course, Cong. Q., March 22, 1986, at 675. To help resolve scientific disputes about the damages caused by acid rain, Congress created the National Acid Precipitation Assessment Program (NAPAP), which spent about $600 million through the end of 1990 (NAPAP, 1989 Annual Report to the President and Congress 7 (June 1990)). Its work had no visible effect on the 1990 legislative debates, however; see Leslie Roberts, Learning from an Acid Rain Program, 251 Science 1392 (1991), and Acid Rain Program: Mixed Review, 252 Science 1302 (1991). Among the reasons offered for NAPAP's lack of impact are its focus on "good science" instead of policy-relevant analysis and its lack of political support from the environmental community.

[25] See Cohen, *supra* note 15, at 36–44; Robert Hanley, Turning Off Acid Rain at the Source, N.Y. Times, December 11, 1983, at A12; Robert W. Crandall, Air Pollution, Environmentalists, and the Coal Lobby, in The Political Economy of Deregulation: Interest Groups in the Regulatory Process (Roger G. Noll & Bruce M. Owen eds. 1983); and the following pages in the indicated annual numbers of the Congressional Quarterly Almanac: 1982, at 425–34; 1983, at 340–41; 1984, at 340–42; 1986, at 137; 1987, at 299–301; 1988, at 142–48.

legislation generally called for reductions of from 6 to 12 million tons of SO_2 emissions per year from 1980 levels, targeted the dirtiest generating units for cleanup, and often involved some variant of the ER ≤ 1.2 constraint that had been applied to new units since 1971. In part because costs of cleanup varied considerably among existing units, these proposals often provided for more flexibility than traditional command and control regulation by, for instance, applying emissions limits at the state level rather than unit by unit.[26] Because the costs of these control strategies would have been heavily concentrated in a few Midwestern states, and projections suggested that electric rates there would have to rise significantly to cover those costs, some of the proposals included a national electricity tax to help to pay for cleanup costs and to "share the pain." Some proposals included mandatory scrubbing, while others did not.

During the 1980s, Midwestern and Appalachian high-sulfur coal-producing states generally opposed *any* new acid rain controls, while Western and Northeastern states opposed both a national electricity tax and any additional scrubbing requirements. Acid rain legislation was effectively blocked in the House by John Dingell (D-Mich.), who became chairman of the powerful House Energy and Commerce Committee in 1981. His main concern was that any legislation amending the Clean Air Act would likely tighten auto emission standards significantly, and he accordingly blocked all such legislation.[27] In the Senate, acid rain legislation was effectively blocked by the majority leader, Robert Byrd (D-W.Va.). West Virginia, with high per capita emissions of SO_2 and high production of high-sulfur coal burned in other states, was potentially a big loser from acid rain legislation. Completing the constellation of major "Just Say No!" forces on acid rain was President Ronald Reagan, who opposed environmental regulation generally.[28]

The political strength of the environmental movement grew dramatically as the decade of the 1980s proceeded, fueled in part by the Reagan administration's apparent intransigence.[29] Population continued to shift to the West and South, and the number of high-sulfur coal miners dwindled as high-

---

[26] E. H. Pechan & Associates, Comparison of Acid Rain Control Bills (EPA Contract No. 68-WA-0038, Work Assignments 94 and 116, OTA Contract Ls-5480.0, November 1989), compare six contemporary acid rain proposals.

[27] See, for instance, Cohen, *supra* note 16, at 29–32.

[28] Crandall, *supra* note 3, discusses other obstacles to assembling a winning pro-control coalition during the 1980s.

[29] The Sierra Club's membership increased more than sixfold between 1980 and 1990 (personal communication with Club officials), and the share of respondents agreeing with the following statement increased from 45 percent to 80 percent between 1981 and 1989 (Roberto Suro, Concern for the Environment, N.Y. Times, July 2, 1989, at A1): "Protecting the environment is so important that requirements and standards cannot be too high, and continuing environmental improvements must be made regardless of cost."

sulfur coal production fell and productivity improved dramatically.[30] The 1988 presidential election was won by George Bush, who had promised to be "the Environmental President" and had advocated looking "to the marketplace for innovative solutions" to environmental problems. George Mitchell (D-Maine), an ardent proponent of acid rain controls, succeeded Robert Byrd as Senate majority leader. Even before Bush's inauguration, staff at EPA, in the vice president's office, and elsewhere in the executive branch began work on a set of proposed amendments to the Clean Air Act that would deal with acid rain, as well as toxic air pollutants, urban smog, and other air quality issues.[31] Work on acid rain was heavily influenced by an emissions-trading proposal that had been circulated during 1988 by the Environmental Defense Fund (EDF). Though there were concerns about both the workability of the EDF proposal and the size of the emissions reductions it required (12 million tons from 1980 levels), relying on tradable permits to control acid rain would respond to Bush's call to look "to the marketplace" and could reduce control costs. Moreover, it was hoped that EDF's support would provide protection against knee-jerk antimarket attacks from other environmental groups. While some EPA staff clearly preferred traditional command and control methods, strong support developed within the agency, and the basic idea of using tradable permits to control acid rain was adopted by the Bush administration without much internal warfare.

The administration's Clean Air proposal was announced in general terms in June 1989, and draft legislation was released the following month. In the House, the administration's bill went to the Committee on Energy and Commerce, still chaired by John Dingell (D-Mich.). The acid rain Title was sent to the Subcommittee on Energy and Power, chaired by Philip Sharp (D-Ind.). Indiana had large emissions from old dirty plants, and while Sharp had earlier joined in supporting some modest acid rain control proposals, he opposed stringent controls targeted at existing plants without significant cost sharing with other regions. He had advocated paying for acid rain abatement through a national electricity tax.

On the Senate side, the administration's bill went to the Subcommittee on Environmental Protection, chaired by Max Baucus (D-Mont.), of the Committee on Environment and Public Works, chaired by Quentin Burdick (D-N.Dak.). Fifteen of the 16 members of the full committee were also

---

[30] Between 1980 and 1990, the average daily employment of miners in Eastern mines (both high-sulfur and low-sulfur) fell from 202,039 to 115,216 (Coal Data (National Coal Association, various years)).

[31] For a contemporary view of this process, see Margaret E. Kriz, Politics in the Air, Nat'l J., May 6, 1989, at 1098.

members of the Environmental Protection Subcommittee, and Burdick was not much interested in environmental policy, so all the action was in the Baucus subcommittee. Montana, a state that both produces and uses low-sulfur coal, was one of the losers in the 1977 amendments.

The Senate and House committees differed substantially in regional composition and support for environmental legislation.[32] Five of 16 senators on Environment and Public Works were from New England, where concerns about acid rain were high. On the House side, however, New Englanders were outnumbered 41 to 2 on Energy and Commerce. While the Senate committee had representation from neither the states with the highest SO_2 emissions nor the largest Eastern coal-producing states, these states were well represented on Energy and Commerce. Only 31 percent of the senators on Environment and Public Works were from states with (old, dirty) Phase I plants, as compared to 56 percent of representatives on Energy and Commerce. As one might expect, the Senate committee had members who were substantially more inclined to support environmental legislation than their counterparts in the House.

In mid-November, after four days of debate and one day of markup, the Senate Committee on Environment and Public Works approved Clean Air legislation written by its staff by a 15–1 vote.[33] The president threatened to veto the committee's bill unless its costs were reduced substantially, and the bill was poorly received on the Senate floor. In an attempt to produce acceptable legislation, the majority leader, Senator Mitchell, convened a set of closed-door sessions involving senators and administration officials beginning in early February. These meetings were open to all senators and their staffs, and states with large stakes in the acid rain Title were well represented when it was discussed.

The Senate negotiators modified the administration's relatively simple rules for determining Phase II allowance endowments. They also brought forward the starting dates of both phases by a year, thus producing greater

---

[32] Joskow & Schmalensee, *supra* note 16, provide more on the points in this paragraph.

[33] At the insistence of Alan Simpson (R-Wyo.), representing a state that both produced and burned large quantities of low-sulfur coal, the committee bill contained a provision purporting to repeal the "percent reduction" provision of the 1977 amendments. This provision was retained in the final legislation, and the EPA was given 3 years to produce a new NSPS. As of January 1998, however, it had not yet done so. The repeal provision requires that any new NSPS allow no unit to emit more than it would have been allowed to emit under the 1978 NSPS. But this requirement is a "Catch-22," since the 1978 NSPS always requires that emissions be less than the sulfur content of the coal burned (the essence of "percent removal"). Thus the only way to ensure that a unit emits no more than it would have been allowed to emit under the 1978 NSPS is to install a scrubber! In addition, we are told that state regulations effectively require scrubbing in areas where new coal-fired plants have been built, so that there has not been strong industry pressure to revise the 1978 NSPS.

emissions reductions in 1995 and 2000 than the administration's proposal.[34] In response to efforts by Robert Byrd (D-W.Va.) and other senators from states producing high-sulfur coal, the incremental 1995 reductions were given back as "bonus" allowances for utilities that installed scrubbers rather than switching to low-sulfur coal in Phase I. The incremental reductions in 2000 were given back over the 2000–2009 period through a number of provisions.

A major issue in these negotiations and, after an agreement between the administration and the Senate leadership was unveiled in early March 1990, on the Senate floor was the so-called Byrd Amendment. This provision would have provided generous financial aid to high-sulfur coal miners whose jobs were eliminated by Clean Air legislation. The administration and the Senate leadership opposed this amendment and prevailed by a single vote.[35]

The bill subsequently developed in the House also modified the administration's simple allocation rules, but it retained the original administration start dates and ceilings for Phase I and Phase II.[36] Like the Senate bill, it provided incentives for scrubbing. A provision authorizing unemployment and job-training benefits for displaced workers was added on the House floor; it was not restricted to miners and had a much smaller price tag than the Byrd Amendment.

The acid rain Title produced by the conference committee was based

---

[34] See Kete, *supra* note 10, at 210.

[35] For discussions of this episode, see Richard E. Cohen, When Titans Clash on Clean Air, Nat'l J., April 7, 1990, at 849; and Phil Kuntz & George Hager, Showdown on Clean-Air Bill: Senate Says "No" to Byrd, Cong. Q., March 31, 1990, at 983. Senator Byrd called on longstanding relationships with his Democratic colleagues and on his power as chairman of the Appropriations Committee, and Democrats voted with him (and against the Senate leadership) 38 to 16. In addition, all Republicans from Midwestern and Appalachian coal-producing states voted for the Byrd Amendment, except for Senator Warner (R-Va.), despite strong administration and Republican leadership opposition. Finally, Senators Cochrane (R-Miss.) and McClure (R-Idaho) voted for the Byrd Amendment, and thus against both the White House and the Republican Senate leadership, even though they represented no high-sulfur coal miners. Senator Symms (R-Idaho) was talked out of doing likewise only in the last minute of voting. Given that these three senators were in the bottom 20 in terms of the AFL-CIO's evaluations of lifetime voting records, it seems unlikely that they were casting pro-labor votes for ideological reasons. Strategic motives are suggested by the facts that these three senators were in the bottom 10 in terms of the League of Conservation Voters' ratings of 1989–90 voting records and that the president had threatened to veto any legislation containing the Byrd Amendment. It is most plausible that these senators hoped that passage of the Byrd Amendment would force the president to carry out his veto threat and thus likely kill new clean air legislation.

[36] For a detailed comparison of the acid rain provisions of the House and Senate bills, see ICF Resources, Inc. (ICF), Comparison of the Economic Impacts of the Acid Rain Provisions of the Senate Bill (S. 1630) and the House Bill (S. 1630) (draft report prepared for the U.S. Environmental Protection Agency, July 1990).

mainly on the Senate bill, while the House prevailed on most of the rest of the legislation.[37] A relatively small provision for aiding displaced workers (Title XI) based on the House bill was added,[38] and the Senate's provisions for allocating allowances were modified.

The provisions of the law allocating allowances in Phase I remained fairly simple, but 8 dense pages of about 30 complex and convoluted provisions were developed to govern Phase II allocations. In order to ensure that the intended constraints on *total* Phase II emissions were satisfied in the face of a rising tide of proposed special interest provisions, work on the Senate/administration bill had quickly incorporated an overarching "ratchet" provision. This provision, which was not controversial and was retained in the final legislation, in effect said that at the end of the day total allocations under (almost) all other provisions would be scaled down to a specified total.[39] This provision had the effect of making negotiations about allowance allocations into a zero-sum game. It also implied that, all else equal, benefits from rules changes that would *decrease* somebody else's allowances would be widely shared. Thus, at least in the negotiations that led up to the passage of the Senate bill, debates about allowance allocations were conducted primarily in terms of proposed rules for *increasing* particular allocations, which were typically supported by arguments about fairness under autarchy.

V. PHASE I ALLOWANCE ALLOCATIONS

Table A of the 1990 CAAA lists the Phase I units and specifies allowances to be allocated to each. Eight of these units were added to table A before the Senate bill was passed in April. Though these additions were justified by technical corrections to earlier work, it is interesting that five of the eight units, accounting for 84 percent of the allowances allocated to these units, were located in Minnesota, New York, and Wisconsin. The two Wisconsin units had been retired in 1988, so that adding them to Phase I

---

[37] See Cohen, *supra* note 15, ch. 10; and Alyson Pytte, A Decade's Acrimony Lifted in the Glow of Clean Air, Cong. Q., October 27, 1990, at 3587.

[38] Of the total authorization of $250 million, less than $29 million had been spent for all displaced workers as of May 1995 (telephone interview, Employment and Training Administration, U.S. Department of Labor).

[39] When the EPA figured out the allocations required by the statute in 1992, the ratchet's operation reduced Phase II allowances by about 9.6 percent from the total implied by strict application of the other allocation provisions in the bill. The "ratchet" had the effect of reducing annual Phase II "basic" allowances from 9.876 to 8.90 million tons and thus, if "bonus" allowances are taken as fixed, of reducing total annual allowances allocated in the first 10 years of Phase II from 10.115 to 9.139 million tons (EPA, *supra* note 14, at 5). The large size of the "ratchet" announced in early 1992 was a great surprise to those involved in the process, most of whom had expected a ratchet of less than 5 percent.

clearly made their owners better off by the value of the allowances they were given. Since all three of these states had significant acid rain legislation on the books by 1990, adding the Minnesota and New York units to Phase I *and* using their 1985 emissions rates to determine their allowance allocations probably made the owners of these units better off as well.

Most commentators describe the annual table A allowance allocations as equal to emissions (in tons) from baseline fuel use and an ER of 2.5 pounds per million Btus.[40] The EPA's NADB reveals that this formula is only approximately correct. Moreover, table A does not fully describe the Phase I allocations. The table A allocations differ by more than 1 percent from those produced by applying this formula to the NADB data, which we will call the *Basic Rule,* in 44 cases. The absolute value of the difference exceeded 1,000 allowances per year for 17 units.[41] Most, but not all, of these differences reflect departures from the administration's original table A proposal. In large part, at least, these differences reflect the fact that the NADB contains more recent data than those employed in computations underlying table A.

Table 2 shows that at the state level, the table A allocations of Wisconsin, Indiana, and Missouri are well above those implied by the 2.5 ton/mmBtu Basic Rule, while Pennsylvania's is noticeably lower. The third column of Table 2 also shows the effects of two "bonus" provisions: Section 404(h), which affected one unit in Iowa, and Section 404(a)(3), which affected all units in Illinois, Indiana, and Ohio except for three plants that sell mainly to Department of Energy uranium-processing plants.[42] This latter provision was added in response to Midwestern pressures for some form of cost sharing—with care taken not to allocate valuable allowances to plants that sold electricity under cost plus arrangements back to federal facilities. It is worth noting as well that representatives from Indiana and Illinois were chairman and ranking member, respectively, of key House subcommittees. Ohio had the highest total emissions of any state in the country, and two representatives on the House Energy and Power Subcommittee, one of

[40] See, for instance, Reinier Lock & Dennis P. Harkawik, eds., The New Clean Air Act: Compliance and Opportunity, at 24 (1991).

[41] This does not count large, almost exactly offsetting differences for units 1 and 2 of Georgia Power's Bowen plant. These differences seem almost certain to reflect some sort of error or the correction of another sort of error.

[42] Hausker, *supra* note 13, at 567, notes that the Midwest bonus provision, added late in conference, was the single breach in the zero-sum barrier imposed by the ratchet provision. A third bonus provision, Section 404(e), would provide Phase I allowances to Union Electric in Missouri and Phase II allowances to both Union Electric and Duke Power. Because of pending litigation, however, no allowances had been issued under this provision by late 1995. Only about 4,000 allowances had been allocated under a final bonus provision, Section 404(f), which rewards using conservation or renewable energy to reduce emissions.

TABLE 2

PHASE I ALLOWANCE ALLOCATIONS BY STATE

State	Basic Rule	Table A Difference	Bonuses	Final Allocation	Absolute/% Difference from Rescaled Basic Rule	Extension Allowances
Alabama	230,947	−7	0	230,940	−10,381/−4.30	3,428
Florida	129,792	3,338	0	133,130	−2,492/−1.84	33,248
Georgia	581,599	1	0	581,600	−26,123/−4.30	0
Illinois	353,191	4,709	36,356	394,256	25,201/6.83	0
Indiana	640,855	9,485	66,724	717,064	47,424/7.08	104,323
Iowa	37,555	2,735	1,350	41,640	2,398/6.11	0
Kansas	4,226	−6	0	4,220	−196/−4.44	0
Kentucky	278,637	−387	0	278,250	−12,903/−4.43	82,587
Maryland	140,066	−526	0	139,540	−6,818/−4.66	7,110
Michigan	42,334	6	0	42,340	−1,896/−4.29	0
Minnesota	4,409	−139	0	4,270	−337/−7.32	0
Mississippi	54,609	1	0	54,610	−2,452/−4.30	0
Missouri	345,101	7,889	0	352,990	−7,612/−2.11	0
New Hampshire	32,207	−17	0	32,190	−1,463/−4.35	0
New Jersey	20,811	−31	0	20,780	−966/−4.44	6,242
New York	147,393	3,587	0	150,980	−3,034/−1.97	11,673
Ohio	863,191	89	96,920	960,200	58,237/6.46	167,442
Pennsylvania	536,121	−1,981	0	534,140	−26,063/−4.65	76,441
Tennessee	386,183	247	0	386,430	−17,100/−4.24	111,374
West Virginia	496,528	1,342	0	497,870	−20,961/−4.04	96,131
Wisconsin	130,004	13,376	0	143,380	7,356/5.55	0
Total	5,455,761	43,709	201,350	5,700,820	0/.0	700,000

NOTE.—Basic Rule allocations are computed by multiplying an emissions rate of 2.5 times baseline fuel consumption, in tons. The Table A Difference is the difference between the table A and Basic Rule allocations. Bonuses are from sec. 404(h) for the George Neal North unit 1 in Iowa and from sec. 404(a)(3) for units in Illinois, Indiana, and Ohio. The second to last column is the final allocation minus (Basic Rule rescaled to same total)/that difference expressed as a percentage of rescaled Basic Rule. The final column gives annual average Phase 1 extension allowances received, from sec. 404(d), after reallocations among utilities.

whom (Thomas Luken, D) had been heavily involved in debates over acid rain legislation proposed earlier in the 1980s.

The second to last column in Table 2 shows a comparison of the Final Allocation in the 1990 law with the Basic Rule allocation scaled up to a total of 5,700,820 tons. None of the differences exceed 10 percent of the Basic Rule benchmark, but at an expected price of $200/ton, a thousand-ton annual difference corresponds to a million dollars a year. The positive differences (gains) are much more concentrated than the negative differences (losses): the top three gainers (Ohio, Indiana, and Illinois) accounted for 93 percent of total gains, while the top three losers (Georgia, Pennsylvania, and West Virginia) accounted for 52 percent of the losses. Only four states have positive differences in excess of 5,000 tons per year, while eight states have negative differences of that magnitude.

One hypothesis that explains some of these differences is that the states that burned more coal than they produced, including Indiana and Ohio, focused their attention on acquiring additional allowances, while the states that produced more than they burned, including Pennsylvania and West Virginia, focused their attention on providing incentives for scrubbing and direct financial benefits for displaced coal miners. However, Georgia, which produced no coal, and Illinois, which produced about twice as much as it burned in 1990, conspicuously fail to fit this pattern.[43]

The last column in Table 2 shows the effects of a final important Phase I provision. In response to pressure from high-sulfur coal states, 3.5 million allowances (the "gain" from moving the start of Phase I from 1996 to 1995) were set aside to encourage the use of "technology" (that is, scrubbers) as an emissions reduction technique in preference to fuel switching. The main beneficiaries of this provision were utilities in Ohio, Tennessee, Indiana, and West Virginia and the high-sulfur coal interests in these and nearby states.[44]

---

[43] Both states had high total emissions and high emissions rates. Georgia had no representation on the Senate Committee on Environment and Public Works or the Senate leadership. On the House side it had nobody on the House Energy and Power Subcommittee and only one junior member (J. Roy Rowland, D) on the full Energy and Commerce Committee. It was represented on the House leadership by the Minority Whip (Newt Gingrich, R). Illinois also had no well-placed representation on the Senate side, but it had the ranking member of the Health and Environment Subcommittee (Edward Madigan, R), a member of both involved subcommittees (Terry Bruce, D), and a third member of the full committee (Cardiss Collins, D). As we discuss below, Georgia fared poorly in both Phase I and Phase II, while Illinois fared well in both phases. Illinois would have appeared to have done even better in Phase I if Illinois Power had applied for scrubber extension allowances, as had been expected when Title IV was being debated.

[44] Again, Georgia got nothing out of the scrubber bonus allowances, but it also had no high-sulfur coal miners to protect. Illinois miners benefited from the scrubbing incentives, and it was generally expected in 1990 that Illinois utilities would apply for a large number

Even though the Phase I allowance allocations have generally been described as following a simple rule, it is clear that the actual allocations were significantly influenced by special interest rent seeking. In addition to the differences between the table A allocations and those implied by the Basic Rule, large special allocations of allowances were given to three of the five states with the highest SO_2 emissions (see Table 1): Ohio, Indiana, and Illinois. All three also had substantial high-sulfur coal mining interests. Pennsylvania, West Virginia, and Kentucky, which had both relatively high aggregate emissions and more important high-sulfur mining interests, were not covered by this special provision. However, these six states plus Tennessee (with emissions just above Kentucky's but few high-sulfur miners) acquired almost all the bonus allowances made available to Phase I units that chose to reduce emissions by scrubbing. Georgia, number 4 in emissions, benefited from neither the special allocation nor the scrubber bonus.

This pattern suggests that Phase I allowances were used partially to compensate three of the high emissions states that were well represented on the key committees. Phase I allowances were also used to subsidize scrubbers in response to high-sulfur coal-mining interests. There is some evidence that the states with important coal-mining interests focused more on increasing scrubber allowances than on securing earmarked allowances. Georgia, which was not represented on the relevant committees, did particularly badly overall in the Phase I allowance allocation process.

VI.   Statutory Provisions for Phase II Allocations

Calculations of a generating unit's Phase II allowance allocations generally begin with "baseline" emissions, determined by the recorded emissions rate for 1985 and average heat input from fuel burned during 1985–87.[45] The simple rule at the core of Phase II allocates allowances equal to each unit's baseline fuel use times the lesser of its actual 1985 emissions rate and 1.2 pounds of SO_2 per million Btu, expressed in tons. The statute contains over 30 individual provisions that specify exactly how Phase II allowances are to be allocated. These rules fall into three general categories.

The first category contains provisions that specify variations from the simple rule above based on fuel type, unit age, unit capacity, and capacity

---

of extension allowances. Illinois Power eventually decided not to install scrubbers because its regulators refused to preapprove such investments for rate-making purposes. Illinois Power then became an important early purchaser of allowances.

[45] Special provisions were included for units that were not in operation in 1985 or were still under construction in 1990 when the Act was passed. Emissions rates for 1985 were used in all other cases because NAPAP (see note 24 *supra*) had constructed particularly good emissions data for that year.

utilization during the base period. These allocation rules were generally advertised as dealing with various "technical issues" associated with the fuel and operating attributes of units in these categories during the base period. These rules include special provisions for units that operated at low capacity factors during the baseline period due to mechanical problems or unusually low demand along with special allocations for small coal plants for which control options were particularly limited and costly. Other "technical arguments" supporting, for example, a special allocation for units that happened to burn lots of gas during the baseline period because gas prices were unusually low during that time, are more difficult to accept as being "non-political." As we show below, the allocation rules in this first category generally shift allowances from relatively dirty states to relatively clean states, especially those with oil/gas generating units.

The second category of allocation rules consists of those rules that are narrowly focused on special interests—either individual states or individual utilities. Table 3 provides the clearest examples. This table was developed by categorizing all Phase II units by applicable allocation rules and then searching for rules that appeared to be narrowly focused on a single state or a small number of generating units. Table 3 should remove any doubt that interest group politics was at work in the development of the U.S. acid rain program. Some of these provisions are clearly the work of influential legislators. Senator Burdick used his chairmanship of the Committee on Environment and Public Works to ensure that his constituents in North Dakota got special allocations for the lignite-fired units that generate electricity there by inserting Section 405(b)(3). In addition, Congressman Dingell seems to have provided regulatory relief for Detroit Edison through Section 405(I)(2).

It is more difficult to relate some of the other provisions in Table 3 directly to well-positioned congressmen from the states that benefited from them. Florida was not represented in the leadership of either House or Senate, and Senator Bob Graham (D-Fla.) and Congressman Michael Bilirakis (R-Fla.) were the only Floridians on the relevant committees. Nonetheless, Senator Graham managed to secure thousands of incremental allowances for Florida through Section 405(I)(1).[46] Section 405(c)(3) originated in the House, even though Springfield, Missouri, was represented by a first-term Republican not

---

[46] See Kete, *supra* note 10, at 207–10. The impact of this provision is capped in the statute at 40,000 allowances annually. Florida may have been treated well in part because it was a large state with competitive races for both senator and governor in prospect for the fall of 1990. (See Table 8 below for the definition of "competitive" used here.) At least one of the other Florida-specific provisions in Table 3 was added to the Senate bill at the insistence of the Republican leadership to give Florida's other senator, Connie Mack (R), something for which he could also claim credit.

TABLE 3

INCIDENCE OF SELECTED SPECIAL PHASE II (2000–2009) PROVISIONS

Section	Coverage	No. of Units, States (Systems) Affected	
404(h)	Phase I units 1990 ER $<$ 1.0, $\geq$60% ER drop since 1980; system ER $<$ 1.0	1	Iowa (Iowa Public Service)
405(b)(3)	Large lignite units with ER $\geq$ 1.2 in a state with no nonattainment areas	5	North Dakota
405(b)(4)	State has $>$30 million KW capacity; unit barred from oil use, switched to coal between 1/1/80 and 12/31/85	4	Florida (Tampa Electric)
405(c)(3)	Small unit, ER $\geq$ 1.2, on line before 12/31/65; system fossil steam capacity $>$250 MW and $<$450 MW, fewer than 78,000 customers	2	Missouri (City of Springfield)
405(c)(5)	Small units with ER $\geq$ 1.2; systems $>$20% scrubbed, rely on small units, have large units expensive to scrub	23	Ohio (Ohio Edison), Pennsylvania (Pennsylvania Power)
405(d)(5)	Oil/gas units awarded a clean coal technology grant as of 1/1/91	1	Florida (City of Tallahassee)
405(f)(2)	Operated by a utility providing electricity, steam, and natural gas to a city and one contiguous county; or state authority serving same area	48	New York (Consolidated Edison, Power Authority of the State of New York)
405(g)(5)	Units coverted from gas to coal between 1/1/85 and 12/31/87 with proposed or final prohibition order	3	Arizona (Tucson Electric), New York (Orange & Rockland Utilities)
405(I)(1)	States with $>$25% population growth 1980–88 and 1988 electric generating capacity $>$30 million KW	134	Florida
405(I)(2)	Large units with reduced actual or allowable emissions meeting five conditions on emissions and growth	6	Florida (Florida Power Company), Michigan (Detroit Edison)

on Energy and Commerce. Section 405(g)(5) was broadened in conference to include Tucson Electric, even though Arizona was not represented on the conference committee.[47] Finally, Section 404(h) originated in the House, even though the only Iowan on Energy and Commerce, Tom Tauke (R), was not on Energy and Power and was campaigning vigorously (though ultimately unsuccessfully) against an incumbent Democratic senator.

[47] Morris Udall (D) of Arizona was appointed to the conference, but specifically to deal with issues other than acid rain; Cong. Record, June 6, 1990, at S-7541.

These examples make it clear that the ability of a utility to obtain favorable Phase II allocation provisions in the statute did not necessarily depend on having one or more of the members of its state's congressional delegation on a key committee or in the leadership. States like Florida were of "partisan" political importance because of the presence of close races for the Senate or governor or their expected importance in the next presidential election. Utilities could also gain influence with influential members of Congress representing other areas through their trade associations, PACs, and political contributions. The existence of these alternative pathways through which legislators can be influenced is consistent with the difficulty scholars have had in finding strong empirical linkages between congressional appropriations and the concentration of interest groups in particular states and the seniority and committee assignments of their representatives in Congress.[48] We encounter similar difficulty in the regression analysis discussed below.

As compared with legislation in other areas, we do not believe that there is anything unusual about the provisions in Table 3. The EPA data simply make it easier to identify beneficiaries of these rules than of, say, functionally equivalent provisions in the tax code. Nor do we believe these are the only "special interest" allocation rules included in Title IV—just the most obvious. For example, Section 405(f)(1) provides special bonuses for oil/gas units with very low emissions rates during the baseline period. Units in over 30 states get some benefit from this provision, but the bulk of the benefits are concentrated in California, Florida, and New York.

The third category of Phase II allocation rules provides for general allocations of bonus allowances to units located in groups of states that fall neatly into the "clean" and "dirty" camps. As we discussed above, Section 405(a)(3) allocates 50,000 additional allowances each year to Phase I units located in 10 "dirty" Midwestern states. Section 406 made 125,000 allowances per year available to units in "clean states," which the governor of any of these states could access at his option in lieu of accepting other bonus allowances to which the units were entitled. (See Table 1 for the definition and list of "clean states.") These allocations clearly reflect efforts to "buy off" two well-organized groups of states with utilities at opposite ends of the dirty/clean spectrum.

VII. ALTERNATIVE ALLOCATION RULES AND THE DISTRIBUTION OF PHASE II ALLOWANCES

Given the number and complexity of Phase II allocation rules, interactions between them, and the global ratchet, it does not appear either practi-

---

[48] See Levitt & Poterba, *supra* note 5, and the references they cite.

TABLE 4

INITIAL PHASE II ALLOWANCE ALLOCATIONS CONSIDERED

ALLOCATION	CODE	CORRELATION WITH STATES' FINAL ALLOCATIONS		DESCRIPTION
		Total	Per Capita	
Proportional Reduction	PR	.882	.811	Baseline emissions ratcheted down by 42.3% to equal total Phase II allowances (i.e., the total in the Final Allocation)
Simple Rule	SR	.989	.985	(1) Units on line before 1986 receive (1985 heat input) × Max (1985 ER, 1.2), expressed in tons; (2) units on line in 1986 or later receive unratcheted basic allowances per Section 405(g); (3) allocations are ratcheted up by 8.5% to equal total Phase II allowances
Base Case	BC	.996	.991	(1) Allowances are allocated using basic provisions in the law that distinguish units by baseline emissions rate, fuel type, and vintage (for units on line in 1986 or later) as described in note 51; (2) allocations are ratcheted down by 1.4% to equal total Phase II allowances
Final Allocation	FA	. . .	. . .	Actual allocation of Phase II allowances, as provided for in the law
Cost Minimization	CM	.956	.887	Allocation of allowances that minimizes estimated total compliance cost in 2005 on the assumption that transactions costs rule out interstate trading; linear state-level marginal cost curves estimated from table A-16 in ICF, *supra* note 36, assuming intercepts are $115, as described in note 52 *infra*

cal or interesting to use the EPA data to try to sort out the effects of each individual provision as we did for Phase I in Table 2. Nor is there any simple, systematic way to tie these provisions to specific interest groups or legislators, since there are no votes to observe either on individual provisions or on the acid rain Title itself in isolation from the rest of the 1990 Amendments. Instead, we have elected to structure our analysis around the allocation patterns produced by the statute and by the four benchmark alternative allocation rules (PR, SR, BC, and CM) defined in Table 4 and discussed in more detail in the next several paragraphs. We perform a variety of direct comparisons in this section and then use hypothetical voting and regression techniques for further analysis in Sections VIII and IX, respectively.

A.   *Alternative Allocations*

The *Proportional Reduction* (PR) allocation is a natural starting point for most academic discussions, though it has been found to lack attractive distributional properties in several contexts.[49] The PR allocation implies that in the absence of interstate trading, all states would reduce their emissions by the same proportion to achieve the Phase II emissions cap. This rule implicitly ignores the fact that some states were already clean, and these states generally faced relatively high abatement costs.[50]

The *Simple Rule* (SR) resembles the core rule of the initial administration bill as well as some earlier proposals. Like those bills, it reflects the maximum emissions rate for new coal sources (ignoring the "percent reduction" requirement) in effect since the 1970 Clean Air Act Amendments. Each unit operating in 1985 is initially allocated allowances equal to its baseline fuel use times the lesser of its actual emissions rate and 1.2, expressed in tons. This allocation rule leads to significantly *lower* aggregate allowances than is provided for by Title IV. Thus, these initial allocations are then ratcheted *up* by 8.5 percent so that total allowances under SR equal the actual Phase II cap. The basic idea is to bring old generating units, which account for the bulk of SO_2 emissions, into conformity with the 1971 NSPS in aggregate. Because the ratchet up from this basic principle to the actual Phase II allocations is so large, following this rule makes it possible to meet the statutory emissions limit by allowing all existing coal units to operate with emissions rates substantially above 1.2 pounds per million Btu on average and to provide all other units with allowances well in excess of their baseline emissions.

The *Base Case* (BC) was produced by using the six basic provisions in the final law that distinguish units by baseline emissions rate, fuel type, and age—what we referred to in Section VI as the first category of allocation rules.[51] Our original idea was that differences between the SR and BC allo-

---

[49] See Tietenberg, *supra* note 1, ch. 5.

[50] See, for instance, Crandall, *supra* note 3, at 27.

[51] Base Case allowances were allocated as follows before ratcheting down, dividing the results of these formulas by 2,000 to convert to tons. (1) All units that began operation in 1985 or earlier and had ER ≥ 1.2 received baseline fuel use (in Btus) × 1.2, following Section 405(b)(1). (2) All units that began operation in 1985 or earlier and had 0.6 ≤ ER < 1.2 received baseline fuel use × min [actual 1985 ER, maximum allowable 1985 ER] × 1.2, following Section 405(d)(2). (3) All other units (with ER < 0.6) that began operation in 1985 or earlier, except units that derived more than 90 percent of their total fuel consumption (on a Btu basis) from gas during 1980–89 (the ">90 percent gas" units), received baseline

cations would have primarily technical rationales, with political influences affecting primarily the difference between BC and the *Final Allocation* (FA) actually employed. As we noted above and will demonstrate below, reality was not so tidy. The high pairwise correlations between FA and each of PR, SR, and BC shown in Table 4 reflect the huge interstate differences in emissions levels.

Finally, we used preenactment, state-level compliance cost estimates from a widely circulated report prepared to inform the legislative process to produce an estimate of the allowance allocation that would have minimized total compliance costs in the absence of interstate trading.[52] Other cost analyses were also developed for and considered in the legislative process and would, of course, imply different cost-minimizing allocations, so the *Cost Minimization* (CM) allocation considered here is more illustrative than definitive. This allocation is of interest both because of actual and perceived market imperfections,[53] and because autarchy was implicitly assumed in much of the actual debate about "fair" allowance allocations. Table 4 shows that the CM allocation is also highly correlated with the FA allocation, again reflecting the importance of baseline interstate differences.

Many in Congress seemed to believe that there would be significant obstacles to interstate allowance trading. It is thus of some interest to use our estimated marginal cost functions, along with consistent estimates of un-

---

fuel use × min [0.6, maximum allowable 1985 ER] × 1.2, following Section 405(d)(1). (4) All >90 percent gas units received baseline fuel use × 1985 ER, following Section 405(h)(1). (5) Units that began operation between 1986 and 1990 received estimated fuel consumption at a 65 percent operating factor × the unit's maximum allowable 1985 ER, following Section 405(g)(1). Finally, (6) all covered units under construction and expected to begin operation after 1990 received estimated fuel consumption at a 65 percent operating factor × min [0.3, the unit's maximum allowable ER], following Sections 405(g)(3) and 405(g)(4).

[52] Table A-16 in ICF, *supra* note 36, contains state-by-state estimates of emissions in 2005 (*a*) with no controls and (*b*) with a common marginal cost of control ($572/ton) that was projected to reduce total emissions to near the actual Phase II cap. These data imply a point on each state's estimated marginal cost of abatement schedule for 2005. To determine those schedules fully, we assume linearity and a common intercept. Table A-16 in ICF, *supra* note 36, gives the total cost of control for the case analyzed, including the cost of reducing utility NO_x emissions by 10.556 million tons. Comparing the total cost of SO_2 control implied by an assumed intercept value with the ICF total cost gives an implied cost per ton of NO_x reductions. An intercept value of $115 gives a cost per ton in the center of the range discussed by ICF, *supra* note 36, at C-12. (Intercept values of $80 and $150 yielded very similar results; see Joskow & Schmalensee, *supra* note 16, table 5.) The CM allocation was then computed by equating estimated marginal costs across states and setting total emissions equal to the Phase II cap. ICF, *supra* note 36, table A-16, projected California and Vermont to have zero SO_2 emissions in 2005 even with no controls; they received zero allowances under CM. At the other extreme, Oregon and the District of Columbia were projected to find it uneconomic to reduce emissions at all, even at an allowance price of $572/ton; their CM allocations equal baseline 2005 emissions.

[53] Stavins, *supra* note 2.

controlled emissions,[54] to estimate the total expected allocation-specific compliance costs in 2005 in the absence of interstate trading. These calculations imply that PR would impose costs about 30 percent above their minimum value, while SR, BC, and FA are estimated to involve total cost between 5 and 10 percent above the minimum. These latter differences seem unlikely to be much above the noise in this exercise. These results suggest that in the presence of transactions costs there was at least a plausible *efficiency* case for rejecting PR in favor of any of the other allocations.[55]

B. Gainers and Losers by Type of Generating Unit

Since utility service areas do not map easily into House districts, and since the Senate had somewhat more influence on the final allowance allocations than the House, states are the natural units of political economic analysis. However, most of the Phase II allocation provisions do not relate directly to states but, rather, to generating units with different attributes. The distribution of different types of generating units among the states is thus the main determinant, as a matter of arithmetic rather than of causality, of the effects of different allocation rules on individual states. To understand the latter effects, we begin with an analysis of how those rules treat generating units with different characteristics.

Table 5 summarizes baselines emissions by and allowances allocated to generating units of various types in Phase II under SR, BC, and FA.[56] Under SR, "dirty" units are allocated allowances equal to only about 40 percent of baseline emissions, while both "moderate" and "clean" units receive allocations above their baselines. If the Phase II allowance allocation process had been used partially to "buy off" the states with many dirty generating units, which were the main targets of the whole acid rain program, we would have expected to see allowances allocated to dirty units to be *increased* as we move from SR to BC and from BC to FA. Table 5 shows exactly the opposite: both moves *decrease* the aggregate allowances of dirty units, particularly large, very dirty units. (Table A units fall in this cate-

[54] From ICF, *supra* note 36, table A-16.

[55] One often-invoked principle of equity is equality of sacrifice. Using the coefficient of variation of states' estimated per capita compliance costs as a measure of inequality of sacrifice, PR is estimated to involve substantially less inequality than the other four allocations (Joskow & Schmalensee, *supra* note 16, table 5). Using this measure, CM and SR have the least inequality of sacrifice and FA the most. While these estimates must clearly be treated with considerable caution, the outcome of the political process suggests that the equity considerations that drove it are not well summarized by equality of sacrifice.

[56] Since the calculations leading to the CM allocation could only be done at the state level, a breakdown of this allocation by unit type is not possible. PR allocations are directly proportional to baseline emissions.

TABLE 5

EMISSIONS AND PHASE II ALLOWANCE ALLOCATIONS BY UNIT TYPE

UNIT TYPE	BASELINE EMISSIONS	IMPLIED INITIAL ALLOWANCE ALLOCATIONS		
		Simple Rule (SR)	Base Case (BC)	Final Allocation (FA)
Dirty: $1.2 \leq$ ER:	13,004	5,375	4,887	4,745
ER ≥ 2.5, ≥ 75 MW	9,451	2,901	2,645	2,412
Other dirty	3,553	2,465	2,242	2,333
Moderate: $.6 \leq$ ER < 1.2	2,793	2,881	3,107	3,186
Clean: ER $< .6$:	363	394	772	864
Coal	298	323	475	510
Oil/gas	61	67	292	303
Gas ($>90\%$)	4	5	4	50
New: Came on line 1986–90	230	250	238	209
Other: Planned, exempt, etc.	305	239	134	135
Total	16,695	9,139	9,139	9,139

NOTE.—Emissions and allowances are expressed in thousands of tons of SO_2. ER is the baseline emissions rate in pounds of SO_2 emitted per million Btu of fuel burned. Baseline emissions generally equal (1985 emissions rate × 1985–87 average fuel use) for all units on line in 1985.

gory.) Moreover, all other unit types on line by 1985 receive allowances under FA that in aggregate exceed their baseline emissions. This pattern is consistent with "We're already clean, don't pick on us!" having been a more effective equity argument than any notion of equal sacrifice. It is also consistent with a desire of senators from the "clean" Western states to pay back the Midwestern and Appalachian states for the mandatory scrubbing provision in the 1977 law.[57] Finally, along with the results of Section V, it is also broadly consistent with high-emissions states being willing to accept fewer Phase II allowances in return for more Phase I allowances.

Clean units do much better under BC than under SR.[58] The higher allocation to clean units mainly represents a gain by clean oil/gas units. The formula involved was nominally a response to an argument that these units had burned an "unusual" amount of gas in the base period, so that their baseline emissions were "abnormally"—and thus "unfairly"—low. In connection with both this provision and the "clean states" provision discussed below, it is instructive to consider the possible role of Senator Ben-

[57] See Margaret E. Kriz, Dunning the Midwest, Nat'l J., April 14, 1990, at 893, on this point.

[58] The lower allocation to "Other" under BC than under SR is an artifact; it primarily reflects a legislative decision to exempt some cogenerators and other units from the program altogether.

nett Johnston (D-La.) in promoting provisions favorable to gas-burning units. Senator Johnston represented a major gas-producing and gas-consuming state and chaired the Energy and Natural Resources Committee. Though this committee had broad oversight authority for federal economic regulation of electric utilities and could have plausibly asserted jurisdiction over aspects of the 1990 legislation, it did not do so. Moreover, it would have been natural for gas-burning electric utilities without more direct influence on the relevant committees to turn to Senator Johnston for assistance.

Differences between BC and FA reflect more than a score of other provisions, some of which appear in Table 3. Their most striking implication in Table 5 is the huge increase in allowances for units burning more than 90 percent gas. This results mainly from the "clean states" provision, Section 406, discussed above. This provision allocated a pool of bonus allowances to units in "clean" states in proportion to generation, not baseline emissions.

Table 5 shows that only the dirtiest large units did less well under FA than under BC, even though their FA endowments were increased by explicit bonuses for Phase I units. Small dirty units (<75 megawatts) receive more allowances under FA than BC because they are explicitly favored in the final legislation. In fact, because of bonuses for low capacity utilization (rationalized, of course, by arguments that the base period was unusual) and the special provisions affecting Florida and North Dakota listed in Table 3, allowances were also higher for large units with baseline emissions rates between 1.2 and 2.5.

C. Gainers and Losers by State

To examine the state-level implications of alternative allocation rules, we compute the differences between the corresponding implied allocations. The computation reveals that a shift from PR to SR would impose costs mainly on a few Midwestern states and provide benefits to most others. In addition, there is a good deal of similarity in the differences between the three most plausible alternative benchmark allocations (SR, BC, and CM) and the actual allocation (FA).[59] Accordingly, Table 6 displays the states with the largest (in absolute value) differences between FA and the average of the SR, BC, and CM allocations.

Table 6 reveals that Pennsylvania, West Virginia, and Kentucky, which all burn dirty coal and are large net producers of dirty coal, did particularly

---

[59] The major exception is Ohio, which receives many fewer allowances under CM than under SR or BC because ICF, *supra* note 36, estimates it to have the lowest abatement costs in the nation.

TABLE 6

STATES WITH LARGEST PHASE II GAINS AND LOSSES VERSUS AVERAGE
BENCHMARK ALLOWANCE ALLOCATION

AVERAGE GAIN			AVERAGE LOSS		
Absolute	Percent	STATE	Absolute	Percent	STATE
61,727	202.03	California*†	93,666	18.17	West Virginia
58,992	27.58	New York†	88,052	13.95	Pennsylvania*
57,126	15.39	Illinois*†	50,057	15.93	Tennessee
29,839	33.87	Louisiana	31,359	7.65	Kentucky
27,460	5.64	Florida	25,759	16.56	Virginia
27,168	20.65	North Dakota†	20,215	34.04	Washington*
19,311	16.33	Wyoming*	19,943	5.89	Alabama
18,590	35.00	Utah	15,687	4.06	Michigan†
18,190	17.26	Minnesota	14,945	2.82	Indiana†
15,515	30.75	Connecticut	13,984	17.18	New Jersey
13,383	11.12	Iowa	12,889	8.09	Maryland
12,678	11.07	Oklahoma	11,351	2.68	Georgia*
11,880	4.30	Missouri*	9,597	5.30	Wisconsin
11,513	18.21	Nebraska	6,194	4.77	Kansas*

NOTE.—Absolute gains and losses are differences between the state's actual (FA) allowance allocation and the average of its allocations under the SR, BC, and CM benchmarks. Percent gains and losses are absolute gains and losses as percentages of the average of the three benchmark allocations.

* States represented in Senate or House leadership. (The other state represented was Maine, which had an average gain of 2,597 (28.22%).)

† States represented in Senate or House committee leadership. (The other states represented were Montana, which had an average loss of 1,621 (5.24%), and Rhode Island, which had an average gain of 1,117 (47.28%).)

poorly in Phase II.[60] One hypothesis that explains this is that these states' congressional delegations focused on obtaining benefits for miners, consistent with what we observe for Phase I allocations, both as direct financial assistance and in the form of incentives to scrub, rather than on obtaining additional Phase II allowances. On the other hand, Illinois, which produced more than twice as much high-sulfur coal as it burned, did well in obtaining allowances in both Phases,[61] while Georgia, which produced no coal, did poorly in both Phases. Ohio and Indiana did much better in Phase I than in Phase II; this may reflect an atypically high valuation of near-term benefits.

Many of the clean states did rather well in Phase II, especially California and Louisiana. These states could focus on Phase II allocations since they had no Phase I units. Similarly, less than 40 percent of utility SO_2 emissions

[60] Recall that they also did poorly in Phase I; see Table 2. In Phase I, however, they did benefit significantly from the bonus allowances for scrubbing.

[61] Illinois' senators occupied no relevant leadership positions; in the House it was represented by the Minority Leader, Robert Michel (R), and by the Ranking Member of the Subcommittee on Health and the Environment, Edward Madigan (R).

in New York and Florida, which also did well in Phase II, were from Phase I units—as compared to over 70 percent in Ohio, Indiana, Illinois, West Virginia, and Georgia. Examination of the Senate and House committee and leadership structures, however, would not suggest that Louisiana or Florida would be winners in this game.[62] Indeed, the two best-positioned congressmen, Chairmen Dingell and Sharp, represented states that wound up doing particularly poorly in Phase II—though Sharp's state, Indiana, did well in Phase I.

Overall, the passage of acid rain legislation aimed at existing dirty units was a loss for the Appalachian and Midwestern coalition that had prevailed in the 1977 debate on SO_2 control. One might have thought that these states, which had the most to lose from this legislation, would have been able to mobilize their well-organized opposition to SO_2 controls and their representation in key leadership positions to obtain a disproportionate share of the allowances, to help to compensate for their high cleanup costs. However, Table 6 reveals that, with a few exceptions, including Illinois and Ohio, the opposite generally occurred. Not only did the states that produced and burned dirty coal lose in the large when they failed to block the passage of an acid rain law, they also generally lost in the small in the contest over the allocation of Phase II allowances. West Virginia and Pennsylvania, historically among the most aggressive opponents of acid rain legislation, were the biggest losers. On the other hand, a broadly distributed set of states that relied primarily on clean coal and gas-fired generation to produce electricity did well relative to these benchmarks. This result is consistent with the Phase II allowance allocation game being one of what Wilson has called "majoritarian politics,"[63] once the 1977 coalition lost its effort to keep the game from being played at all.

[62] New York and California do not seem likely winners either. New York was represented in the relevant leadership only by the ranking member on Energy and Commerce, Congressman Norman Lent (R). Lent was not generally thought to be nearly as powerful as Chairman Dingell, and Lent's district was not served by Consolidated Edison. California was represented here by Henry Waxman (D), Chairman of Energy and Commerce's Subcommittee on Health and the Environment. Chairman Waxman was primarily concerned with (and only had jurisdiction over) other parts of the 1990 legislation. The Senate majority whip, Alan Cranston (D-CA) took no visible part in the administration-Senate negotiations. California's other senator, Pete Wilson (R), was active in those negotiations, but his focus was on auto-related provisions. As we noted above, some of Louisiana's success in the Phase II "game" may reflect the efforts of Senator Bennett Johnston (D), who had some power in this setting because he chaired the Energy and Natural Resources Committee. California's significant gain on clean oil/gas units would then have been in part a byproduct of Senator Johnston's efforts on behalf of similar units in Louisiana.

[63] James Q. Wilson, The Politics of Regulation, in The Politics of Regulation (J. Q. Wilson ed. 1980).

VIII. Hypothetical Votes on Phase II Allocations

As is often the case with complex legislation, the details of Title IV were largely worked out behind closed doors. There was never a recorded vote on any aspect of allowance allocations. Since it is very difficult to deny a determined minority, let alone a majority, the right to offer an amendment on the Senate floor, the lack of *any* votes suggests, at least, that FA was some sort of majority rule equilibrium.[64]

One can explore quantitatively the plausibility of this notion by making some assumptions about voting behavior and seeing how obvious alternatives would have fared in hypothetical votes.[65] Because it is impossible to define the relevant set of alternatives rigorously or to defend ignoring linkages between allowance allocations and other issues in this and other legislation, this approach cannot provide a rigorous test of any hypothesis.[66] Nonetheless, it is interesting to see what can be learned by a simple analysis of hypothetical votes among the alternative Phase II allocations defined in Table 4.

The results of a number of simulated votes are contained in Table 7. It is assumed here that senators and representatives vote for the alternative giving their state more allowances—but only if the difference is noticeable. Given the complexity of the Phase II allocation process, states in which actual differences are relatively small could easily have gotten the sign wrong in the heat of debate. Moreover, as others have observed, if constituents are

---

[64] To be clear, since there is an alternative allocation with the same total number of allowances that can defeat any proposed allocation, there is no majority rule equilibrium in a game in which vectors of unit-specific allocations compete for votes. (*Proof:* Let X be a proposed equilibrium vector of unit-specific allocations, and let $W(X)$ be the set of elements of X that correspond to units represented (in whatever sense is relevant) by any arbitrary majority of legislators. Let X' be a vector formed from X by increasing all elements in $W(X)$ by ϵ and decreasing all other elements by the common amount necessary to equate the sum of the elements of X' to the sum of the elements of X. Then X' defeats X under majority rule, so X is not an equilibrium.) However, any votes would not have been on allowance vectors but, rather, on a limited set of alternative allocation rules. (Similarly, tax legislation is about the rules in the tax code, not the vector of real after-tax household incomes.) As our discussion should have made clear, significant analytical effort would have been required to determine the incidence of alternative systems of rules, putting proposed amendments to a bill on the floor at a significant disadvantage.

[65] We are unaware of any previous applications of this technique, though we would not be surprised to learn that some exist.

[66] On its face, for instance, dropping the special treatment of North Dakota lignite plants (Section 405(b)(3)) would seem to be a clear winner: one small state loses and all others win. But the others do not win much, and Senator Burdick, the powerful chairman of the Environment and Public Works Committee, would have been furious at the amendment's sponsors and supporters.

TABLE 7

RESULTS OF SIMULATED VOTES ON PHASE II ALLOWANCE ALLOCATION CHANGES

CHANGE AND VOTING TEST	STATES DROPPED	SENATE			HOUSE			ELECTORAL VOTES		
		Yea	Nay	Margin	Yea	Nay	Margin	Yea	Nay	Margin
PR → SR:										
None	0	70	24	46	303	126	177	379.5	147	232.5
|Δ| ≥ 5%	3	68	20	48	302	102	200	376.5	120	256.5
|Δ| ≥ 10%	7	62	18	44	257	99	158	327.5	115	212.5
PR → CM:										
None	0	62	32	30	235	194	41	300.5	226	74.5
|Δ| ≥ 5%	1	60	32	28	228	194	34	292	226	66
|Δ| ≥ 10%	6	54	28	26	199	184	15	258	212	46
SR → BC:										
None	0	48	46	2	220	209	11	274.5	252	22.5
|Δ| ≥ 5%	15	40	24	16	178	91	87	223.5	115.5	108
|Δ| ≥ 10%	31	28	6	22	147	3	144	178.5	9	169.5
SR → FA:										
None	0	50	44	6	209	220	−11	261	265.5	−4.5
|Δ| ≥ 5%	15	40	24	16	170	113	57	212.5	139	73.5
|Δ| ≥ 10%	22	34	18	16	158	75	83	194	92.5	101.5
BC → FA:										
None	0	42	52	−10	207	222	−15	251	275.5	−24.5
|Δ| ≥ 5%	19	28	28	0	138	106	32	170	136.5	33.5
|Δ| ≥ 10%	34	18	8	10	39	24	15	56	35.5	20.5
CM → FA:										
None	0	48	46	2	242	187	55	290.5	236	54.5
|Δ| ≥ 5%	7	40	40	0	197	168	29	236.5	210.5	26
|Δ| ≥ 10%	13	38	30	8	193	111	82	230.5	142.5	88

NOTE.—For each change, congressional delegations or electors of states that gain enough to pass the voting test indicated are assumed to vote yea; delegations/electors of states that lose enough are assumed to vote nay. The average of 1988 and 1992 electoral votes was used to tabulate the final three columns.

not much affected,[67] legislators may be free to indulge their own preferences—which may depend on ideology, logrolling, PAC contributions, or
a host of other factors. We have assumed three different thresholds of concern: any change at all, any change above 5 percent in absolute value, and
any change above 10 percent in absolute value. Those legislators whose
states' allowance changes do not pass the relevant threshold are assumed to
divide their votes evenly; for the sake of clarity they are simply omitted
from the vote counts in Table 7. For the sake of completeness we have applied the same calculations to electoral votes (including those of the District
of Columbia).

Table 7 makes clear that PR is a political nonstarter as well as potentially
expensive (Section VIIA above): a change from PR to SR or to CM passes
overwhelmingly in both Houses under any of our thresholds of concern.
There are just too many relatively clean states that would suffer under PR
for it to gather a majority against any alternative that concentrates the pain
in a smaller number of dirty states. This is consistent with SR being at the
core of most proposals made during the 1980s and with those proposals
having been blocked from passage by powerful legislators from states that
this change makes worse off, as discussed above. Once these legislators
could no longer simply block acid rain legislation, majoritarian politics increased their pain by reducing the allowances below those they would have
received under proportional reduction. This is also broadly consistent with
the ultimate rejection of efforts to fashion a cost-sharing program built
around a national tax on electricity, a possibility that was seriously discussed during the 1980s. Such a tax would, of course, have benefited precisely those states that lose from a shift from PR to SR, BC, or CM.

A change from SR to BC also passes both Houses, as well as the electoral college. Note that its margin increases uniformly as we impose a
stricter voting test. The actual allocation of allowances (FA) defeats CM in
the House and electoral college and generally wins in the Senate as well.
On the other hand, if we assume that every loss of allowances, no matter
how relatively or absolutely small, leads to a ''Nay'' vote, FA fails in the
Senate against BC and in the House against both BC and SR. When even
a 5 percent threshold of significance is imposed, however, FA beats both
alternatives easily in the House, easily beats SR in the Senate, and needs
only a nudge to beat BC in the Senate.

On the whole, Table 7 supports the notion that the Phase II allowance
allocation provisions were crafted with sufficient (implicit or explicit) concern for their viability on the floors of both chambers to make them no less

---

[67] See, for instance, Kalt & Zupan, *supra* note 6.

attractive than at least some obvious alternatives. If this had not been the case, one would expect to have seen votes involving alternative allocation provisions.

IX. ESTIMATING POLITICAL DETERMINANTS OF ALLOWANCE ALLOCATIONS

Our analysis thus far does not suggest that the Phase II allowance allocations can be easily explained by a small number of "standard" political economy variables. We appear to be dealing with a process of majoritarian politics (once the dam holding back acid rain legislation was broken) combined with a number of special interest provisions to satisfy narrow constituencies. Committees of jurisdiction were not unimportant in the legislative process, but, particularly in the Senate and in conference, issue-specific groups of legislators played critical roles.[68]

Because an abundance of quantitative information is available here, we can use regression analysis to examine whether and how variables measuring the importance of various interest groups, the presence of senators and congressmen in leadership positions, and competitive races for Senate, governor, and/or president in particular states help explain the observed allowance allocation in ways consistent with various theories of distributive politics. This analysis is similar in spirit (and results) to the extensive literature that relates congressional appropriations to various political variables (and that fails to find strong support for any simple theories of distributive politics).[69]

As above, our analysis concentrates on the Phase II allocation for years 2000—2009, both because it is more complex and important (in expected dollar terms) than the Phase I allocation and because it involves a larger sample size. Because of the importance of complex interstate differences in initial conditions, we focus on explaining *differences* between the states' actual allocations (FA) and the average of the allocations implied by our three benchmarks: SR, BC, and CM. (See Table 6 above.) This variable is defined as ΔPHASEII in Table 8.[70]

We focus on differences in numbers of allowances because allowances are homogeneous property rights that should have the same market value no matter to whom they are given. Therefore, the political cost of getting

[68] Cohen, *supra* note 16, stresses that this bill was not atypical of recent experience in this last regard.

[69] See, for instance, the references cited in note 5, *supra.*

[70] Joskow & Schmalensee, *supra* note 16, describe the generally minor differences between the results for this average variable and those obtained for each of the three differences involving individual benchmark allocations.

an incremental allowance for one's own constituents should not depend heavily on the state in which they happen to reside. Nonetheless, we performed a number of experiments involving percentage and per capita differences, without obtaining results qualitatively different from those reported below.

As Table 8 describes, we employed several exogenous variables intended to capture interstate variations in the importance of interest groups involved in debates about acid rain legislation. These include a variable that measures projected job loss in the coal-mining industry as a result of the legislation (HSMINERS),[71] variables that distinguish between clean and dirty states with different levels of SO_2 emissions (EMISSIONS) and different emissions rates (EMRATE),[72] and a variable designed to measure interest in relying on scrubbers by applications for Phase I extension allowances to support scrubber investments (PH1EXT).

One might expect that states for which HSMINERS is large would be very interested in obtaining allowances as compensation for losses of mining jobs. On the other hand, allowances are given to electric utilities, not miners. It is thus at least equally plausible, particularly in light of some of the results of Section VII, that representatives of these states would have neglected the pursuit of allowances in favor of seeking aid for displaced miners and/or attempting to strengthen incentives to scrub. Thus while states with high values of HSMINERS cared more than others about the acid rain program, it is unclear whether that concern should be expected to produce more or fewer Phase II allowances.

We would expect EMISSIONS and/or EMRATE to have positive coefficients if the "dirty" states were able to use the Phase II allocation process to make up for some of what they lost through passage of acid rain legislation aimed at existing dirty plants. Negative coefficients, on the other hand, would be consistent with clean states having been able to use the allocation process to their advantage—the pattern suggested by Section VII. Finally, we would expect PH1EXT to be negative if the states interested in scrub-

---

[71] Two other conceptually weaker mining-related variables were computed. (1) Except for Kentucky and West Virginia, which are divided into two regions each, ICF, *supra* note 36, projections of mining job losses are based on state-level net employment changes, rather than gross flows out of high-sulfur mining. (2) Aid actually received by May 1995 under the displaced worker provision (Title XI) that was pushed hard by mining-state representatives (see Section 4, above) amounted to less than $29 million and could not have been well anticipated in 1990. Both these variables were highly correlated with HSMINERS, and neither outperformed it significantly in regressions.

[72] We also considered using emissions from or allowances given to Phase I units as independent variables, but both were almost perfectly correlated with EMISSIONS ($\rho = 0.96$). The share of state emissions accounted for by Phase I plants did not suffer from this infirmity, but its coefficient never approached statistical significance in any experiment.

TABLE 8

VARIABLES EMPLOYED IN PHASE II REGRESSION ANALYSIS

Variable	Mean	Max	Min	SD	Description
ΔPHASEII	.00	61.7	−93.7	28.4	Difference between actual (FA) Phase II allowances and the average of allocations under SR, BC, and CM, thousands of tons per year from 2000 to 2009
HSMINERS	1.18	21.6	0	3.64	Estimated number of miners of high-sulfur coal, thousands: product of (fraction of 1992 demonstrated reserves with >1.68 lbs. sulfur per million Btu [from U.S. Energy Information Admin., U.S. Coal Reserves: An Update by Heat and Sulfur Content (DOE/EIA-0529, 1992), table C-1]) and (average daily employment of coal miners in 1990 [from National Coal Assn., Coal Data 1994, at 11–20])
EMISSIONS	348	2,303	.16	473	Baseline SO_2 emissions, thousands of tons
EMRATE	1.49	4.20	.01	1.03	State average SO_2 emission rate from fossil-fueled electric generating units, pounds per million Btu of fuel burned
PHIEXT	16.6	190	0	42.1	Phase I extension allowances requested for generating units in the state, average per year from 1995 to 1999, thousands of tons
SEN	.27	1	0	.45	Competitive Senate election dummy variable: equals one if state has a competitive Senate race in 1990 (races labeled "Best Bets" or noncompetitive in Nat'l J., March 17, 1990, were excluded), zero otherwise
GOVEV	6.14	50.5	0	9.95	Competitive and important governor's election: product of (a dummy variable for competitive governors race, constructed like SEN) and (the average of the state's 1988 and 1992 electoral votes)

72

continued overleaf

SWINGEV	10.0	48.2	.65	8.85	Important swing state: product of {[1 − |RPCT − 53.4|/50], where RPCT is the percentage of the state's popular vote cast for Bush in the 1988 Presidential election, and 53.4 is the sample mean of RPCT} and {the average of the state's 1988 and 1992 electoral votes}
HLEAD	.10	1	0	.31	Number of House leadership slots (5 total) filled by the state's delegation
HCR	.12	2	0	.39	Number of House committee (Energy and Commerce) and subcommittee (Energy and Power, Health and Environment) chairmanships and ranking member slots (6) filled by the state's delegation
HCOMM	1.35	8	0	1.84	Number of House committee (Energy and Commerce) slots (43) plus number of subcommittee (Energy and Power) slots (22) filled by the state's delegation
SLEAD	.08	1	0	.28	Number of Senate leadership slots (4) filled by the state's delegation
SCR	.06	1	0	.24	Number of Senate committee (Environment and Public Works) and subcommittee (Environmental Protection) chairmanships and ranking member slots (4) filled by the state's delegation
SSUB	.29	1	0	.46	Number of Senate subcommittee (Environmental Protection) slots (14) filled by the state's delegation
ΔPHASEI	.00	58.2	−26.1	13.7	Actual Phase I allowances minus allocation under rescaled Basic Rule (from Table 2), thousands of tons per year

NOTE.—Except as noted, data are from EPA (principally the NADB) and standard references on U.S. politics. Sample size = 48: Alaska, Hawaii, and Idaho are excluded from the sample, as from the acid rain program, and the District of Columbia is included.

bing (either because it was the least-cost control option or because of pressures to save high-sulfur coal miners' jobs) gave up Phase II allowances in exchange for greater scrubber incentives during Phase I.

We also computed two sets of more narrowly defined "political" variables. In the spirit of models of partisan distributive politics, variables in the first set are designed to measure states' electoral importance when the 1990 legislation was being considered. These variables include a dummy variable indicating whether there was a competitive election for the Senate expected in 1990 (SEN), the national importance of an upcoming competitive governor's race (GOVEV), and a variable that measures the importance of a state as a "swing state" in the 1988 presidential election (SWINGEV). Since 1990 was an election year, it seems plausible that states would have had more clout in the zero-sum allowance allocation game if they had a competitive senatorial race (SEN) or if they were an important state with a competitive gubernatorial race (GOVEV). It also seems plausible that important states that were swing states in the 1988 presidential race (SWINGEV) would have extra bargaining strength.[73] If these electoral importance variables influenced allocations, they should have positive signs. Since the issues in the acid rain program, and in the allowance allocation process in particular, did not reflect a clear split between Democrats and Republicans, we have not included variables measuring party affiliations or ideological ratings of each state's legislators.

The second set of political variables reflects the nonpartisan distributive politics literature, which implies that the ability of an individual legislator or a group of legislators with similar interests to affect acid rain legislation depends, in part, on whether they occupy positions on key committees or subcommittees or hold leadership positions that provide special influence over the provisions of the bill reported to the Senate or the House floor.[74] The variables in this second set include the number of House and Senate leadership posts (HLEAD and SLEAD), the number of House and Senate committee and subcommittee chairmanships and ranking member slots filled by a state's representatives (HCR and SCR), and the number of committee and/or subcommittee slots filled by a state's representatives in the

---

[73] One might also suspect that rich states would have more clout, all else being equal (perhaps because of the presence of campaign contributors), but income per capita had essentially no explanatory power in any equation.

[74] See Barry Weingast & M. Moran, Bureaucratic Discretion or Congressional Control, 91 J. Pol. Econ. 765 (1983); Barry Weingast & W. J. Marshall, The Industrial Organization of Congress; Or, Why Legislatures, Like Firms, Are Not Organized as Markets, 96 J. Pol. Econ. 132 (1988); Kenneth A. Shepsle & Barry R. Weingast, When Do Rules of Procedure Matter? 46 J. Pol. 206 (1984), and The Institutional Foundations of Committee Power, 81 Am. Pol. Sci. Rev. 85 (1987).

House and Senate (HCOM and SSUB). The leadership in the House (HLEAD) and Senate (SLEAD) generally has seats at any negotiating table about which they care. Committee membership and, especially, chairmanship or service as the ranking minority member can convey issue-specific influence via agenda control.

As we discussed in Section IV, on the House side both the Energy and Commerce Committee (chaired by Congressman Dingell) and two of its subcommittees played important roles in the Clean Air process, though only one of the subcommittees (chaired by Congressman Sharp) dealt with the acid rain program explicitly. Thus HCR counts all chairmen and ranking members involved in Clean Air, while HCOMM gives extra credit for membership on the subcommittee that dealt with the acid rain program. On the Senate side the process was very different. The Senate bill was essentially written in negotiations with the administration in early 1990. While Senator Baucus generally chaired the negotiation sessions, Senator Mitchell assumed the chair at key moments and was heavily involved throughout the process. Similarly, while most senators in the room at any one time were likely to be members of Senator Baucus's Subcommittee on Environmental Protection, the sessions were open to all senators, and many nonmembers participated personally on issues with which they were particularly concerned and had staff in regular attendance. The variables SCR and SSUB attempt to reflect the essential elements of this process.[75] We would expect all the congressional control variables in this second set to have positive coefficients.

Some of our regressions also included ΔPHASEI, a variable, taken from Table 2, that measures how well or poorly a state did in the Phase I allocation process relative to the ER = 2.5 benchmark.[76] Our idea here is that states that did relatively well in Phase I for reasons not reflected in our Phase II independent variables might also have done well in Phase II, reflecting the same unobserved political forces. This variable is clearly endogenous, and its coefficient cannot be given an unambiguous structural interpretation.[77]

---

[75] Idaho, with one subcommittee member, Steve Symms (R), was excluded from our sample because it had no fossil-fueled generating units and was thus not included in the allowance allocation process.

[76] This variable does not reflect actual or anticipated extension (scrubber bonus) allowances; it is from the second-last column in Table 2.

[77] Several additional variables were employed in a variety of unsuccessful experiments. One might expect that representatives of states with high electricity rates or expecting to need large numbers of allowances to accommodate growth would both be particularly interested in obtaining incremental allowances and particularly able to argue effectively for them, especially in light of Florida's ability to obtain Section 405(I)(1), but a range of experiments failed to support either hypothesis. (We used the product of the 1980–90 population growth

Table 9 presents illustrative estimation results for a series of equations in which ΔPHASEII is the dependent variable and alternative combinations of the three sets of variables discussed above are the independent variables. In the equation described in the first column of Table 9, as in all other equations estimated with a large number of plausible independent variables, most coefficients are not significantly different from zero.

Several "political" variables in that equation never had significant coefficients in any specification, and we drop them from further consideration. One of these was SEN, even though all of SEN's correlations with the other independent variables were less than 0.25. In addition, neither HCOMM nor SSUB ever had significant coefficients, perhaps reflecting the general decline in the importance of committees and the concomitant rise in the importance of other issue-specific groups stressed by Cohen.[78] The coefficient of SCR was never significant, even though that of HCR was positive and significant in all specifications.

Finally, the coefficient of HLEAD was generally negative and sometimes significant. Four of the five House leadership slots were filled by representatives from Georgia, Illinois, Missouri, and Pennsylvania—all high-emissions states. (The correlation of HLEAD with EMRATE is 0.44.) It seems most likely that there is no real "leadership effect," since a negative effect is implausible and SLEAD never had a positive and significant coefficient. The negative HLEAD coefficient simply tells us that "dirty" states did poorly in Phase II allocations despite being well represented in the House leadership. Accordingly, we drop both HLEAD and SLEAD from further consideration.

Dropping the variables just discussed leads us to the second equation in Table 9. That equation has two groups of independent variables, with high intragroup correlations and low intergroup correlations. The first group consists of four variables that we think of as measuring "dirtiness": HSMINERS, EMISSIONS, EMRATE, and PHIEXT. The lowest of the six pairwise correlations among these variables is 0.38, and the second-lowest is 0.49. The second group consists of three variables that we think of as measuring political/electoral "clout": GOVEV, SWINGEV, and HCR. The

---

rates and baseline emissions as a measure of growth-related allowance "needs.") Optimistic economists might expect that states with high baseline average or marginal costs would be both eager and able to obtain incremental allowances, all else being equal, but coefficients of such variables (based on ICF, *supra* note 36, as above) never approached statistical significance. Finally, we attempted to measure the importance of two other Clean Air issues, ozone nonattainment and alternative fuels, that might have been involved in cross-Title deals. Specifically, variables measuring the percentage of each state's population in severe or extreme ozone nonattainment areas and each state's production of corn and natural gas (inputs into alternative fuels) never had significant and sensible coefficients in any specification.

[78] Note 16 *supra*.

MARKET-BASED ENVIRONMENTAL POLICY   77

TABLE 9

PHASE II REGRESSION RESULTS

Independent Variable	Dependent Variable = ΔPHASEII					
Constant	−4.032	5.142	1.746	4.094	−2.646	−5.412
	(10.55)	(8.770)	(3.618)	(7.810)	(3.983)	(5.386)
HSMINERS	−.043	−.814	. . .	. . .	. . .	−2.660*
	(1.194)	(1.088)				(.976)
EMISSIONS	−.0311	.023	. . .	. . .	. . .	. . .
	(.0220)	(.020)				
EMRATE	1.400	−4.642	. . .	−9.054*	. . .	. . .
	(6.534)	(5.849)		(3.708)		
PHIEXT	−.604*	−.421*	−.334*	. . .	−.466*	. . .
	(.198)	(.158)	(.078)		(.065)	
SEN	−4.594	. . .	. . .	. . .	. . .	. . .
	(9.026)					
GOVEV	.393	.555	. . .	. . .	. . .	. . .
	(.593)	(.530)				
SWINGEV	−1.012	−.522	. . .	.942*	1.039*	.854*
	(1.030)	(.731)		(.433)	(.299)	(.404)
HLEAD	−22.79	. . .	. . .	. . .	. . .	. . .
	(15.02)					
HCR	30.67*	27.82*	30.47*	. . .	. . .	. . .
	(14.24)	(12.68)	(8.328)			
HCOMM	3.923	. . .	. . .	. . .	. . .	. . .
	(3.894)					
SLEAD	.788	. . .	. . .	. . .	. . .	. . .
	(13.84)					
SCR	9.549	. . .	. . .	. . .	. . .	. . .
	(13.85)					
SSUB	9.481	. . .	. . .	. . .	. . .	. . .
	(8.183)					
ΔPHASEI	. . .	. . .	. . .	. . .	1.140*	.745*
					(.200)	(.260)
R^2	.538	.461	.403	.184	.630	.379
SE	22.67	22.58	22.40	26.20	17.83	23.11

NOTE.—Standard errors are in parentheses. Sample size = 48.
* Significant at 5%.

lowest of the three pairwise correlations among these variables is 0.58. Within each of these groups, the different variables are conceptually quite distinct. If their performance in regression experiments could also be clearly distinguished, it might be possible to base a structural story on the results. These data, however, are not so kind.

Note first that in the second equation in Table 9, only one variable from each of these two groups has a coefficient that is significant at the 5 percent level. Similarly, in the 18 equations (not shown) with two variables from each group, at most one from each group is significant. In the 12 regressions with only one variable from each of these groups, however, all "dirtiness" coefficients are negative, all "clout" coefficients are positive, all 24 slope coefficients are significant at 5 percent, and 16 are significant at 1 percent. The third and fourth columns in Table 9 show the specifications within this set with the highest and lowest values of R^2, respectively.

These results provide strong evidence that "dirty" states tended to do poorly relative to our benchmarks in Phase II, while states with "clout" tended to do well. Unfortunately, high correlations within our two groups of independent variables make it impossible to use these data to determine with any confidence what elements or aspects of "dirtiness" and "clout" were most important. We are thus unable to discriminate among a large number of plausible structural hypotheses.

We ran the same set of 12 regressions just discussed using ΔPHASEI as the dependent variable and restricting the sample to the 21 Phase I states. All coefficients of both "dirtiness" and "clout" variables were *positive*, though only one of each was significant at 5 percent. These results at least suggest that the dirtiest states concentrated on Phase I, where they did relatively well on average, at the expense of Phase II, where they fared less well. These results also suggest that the "clout" variables are at least correlated with the ability to affect the legislative process positively—at least in the context of acid rain in 1990.

Finally, we re-ran the 12 regressions with one "dirtiness" variable and one "clout" variable on the right, adding ΔPHASEI as a third independent variable. All coefficients of "dirtiness" variables were negative and significant at 5 percent; all coefficients of "clout" variables were positive and significant; and all coefficients of ΔPHASEI were positive and significant. The last two columns of Table 9 show the specifications among these 12 with the highest and lowest R^2 values, respectively. These results suggest that states that managed to do well in Phase I for reasons not correlated with our "dirtiness" and "clout" variables also did well in Phase II. Unfortunately, there seems to be no way to use these data to tell what sorts of forces this effect might reflect, and the complex legislative history summarized above provides no obvious candidates.

This analysis suggests four tentative conclusions. First, and perhaps most important, there does not appear to be any simple, structural theory of distributive politics that is well supported by the data. In particular, the failure of most congressional leadership and committee membership variables seems inconsistent with theories in which power over most legislation is concentrated in the hands of a few people who happen to occupy key positions. This result does not in any sense refute the literature that emphasizes the role of committees, subcommittees, and leadership positions in congressional behavior, however. After all, Congressman Dingell and Senator Byrd

managed to block Clean Air legislation for a decade, with the help of a
Republican president opposed to new environmental legislation. But, once
acid rain legislation got through the gate, the distribution of influential committee assignment and leadership positions did not help much in predicting
allowance allocations. As our discussion of Table 3 indicates, some legislators with key committee posts clearly used them to benefit their constituents
through the allocation process, but others did not, and several states without
obvious influence on the relevant committees or in the leadership did quite
well.

Second, there is good evidence that "dirty" states—those on average
with many high-sulfur coal miners, high total emissions and emissions
rates, and much interest in using scrubbing to comply with Phase I emissions limits—did relatively poorly in the Phase II allowance allocation
game, all else equal. There is weak evidence suggesting that the very dirtiest states did relatively well in Phase I, suggesting in turn a willingness to
give up Phase II allowances to obtain Phase I allowances from states less
concerned with Phase I compliance. Third, there is strong evidence that
states with political "clout"—because they were large states that were
swing states in the 1988 presidential election, or because they were large
states that happened to have competitive gubernatorial campaigns in 1990,
or because they had representatives in the House Energy and Commerce
leadership—tended to do well in Phase II, and weak evidence that they also
did well in Phase I, all else equal.[79]

Finally, there is strong evidence that states that did well relative to our
Phase I benchmark, holding "dirtiness" and "clout" constant, also did
well in Phase II. In a way, this just reaffirms our first tentative conclusion:
something not captured by any of our "dirtiness" and "clout" variables
produced positive results in both phases. We do not know whether this factor primarily reflects differences in legislators' effectiveness, logrolling on
issues outside the acid rain Title (or even completely outside the Clean Air

---

[79] At the suggestion of an editor, we ran a number of regressions using as dependent variables SUM = $D(\Delta PHASEII) + \Delta PHASEI$ and DIF = $D(\Delta PHASEII) - \Delta PHASEI$, where
$D = (1.05)^{-5}$ is a discount factor reflecting the 5 years between the starts of Phases I and II.
As before, at most one "dirtiness" and one "clout" variable was significant at the 5 percent
level in any one regression. In both SUM and DIF regressions involving one variable from
each group (12 regressions each), all "dirtiness" coefficients were negative and all "clout"
coefficients were positive. In the SUM regressions, none of the "dirtiness" coefficients and
eight of the "clout" coefficients were significant. In the DIF regressions, all of the "dirtiness" coefficients were significant, along with six of the "clout" coefficients. These results
are consistent, at least, with the notions that the "dirtiest" states gave up Phase II allowances
in exchange for Phase I allowances and that "clout" was valuable. Mechanically, however,
these results reflect the high correlations between $\Delta PHASEII$ and both SUM ($\rho = 0.91$) and
DIF ($\rho = 0.80$).

bill), or other effects. Whatever this factor reflects, it appears likely from our earlier work that Illinois had it and Georgia did not.

We do not believe that these regression results should be interpreted as implying that interest group politics, congressional influence, or considerations of state and federal electoral politics did not play an important role in the allocation of SO_2 allowances. Our earlier discussion shows that there is clearly evidence of rent-seeking behavior and congressional influence at work. However, these effects are apparently too subtle and too complex to be captured in any but the crudest way in this kind of summary regression analysis. This is consistent with the results of related work analyzing congressional appropriations.

X. CONCLUSIONS

Environmental regulation is an excellent example of interest group politics mediated through legislative and regulatory processes. The history of federal regulations governing power plant emissions of SO_2 represents, in many ways, a classic case. Concentrated and well-organized interests in a few states that produced and burned high-sulfur coal were able to shape the Clean Air Act Amendments of 1970 and, particularly, 1977 to protect high-sulfur coal and impose unnecessary costs on large portions of the rest of the country. During most of the 1980s, the Midwestern and Appalachian utility and mining elements of this coalition managed to use their control over key congressional leadership positions, combined with presidential opposition to new environmental legislation, to block new acid rain legislation. However, once it became clear that acid rain legislation was likely to be enacted as part of a larger reform of the Clean Air Act, our analysis indicates that this coalition was unable to avoid appreciable control costs by obtaining a disproportionate share of emissions allowances.

With regard to Phase I allowances (apart from scrubber bonuses), three of the states with the greatest emissions and cleanup requirements (Ohio, Indiana, and Illinois) did relatively well compared to other states, while four others (Pennsylvania, West Virginia, Kentucky, and Georgia) did relatively poorly. Aside from Illinois, the utilities and, indirectly, high-sulfur coal miners in these states benefited from bonus allowances allocated to Phase I units that scrubbed. However, aside from Illinois, the traditional coalition of high-sulfur coal producers and high-sulfur coal users were not able to claw back a disproportionate share of Phase II allowances. Indeed, they lost even more during the legislative allocation process than they would have if several simple alternative allocation rules had been utilized. Specifically, the relatively larger number of clean states with little to gain per capita were more successful in Phase II than the relatively small number of ''dirty'' states with much to lose per capita.

If anything, the resulting allocation of Phase II allowances appears more to be a majoritarian equilibrium than one heavily weighted toward a narrowly defined set of economic or geographical interests. It is not strongly consistent with the predictions of standard models of interest group politics or of congressional control. In some cases, influential senators and congressmen managed to capture special benefits for their constituents. In other cases, particular states did much better (or much worse) in the allocation process than might have been predicted by simple theories of distributive politics. On average relatively "dirty" states did poorly in Phase II (perhaps because they were more concerned with Phase I and benefits for miners), while states with political "clout" did relatively well in both Phases. These results do not have great explanatory power, however, and we can only conclude that the fight to grab allowances, within a range of allocations that could not be easily defeated in the Senate or House, reflects both a more complex and a more idiosyncratic pattern of political forces than one might expect from previous work on the political economy of clean air.

Of course, none of this takes away from the fact that Title IV of the 1990 Clean Air Act Amendments put in place a major long-term program to reduce pollution using an innovative tradable emissions permit system. At least in theory, the allowance system gives utilities enormous flexibility in meeting aggregate emissions reductions goals and may thus allow them to meet those goals at much lower cost than under traditional command and control approaches. Demonstrating this theory in the large-scale acid rain program may lead to fundamental changes in environmental policies and significant reductions in their costs.

BIBLIOGRAPHY

Ackerman, Bruce A., and Hassler, William T. *Clean Coal and Dirty Air.* New Haven, Conn.: Yale University Press, 1981.

Baron, David P. "Distributive Politics and the Persistence of Amtrak." *Journal of Politics* 52 (1989): 883–913.

Cohen, Richard E. "When Titans Clash on Clean Air." *National Journal* (April 7, 1990): 849–50.

Cohen, Richard E. *Washington at Work: Back Rooms and Clean Air.* New York: Macmillan, 1992.

Crandall, Robert W. "Air Pollution, Environmentalists, and the Coal Lobby." In *The Political Economy of Deregulation: Interest Groups in the Regulatory Process,* edited by Roger G. Noll and Bruce M. Owen. Washington, D.C.: American Enterprise Institute, 1983.

Crandall, Robert W. "An Acid Test for Congress?" *Regulation* 8 (September/December 1984): 21–28.

Davis, Joseph A. "Acid Rain to Get Attention as Reagan Changes Course." *Congressional Quarterly* (March 22, 1986): 675–76.

Hahn, Robert W., and Hester, Gordon L. "Marketable Permits: Lessons for Theory and Practice." *Ecology Law Review* 16 (1989): 361–406.

Hahn, Robert W., and Noll, Roger G. "Barriers to Implementing Tradeable Air Pollution Permits: Problems and Regulatory Interactions." *Yale Journal on Regulation* 1 (1983): 63–91.

Hanley, Robert. "Turning Off Acid Rain at the Source." *New York Times* (December 11, 1983): A12.

Hausker, Karl. "The Politics and Economics of Auction Design in the Market for Sulfur Dioxide Pollution." *Journal of Policy Analysis and Management* 11 (1992): 553–72.

ICF Resources Incorporated (ICF). "Comparison of the Economic Impacts of the Acid Rain Provisions of the Senate Bill (S. 1630) and the House Bill (S. 1630)." Draft Report Prepared for the U.S. Environmental Protection Agency. Washington, D.C., July 1990.

Joskow, Paul L., and Schmalensee, Richard. "The Political Economy of Market-Based Environmental Policy: The U.S. Acid Rain Program." MIT Center for Energy and Environmental Policy Research Working Paper 96-003. Cambridge, Mass.: MIT, March 1996.

Joskow, Paul L.; Schmalensee, Richard; and Bailey, Elizabeth M. "The Market for Sulfur Dioxide Emissions." *American Economic Review,* forthcoming.

Kalt, Joseph P., and Zupan, Mark. "Capture and Ideology in the Economic Theory of Politics." *American Economic Review* 74 (1984): 243–77.

Kete, Nancy. *The Politics of Markets: The Acid Rain Control Policy in the 1990 Clean Air Act Amendments.* Unpublished dissertation, Johns Hopkins University, 1992.

Kiel, Lisa J., and McKenzie, Richard B. "The Impact of Tenure on the Flow of Federal Benefits to SMSAs." *Public Choice* 41 (1983): 285–93.

Kriz, Margaret E. "Politics in the Air." *National Journal* (May 6, 1989): 1098–1102.

Kriz, Margaret E. "Dunning the Midwest." *National Journal* (April 14, 1990): 893–97.

Kuntz, Phil, and Hager, George Hager. "Showdown on Clean-Air Bill: Senate Says 'No' to Byrd." *Congressional Quarterly* (March 31, 1990): 983–87.

Levitt, Steven D., and Poterba, James M. "Congressional Distributive Politics and State Economic Performance." *Public Choice,* forthcoming.

Lock, Reinier, and Harkawik, Dennis P., eds. *The New Clean Air Act: Compliance and Opportunity.* Arlington, Va.: Public Utilities Reports, 1991.

National Acid Precipitation Assessment Program. *1989 Annual Report to the President and Congress.* Washington, D.C.: U.S. Government Printing Office, June 1990.

National Economic Research Associates, Inc. *Key Issues in the Design of NO_x Emission Trading Programs to Reduce Ground-Level Ozone.* EPRI TR-104245. Palo Alto, Cal.: Electric Power Research Institute, July 1994.

Noll, Roger G. "Economic Perspectives on the Politics of Regulation." In *Handbook of Industrial Organization,* vol. 2, edited by R. Schmalensee and R. D. Willig. Amsterdam: Elsevier, 1989.

Pashigian, B. Peter. "The Effects of Environmental Regulation on Optimal Plant Size and Factor Shares." *Journal of Law and Economics* 27 (1984): 1–28.

Pashigian, B. Peter. "Environmental Regulation: Whose Self-Interests Are Being Protected?" *Economic Inquiry* 23 (1985): 551–84.

Pechan, E. H., & Associates, *Comparison of Acid Rain Control Bills.* EPA Contract No. 68-WA-0038, Work Assignments 94 and 116, OTA Contract L3-5480.0. Washington, D.C.: E. H. Pechan & Associates, November 1989.

Peltzman, Sam. "How Efficient Is the Voting Market?" *Journal of Law and Economics* 33 (1990): 27–63.

Pytte, Alyson. "A Decade's Acrimony Lifted in the Glow of Clean Air." *Congressional Quarterly* (October 27, 1990): 3587–92.

Roberts, Leslie. "Learning from an Acid Rain Program." *Science* 251 (March 15, 1991): 1302–5.

Roberts, Leslie. "Acid Rain Program: Mixed Review." *Science* 252 (April 19, 1991): 371.

Shepsle, Kenneth A., and Weingast, Barry R. "When Do Rules of Procedure Matter?" *Journal of Politics* 46 (1984): 206–21.

Shepsle, Kenneth A., and Weingast, Barry R. "The Institutional Foundations of Committee Power." *American Political Science Review* 81 (1987): 85–104.

Stavins, Robert N. "Transaction Costs and Tradeable Permits." *Journal of Environmental Economics and Management* 29 (1995): 133–48.

Suro, Roberto. "Concern for the Environment." *New York Times* (July 2, 1989): A1.

Tietenberg, Thomas H. *Emissions Trading: An Exercise in Reforming Pollution Policy.* Washington, D.C.: Resources for the Future, 1985.

U.S. Environmental Protection Agency (EPA), Acid Rain Division. *Technical Documentation for Phase II Allowance Allocations.* Washington, D.C.: U.S. Government Printing Office, March 1993.

U.S. Environmental Protection Agency (EPA). *National Air Pollutant Emission Trends, 1900–1993.* EPA-454/R-94-027. Washington, D.C.: U.S. Government Printing Office, October 1994.

U.S. General Accounting Office (GAO). *An Analysis of Issues concerning "Acid Rain."* GAO/RCED-85-13. Washington, D.C.: U.S. Government Printing Office, December 1984.

U.S. General Accounting Office (GAO). *Allowance Trading Offers an Opportunity to Reduce Emissions at Less Cost.* GAO/RCED-95-30. Washington, D.C.: U.S. Government Printing Office, December 1994.

Weingast, Barry, and Marshall, W. J. "The Industrial Organization of Congress; Or, Why Legislatures, Like Firms, Are Not Organized as Markets." *Journal of Political Economy* 96 (1988): 132–63.

Weingast, Barry, and Moran, M. "Bureaucratic Discretion or Congressional Control? Regulatory Policymaking by the Federal Trade Commission." *Journal of Political Economy* 91 (1983): 765–800.

Wilson, James Q. "The Politics of Regulation." In *The Politics of Regulation,* edited by J. Q. Wilson. Cambridge, Mass.: Harvard University Press, 1980.

[13]

THE CHOICE OF REGULATORY INSTRUMENTS IN ENVIRONMENTAL POLICY

*Nathaniel O. Keohane**

*Richard L. Revesz***

*Robert N. Stavins****

I. INTRODUCTION

The design of environmental policy requires answers to two central questions: (1) what is the desired level of environmental protection?; and (2) what policy instruments should be used to achieve this level of protection? With respect to the second question, thirty years of positive political reality in the United States has diverged strikingly from the recommendations of normative economic theory. The purpose of this Article is to explain why.

Four gaps between normative theory and positive reality merit particular attention. First, so-called "command-and-control" instruments (such as design standards requiring a particular technology's usage, or performance standards prescribing the maximum amount of pollution that a source can emit)[1] are used to a significantly greater degree than "market-based" or "economic-incentive" instruments (principally pollution taxes or charges[2] and systems of trade-

---

* Ph.D. student in Political Economy and Government, Harvard University. B.A., Yale University, 1993.

** Professor of Law, New York University School of Law. J.D., Yale Law School, 1983; M.S., Massachusetts Institute of Technology, 1980; B.S.E., Princeton University, 1979.

*** Professor of Public Policy, John F. Kennedy School of Government, Harvard University, and University Fellow, Resources for the Future. Ph.D., Harvard University, 1988; M.S., Cornell University; B.A., Northwestern University. Helpful comments on a previous version of the Article were provided by: David Charny, Cary Coglianese, John Ferejohn, Don Fullerton, Robert Hahn, James Hamilton, Robert Keohane, David King, Lewis Kornhauser, Robert Lowry, Roger Noll, Kenneth Shepsle, and Richard Stewart. Financial support was provided by the Dean's Research Fund, John F. Kennedy School of Government, and the Filomen D'Agostino and Max E. Greenberg Research Fund at the New York University School of Law. The authors alone are responsible for any errors.

1. Performance standards could specify an absolute quantity of permissible emissions (that is, a given quantity of emissions per unit of time), but more typically these standards establish allowable emissions in proportional terms (that is, quantity of emissions per unit of product output or per unit of a particular input). This Article uses the term "standard" to refer somewhat generically to command-and-control approaches. Except where stated otherwise, the Article refers to proportional performance standards.

2. The development of the notion of a corrective tax on pollution is generally

313

able permits[3]), despite economists' consistent endorsement of the latter.

At least in theory, market-based instruments minimize the aggregate cost of achieving a given level of environmental protection,[4] and provide dynamic incentives for the adoption and diffusion of cheaper and better control technologies.[5] Despite these advantages, market-based instruments have been used far less frequently than command-and-control standards.[6] For example, the cores of the Clean Air Act ("CAA")[7] and Clean Water Act ("CWA")[8] consist of federally prescribed emission and effluent standards, set by reference to the levels that can be achieved through the use of the "best available technology."[9]

Second, when command-and-control standards have been used, the required level of pollution abatement has generally been far more stringent for new pollution sources than for existing ones,

---

credited to Pigou. *See generally* ARTHUR CECIL PIGOU, THE ECONOMICS OF WELFARE (1920).

3. John Dales initially proposed a system of tradeable permits to control pollution. *See generally* JOHN H. DALES, POLLUTION, PROPERTY, & PRICES (1968). David Montgomery then formalized this system. *See generally* W. David Montgomery, *Markets in Licenses and Efficient Pollution Control Programs*, 5 J. ECON. THEORY 395 (1972). However, much of the literature can be traced back to Ronald Coase. *See* Ronald H. Coase, *The Problem of Social Cost*, 3 J.L. & ECON. 1, 39–44 (1960).

4. As is well known, a necessary condition for the achievement of such cost-minimization is that the marginal costs of abatement be equal for all sources. *See* WILLIAM J. BAUMOL & WALLACE E. OATES, THE THEORY OF ENVIRONMENTAL POLICY 177 (1988). In theory, pollution taxes and systems of marketable permits induce this effect, at least under specified conditions.

5. Market-based systems can provide continuous dynamic incentives for adoption of superior technologies, since under such systems it is always in the interest of firms to clean up more if sufficiently inexpensive cleanup technologies can be identified. *See* Scott R. Milliman & Raymond Prince, *Firm Incentives to Promote Technological Change in Pollution Control*, 17 J. ENVTL. ECON. & MGMT. 247, 257–61 (1989); Adam B. Jaffe & Robert N. Stavins, *Dynamic Incentives of Environmental Regulation: The Effects of Alternative Policy Instruments and Technology Diffusion*, 29 J. ENVTL. ECON. & MGMT. S43, S43–S46 (1995).

6. OFFICE OF TECH. ASSESSMENT, TECH. ASSESSMENT BOARD OF THE 103D CONGRESS, ENVIRONMENTAL POLICY TOOLS: A USER'S GUIDE 27–28 (1995).

7. *See* 42 U.S.C. § 7411(a),(b) (1994).

8. *See* 33 U.S.C. §§ 1311(b), 1316 (1994).

9. We use this label as a generic one. The various statutory schemes employ somewhat different formulations. *See, e.g.*, 33 U.S.C. § 1311(b)(1)(A) (1994) ("best practicable control technology"); *id.* § 1311(b)(2)(A) ("best available technology"); *id.* § 1316(a)(1) ("best available demonstrated control technology"); 42 U.S.C. § 7411(a)(1) (1994) ("best system of emission reduction"); *id.* § 7479(3) ("best available ·control techonology").

possibly worsening pollution by encouraging firms to keep older, dirtier plants in operation.[10]

The federal environmental statutes further these disparities by bifurcating the regulatory requirements that apply to new and existing sources. For example, under the Clean Air Act, emission standards for new sources are set federally, whereas the corresponding standards for existing sources are set by the states.[11] Similarly, the CAA's Prevention of Significant Deterioration ("PSD") program,[12] which applies to areas with air that is cleaner than the National Ambient Air Quality Standards ("NAAQS"),[13] imposes additional emission standards only on new sources.[14] The Clean Water Act sets effluent limitations for both new and existing sources, but these limitations are governed by different statutory provisions.[15]

Third, in the relatively rare instances in which they have been adopted, market-based instruments have nearly always taken the form of tradeable permits rather than emission taxes,[16] although economic theory suggests that the optimal choice between trade-

---

10. New plants ought to have somewhat more stringent standards because their abatement costs are lower, although such standards should be linked with actual abatement costs, not with the proxy of plant vintage. When new source standards are sufficiently more stringent, however, they can give rise to an "old-plant" effect, precluding plant replacements that would otherwise take place. *See* Matthew D. McCubbins et al., *Structure and Process, Politics, and Policy: Administrative Arrangements and the Political Control of Agencies*, 75 VA. L. REV. 431, 467 (1989); Richard B. Stewart, *Regulation, Innovation, and Administrative Law: a Conceptual Framework*, 69 CAL. L. REV. 1259, 1270–71 (1981). Empirical evidence shows that differential environmental regulations lengthen the time before plants are retired. *See* Michael T. Maloney & Gordon L. Brady, *Capital Turnover and Marketable Pollution Rights*, 31 J.L. & ECON. 203, 206 (1988); Randy Nelson et al., *Differential Environmental Regulation: Effects on Electric Utility Capital Turnover and Emissions*, 75 REV. ECON. & STAT. 368, 373 (1993).

11. *Compare* 42 U.S.C. § 7411(a), (b) (1994) (defining federal standards for new sources) *with id.* § 7410(a) (requiring state plans for existing sources).

12. *See* 42 U.S.C. §§ 7470–7479 (1994).

13. *See id.* § 7471.

14. *See id.* § 7475(a).

15. *Compare* 33 U.S.C. § 1316 (1994) (prescribing standards for new sources) *with id.* § 1311(b) (setting standards for existing sources).

16. Taxes (so-called unit charges) have been used in some communities for municipal solid waste collection. *See* OFFICE OF TECH. ASSESSMENT, *supra* note 6, at 119–21. Gasoline taxes serve primarily as revenue-raising instruments, rather than environmental (Pigouvian) taxes per se. Interestingly, the European experience is the reverse: environmental taxes are far more prevalent than tradeable permits, although the taxes employed have typically been too low to induce much pollution abatement. *See* Richard B. Stewart, Economic Incentives for Environmental Protection: Opportunities and Obstacles 42 (1996) (unpublished manuscript, on file with New York University). A more comprehensive

able permits and emission taxes is dependent upon case-specific factors.[17] Moreover, the initial allocation of such permits has been through "grandfathering," or free initial distribution based on existing levels of pollution,[18] rather than through auctions, despite the apparently superior mechanism of auctions.[19] Despite diversity of

---

positive analysis of instrument choice than we provide here would seek to explain this difference between the European and U.S. experiences.

17. With perfect information, tradeable permits sold at auction have the same effect as a tax. Under conditions of uncertainty, the relative efficiency of tradeable permits and fixed tax rates depends upon the relative slopes of the relevant marginal benefit and marginal cost functions. *See* Martin L. Weitzman, *Prices v. Quantities*, 41 REV. ECON. STUD. 477, 485–90 (1974); Gary W. Yohe, *Towards a General Comparison of Price Controls and Quantity Controls Under Uncertainty*, 45 REV. ECON. STUD. 229, 238 (1978); Robert N. Stavins, *Correlated Uncertainty and Policy Instrument Choice*, 30 J. ENVTL. ECON. & MGMT. 218, 219–25 (1996).

In theory, a hybrid system that incorporates aspects and attributes of both a simple linear tax or a simple tradeable permit system will be preferable, under conditions of uncertainty, to either alone. *See* Marc J. Roberts & Michael Spence, *Effluent Charges and Licenses Under Uncertainty*, 5 J. PUB. ECON. 193, 196–97 (1976); LOUIS KAPLOW & STEVEN SHAVELL, ON THE SUPERIORITY OF CORRECTIVE TAXES TO QUANTITY REGULATION 12–14 (National Bureau of Econ. Research Working Paper No. 6251, 1997).

18. Mandated by the Clean Air Act amendments of 1990, the sulfur dioxide ("SO_2") allowance program (a tradeable permit program to reduce acid rain) provides for annual auctions in addition to grandfathering. However, such auctions involve less than three percent of the total allocation. *See* ELIZABETH M. BAILEY, ALLOWANCE TRADING ACTIVITY AND STATE REGULATORY RULINGS: EVIDENCE FROM THE U.S. ACID RAIN PROGRAM 4 (Mass. Inst. of Tech. Working Paper No. MIT-CEEPR 96-002, 1996). These auctions have proven to be a trivial part of the overall program. *See* PAUL L. JOSKOW ET AL., AUCTION DESIGN AND THE MARKET FOR SULFUR DIOXIDE EMISSIONS 27–28 (National Bureau of Econ. Research Working Paper No. 5745, 1996).

19. With perfect information and no transactions costs, trading will result in the economically efficient outcome independently of the initial distribution of permits. *See* W. David Montgomery, *Markets in Licenses and Efficient Pollution Control Programs*, 5 J. ECON. THEORY 395, 409 (1972); Coase, *supra* note 3, at 15; Robert W. Hahn & Roger G. Noll, *Designing a Market for Tradeable Emission Permits*, *in* REFORM OF ENVIRONMENTAL REGULATION 120–21 (Wesley Magat ed., 1982). Under more realistic scenarios, however, there are compelling arguments for the superiority of auctioned permits. First, auctions are more cost-effective in the presence of certain kinds of transactions costs. *See* Robert N. Stavins, *Transaction Costs and Tradeable Permits*, 29 J. ENVTL. ECON. & MGMT. 133, 146 (1995). Second, the revenue raised by an auction mechanism can be used to finance a reduction in some distortionary tax. *See* LAWRENCE H. GOULDER ET AL., REVENUE-RAISING VS. OTHER APPROACHES TO ENVIRONMENTAL PROTECTION: THE CRITICAL SIGNIFICANCE OF PRE-EXISTING TAX DISTORTIONS 1 (National Bureau of Econ. Research Working Paper No. 5641, 1996). Instruments that restrict pollution production (such as tradeable permits) can create entry barriers that raise product prices, reduce the real wage, and exacerbate preexisting labor supply distortions. However, this effect can be offset if the government auctions the permits, retains the scarcity rents, and recycles the revenue by reducing distortionary labor taxes. *See* Don Fullerton & Gilbert Metcalf, Environmental Regulation in a Second-Best World 6, 25 (1996) (unpublished manuscript, on file with authors). Third, auctions provide greater incentives for firms to develop substitutes for regulated products, by requiring firms to pay for permits rather than giving them rents. *See* Robert W. Hahn & Albert M. McGartland, *The Political Economy of Instrument Choice: An Examination of the U.S. Role in Implementing the Montreal Protocol*, 83 Nw.

available market-based instruments (taxes, revenue-neutral taxes, auctioned permits, and grandfathered permits)[20] and the numerous tradeoffs that exist in normative economic terms, the U.S. experience has been dominated by one choice: grandfathered permits.

Notably, the acid rain provision of the Clean Air Act allocates, without charge, marketable permits for sulfur dioxide emissions to current emitters.[21] Similarly, grandfathered marketable permits are created by the offset mechanism of the nonattainment provision of the CAA.[22] This mechanism permits existing sources to reduce their emissions and sell the resulting reduction to new sources attempting to locate in the area.[23]

Fourth and finally, there has been a conceptual gap between prior and current political practice. In recent years, the political process has been more receptive to market-based instruments,[24]

U. L. REV. 592, 604 (1989). Fourth, the revenue raised by auctions may provide administrative agencies with an incentive to monitor compliance. *See* Bruce A. Ackerman & Richard B. Stewart, *Reforming Environmental Law*, 37 STAN. L. REV. 1333, 1344-46 (1985). Fifth, grandfathering, if accepted as general practice, could lead unregulated firms to increase their emissions in order to maximize the pollution rights that they obtain if there is a transition to a market-based system. *See* Donald N. Dewees, *Instrument Choice in Environmental Policy*, 21 ECON. INQUIRY 53, 62-63 (1983).

20. In a straightforward scheme of effluent taxes, a constant tax is levied on each unit of pollution. In a revenue-neutral framework, the tax revenues are then rebated to the payors, by some method other than the amount of their pollution. In marketable permit schemes, the initial allocation can be performed through an auction, or through grandfathering. In a deterministic setting and abstracting from a set of other issues, a revenue-neutral emission tax can be designed which is equivalent to a grandfathered tradeable permit system. Likewise, under such conditions, a simple emission tax will be roughly equivalent to an auctioned permit system.

21. *See* 42 U.S.C. § 7651(b) (1994). The amount of the allocation is capped in Phase I, which is currently in effect, at 2.5 pounds of sulfur dioxide per million BTUs of fuel input consumed. In Phase II, which goes into effect in the year 2000, the cap will be 1.2 pounds of sulfur dioxide per million BTUs of fuel input consumed. *See* Paul L. Joskow & Richard Schmalensee, *The Political Economy of Market-based Environmental Policy: The 1990 U.S. Acid Rain Program*, 41 J.L. & ECON. (forthcoming April 1998) (manuscript at 94-95, on file with authors).

22. *See* 42 U.S.C. § 7503(a)(1)(A) (1994).

23. *See id.* at § 7503(c)(1).

24. Beginning in the 1970s, the U.S. Environmental Protection Agency ("EPA") allowed states to implement trading schemes, as alternatives to command-and-control regulation, in their State Implementation Plans under the Clean Air Act. *See* Robert W. Hahn, *Economic Prescriptions for Environmental Problems: How the Patient Followed the Doctor's Orders*, J. ECON. PERSP., Spring 1989, at 95, 101. More significantly, tradeable permit systems were used in the 1980s to accomplish the phasedown of lead in gasoline. *See* SUZI KERR & DAVID MARÉ, EFFICIENT REGULATION THROUGH TRADEABLE PERMIT MARKETS: THE UNITED STATES LEAD PHASEDOWN 3-6 (U. Md. C. Park Working Paper No. 96-06, 1997). Moreover, such systems facilitated the phasedown of ozone-depleting

even though they continue to be a small part of the overall portfolio of existing environmental laws and regulations. After being largely ignored for so long, why have incentive-based instruments begun to gain acceptance in recent years?

Commentators have advanced various explanations for the existence of these four gaps between normative theory and positive reality. While some explanations emerge from formal theories, others take the form of informal hypotheses, purporting to explain certain aspects of environmental policy, but not as a part of a formal theory of political behavior. This Article reviews, evaluates, and extends these explanations. Moreover, this Article places these disparate explanations within the framework of an equilibrium model of instrument choice in environmental policy, based upon the metaphor of a political market.

Informed by intellectual traditions within economics, political science, and law, this framework organizes and synthesizes existing theories and empirical evidence about observed departures of normative prescription from political reality. The scope of the Article, however, is limited in a number of respects. The emphasis is on the control of pollution rather than the management of natural resources. The Article treats Congress, rather than administrative agencies, as the locus of instrument choice decisions; it views legislators (rather than regulators) as the "suppliers" of regulation.[25] Moreover, the Article focuses exclusively on the choice among the policy instruments used to achieve a given level of environmental protection, ranging from tradeable permits to taxes to standards. It does not explore the related issues of how the level of protection is chosen or enforced. Nor does it address why Congress chooses to delegate authority to administrative agencies in the first place.[26] Finally, the Article's outlook is positive, not normative: it seeks to

---

chloroflourocarbons ("CFCs") and are projected to cut nationwide SO_2 emissions by 50% by the year 2005, *see* OFFICE OF AIR RADIATION, U.S. ENVIRONMENTAL PROTECTION AGENCY, 1995 COMPLIANCE RESULTS: ACID RAIN PROGRAM 10–11 (1996), as well as achieving ambient ozone reductions in the northeast and implementing stricter local air pollution controls in the Los Angeles metropolitan region.

25. We do not intend, however, to deny the importance of executive branch departments and administrative agencies, such as the EPA. For example, the intra-firm emission trading programs of the 1970s were largely the direct creation of EPA.

26. *See generally* Morris P. Fiorina, *Legislative Choice of Regulatory Forms: Legal Process or Administrative Process?*, 39 PUB. CHOICE 33 (1982).

understand why the current set of tools exists, rather than which tools are desirable.

Part II of the Article reviews the relevant intellectual traditions in economics, political science, and law. Part III presents the key features of our equilibrium framework. Part IV considers the demand for environmental policy instruments, while Part V examines the supply side. Finally, Part VI presents some conclusions.

II. INTELLECTUAL TRADITIONS

Positive theories of policy instrument choice find their roots in the broader study of government regulation, a vast literature which has been reviewed elsewhere.[27] For the purposes of this Article, the literature can be divided into three approaches for explaining government regulation: demand-driven explanations, supply-driven explanations, and explanations incorporating the interaction between demand and supply.

A. Demand-Side Analyses

Explanations that focus heavily on the demand for regulation are grounded largely in economics. Not surprisingly, economists have generally concentrated on the demand for economic (rather than social) regulation, devoting most attention to the interests of affected firms. The "economic theory of regulation," initiated by George Stigler[28] and developed further by Richard Posner,[29] Sam Peltzman,[30] and Gary Becker,[31] suggests that much regulation is not imposed on firms but rather demanded by them, as a means of harnessing the coercive power of the state to restrict entry, support

---

27. *See generally* Thomas Romer & Howard Rosenthal, *Modern Political Economy and the Study of Regulation, in* PUBLIC REGULATION: NEW PERSPECTIVES ON INSTITUTIONS AND POLICIES 73 (Elizabeth E. Bailey ed., 1987).

28. *See generally* George J. Stigler, *The Theory of Economic Regulation*, 2 BELL J. ECON. 3 (1971).

29. *See generally* Richard A. Posner, *Theories of Economic Regulation*, 5 BELL J. ECON. 335 (1974).

30. *See generally* Sam Peltzman, *Toward a More General Theory of Regulation*, 19 J.L. & ECON. 211 (1976).

31. *See generally* Gary S. Becker, *A Theory of Competition Among Pressure Groups for Political Influence*, 98 Q.J. ECON. 371 (1983).

prices, or provide direct cash subsidies.[32] A related strand of literature has likewise emphasized rent-seeking behavior.[33]

In a number of these economic analyses, the supply side (i.e., the political process itself) is virtually ignored.[34] One paper typifying this demand-driven approach has examined private industry's preferences for regulation and has simply assumed that those policy preferences will prevail.[35] Similarly, another model of the resource allocation decisions of competing interest groups has assumed that the policy outcome depends solely on the relative pressures exerted by interest groups.[36]

Even when they model political processes, economic explanations of regulation have often remained driven by the demand of firms. In Stigler's analysis[37] and Peltzman's elaboration,[38] the state enacts the program of the industry (or, more generally, of the interest group) offering the most resources to the governing party; in other words, regulation goes to the "highest bidder."[39] Thus, private industry will tend to be regulated where and when the benefits to firms from government regulation are highly concentrated, but the costs are widely dispersed.[40] The "government" sim-

---

32. Stigler's influential paper has been characterized as breaking with a previously dominant view (among economists) that regulation is initiated to correct market imperfections. *See* Stigler, *supra* note 28, at 3; *see also* Posner, *supra* note 29, at 343. It is worth noting that as far back as E.E. Schattschneider, political scientists recognized the importance of economic interests among groups pressuring Congress. *See* E.E. SCHATTSCHNEIDER, POLITICS, PRESSURES, AND THE TARIFF 4 (1935). The "capture theory of regulation" in political science was already well developed by the time of Stigler's work. Stigler's main contribution was less his recognition that economic interests will seek favorable regulation than his introduction of that insight into the economics literature and his application of economic models of behavior (i.e., treating political parties as resource maximizers) to explain policy formulation.

33. *See generally* JAMES M. BUCHANAN & GORDON TULLOCK, THE CALCULUS OF CONSENT (1962); Gordon Tullock, *The Welfare Cost of Tariffs, Monopolies, and Theft*, 5 W. ECON. J. 224 (1967).

34. *See generally* JEAN-JACQUE LAFFONT & JEAN TIROLE, A THEORY OF INCENTIVES IN PROCUREMENT AND REGULATION (1993); Romer & Rosenthal, *supra* note 27.

35. *See* James M. Buchanan & Gordon Tullock, *Polluters' Profits and Political Response: Direct Controls Versus Taxes*, 65 AM. ECON. REV. 139, 142 (1975).

36. *See* Becker, *supra* note 31, at 392.

37. *See* Stigler, *supra* note 28, at 12.

38. *See* Peltzman, *supra* note 30, at 214.

39. The Stigler-Peltzman model is essentially a policy auction. *See* Stigler, *supra* note 28, at 12–13; Peltzman, *supra* note 30, at 212.

40. Peanut regulation provides an excellent example of the effect of concentrated benefits and diffuse costs. Quotas, import restrictions, and price supports combined in 1982-1987 to transfer an average of $255 million a year from consumers to producers, with a deadweight loss of $34 million. The annual cost to each consumer was only $1.23; each peanut farmer, on the other hand, gained $11,100. Peanut farmers clearly had an

ply acts to maximize an exogenous "political support function" and thus caters to the more powerful group. Following a conceptually similar tack, another model pictures a single policymaker's decision as responding to a weighted sum of industry interests and environmental interests.[41]

Political actors are included in these analyses, but they are treated as economic agents reacting somewhat mechanically to the resources or the demands of interest groups. In many cases, as in the Stigler-Peltzman model, they have no interest other than collecting political contributions. Moreover, government is treated as a monolith, controlled by a single political party, with regulatory agencies and legislatures combined into a single unit. These accounts leave no room for constituency pressures, variation among legislators, slack between legislative direction and the actions of administrative agencies, or other supply-side phenomena.

B. Supply-Side Analyses

By contrast, political scientists and economists studying the supply side of regulation (and of legislation more generally) have focused on the voting behavior of legislators and the institutional structure of the legislature. The approach typically used by political scientists to explain voting behavior is based upon interview and survey data. On the basis of these sources, Congressmen are seen to be most influenced by colleagues and constituents in deciding how to vote.[42] An alternative approach analyzes roll-call data to estimate the relative importance of ideology, constituent interests, and interest groups in legislative voting.[43] One study found that legislators base their votes not only on the economic interests of their constituents (as the economic theory of regulation as-

---

incentive to preserve the program, while any individual consumer had little to gain from dismantling it. *See* W. KIP VISCUSI ET AL., ECONOMICS OF REGULATION AND ANTITRUST 331 (1995).

41. *See generally* Robert W. Hahn, *The Political Economy of Environmental Regulation: Towards a Unifying Framework*, 65 PUB. CHOICE 21 (1990).

42. *See* JOHN W. KINGDON, CONGRESSMEN'S VOTING DECISIONS 17 (1989).

43. *See generally* Joseph P. Kalt & Mark A. Zupan, *Capture and Ideology in the Economic Theory of Politics*, 74 AM. ECON. REV. 279 (1984); James B. Kau & Paul H. Rubin, *Self-Interest, Ideology, and Logrolling in Congressional Voting*, 22 J.L. & ECON. 365 (1979); Sam Peltzman, *Constituent Interest and Congressional Voting*, 27 J.L. & ECON. 181 (1984).

sumes), but also on their ideologies.[44] Some scholars, notably Michael Munger and his colleagues, have sought to explain voting behavior by explicitly linking it to campaign contributions.[45] However, just as the Stigler-Peltzman model incorporates politicians but remains fundamentally demand-driven, their approach acknowledges the role of interest groups but is driven by supply-side factors. Some mention is made of the costs to legislators of supplying legislation to interest groups, but the models focus on estimating a "supply price" determined solely by the characteristics of legislators.[46]

A second line of inquiry on the supply side has investigated the role of institutional structure in the legislature. The policy outcome in Congress depends not only on the voting preferences of individual legislators, but also on features such as decision rules, the order of voting, and especially the powers of committees (and their chairmen) to control the agenda of the legislature.[47] Further, expectations of subsequent problems of overseeing implementation of regulatory policy by administrative agencies may influence legislators in their choice of regulatory procedures and instruments.[48]

C. Equilibrium Analyses

Compared to the above, relatively few works have taken an equilibrium approach by considering the interaction of the supply and demand for regulation. Those considering such linkages have

---

44. *See* Kalt & Zupan, *supra* note 43, at 298. Their econometric analysis has been criticized by John Jackson and John Kingdon. *See* John E. Jackson & John W. Kingdon, *Ideology, Interest Group Scores, and Legislative Votes*, 36 AM. J. POL. SCI. 805, 806 (1992).

45. *See generally* Arthur T. Denzau & Michael C. Munger, *Legislators and Interest Groups: How Unorganized Interests Get Represented*, 80 AM. POL. SCI. REV. 89 (1986); *see also* Kevin B. Grier & Michael C. Munger, *Comparing Interest Group PAC Contributions to House and Senate Incumbents, 1980–1986*, 55 J. POL. 615, 625–40 (1993).

46. In empirical studies of interest group contributions, a number of researchers seem to have in mind a "market model" of interest group contributions to legislators where interest groups offer campaign contributions and votes in return for political support. *See* Jonathan I. Silberman & Garey C. Durden, *Determining Legislative Preferences on the Minimum Wage: An Economic Approach*, 84 J. POL. ECON. 317, 328 (1976); Garey C. Durden et al., *The Effects of Interest Group Pressure on Coal Strip-Mining Legislation*, 72 SOC. SCI. Q. 239, 249 (1991).

47. *See generally* Kenneth A. Shepsle & Barry R. Weingast, *Positive Theories of Congressional Institutions*, 19 LEGIS. STUD. Q. 149 (1994) (reviewing recent literature on congressional institutions).

48. *See* Matthew D. McCubbins et al., *Administrative Procedures as Instruments of*

typically focused on the role of campaign contributions. Several researchers have modeled campaign contributions from profit-maximizing firms to vote-maximizing politicians,[49] where candidates choose optimal policy positions that balance the need to get votes (by moving towards the policy preferences of voters) and the need to secure campaign funds (by moving towards the preferences of contributors).[50] In a similar vein, some analysts have employed game-theoretic models to link campaign contributions by interest groups and policy positions adopted by legislators.[51]

One group considered legislative outcomes directly, modeling the determination of campaign contributions, legislators' floor votes, and constituents' votes, but without advancing a theoretical model of legislative behavior.[52] Another researcher has explicitly considered the interaction of interest group demand and the legislative supply of policy instruments.[53] In his model, the choice of regulatory instrument is the equilibrium of a game between interest groups (who choose how much to allocate to lobbying in support of their preferred instrument) and legislators (who vote for the instrument that maximizes their support, taking into account the contributions from the interest groups).

Despite the relative scarcity of equilibrium models of positive political economy, the metaphor of a "political market" has frequently been employed in the public choice literature. The works using the market metaphor seem to have had three distinct markets in mind. One market is the market for votes *within* a legislature: legislators are at once demanders and suppliers of votes as they engage in vote trading and logrolling.[54] Other market models focus

---

Political Control, 3 J.L. Econ. & Org. 243, 252–53 (1987); McCubbins et al., *supra* note 10, at 481.

49. *See generally* Uri Ben-Zion & Zeev Eytan, *On Money, Votes, and Policy in a Democratic Society*, 17 Pub. Choice 1 (1974).

50. Bental and Ben-Zion extend the model to consider the case where politicians derive utility from adopting a platform close to their personal policy preferences. *See* Benjamin Bental & Uri Ben-Zion, *Political Contribution and Policy—Some Extensions*, 24 Pub. Choice 1, 1–4 (1975).

51. *See* David Austen-Smith, *Interest Groups, Campaign Contributions, and Probabilistic Voting*, 54 Pub. Choice 123, 128–34 (1987).

52. *See* James B. Kau et al., *A General Equilibrium Model of Congessional Voting*, 97 Q.J. Econ. 271, 288–89 (1982).

53. *See* Jose Edgardo L. Campos, *Legislative Institutions, Lobbying, and the Endogenous Choice of Regulatory Instruments: A Political Economy Approach to Instrument Choice*, 5 J.L. Econ. & Org. 333, 348–49 (1989).

54. In a "logroll," or vote trade, several legislators might arrange to vote for each

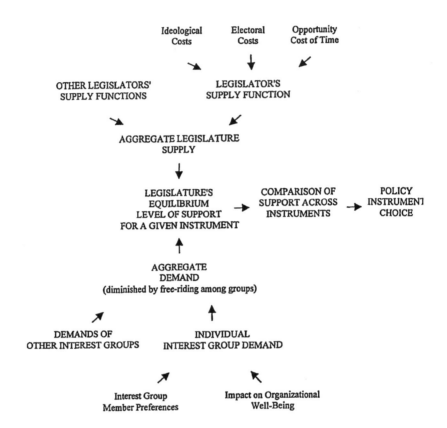

Figure 1

An Equilibrium Framework for Examining the Political Market

on the distribution of wealth resulting *from* legislation: the demanders are the beneficiaries of legislation and the suppliers are the
losers, with politicians serving as brokers between the two groups.[55]
This Article employs what is perhaps the most prevalent concep-

---

others' bills, so that each legislator secures her most preferred outcome in return for
supporting other legislators' bills (which she may oppose only slightly if at all). For
example, a series of public works projects might prompt a logroll, since each in the series
matters a great deal to the representative whose district receives the funds, but is
insignificant to other legislators.

55. *See* PUBLIC CHOICE THEORY at xviii (Charles K. Rowley ed., 1993).

tion of the "political market," one which focuses on the exchange between legislators and constituents or interest groups.[56]

The remainder of this Article develops a new model of a political market involving legislators, constituents, and interest groups in the context of instrument choice in environmental policy. This market framework supplements existing work by simultaneously considering the demand for regulation, the supply of regulatory options, and the equilibrium outcome, that is, the choice of policy instrument in the legislature. In this way, the Article strives to synthesize prior research from the demand side and supply side, using it as a foundation for our own equilibrium framework. This Article also seeks to suggest a richer sense of the supply side than is found in existing equilibrium models,[57] incorporating legislator ideology as well as a fuller description of the opportunity costs of supplying legislation.[58]

III. A Market Framework for Examining Instrument Choice

To develop a framework within which various existing positive political economy theories can be synthesized, consider a "political market" embodied in a legislature and focused on a single "commodity," namely legislators' support for a given instrument in a specific policy context.[59] A schematic view of this political market is provided in Figure 1. Demand for various degrees of support

---

56. In previous work, the identity of demanders and suppliers has varied; the market has been in electoral votes (with legislators "paying" for votes with legislation) and in legislation (with voters paying for the policies with their votes). Peltzman, for one, was clear that the demanders were constituents and the suppliers legislators: "[t]he essential commodity being transacted in the political market is a transfer of wealth, with constituents on the demand side and their political representatives on the supply side." *See* Peltzman, *supra* note 30, at 212. In this Article's framework, the market is in units of effective political support (for particular public policies).

57. *See, e.g.*, Campos, *supra* note 53, at 338–48.

58. As noted above, Congress is seen as the locus of policy instrument choice. Extending the framework to cover regulatory agencies and the courts would introduce several interesting but complex issues. For regulatory agencies, for example, it is important to deal with issues such as the principal-agent relationship between the agency and Congress; the degree and nature of congressional oversight; the possibly conflicting goals of the agency head and career bureaucrats; the objective function of the bureaucrats (for example, job security, power, protection of expertise); and the way in which policy demanders provide payoffs to the agency.

59. "Specific policy context" simply refers to the fact that the demand for instru-

comes from diverse interest groups, including environmental advocacy organizations, private firms, and trade associations. The currency in this market takes the form of resources (monetary and other contributions, and/or endorsements or other forms of support) that can facilitate legislators' reelections. The aggregation of these individual demands is not a simple sum, because the public good nature of regulation means that interest groups can free-ride on the demands of others.

Next, it is assumed that each individual legislator seeks to maximize her expected utility, which involves the satisfaction that comes from being a member of the legislature, now and in the future. The result is the legislator's political-support supply function, the shape of which is determined by her ideological predisposition, her perception of her constituents' preferences, and the increasing opportunity cost of providing additional support for the policy instrument (in terms of expended effort, foregone future electoral votes in her home district, and discomfort associated with departures from her ideology). Since each legislator supplies units of a homogeneous product called "effective support" (at differing costs), the individual legislators' supply functions combine to yield an aggregate supply function at the level of the legislature.

Thus, for each instrument, a competitive equilibrium in the legislature is given by the intersection between the aggregate political-support supply function and the aggregation of relevant demands.[60] Levels of effective support provided by individual members of the legislature are hence equivalent to the amounts they are willing to provide at the competitive equilibrium "price," the points of intersection of their supply functions with the infinitely elastic demand they face. The aggregate support is simply the sum over legislators of their individual levels of effective support. The legislative outcome, i.e., the choice of a policy instrument, then depends upon the relative degrees of support generated for alternative policy instruments.

---

ments and the supply of instrument options are both linked to the specific environmental problems for which the instruments are being considered. Also, as discussed below, the legislature in this framework selects a policy instrument from among a range of options, including alternative policy instruments plus the status quo.

60. It is implicitly assumed that the effective support provided by individual legislators can be observed. This is a reasonable assumption in many but not all situations. Future work should explicitly incorporate this uncertainty.

The following sections describe the political market's commodity and currency, and then turn to more detailed expositions of the origins of regulatory demand and supply, respectively. Finally, the Article discusses the nature of political market equilibria and the legislative outcomes that result.

A. The Political Market's Commodity and Currency

Each legislator supplies some degree of support for a given regulatory instrument. Interest groups seek to secure support from legislators in the political market. The commodity of support is seen to be *homogeneous* among legislators. That is, the support produced by one legislator is equivalent to (a perfect substitute for) support produced by any other legislator. This commodity may be characterized as "effective support."[61] It is a measure of impact (output), not of effort (input).

---

61. It might be argued that interest groups ultimately care about votes, which at the level of an individual legislator reduces to a binary variable. But there are several reasons to focus on support, rather than on votes alone. First, this approach facilitates comparisons among several instruments, since the outcome of the legislative process is the instrument that garners the most effective support. Second, empirical analysis has largely failed to link campaign contributions with legislators' votes, see Richard L. Hall & Frank W. Wayman, *Buying Time: Moneyed Interests and the Mobilization of Bias in Congressional Committees*, 84 AM. POL. SCI. REV. 797, 813 (1990), while campaign contributions have been found to be highly correlated with legislators' participation in committees, itself closely linked with the notion of "effective support[.]" *See* Grier & Munger, *supra* note 45, at 641; Jonathan I. Silberman & Garey C. Durden, *Determining Legislative Preferences on the Minimum Wage: An Economic Approach*, 84 J. POL. ECON. 317, 326–27 (1976). Third, the fate of most prospective legislation is determined before it reaches the floor for a vote. The agenda-setting powers of committees make them virtual arbiters of whether or not bills reach the floor for voting. *See* Kenneth A. Shepsle & Barry R. Weingast, *The Institutional Foundations of Committee Power*, 81 AM. POL. SCI. REV. 85, 87 (1987). Once a bill reaches the floor, norms of deference may lead many members of Congress to follow committee recommendations, either because of implicit logrolls among committees, see Barry R. Weingast & William J. Marshall, *The Industrial Organization of Congress, or, Why Legislatures, like Firms, Are Not Organized as Markets*, 96 J. POL. ECON. 132, 157–58 (1988), or because of recognition of committees' greater expertise. *See* KINGDON, *supra* note 42, at 133.

Votes of committee members are usually less critical than the intensity of members' support. *See* Richard L. Hall, *Participation and Purpose in Committee Decision Making*, 81 AM. POL. SCI. REV. 105, 105–06 (1987); DAVID R. MAYHEW, CONGRESS: THE ELECTORAL CONNECTION 92 (1974). Hence, securing the support of a relatively small number of legislators (each of whom is a highly efficient producer of effective support) may be the primary goal of interest groups, even though the groups ultimately care about the outcome of floor votes. This reality is captured by the above framework, with its focus on levels of "effective support."

To be sure, different legislators require different amounts of effort to produce a unit of effective support. These variations in productivity are due to such factors as the size and effectiveness of members' staffs, their seniority, their committee assignments, and their leadership positions, including committee chairs. Moreover, a legislator's effort may encompass a much larger range of activities than simply voting for a given instrument: among other things, a legislator might hold hearings, attend committee markup meetings, draft or sponsor legislation, insert statements into committee reports, propose amendments, seek to influence colleagues, or make behind-the-scenes deals.[62]

The political currency in this market is seen as the resources necessary for the legislator's reelection: not only votes, but also monetary and other contributions.[63] An environmental interest group, for example, may publicly endorse a candidate for office, or may volunteer time and effort to mobilize votes in a legislator's district. Other forms of "payment" to legislators (such as time spent drafting legislation or policy information for the legislator) are also valued by a legislator seeking reelection, since association with the interest group may increase the legislator's support, and the time saved by the legislator may be spent on activities that generate home district votes. Incorporating home district votes, financial contributions, and nonmonetary contributions in the currency of "resources," the model adopts a monetary numeraire for convenience.

---

62. One set of researchers describes the range of services legislators can offer interest groups. *See* Denzau & Munger, *supra* note 45, at 91. Another group analyzes a similar measure of legislator participation, which they call "political support effort." *See* Silberman & Durden, *supra* note 61, at 318. Notably, these models generally treat as an output what in this framework is an input: namely, the effort exerted by the legislator to produce effective support. The above framework incorporates differences among legislators in effectiveness and productivity into the supply side (production of effective support) rather than the demand side (demand of interest groups for support from different legislators). For further discussion of the ways in which members of Congress participate in policy making, especially in committee, see Hall, *supra* note 61, at 106–08; RICHARD L. HALL, PARTICIPATION IN CONGRESS 40–48 (1996); Hall & Wayman, *supra* note 61, at 804–15.

63. Monetary contributions can be used to finance advertising campaigns, literature production and distribution, and other activities that increase the probability of a legislator being reelected.

B. Origins of Demand for Environmental Policy Instruments

The Article now explores the nature of demand by firms and individuals, dividing the latter category into three overlapping groups (consumers, workers, and environmentalists), and then considers the role of interest groups in the political market.[64]

1. Firms and Individuals

Firms are affected by environmental regulation through the costs they incur to produce goods and services. Consider a price-taking firm[65] that wishes to maximize its profit from producing a single product and that employs a set of factors in its production, each of which has some cost associated with it. One of these input factors is the set of relevant features of the regulatory environment. In seeking to maximize profits, the firm chooses levels of all its inputs, including the efforts it puts into securing its desired regulatory environment. By solving this maximization problem, the firm derives its demand functions for all its inputs, including its demand for the environmental policy instrument. In this simple model, individual firms have a decreasing marginal willingness to pay to secure particular policy instruments.[66] At a minimum, a firm's demand for a policy instrument is a function of output and input prices, including the "price of legislators' support."[67]

---

64. Of course, individuals and interest groups also play a role on the "supply side" of the political market by affecting legislators' electoral prospects. Individuals vote, while interest groups may spend resources to influence that vote directly (for example, by disseminating information about a legislator's voting record on an issue). Stated in terms of our framework, individuals and interest groups not only exhibit a demand function, but also may also shift legislators' supply functions. *See infra* Part III.C. This Article attempts to draw a conceptual distinction between these two facets of individual and interest group involvement.

65. In a competitive market economy, individual firms cannot independently set the price that they will charge (only monopolists can do this); rather, they must accept or "take" the price given by the competitively determined supply-demand equilibrium, and then decide how much to supply at that price.

66. The maximized objective function is the firm's profit function. Hotelling's Lemma (a basic microeconomic theorem) establishes that the factor demand functions are downward sloping as long as the profit function is convex.

67. This stylized framework implicitly assumes that firms are profit-maximizing (or cost-minimizing) atomistic units, and thus that there is no significant principal-agent slack between managers and shareholders. There is little doubt that this assumption departs from reality in many cases, but we leave its investigation to future research.

330   *Harvard Environmental Law Review*   [Vol. 22

The choice of environmental policy instruments can also have an effect on individuals. For example, individuals can be affected by the level of environmental quality that results from the use of a particular instrument,[68] or by the costs of environmental protection as reflected in the prices of the goods and services they buy. Individuals might even derive some direct utility from knowing that a particular type of policy instrument was employed. These effects can be reflected in a utility function, which the consumer maximizes subject to a budgetary constraint. The result is a set of demand functions for all private and public goods, including demand functions for any environmental policy instruments that affect the individual's utility either directly or indirectly. Thus, like firms, individuals can have a decreasing marginal willingness to pay to secure particular policy instruments.[69] Their demand for a policy instrument is a function of their income and of the relative prices of relevant goods, including the price of securing support for their preferred instrument.

Moreover, individuals can be categorized as "consumers," "environmentalists," and "workers"; these three categories are neither mutually exclusive nor exhaustive. Individuals are "consumers" to the degree that the choice of environmental policy instrument affects them through its impact on the prices of goods and services, "environmentalists" to the degree that they are affected by the impact of instrument choice on the level of environmental quality, and "workers" to the degree that they are affected by environmental

---

68. Although attention has been restricted at the outset to the policy instruments used to achieve a given level of protection, the choice of cost-effective instruments can lead to the adoption of more stringent environmental standards, as noted below.

69. The maximized utility function is the individual's indirect utility function. By Roy's Identity (a basic microeconomic truism), the demand functions are derived as downward sloping, as long as the utility function has the usual properties. It is possible that over a certain region the demand function will be increasing. For example, a unit of support for an instrument will be virtually worthless at very low levels of support, since adoption of that instrument will be extremely unlikely. Assume, however, that the demand function is decreasing over the politically relevant range, in which adoption of the instrument is a realistic possibility. It might be argued that if a legislature were composed of a single legislator and there was perfect information, demand functions for political support would (in the case of support relevant for voting) be a step function with a single step: interest groups would have no willingness-to-pay below some level of (adequate) support, and no willingness-to-pay above a sufficient level of support. But in a multi-member body, more support from individual legislators can always be worth something, and if there is uncertainty about how much support is sufficient, the demand function is likely to be downward sloping over at least some range.

policy through its impact on the demand for labor, and hence their wages.

2. Interest Groups

Because there are significant costs of lobbying and because the target of demand (i.e., the public policy) is a public good,[70] an individual and even a firm will receive relatively small rewards for any direct lobbying efforts. For individuals, the marginal costs of lobbying are likely to outweigh the perceived marginal benefits over much of the relevant range of lobbying activity, such that individuals will undersupply lobbying, hoping instead to free ride on the efforts of others. Although some large firms maintain offices in Washington, D.C., to facilitate direct lobbying of Congress, most of the demand for public policies from both firms and individuals is transmitted through organized interest groups.

The free-riding problem standing in the way of individual lobbying efforts can also be a significant obstacle to the formation of interest groups.[71] For an interest group to organize, it must overcome the free-riding problem by offering its members enough benefits to make the costs of membership worthwhile. For a citizen group, such as an environmental advocacy organization, these benefits are likely to include: "material incentives," such as newsletters, workshops, or gifts; "solidary incentives," namely the benefits derived from social interaction; and "purposive incentives," such as the personal satisfaction derived from membership in an organization whose activities one supports.[72]

Among citizen groups, taxpayer and consumer organizations may face greater free-riding problems than environmental groups:[73]

---

70. Regulation may not always be nonexclusive. Loopholes, narrowly applying clauses in statutes, and bureaucratic exemptions can all afford special treatment for some firms or narrowly defined categories of consumers. This possibility may provide enough incentive for some individual firms to lobby.

71. *See* MANCUR OLSON, THE LOGIC OF COLLECTIVE ACTION: PUBLIC GOODS AND THE THEORY OF GROUPS 43–44 (1965).

72. *See* LAWRENCE S. ROTHENBERG, LINKING CITIZENS TO GOVERNMENT: INTEREST GROUP POLITICS AT COMMON CAUSE 66 (1992); JAMES Q. WILSON, POLITICAL ORGANIZATIONS 33–35 (1995).

73. Notably, labor unions are able to overcome free-riding problems through mandatory dues payments. *See* OLSON, *supra* note 71, at 76; WILSON, *supra* note 72, at 119. To the extent that these funds are used for lobbying efforts, unions might be expected to be especially well-represented in the political arena. Yet, since unions dedicate most of

their lobbying actions are likely to have an even wider range of potential beneficiaries; they may be able to offer fewer material incentives; and they lack the compelling moral mission that may drive the purposive incentives motivating members of environmental groups.

To overcome their own set of free-rider problems, trade associations can offer a range of benefits to member firms that non-members do not enjoy, including: influence over policy goals; information on policy developments; reports on economic trends; and participation in an annual convention.[74] Compared with citizen groups, trade associations may have significant advantages in overcoming free-riding: they are usually smaller, making the contributions of each member more significant; and even substantial annual dues may be negligible costs for member firms.[75] Hence, private industry interests may be over-represented in the political process relative to citizen groups.

Importantly, interest groups do not simply aggregate the political demands of their members. Indeed, an interest group's utility maximization function may diverge significantly from those of its members as a result of a principal-agent problem: the members (and donors) are principals who contract with their agent—the interest group (or, more precisely, its professional staff)—to represent their views to the legislature.[76] As in many such contractual relationships, the output exerted by the agents may not be directly observable or controllable by the principal. This principal-agent problem is probably far more serious for environmental advocacy groups than for private industry trade associations.[77]

---

their campaign contributions to securing favorable labor policy, unions as a group have only rarely been influential (or even active) in environmental policy debates.

74. *See* OLSON, *supra* note 71, at 139–41.

75. *See* WILSON, *supra* note 72, at 144.

76. In the typical principal-agent relationship, the principals (in this case, the firms) know their own interests and wish to ensure that the agent (here the trade association) acts in accordance with those interests. It is conceivable, however, that interest group staff may be leading the charge for policy changes that will benefit member firms, while those firms remain largely ignorant about the policy issues at stake. *See* RAYMOND A. BAUER ET AL., AMERICAN BUSINESS AND PUBLIC POLICY 331 (1963).

77. An environmental organization may have a hundred thousand members or more scattered across the country, paying scant attention to the operational priorities of the organization (let alone the details of its day-to-day activities). Trade associations, on the other hand, may be dominated by a large producer, with an incentive to monitor the association's activities, and their boards of directors may be made up of executives from member firms. Moreover, trade associations have many fewer members, and therefore the

Principal-agent slack between what the members want and what the interest group actually does arises because the organization's staff has its own self interests. A trade association, for example, may not only want to maximize the profits of its member firms; it may also seek to expand its membership or to increase revenue from member dues. Similarly, the objective function of an environmental group may include not only the level of environmental quality, but also factors such as membership size, budget, and reputation among various constituencies that affect the organization's health and viability.[78]

With these competing interests and constraints in mind, an interest group must decide how to allocate its scarce resources as it lobbies the legislature for its preferred outcome. The total benefits to an interest group of the legislature's support for an instrument rise with the degree of support offered, but there are decreasing marginal returns. As in the case of individuals and firms, a unit increase in support when the legislature is already very favorably disposed to one's position is worth less than a unit increase in support by a lukewarm or previously unsupportive legislature. This characteristic produces a downward-sloping demand function: an interest group's marginal willingness-to-pay for support decreases as the legislature's total support increases.

C. Origins of Supply of Environmental Policy Instruments

The Article now considers a legislator who derives utility from a number of relevant interests: making public policy, doing good things for the country or for her district, satisfying ideological beliefs, having prestige and the perquisites of office, and so on. To continue getting utility from these factors, the legislator must be

---

stake of each in the organization is greater, and monitoring is more likely to be worthwhile. On the other hand, trade associations have their own set of problems. Among these are the possible necessity of obtaining an expression of consensus from member firms prior to undertaking specific lobbying efforts.

78. One researcher treats the agency problem in environmental groups extensively, arguing that, because members and patrons cannot observe the outputs or effort of their agents directly, they must instead make funding and membership decisions based on a group's inputs: its expenditures on lobbying, member materials, advertising, and fund raising. *See* Robert C. Lowry, The Political Economy of Environmental Citizen Groups 94–96 (1993) (unpublished Ph.D. dissertation, Harvard University) (on file with the Harvard University Library).

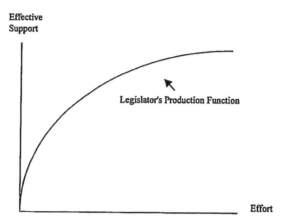

Figure 2
Political-Support Production Function

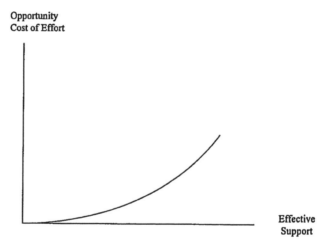

Figure 3
Political-Support Cost Function

reelected. Assuming that legislators seek to maximize their expected utility, a legislator will choose her level of support for a proposed policy instrument based on the effort required to provide that support, the inherent satisfaction she derives from providing that level of support, and the effects her position will likely have on her chances of reelection.[79]

Accordingly, the legislator's supply function consists of three components: (1) the opportunity cost of efforts required to provide a given degree of support for a policy instrument; (2) the psychological cost of supporting an instrument despite one's ideological beliefs;[80] and (3) the opportunity cost (in terms of reduced probability of reelection) of supporting an instrument not favored by one's electoral constituency in terms of reduced probability of reelection.[81]

The first component emerges from the individual legislator's productivity in providing support. As indicated in Figure 2, the legislator's input is "effort"[82] and the relevant output is "effective support." Some legislators may produce "effective support" more efficiently with a given amount of effort thanks to the size and effectiveness of their staffs, their seniority in the legislature, and their membership and leadership on relevant committees. By placing a value on the opportunity cost of time and effort, an opportunity cost function can be derived (Figure 3), and from that, the related marginal opportunity cost of effort, represented by the upward-sloping line emanating from the origin in Figure 4.[83]

---

79. This notion of legislators' goals is consistent with other descriptions of Representatives as having three basic objectives: reelection, influence within the House, and good public policy. *See* RICHARD F. FENNO, JR., HOME STYLE: HOUSE MEMBERS IN THEIR DISTRICTS 137 (1978). In our framework, "influence within the House" and "good public policy" are combined in "being a legislator." If the legislator wishes to continue to be a legislator in the future, she will also value reelection.

80. If supporting the instrument is consistent with one's ideological beliefs, then this is a "negative cost," i.e., a benefit.

81. This is also a "negative cost" (benefit) if supporting the instrument is consistent with one's constituents' positions.

82. This includes the use of other resources, but may be thought of as being denominated in units of time.

83. In the face of the overwhelming claims on her time and resources—both in Washington and in her home districts—a member's time and effort carries a significant opportunity cost. *See* BAUER, *supra* note 76, at 412–13; KINGDON, *supra* note 42, at 216; FENNO, *supra* note 79, at 141. Effort invested in providing support for one bill could have been spent working on other legislation that would satisfy ideological goals, reflect voters' objectives, and/or attract votes, dollars, and other resources; or visiting the home district and supplying constituency services such as help in dealing with the bureaucracy. *See*

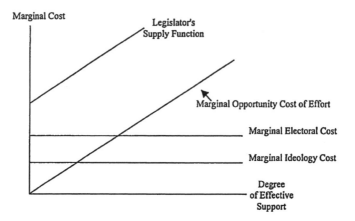

Figure 4
Opportunity Costs and the Supply of Political Support
by an Individual Legislator

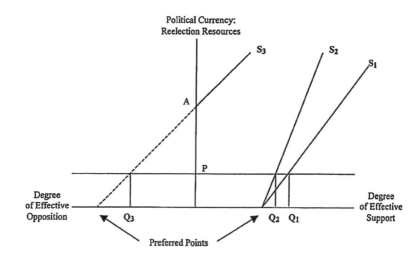

Figure 5
Supplies of Political Support by Individual Legislators

Next, assuming that a legislator derives disutility from acting inconsistently with her ideology, the psychological cost of supporting a policy inconsistent with one's ideological beliefs can be introduced into the framework. As suggested above, this cost would be negative (a benefit) if one were ideologically predisposed to favor the particular policy. In either case, it is conceivable that these marginal psychological costs might be increasing or decreasing (in absolute value) with the degree of support, but for ease of presentation we portray this marginal cost as constant in Figure 4. In this case, the legislator's ideology has no effect on the slope of the combined marginal cost function; rather, ideology shifts the function upwards (for inconsistency with ideology) or downwards (for consistency with ideology).

Finally, the framework incorporates the third component of the legislator's supply function: the opportunity cost corresponding to the reduced probability of reelection given the support of an instrument not favored by one's electoral constituency. Lost votes from constituents unhappy with the legislator's position would directly affect the legislator's chances of reelection, whereas protest and grassroots efforts by interest groups unhappy with the legislator's position could indirectly affect constituents' assessment of the legislator.[84] Again, this is a "negative cost" if supporting the instrument is consistent with one's constituents' positions.[85] As with ideological costs, although these marginal electoral opportunity costs could be increasing or decreasing with the level of the legislator's support, they are drawn as constant (and positive) in Figure 4, to keep things simple.[86]

Accordingly, the overall (individual) marginal cost function, or the legislator's supply-of-support function, is simply the vertical

---

Denzau & Munger, *supra* note 45, at 92–96; Grier & Munger, *supra* note 45, at 618. Note that the marginal cost function is assumed in the figure to be linear, simply to keep the explication simple.

84. Members of Congress tend to take into account the preferences of the people who voted for them, i.e., their "supporting coalition," *see* KINGDON, *supra* note 42, at 60, or their "reelection constituency[,]" *see* FENNO, *supra* note 79, at 8. A conservative legislator whose reelection constituency is anti-regulatory, for example, will not be affected by a minority group of environmentalists calling for command-and-control regulation.

85. Departing from the preferences of constituents reduces the probability of the legislator's reelection. This reduced probability can be evaluated in terms of the resources required to maintain a constant probability of reelection.

86. Figure 4 represents both ideological costs and electoral costs as being positive; support for the policy is essentially inconsistent both with the legislator's own ideology

summation of these three components: opportunity costs of effort, ideological costs, and constituency costs (Figure 4). The amount of support for a policy instrument that a legislator would supply in the absence of any contributions helpful to advancing the member's goals (including her reelection) is represented in Figure 5 as the "preferred point," the intersection of the supply function with the horizontal axis. In this framework, the legislator can be induced to offer progressively greater degrees of support from this preferred point through offers of "political compensation" that offset the legislator's respective opportunity costs.

Thus, the legislator has an upward-sloping marginal opportunity-cost or supply function, beginning at her preferred degree of support along the horizontal axis. The intersection of the supply function with the horizontal axis can take place at either a positive or a negative degree of support (see S_1 and S_3, respectively, in Figure 5). A politician who is strongly opposed to a given instrument will have a supply function with a negative intercept on the horizontal axis (and a positive intercept on the vertical axis). For such a legislator, a positive, non-marginal shadow price[87] of political compensation is required for any positive degree of support to be forthcoming (see point A in Figure 5).

The legislator's supply function is affected by several exogenous factors. First, an exogenous increase in the negative impact of a given instrument on a legislator's constituents (for example, the construction in the legislator's district of a new factory that would have to pay pollution taxes) may increase the legislator's opportunity costs of supporting that instrument. Conversely, an exogenous increase in the benefits of an instrument to the legislator's constituents (for example, the expansion of a firm in the district that produced a mandated abatement technology) would decrease the legislator's opportunity costs.

Second, the position of the legislator's political party is also relevant. Parties supply funds and organizational support in reelection campaigns. Moreover, leadership posts in the party offer op-

---

and her constituents' preferences. It is not inconceivable that these could be of opposite sign, but in a representative democracy, that would be the exception, not the rule. As stated by one author, "'If your conscience and your district disagree too often,' members like to say, 'you're in the wrong business.'" FENNO, *supra* note 79, at 142.

87. The shadow price refers to the implicit price or the marginal valuation of the good or service in question.

portunities for increased effectiveness in the legislature. Obviously, parties are likely to be more generous with legislators who are loyal.[88]

Third, the actions of other legislators will have a bearing on the costs of supplying support thanks to the possibilities for vote trading. For example, one legislator may care a great deal about the chosen level of environmental protection, while having only a slight preference for standards over taxes; another legislator may care less about the exact level but have a strong preference for taxes over standards, given her own market-oriented ideology. In a logroll, both legislators could gain from vote trading, with such a logroll affecting both legislators' costs of supplying support for a given instrument.

Fourth and finally, it is both the intent and the consequence of some lobbying activities to shift legislators' supply functions. In other words, in addition to being the primary demanders for alternative forms of regulation, organized interest groups can also play a role in determining the position and shape of legislators' supply functions. Lobbyists might attempt to: affect a legislator's ideologically based perception of the merits of a proposed policy instrument;[89] affect a legislator's perceptions of her constituents' policy preferences;[90] and/or affect a legislator's effort-support production function through provision of information or technical support.[91]

D. Formation of Equilibria and Legislative Outcomes

Up to this point, this Article has focused on the origins of supply and demand for a single policy instrument. However, in many contexts, there will be a *set* of possible instruments considered for achieving a given policy goal: for example, a standard, a tax, and a system of tradeable permits. In addition, there will exist the possibility of doing nothing, i.e., maintaining the status quo. Hence if N alternative instruments are under consideration, then

---

88. Party leaders may conceivably also become effective demanders for policy instrument support by offering various resources to legislators in exchange for support, in which case the parties are essentially functioning as interest groups.

89. *See* KINGDON, *supra* note 42, at 141–42.

90. *See* David Austen-Smith & John R. Wright, *Counteractive Lobbying*, 38 AM. J. POL. SCI. 25, 29–30 (1994).

91. *See* BAUER, *supra* note 76, at 354–57.

there will be N+1 possible choices of action.[92] Each option can define a "political market" for effective support.[93] On the demand side, each policy instrument may have an associated set of interest groups seeking to secure support for it. Moreover, on the supply side, each policy instrument gives rise to its own set of legislator supply functions.[94]

The legislative outcome is the choice of one of the N+1 alternatives arising from the interactions of interest groups' demands for and legislators' supplies of support for alternative instruments. The degree of aggregate support for each instrument results from an equilibrium established in the legislature, and the outcome in the legislature favors the policy instrument with the greatest degree of total support.

The following sections examine the component parts of this process. First, the nature of the aggregation of demand for a policy instrument across interested individuals and groups, and the aggregation of supplies of support for a policy instrument across members of the legislature, is considered. Then, the formation of equilibria in the legislature for alternative policy instruments and the consequent choice of political outcome is examined. Finally, alternative approaches to modeling this political market are discussed.

1. Aggregation of Demand for Policy Instrument Support

Typically, more than one interest group will be pressing for support from the legislature. How is such interest group demand to be aggregated? In the classic model associated with Stigler[95] and Peltzman,[96] the "winner takes all": the highest bidder wins and gains control over regulation. In another model, competing interest groups participate in a zero-sum game along a single dimension: one group is taxed, the other subsidized, and each tries to improve

---

92. The choice set of instruments is simply taken as given. Important questions remain regarding how it is determined, but these are beyond the scope of this Article.

93. An interest group can demand and a legislator can supply support for more than one instrument. Although this may at first seem counterintuitive, recall that each legislator's supply function for a given instrument may include the possibility of opposition.

94. A single legislator may be more efficient at producing support for one instrument than for another and may even have different ideological attitudes towards different instruments. Moreover, the preferences of her reelection constituency may vary across instruments.

95. *See* Stigler, *supra* note 28, at 12–13.

96. *See* Peltzman, *supra* note 30, at 212.

its lot at the expense of the other.[97] In an actual legislature, interest groups may be opposed to one another or aligned in support of the same instrument.

The most obvious approach for aggregating the demand functions of interest groups might be simply to sum, at each level of willingness-to-pay, the degrees of support that each group demands at that price. Such demand aggregation makes sense for private goods, but the support the legislature provides is essentially a public good. Hence, an efficient approach might involve taking a given level of support and vertically summing what each interest group is (marginally) willing to pay for that degree of support. But such an efficient approach is unlikely to reflect positive reality, as long as free-rider problems among interest groups exist. Therefore, the aggregate demand thus calculated represents the upper bound of actual aggregate demand, that is, the demand experienced in the absence of free-riding.

2. Aggregation of Supply of Policy Instrument Options

In this framework, the degree of support by individual legislators is denominated in terms of homogenous units of "effective support," with differences among legislators already incorporated into the underlying production functions with respect to individual marginal opportunity costs of effort (as well as individual marginal ideological and electoral costs). Therefore, the legislature's supply function can be derived by horizontally summing the supply functions of individual legislators. As noted above, some legislators' supply functions may extend to the left of the vertical axis (for example, S_3 in Figure 5), corresponding to opposition to the instrument in question. Therefore, when the individual legislator supply functions are horizontally added, the aggregate supply function for the legislature represents the relevant net supply of support. Like the supply function for an individual legislator, the aggregate supply function for some instruments may intersect the vertical axis at a positive price.

---

97. *See* Becker, *supra* note 31, at 373–76.

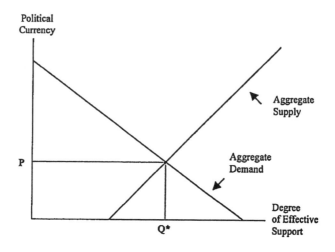

Figure 6
Aggregate Demand and Aggregate Supply of Political Support
and the Formation of a Legislative Equilibrium

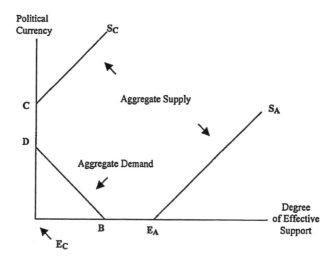

Figure 7
Degenerate Cases in the Political Market

3. Equilibrium Support in the Legislature for a Policy Instrument

The model treats the legislature as a competitive market for the support of policy instruments. Given the homogeneity of the commodity demanded and supplied, the number of members in the two houses of Congress, and the number of active interest groups, perfect competition is a reasonable first approximation. Under that assumption, the equilibrium, aggregate level of "effective support" provided for the policy instrument is the level for which aggregate supply equals aggregate demand (Q* in Figure 6). This level is associated with a shadow price (P in Figure 6) representing the aggregate marginal willingness to pay for support in the legislature's equilibrium.

There are two cases of interest in which the aggregate supply and demand functions do not intersect in the politically relevant positive orthant, the northeast part of the graph where both price and quantity are positive. In one case, the demand function intersects the horizontal axis to the left of the legislature's "aggregate preferred point" (see the gap between points B and E_A in Figure 7). In that instance, the maximum support demanded in aggregate by interest groups (at zero price) is lower than the amount that the legislature would provide on its own. In this case of "excess supply," it is reasonable to assume that the legislature would provide support at its preferred point (E_A). With the likelihood of free-riding among interest groups, it would not be surprising if the aggregate demand by interest groups often fell short of the support a strongly committed legislature would provide absent any lobbying. In the above case, the competitive equilibrium price is zero, with each legislator providing support at her own preferred point.

A second special case arises when a legislature so strongly opposes a policy that its upward-sloping aggregate supply function intersects the vertical axis at a positive price (point C in Figure 7). In this case, the supply function could conceivably lie entirely above the interest groups' aggregate demand function. The political price that such a legislature would require for a positive degree of support is simply greater than the interest groups' overall reservation price for obtaining such support (point D in Figure 7).

In this competitive political market framework, an individual legislator will tend to supply support for a particular policy instrument up to the point where her marginal opportunity costs of doing

The Political Economy of Environmental Regulation

so are equivalent to the infinitely elastic demand for support she faces from interest groups, represented by the horizontal line through the point P in Figure 5 (derived from the equilibrium in Figure 6). Thus, a set of legislators with supply functions represented by S_1, S_2, and S_3 (Figure 5), would provide effective support of Q_1, Q_2, and Q_3, respectively.

The legislator with supply function S_3 provides a negative level of support, i.e., opposition. An interest group might benefit from contributing to this legislator in the hope of reducing her degree of active opposition,[98] just as it can benefit by increasing the support of a "friendly" legislator. It would take a level of demand (and political compensation) equivalent to point A in Figure 5 to move this same legislator to a position of inaction or indifference. On the other hand, legislators such as those represented by S_1 and S_2 in Figure 5 derive benefits (negative costs) from supporting an instrument, no matter what the position of relevant interest groups. Not surprisingly, such friendly legislators supply even greater levels of support in response to interest group demand.

4. Legislative Outcomes

The previous section discussed the equilibrium level of support for a policy instrument by a single legislator. The next step, then, is to ask how these individual levels of support translate into policy outcomes. One could imagine summing the individual levels of support across legislators to find the aggregate support for an instrument. Such an approach is insufficient, however, because it ignores institutional processes (for example, various kinds of voting rules) that influence collective decisions. In moving from individual support to policy outcomes, therefore, the analysis must take institutional features of the legislature into account.

First, the committee structure of Congress (especially in the House of Representatives) gives different legislators widely different levels of influence over policy.[99] Thus, legislators vary greatly

---

98. Hall and Wayman examine legislator participation in committees, and argue that interest groups give contributions to "hostile" legislators in order to reduce their participation, i.e., their opposition. *See* Hall & Wayman, *supra* note 61, at 803.

99. Norms of deference, backed up by repeated interactions and the threat of retaliation, give members of committees and subcommittees significant influence over policies under their jurisdiction. *See* Shepsle & Weingast, *supra* note 61, at 88–89;

in the effectiveness of the support they can supply for a given instrument. However, with the framework's focus on degrees of *effective* support, this reality is already incorporated (through the political support production functions) and has no effect on the appropriate aggregation; it remains one of simple summation of individual equilibria.

Second, legislative outcomes are affected by voting rules. The number of votes necessary for passage (taking into account the veto power of the executive) determines the level and distribution of support needed to pass a bill.[100] Furthermore, the order of voting on amendments and the nature of the final vote also affect the outcome.[101] The question is then how support translates into votes. Whereas the model's "degree of support" is a continuous variable, it produces a binary variable: a vote. Any empirical implementation of this framework would need to address this linkage.[102] For the purposes of this Article, focus can be confined to the reality that, in general, the policy instrument chosen will be the alternative garnering the greatest aggregate support.

5. Alternative Equilibrium Frameworks

Alternative conceptual frameworks of the political market are possible. One potential approach would give greater emphasis to the differences existing among individual legislators in terms of

Weingast & Marshall, *supra* note 61, at 158. Agenda-setting or "gate keeping" powers give committees the right to send bills to the floor or table them in committee. Standing committees are also heavily represented on the conference committees that are established to reconcile differences between the chambers before final passage. Power is particularly concentrated in the hands of committee chairs, who hold sway over the committees' agendas and the bills reported to the floor. Given the importance of committee composition, policy outcomes may differ markedly from the preferences of the legislature as a whole; given low committee turnover and the importance of seniority, the status quo may persist long after support in the full legislature has ebbed. *See* Kenneth A. Shepsle & Barry R. Weingast, *Political Solutions to Market Problems*, 78 AM. POL. SCI. REV. 417, 429 (1984).

100. In the U.S. Congress, a bill needs a bare majority in the House of Representatives, but may have to clear a higher hurdle in the Senate to bring closure to debate. If the President vetoes the bill, of course, two-thirds majorities in both houses are required to enact legislation.

101. If modified by successful amendments, a bill will be considered in opposition to the status quo in the final vote. This arrangement favors the status quo and requires that each bill be compared ultimately with the status quo rather than with other alternatives.

102. Discrete-choice econometric models theoretically based on the existence of an unobserved latent variable are obvious candidates.

the nature of support they can provide. Thus, instead of quantifying support in terms of perfectly homogenous units of "effective support," the "uniqueness" of support from any single legislator (particularly from powerful members of the legislature) would be interpreted as leading to a set of monopoly political markets, rather than to a single competitive political market.

At one extreme, each member of the legislature is assumed to be a monopoly supplier of her unique type of support and is thus facing a downward-sloping demand for her support. As such, there would exist a set of monopoly equilibria, one for each member of the legislature. In their respective equilibria, each member equates her marginal cost (individual supply function) with the "marginal revenue" function associated with the policy demands she faces, and determines her equilibrium (and utility-maximizing) level of support.

The extreme case of multiple monopoly suppliers appears less reasonable than the perfectly competitive case as an approximation of political reality. However, it does illustrate the potential for alternative models of imperfect competition that may be superior for capturing important characteristics of political markets. Various models of cooperative and noncooperative oligopoly might capture significant elements of legislative relationships.[103] Such explorations will not be dealt with here. Instead, in order to develop a conceptual framework within which existing political economy theories can be organized and synthesized, the basic competitive framework is examined further.

IV. DEMAND FOR ENVIRONMENTAL POLICY INSTRUMENTS

Demand-side explanations for the choice among environmental policy instruments can be separated into four sectors of regulatory demand: firms, environmentalists, labor, and consumers.

---

103. For example, the respective roles played by committee chairs and members may be modeled as a monopolist operating in the context of a competitive fringe.

A. Firms

Firms tend to demand the policy instruments promising the highest profits (or the lowest losses) from regulation. While all environmental regulation imposes costs of compliance on firms, not all instruments impose the same costs to achieve a given regulatory goal. Positive political economy explanations of firm demand for environmental regulation can be divided into three principal categories: firm preferences for particular instruments given lower aggregate costs of compliance compared to the industry as a whole; the presence of rents and entry barriers; and differential costs of compliance across firms in a given industry.[104]

1. Lower Aggregate Costs to an Industry as a Whole

All else being equal, firms will tend to prefer regulatory instruments with lower aggregate costs for the industry as a whole. As market-based approaches are likely more cost-effective than command-and-control instruments, the above would suggest that private industry as a whole would generally prefer market-based approaches. However, a crucial distinction exists between the aggregate cost for society and the aggregate cost for private industry. By definition, cost-effective instruments minimize costs to society; they may however vary in proportion of costs imposed on polluters. Accordingly, the use of market-based instruments does not guarantee that firms' compliance costs will be less than the compliance costs of command-and-control regulation.

---

104. There are other plausible explanations for firms' preferences. Firms may simply support the continuation of the status quo, which is generally the command-and-control approach, because replacing familiar policies with new instruments can mean that existing expertise within firms becomes less valued. *See* STEVEN P. KELMAN, WHAT PRICE INCENTIVES? 118–22 (1981); Stewart, *supra* note 16, at 40. For example, lobbyists—the agents in a principal-agent relationship—may be rationally expected to resist the dissipation of their human capital. *See* Robert W. Hahn & Robert N. Stavins, *Incentive-based Environmental Regulation: A New Era from an Old Idea*, 18 ECOLOGY L.Q. 1, 24 (1991). It has also been suggested that market-based instruments may be opposed simply because they are not well understood, and there is at least anecdotal evidence that this has been the case. *See* KELMAN at 96, above; W.P. Welch, *The Political Feasibility of Full Ownership Property Rights: The Case of Pollution and Fisheries*, 16 POL'Y SCI. 165, 175 (1983). Such lack of understanding can also affect the supply side, and we discuss this later.

It would then follow that firms would oppose regulatory instruments that shift a greater cost burden onto industry. For instance, the virtually unanimous opposition by private industry to pollution taxes results from the fact that, under such schemes, firms pay not only their private costs of compliance, but also the costs of tax payments to the government for any residual emissions.[105] Similarly, under tradeable permit schemes, firms bear equivalent costs if the initial distribution of the permits is through an auction. In contrast, under a tradeable permit scheme with grandfathered permits, existing firms do not bear any cost for their residual emissions.[106]

The above suggests that private industry as a whole would prefer grandfathered permits *and* standards to other instruments, since grandfathered permits are cost-effective and the burden placed on industry (at least on existing firms) is minimized. Emissions standards are usually worse for industry in terms of the total-cost criterion, but are likely to be preferred by firms to auctioned permits or taxes.

2. Generation of Rents and Erection of Entry Barriers

Certain types of regulations can actually augment firms' profits through the generation of rents and the erection of entry barriers. In general, firms earn rents if a regulatory instrument drives price above average cost. Assume the case of a command-and-control standard that sets an allowable level of aggregate pollution for each firm, where firms can meet the standard only by reducing output.[107] Assume further that the industry is initially made up of many identical firms, each facing an identical demand, with classical

---

105. On this point, *see* KELMAN, *supra* note 104, at 120; *see also* FRANK S. ARNOLD, ECONOMIC ANALYSIS OF ENVIRONMENTAL POLICY AND REGULATION 227 (1995); ROBERT W. CRANDALL, CONTROLLING INDUSTRIAL POLLUTION 70 (1983); Robert W. Hahn & Roger G. Noll, *Environmental Markets in the Year 2000*, 3 J. RISK UNCERTAINTY 351, 359 (1990). Actually, firms pay less than the full amount of the tax, since a share is passed on to consumers.

106. Grandfathering distributes the rents from permits to firms that participate in the initial allocation, in contrast with an auction. *See* Donald N. Dewees, *Instrument Choice in Environmental Policy*, 21 ECON. INQUIRY 53, 59 (1983); Gary W. Yohe, *Polluters' Profits and Political Response: Direct Control Versus Taxes: Comment*, 66 AM. ECON. REV. 981, 981 (1976).

107. *See* James M. Buchanan & Gordon Tullock, *Polluters' Profits and Political Response: Direct Control Versus Taxes*, 65 AM. ECON. REV. 139, 140 (1975).

average and marginal cost functions. In the absence of regulation, each firm would produce at the intersection of its marginal and average cost curves, making zero profits. The environmental standard reduces total production and therefore raises price along the aggregate demand curve. If the environmental restriction is not exceptionally severe, the new price will be above average cost for all firms. Firms, therefore, earn rent: the difference between the price they receive for their product and their cost of production. If entry is prohibited, existing firms will continue earning rents into the future; even if not, rents will last until enough new firms enter to reestablish competitive equilibrium at the new price. Hence, in the above model, firms may prefer standards to no regulation at all, and firms will prefer standards to taxes, since a tax charges for a resource that otherwise would be free.[108]

Firms, however, are not limited to the single response of cutting output. They can also reduce emissions by adopting new technologies or by changing their input mix. In this more general and realistic scenario, depending on the stringency of the standards and other factors, command-and-control standards can still have the effect of providing rents to regulated firms.[109] Here, too, under certain conditions, firms may prefer command-and-control standards to no regulation at all.[110]

It is important to note that the enhanced industry profitability resulting from rents will be sustainable over the long term *only* in the presence of entry restrictions. Thus, firms regulated by a rent-generating instrument, such as command-and-control standards, will

---

108. Even if the restriction is severe enough to impose losses on firms, they will prefer standards to taxes, which impose new costs. In the long run, under a tax scheme, firms will exit the industry until a new zero-profit equilibrium is reached; in the short term, firms will lose money. The tax reduces each firm's present value of income, whether it remains in the industry or exits. Firms will therefore oppose the introduction of pollution taxes.

109. *See* Michael T. Maloney & Robert E. McCormick, *A Positive Theory of Environmental Quality Regulation*, 25 J.L. & ECON. 99, 105 (1982).

110. Pollution restrictions raise both the average and marginal cost curves. Each firm will produce at the level where restricted marginal cost intersects the per-firm demand curve. If the minimum average cost under regulation is to the left of this point, the price (marginal cost) will exceed average cost, and firms will earn rents. Maloney and McCormick identified three conditions that are sufficient for regulation to enhance producer profits: (1) output under regulation corresponds to some cost-minimizing level of output in the absence of regulation; (2) pollution increases with output; and (3) average costs increase more at higher levels of output under regulation. *See id.* at 104. The necessary and sufficient condition for higher profits is that the intersection of average and marginal cost under regulation lie to the left of the firm's demand curve.

benefit if that instrument is linked to a mechanism that imposes barriers to entry. In theory, such a mechanism might prohibit new entry outright; a more politically feasible approach would impose higher costs on new entrants.[111]

The above body of theory explains why private firms (and their trade associations) may have a strong preference for command-and-control standards, which may create rents, and especially for considerably more stringent command-and-control standards for new pollution sources, which create barriers to entry.[112] The indication that firms would support this form of regulation begins to explain the prevalence of such instruments in U.S. environmental law. Furthermore, the theory indicates that, under certain conditions, the regulated industry would be better off than without regulation.

Although the theoretical arguments are strong, there are no conclusive empirical validations of these demand-side propositions. Direct empirical tests of firm demand for regulatory instruments (such as analyses of resources devoted to lobbying for such instruments as a function of firms' stakes in an issue) are virtually nonexistent. Instead, most empirical work in this area simply seeks to measure the benefits an industry receives under regulation. Thus, the work examines not instrument demand itself, but rather the presumed product of such demand.[113]

The above discussion also provides a positive political economy explanation for why market-based instruments have virtually

---

111. *See* Stigler, *supra* note 28, at 3, 5; Eric Rasmusen & Mark Zupan, *Extending the Economic Theory of Regulation to the Form of Policy*, 72 PUB. CHOICE 167, 187–89 (1991).

112. Other barriers to entry result, for example, from the permitting requirements for new sources under the PSD and non-attainment programs under the Clean Air Act, as well as by non-attainment programs' offset requirements for new sources. The positive significance of scarcity rents as a major explanation for the prevalence of particular forms of environmental regulation has important normative implications as well. This is because, in the presence of pre-existing tax distortions, the distribution of these rents can have efficiency implications. *See* Fullerton & Metcalf, *supra* note 19, at 44–45. It is ironic that the mechanism that facilitates political acceptance of some environmental policies (transmission of scarcity rents to the regulated sector) may also undo some or all of the welfare gains that would have been forthcoming.

113. Several researchers employed financial market event analysis in two regulatory cases to test whether the value of regulated firms (measured by stock market prices) was positively affected by the announcement of regulation, as the economic theory of regulation would suggest. They found that cotton dust standards promulgated by the U.S. Occupational, Safety, and Health Administration ("OSHA") raised the asset value of cotton producers, which is consistent with the notion that regulation increased firms' profits by

always taken the form of grandfathered tradeable permits, or at least why private firms should be expected to have strong demands for this means of permit allocation. In tradeable permit schemes, grandfathering not only conveys scarcity rents to firms, since existing polluters are granted valuable economic resources for free, but also provides entry barriers, in that new entrants must purchase permits from existing holders.[114]

The preceding discussion does not provide a compelling explanation for the prevalence of command-and-control standards over grandfathered tradeable permits. In principle, either instrument could provide sustainable rents to existing firms. The theory needs to be extended to explain this phenomenon.

3. Differential Costs across Firms in an Industry

An alternate explanation for the landscape of environmental policy instruments arises from the existence of differential costs of environmental compliance across firms. Due to this heterogeneity, a firm may support policy instruments that impose costs on it, as long as those costs affect it less than the industry average, giving it a competitive advantage.[115] For example, firms which could reduce lead content at relatively low costs (thanks to large refineries) tended to support the tradeable permit system by which the leaded content of gasoline was reduced in the 1980s,[116] while firms with less efficient, smaller refineries were vehemently opposed.[117] Other

---

creating rents. *See* Maloney & McCormick, *supra* note 109, at 122. However, a more comprehensive study reached the opposite conclusion. *See* John S. Hughes et al., *The Economic Consequences of the OSHA Cotton Dust Standards: An Analysis of Stock Market Price Behavior*, 29 J.L. ECON. 29, 58–59 (1986).

114. One research group provided anecdotal evidence for rent-seeking in the decision making process over EPA's implementation of the Montreal Protocol restricting the use and production of CFCs. *See* Hahn & McGartland, *supra* note 19, at 601–10. They argue that a rent-seeking model explains the positions of large producers supporting grandfathered tradeable permits and opposing other implementation schemes, including an auction proposal. *See id.*

115. *See* ROBERT A. LEONE & JOHN E. JACKSON, STUDIES IN PUBLIC REGULATION 231, 247 (Gary Fromm ed. 1981); Sharon Oster, *The Strategic Use of Regulatory Investment by Industry Sub-groups*, 20 ECON. INQUIRY 604, 606 (1982).

116. *See* KERR & MARÉ, *supra* note 24, at 31.

117. *See* Small Refiner Lead Phasedown Task Force v. EPA, 705 F.2d 506, 514 (D.C. Cir. 1983) (discussing small refineries' opposition). Another example of such intra-industry differentials, and the resulting splintering of lobbying strategy, occurred when the National Coal Association ("NCA") divided over the question of scrubber requirements in clean air legislation. A universal scrubber requirement would have preserved demand for eastern

empirical work, however, has cast doubt on the proposition that firms advocate instruments based on inter-industry or intra-industry transfers.[118]

Another form of cost differential arises as a result of barriers to entry. It is important to maintain the distinction between the entry of new firms and the expansion of existing firms. Entry barriers from environmental regulation generally apply to both situations. Within an industry, firms with no plans to expand would derive greater benefit from entry barriers, potentially discouraging further growth by their competitors.

Conversely, firms with ambitious expansion plans relative to their existing operations would benefit from weaker barriers. Such firms would also try to structure barriers in a manner giving them an advantage relative to newcomers. For example, the "bubble" program of the Clean Air Act creates barriers that are less onerous for existing firms because firms are allowed to engage in intra-firm emissions trading.[119] Under this program, a firm can reduce the emissions of an existing source by an amount at least equal to the emissions of the new source, instead of having to take the more costly step of meeting the command-and-control standard otherwise applicable to new sources.[120] The CAA's banking policies, which allow intra-firm trading across time periods, also make expansion by an incumbent easier than entry by a new firm.

---

coal, which had higher sulfur content than its cleaner western competition. The NCA split between eastern and western coal producers and stayed out of the debates leading up to the 1977 Clean Air Act Amendments. *See* BRUCE A. ACKERMAN & WILLIAM T. HASSLER, CLEAN COAL/DIRTY AIR 31 (1981). Similarly, the largest producers of CFCs (DuPont and Imperial Chemical Industries) supported a ban on CFCs mainly because they were the firms best able to develop substitutes. *See* Kenneth A. Oye & James H. Maxwell, *Self-Interest and Environmental Management, in* LOCAL COMMONS AND GLOBAL INTERDEPENDENCE: HETEROGENEITY AND COOPERATION IN TWO DOMAINS 191, 198 (Robert O. Keohane & Elinor Ostrom eds., 1995).

118. Several researchers found that legislators with a paper producer in their districts voted against water pollution control legislation, regardless of whether the producer stood to gain or lose relative to its competitors. *See* LEONE & JACKSON, *supra* note 115, at 247. These authors note that firms may oppose regulation out of uncertainty concerning how the legislation will be implemented, since cost predictions depend on subsequent rulemaking decisions by administrative agencies. *Id.* at 248.

119. *See* 51 Fed. Reg. 43,814, 43,830 (1986). The bubble program typically permits only geographically contiguous trades. Thus, even among existing firms with expansion plans, the benefits of the program depend on where the expansion is contemplated.

120. Inter-firm trading (as opposed to only intra-firm trading) would eliminate this advantage. *See* 51 Fed. Reg. 43,814, 43,847–48 (1986).

The mechanism for allocating tradeable permits might also produce different winners and losers within an industry. Under a grandfathering scheme that allocates permits on the basis of emissions at the time of the scheme's establishment, firms investing in pollution abatement prior to regulation stand to lose relative to their more heavily polluting competitors.[121] Although such investing and expanding firms might conceivably prefer the allocation of permits by means of an initial auction,[122] smaller firms often prefer grandfathering out of concern that auctions will be dominated by larger players.[123]

B. Environmental Organizations

As noted above, the utility of an environmental advocacy group will probably be affected by both the organization's well-being and the level of environmental quality. First, organizational well-being may be measured partly by budgetary resources, which are a function of donor contributions. This financial concern can affect an organization's demand for specific policy instruments if such support attracts members, persuades donors to make contributions, or, more broadly, increases the visibility and prestige of the organization. Hence, an organization's demand for a given policy instrument is likely to be affected by several factors, all else being equal:

---

121. *See* Hahn & Noll, *supra* note 105, at 359.

122. Some supporting evidence is provided by the establishment of a market in takeoff and landing slots at the nation's busiest airports. Since 1968, peak-hour takeoffs and landings have been restricted at LaGuardia, John F. Kennedy, O'Hare, and Washington National Airports. Until 1986, these slots were allocated by a scheduling committee composed of the airlines using a given airport. In that year, the Federal Aviation Administration ("FAA") replaced the committee allocation system with a system of grandfathered tradeable permits. *See Government Policies on the Transfer of Operating Rights Granted by the Federal Government: Hearings before the Subcomm. on Aviation of the House Comm. on Pub. Works and Transp.*, 99th Cong. 2–4 (1985) (statement of Rep. Norman Y. Mineta). In the months before the proposal was to go into effect, Congress held hearings and considered whether to overrule the FAA. At the hearings, large airlines, which already held most of the slots, supported grandfathering. *See, e.g., id.* at 55–56 (statement of Robert L. Crandall, CEO, American Airlines); *id.* at 96 (statement of Steven G. Rothmeier, CEO, Northwest Airlines). In contrast, upstart airlines looking to expand but having few slots, such as People Express, Republic, and Western, vigorously opposed grandfathering, calling for a large percentage of existing slots to be auctioned or distributed by lottery. *See, e.g., id.* at 71 (statement of Robert E. Cohn, CEO, People Express); *id.* at 372 (statement of A.B. Magary, Marketing VP, Republic Airlines).

123. *See* Hahn & McGartland, *supra* note 19, at 606. Similarly, since the transition to a grandfathered-permits system is likely to involve less uncertainty than an auction, it might receive disproportionate support from risk-averse firms. *Id.* at 605.

the likelihood that the instrument will be chosen by policymakers;[124] the degree to which the organization is clearly identified with supporting the instrument; the magnitude of potential funding gains from distinguishing the organization from other environmental groups; and the ability to offer donors and members a compelling environmental quality argument in support of the instrument.

A prominent example is provided by the Environmental Defense Fund's ("EDF") enthusiastic and effective support of the SO_2 allowance trading system adopted as part of the Clean Air Act Amendments of 1990. With the Bush Administration eager to back up the President's claim of being "the environmental President," and with key senior staff in the Administration having strong predispositions to the use of market-based approaches, the proposal had a strong chance of success. EDF had already become a champion of market-based approaches to environmental protection in other, less nationally prominent, domains. Now it faced an opportunity to strengthen that position and solidify its reputation as a pragmatic environmental organization willing to adopt new strategies involving less confrontation with private industry. By supporting tradeable permits, EDF could seize a market niche in the environmental movement, distinguishing itself further from other groups. Importantly, EDF was able to make a powerful argument for tradeable permits on environmental, as opposed to economic, grounds: the use of a cost-effective instrument would make it politically possible to achieve greater reductions in sulfur dioxide emissions than would otherwise be the case.[125]

EDF is an outlier in this realm. Most environmental advocacy groups have been relatively hostile towards market-based instruments. This should not be terribly surprising. Because of their interest in strengthening environmental protection, environmental organizations might be expected to prefer command-and-control approaches to market-based schemes for philosophical, strategic, and technical reasons. On philosophical grounds, environmentalists

---

124. There is an important distinction between advocacy groups' strategic and tactical decisions. An environmental organization's strategic decision to express demand for a policy instrument and get it on the agenda for consideration tends to be positively related to perceived probability of success, whereas the tactical decision to express demand for an instrument already on the agenda may well be negatively related to probability of success.

125. *See* Hahn & Stavins, *supra* note 104, at 33 n.180.

have portrayed pollution taxes and tradeable permits as "license[s] to pollute[.]"[126] Moreover, they have voiced concerns that damages from pollution—to human health and to ecological well-being—are so difficult or impossible to quantify and monetize that the harm cannot be calculated through a marginal damage function or captured by a Pigouvian tax rate.[127]

Second, environmental organizations may oppose market-based schemes on strategic grounds. Once implemented, permit levels and tax rates may be more difficult to alter than command-and-control standards. If permits are given the status of "property rights," an attempt to reduce pollution levels in the future may meet with "takings" claims and demands for government compensation.[128] This concern, however, can be alleviated by an explicit statutory provision (like that contained in the acid rain provisions of the Clean Air Act Amendments of 1990) stating that permits do not represent property rights,[129] or by "sunset" provisions that specify a particular period of time during which a permit is valid.

Likewise, in the case of pollution taxes, if increased tax rates become desirable in response to new information about a pollutant or about the response of firms to the existing taxes, adjustment may be unlikely because raising tax rates is politically difficult. Furthermore, taxes have long been treated as "political footballs" in the United States (as in the recent case of efforts to reduce gasoline taxes). Hence, environmental organizations might oppose pollution taxes out of fear that they would be reduced or eliminated over time. A related strategic reason for environmentalists' opposition of tax instruments is that a shift from command-and-control to tax-based environmental regulation would shift authority from environment committees in the Congress, frequently dominated by pro-environment legislators, to tax-writing committees, which are generally more conservative.[130]

Third, environmental organizations may object to decentralized instruments on technical grounds. Although market-based in-

---

126. *See* KELMAN, *supra* note 104, at 44. This criticism overlooks the fact that under conventional command-and-control regulations, firms receive these same licenses to pollute for free. *See* Hahn & Stavins, *supra* note 104, at 37.

127. *See* KELMAN, *supra* note 104, at 54–55.

128. *See* Hahn & Noll, *supra* note 105, at 359.

129. *See* 42 U.S.C. § 7651b(f) (1994).

130. *See* KELMAN, *supra* note 104, at 139–42. Note that these strategic arguments refer, for the most part, to pollution taxes, not to market-based instruments in general.

356   *Harvard Environmental Law Review*   [Vol. 22

struments are theoretically superior in terms of cost-effectiveness, problems may arise in translating theory into practice.[131] For example, an emission tax or tradeable permit scheme can lead to localized "hot spots" with relatively high levels of ambient pollution.[132] While this problem can be addressed in theory through the use of permits or charge systems that are denominated in units of environmental degradation, the design of such systems might be perceived as excessively cumbersome.[133]

C. Labor

Since unions generally seek to protect jobs, they might be expected to oppose instruments likely to lead to plant closings or other large industrial dislocations. Under a tradeable permit scheme, for example, firms might close their factories in heavily polluted areas, sell permits, and relocate to less polluted areas, where permits are less expensive.[134] In contrast, command-and-control standards have generally been tailored to protect aging plants. The threat of factory dislocation is a likely explanation of support from northern, urban members of Congress for the PSD policy in clean air regulation, which has discouraged movement of industry out of urban areas in the northeast into high-quality air sheds in the South and West.[135] Depending on the tradeoffs between job creation and preservation effects, labor might support stricter command-and-control standards for new sources.[136]

Indeed, one reason environmental groups such as EDF have endorsed the tradeable permits approach is that it promises the cost savings of taxes without the drawbacks that environmentalists associate with tax instruments.

131. *See* Robert W. Hahn & Robert L. Axtell, *Reevaluating the Relationship Between Transferable Property Rights and Command-and-Control Regulation*, 8 J. REG. ECON. 125, 126–27 (1995).

132. *See* Richard L. Revesz, *Federalism and Interstate Environmental Externalities*, 144 U. PA. L. REV. 2341, 2412 (1996).

133. *See id.* at 2412–14.

134. *See* Hahn & Noll, *supra* note 105, at 358.

135. *See, e.g.*, CRANDALL, *supra* note 105, at 127–29 (1983); B. Peter Pashigan, *Environmental Regulation: Whose Self-Interests Are Being Protected?*, 23 ECON. INQUIRY 551, 552–53 (1985).

136. There are other examples of labor concern over the choice of environmental policy instruments. In the 1977 debates over amendments to the Clean Air Act, eastern coal miners' unions fought to include a command-and-control standard that effectively required scrubbing, thereby seeking to ensure continued reliance on cheap, high-sulfur coal from the east, over cleaner western coal. *See* ACKERMAN & HASSLER, *supra* note 117, at

D. Consumers

To the extent that consumer groups have preferences among environmental policy instruments, one might expect them to favor those instruments that minimize any increases in the prices of consumer goods and services; this would seem to suggest cost-effective (hence, market-based) instruments over command-and-control.[137] In practice, however, these groups typically have not expressed strong demand for environmental policies. As mentioned above, free-riding and limited information are likely to present greater obstacles for consumer organizations than for environmental groups, especially on environmental issues. Thus demand from consumer groups for environmental policy instruments is likely to be muted. Moreover, environmental policy may lie outside the core concerns of consumer groups' constituents. Indeed, when consumer groups do get involved, it may be on "consumer health and safety" issues, where their interests are aligned with those of environmentalists. Calls for cost-effective policies might also be voiced by taxpayer organizations, but again, the minutiae of instrument choice lie outside the scope of these groups' primary concerns. Hence, environmental groups are unlikely to face significant opposition from other public interest organizations.

V. SUPPLY OF ENVIRONMENTAL POLICY INSTRUMENTS

There are several plausible positive political economy explanations for the nature of the supply of environmental policy instruments. First, legislators and their staffs are thought to be predisposed by their predominantly legal training to favor command-and-

---

31. Likewise, in the debates over the SO_2 allowance trading system in the 1990 amendments to the CAA, the United Mine Workers opposed the system because it would create incentives for the use of low-sulfur coal from largely non-unionized mines in Wyoming's Powder River Basin over high-sulfur coal from eastern, unionized mines. *See Clean Air Reauthorization: Hearing Before the Subcomm. on Energy and Power of the House Comm. on Energy and Commerce*, 101st Cong. 455–56 (1989) (statement of Richard L. Trumka, President, United Mine Workers).

137. It is also possible to distinguish among types of market-based instruments and types of command-and-control instruments, given that any environmental policy instrument that generates privately retained scarcity rents (such as new source performance standards, grandfathered tradeable permits, and others) also raises consumer prices, relative to a policy that does not generate such rents. *See* Fullerton & Metcalf, *supra* note 19, at 44.

control approaches to regulation.[138] Similarly, legislators may need to spend time learning about unfamiliar policy instruments before they can provide substantial support, thereby giving rise to a status quo bias in favor of the current regime of command-and-control regulation.[139] Both these effects may become weaker in the coming years, as a result of the increasing understanding of economics among lawyers as well as among legislators and their staffs.[140]

Second, ideology plays a significant role in instrument choice. A conservative lawmaker who generally supports the free market might be predisposed to support market-based instruments; a legislator with more faith in government and less faith in the private sector might, all else being equal, prefer a command-and-control approach. A 1981 survey of congressional staff members found that support and opposition to effluent charges was based largely on ideological grounds.[141] For example, Republicans who supported the concept of pollution charges offered assertions such as "I trust the marketplace more" or "less bureaucracy" is desirable, without any real awareness or understanding of the economic arguments for market-based programs.[142] Likewise, Democratic opposition was

---

138. *See* ALLEN V. KNEESE & CHARLES L. SCHULZE, POLLUTION, PRICES, AND PUBLIC POLICY 116–17 (1975).

139. *See id.* at 114–15. This argument assumes that a legislator (or at least her staff) needs to understand an instrument in order to support it. Although such understanding might not be a precondition for voting in favor of the instrument, it is more important for other forms of support, such as insertion of a statement into the legislative history, efforts to get a bill through committee, or attempts to persuade other legislators. Moreover, a lack of understanding may hurt the legislator in her reelection campaign if the press or an opponent seeks to make it an issue. Thus, the greater the prominence of an issue, the more important it will be for a legislator to have a compelling rationale for her position. Responding to this need, interest groups may supply legislators with justifications for supporting given policies. *See, e.g.,* FENNO, *supra* note 79, at 141–43; KINGDON, *supra* note 42, at 46–48.

140. *See* Hahn & Stavins, *supra* note 104, at 31, 36. Thus, outreach efforts by economists and others may be thought to have both demand-side and supply-side effects. On the demand side, increased understanding of market-based instruments may have increased the demand for these instruments by various interest groups. On the supply side, increased understanding reduces learning costs for legislators. Since both effects translate into rightward shifts of the respective functions, the outcome is unambiguous in terms of increased degrees of support.

Economists have also played a sometimes significant role as advocates of market-based instruments on efficiency grounds, not only in aspects of environmental policy (such as the U.S. acid rain program) but also in other policy areas, such as the allocation of airport landing spots and the broadcast spectrum. Economists therefore might be seen as acting as "policy entrepreneurs" outside of the interest group-politician nexus (i.e., outside of the strict supply-and-demand framework posited here). *See id.* at 41.

141. *See* KELMAN, *supra* note 104, at 100.

142. *See id.* at 100, 104.

largely based upon analogously ideological factors, with little or no apparent understanding of the real advantages or disadvantages of the various instruments.[143]

Third, constituents react to their perceptions of the costs and benefits to themselves and others of a particular policy, regardless of the real costs and benefits.[144] The more visible the benefits, the greater the demand for an instrument; the more visible the costs, the greater the opposition and thus the political costs to the legislator. The importance of perceived costs and benefits is a consequence of the limited information most voters have about the details of public policy.[145] Hence, politicians are likely to prefer command-and-control instruments because they tend to hide the costs of regulation in the price increases passed on to consumers.[146] In contrast, though they impose lower total costs, market-based instruments generally impose those costs directly, in the form of effluent or permit charges.[147] Grandfathered permits fare better on the visibility criterion than auctioned permits or taxes, because no money is exchanged at the time of the initial allocation.[148]

---

143. *See id.* at 100–01.

144. *See, e.g.,* Matthew D. McCubbins & Terry Sullivan, *Constituency Influences on Legislative Policy Choice,* 18 QUANTITY & QUALITY 299, 301–02 (1984); Robert W. Hahn, *Jobs and Environmental Quality: Some Implications for Instrument Choice,* 20 POL'Y SCI. 289, 299 (1987).

145. A rational voter will choose to remain ignorant on most issues, because the costs of gathering information are likely to outweigh the nearly insignificant benefits from voting knowledgeably. *See* ANTHONY DOWNS, AN ECONOMIC THEORY OF DEMOCRACY 212–13 (1957). In contrast, organized interest groups with large stakes in an issue are likely to be well-informed and thus overrepresented in the political process. These issues raised by asymmetric information are particularly relevant to instrument choice, because votes on instrument choice are often much more technical than votes on policy goals, and therefore attract even less attention from average voters. *See generally* James T. Hamilton, *Taxes, Torts, and the Toxics Release Inventory: Congressional Voting on Instruments to Control Pollution,* 35 ECON. INQUIRY 745 (1997).

146. *See* McCubbins & Sullivan, *supra* note 144, at 306. The point that politicians prefer, all else being equal, regulatory instruments with "invisible" associated costs is related to the more general notion that legislators may seek to disguise transfers to special interests. *See* Stephen Coate & Stephen Morris, *On the Form of Transfers to Special Interests,* 103 J. POL. ECON. 1210, 1212 (1995).

147. The potential government revenue offered by auctions and taxes is likely to be politically attractive. *See* Hahn & McGartland, *supra* note 19, at 608–09.

148. One commentator emphasized the importance of observable costs and benefits in explaining why Wisconsin chose a largely state-funded pollution-credit program over an effluent charge. *See* Hahn, *supra* note 144, at 299. The instrument offered visible job creation, by favoring the construction of new facilities, at the expense of diffuse, less visible costs to widely distributed third parties. In contrast, the market-based alternative would have appeared to sacrifice jobs while its cost-saving benefits would have been less evident. *See id.* at 299–300.

Fourth, voters' limited information may also lead politicians to engage in symbolic politics: the use of superficial slogans and symbols to attract constituent support, even when the policies actually implemented are either ineffectual or inconsistent with the symbols employed. Such symbolism offers the legislator political benefits at little opportunity cost. Command-and-control instruments are likely to be well suited to symbolic politics, because strict standards, as strong statements of support for environmental protection, can be readily combined with less visible exemptions.[149] Congress has on several occasions passed environmental laws with strict compliance standards, while simultaneously including lax or insufficient enforcement measures.[150] Tradeable permits and taxes do not offer the powerful symbolic benefits of declaring strict standards. Moreover, it may be difficult to have market-based instruments which simultaneously "exempt" certain parties or which are "loosely" enforced.[151]

Fifth, if politicians are risk averse, they will prefer instruments involving more certain effects.[152] With respect to environmental policy instruments, uncertainty is likely to arise with respect to the distribution of costs and benefits among the affected actors and to the implementation of the legislative decision by the bureaucracy. The flexibility inherent in permits and taxes creates uncertainty about distributional effects and local levels of environmental quality.[153] Typically, legislators are more concerned with the distribution of costs and benefits than with a comparison of total benefits and costs.[154] For this reason, aggregate cost-effectiveness, perhaps the major advantage of market-based instruments, is likely to play a less significant role in the legislative calculus than whether a

---

149. *See* Hahn & Noll, *supra* note 105, at 361. Of course, the reliance on voter ignorance may be countered by better informed interest groups.

150. *See id.*

151. *But see* Joskow & Schmalensee, supra note 21 (examining Congressional attempts to confer benefits on particular firms within the context of the SO_2 allowance trading program).

152. *See* Matthew D. McCubbins et al., *Structure and Process, Politics and Policy: Administrative Arrangements and the Political Control of Agencies*, 75 VA. L. REV. 431, 437 n.22 (1989) ("Legislators are likely to behave as if they are risk averse, even if they are personally risk neutral, if their constituents punish unpredictable policy choices or their reelection probability is nearly unity.").

153. *See* Matthew D. McCubbins & Talbot Page, *The Congressional Foundations of Agency Performance*, 51 PUB. CHOICE 173, 178 (1986).

154. *See* Hahn & Stavins, *supra* note 104, at 38–41.

politician is getting the best deal possible for her constituents.[155] Moreover, politicians are likely to oppose instruments (such as tradeable permit schemes) that may induce firms to close business and relocate elsewhere, leading to localized unemployment.[156] Although there will be winners as well as losers from such relocation, potential losers are likely to be more certain of their status than potential gainers. This asymmetry creates a bias in favor of the status quo.[157]

Sixth, command-and-control instruments offer Congress greater control with respect to the implementation of legislative outcomes by administrative agencies. To ensure that the interests of the winning coalition are protected in implementation, Congress may effectively prescribe administrative rules and procedures that favor one group over another.[158] In theory, such a practice protects intended beneficiaries of legislation by constraining the scope of subsequent executive intervention in implementation.[159] If stacking the deck is an important aspect of policymaking, it is more likely to be successful in the context of command-and-control legislation. Market-based instruments leave the allocation of costs and benefits

---

155. *See* Kenneth A. Shepsle & Barry Weingast, *Political Solutions to Market Problems*, 78 AM. POL. SCI. REV. 417, 418–20 (1984).

156. *See* Hahn & Noll, *supra* note 105, at 358. Tradeable permits are more likely to be adopted in cases where the industry to be regulated is relatively dispersed and has relatively homogeneous abatement costs. *See id.* at 363–64. But such homogeneity also means that the gains from a market-based approach are more limited.

157. The Clean Air Act Amendments of 1977 provide an example of legislation built upon such compromises. *See id.* at 361–62. Stringent standards for urban non-attainment areas were offset by industry-specific exemptions and by measures preventing relocation of urban factories to less polluted areas, the so-called PSD policy described above. *See id.* at 361. The winning coalition would likely not have held up under a tradeable permit scheme, which would have allowed rust belt firms to purchase pollution permits from firms in cleaner areas and thus to relocate. *See id.* On the other hand, a tradeable permit scheme that prevented interregional trading could presumably have protected northern factory jobs just as well.

For the same reason, grandfathering of tradeable permits is more likely to attract a winning coalition than auctions, since grandfathering allows leeway in rewarding firms and distributing the costs and benefits of regulation among jurisdictions. Several prominent researchers have examined the political process of allocating SO_2 emissions permits in the 1990 amendments to the Clean Air Act. *See* Joskow & Schmalensee, *supra* note 21. Their focus was on empirically measuring the role of interest group politics and rent-seeking in how those permits were allocated, but another point is made clear by their work: allocating permits by grandfathering can produce fairly clear "winners" and "losers" among firms and states. *See id.* An auction, on the other hand, would allow no such political maneuvering.

158. *See* McCubbins et al., *supra* note 152, at 244.

159. *See id.* at 261–62.

298

up to the market, treating polluters identically.[160] Standards, on the other hand, open up possibilities for stacking the deck, by building protections in favor of particular constituencies.[161] For example, Congress might favor industry by placing the burden of proof in standard-setting on the administrative agencies, or alternatively help out environmental groups by including citizen-suit provisions allowing legal action to impel standards enforcement.

Seventh, bureaucrats are less likely to undermine the legislative decision if their preferences over policy instruments are accommodated. Administrative decisionmakers are likely to oppose decentralized instruments on several grounds: they are familiar with command-and-control approaches; market-based instruments may not require the same kinds of technical expertise that agencies have developed under command-and-control regulation; and market-based instruments imply a scaled-down role for the agency by shifting decisionmaking from the bureaucracy to private firms, undermining the agency's prestige and its staff's job security.[162]

VI. CONCLUSIONS

This Article has attempted to synthesize the seemingly diverse strands of the positive political economy literature by viewing them as relating to component parts of a political market framework. In this framework, interest groups have demands for particular instruments. Legislators, in turn, provide political support for such instruments. The demands of the various interest groups are aggregated, as are the supplies of support from individual legislators. The interaction of such aggregate demand and supply produce a legislature's equilibrium level of aggregate support, with each member simultaneously determining her effective support level. The effective support levels of the various legislators are combined, in an institutional context, to produce the legislature's choice of policy instrument.

This framework is far from complete, since it focuses on the decisions of individual legislators, while leaving unanswered those questions of how individual (and continuous) legislator support

---

160. *See* Hahn & Noll, *supra* note 105, at 362.
161. *See id.*
162. *See* Hahn & Stavins, *supra* note 104, at 14, 21.

translates into binary votes and how such support or votes are aggregated to the level of the legislature. For example, the model does not deal with the nature of competition among legislators, only briefly considers the role that congressional committees and other institutions play in structuring and influencing instrument choice, and does not explain how instrument choices are framed. Likewise, this is only a competitive legislative model as a first approximation; alternative approaches were discussed briefly. These issues represent promising avenues for extending this framework and building a workable model of instrument choice.

This Article takes a modest step toward a unified framework for positive analysis of policy instrument choice. This framework may permit greater understanding than approaches that focus almost exclusively on one component of the problem at a time. Thus, for example, if one considers only the benefits that a particular industry derives from a proposed regulatory program, one might conclude that a program will be forthcoming if the benefits are sufficiently high. Attention to questions of supply shows why this might not be the case. If the legislature prefers the status quo to the instrument demanded by the interest group, and if the legislature's aggregate supply function is sufficiently inelastic, there may be no equilibrium under which the legislature provides positive support for the demanded instrument. Indeed, the supply function of such a legislature might be above the industry demand function everywhere in the politically relevant domain. Similarly, whether a large shift in the demand for a particular instrument resulting from exogenous factors causes a comparable shift in the actual support provided by the legislature depends on the elasticity of supply. There will be relatively little change in equilibrium support if supply is inelastic, but a far larger change if supply is elastic.

This framework helps us to organize and synthesize available explorations of the four gaps which introduced the Article: three gaps between economic prescription and political reality and one gap between past and current political practices. With respect to the first—the predominance of command-and-control over market-based instruments despite the economic superiority of the latter—firms are likely to prefer command-and-control standards to auctioned permits and taxes. Standards produce rents, which can be sustainable if coupled with sufficiently more stringent requirements for new sources. In contrast, auctioned permits and taxes require firms to pay not only abatement costs to reduce pollution to a specified level, but also costs of polluting up to that level. Environmental interest groups are also likely to prefer command-and-control instruments, for philosophical, strategic, and technical reasons.

On the supply side, command-and-control standards are likely to be supplied more cheaply by legislators for several reasons: the training and experience of legislators may make them more comfortable with a direct standards approach than with market-based approaches; the time needed to learn about market-based instruments may represent significant opportunity costs; standards tend to hide the costs of pollution control while emphasizing the benefits; and standards may offer greater opportunities for symbolic politics. Finally, at the level of the legislature, command-and-control standards offer legislators a greater degree of control over the distributional effects of environmental regulation. This feature is likely to make majority coalitions easier to assemble, because legislative compromise is easier in the face of less uncertainty, and because the winning coalition can better guarantee that its interests will be served in the implementation of policy.

The second gap—that when command-and-control standards have been used, the standards for new sources have been far more stringent than those for existing sources, despite the potentially perverse incentives of this approach—can also be understood in the context of this market framework. Demand for new source standards comes from existing firms, which seek to erect entry barriers to restrict competition and protect the rents created by command-and-control standards. In turn, environmentalists often support strict standards for new sources because they represent environmental progress, at least symbolically. On the supply side, more stringent standards for new sources allow legislators to protect existing constituents and interests by placing the bulk of the pollution control burden on unbuilt factories.

Many of these same arguments can also be used to explain the third gap—the use of grandfathered tradeable permits as the exclusive market-based mechanism in the United States, despite the disadvantages of this allocation scheme. Like command-and-control standards, tradeable permits create rents; grandfathering distributes those rents to firms, while auctioning transfers the rents to government. Moreover, like stringent command-and-control standards for new sources, but unlike auctioned permits or taxes, grand-fathered permits give rise to entry barriers. Thus, the rents con-veyed to the private sector by grandfathered tradeable permits are, in effect, sustainable.

Moreover, grandfathered tradeable permits are likely to be less costly for legislators to supply. The costs imposed on industry are less visible and less burdensome for grandfathered permits than for auctioned permits or taxes. Also, grandfathered permits offer a greater degree of political control over the distributional effects of regulation, facilitating the formation of majority coalitions. In both these respects, grandfathered permits are somewhat analogous to command-and-control standards.

The fourth and final gap—between the recent rise of the use of market-based instruments and the lack of receptiveness such schemes had encountered in the past—can be credited to several factors. These include: the increased understanding of and famili-arity with market-based instruments; niche-seeking by environmental groups interested in both environmental quality and organizational visibility; increased pollution control costs, which create greater demand for cost-effective instruments; attention to new, unregu-lated environmental problems without constituencies for a status quo approach; and a general shift of the political center toward a more favorable view of using the market to solve social problems. Overall, the image is one of both demand and supply functions for market-based instruments shifting rightward, leading to greater de-grees of political support for these market-based instruments over time.[163]

Although some of the current preferences for command-and-control standards simply reflects a desire to maintain the regulatory status quo, the aggregate demand for a market-based instrument is likely to be greatest (and the opportunity costs of legislator support is likely to be least) when the environmental problem has not previously been regulated.[164] Hence, the prospects may be promis-ing with respect to the introduction of such market-based instru-ments for new problems, such as global climate change, rather than

---

163. It is also possible that changes in some of the institutional features identified above have affected individual legislators' degrees of support. For example, changes may have occurred that led to particular legislators taking on important committee positions, thus changing their production functions, and hence their opportunity costs.

164. *See* Hahn & Stavins, *supra* note 104, at 42.

for existing, regulated problems, such as abandoned hazardous waste sites.

Such a market framework can generate empirical work on the positive political economy of instrument choice for environmental regulation. So far, most of the academic work in this area has been theoretical; very few arguments have been subjected to empirical validation. Several of the existing empirical studies have addressed the question of why firms might support particular instruments, rather than whether firms actually provide such support. No empirical studies have constructed demand functions by determining how much firms actually are willing to pay (in the form of lobbying expenses and campaign contributions, for example) to secure particular outcomes. Similarly, no work has sought to determine the nature of demand by interest groups other than industry. In particular, the motives of environmental organizations merit more consideration. This Article discussed the possible self-interested motives of such organizations, and how their demands for particular policy instruments may be motivated by niche-seeking. Whether their expenditures in the political process comport with this theory remains essentially untested.

On the supply side, substantial impediments to empirical work remain. Existing studies have primarily attempted to determine the factors that affect legislative votes on particular programs.[165] In recent years, however, Congress has enacted a greater proportion of legislation by voice vote, rather than recorded vote. There has also been a shift from votes on comparatively narrow bills to votes on omnibus bills, which make it virtually impossible to determine a legislator's actual position with respect to specific components. Thus, the relative dearth of new data makes it difficult to perform studies of legislative voting behavior.

Legislative voting studies also share a substantial problem: distinguishing votes that reflect a legislator's true views about a bill from votes cast as part of an implicit or explicit logrolling trade, in which a legislator votes in favor of a program that she otherwise opposes in order to obtain a more valuable quid pro quo.[166] Moreover, as argued above, a vote constitutes only one

---

165. *See generally* Hamilton, *supra* note 145; *see also* Pashigan, *supra* note 135, at 551–54.
166. *Compare* Kau & Rubin, *supra* note 43, at 380–81 (attempting to measure the

component of the support that a legislator can extend to a bill. But the other components of support are less well suited to quantitative analysis.[167] Thus, in some cases, the best way to explore empirically the supply side of the equilibrium framework may be through detailed case studies of the legislative decisionmaking process.[168]

The market model will, in the end, be an imperfect and incomplete description of political behavior. But there are real advantages to considering instrument choice within this framework, and from developing more fully the details of the market model and its implications. The ultimate test of the usefulness of such a framework will be the extent to which it enables reliable predictions of the choices legislatures make, and the extent to which it facilitates the design of policy instruments that are both economically rational and politically successful.

---

importance of logrolling with a conditional probability model that examined votes as a function of one another) *with* Jackson & Kingdon, *supra* note 44, at 807 (criticizing aspects of Kau and Rubin study).

167. A pattern of votes on a series of amendments may be used as a proxy for a continuous underlying support variable, overcoming this problem. *See* Silberman & Durden, *supra* note 61, at 322–27. Such series of closely related votes, however, are rarely available, particularly in the case of instrument choice. A different approach has examined the relationship between campaign contributions and degrees of participation in committee activities. *See* Hall & Wayman, *supra* note 61, at 805–09.

168. *See generally* ACKERMAN & HASSLER, *supra* note 117.

[14]

RAND Journal of Economics
Vol. 30, No. 1, Spring 1999
pp. 137–157

Toward a political theory of the emergence of environmental incentive regulation

Marcel Boyer*

and

Jean-Jacques Laffont**

This article makes some steps toward a formal political economy of environmental policy. Economists' quasi-unanimous preference for sophisticated incentive regulation is reconsidered. We recast the question of instrument choice in the general mechanism design literature within an incomplete contract approach to political economy. We show why "constitutional" constraints on the instruments of environmental policy may be desirable, even though they appear inefficient from a standard economic viewpoint. Their justification lies in the limitations they impose on the politicians' ability to distribute rents. Insights are provided on the emergence of incentive mechanisms in environmental regulation.

1. Introduction

■ A large number of instruments have been considered to regulate polluting activities: Pigouvian taxes, quotas, subsidies for pollution reduction, marketable emission permits,[1] deposit refund systems (see Bohm (1981)), assignments of legal liabilities,[2] etc. As a result, the choice of policy instruments has become one of the major questions debated in environmental economics. Cropper and Oates (1992) devote a large part of their survey to this question. See also Segerson (1996) and Lewis (1996). Most of the discussion has taken place within the benevolent social maximizer paradigm. Starting with Buchanan and Tullock (1975), the necessity of looking for political economy explanations of the choice of instruments has been recognized.[3] However, dissatisfaction remains. Hahn

---

* CIRANO, École Polytechnique de Montréal, University of Montreal; boycrm@cirano.umontreal.ca.
** IDEI and GREMAQ, Université de Toulouse I, France; laffont@cict.fr.

We would like to thank Tracy Lewis, Patrick González, Larry Jones, two anonymous referees, Editor Glenn Ellison, and participants in the Canadian Economic Theory Conference (Toronto 1997), Boston College 1997 Microeconomic Workshop, GREEN-CIRANO Conference on the Environment (Québec 1997), and Econometric Society Meeting (Chicago 1998) for their comments. Financial support from the Social Science and Humanities Research Council (Canada) and the Mattei Foundation (Italy) is gratefully acknowledged.

[1] Crocker (1966) and Dales (1968a, 1968b) first proposed marketing emission permits.

[2] There is a large literature on this topic; see in particular Segerson (1995) and Boyer and Laffont (1996, 1997) and the references therein. See also Gupta, Van Houtven, and Cropper (1996) for an empirical analysis of EPA's decisions on the cleanup of Superfund sites.

[3] Beyond the debate about the Buchanan-Tullock article (Yohe, 1976; Dewees, 1983; and Coelho, 1976), see also Boyer (1979), Noll (1983), McCubbins, Noll, and Weingast (1989), Hahn (1990), and Hahn and McGartland (1989).

Copyright © 1999, RAND   137

(1990) writes: "There is yet no satisfactory theory about the emergence of incentive based mechanisms" (p. 22). Lewis (1996) concludes his survey as follows: "I see the next progression in [environmental regulation] as being a positive analysis asking which kind of environmental policies will be implemented under information and distribution constraints when special interests try to intervene to affect policy" (p. 844).

The purpose of this article is to provide some preliminary steps in the construction of a formal political economy of environmental economics (see also Laffont (1996)). Economists' general preferences for sophisticated incentive mechanisms is reconsidered in a political economy approach resting on two main features: private information of economic agents, which explains the rents accruing to them as functions of policy choices, and the incomplete contract nature of constitutions, which explains the need for politicians as residual decision makers.

Incomplete information is by now well understood as being a major obstacle to first-best efficient regulation. Starting with Loeb and Magat (1979), regulation of natural monopolies has been modelled as a principal-agent problem. When contracting is unconstrained, the revelation principle then states that any type of regulation is equivalent to a revelation mechanism. (See also Baron and Myerson (1982) and Guesnerie and Laffont (1984).) In such a mechanism, agents communicate truthfully their private information to the regulator, who then recommends proper actions. The requirement of incentive compatibility puts constraints on the actions that can be implemented.

It is only recently that this framework has been extensively developed for environmental economics.[4] A revelation mechanism can be viewed as a command and control instrument and yet is clearly optimal here: once an optimal revelation mechanism has been obtained, the question of its implementation by various economic instruments or institutions, such as regulatory proceedings, taxes, and markets, arises— but by definition those institutions then implement the same allocation as the command and control approach (see Laffont (1994) for an example).

In such a framework the question of instrument choice is empty. Such a question often arose in the literature because authors were not careful enough in defining their instruments. For example, Yohe (1976) correctly shows that the alleged difference between quotas and price controls in Buchanan and Tullock (1975) disappears when instruments are appropriately defined. He writes: "When the equivalent quantity control is properly specified, both the economist's general preference for taxation and the regulatee's general preference for quotas will disappear" (p. 981).

Two types of meaningful comparisons of instruments are then possible. In the first type, one considers constraints on instruments (the analysis should explain the origin of these constraints), and various constrained instruments can be compared. This is the essence of Weitzman's (1975) comparison of prices and quantities in a situation where asymmetric information calls for nonlinear prices as optimal instruments, as Roberts and Spence (1976) pointed out. Another example is the case of nonconvexities due to negative externalities. (See Starrett (1972) and Baumol and Bradford (1972).) There, quotas are equivalent to nonlinear taxes. Pigouvian (linear) taxes are then dominated by quotas. Similarly, taxes and subsidies that are equivalent when they are accompanied with appropriate lump-sum transfers differ in their absence with respect to the long-run entry and exit decisions of firms. See Kamien, Schwartz, and Dolbear (1966), Bramhall and Mills (1966), Kneese and Bower (1968), and Dewees and Sims (1976) for further discussion.

---

[4] See Baron (1985a), Laffont (1994), and Lewis (1996). Early applications were essentially reinterpreting Groves mechanisms by treating environmental externalities like public goods. See, for example, Dasgupta, Hammond, and Maskin (1980).

In the second type, one considers instruments that could be equivalent in the complete contracting framework and introduces imperfections elsewhere in the economy that cannot be corrected by the regulator (then one must give a good explanation of the regulator's inability). This is the case in Buchanan's (1969) example of a polluting monopolist when the subsidies required to correct the monopolistic behavior are not available. Then, the Pigouvian tax is clearly dominated by a quota that implements the second-best tax, as devised for example by Lee (1975) and Barnett (1980), and which depends on the firm's market power.

A systematic analysis of instrument choice should then be conducted in well-defined second-best frameworks, which are all methodological shortcuts of an incomplete contract analysis. Constraints such as limited commitment, renegotiation-proof commitment, collusion, favoritism, and multiprincipal structures[5] should be considered. Political economy constraints can also be viewed as a special case of this methodology. The lack of finely tuned constitutional control of the politicians (the incomplete contract feature) who have private agendas introduces inefficiencies in the regulatory decision process. It may then become desirable to impose constraints on politicians that favor particular instruments or to force the use of apparently crude instruments.

Section 2 presents the basic model we use, which is a simple model of regulation of a polluting monopolist who is privately informed of the cost of realizing a public project. The asymmetric information about the firm's technology explains that a rent will have to be given up to those who have stakes in the firm. The choice of an environmental policy affects this rent. We derive as a benchmark the environmental policy that maximizes expected social welfare.

Section 3 takes as given the delegation of environmental policy to political majorities. Since the majorities will have different stakes in the informational rent of the firm, the delegation of environmental policy to politicians will enable them to pursue their private agendas, that is, to favor the agents who belong to their majority. As majorities change, this induces an excessive fluctuation of policies. Restricting the instruments used in environmental policy becomes a way to restrict this excessive fluctuation, at the cost of a lack of flexibility. More specifically, we compare the policy consisting in the choice of a single pollution level, a typical command and control regulation, with the policy consisting in the choice of a menu of pollution-transfer pairs, a typical incentive regulation. We determine the conditions under which the higher discretion associated with the second policy is compensated by its greater efficiency potential.

Section 4 explores the foundation of the delegation of environmental policy to politicians. Since a constitution is a rather incomplete contract, a policy choice at the constitutional level necessarily has little flexibility. On the contrary, politicians can use their current detailed knowledge of the economy to choose their policy but in so doing will pursue their private agendas. Taking the social cost of public funds—which should be viewed as a proxy for the economic outlook—as the variable that the politicians but not the constitution will be able to make their policy choice contingent on, we characterize the conditions under which the environmental policy conducted by changing majorities is superior to a social-welfare-maximizing but inflexible environmental policy imposed by the constitution.

Section 5 extends the model to a situation where two types of interest groups, stakeholders in the firm and environmentalists, may benefit from the capture of the government through the size of informational rents that the regulation mechanisms

---

[5] See Baron (1985b) for an early study of the distortions due to the uncoordinated activities of two regulators.

© RAND 1999

leave them. The distortions due to the political process are studied in this more general model, as well as the impact of the dynamics of reelection based on campaign contributions. The comparison of instruments is extended to this case. We find that the competition of interest groups may kill otherwise desirable reforms toward more sophisticated regulation by raising the stakes of political conflict, a kind of negative rent-seeking effect. Concluding comments are gathered in Section 6. All proofs are in the Appendix.

2. The basic model

■ We consider a natural monopoly to which is delegated the realization of a public project that has social value S and costs $C(\beta, d)$, where d is the level of pollution accompanying the completion of the project and β is a cost characteristic that is private information of the firm. For a given pollution level, β measures the efficiency of the firm in realizing the project, a higher β meaning a higher cost. For a given β, we assume that allowing more pollution reduces cost.

Two alternative assumptions are then possible on the cost of reducing pollution. The more efficient the firm is, either the more efficient it is in also reducing pollution or the less efficient it is in that regard. In terms of a general cost function $C(\beta, d)$, if we assume $C_\beta > 0$, we have the choice between $C_{\beta d} < 0$ and $C_{\beta d} > 0$. We will assume $C_{\beta d} < 0$ because, with a one-dimensional asymmetry of information, the positive correlation between ability to produce and ability to reduce pollution seems more compelling than the alternative assumption and leads to more striking results. However, we will point out how our results change with the alternative assumption $C_{\beta d} > 0$. To obtain explicit solutions and carry out numerical simulations, we choose a specific cost function corresponding to $C_{\beta d} < 0$, namely $C(\beta, d) = \beta(K - d)$, where K is a constant. We assume that β can take two values $\{\underline{\beta}, \overline{\beta}\}$, with $\Delta\beta = \overline{\beta} - \underline{\beta}$ and $\nu = \text{Prob}\{\beta = \underline{\beta}\}$.

Let t be the compensatory monetary transfer from the regulator to the firm, which then has a rent equal to

$$U = t - \beta(K - d).$$

The social disutility of pollution is $V(d)$ (with $V' > 0$, $V'' > 0$). If $1 + \lambda$, with $\lambda > 0$, is the social cost of public funds due to the need for using distortionary taxation to raise public funds,[6] the consumers' welfare is

$$CS = S - V(d) - (1 + \lambda)t.$$

The utilitarian social welfare is then

$$W = CS + U = S - V(d) - (1 + \lambda)\beta(K - d) - \lambda U. \tag{1}$$

We assume that S is large enough to make the realization of the project always desirable. Under complete information, a benevolent social welfare maximizer would set $V'(d) = (1 + \lambda)\beta$ and $t = \beta(K - d)$ to nullify the rent of the firm that is socially costly because $\lambda > 0$. The chosen pollution levels would depend on λ and β.

---

[6] The mean value of λ is nonnegligible and considered to be of the order of .3 in developed countries and higher in developing ones. See Jones, Tandon, and Vogelsang (1990) for the empirical evidence.

© RAND 1999.

Under incomplete information about β, the firm's individual-rationality and incentive-compatibility constraints must be taken into account. Only the type-$\underline{\beta}$ firm receives a rent that is equal to

$$\underline{U} = \Delta\beta(K - \overline{d}),$$

where $\overline{d}$ is the pollution level requested from the less efficient type firm by the separating regulation mechanism $((\underline{t}, \underline{d}), (\overline{t}, \overline{d}))$. The firm of type $\underline{\beta}$ can always pretend to be of type $\overline{\beta}$ and realize the project with a pollution level of $\overline{d}$ at a cost of $\underline{\beta}(K - \overline{d})$; since it is entitled to a transfer $t(K - \overline{d}) \geq \overline{\beta}(K - \overline{d})$, it realizes a profit (rent) of at least $(\overline{\beta} - \underline{\beta})(K - \overline{d})$, a decreasing function of $\overline{d}$, which must then be a lower bound on its welfare or profit when it acts according to its real type. (See Laffont and Tirole (1993).) Note that this rent decreases with the pollution level of the inefficient firm.[7]

The optimal pollution levels obtained from the maximization of the expected value of social welfare (1) under the informational constraint on β can be characterized by the following program:

$$\max_{(\underline{d}, \overline{d})} W(\underline{d}, \overline{d}) = [\nu(S - V(\underline{d}) - (1 + \lambda)\underline{\beta}(K - \underline{d}) - \lambda\Delta\beta(K - \overline{d}))$$

$$+ (1 - \nu)(S - V(\overline{d}) - (1 + \lambda)\overline{\beta}(K - \overline{d}))], \tag{2}$$

yielding

$$V'(\underline{d}^*) = (1 + \lambda)\underline{\beta} \tag{3}$$

$$V'(\overline{d}^*) = (1 + \lambda)\overline{\beta} + \lambda\frac{\nu}{1 - \nu}\Delta\beta.$$

3. Controlling the discretionary power of politicians through constraints on the choice of instruments

■ We have a continuum $[0, 1]$ of agents in the economy. Let α represent each period the measure of consumers who do not share the firm's rent, the nonstakeholders, and let $1 - \alpha$ be the measure of those who share the rent, that is, the stakeholders. Let α be drawn independently each period, taking the value $\alpha^* \in (\frac{1}{2}, 1)$ with probability $\frac{1}{2}$ and $1 - \alpha^*$ with probability $\frac{1}{2}$. When $\alpha = \alpha^*$, the nonstakeholders majority, of measure α^*, is in power; when $\alpha = 1 - \alpha^*$, the stakeholders majority is in power and the measure of this majority is also α^*.

We will assume that politicians have the discretion of using their private information about the economy as exemplified here by the value of λ, the social cost of public funds, whose distribution is common knowledge but whose value is either observed only by the government (the majority in power) or is commonly observed *ex post* but cannot be made verifiable by a court. We consider the value of λ either to be a proxy for specific economic conditions that the government in power is better

---

[7] This feature, which follows from our assumptions on the cost function ($C_\beta > 0$, $C_{\beta d} < 0$), will imply that to reduce the costly rent of the efficient firm, one should let pollution increase. However, this striking result would be reversed with the alternative assumptions ($C_\mu > 0$, $C_{\beta d} > 0$) as in $C(\beta, d) = K - d/\beta$, or ($C_\beta < 0$, $C_{\beta d} < 0$) as in $C(\beta, d) = K - \beta d$.

© RAND 1999.

equipped to observe (from confidential reports of the public service bureaucracy, for example) or to refer to complex economic conditions that cannot be written in a constitutional contract. The constitutional convention may, on the other hand, impose constraints on the choice of instruments for pollution abatement.

We want to compare two instruments. The first one is a menu of contracts (abatement levels and associated transfers) offered to the firm. The second one is a single abatement level based on $E\beta$, the expected value of β, and imposed on both types of firm. The first instrument corresponds to a rather sophisticated incentive regulation of the firm. In the first case, we let the political majorities decide on the menu of abatement levels and transfers; in the second case, they are constrained to a unique level. In each case they can use their private information on λ.

Let us consider first the sophisticated separating mechanism. If $\alpha = \alpha^*$, we have majority 1, which maximizes the welfare of nonstakeholders, who benefit from the project, suffer from the pollution externality, and must pay taxes to finance the realization of the project (the cost of the project plus the rent of the firm), namely

$$\alpha^*(S - V(d) - (1 + \lambda)t) = \alpha^*(S - V(d) - (1 + \lambda)\beta(K - d) - (1 + \lambda)U), \quad (4)$$

thus overestimating in comparison with (1) the social cost of the firm's rent, since $1 + \lambda > \lambda$.[8] Similarly, if $\alpha = 1 - \alpha^*$, majority 2 maximizes the welfare of stakeholders, who are similar to type 1 agents except that they share the firm's rent, namely

$$\alpha^*(S - V(d) - (1 + \lambda)t) + U \quad (5)$$

$$= \alpha^*\left(S - V(d) - (1 + \lambda)\beta(K - d) - \left(1 + \lambda - \frac{1}{\alpha^*}\right)U\right),$$

thus underestimating the social cost of the firm's rent, since $1 + \lambda - 1/\alpha^* < \lambda$.[9]

Majority 1 maximizes over the pollution levels the expected value of the welfare of nonstakeholders given by (4) under incentive and participation constraints of the firm; that is, it solves

$$\max_{(\underline{d}, \bar{d})} W^1(\underline{d}, \bar{d}) = \alpha^*[\nu(S - V(\underline{d}) - (1 + \lambda)\underline{\beta}(K - \underline{d}) - (1 + \lambda)\Delta\beta(K - \bar{d}))$$
$$+ (1 - \nu)(S - V(\bar{d}) - (1 + \lambda)\bar{\beta}(K - \bar{d}))]. \quad (6)$$

Hence

$$V'(\underline{d}_1) = (1 + \lambda)\underline{\beta} \quad (7)$$

$$V'(\bar{d}_1) = (1 + \lambda)\bar{\beta} + (1 + \lambda)\frac{\nu}{1 - \nu}\Delta\beta,$$

with associated transfers given by $\bar{t} = \bar{\beta}(K - \bar{d}_1)$ and $\underline{t} = \underline{\beta}(K - \underline{d}_1) + \Delta\beta(K - \bar{d}_1)$. Majority 2 similarly maximizes $W^2(\underline{d}, \bar{d})$, the expected value of stakeholders given by (5). This leads to

---

[8] This formulation presumes that the majorities cannot change the funding of firms through indirect taxation that is uniformly spread across all agents.

[9] We assume that $1 + \lambda - 1/\alpha^* > 0$. Otherwise, we would have to take into account the agents' individual-rationality constraints, since majority 2 would like to make U as large as possible.

$$V'(\underline{d}_2) = (1 + \lambda)\underline{\beta} \tag{8}$$

$$V'(\overline{d}_2) = (1 + \lambda)\overline{\beta} + (1 + \lambda - 1/\alpha^*)\frac{\nu}{1 - \nu}\Delta\beta.$$

We obtain (assuming that each majority is in power half the time) the expected social welfare

$$E_{\lambda\alpha}W(\underline{d}, \overline{d}) = \frac{1}{2}E_\lambda W(\underline{d}_1, \overline{d}_1) + \frac{1}{2}E_\lambda W(\underline{d}_2, \overline{d}_2), \tag{9}$$

where $W(\underline{d}_m, \overline{d}_m)$ is the expected level, with respect to the firm's type, of social welfare (1) evaluated at pollution levels chosen by majority m as a function of λ.

Comparing (3), (7), and (8), we observe that the pollution level of the more efficient firm is optimal whatever the majority in power, since $\underline{d}_1 = \underline{d}_2 = \underline{d}^*$. But the pollution level of the less efficient firm is either too large (under a nonstakeholders majority government) or too low (under a stakeholders majority government): $\overline{d}_1 > \overline{d}^* > \overline{d}_2$. These apparently surprising distortions need some explanation. Since both majorities take fully into account the social cost of pollution $V(d)$, they differ only in their treatment of the informational rent accruing to the stakeholders of the more efficient firm. Majority 1 (nonstakeholders) overvalues the social cost of the firm's informational rent (it uses a weight of $(1 + \lambda)$ instead of λ) because it does not share any of that rent. For that majority, the cost of inducing abatement from the less efficient firm, which is the source of the rent of the more efficient firm, is therefore larger than its social cost net of the rent. Majority 1's regulation leads therefore to a larger-than-optimal level of pollution from the less efficient firm because it does not value the positive effect of a more stringent abatement level $\overline{d}$ on the efficient firm's rent. On the other hand, majority 2 (stakeholders) undervalues the social cost of the firm's informational rent (it uses a weight of $(1 + \lambda - 1/\alpha^*) < \lambda$) because it captures the totality of that rent. For that majority, the net cost of inducing abatement is smaller than its social cost. Majority 2's regulation thus leads to a smaller-than-optimal level of pollution from the less efficient firm.

We now consider the case of a nondiscriminating pollution-abatement mechanism that the constitutional convention may impose on the politicians. The latter then have a more limited discretion for promoting the interests of their constituency. Each majority can now select a single abatement level only, not a menu of pollution abatement and transfer levels.

If the nonstakeholders majority is in power, it now solves

$$\max_d W^1(d) = \alpha^*[S - V(d) - (1 + \lambda)E\beta(K - d) - \nu(1 + \lambda)\Delta\beta(K - d)], \tag{10}$$

yielding

$$V'(d_1) = (1 + \lambda)E\beta + (1 + \lambda)\nu\Delta\beta = (1 + \lambda)\overline{\beta}. \tag{11}$$

Similarly, the stakeholders majority chooses a pollution level d_2 characterized by

$$V'(d_2) = (1 + \lambda)E\beta + (1 + \lambda - 1/\alpha^*)\nu\Delta\beta = (1 + \lambda)\overline{\beta} - \frac{1}{\alpha^*}\nu\Delta\beta. \tag{12}$$

© RAND 1999.

Again, $d_2 < d^* < d_1$, where d^* is the optimal nondiscriminating pollution-abatement level under the same informational constraints. The latter pollution-abatement level solves

$$\max_d W(d) = S - V(d) - (1 + \lambda)E\beta(K - d) - \nu\lambda\Delta\beta(K - d),$$

yielding $V'(d^*) = (1 + \lambda)E\beta + \lambda\nu\Delta\beta = (1 + \lambda)\bar{\beta} - \nu\Delta\beta$.

We obtain an expected social welfare level given by (assuming that each majority is in power half the time)

$$E_{\lambda\alpha}W(d) = \frac{1}{2}E_\lambda W(d_1) + \frac{1}{2}E_\lambda W(d_2), \tag{13}$$

where $W(d_m)$ is the social welfare (1) evaluated at the single pollution level chosen by majority m as characterized by (11) and (12).

The emergence of the separating delegated incentive mechanism (DIM) hinges on its *ex ante* comparison with the delegated pooling mechanism (DPM) obtained above. We carry out this comparison for small asymmetries of information represented by $\Delta\beta$.

Proposition 1. For $\bar{\beta}$ close enough to β, we have $E_{\lambda\alpha}W(\underline{d}, \bar{d}) > E_{\lambda\alpha}W(d)$, that is, the delegated incentive mechanism chosen by the political majorities dominates the delegated pooling mechanism selected by political majorities if and only if

$$\text{var}(\lambda) > H(\nu, \alpha^*, E\lambda) \equiv -\nu^2 \left(\frac{\alpha^* - \frac{1}{2}}{\alpha^{*2}} \right) - 1 + 2\nu - 2(1 - \nu)E\lambda - (E\lambda)^2. \tag{14}$$

In this context of political delegation,[10] the emergence of the sophisticated separating incentive mechanisms discriminating between the pollution abatement levels requested from the different firms, will be associated with increases in $E\lambda$, var(λ), and α^*, and with decreases in ν. A small α^* that is close to ½ corresponds to the case where political agendas differ the most from social welfare; then, pooling is favored to decrease the discretionary pursuit of private agendas. When $E\lambda$ or var(λ) are large, the larger sensitivity of the separating incentive mechanism dominates. Increases in ν have two effects. A larger ν implies a strong concern for rents accruing to the firm with probability ν but also larger distortions from social welfare maximization in the objective function of the majorities, since

$$W(\underline{d}_1, \bar{d}_1) = \frac{W^1(\underline{d}_1, \bar{d}_1)}{\alpha^*} + \nu\Delta\beta(K - \bar{d}_1) \tag{15}$$

$$W(\underline{d}_2, \bar{d}_2) = \frac{W^2(\underline{d}_2, \bar{d}_2)}{\alpha^*} + \left(1 - \frac{1}{\alpha^*} \right)\nu\Delta\beta(K - \bar{d}_2). \tag{16}$$

It turns out that the second distortions are larger and therefore a large ν favors a nondiscriminating policy (DPM).

---

[10] Our analysis extends the results of Holmström (1984) on delegation to a multiagent framework in which one agent is selected (by a majority rule) and delegated the collective decision within the constraints imposed by the constitution.

Increases in the asymmetry of information $\Delta\beta$ have *a priori* an ambiguous effect: the greater ability of discriminating mechanisms to extract rents must be compared with the negative effects of political discretion. However, for a quadratic $V(\cdot)$ function, social welfare is quadratic in $\overline{\beta}$. We can then derive the global superiority of the pooling mechanism or the sophisticated separating mechanism from Proposition 1 and the fact that all welfare levels coincide at $\overline{\beta} = \underline{\beta}$.[11] For more general $V(\cdot)$ functions, the increase in $\overline{\beta}$, which is favorable to letting the majorities choose separating mechanisms, may lead to the superiority of that mechanism over the pooling mechanism even when $\text{var}(\lambda) < H(\cdot)$, that is, even when the pooling mechanism dominates when $\overline{\beta}$ is close to $\underline{\beta}$. On the other hand, if separation (DIM) dominates for small $\Delta\beta$, it dominates always. Figure 1 provides an example where $\text{var}(\lambda) = 0 < H(\cdot) = .08$ and yet the separating incentive mechanism chosen by the political majorities dominates the delegated pooling mechanism selected by political majorities when $\overline{\beta}$ is large enough.

Majorities can favor their respective constituency by choosing menus of pollution levels and transfers that maximize their respective welfare functions, yielding the delegated separating incentive regulation regime. Proposition 1 compared this delegation of powers to a constitutional requirement that the majorities select a unique pollution abatement level to be imposed on all firms. One can take a more positive approach to constitutional reform and wonder if moving toward the use of an incentive mechanism with delegated discretion may emerge from unanimous *ex ante* consent and not simply by appealing to social welfare maximization under the veil of ignorance. For this purpose we can compare *ex ante* the per-capita welfare of the two types of agents in a DIM and a DPM. We obtain the following proposition.

Proposition 2. For $\overline{\beta}$ close to $\underline{\beta}$, majority 1 prefers the optimal DIM over the optimal DPM if and only if

$$\text{var}(\lambda) > H^1(\nu, \alpha^*, E\lambda) \equiv \frac{1}{2}\frac{\nu^2}{\alpha^{*2}} - 1 - 2E\lambda - (E\lambda)^2, \tag{17}$$

while majority 2 does if and only if

$$\text{var}(\lambda) > H^2(\nu, \alpha^*, E\lambda) \equiv 2\frac{\nu}{\alpha^*} - \frac{1}{2}\frac{\nu^2}{\alpha^{*2}} - 1 - 2\left(1 - \frac{\nu}{\alpha^*}\right)E\lambda - (E\lambda)^2. \tag{18}$$

Comparing $H^1(\cdot)$, $H^2(\cdot)$, and $H(\cdot)$, we obtain directly the following corollary, given here without proof.

Corollary 1. We have

$$H^1(\nu, \alpha^*, E\lambda) < H(\nu, \alpha^*, E\lambda) < H^2(\nu, \alpha^*, E\lambda). \tag{19}$$

The nonstakeholders (majority 1) are more active proponents of delegating discretionary power to politicians over environmental policy, that is, of a DIM scheme, than are the stakeholders (majority 2). Majority 1 prefers a DIM scheme as soon as the variance of λ reaches the threshold $H^1(\cdot)$, while majority 2 will still prefer to stick to the DPM scheme until the variance of λ has reached the higher threshold $H^2(\cdot)$. Indeed, the net cost of pollution abatement is higher for majority 1 (because they do not benefit from

---

[11] The first derivatives of the expected welfare functions with respect to $\overline{\beta}$, evaluated at $\overline{\beta} = \underline{\beta}$, are negative and equal. If $V(d)$ is quadratic, then the second derivatives are independent of $\overline{\beta}$.

© RAND 1999.

FIGURE 1

THE DIFFERENTIAL EXPECTED WELFARE

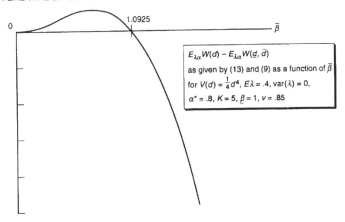

the informational rent of higher abatement) and therefore raises the value of the more efficient pollution-abatement incentive mechanism DIM above that of the cruder DPM as soon as $H'(\cdot)$ is reached. If unanimous approval is needed for constitutional reform in favor of a sophisticated separating incentive mechanism with delegated discretion, it will happen less often than is socially desirable because $H^2(\cdot) > H(\cdot)$, that is, because of the resistance of the stakeholders in the firm's rent.

4. Delegating discretionary power to politicians or not

■   The gain from delegating discretionary power to politicians comes from the use they can make of their information, here their knowledge of λ, the social cost of public funds. The cost of such delegation is the excessive fluctuation of their decisions $(\underline{d}, \bar{d})$ as a function of λ, as private agendas are taken into account by successive majorities. Alternatively, the constitutional convention may decide not to delegate such discretionary power but instead impose an incentive mechanism $((\underline{t}^p, \underline{d}^p), (\bar{t}^p, \bar{d}^p))$ determined at the constitutional level to maximize expected social welfare. This incentive mechanism can be characterized as the solution to the social welfare-maximization program

$$\max_{(\underline{d},\bar{d})} W(\underline{d}, \bar{d}) = \nu(S - V(\underline{d}) - (1 + E\lambda)\underline{\beta}(K - \underline{d}) - (E\lambda)\Delta\beta(K - \bar{d})) \tag{20}$$

$$+ (1 - \nu)(S - V(\bar{d}) - (1 + E\lambda)\bar{\beta}(K - \bar{d})),$$

yielding

$$V'(\underline{d}^p) = (1 + E\lambda)\underline{\beta} \tag{21}$$

$$V'(\bar{d}^p) = (1 + E\lambda)\bar{\beta} + (E\lambda)\frac{\nu}{1 - \nu}\Delta\beta.$$

The pollution levels $\underline{d}^p$ and $\bar{d}^p$ now depend on $E\lambda$.

© RAND 1999.

At the constitutional level, the choice is then between imposing a separating incentive regulation mechanism that maximizes expected social welfare on the basis of
the expected value $E\lambda$, a mechanism that we shall call a constitutional incentive mechanism (CIM), or delegating to the political majorities the choice of a separating incentive
regulation mechanism that will then be a function of the value of λ, that is, the delegated
incentive mechanism DIM. In the latter case, the choice of pollution-regulation mechanisms will reflect private agendas. The emergence of the latter delegated incentive
mechanism, which depends on λ, hinges on its *ex ante* comparison with the former
constitutional incentive mechanism.

Proposition 3. The difference in expected welfare between the CIM and the DIM
converges to zero as $\Delta\beta \to 0$ and $var(\lambda) \to 0$. For a given $\Delta\beta$, the CIM dominates if
$var(\lambda)$ is small. For a given $var(\lambda)$, the DIM dominates if $\Delta\beta$ is small.

Clearly, the CIM will dominate the DIM chosen by the majorities when the vari-
ance of λ is small for a given level of asymmetric information, as represented by $\Delta\beta$.
Indeed, the CIM is optimal when $var(\lambda) = 0$, whereas the DIM is not. By continuity,
for low levels of the variance in λ, allowing political majorities to use the observed
value of λ in choosing *ex post* an incentive mechanism generates little social value but
does generate a significant social cost given the pursuit of private agendas. As $var(\lambda)$
increases, the value of adjusting policies to the realized value of λ increases, and
therefore it may eventually become better to give political majorities greater latitude
in setting policies and choosing the mechanism.

Similarly, the delegation of authority to politicians will be socially valuable and
indeed optimal if $\Delta\beta = 0$ for a given variance in λ. By continuity, for small values of
$\Delta\beta$, the delegation of authority allows the politicians to fine tune the choice of the
incentive mechanism to the realized value of λ, while the pursuit of their private agendas generates little unwarranted distortions in pollution abatement. Since $\Delta\beta$ is small,
maximizing any majority objective function is almost equivalent to maximizing the
social welfare function, because there are (almost) no rents. Again, as $\Delta\beta$ increases,
for the same given variance of λ, one expects that the distortions generated by the
pursuit of private agendas will eventually exceed the benefit of fine tuning the incentive
abatement mechanism chosen by the majorities and will therefore lead to the dominance
of the CIM.

5. Multiple privately informed interest groups

■   In the previous sections we have seen how the delegation of environmental policy
to politicians enables them to distribute informational rents to interest groups. In this
section we want to explore the extent to which reelection concerns and competing
interest groups may mitigate the distortions in the allocation of resources that politicians
might find profitable. For this purpose, we extend the model by introducing, in addition
to reelection concerns of majorities, first the financing of political coalitions or majorities through campaign contributions, and second an information asymmetry regarding
the damages of pollution. In the same way as β is private information of stakeholders,
the disutility of pollution is now assumed to be $V(\theta, d)$, with $\theta \in \{\underline{\theta}, \overline{\theta}\}$, $\Delta\theta = \overline{\theta} - \underline{\theta}$,
and $\mu = \text{Prob}(\underline{\theta})$.[12] The parameter θ is private information of the environmentalists
who suffer the pollution damage; we assume that $V_{\theta} > 0$ and $V_d > 0$. Two assumptions
are then possible regarding the value of pollution abatement: either $V_{\theta d} > 0$ or $V_{\theta d} < 0$.
In the first case, the more sensitive the environmentalists are to pollution (larger θ),

---

[12] As for β, the value of θ is assumed to be drawn anew every period.

the less efficient they are in finding ways to reduce their suffering from pollution, and vice versa in the second case. We will assume here that $V_{\theta d} > 0$, more precisely that $V(\theta, d) = \theta V(d)$, because it seems more compelling to us and also leads to more striking results.

We maintain our assumption that environmentalists (the new majority 1) have no stake in the polluting firm, but we now assume that they will be compensated for the cost of pollution. This compensation assumption should be interpreted as a shortcut reduced-form formulation of a political constraint on the level of hardship that a majority can impose on the agents of the other majority; this assumption can also be interpreted as a threshold under which civil disobedience would be triggered. Since θ is private information of the environmentalists and since the latter will now be compensated for the cost of pollution, they will be able to capture an informational rent. Together with our assumption $V_{\theta d} > 0$, this will lead environmentalists to favor higher pollution levels, which provide them with higher informational rents. Their informational rent is

$$U_1 = s - \theta V(d),$$

where s is the transfer from the government. The stakeholders who do not suffer the pollution damage have an informational rent of

$$U_2 = t - \beta(K - d).$$

The taxpayers, who are now distinct from stakeholders and environmentalists, have utility

$$U_3 = S - (1 + \lambda)(t + s).$$

The environmentalists of type $\underline{\theta}$ can always pretend to be of type $\overline{\theta}$ and let the government implement the project with a pollution level of $\overline{d}$ at a cost to them of $\underline{\theta} V(\overline{d})$; since they are entitled to a transfer $t(\overline{d}) \geq \overline{\theta} V(\overline{d})$, they then capture a rent of $(\overline{\theta} - \underline{\theta})V(\overline{d})$, an increasing function of $\overline{d}$.[13]

Assuming that each group of measure one (environmentalists, stakeholders, taxpayers) represent ⅓ of the population, utilitarian social welfare is

$$W = U_1 + U_2 + U_3 = S - (1 + \lambda)(\beta(K - d) + \theta V(d)) - \lambda(U_1 + U_2). \quad (22)$$

Under complete information the optimal pollution is now characterized[14] by $\theta V'(d) = \beta$. Under incomplete information a revelation mechanism is now a triple $\{d(\beta, \theta), t(\beta, \theta), s(\beta, \theta)\}$. The relevant incentive-compatibility and individual-rationality constraints are, for the stakeholders and the environmentalists respectively,

---

[13] This feature, which follows from our assumptions $V_\theta > 0$, $V_d > 0$, and $V_{\theta d} > 0$, will imply that to reduce the costly rent of the less sensitive environmentalists, one should favor a pollution reduction. However, this result would be reversed with the alternative assumptions ($V_{\theta d} < 0$) as in $V(\theta, d) = \theta(A + d/\theta^2)$ with $A > d/\theta^2$.

[14] Having an individual-rationality constraint for the environmentalists amounts to and should be interpreted as assuming that they are indemnified at a social cost of $(1 + \lambda)$. This is why we now obtain $\theta V'(d) = \beta$ instead of $\theta V'(d) = (1 + \lambda)\beta$.

© RAND 1999

$$E_{\theta}\{t(\underline{\beta}, \theta) - \underline{\beta}(K - d(\underline{\beta}, \theta))\} \geq E_{\theta}\{t(\overline{\beta}, \theta) - \underline{\beta}(K - d(\overline{\beta}, \theta))\}$$

$$E_{\theta}\{t(\overline{\beta}, \theta) - \overline{\beta}(K - d(\overline{\beta}, \theta))\} \geq 0$$

$$E_{\beta}\{s(\beta, \underline{\theta}) - \underline{\theta}V(d(\beta, \underline{\theta}))\} \geq E_{\beta}\{s(\beta, \overline{\theta}) - \underline{\theta}V(d(\beta, \overline{\theta}))\}$$

$$E_{\beta}\{s(\beta, \overline{\theta}) - \overline{\theta}V(d(\beta, \overline{\theta}))\} \geq 0.$$

Assuming Bayesian Nash behavior of stakeholders and environmentalists, the revelation mechanism that maximizes expected social welfare

$$W(\vec{d}) = E_{\mu, \nu}[S - (1 + \lambda)(\beta(K - d) + \theta V(d))] - \lambda\mu\underline{U}_1 - \lambda)\nu\underline{U}_2 \qquad (23)$$

under the above incentive- and individual-rationality constraints is characterized by[15]

$$\underline{\theta}V'(d(\underline{\beta}, \underline{\theta})) = \underline{\beta}$$

$$\left(\overline{\theta} + \frac{\lambda}{1 + \lambda}\frac{\mu}{1 - \mu}\Delta\theta\right)V'(d(\underline{\beta}, \overline{\theta})) = \underline{\beta}$$

$$\underline{\theta}V'(d(\overline{\beta}, \underline{\theta})) = \overline{\beta} + \frac{\lambda}{1 + \lambda}\frac{\nu}{1 - \nu}\Delta\beta$$

$$\left(\overline{\theta} + \frac{\lambda}{1 + \lambda}\frac{\mu}{1 - \mu}\Delta\theta\right)V'(d(\overline{\beta}, \overline{\theta})) = \overline{\beta} + \frac{\lambda}{1 + \lambda}\frac{\nu}{1 - \nu}\Delta\beta.$$

(24)

Let us assume that the two interest groups use a share of their informational rent as campaign contributions to influence politicians. We consider a two-period model. In period 2, majority 1 is able to favor the interests of environmentalists by maximizing the sum of taxpayers' utility and environmentalists' utility,

$$W^1(\vec{d_1}) = W(\vec{d_1}) - \nu\underline{U}_2, \qquad (25)$$

that is, by not including in its objective function the informational rent of the stakeholders, where $\vec{d_1} = (d_1(\underline{\beta}, \underline{\theta}), d_1(\underline{\beta}, \overline{\theta}), d_1(\overline{\beta}, \underline{\theta}), d_1(\overline{\beta}, \overline{\theta}))$. Similarly, if elected, majority 2 is able to favor the interests of the stakeholders of the firm by maximizing the sum of taxpayers' utility and stakeholders' utility,

$$W^2(\vec{d_2}) = W(\vec{d_2}) - \mu\underline{U}_1, \qquad (26)$$

that is, by not including the informational rent of the environmentalists.

Let us assume that each majority makes campaign contributions C_1 and C_2 as a fixed proportion ζ, assumed equal for both majorities, of their average rents: $C_1 = \zeta\mu\underline{U}_1$ and $C_2 = \zeta\nu\underline{U}_2$, with

$$\underline{U}_1 = \Delta\theta[\nu V(d(\underline{\beta}, \overline{\theta})) + (1 - \nu)V(d(\overline{\beta}, \overline{\theta}))]$$

and

---

[15] On the left appear the adjusted (due to information asymmetry) marginal social values of pollution abatement and on the right the adjusted marginal social costs of pollution abatement in the different cases (θ, β).

© RAND 1999.

$$\underline{U}_2 = \Delta\beta[\mu(K - d(\overline{\beta}, \underline{\theta})) + (1 - \mu)(K - d(\overline{\beta}, \overline{\theta}))].$$

These campaign contributions affect the probability of winning the election that follows. For majority 1, the probability of winning is assumed to be

$$\Psi = \frac{1}{2} + \frac{1}{2}g\zeta(\mu\underline{U}_1 - \nu\underline{U}_2), \tag{27}$$

where g is a parameter representing the importance of campaign contributions in the electoral process. The stake of winning the election for period 2 is, for majority 1, $E^1(\overrightarrow{d_1}, \overrightarrow{d_2}) = W^1(\overrightarrow{d_1}) - W^1(\overrightarrow{d_2})$ and, for majority 2, $E^2(\overrightarrow{d_1}, \overrightarrow{d_2}) = W^2(\overrightarrow{d_2}) - W^2(\overrightarrow{d_1})$. Hence, majority 1 maximizes

$$W^1(\overrightarrow{d_1}) + \delta\Psi E^1(\overrightarrow{d_1}, \overrightarrow{d_2}), \tag{28}$$

leading to

$$\underline{\theta}V'(\hat{d}_1(\underline{\beta}, \underline{\theta})) = \underline{\beta}$$

$$\left(\overline{\theta} + \frac{\lambda}{1 + \lambda}\frac{\mu}{1 - \mu}\Delta\theta - \frac{1}{2}\frac{\delta E^1 g\zeta\Delta\theta\mu}{(1 + \lambda)(1 - \mu)}\right)V'(\hat{d}_1(\underline{\beta}, \overline{\theta})) = \underline{\beta}$$

$$\underline{\theta}V'(\hat{d}_1(\overline{\beta}, \underline{\theta})) = \overline{\beta} + \frac{\lambda}{1 + \lambda}\frac{\nu}{1 - \nu}\Delta\beta \tag{29}$$
$$+ \frac{1}{2}\frac{\delta E^1 g\zeta\Delta\beta\nu}{(1 + \lambda)(1 - \nu)}$$

$$\left(\overline{\theta} + \frac{\lambda}{1 + \lambda}\frac{\mu}{1 - \mu}\Delta\theta - \frac{1}{2}\frac{\delta E^1 g\zeta\Delta\theta\mu}{(1 + \lambda)(1 - \mu)}\right)V'(\hat{d}_1(\overline{\beta}, \overline{\theta})) = \overline{\beta} + \frac{\lambda}{1 + \lambda}\frac{\nu}{1 - \nu}\Delta\beta$$
$$+ \frac{1}{2}\frac{\delta E^1 g\zeta\Delta\beta\nu}{(1 + \lambda)(1 - \nu)}.$$

Let $\overrightarrow{\hat{d}_1} = (\hat{d}_1(\underline{\beta}, \underline{\theta}), \hat{d}_1(\underline{\beta}, \overline{\theta}), \hat{d}_1(\overline{\beta}, \underline{\theta}), \hat{d}_1(\overline{\beta}, \overline{\theta}))$.[16] In comparison with the static case, the environmentalist majority increases the pollution levels in all cases, except in the case $(\underline{\beta}, \underline{\theta})$. The reason is that it now wishes not only to decrease, as in the static case, the stakeholders' rent (with respect to the social optimum) because it undervalues this rent in its objective function, but also to increase its own rent in order to increase its probability of winning the election through campaign contributions and furthermore to decrease even further the stakeholders' rent for the same reason.

We obtain symmetric results for the stakeholders majority choosing $\overrightarrow{\hat{d}_2}$. In comparison with the static case, the stakeholders majority decreases the pollution levels in all cases except the case $(\underline{\beta}, \underline{\theta})$. The reason is similar to the one for which the environmentalist majority increased the pollution levels. Recalling the social welfare function $W = U_1 + U_2 + U_3$, let

$$E_{\lambda\alpha}\hat{W}(\overrightarrow{d}) = \frac{1}{2}E_\lambda W(\overrightarrow{\hat{d}_1}) + \frac{1}{2}E_\lambda W(\overrightarrow{\hat{d}_2}). \tag{30}$$

---

[16] One should note that the second-period pollution levels can be obtained from (29) with $\delta = 0$.

© RAND 1999

The above delegated incentive mechanism with two specific interest groups (DIM2) is to be compared with a constitutional pooling mechanism that determines a unique welfare-maximizing pollution abatement level as a function of λ but is common to all firms and environmentalists (or specific values of β and θ) and common to all majorities in power, that is, a CPM2 regulation.[17] This comparison creates a real tradeoff between the simplicity of the constitution and the distortions created by the political delegation and the use of separating mechanisms by majorities even in the simple limit case of var(λ) = 0. The same type of results would be obtained by comparing the performance of the DIM2 with reelection concerns to that of the CIM, characterized in Section 4, when var(λ) > 0. The latter can be characterized as follows:

$$\max_{d} W(d) = S - (1 + \lambda)(E\beta(K - d) + E\theta V(d)) - \lambda\mu\Delta\theta V(d) - \lambda\nu\Delta\beta(K - d), \quad (31)$$

yielding

$$\left(E\theta + \frac{\lambda}{1 + \lambda}\mu\Delta\theta\right)V'(\hat{d}) = \left(E\beta + \frac{\lambda}{1 + \lambda}\nu\Delta\beta\right), \quad (32)$$

leading to

$$E_\lambda W(\hat{d}). \quad (33)$$

The use of sophisticated delegated incentive schemes (DIM2) leads to two additional sources of distortions. First, campaign contributions are losses from a welfare point of view, and second, incentive distortions are reinforced. In a situation where the CPM2 scheme given by (32) is dominated in the static case by a DIM2 scheme,[18] we may expect that it will dominate the latter for g, ζ or δ large enough. Figure 2 provides such an example. Curve A illustrates the basic case ($\underline{\beta} = 1$, $\overline{\beta} = 1.5$, $\underline{\theta} = 1$, $\overline{\theta} = 1.5$) in which, for large-enough values of δ, the CPM2 scheme dominates the sophisticated DIM2 scheme. Curve B illustrates the same basic case except that $\overline{\beta} = 1.7$; it shows that as the informational asymmetry $\Delta\beta$ is increased, the domination of the CPM2 scheme occurs for values of δ larger than 5.35. Curve C illustrates the same basic case except that $\overline{\theta} = 1.7$; it shows again that as the informational asymmetry $\Delta\theta$ is increased, the domination of the CPM2 scheme occurs for values of δ larger than 7.15.

In this context, the emergence of sophisticated delegated incentive mechanisms (DIM2) would therefore be associated with *decreases* in δ, a measure of the desire of politicians to remain in power over time, with *decreases* in g, a measure of the importance of campaign contributions in the electoral process, and with *decreases* in ζ, a measure of the willingness of agents to make campaign contributions out of their informational rents. Hence, the long-term objectives of politicians, together with the private financing of electoral campaigns, favor simple command and control schemes over more sophisticated delegated separating incentive mechanisms.

This negative effect of reelection concerns would be mitigated by a reputation effect if taxpayers punish politicians who pursue excessively their private agendas. This reputation effect would appear if, for instance, the reelection probability of a given majority depended also on the difference between its chosen menu of pollution levels

---

[17] The pure effect of the discount factor δ on the emergence of an incentive mechanism could be analyzed, in light of Proposition 2, by comparing DIM2 and DPM2, which are both influenced by δ.

[18] The static regulation values for the CPM2 can be obtained from (29) with $\delta = 0$.

© RAND 1999.

FIGURE 2

THE DIFFERENTIAL EXPECTED WELFARE

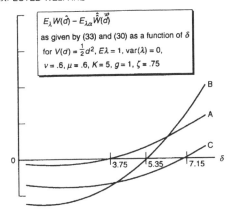

and the policy that would maximize social welfare. When in power, a majority would trade off in the first period the pursuit of its first-period gain and the impact of this pursuit on the probability of being reelected in the second period. Reelection considerations would then lead to conflicting influences. If pursuing excessively private agendas today is costly for the next election (through reputation effects and a better social control), then more sophisticated environmental policies may emerge as socially optimal. On the other hand, if the campaign contributions favoring reelection are important (large g) and significantly related (large ζ) to the informational rents of the various interest groups, politicians are led to greater distortions to favor even more the interest groups supporting them. The presence of multiple interest groups may therefore transform valuable reforms toward delegated incentive mechanisms into undesirable reforms if these powerful mechanisms raise the stake of political conflicts, generating additional distortions.

6. Conclusion

■ We have interpreted the political economy of environmental policy as an analysis of the economic implications of politicians' discretion in pursuing the private agendas of their electoral base: some voters are more concerned than others by pollution, some voters have stakes in the informational rents of the polluting firms.

Sophisticated environmental policy depends on nonverifiable variables that cannot be contracted upon in the constitution. So it must be delegated to politicians, creating an incentive problem when politicians' motivations are to stay in power by pleasing to a certain degree a majority of voters rather than by strictly maximizing social welfare. In this article we have studied the severity of this incentive problem. We have shown that the larger the social cost of public funds is (larger $E\lambda$) and the greater the variability of economic variables (var(λ), $\Delta\beta$, $\Delta\theta$) is, the more valuable flexibility is and therefore the greater the delegation of authority to politicians should be. However, the thinner the majorities are (the lower α^* is) or the larger the informational rents are (the larger ν and/or the larger μ are), the more the politicians' objectives are biased away from

© RAND 1999.

maximizing social welfare, providing a justification of cruder environmental policies that leave them less discretion.

The reelection mechanism we considered here depends solely on campaign contributions modelled as a given percentage of rents. When this is added to the waste of campaign contributions themselves, it favors giving up sophisticated policies that become costly political stakes. In this case, a longer-term view in politics (larger δ) does not favor the emergence of sophisticated market-based or incentive mechanisms.

The approach developed in this article could be extended to other types of social and economic regulations. It should also be broadened by considering more detailed and realistic electoral processes and by introducing various institutions (bureaucracy, courts, etc.) that mitigate the incentive problems associated with the delegation of public policy responsibilities to political majorities. (See in particular Breyer (1993) and Pollak (1995).)

Appendix

■   Proofs of Propositions 1–3 follow.

Proof of Proposition 1. To compare the two schemes, DPM and DIM, we first note that the two expected welfare functions evaluated at $\overline{\beta} = \beta$ are equal (equations (7), (8), (11), and (12) all give the same values) and that their first derivatives with respect to $\overline{\beta}$ evaluated at $\overline{\beta} = \beta$ are negative and equal. Hence, we compare the DPM and DIM schemes by computing the second derivatives of the expected social welfare with respect to $\overline{\beta}$ at $\overline{\beta} = \beta$. Consider first the case of the DIM scheme, where separating incentive mechanisms are chosen by the political majorities. Social welfare when majority 1 decides, $W(\underline{d}_1, \overline{d}_1)$, can be written from (1) and (4) as

$$W(\underline{d}_1, \overline{d}_1) = \frac{W^1(\underline{d}_1, \overline{d}_1)}{\alpha^*} + \nu\Delta\beta(K - \overline{d}_1),$$

where $W^1(\cdot, \cdot)$ is the objective function of majority 1. Using the envelope theorem for $W^1(\underline{d}_1, \overline{d}_1)$, we have

$$\frac{dW(\underline{d}_1, \overline{d}_1)}{d\overline{\beta}} = -(1 + \lambda - \nu)(K - \overline{d}_1) - \nu\Delta\beta\frac{d\overline{d}_1}{d\overline{\beta}},$$

where from (7),

$$\frac{d\overline{d}_1}{d\overline{\beta}} = \frac{1 + \lambda}{(1 - \nu)V''(\overline{d}_1)}$$

and therefore

$$\frac{d^2W(\underline{d}_1, \overline{d}_1)}{d\overline{\beta}^2} = \frac{(1 + \lambda - 2\nu)(1 + \lambda)}{(1 - \nu)V''(\overline{d}_1)}.$$

Similarly, when majority 2 decides, we have

$$W(\underline{d}_2, \overline{d}_2) = \frac{W^2(\underline{d}_2, \overline{d}_2)}{\alpha^*} + \left(1 - \frac{1}{\alpha^*}\right)\nu\Delta\beta(K - \overline{d}_2),$$

yielding

$$\frac{dW(\underline{d}_2, \overline{d}_2)}{d\overline{\beta}} = -(1 + \lambda - \nu)(K - \overline{d}_2) - \left(1 - \frac{1}{\alpha^*}\right)\nu\Delta\beta\frac{d\overline{d}_2}{d\overline{\beta}},$$

where from (8)

© RAND 1999.

$$\frac{d\bar{d}_2}{d\bar{\beta}} = \frac{1 + \lambda - \nu/\alpha^*}{(1 - \nu)V''(\bar{d}_2)}$$

and therefore

$$\frac{d^2W(\bar{d}_2, \bar{d}_2)}{d\bar{\beta}^2} = \frac{(1 + \lambda - \nu/\alpha^*)}{(1 - \nu)V''(\bar{d}_2)}\left(1 + \lambda + \frac{\nu}{\alpha^*} - 2\nu\right).$$

Hence the expected second derivative at $\bar{\beta} = \underline{\beta}$ (implying that $\bar{d}_1 = \underline{d}_1 = (1 + \lambda)\underline{\beta}$) in the case of the DIM (assuming that each majority is in power half the time) is given by

$$\frac{d^2E_{\lambda a}W(\underline{d}, \bar{d})}{d\bar{\beta}^2}\bigg|_{\bar{\beta}=\underline{\beta}} = \frac{\nu^2\left(\dfrac{\alpha^* - \dfrac{1}{2}}{\alpha^{*2}}\right) + 1 - 2\nu + 2(1 - \nu)E\lambda + (E\lambda)^2 - \text{var}(\lambda)}{(1 - \nu)V''(d^0)},$$

where $V'(d^0) = (1 + \lambda)\underline{\beta}$.

Consider now the DPM scheme, where the political majorities are restricted to choosing a single abatement level as a function of λ. We obtain from (11) and (12)

$$\frac{dd_1}{d\bar{\beta}}\bigg|_{\bar{\beta}=\underline{\beta}} = \frac{1 + \lambda}{V''(d^0)}$$

and

$$\frac{dd_2}{d\bar{\beta}}\bigg|_{\bar{\beta}=\underline{\beta}} = \frac{1 + \lambda - \dfrac{\nu}{\alpha^*}}{V''(d^0)}.$$

The social welfare when majority 1 is in power is given by

$$W(d_1) = \frac{W^1(d_1)}{\alpha^*} + \nu\Delta\beta(K - d_1),$$

and, similarly, the social welfare when majority 2 is in power is given by

$$W(d_2) = \frac{W^2(d_2)}{\alpha^*} + \left(1 - \frac{1}{\alpha^*}\right)\nu\Delta\beta(K - d_2).$$

Hence,

$$\frac{dW(d_1)}{d\bar{\beta}} = -(1 + \lambda - \nu)(K - d_1) - \nu\Delta\beta\frac{dd_1}{d\bar{\beta}}$$

and

$$\frac{dW(d_2)}{d\bar{\beta}} = -(1 + \lambda - \nu)(K - d_2) - \left(1 - \frac{1}{\alpha^*}\right)\nu\Delta\beta\frac{dd_2}{d\bar{\beta}}.$$

We therefore obtain

$$\frac{d^2W(d_1)}{d\bar{\beta}^2}\bigg|_{\bar{\beta}=\underline{\beta}} = (1 + \lambda - 2\nu)\frac{(1 + \lambda)}{V''(d^0)}$$

and

© RAND 1999.

$$\frac{d^2W(d_2)}{d\overline{\beta}^2}\bigg|_{\overline{\beta}-\underline{\beta}} = \left(1 + \lambda + \frac{\nu}{\alpha^*} - 2\nu\right)\frac{\left(1 + \lambda - \frac{\nu}{\alpha^*}\right)}{V''(d_0)}.$$

Hence the expected second derivative at $\overline{\beta} = \underline{\beta}$ in the case of a DPM scheme (assuming again that each majority is in power half the time) is given by

$$\frac{d^2E_{\lambda\alpha}W(d)}{d\overline{\beta}^2}\bigg|_{\overline{\beta}-\underline{\beta}} = \frac{\nu^2\left(\dfrac{\alpha^* - \dfrac{1}{2}}{\alpha^{*2}}\right) + 1 - 2\nu + 2(1 - \nu)E\lambda + (E\lambda)^2 + \text{var}(\lambda)}{V''(d^0)}.$$

Therefore, the second derivative of the expected social welfare under the DPM scheme is $(1 - \nu)$ times the second derivative of the expected social welfare under the DIM scheme as given above. Those derivatives are of the sign of the numerator, which is positive if and only if (14) holds. If $\text{var}(\lambda) > H(\cdot)$, the DIM dominates the DPM for $\overline{\beta}$ close to $\underline{\beta}$ and vice-versa if $\text{var}(\lambda) < H(\cdot)$.   *Q.E.D.*

Proof of Proposition 2. We want to compare the expected welfare of each majority under a DPM imposed by the constitution and under a DIM to determine the eagerness of each majority to support the latter constitutional rule. So we want to compare in per-capita terms

$$E_{\lambda\alpha}W^1(d) - E_{\lambda\alpha}W^1(\underline{d}, \overline{d})$$

and

$$E_{\lambda\alpha}W^2(d) - E_{\lambda\alpha}W^2(\underline{d}, \overline{d})$$

for $\overline{\beta}$ close to $\underline{\beta}$. First note that both differences and their first derivatives with respect to $\overline{\beta}$ vanish at $\Delta\beta = 0$. So we consider second derivatives. Straightforward computations (the proof follows steps similar to those in the proof of proposition 1; details are available from the authors) lead to

$$E_{\lambda\alpha}\frac{\partial^2 W^1(d)/\alpha^*}{\partial\overline{\beta}^2} - E_{\lambda\alpha}\frac{\partial^2 W^1(\underline{d}, \overline{d})/\alpha^*}{\partial\overline{\beta}^2} \quad \text{if and only if } \text{var}(\lambda) > H^1(\nu, \alpha^*, E\lambda)$$

and, similarly,

$$E_{\lambda\alpha}\frac{\partial^2 W^2(d)/\alpha^*}{\partial\overline{\beta}^2} - E_{\lambda\alpha}\frac{\partial^2 W^2(\underline{d}, \overline{d})/\alpha^*}{\partial\overline{\beta}^2} \quad \text{if and only if } \text{var}(\lambda) > H^2(\nu, \alpha^*, E\lambda).$$

Q.E.D.

Proof of Proposition 3. Clear from the text.

References

BARNETT, A.H. "The Pigouvian Tax Rule Under Monopoly." *American Economic Review*, Vol. 70 (1980), pp. 1037–1041.

BARON, D.P. "Regulation of Prices and Pollution Under Incomplete Information." *Journal of Public Economics*, Vol. 28 (1985a), pp. 211–231.

———. "Noncooperative Regulation of a Nonlocalized Externality." *RAND Journal of Economics*, Vol. 16 (1985b). pp. 553–568.

——— AND MYERSON, R.B. "Regulating a Monopolist with Unknown Costs." *Econometrica*, Vol. 50 (1982), pp. 911–930.

BAUMOL, W.J. AND BRADFORD, D.F. "Detrimental Externalities and Non-Convexity of the Production Set." *Economica*, Vol. 39 (1972), pp. 160–176.

BOHM, P. *Deposit-Refund Systems: Theory and Applications to Environmental, Conservation, and Consumer Policy.* Washington, D.C.: Johns Hopkins University Press, 1981.

BOYER, M. "Les effects de la réglementation." *Canadian Public Policy / Analyse de Politiques*, Vol. 4 (1979), pp. 469–474.

© RAND 1999

156 / THE RAND JOURNAL OF ECONOMICS

—— AND J.-J. LAFFONT "Environmental Protection, Producer Insolvency and Lender Liability." In A. Xepapadeas, ed., *Economic Policy for the Environment and Natural Resources*. Brookfield, Vt.: Edward Elgar, 1996.

—— AND ——. "Environmental Risks and Bank Liability." *European Economic Review*, Vol. 41 (1997), pp. 1427–1459.

BRAMHALL, D.F. AND MILLS, E.S. "A Note on the Asymmetry Between Fees and Payments." *Water Resources Research*, Vol. 2 (1966), pp. 615–616.

BREYER, S.G. *Breaking the Vicious Circle: Toward Effective Risk Regulation*. Cambridge, Mass.: Harvard University Press, 1993.

BUCHANAN, J.M. "External Diseconomies, Corrective Taxes, and Market Structure." *American Economic Review*, Vol. 59 (1969), pp. 174–177.

—— AND TULLOCK, G. "Polluters' Profits and Political Response: Direct Control Versus Taxes." *American Economic Review*, Vol. 65 (1975), pp. 139–147.

COELHO, P.R.P. "Polluters' Profits and Political Response: Direct Control Versus Taxes: Comment." *American Economic Review*, Vol. 66 (1976), pp. 976–978.

CROCKER, T. "The Structuring of Atmospheric Pollution Control Systems." In H. Wolozin, ed., *The Economics of Air Pollution*. New York: W.W. Norton, 1966.

CROPPER, M.L. AND OATES, W. "Environmental Economics: A Survey." *Journal of Economic Literature*, Vol. 30 (1992), pp. 675–740.

DALES, J.H. "Land, Water and Ownership." *Canadian Journal of Economics*, Vol. 1 (1968a), pp. 797–804.

——. *Pollution, Property and Prices*. Toronto: University of Toronto Press, 1968b.

DASGUPTA, P., HAMMOND, P., AND MASKIN, E. "On the Imperfect Information and Optimal Pollution Control." *Review of Economic Studies*, Vol. 47 (1980), pp. 857–860.

DEWEES, D.N. "Instrument Choice in Environmental Policy." *Economic Inquiry*, Vol. 21 (1983), pp. 53–71.

—— AND SIMS, W.A. "The Symmetry of Effluent Charges and Subsidies for Pollution Control." *Canadian Journal of Economics*, Vol. 9 (1976), pp. 323–331.

GUESNERIE, R. AND LAFFONT, J.-J. "A Complete Solution to a Class of Principal-Agent Problems with an Application to the Control of a Self-Managed Firm." *Journal of Public Economics*, Vol. 25 (1984), pp. 329–369.

GUPTA, S., VAN HOUTVEN, G., AND CROPPER, M. "Paying for Permanence: An Analysis of EPA's Cleanup Decisions at Superfund Sites." *RAND Journal of Economics*, Vol. 27 (1996), pp. 563–582.

HAHN, R.W. "The Political Economy of Environmental Regulation: Towards a Unifying Framework." *Public Choice*, Vol. 65 (1990), pp. 21–47.

—— AND MCGARTLAND, A.M. "The Political Economy of Instrument Choice: An Examination of the U.S. Role in Implementing the Montreal Protocol." *Northwestern University Law Review*, Vol. 83 (1989), pp. 592–611.

HOLMSTRÖM, B. "On the Theory of Delegation." In M. Boyer and R.E. Kihlstrom. eds., *Bayesian Models in Economic Theory*. New York: North-Holland, 1984.

JONES, L.P., TANDON, P., AND VOGELSANG, I. *Selling Public Enterprises*. Cambridge, Mass.: MIT Press, 1990.

KAMIEN, M.L., SCHWARTZ, N.L., AND DOLBEAR, F.T. "Asymmetry Between Bribes and Charges." *Water Resources Research*, Vol. 2 (1966), pp. 147–157.

KNEESE, A.V. AND BOWER, B.T. *Managing Water Quality: Economics, Technology, Institutions*. Baltimore: Johns Hopkins University Press, 1968.

LAFFONT, J.-J. "Regulation of Pollution with Asymmetric Information." In C. Dosi and T. Tomasi, eds., *Nonpoint Source Pollution Regulation: Issues and Analysis*. Dordrecht: Kluwer Academic, 1994.

——. "Industrial Policy and Politics." *International Journal of Industrial Organization*, Vol. 14 (1996), pp. 1–27.

—— AND TIROLE, J. *A Theory of Incentives in Procurement and Regulation*. Cambridge, Mass.: MIT Press, 1993.

LEE, D.R. "Efficiency of Pollution Taxation and Market Structure." *Journal of Environmental Economics and Management*, Vol. 2 (1975), pp. 69–72.

LEWIS, T.R. "Protecting the Environment When Costs and Benefits Are Privately Known." *RAND Journal of Economics*, Vol. 27 (1996), pp. 819–847.

LOEB, M. AND MAGAT, W.A. "A Decentralized Method for Utility Regulation." *Journal of Law and Economics*, Vol. 22 (1979), pp. 399–404.

MCCUBBINS, M.D., NOLL, R.G., AND WEINGAST, B.R. "Structure and Process, Politics and Policy: Administrative Arrangements and the Political Control of Agencies." *Virginia Law Review*, Vol. 75 (1989), pp. 431–482.

NOLL, R. "The Political Foundations of Regulatory Policy." *Journal of Institutional and Theoretical Economics*, Vol. 139 (1983), pp. 377–404.

POLLAK, R.A. "Regulating Risks." *Journal of Economic Literature*, Vol. 33 (1995), pp. 179–191.

ROBERTS, M.J. AND SPENCE, M. "Effluent Charges and Licenses Under Uncertainty." *Journal of Public Economics*, Vol. 5 (1976), pp. 193–208.

SEGERSON, K. "Liability and Penalty Structures in Policy Design." In D.W. Bromley, ed., *Handbook of Environmental Economics*. Cambridge, Mass.: Basil Blackwell, 1995.

———. "Issues in the Choice of Environmental Policy Instruments." In J.B. Braden, H. Folmer, and T.S. Ulen, eds., *Environmental Policy with Political and Economic Integration* Brookfield, Vt.: Edward Elgar, 1996.

STARRETT, D.A. "Fundamental Nonconvexities in the Theory of Externalities." *Journal of Economic Theory*, Vol. 4 (1972), pp.180–199.

WEITZMAN, M.L. "Prices vs. Quantities." *Review of Economic Studies*, Vol. 41 (1975). pp. 477–491.

YOHE, G.W. "Polluter's Profits and Political Response: Direct Control Versus Taxes: Comment." *American Economic Review*, Vol. 66 (1976), pp. 981–982.

© RAND 1999.

[15]

ELSEVIER

Ecological Economics 31 (1999) 123–138

ECOLOGICAL
ECONOMICS

www.elsevier.com/locate/ecolecon

ANALYSIS

No chance for incentive-oriented environmental policies in representative democracies? A Public Choice analysis[☆]

Friedrich Schneider [a,*], Juergen Volkert [b]

[a] *Institute of Economics, Johannes Kepler University of Linz, Altenbergerstraße 69, 4040 Linz/Auhof, Austria*
[b] *Institute for Applied Economic Research Tübingen, Ob dem Himmelreich 1, D-72074 Tübingen, Germany*

Received 2 February 1998; received in revised form 2 April 1999; accepted 16 April 1999

Abstract

Using the Public Choice approach, this paper gives an explanation as to why in representative democracies, in which political entrepreneurs attempt to maximize utility, an incentive-oriented environmental policy has hardly any chance of being implemented. We discuss two main aspects: first, the reasons which make it difficult to enforce any kind of environmental policy in the competitive political environment. And second, why such a policy—if it can be implemented at all—is very often enacted with inefficient instruments. In order to give a satisfactory explanation of these 'execution deficits', we differentiate between voters', politicians', interest groups', and bureaucracies' behavior to show that there are conflicts with other policies, and that individual rationality may be the greatest obstacle in implementing most incentive-oriented environmental policies. In the final section we provide five suggestions for overcoming these difficulties. © 1999 Elsevier Science B.V. All rights reserved.

Keywords: Incentive; Environmental policies; Democracy; Public Choice

1. Introduction

Apart from traditional economic studies of the effects of environmentally-oriented policies, it is important to analyze the implementation of these policies, such as taxes on fossil fuels or harmful (CO_2–) emissions, in representative democracies (There are numerous studies for Austria and Germany on this topic which will not be explored here, e.g. Schneider, 1993, 1994a; DIW (Deutsches Institut für Wirtschaftsforschung), 1994; Köppl et al., 1995; Schneider and Stiglbauer, 1995). By using the Public Choice approach we will analyze the possibilities of environmentally-oriented policy measures. We discuss two main aspects: first, the reasons which make it difficult to enforce any kind of environmental

---

[☆] This is a revised version. A first version was presented at the IIPF Meeting in Kyoto, Japan, August 25–28th, 1997.

* Corresponding author. Tel.: +43-732-2468210/211; fax: +43-732-2468209.

E-mail addresses: friedrich.schneider@jk.uni-linz.ac.at (F. Schneider), juergen.volkert@iaw.edu (J. Volkert)

0921-8009/99/$ - see front matter © 1999 Elsevier Science B.V. All rights reserved.
PII: S0921-8009(99)00047-6

124 F. Schneider, J. Volkert / Ecological Economics 31 (1999) 123–138

policy in the competitive political environment. And second, why such a policy—if it can be implemented at all—is very often enacted with inefficient instruments. We show that there are quite a number of incentives for political decision makers to implement command-and-control approaches instead of market-based environmental policies, even where those are economically and ecologically more efficient. Therefore, we will focus on the interaction among voters, politicians, interest groups, and the bureaucracy, especially concentrating on the individual (self-interested) preferences of the various actors within the framework of environmentally-oriented economic policies.

In our analysis we use the Public Choice approach. This implies that the state is not intended to be a homogenous body with uniform goals (i.e. welfare maximizing). Instead, all types of political decision makers should follow their own goals (methodological individualism). Therefore, we will focus on the interaction among voters, politicians, interest groups, and the bureaucracy, especially concentrating on the individual (self-interested) preferences of the various actors within the framework of environmentally-oriented economic policies. To state that people maximize their utility and follow their own goals does not mean that they must be selfish in the very narrow sense of the word. Altruism can easily be included.[1] However, Public Choice analysis tries to propose institutions and incentive structures which can function without the assumption that all people are necessarily altruistic. From the Public Choice perspective, it is not surprising that, specifically in representative democracies, numerous well-founded suggestions (from a purely traditional economic point of view) for the ecologizing of the tax system have been made; but so far, hardly any incentive-oriented concepts have been enacted. Additionally, most studies do not investigate why decision makers have not adopted important measures that numerous economic studies propose, which widen our social market economy into an ecological social market economy. From the traditional economic perspective, environmental policy is shaped by the omission and inefficient use of instruments.

In order to give a satisfactory explanation of this 'execution deficit' within the framework of Public Choice theory, we differentiate between the behavior of voters, politicians (or governments), interest groups, and bureaucracies. (According to the authors' knowledge, a small number of studies deal with Public Choice aspects of environmental policies, e.g. Holzinger, 1987; Frey, 1992; Horbach, 1992; Frey and Kirchgaessner, 1994; Weck-Hannemann, 1994; Gawel, 1995a; Kurz and Volkert, 1995, 1997.) With the help of the above differentiation, we explain why very little happens currently, or can be accomplished, toward ecologizing the economic system.

In Section 2 some basic interactions of the most important 'players', with respect to incentive-oriented ecological policies in representative democracies, are discussed. Section 3 examines voters' support for environmental economic policy. There are two lines of arguments: first, the conflict between environmental goals and other economic goals, such as full employment; and second, the character of public goods and the possibilities of free rider behavior. Section 4 considers the chances of an environmentally-oriented policy being carried out from the perspective of incumbent candidates. Sections 5 and 6 examine interest groups' and administrations' influence on environmental policy. The paper ends with suggestions in Section 7 for overcoming some of the major problems.

2. The interaction of the most important 'players' with respect to incentive-oriented ecological policies in representative democracies

Various actors (governments, bureaucracies, voters, interest groups, etc.) are involved in the formulation of environmental economic policies. In Fig. 1 the major interactions among the actors in a representative democracy as well as the sec-

[1] Altruism is usually modeled by utility-interdependences. That means that the individual utility is increased if other individuals (or generations) are favored by political decisions. By helping or contributing to the welfare of others the individual is therefore maximizing his utility as well as that of others.

F. Schneider, J. Volkert / Ecological Economics 31 (1999) 123–138

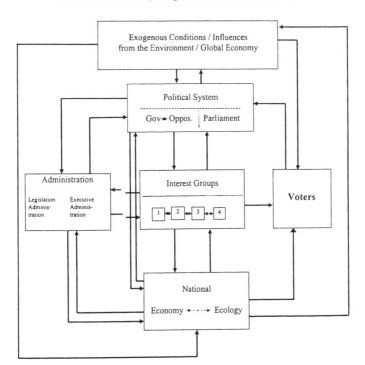

Fig. 1. A politico-economic model of the interaction of incentive-orientated ecological policies.

tions of our analysis which discuss each kind of interaction are shown.

As a starting point, and an illustrative example for our analysis, we examine a parliamentary system. Some aspects are, therefore, different in other systems of government, as in the US. But this does not mean that all key points would differ from our analysis. Instead we try to mention some of the main differences, even if a detailed comparison lies far beyond the scope of this paper.

The voters are influenced by the exogenous conditions from the global and national environment and economy as well as the actions of interest groups. Most likely, the voters will make their evaluation of government performance on ecological and (short-term) economic conditions, especially if general elections are close. The sur-

vival of government is influenced by voters' decisions at general elections.[2] Consequently, in order to get re-elected, a government will pursue a policy which favors a majority of voters, and will closely interact (and cooperate) with the administration and some interest groups. A close interaction also takes place between the administration and the interest groups because both depend on the national economy/ecology as well as on the exogenous conditions from the environment and global economy. The interest groups will form coalitions with various types of administrations in

[2] This applies especially to a parliamentary system of government. Nevertheless, quite a number of aspects apply to other systems of government as well, such as the US: the 'survival of government' and its implications could stand for the survival of the president as well as of the elected members of other political institutions.

126   *F. Schneider, J. Volkert / Ecological Economics 31 (1999) 123–138*

order to reach their self-interested goals. They have a preference for 'administrative-ecological rules' over the use of incentive-oriented instruments, a preference which is also in the interest of the various administrations. In the next sections, a detailed politico-economic analysis of the various actors is undertaken.

3. Voters: plenty of spectators but no advocates of an ecologically-oriented economic policy?

In this section we discuss the influence of voters on the political system and its consequences on the realization of incentive-oriented policies. Moreover, we ask how voters' dependence on exogenous conditions affects this influence (Fig. 1).

Due to an increased sensitivity to environmental issues by over two-thirds of the citizens, the approval of a majority of Austrian and German voters for the implementation of sustainable economic policies is becoming more and more realistic. This is shown in the results of several surveys made in the 1980s and 1990s in Germany and Austria, from which one can derive that Austrian and German voters consider environmental problems increasingly important. They label these issues extremely high, second only to unemployment (see for example, the survey results of the IMAS Institute (IMAS, 1995, 1996) published at regular intervals in Austria, and see Horbach (1992) regarding the development in Germany). Based on this, one can propose the hypothesis that the likelihood of the enactment of environmental economic policies is rising. However, it should be taken into account that ecological goals 'compete' with other interests (e.g. pure economic goals) of the voters.

The question arises: who would bear the costs of environmental policies? If price elasticity is low, the consumers can be assumed to bear most of the costs. This implies that the majority of voters directly pay for such a policy. But what if price elasticity is high and only a small part of the burden can be passed to the consumers? The producers, including owners as well as workers, have to bear the costs. From this it follows that

the resistance to environmental programs should be higher in regions with a high share of producer interests, which oppose such a policy, because a higher burden can lead to lower profits, wages, and employment in these regional sectors.

In Germany, empirical evidence for such a trade-off between the reduction of unemployment and ecological goals was found. Horbach (1992) points out that in regions with a high unemployment rate, environmental parties receive fewer votes in elections than in other regions. Furthermore, Horbach (1992) shows in an empirical study of Germany that the more important the chemical and steel industries are in a certain region, the worse the election chances are for environmental parties whose ecological economic policy programs could weaken the position of these industries. Citizens voting out of self-interest are, therefore, an obstacle to the approval of any kind of environmental policy.[3] This implies that too little may be done, especially in those regions where environmental policy is needed the most.

New arguments have emerged in the recent international discussion on the double dividend. The implementation of incentive-oriented environmental tax policies need not be accompanied by an increase, but by a shift in the tax burden. In such a case there is no immediate trade-off between fighting unemployment and enforcing stricter environmental policies (OECD, 1997). It can be shown that an environmental tax generates a large number of winners among different economic sectors and firms with comparatively small gains. This implies that there should be a large group in favor of the tax alternative. On the other hand, there are a few definite losers among the firms whose economic position deteriorates quite substantially (Fiederer, 1998; Schneider, 1998). At first sight, politicians might be expected to enact such a tax alternative in response to the preferences of the majority of voters instead of caring for the minority of losers. But such an expectation would neglect important results of Public Choice

---

[3] In Sections 4–6 we show that despite these general obstacles, political decision makers tend to favor command-and-control regulation and not market-based policies even if the latter are more efficient.

F. Schneider, J. Volkert / Ecological Economics 31 (1999) 123–138   127

theory. One of Buchanan's and Tullocks' (1996/ 1997, S. 36) main arguments against the distributive attractiveness of a tax alternative still holds for the actual double dividend discussion:

> ... a small, concentrated, identifiable, and intensely interested pressure group may exert more influence on political choice making than the much larger majority of persons, each of whom might expect to secure benefits in the second order of smalls...

Even if a double dividend would allow the fighting of unemployment by enforcing stricter environmental policies in the economy as a whole, there would still exist a political trade-off between the fighting of unemployment in small, intensely interested, and highly influential pressure groups of potential losers and an incentive-based environmental policy.

Even if voters' self-interests are in favor of environmental policies, there are at least two prerequisites before a noticeable pressure toward ecologizing the economy can be reached.

1. Considerable time-lags between changes in voters' ecological preferences, political actions and ecological improvements must not occur.
2. Citizens have to be well-informed about the consequences of the ecological problems.

Time-lags may cause inefficient results (i.e. when policy reactions against dangerous ecological developments come too late to prevent ecological damage with serious long-term consequences), and ecologically-oriented economic policies are characterized by high complexity, making it difficult to calculate the present and future consequences of such policies. Therefore, individual voters who want to evaluate such a policy need a relatively high level of education, otherwise they cannot calculate the current and future effects of the political parties' various ecological programs. It is, therefore, not surprising that not only the good economic performance of a country, but also a high educational level among voters, has a positive influence on the election results of strongly ecologically-oriented parties (Schneider and Volkert, 1997). In addition to a well-educated

body of voters, significant support for ecologically-oriented economic policy requires sufficient information about the ecological problems and the state of the environment as a whole. In contrast to these rather restrictive prerequisites of successful ecological policies, the effects of being unemployed can be calculated quite easily by most voters.

Let us now suppose that these first obstacles have been overcome. Even in such a situation, only some of the necessary ecological measures will gain substantial support by a majority of the voters. Citizens will vote for ecological measures which provide utility in the form of private (or at least club) goods, such as more restrictive ecological standards for producers in the neighborhood (concerning bad smells or the reduction of noise). However, other important ecological goals, from which a great number of people (scattered over the whole world) or even the future generations will benefit, take the form of public goods. Sustainability in a global context, with all its various worldwide implications, is just such a public good. In such a case, a voter who behaves in a utility-maximizing way has little incentive for casting his/her vote for the approval of such an environmental/economic policy. Instead, most voters' investment motive favors those political parties which most strongly represent his/her own self interests (i.e. job security). Therefore, a large group of voters may act as free riders, leaving the votes for the approval of the environmental policy up to others. This means that the goal of improving the environment must compete for votes with self-interested economic goals having much less of a public good character. For example, one's own employment situation will have a much higher priority than ecological economic policy, even though such policy is, by nature, beneficial for the general welfare of all voters.

Consequently voters care more about the economic short-term development (unemployment, disposable income, etc.) than about the ecological situation (Paldam, 1991; Schneider, 1994b). Such a behavior can delay or even prevent the approval of ecologically-oriented policies by the majority of voters. Even when a citizen is to some extent altruistic, well-educated, and informed, it is not

128   *F. Schneider, J. Volkert / Ecological Economics 31 (1999) 123–138*

obvious that he/she as a (long-term oriented) 'rational' voter will support ecologically-oriented economic policies in general elections. He/she may believe that his/her influence on the electoral outcome is so minimal that he/she cannot change the actual political situation with the help of his/her vote.

It should therefore be taken into consideration that the 'consumption motive' is important regarding the participation of voters in general elections. The voting act itself often contributes to voters' utility, independent of the election outcome. Such is the case when the voter is acting in accordance with 'civic duties'. It is also possible that voting in general elections expresses the individual's satisfaction derived simply from participating in the political process (similar to the satisfaction which these voters get by participating in political discussions or by supporting certain politicians (Brennan and Lomasky, 1983). On the basis of the very weak individual influence on the outcome of the election, it must also be taken into account that voters will generally be poorly informed about the issues at general elections and will, therefore, prepare their voting decisions on easily available information. If the voters' information about environmental issues, such as sustainability, could be improved, then the election mechanism could serve as a suitable instrument for revealing preferences for the environmental policy measures. One reason for this is the independence of the consumption motive from the voting act, as well as the extremely low influence of individually cast votes on the election outcome. Because of this, individual preferences can be revealed without 'danger'. Kirchgaessner (1996a,b,c) argues that supporting the moral arguments of green parties is relatively 'cheap' in an election and can therefore be expected as a special form of 'ethical voting' (Mueller, 1989). In this way, it is possible for a voter, in accordance with his/her actual preferences, to vote for radical and costly ecological reform measures because there will be no immediate consequences, such as higher individual tax burdens, from his vote alone.

High-publicity activities, such as those of the Club of Rome regarding the limits of growth or the focus of certain technological environmental policy issues, have been successful steps toward a reduction of the information deficit. On the whole, Horbach (1992) shows empirically that such activities have a positive effect on the sensitivity of voters to environmental problems as well as a significant positive influence on the realization of environmental policy measures in Germany.

To summarize the remarks about voter behavior: in many situations a majority of voters will not vote in favor of an environmental program if they are not well-informed about it. Another obstacle in the realization of ecologically oriented policies is that these or many of these programs provide benefits only in the form of public goods in future times, but have immediate cost (i.e. a higher tax burden).

4. Can politicians win elections with environmental programs?

This section refers to the incentives within the political system (Section 2). We discuss two main questions:

1. Do politicians have incentives to implement a sufficient level of environmental measures?
2. Are the existing incentives leading toward efficient environmental policies?

We begin with the discussion of the first question. If we consider the self-interested behavior of utility-maximizing politicians (e.g. politicians who are, at least at certain time intervals, primarily interested in being re-elected), the chances of ecologically oriented economic policy being implemented are poor. This hypothesis is supported by the fact that most environmental policies come quite easily into conflict with the preferences of politicians seeking re-election. These politicians favor economic policy measures which provide a majority of voters with immediate and noticeable utility gains, such as increased transfer payments. Moreover, the costs of these measures are either not visible for the average voter (e.g. by an increased state debt) or come into effect in future times (Schneider, 1994b; Volkert, 1996). The long-term effective utility gain of an ecological oriented economic policy can hardly be used for winning a

F. Schneider, J. Volkert / Ecological Economics 31 (1999) 123–138

129

majority in a general election because future generations will receive most of the benefit from such policies. In addition, incentive-oriented environmental policy measures may burden the current generation (voters/taxpayers) with quite extensive cost increases or even rising unemployment in the short term (a fact which reduces the chances for realizing ecological economic policy through the political process even further). It is very likely that potential losers from ecological policies will organize a voting campaign against these policies because they are frustrated with an increased (tax) burden or other economic disadvantages, such as job losses or consumption reduction. The threat of job loss is especially important in this context because it is an issue which can be presented by a coalition between employers and employees in the affected production area. Such powerful coalitions will influence the behavior of politicians, making them either hesitate to implement the necessary environmental measures or even reject them.

One indicator of the low level of interest in environmental and/or sustainable economic issues of incumbent candidates is the fact that one can realize only a few election cycles in environmental policy. These cycles are observable, but also noticeably weaker than in other traditional economic policy fields such as increased government spending (Frey, 1992; Horbach, 1992). In these short-term oriented areas, more votes can be won than can with long-term ecologically oriented economic policy programs.

Since an ecologically oriented economic policy is less attractive to incumbent candidates, they will give low priority to this issue. This tendency is strengthened by the fact that the expansion of state activities is limited because these activities quickly stretch the public budgets to their financial limits. In such a situation, it is natural for utility-maximizing politicians to reduce subsidies or restrict programs in environmental fields because their re-election chances are least affected by such measures.

But even if the level of environmental activities may be too low, the question arises whether the remaining policies in this field are at least carried out in an efficient way. With respect to the use of

economic instruments, it can be observed that self-interested politicians strongly prefer 'vote-maximizing' instruments, such as tax rate reductions or increasing transfer payments (see Pommerehne and Schneider (1978, 1983) and Schneider (1994b) for a detailed discussion on instruments used for securing re-election by utility-maximizing politicians). The resulting benefits of such policies can be directly associated with the responsible politician(s). With respect to incentive-oriented environmental policies, this direct link is often missing, and hence, we observe the tendency of politicians to choose instruments which are 'inefficient' in the traditional economic sense. The reason for this is that the re-election criteria of highly visible and immediately effective measures with postponed costs are more likely to be fulfilled by using regulations (i.e. standards) or, to a lesser extent, subsidies for environmental issues than by using the instrument of environmental taxes or tradeable permits. Incentive-oriented instruments are inefficient for the politicians' re-election goals because the utility gains from these instruments are postponed until future times and will only be partially attributed to the current government. In contrast, the government will be immediately held responsible for an increased tax burden and the negative economic consequences (e.g. rising unemployment) induced by those instruments.

We can summarize that the level of environmental activities may be too low due to the incentive structure of incumbent candidates (Coates, (1996) discusses the role of campaign contributions in the US).[4] While command-and-control instruments lead to immediate results, the effectiveness of economic instruments is based on new or different incentives. Because it takes time until

---

[4] This argument refers especially to parliamentary democracies. In other systems of government, such as the US, campaign contributions play a much more important role than in parliamentary democracies. Coates (1996) shows that campaign contributions alter the position of the recipients in the US House of Representatives toward wilderness and other environmental issues. However, there are more incentives to support policies which affect private goods and private rent-seeking outcomes than to contribute in favor of a public good like environmental improvements.

130   *F. Schneider, J. Volkert / Ecological Economics 31 (1999) 123–138*

a sufficient number of decision makers have adapted their strategies to the new incentives, the ecological effects often come too late for incumbent candidates. The costs of command-and-control instruments as well as those of incentive-oriented instruments can be postponed. However, the costs of command-and-control instruments which can result in general economic inefficiencies are less visible than costs, such as higher taxes or an increased debt burden.

5. Lobbying for and against incentive-oriented environmental policies

In this section we discuss the influence of interest groups on the political system and the consequences for environmental policies (Fig. 1). As in the preceding section, we discuss first if political decision makers, such as members of lobbying groups, have incentives to implement a sufficient level of environmental measures. Second, we ask if the existing incentives lead toward efficient environmental policies.

The great importance of well-organized and well-informed interest groups is derived from the fact that the environmental legislation requires a large volume of specialized information before it is passed. This information is only obtainable with the assistance of interest groups. If the information from the various interest groups is equally reliable, the question as to which group will be able to achieve the strongest effect with their information, and thereby have the strongest influence in the political arena, turns out to be decisive in the behavior of the interest groups. The answer to this question depends on the successful organization of the group members' individual interests as well as on the specific effectiveness of each interest group in carrying out its lobbying activities.

The members of environmental groups have very heterogeneous interests, making the organizational costs sharply rise with an increasing number of members. Second, future generations, who are the major beneficiaries of ecological or sustainable policies, must be taken into account; however, they are unable to contribute to the actual group activities, such as the financing of the various lobbying activities. This 'disadvantage' strongly increases the organizational and lobbying costs for the current members of interest groups favoring environmental policies. Third, at the beginning of their work, environmental interest groups often face the lack of a sufficient infrastructure, which is necessary for successful lobbying in the political arena.

The relatively high costs of 'green' interest groups will only be accepted by their members if these costs are clearly lower than the expected 'rents' or 'utility gains' which the group members try to achieve by their lobbying activities. From an economic perspective, however, there are further difficulties. Those rents can only be considered as 'relevant' additional rents from environmental policies when the group members benefit almost exclusively from them. This means that if the environmental interest group succeeds in attaining highly efficient lobbying and, finally, implementation of efficient environmental policies, every citizen will benefit from this policy. The results of environmental policy are often public goods: everybody receives the whole benefits (like less air pollution, better climate, etc.). There is no necessity to divide these benefits because they accrue to anyone. The crucial problem in very large groups of potential beneficiaries is that everybody benefits without any difference between those who have contributed to the results and free-riders who have not. A well-known result of the theory of collective action is the difficulty of achieving an efficient organization of very large interest groups which cannot monitor and sanction such a free-rider behavior (Olson, 1968, 1985; Schneider, 1985; Mueller, 1989).

From the Public Choice perspective, environmental groups must take high organizational and lobbying costs into account when working toward the long-term goal of ecologically oriented economic policies. These activities often do not yield the necessary high profits or utility gains until some time in the future; and moreover for the individual, this achievement has the character of a public good.

If one considers the position of more traditional interest groups (e.g. the producers), not all of

F. Schneider, J. Volkert / Ecological Economics 31 (1999) 123–138 131

them are necessarily against environmental policies. Environmental protection industries might benefit from environmental policies through additional business. Hence, it is obvious that the success of their lobbying is dependent, among other factors, upon the extent to which changes along the lines of a sustainable development have already taken place. Horbach (1992) shows that the passing of extensive environmental protection legislation becomes possible when environmental protection industries make up a considerable share of economic production and employ a significant number of workers. An accelerated speed of environmental policy activities will be easier to attain when these industries form an interest group, thereby creating a counterbalance to those interest groups which oppose environmental policies.

Aside from the environmental protection industries, most other traditional industries oppose environmental policies. Most of these interest groups have the advantage that their size is smaller than those groups which benefit from environmental policy. Therefore, they face lower organizational and lobbying costs and do not experience free rider behavior to a great extent. If these interest groups succeed in providing information which is used in the political arena to weaken environmental policies, the short-term benefits from such lobbying activities are much higher than the 'pure consumption utility' for the individual group member.[5] These benefits can be interpreted as a return on investment in the political arena, whose absolute value can be calculated from the value of the gained monetary advantages.

There are five main reasons why interest groups, which oppose most environmental policies and which combine both employer and employee interests, not only are better organized, but are also better able to achieve their self-interested goals:

1. In contrast to environmental interest groups, the respective industry and business associa-

tions usually have sufficient financial backing, which is used for efficient lobbying.[6]

2. Producers themselves are closest to the origin of environmental problems in the production sector. That is the reason for substantial information asymmetries. Therefore 'green' groups often have difficulties in getting information about pollution effects as well as about the feasibility of alternative technologies. This lack of sufficient information in discussions with well-informed industry groups, who can filter the relevant information according to their own intentions, makes the environmental groups' task even harder.

3. Based on this information asymmetry, industry and business associations often have considerable influence on public opinion through their own publications as well as through their effect on the media.[7]

4. The 'market power' of these interest groups is a crucial factor in the achievement of their goals in the political arena. It is not only important in the goods and services market, but in the labor market as well, especially in the form of the threat of transferring production abroad.

5. Quite often these associations gain personal representation in legislative institutions (parliament and committees) which makes it possible for them to postpone or even reject environmental issues.

Above all, individual representatives of industrial and business interest groups are able to influence legislative proposals in their early stages through active lobbying in hearings and other

---

[5] That is, information about subsidies for an environmentally compatible policy, or strategies for the reduction of cost burdens from environmental policies.

[6] While this aspect is decisive in parliamentary democracies, the ability to make campaign contributions is another major point, as in the US (Coates, 1996). However, in parliamentary democracies, campaign contributions are less important.

[7] The considerable influence on the public opinion is a result of informational advantages, the solid financial background, and the specialized lobby organizations which face very good conditions for successful activities. However, one should note that environmental groups are nowadays sometimes better represented in the media than their opponents because of spectacular actions (for example, Greenpeace vs. Shell in fall 1995).

parliamentary committees. For that purpose, they provide detailed information about environmental measures. This has the effect of linking together lobbyists and members of legislative bodies. As a result of this relationship, arrangements are made between the political administrative system and 'private' interest groups of the economy. In Germany, such agreements have become common practice in more than 50 industrial committees and 'voluntary self-obligations' (for example, the obligation in the automobile industry to produce cars with a '3-l engine'), as well as in several hundred committees for the definition of the 'best available technology' (Maier-Rigaud, 1996; Helbig and Volkert, 1999) (the legitimacy of interest groups, not only in this field, would be a promising topic for further research, but this would go far beyond the mainly positive analysis that we present in this context). Due to this successful lobbying, the efficiency of environmental policies is reduced. Consider, for example, the compromises which are made in the form of modifications benefiting influential polluter interests in Germany. These compromises are only argued as being 'economically tolerable'. However, this catchword is quite often only a political 'excuse' instead of an overall well-sounded economic argument (Sandhövel (1994a) mentions the *Bund der Deutschen Industrie* (BDI) and the *Deutsche Industrie- und Handelstag* (DIHT) as two especially influential producer interest groups).

From the Public Choice perspective it is obvious that industry groups, who are directly affected by environmental policy measures, prefer the instrument of setting fixed standards to other environmental incentive-oriented instruments. A major reason for the preference of this instrument is that industries only have to make sure they do not to reach the limits of these emission standards. The outcome is that all emissions which remain below the limit are free of charge. Furthermore, defining these standards often provides affected industries considerable leeway for manipulating the environmental policy measures. For example, negotiations can be held regarding specific technical standards which can lead to exemptions (loopholes) for the affected firms. Since the information from affected companies on

pollution prevention technologies and costs is more detailed and more precise (but quite often one-sided), such agreements (compromises) are mainly made in the interest of the (private) producers. In comparison to other policy instruments (i.e. ecological taxes) exemptions can also be more easily carried out when standards are employed. Also, in many cases, a further tightening of standards would prove to be difficult and ineffective because administrative controls are unable to monitor and sanction violations of these tightened standards. Therefore, the additional cost to companies of preventing pollution increases to a lesser extent the more difficult the control becomes and the higher current level of environmental protection measures. Furthermore, standards can lead to market entry barriers if potential competitors produce with different technologies, which results in a large rent-seeking potential for old emitters.

The preference of interest groups for administrative environmental regulations has also been found in surveys of the affected companies. According to Horbach (1992) two-thirds of the German companies favor standards, whereas only one-third favor levies or taxes. It is interesting that those companies who argue in favor of standards estimate that environmental standards are easier to fulfill and cause fewer conflicts and costs than environmental taxes. This statement can also be seen as an indicator of the significant leeway that is gained when environmental standards are used. Therefore, the interest groups' preferences for administrative environmental regulations are not surprising. One reason for this is that in Germany much less leeway results from the use of environmental taxes. The broader acceptance of US industry for market-based mechanisms may, therefore, be caused by the different regulatory structures.[8] The USA tends to be more rigid and transparent, but in Germany, enterprises and industries have many more possibilities to manipulate the outcome of command-and-control instruments. The institutional setting of environmental bureaucracies is, therefore, of great impor-

---

[8] We thank an anonymous referee for this important remark.

F. Schneider, J. Volkert / Ecological Economics 31 (1999) 123–138 133

tance in the direction of lobbying activities (Jaedicke et al., 1993) (Section 6).[9]

6. Public administrations' resistance against incentive-oriented environmental policies

The political influence of producer and other interest groups is not only relevant in the legislative arena, but also at the administrative level of the political system. This is most important because the influence of the public administration, such as in Germany, has continuously increased due to the shifting of executive power. This is especially true in the course of the preparation and early implementation of environmental policy programs.

Administrators necessarily play a significant role in setting environmental regulations. In the preceding section we asked how this affects environmental policy in general and whether the efficiency of such a policy is influenced by bureaucratic activities.

Since most public administrations have a superior knowledge due to intense contacts with the affected interest groups and industries, the bureaucracy has acted more and more often as a generator of momentum and as a mediator for organized interest group preferences. The task of the legislation has increasingly been reduced to the mere legitimization of those programs whose contents have already been (pre)structured by the administration. Furthermore, lower levels of environmental administrations have been growing in influence on the concrete structure of complex environmental programs. In Germany, for example, the industrial inspection board (Gewerbeaufsichtsamt) and community environmental agencies (Umweltämter) have become more and more important in the realm of permission, control, sizing, and sanctioning of environmental-politically relevant activities (Horbach, 1992; Gawel, 1995a).

The empirical studies of Holzinger (1987) demonstrate that German environmental administrations are not completely bound to instructions and do not fully act according to the legislation's decisions in order to fulfill the legislator's environmental goals. Holzinger's studies reveal that bureaucrats follow their own interests, whereas goals such as 'economic efficiency' and 'overall economic cost optimization' are of only minor importance for the employees of German environmental administrations. Environmental authorities are vitally interested in environmental policy measures, which are labor- and resource-intensive. If they succeed in applying such policies, they can grow quickly. As a result, they are able to increase their number of employees, and each year they have a larger budget at their disposal. The result of this is that the environmental administrations will try to implement those environmental policy measures which require high administrative controls.

Using the theories of bureaucracy from Niskanen (1971) and of Migué and Bélanger (1974), one can analyze the consequences of these goals of budget maximization and/or optimal discretionary budgets. According to the study by Holzinger (1987), about 76% of all surveyed employees working in environmental authorities in Germany demand an increase of their budgets in combination with additional responsibility.

If the goal of budget maximization in a given surrounding is difficult to achieve for the environmental administration, then, according to Migué and Bélanger (1974), the administration will pursue the objective of expanding their discretionary budget. According to Gawel (1994, 1995b), 49% of surveyed employees in German environmental administrations wanted political authorities to regulate as little as possible so that the environmental authorities had the greatest possible discretionary budget for their own decisions. Only 36% favored a clear regulation of environmental procedures. Discretionary budgets are also necessary in order to meet the demands of those lobbies for which the different environmental sections of German ministries have become even more important than the parliament.

In spite of these normal day-to-day cooperations, a number of conflicts can arise between the administrations and interest groups. For example,

---

[9] Apart from the leeway that command-and-control instruments provide in Germany, it is also the fact that the total amount of emission is subject to costs, which leads to the companies' rejection of environmental taxes. Strong resistance by interest groups to environmental taxes has also been observed in Switzerland.

according to almost 50% of surveyed enterprises in the German iron and steel industry, the intensive cost burden due to planned environmental protection measures caused conflicts with the respective executive administrations. According to Sandhövel (1994b) and Ullmann (1982), the same sector, however, reaches most 'compromises per firm' with environmental authorities. These compromises are reached in spite of the generally weak bargaining position of the administrations. As empirical studies for Germany show, there is little incentive from the perspective of the environmental bureaucracies to engage in lengthy, formal, and/or legal confrontations with affected companies and their interest groups because, in doing so, funding is tied up and can no longer be used in pursuing the goal of additional employees. Moreover, environmental bureaucracies quite often have poor labor resources (especially in regions with a large share of ecologically harmful industries), which significantly reduces their chances for successful negotiations with well-organized producer interests (see Horbach (1992) for a survey of the relevant studies).

The asymmetrical distribution of bargaining power between firms and environmental authorities results in compromises in environmental standards and in allowances concerning the best available technology. Further indicators of the rather weak bargaining position of environmental authorities in (potential) confrontations with producer interests are the comparatively low sanctions as well as the relatively mild punishments. In Germany, sanctions are only carried out against approximately 5% of firms which, due to environmental regulations, need business permits. According to the environmental administrations, the reason for this stems in no way from the widespread adherence to existing regulations, but rather the difficulty of gathering proof, the high administrative costs of investigations, the desire to avoid damaging the relationship with the addressee, and the insufficient infrastructure of the penal system. Considering the small number of prosecuted violations, the low amount of the applied official sanctions is even more surprising, and can be explained due to the weak position of the administration. In the German city of Kiel,

for example, 714 prosecuted violations of environmental protection regulations resulted in only about \$40 000 in fines, approximately \$55 per case (see Volkert (1996) regarding the weak position of environmental authorities).

Despite the weak bargaining position of the bureaucracies, some measures can be carried out. The reason for this is that conflicts between potentially affected firms and the administration in Germany mainly occur with respect to the intensity of the environmental policy measures, but less often with respect to the type of instruments to be used. The incentive structure of bureaucracies has many similarities to the incentive structure of business associations with respect to the preferences of certain policy instruments. For example, administrations also prefer the use of environmental standards which can only be supervised with labor- and resource-intensive execution efforts, allowing them to expand their budgets. Moreover, standards have relatively high discretionary regulatory requirements such as for example

- a formulation of an exact definition of the given environmental goal and consideration of the best available technology,
- definition of sanction threats,
- determination of minimum requirements, and
- definition of control and observation rights.

These high-discretionary regulatory requirements increase the influence of bureaucracies. The discretionary budget pursued by the employees of environmental authorities is extended even further by the setting of standards when negotiations are held with the affected industries or interest groups. Furthermore, standards are characterized by a certain amount of rigidity, which is desirable from the bureaucratic point of view because it lowers transaction costs. Lastly, because of the high demand for information often caused by the setting of environmental standards, further budget increases can be justified.

In Germany, on the one hand, the incentive structure of bureaucracies has many similarities to the incentive structure of business associations with respect to the preferences of certain policy instruments; bureaucracies in Germany have extensive leeway when implementing command-and-control instruments. Industry groups in Germany, therefore, also favor these kinds of instruments because any producer can achieve special treatment and exemptions which are out of reach if market-based economic instruments are implemented. On the other hand, in countries where the administration is bound to stricter regulation and has much less leeway, like the US, industry groups may favor market-based instruments which impose lower transaction costs. Moreover, the potential rents which can be gained by each enterprise are not sufficient to lead to a preference for command-and-control instruments. Therefore, an institutional setting like the US can lead to a conflict between business associations who prefer more efficient market-based instruments and administrators with a preference for command-and-control instruments. But in an institutional setting like in Germany, there is a clear preference of most business associations and administrations for command-and-control instruments. The only conflict is whether an environmental policy should be implemented at all.

In addition to standards, subsidies are another instrument preferred by environmental administrations. They are attractive for the employees of administrations and for the politicians as well because they can often be used in vote-maximizing strategies. The granting of subsidies, which are often (co-)determined by the environmental authorities, can reduce environmental damage through benefits instead of burdens, and costly confrontations with the affected industries can be avoided. One must, however, take into consideration that the use of environmental subsidies can only be ecologically successful if enough financial means are shifted away from budgets of other administrations or if additional revenues are available. But because ecologically oriented policies are relatively unattractive for incumbent candidates these instruments will not take a dominant position in comparison to the instrument of environmental standards.

The evaluation of ecological taxes from the perspective of environmental administrations is completely different. While standards can only exist with high labor costs and other expenditures, the use of taxes requires much less expenditure and less staff. Hence, a budget increase or rise in the importance of environmental authorities is less likely to occur than with the use of standards. Furthermore, the change from the current system of environmental standards to a system of taxes would require a high degree of flexibility in the environmental agencies. One should also note that establishing an ecological tax system requires large amounts of information on producers' pollution prevention costs, which may not be easily available to the administrations. In contrast to the use of taxes, the information requirement which an environmental authority would face with the use of tradeable permits is notably smaller because almost no information on companies' marginal pollution costs is required. Detailed information is only necessary for the tolerable total burden, for the 'correct' total emission amount derived from it, and for the estimation of the economic effects of such tradeable permits.

Using tradeable permits would increase the economic efficiency of the executing administrations, but for the administrations this is no advantage. First, the obviously lower information requirements make it rather difficult to justify a large official budget. And second, the gained discretionary budget is very small compared to the use of standards. It is also questionable if the additional revenues from tradeable permits could be spent by the environmental administration. Furthermore, it should be noted that the instrument of tradeable permits is the least well-known and least established instrument in German speaking countries. This can explain the strong resistance of state administrations to the use of tradeable permits, which are often, from an economic point of view, highly efficient environmental policy instruments. These considerations are supported by surveys in which German bureaucrats gave the poorest evaluation of all environmental policy instruments to tradeable permits (Holzinger, 1987; Horbach, 1992).

7. Concluding remarks

Public Choice theory assumes that political entrepreneurs are self-interested utility maximizers. Consequently, an environmentally incentive-oriented policy has hardly any chance of being implemented. It is, therefore, not surprising that a significant 'execution' deficit can be observed. In this paper various difficulties which could hinder the establishment of ecologically oriented policies have been discussed. These include the public goods character of environmental measures, the fact that the costs of environmental measures show up immediately and the benefits much later, and widespread preferences for the use of standards. Perhaps some of them can be overcome with the help of the following suggestions, which are only rough ideas and need further elaboration.

7.1. Decentralized environmental policy according to the principle of subsidiarity

The principle of subsidiarity should be used more extensively in environmental policy. According to the principle of subsidiarity, each environmental task shall be fulfilled by the smallest or most decentralized unit. Following this principle, the costs/utilities of many environmental measures could be more effectively 'localized and accredited' to the affected parties if they were divided into small distinct units. This is necessary because the environmental situation, the attitude of the affected parties toward the environment, and the economic policy measures differ strongly over the regions. Another aspect is that the subsidiarity principle is necessary in order to be able to design an environmental policy according to voters' preferences. Moreover, information costs for voters are lower if environmental policies are decentralized. As we have seen in Section 3, only sufficiently informed citizens will vote in favor of environmental policy. Making information cheaper in a decentralized policy according to the principle of subsidiarity is, therefore, very important (especially for environmental policies). Moreover 'green' groups face fewer problems to become organized and sufficiently informed if their lobbying activities can be restricted to a certain region with a smaller number of producers as well

as a much smaller number of people who are potential beneficiaries of environmental policies.

7.2. Referenda—an institutional progress

Even in a decentralized environmental policy, the individual voter/taxpayer in representative democracies has few possibilities to directly influence ecologically-oriented policy measures. This difficulty can be overcome by introducing direct voting (i.e. the use of a referendum). In the case that the environmental measure is accepted by the voters in a referendum, politicians have a much better legitimization for the implementation of measures than without voters' approval. The importance of referenda for environmental policies is a result of various factors. In a direct democracy, people can act as agenda-setters and make decisions about alternatives which are not attractive for incumbent candidates because, for one reason, they are opposed by highly influential pressure groups. This implies that an environmental policy, in general, as well as market-based instruments, which are hard to enforce in political competition, have better chances in referenda than in the normal process of a parliamentary democracy. Moreover, referenda can initiate a discussion process among the voters which supplies them with more information, makes them evaluate the possible alternatives in more detail, and possibly changes their attitude. And, as the experience in Switzerland shows, politicians are also more tightly bound to voters' preferences if they know that one-sided measures in favor of influential interest groups can be abolished by direct democracy (Frey, 1994). (As noted by Kirchgaessner, 1996a,b, strong resistance by interest groups to environmental taxes has been observed in Switzerland.) Decision makers will, therefore, pay more attention to topics like environmental policies, which are less attractive as (re-)election goals but important for the majority of the citizens. In the case that an environmental measure is accepted by the voters in a referendum, politicians have a more legitimate reason for the implementation of such measures than without voters' approval.

7.3. Compensation by general tax reductions

The chances for an incentive-oriented environmental policy can, under certain conditions, be improved by compensating the additional burden of ecological taxes and tradeable permits through general tax reductions. In this way, voters' resistance against ecological activities, which tend to increase the citizens' burden immediately without raising utilities in the near future, could be reduced. Politicians' view that an economically efficient environmental policy, which increases voters' burden immediately for the sake of long-term improvements, is not attractive at all could be solved by financing the programs with debt. [10]

7.4. Tying ecological tax revenues to environment-related instruments

Another political suggestion is the strengthening of the position of ecologically sensitive producers. One could give up the non-affectation principle in the area of (future) environmental levies and taxes. As a result, these additional revenues can directly be used to finance environmental policy projects. Examples for this, according to Cansier and Krumm (1997), are the SO_2-, NO_x-, and CO_2-taxes, which are levied in France, the Netherlands, and in Scandinavia. The revenue from these taxes can be used in environmental projects or to subsidize companies which apply advanced pollution prevention technologies. If ecological tax revenues are tied closely to environment-related expenditures it would be difficult for rent seekers to gain these revenues. The result would be a more solid financial background for environmental policy with steadier flows of disposable revenues.

It should be noted that these suggestions might help to overcome the above-mentioned difficulties in implementing incentive-oriented policies in rep-

resentative democracies, however, a detailed analysis of how these suggestions can be realized is missing, and is left for further research.

References

Brennan, G., Lomasky, L., 1983. Institutional aspects of 'merit goods' analysis. Finanzarchiv 41, 185–206.

Cansier, D., Krumm, R., 1997. Air pollutant taxation: an empirical survey. Ecol. Econ. 23, 59–70.

Coates, D., 1996. Jobs versus wilderness areas: the role of campaign contributions. In: Congleton, R.D. (Ed.), The Political Economy of Environmental Protection. Analysis and Evidence. Ann Arbor Science Publications, Ann Arbor, pp. 69–95.

DIW (Deutsches Institut für Wirtschaftsforschung), 1994. Ökosteuer-Sackgasse oder Königsweg. DIW, Berlin.

Fiederer, H.J. 1998. Auswirkungen einer ökologischen Steuerreform auf die Abgabenbelastung von Unternehmen, Gutachten im Auftrag des Ministeriums für Umwelt und Verkehr Baden-Württemberg, IAW-Forschungsbericht, Serie B, Nr. 12, Tübingen.

Frey, B.S., 1992. Umweltökonomie, 3rd ed. Vandenhoek and Ruprecht, Goettingen.

Frey, B.S., 1994. Direct democracy: politico-economic lessons from Swiss experience. Am. Econ. Rev. 84 (2), S338–342.

Frey, B.S., Kirchgaessner, G., 1994. Demokratische Wirtschaftspolitik: Theorie und Anwendung, 2nd ed. Vahlen, Munich.

Gawel, E., 1994. Umweltpolitik zwischen Verrechtlichung und Ökonomisierung. ORDO 45/1, 63–103.

Gawel, E., 1995a. Zur Politischen Ökonomie von Umweltabgaben. Mohr (Siebeck), Tuebingen Walter Eucken Institut Freiburg, Vorträge und Aufsätze Nr. 146.

Gawel, E., 1995b. Bürokratie, Theorie und Umweltverwaltung: Ökonomische Einsichten in verwaltungsrechtliches Handeln im Umweltschutz. Z. Angewandte Umweltforschung 8/1, 79–89.

Helbig, J., Volkert, J., 1999. Freiwillige Standards im Umweltschutz. Physica/Springer, Heidelberg.

Holzinger, K., 1987. Umweltpolitische Instrumente aus der Sicht der Bürokratie: Versuch einer Anwendung der ökonomischen Theorie der Bürokratie. Vahlen, Munich.

Horbach, J., 1992. Neue Politische Ökonomie und Umweltpolitik. Fischer, Frankfurt (Main).

IMAS, 1995. Umfrageberichte von IMAS-International. IMAS, Khevenhüllerstrasse 14, 4020 Linz, Austria.

IMAS, 1996. Umfrageberichte von IMAS-International. IMAS-International, Khevenhüllerstrasse 14, 4020 Linz, Austria.

Jaedicke, W., Kern, K., Wollmann, H., 1993. Internationaler Vergleich von Verfahren zur Festlegung von Umweltstandards. Institut für Stadtforschung und Strukturpolitik (IfS) im Auftrag des Umweltbundesamtes, Berlin.

---

[10] Another reason to propose debt financing of long-term ecological measures can be the wish to preserve intergenerational justice. This is another line of argument which critically depends on the (ir-)relevant question of Ricardian equivalence theorem, which is independent of the reasons which result from our Public Choice analysis.

Kirchgaessner, G., 1996a. Probleme internationaler Umweltpolitik. Z. Angewandte Umweltforschung 8/96, 157–172.

Kirchgaessner, G., 1996b. Nachhaltigkeit in der Umweltnutzung. Einige Bemerkungen. Department of Economics, St. Gallen University, St. Gallen Discussion Paper No. 9608, April 1996.

Kirchgaessner, G., 1996c. Bemerkungen zur Minimalmoral. Z. Wirtschafts. Sozialwissenschaften 116 (2), 223–251.

Köppl, A., Kratena, K., Pichel, C., Schebeck, F., Schleicher, S.t., Würger, M., 1995. Makroökonomische und sektorale Auswirkungen einer umweltorientierten Energiebesteuerung in Österreich. WIFÖ—Österreichisches Institut für Wirtschaftsforschung, Vienna, Austria.

Kurz, R., Volkert, J., Helbig, J., 1995. Ordnungspolitische Grundfragen einer Politik der Nachhaltigkeit: Schlußbericht an das Bundesministerium für Wirtschaft, Studie. Institut für Angewandte Wirtschaftsforschung, Tuebingen.

Kurz, R., Volkert, J., 1997. Konzeption und Durchsetzungschancen einer ordnungskonformen Politik der Nachhaltigkeit. Francke, Tuebingen.

Maier-Rigaud, G., 1996. Für eine ökologische Wirtschaftsordnung, Jahrbuch für Ökologie, 1996.

Migué, J.-L., Bélanger, G., 1974. Toward a General Theory of Managerial Discretion. Public Choice, 17, 27–43.

Mueller, D.C., 1989. Public Choice II: A Revised Edition of Public Choice. Cambridge University Press, Cambridge, MA.

Niskanen, W.A., 1971. Bureaucracy and Representative Government. Aldine Atherton, Chicago.

OECD, 1997. Environmental Policies and Employment, Paris.

Olson, M., 1968. Die Logik des kollektiven Handelns. Mohr (Siebeck), Tuebingen.

Olson, M., 1985. Aufstieg und Niedergang von Nationen: Ökonomisches Wachstum, Stagflation und soziale Starrheit. Mohr (Siebeck), Tuebingen.

Paldam, M., 1991. How robust is a vote function? A study of 17 nations over four decades. In: Norpott, H., Levis-Beck, M.S., Lafay, J.D. (Eds.), Economics and Politics: The Calculus of Support. Michigan University Press, Ann Arbor, MI, pp. 138–164.

Pommerehne, W.W., Schneider, F., 1978. Fired illusion, political institutions and local public spending. Kyklos 31/3, 381–408.

Pommerehne, W.W., Schneider, F., 1983. Does government in a representative democracy follow a majority of voters'

preferences? An empirical examination. In: Hanusch, H. (Ed.), Anatomy of Government Deficiencies. Springer, Heidelberg, pp. 61–84.

Sandhövel, A., 1994a. Marktorientierte Instrumente der Umweltpolitik. Die Durchsetzbarkeit von Mengen- und Preislösungen am Beispiel der Abfallpolitik. Westdeutscher, Opladen.

Sandhövel, A., 1994b. Ministerialverwaltung und die Durchsetzbarkeit von Mengen- und Preislösungen. Z. Umweltpolitik Umweltrecht 2, 225–240.

Schneider, F., 1985. Der Einfluß von Interessengruppen auf die Wirtschaftspolitik: Eine empirische Untersuchung für die Schweiz. Haupt, Bern.

Schneider, F., 1993. Energiepolitik in Österreich, vol. 1. Trauner, Linz.

Schneider, F., 1994a. Energiepolitik in Österreich, vol. 2. Trauner, Linz.

Schneider, F., 1994b. Public choice—economic theory of politics: a survey in selected areas. In: Brandstätter, H., Güth, W. (Eds.), Essays on Economic Psychology. Springer, Heidelberg, pp. 177–192.

Schneider, F. 1998. Induzieren ökologische Steuerreformen einen Lenkungseffekt oder nur volle Staatskassen? Einige volkswirtschaftliche Überlegungen, IAW-Mitteilungen, 26. Jg., Heft 3.

Schneider, F., Stiglbauer, A.M., 1995. Makroökonomische Auswirkungen verschiedener Energiesteuermodelle in Österreich. Wirtschaftspolitische Blätter 42/2, 121–126.

Schneider, F., Volkert, J., 1997. Die Realisierung ökologischorientierter Wirtschaftspolitik—eine Unmöglichkeit? Überlegungen aus Sicht der Neuen Politischen Ökonomie. In: Behrends, S. (Ed.), Ordnungskonforme Wirtschaftspolitik in der Marktwirtschaft. Duncker and Humblot, Berlin, pp. 567–589.

Ullmann, A.A., 1982. Industrie und Umweltschutz. Implementation von Umweltschutzgesetzen in deutschen Unternehmen. Campus, WZB-Arbeitsberichte. Frankfurt (Main).

Volkert, J. (1996), Durchsetzungsprobleme effizienter wirtschaftspolitischer Entscheidungsregeln und Maßnahmen: Das Beispiel der Umweltpolitik, IAW-Mitteilungen, Institut für Angewandte Wirtschaftsforschung Tübingen, 24. Jg., Volume 3.

Weck-Hannemann, 1994. Die politische Ökonomie der Umweltpolitik. In: Hackl, F., Pruckner, G. (Eds.), Einführung in die Umweltpolitik. Vahlen. Munich, pp. 102–117.

Part III
Setting the Level of Government to be Delegated Responsibility

[16]

ENVIRONMENTAL GOVERNANCE IN FEDERAL SYSTEMS: THE EFFECTS OF CAPITAL COMPETITION AND LOBBY GROUPS

PER G. FREDRIKSSON AND NOEL GASTON*

We argue that centralized and decentralized environmental governance yield equivalent environmental regulations. We model worker, environmental, and capital owner lobby groups that seek influence by offering political contributions. Worker lobbying in the decentralized case has an effect on environmental regulations identical to that of capital owner lobbying in the centralized case. This is because the aggregate effects of environmental regulations on income are equivalent under the two institutional designs. Whereas workers carry the full burden in the decentralized case when capital competition occurs, the burden is shared with the capital owners in the centralized case. We present evidence consistent with our theory. (JEL Q28, F21, R38, D72, D78)

I. INTRODUCTION

As the demand for efficient environmental policies increases, the ambit of political power in a federation must be determined. Cumberland [1981] suggests that uniform federal rules avoid the economic competition between jurisdictions in order to attract investment that may result in an excessively low environmental quality. As discussed by Burtraw and Portney [1991], central decision making may be highly inefficient, however, because federal regulations fail to take into account the heterogeneity of local environ-

ments.[1] This article develops a theory of decentralized and centralized environmental policy making in federal systems that incorporates the political forces determining the outcomes under the two alternative regulatory designs.

The empirical evidence on the effects of interjurisdictional capital competition on environmental policies is inconclusive and mainly anecdotal. Esty [1996] gives an overview of the available evidence and finds that "rent-seeking behavior undoubtedly affects national as well as state environmental policy making, but there is no evidence that public decision-making is systematically more distorted at the federal level than at state and local levels."[2] In a study of packaging waste regulation in the European Union (EU), Paul [1994/95] describes how the move from decentralized to centralized regulation "remains controversial. Some Greens bitterly criticize the directive as a sellout to industry. It is true that industry aggressively lobbied Parliament to stop the efforts of the Greens to tighten the directive" and that

*We would like to thank Torbjörn Becker, Thomas Crocker, Matthew Emeny, Wilfred Ethier, Kevin Grier, Robert Inman, Paul Kleindorfer, William Oakland, Jonathan Pincus, Kamal Saggi, and participants at presentations at the Universities of Calgary, Central Florida, and Maryland, as well as at George Washington University, Southern Methodist University, and the Eighth Annual EAERE Conference held at Tilburg University. An anonymous referee and the editor, John Lott, provided comments that lead to substantial improvements in the paper. Gian Maria Milesi-Ferretti kindly provided data on capital controls. The first author gratefully acknowledges financial support from the Swedish International Development Cooperation Agency (Sida). The opinions expressed are those of the authors and not those of the World Bank or Sida. The usual disclaimers apply.

Fredriksson: Consultant, The World Bank, Washington, D.C., Phone-202-473-7341, Fax-202-522-1735, E-mail pfredriksson@worldbank.org; and Lecturer, University of Adelaide, Adelaide, South Australia

Gaston: Professor of Economics, Bond University, Gold Coast, Australia, Phone 61-7-5595-2220, Fax 61-7-5595-1160, E-mail Noel_Gaston@Bond.edu.au

1. Examples of decentralized and centralized environmental governance in the United States are the *Clean Air Act* of 1970, which sets uniform national standards for air quality, and the *Clean Water Act* which was enacted in 1972 and allows states to determine their own standards for water quality (Oates [1996]).

2. However, Esty [1996, 650] goes on to argue that "...given the general popular indifference to many state and local environmental decisions, as well as greater media attention to federal-level activities, one might suggest precisely the opposite."

Economic Inquiry
(ISSN 0095-2583)
Vol. 38, No. 3, July 2000, 501–514

©Western Economic Association International

"[i]t is tempting to describe this debate as one more example in which the regulatory authority was captured by industry."[3] Evidently, the move to centralized regulation stimulated industry lobbying.

The present paper provides an explanation for why industry lobbying may be stronger at the federal level and discusses the implications for environmental policy under decentralized and centralized environmental policy making.[4] The current literature lacks a formal comparison of politically determined environmental regulations under the different institutional arrangements that may exist in federal systems.[5] While we couch our argument in terms of environmental policy-making that could be undertaken either at the national level or at lower levels in a federal structure, we believe that the central ideas extend to regulatory policy carried out at both the highest and lowest levels of

multi-country federations such as the EU.[6] Extensions of our theory may apply more generally to several forms of regulation, for example, worker safety standards and product liability legislation, as well as to firm taxation.

A key concern of environmental policy makers in federal systems is interjurisdictional capital mobility. We model a decentralized system of regulation with a mobile capital stock. Consideration of the effects of environmental regulations on capital is important; van Beers and van den Bergh [1997] find no significant negative effect of environmental regulation on export flows in polluting industries except when restricting their data to sectors with high capital mobility.[7] Moreover, Revesz [1992] argues that the fear of capital competition explains why the Clean Air Act in the United States is a federal regulation.[8] While capital mobility is a relevant consideration at the sectoral level, we argue that at the federal or national level, the capital stock can be viewed as (relatively) fixed.[9]

3. We describe Paul's empirical findings in greater detail in section IV below. Esty and Geradin [1998] report that in the mid-1990s, the EU faced strong political pressure from several industry lobbies to revise the legislative framework on waste and biotechnology and to substitute binding legislation for voluntary environmental agreements. Revesz [1992] reports that eight Northeastern states in the United States adopted environmental regulations more stringent than the corresponding federal regulations. This suggests that the political pressures at the federal level may have been relatively greater.

4. The issue of institutional design is highly contentious, see for example, Stewart [1990], Revesz [1992], and Esty [1996].

5. Oates and Schwab [1988] study decentralized policy making under majority rule voting and show that environmental policy is distorted by politics. Rauscher [1994] studies "ecological dumping" in a model with jurisdictionally immobile and intersectorally mobile factors of production. The export industry lobby's objective is to maximize output and the government cares about both output and welfare. Rauscher finds that the export industry has ambiguous lobbying incentives. Markusen, Morey, and Olewiler [1993] analyze the effects of environmental regulations on firm location decisions in a model of imperfect competition. Both plant location and market structure are shown to depend on environmental policy. Chao and Yu [1997] study the interaction of capital taxes, international tax credits, government spending, and environmental policy. They predict that due to the ability of capital to simply relocate across borders, lax environmental policies aimed at mitigating capital outflows will emerge. Fredriksson [2000] compares centralized and decentralized designs of the process for the siting of hazardous waste facilities in federal systems. The centralized system yields a lower level of treatment capacity because of free-riding problems.

6. However, we abstract from the issue of tax competition and local public goods provision (see Wilson [1986], Wildasin [1988], and Edwards and Keen [1996], for example).

7. The existing evidence on the effects of environmental regulation on plant location is somewhat mixed, see Jaffe et al. [1995]. Bartik [1992] found a small but significant adverse effect of state environmental regulations on small firm start-up attempts. In a study of foreign multinationals, Friedman, Gerlowski, and Silberman [1992] examined the effects on plant location of environmental stringency, measured as the ratio of state pollution abatement capital expenditures to state manufacturing gross product. Aggregating all foreign firms, the effect on plant investments was negative but insignificant. However, when considering Japanese companies only, the effect was negative and significant.

8. Pashigian [1985] shows that the Federal prevention of significant deterioration policy in the United States was the result of regional competition between the Northern states and those of the South and West. The latter two regions had superior air quality, so that the more stringent regulations aided the North in restricting the loss of its mobile factors. This could also explain why, under the Reagan administration in the early 1980s, industry showed little interest in decentralization of stationary industrial pollution source policies (see Crandall [1983, 145]).

9. Agglomeration benefits or ready access to the national market may explain why firms wish to produce within the borders of a federation. In addition, the national market may be protected by trade barriers, which further increase the incentive to be located within the federation. See also Feldstein and Horioka [1980] and Gordon and Bovenberg [1996].

It is now well known that policy outcomes may be distorted when the decision-making authority is subject to political pressure exerted by special interests. In our model, a lobby group representing labor interests seeks to increase or secure the capital base in its own jurisdiction by obtaining a lax regulation of pollution from production. Naturally, this effort is opposed by the environmental lobby group. Capital owners have an incentive to lobby against environmental regulation only when the aggregate national capital stock is fixed and the return to capital then depends on the level of environmental regulation.[10] On the other hand, when owners can move capital to jurisdictions in which the rate of return is higher, there is no need to expend valuable resources on influencing environmental policy.

A novel finding of our model is that environmental regulation is likely to be independent of institutional design. Capital competition in a decentralized regime has an equivalent effect on government policy making, as does capital owner lobbying in the centralized case. Essentially, since capital flight does not occur in the centralized case, workers reduce their lobbying effort compared to the decentralized case. This decrease in workers' political pressure is replaced by capital owner lobbying instead. We present anecdotal and econometric evidence as well as voting records on environmental policy in support of our theory.

The paper is organized as follows. Section II outlines the model and briefly character-

izes the political equilibrium. Section III presents the results for the decentralized and centralized systems, and studies the impact on environmental policy of lobbying by capital owners. Section IV discusses empirical support for our model and presents evidence from U.S. state legislatures, congressional and senate voting records on environmental policy, and econometric evidence using cross-country data on capital controls. Section V concludes.

II. A MODEL OF ENVIRONMENTAL REGULATION

Consider an economy with a large number of jurisdictions, in each of which a large number of individuals live and work. Further, each jurisdiction contains one firm that produces a private good, Q, for a perfectly competitive national market. Production requires inputs of capital (K), labor (L), and polluting waste emissions (θ); the last is treated as a non-purchased input. There is no spillover of pollution into other jurisdictions. The production technology exhibits constant returns to scale, is concave and increasing in all inputs, and is twice continuously-differentiable:

$$(1) \qquad Q = F(K, L, \theta).$$

In the case of decentralized environmental governance, the local authority sets the standard for environmental quality; more specifically, it determines the aggregate waste emissions for its jurisdiction. By linear homogeneity, (1) can be rewritten as

$$(2) \qquad Q = Lf(k, \alpha),$$

where $k = K/L$ is the capital-labor ratio and $\alpha = \theta/L$ is the emissions–labor ratio. Suppressing arguments and using subscripts to denote partial derivatives, the marginal products of capital, emissions, and labor are given by f_k, f_α, and $(f - kf_k - \alpha f_\alpha)$, respectively. The marginal products are diminishing, i.e., $f_{kk} < 0, f_{\alpha\alpha} < 0$, and we assume that $f_{k\alpha} > 0$, i.e., increases in α raise the marginal product of capital.

While labor is immobile, the capital stock is assumed to be perfectly mobile between

---

10. Ulph [1996] notes that for countries that wish to impose tighter environmental regulations than their strategic competitors there is policy pressure to impose countervailing tariffs on imports on countries with laxer environmental standards. Needless to say, the policy pressure comes from the industries in the traded goods sector. A qualitatively similar set of issues arise with respect to the setting of uniform minimum wages and other health and safety regulations affecting labor in an economic union such as the EU (as well as a free trade area such as NAFTA). For example, "[s]ome argue that the failure to require any minimum standard will lead to unfair competition, the exploitation of workers abroad, and ultimately a decline in a nation's own minimum wage standard as the nation seeks to keep jobs fleeing abroad. Others argue, however, that attempts to require trading partners to increase their minimum wages do not reflect concern for the welfare of workers abroad, but are really protectionist attempts to preserve employment at home" Ehrenberg [1994, 44–45].

jurisdictions but immobile internationally.[11] This implies that the rate of return on capital, denoted by r, is equalized across all jurisdictions. This feature of our model is central for the comparison of the effects of centralized versus decentralized policy making. A local policy maker is concerned about the impact of more stringent local environmental standards on investment and capital flows from their jurisdiction. A national policy maker sets a uniform environmental code and need not be concerned with capital flight. In the latter case, however, the return to capital depends on the stringency of environmental standards.

We assume that there are three types of individuals in the jurisdiction: workers, environmentalists, and capital owners. While the first two groups are always present in each jurisdiction, this may not be true for the last group. However, for production to occur, at least one of the jurisdictions has capital owners residing within its borders. Normalizing the population in each jurisdiction (or in the economy, when appropriate) to unity, let β^W, β^E, and β^K represent the proportion of the population that are workers, environmentalists, and capital owners, respectively.

The income of environmentalists is exogenously determined, e.g., gained from employment in white-collar jobs unaffected by environmental policy. Workers supply one unit of labor and are paid a wage equal to the gain from employing an additional worker. This is equal to the sum of the marginal product of labor plus the additional output arising from the increase in allowable pollution emissions, αf_α, hence, wage income is

(3) $w = f - k f_k .$

All individuals gain utility from consuming the polluting good, but environmentalists also suffer disutility from the pollution associated with production. Individuals are assumed to have additively separable utility functions of the form

(4) $U^i = c^i - \lambda^E \theta ,$

11. See Gordon and Bovenberg [1996]. Alternatively, one might think of jurisdictions as countries between which capital flows freely. Globally, of course, capital is fixed.

where $i = W, E$, and K index workers, environmentalists, and capital owners, respectively, and $\lambda^E = 1$ for environmentalists (and 0, otherwise).

We assume that the workers, environmentalists, and capital owners in at least some of the jurisdictions have sufficient incentives to overcome free-rider problems and form lobby groups. Following Grossman and Helpman [1994], the organized lobby groups offer political contribution schedules $C^i(\alpha)$, $i = W, E, K$, that relate prospective contributions to the environmental policy chosen by the government. The gross welfare functions for the lobby groups are given by

(5)
$$V^W(\alpha) \equiv \beta^W(f - k f_k)$$
$$V^E(\alpha) \equiv Y^E - \beta^E \theta$$
$$V^K(\alpha) \equiv Kr ,$$

where Y^E denotes the aggregate income of environmentalists.

The government is assumed to derive utility from a weighted sum of campaign contributions and aggregate social welfare, i.e.,

(6)
$$V^G(\alpha)$$
$$\equiv \sum_{i = W, E, K} [aV^i(\alpha) + \delta^i C^i(\alpha)],$$

where $a \geq 0$ represents the weighting that the government places on the social welfare relative to the campaign contributions of lobby groups, and δ^i is an indicator variable which takes a value of 1 if lobby group i is organized, and 0 otherwise.[12]

The Political Equilibrium

The equilibrium emissions standard is determined as the outcome of a two-stage, noncooperative game. In stage one, each lobby group offers the government a schedule that promises a specific contribution for each feasible choice of emissions regulation.

12. Political contributions can be used by a government to sway voters' preferences (by campaign advertising, pre-election public spending, etc.) and so to increase the prospect of re-election. The average welfare of the community also affects re-election chances because disgruntled voters are more likely to vote for the political opposition (see Grossman and Helpman [1994]).

In the second stage, the government selects a policy and collects the associated contributions from the lobby groups.

When the policy maker's welfare function is described by equation (6), Grossman and Helpman [1994] show that they actually end up maximizing a weighted sum of the interest groups' objective functions, i.e.,

$$(7) \quad V^G(\alpha) = \sum_{i=W,E,K} (a + \delta^i)V^i(\alpha).$$

Assuming an interior solution, the first-order condition is

$$(8) \quad \sum_{i=W,E,K} (a + \delta^i)V_\alpha^i(\alpha) = 0.$$

Equation (8) represents the characterization of the equilibrium emissions–labor ratio for each jurisdiction. If all or no groups are organized, note that equation (8) implicitly defines the emissions standards set by a utilitarian social planner. If one or two of the three groups fail to organize, then political distortions arise, in a similar fashion to Grossman and Helpman [1994].

III. THE EFFECTS OF LOBBYING AND CAPITAL COMPETITION

Decentralized Regulation

The effect of a change in the pollution emissions ratio on the gross welfare of workers is simply

$$(9) \quad V_\alpha^W(\alpha) = \beta^W f_\alpha > 0.$$

Recall that the jurisdictional capital stock is mobile and adjusts until $f_k = r$. Thus, labor unambiguously gains from an easing of the emissions policy (i.e., a higher α). The wage effect of a policy change is simply equal to the marginal product of emissions weighted by the number of workers in the jurisdiction.

By determining the impact of a policy change on those individuals who do not earn wage income but are affected by changes in local environmental quality, we are able to consider the opposing interests of different groups within a community and allow for an explicit characterization of their environ-

mental policy preferences. Since the environmentalists' income is exogenous, the partial derivative of the environmentalists' welfare with respect to a small change in policy is

$$(10) \quad V_\alpha^E(\alpha) = -\beta^E \beta^W < 0,$$

noting that $\beta^W = L$.

Equations (9) and (10) indicate the direction and strength of lobbying activity for labor and environmentalists, respectively. In the decentralized case, the capital owners respond to a policy change by moving their capital and thus the rate of return on capital can be treated as exogenous. Since lobbying is likely to be a costly exercise, the capital owners have no incentive to organize a lobby group when capital is perfectly mobile.

The interaction of the various political pressures and the actions of the government help to determine the policy outcome. Equations (9) and (10) can be substituted into equation (8) to yield a condition for the equilibrium emissions policy. Specifically, we find that in equilibrium,

$$(11) \quad \beta^W\big((a + \delta^W)f_\alpha - (a + \delta^E)\beta^E\big)$$
$$= 0.$$

Note that when both lobby groups are organized, or both not organized, i.e., $\delta^W = \delta^E$, then $f_\alpha = \beta^E$. In equilibrium, the local policy maker selects an emissions policy so that the marginal product of emissions, f_α, equals the number of environmentalists in that jurisdiction. The environmental policy is efficient because the marginal benefit of increased pollution is equal to its marginal social cost. From equation (9), the gross gain to society from a rise in α is the increase in aggregate wage income allowed by higher waste emissions. The cost of greater pollution is borne entirely by the environmentalists, as they are the only group who suffer disutility from the rise in pollution associated with an increase in α.

Overall, the decentralized policy outcome is efficient as long as either both or neither of the lobby groups are organized. This contrasts with Oates and Schwab [1988] in which the policy outcome with a heterogeneous community is *always* sub-optimal.[13] When both lobbies are organized, the policy outcome is efficient since the political pressure of one lobby is effectively offset by the other.

Regulation with Immobile Capital

We now turn to the case in which capital does not cross national borders. Not only is this a standard assumption in the literature, but Feldstein and Horioka [1980] and Gordon and Bovenberg [1996] document the considerable amount of evidence supporting the notion of international capital immobility.

With immobile capital, the only effect on wage income of a change in the pollution regulation is the direct effect, i.e., that resulting from the effect of a change in α on the marginal product of labor. The aggregate effect of a change in the pollution emissions ratio on labor is therefore

$$(12) \quad V_\alpha^W(\alpha) = \beta^W(f_\alpha - kf_{k\alpha}).$$

Compare equations (12) and (9), noting that the effect of eased standards on the welfare of labor is now smaller. This is due to the fact that with a uniform national standard, capital no longer flows to jurisdictions with relatively lower emissions standards.

A useful characterization of the equilibrium emissions standard is given Proposition 1 which summarizes the key results so far (Proofs are left to the Appendix).

PROPOSITION 1. *Regulation without lobbying by capital owners.*

(i) *In equilibrium, the emissions regulation satisfies*

$$\alpha^* = [(a + \delta^W)\psi^*w^*]/[(a + \delta^E)\beta^E],$$

where $\psi^* = \alpha^*w_\alpha^*/w^*$, with

$$w_\alpha^* = \begin{cases} f_\alpha, & \text{if capital is mobile} \\ f_\alpha - kf_{k\alpha}, & \text{otherwise.} \end{cases}$$

(ii) *Ceteris paribus, the equilibrium emissions regulation α^* is weaker:*
  (a) *the higher is the emissions standard elasticity of wage income, ψ^*,*
  (b) *the higher is the labor income, w^*,*
  (c) *given the existence of a worker lobby group, $\delta^W = 1$;*
  and is stronger:
  (d) *the greater the number of environmentalists in the jurisdiction, β^E,*
  (e) *given the existence of an environmental lobby group, $\delta^E = 1$.*

(iii) *When only labor and environmentalists lobby, α^* is stronger if environmental governance is centralized.*

Interpretation:
  (a) In equilibrium, the more elastic wage income is with respect to the emissions level, the more workers are directly affected by a given change in the regulation. A higher equilibrium value of ψ^* means that a less stringent environmental regulation will have a greater positive impact on wages. This raises the benefit of such a policy to labor and makes a less stringent emissions standard more attractive to the government;
  (b) A higher level of wage income implies that the emissions standard will be weaker, ceteris paribus. For a given change in policy, the larger the initial wage level, the greater the effect on output and wage income.
  (c) The existence of a worker lobby group raises the influence of worker concerns;
  (d) Similarly, the larger the number of environmentalists, the greater the pressure exerted on the policy maker to choose a more stringent environmental policy;
  (e) The existence of an environmental lobby group raises the influence of environmental concerns.

More importantly, note that ψ^* is *lower* in the centralized case with immobile capital compared to the decentralized case with mobile capital. In particular, when capital is immobile, the impact on wage income caused by a relaxed environmental standard is smaller. Consequently, emissions regulations are more stringent at the national level.

---

13. Oates and Schwab [1988] study a model of local jurisdictions with mobile capital, capital taxation, environmental standards, and majority voting. They find that interjurisdictional competition is efficiency-enhancing except when the local government is a budget-maximizer or if the population is extremely heterogeneous. In our model there is no discontinuity when either population group increases from, say, 49%–51% of the population. This implies a small change in the level of regulation.

With policy coordination, aggregate social welfare is maximized and the equilibrium emissions policy is Pareto optimal in the sense that some individuals would lose if the policy were to deviate from that described in Proposition 1. However, the efficiency condition is qualitatively different from the case in which interjurisdictional competition and the fear of capital flight yield a lower level of environmental protection. When capital is immobile, the national policy maker is able to exploit this fact by setting a stricter environmental regulation.

Lobbying by Capital Owners

We now consider the impact of capital owners who may lobby the central government. Clearly, there is no such incentive in the decentralized case since the available rate of return is equalized globally, but it does exist in the centralized case when capital is immobile. This insight is straightforward; the owners of *any* immobile factor whose return is affected by a policy intervention have an incentive to influence the direction of that policy. In our model, we assume that free-rider problems can be overcome and that factor owners form lobby groups.

When policy is determined at the federal level and capital is fixed at the national level and, by implication, immobile internationally, the return to capital is affected by changes in α. The welfare of capital owners now plays a role in the aggregate social welfare function. Treating the national capital stock K parametrically, the effect of α on the aggregate welfare of capital owners equals

(13) $\qquad V_\alpha^K(\alpha) = \beta^W k f_{k\alpha} > 0.$

Easing environmental regulations unambiguously increases the welfare of capital owners.

We now show that when all groups lobby, the optimal emissions standard is equal to the regulation for the decentralized case. First, the characterization of the political equilibrium needs to be modified to allow for capital owner lobbying. This simply involves adding $(a + \delta^K)$ times equation (13) to

equation (8). For $i = E, W, K$, substitution yields

(14) $\qquad \beta^W((a + \delta^W)(f_\alpha - kf_{k\alpha})$
$\qquad\qquad - (a + \delta^E)\beta^E$
$\qquad\qquad + (a + \delta^K)kf_{k\alpha}) = 0.$

Clearly, when $\delta^E = \delta^W = \delta^K$ we have $f_\alpha = \beta^E$, i.e., the efficiency condition under decentralized decision-making. Thus, capital owner lobbying reintroduces an effect similar to that of capital competition in the decentralized case.

Note that lobbying by capital owners *must* yield a weaker policy. Rearranging equation (14), the political equilibrium is characterized in the following Proposition:

PROPOSITION 2. *Centralized case with lobbying by capital owners.*

Assume that all individuals are organized into lobby groups. Then
  (i) *the equilibrium emissions regulation under centralized policy making, α^o, satisfies*

(15) $\qquad \alpha^o = [(a + \delta^W)\psi^o w^o$
$\qquad\qquad + (a + \delta^K)\gamma^o\pi^o]/$
$\qquad\qquad [\beta^E(a + \delta^E)]$

where, $\psi^o = \alpha^o w_\alpha^o/w^o$, $\pi^o = kf_k = f - w^o$, *and* $\gamma^o = \alpha^o \pi_\alpha^o/\pi^o$.
  (ii) *the emissions regulations under decentralized and centralized governance are equivalent.*

As before, the political determination of α is driven by the impact of the regulation on environmentalist and labor interests. For example, the lower the emissions standard elasticity of marginal labor productivity, ψ^o, i.e., when the impact on labor income of environmental regulation is less, the stricter the resulting regulation. What is different about Proposition 2 is the existence of lobbying by capital owners. Since centralized policy making does not induce flows of capital between jurisdictions, the returns to capital owners are influenced by the emissions regulation. The impact on capital owners is captured by the second term in the numerator of equation (15). First, the lower the emissions standard elasticity of marginal capital productivity, γ^o, i.e., the smaller the effect on capital income, the stricter the regulation. Secondly, this effect is weighted by π^o, capital owner profitability.

In equilibrium, the effects of the emissions standard on all constituents are internalized by the government's welfare maximization. Interestingly, the resulting policy outcome is equivalent to the efficient decentralized case with capital competition, even though capital is immobile. This is due to the fact that the total income effect of the regulation is equal in both cases. In the decentralized case, the capital owners can move capital between jurisdictions and labor bears the full burden of adjustment. In the centralized case, labor and capital owners share the costs of environmental regulation. The capital owners' burden in the centralized case is equivalent to the effect of capital flight on workers in the decentralized case.[14]

IV. DISCUSSION AND EMPIRICAL EVIDENCE

The preceding section examined two institutional settings in which the pollution associated with industrial production is regulated. In a decentralized setting, environmental regulations are primarily shaped by the influence of environmental and labor interest groups. That is, environmental regulations are politically determined and are therefore likely to be influenced by special interests. However, capital owners are unlikely to engage in costly lobbying activities if they can move some or all of their capital to other jurisdictions with more lenient environmental standards. The concomitant capital competition is often thought to engender a "race to the bottom" in industry regulatory policies. If capital is immobile, however, federal or central policy makers may be able to stiffen the regulation of industry without the fear of capital flight. The relative immobility of capital is a linchpin for the traditional support for federal environmental regulations and the proposals to eliminate "downward competition in environmental policy" by harmonizing environmental regulations,

as discussed by Ulph [1995] and Esty and Geradin [1998].[15] However, the owners of immobile factors of production will generally have an incentive to lobby the government for more favorable regulations. Finally, in a fashion similar to Persson and Tabellini [1992], the immobility which leaves capital exposed to stricter regulation of its production may be offset by a "lobbying effect" that creates increased political pressure for more lenient regulation. Overall, the stringency of environmental policy is completely independent of institutional design.

We now consider existing evidence that bears upon these features and we also present some empirical results pertinent to the principal themes of our model. Ideally, the most direct test of our model would be facilitated by an institutional shift in which environmental governance were suddenly centralized. Rather than regulations becoming more stringent, on the basis of our model we would predict that "new" centralized regulations would be similar to the "average" stringency of regulations that had existed in the decentralized level. The study of packaging waste regulation in the European Union, discussed by Paul [1994/95], comes closest to providing this type of experiment. He describes how the EU moved from decentralized regulation to a centralized directive in 1994. There were five-year recycling targets of 25–45% for total packaging waste, a 15% recycling rate for each type of material, and a prohibition of national requirements above 45%. The EU directive was less stringent than the existing German, Danish, and Dutch laws, but was significantly stricter than the existing Greek, Irish, and Portuguese requirements. The preagreement national recycling rates for the EU members are given in Table I.

Golub [1996] describes how the initial proposal immediately came under political fire from various industry groups and how

---

14. Our result is qualitatively similar to the key finding in Persson and Tabellini [1992]. In a model of tax competition, they show that an "economic effect" which causes downward pressure on rates of capital taxation is offset by a "political effect" manifested by a leftward shift in voters' preferences.

15. While a recent OECD report has argued for "some convergence" of the requirements and standards for the pollution associated with the production process ("non-product related PPM's") it also notes that "[h]armonization of non-product related PPM requirements may be less desirable or feasible in the case of local environmental problems. Because environmental conditions and preferences differ widely among countries, environmental process-related requirements for local problems may be best tailored to local circumstances." (Quoted by Ulph [1995, 4]).

TABLE I
European Union National Recycling Rates (%)

	Paper and Board (1990)	Aluminum (1987)	Glass (1993)
Belgium	36*	4	55
Denmark	35	31	64
France	46	25	46
Germany	40	31	65
Greece	21	25**	27
Ireland	3	na	29
Italy	25	36	52
Netherlands	50	47	76
Portugal	39	4	29
Spain	51	28	29
United Kingdom	31	19	29
Average	34	25	46

Source: Golub (1996).

Notes: No data were available for Luxembourg, or for aluminum recycling in Ireland. * denotes (1988), ** denotes (1990).

the new drafts of the regulations were successively less demanding, until the directive described above was finally adopted.[16] The adopted targets were significantly lower than the targets initially proposed by the EU Commission.[17]

In a similar vein, the centralization of environmental policy may simply reify an existing pattern of environmental policies. For example, consider the 1987 Montreal Protocol. It may have achieved considerably less that many observers believe (or hope). According to the U.S. Environmental Protection Agency [1988] (cited by Barrett [1994]),

16. The trade and industry representatives consisted of three highly successful pressure groups: the packaging legislation ad hoc group, the packaged consumer goods industries coordination group, and the packaging chain forum (see Golub [1996]).

17. Among the original targets were a mandatory minimum "recovery" (i.e., reuse, recycling, composting, regeneration, and recovery of energy) rate of 60% (by weight) for all packaging waste materials within five years, set to increase to 90 percent after ten years; a mandatory minimum recycling (includes reuse, composting and regeneration) rate of 40% (by weight) for each type of packaging material within five years, rising to 60% after ten years; minimization of the final disposal of packaging waste (by landfill or incineration without energy recovery) to a maximum of 10% (by weight) of packaging waste after 10 years. In sum, after 10 years, 60% of packaging waste would have to be recycled, 30% recovered but not recycled, and 10% disposed of in other ways.

the benefit to the United States from ratifying this treaty (originally requiring a 50% reduction of hard CFC consumption and production) was $3,575 billion, and a unilateral cut of the same magnitude would yield a benefit of $1,373 billion. These figures should be compared to the projected cost of $21 billion. Barrett [1994] provides a model that supports the conclusion that the Protocol may merely have codified what would have occurred in a noncooperative equilibrium. This view is consistent with the findings of Murdoch and Sandler [1997], who find that CFC cutbacks between 1986 and 1989 in a sample of 61 countries were in excess of the cutbacks required by the Protocol. It appears that industry lobbying may have played an important role in the design of this agreement. Haas [1992] quotes the chairman of an industry interest group, the Alliance for a Responsible CFC Policy, who stated in 1986 that "We do not believe the scientific information demonstrates any actual risk from current CFC use of emissions." However, later in the same year, the major CFC producer, DuPont, made a switch in favor of CFC controls which undermined the remaining firms' position. In 1988, DuPont announced that CFC production would be phased out by the year 2000. The initial change in DuPont's position has been widely credited for making the Protocol possible, as argued by Benedick [1991] and Haas [1991].

We now turn to cross-country patterns in environmental policy and attempt to more explicitly assess the impact of capital controls on the stringency of environmental policy. An implication of our model is that capital controls should have no effect on the stringency of environmental policy, i.e., there are offsetting political changes that mitigate an associated rise in the stringency of environmental policy when capital controls are put in place. Underlying our test is the presumption that in the absence of capital controls, the capital stock is mobile.

Table II presents some representative regression specifications that build on a reasonably standard model for the stringency of environmental regulations. The index of environmental regulations and enforcement, *STRINGENCY*, developed by Dasgupta *et al.*

[1995] for the industry sector for a total of 31 countries, measures policies addressing air, water, land, and living resources. Briefly, a standard model predicts that stringency should increase with real GDP per capita, i.e., environmental quality is a normal good.[18] In addition, the more people there are in urban centers, the greater is the exposure to industrial pollution and thus the marginal disutility of pollution, so *STRINGENCY* should be positively related to *URBAN*. Also, recent research by, e.g., Congleton [1992], Murdoch and Sandler [1997], and Fredriksson and Gaston [2000], indicates that greater political freedoms give rise to stronger pressure for stricter environmental policies. Our dummy variable *RIGHTS* takes a value of one if a country is classified as having political freedoms, zero otherwise. The variable is

18. See, e.g., Shafik [1994], Antle and Heidebrink [1995], Grossman and Krueger [1995].

TABLE II
The Effect of Capital Controls on the Stringency of Environmental Regulations

Variable	Label	Mean (Std. Dev.)	(1)	(2)	(3)	(4)	(5)	(6)
STRINGENCY	Stringency of Regulations (Industry)	113.26 (39.81)						
GDPPC	GDP per capita, thousands $US (1987)	3.80 (6.77)	0.026† (0.014)	0.018* (0.006)	0.016* (0.007)	0.022* (0.008)	0.027* (0.013)	0.017* (0.006)
URBAN	Urbanization % (1990)	44.80 (23.34)	0.008* (0.002)	0.008* (0.002)	0.008* (0.002)	0.008* (0.002)	0.008* (0.002)	0.008* (0.002)
RIGHTS	Political Rights	0.39 (0.50)	0.122 (0.088)	0.151† (0.079)	0.135 (0.084)	0.139† (0.079)	0.135 (0.079)	0.146† (0.077)
CC1	Capital Control Type 1	0.29 (0.46)	0.055 (0.074)	0.045 (0.068)	*	*	*	*
CC2	Capital Control Type 2	0.74 (0.44)	−0.066 (0.113)	*	−0.041 (0.106)	*	*	*
CC3	Capital Control Type 3	0.90 (0.30)	0.070 (0.201)	*	*	0.118 (0.163)	*	*
CC4	Capital Control Type 4	0.87 (0.34)	0.133 (0.288)	*	*	*	0.186 (0.232)	*
Intercept			4.032* (0.282)	4.190* (0.071)	4.240* (0.114)	4.078* (0.163)	4.011* (0.251)	4.204* (0.067)
Adj. R-sq.			0.754	0.772	0.770	0.773	0.774	0.777
F			14.107	26.452	26.103	26.568	26.714	35.885

Sources: STRINGENCY: Dasgupta *et al.* [1995]; *GDPPC* ($US [1987]: World Bank [1992]; *URBAN* [1990]: World Bank [1998]; *RIGHTS*: Freedom House [1993]; *CC1-CC4*: International Monetary Fund [1998]. Data are available from the authors upon request.

Notes: Observations for 31 countries. Columns labelled (1)–(6) contain OLS estimates (standard errors). Dependent variable is natural logarithm of *STRINGENCY*.

*Significance at 5% level.

†Significance at 10% level.

based on a classification of freedoms in countries. Finally, and most importantly for our purposes, we augment this model with various measures of capital controls used by Grilli and Milesi-Ferretti [1995]. We use four different measures for the year 1990; the dummies take the value of one if a restriction is in place, and zero otherwise. CC1 measures the existence of multiple exchange rate practices; CC2 measures restrictions on current account transactions; CC3 measures restrictions on capital account transactions; and CC4 indicates whether or not exporters need to surrender exports proceeds. Our theory predicts that they should not affect STRINGENCY, because we expect environmental stringency to be independent of capital mobility.

Table II indicates that the estimated models yield sensible results for the standard variables. There is strong support for the expected effects of per capita income and urbanization on environmental stringency and moderate support for the view that political and civil freedoms lead to greater political support for policies that protect the environment. However, the capital control measures lack statistical significance, when entered either individually or jointly.[19] Hence, greater restrictions on capital are not associated with the stringency of environmental policies. We interpret these findings as providing support, albeit somewhat indirect, for our model's predictions.

The question remains, of course, about effects of environmental policy on industry and the consequent incentives for capital and industry to lobby for more favorable environmental regulations and policies. Fortunately, anecdotal evidence is strong. For example, in 1997 the provincial government in Ontario, Canada, amended the majority of its statutes concerned with the environment or natural resources to make them less stringent. The main beneficiaries were the agribusiness, forestry, home-building, and mining industries, according to Esty and Geradin [1998]. These industries can be classified as sectors with relatively immobile capital. In comparing the United States and the EU, Kimber [1995, 1,688] argues that "opposition

to central regulation makes it difficult to enact central measures at all or of sufficient stringency to protect the environment adequately." At the same time, she also argues for centrally established policies. For Germany, Rose-Ackerman [1995] finds that farmers and the chemical industry have virtual "veto power" over environmental policy (organic and inorganic chemicals industries are classified as having immobile capital stocks by UNIDO [1982]). Similarly, Bosso [1987] and Cropper et al. [1992] report that for the United States, pesticide manufacturers and farmers have had a significant impact on the regulation of pesticides in agriculture.

Finally, we present two separate pieces of evidence that suggest that environmental policy and the level of pollution may both be independent of institutional design. First, consider evidence from the U.S. state legislatures and congressional and senate voting records on environmental policy. The following data for roll calls on environmental bills in state legislatures and in the U.S. Senate and House are reported by Calvert [1989]. They are for Mean Support Scores which index the tendency for U.S. legislators to vote in support of policies that protect the environment. Specifically, the data are for

i. State House and Senate votes by Democrats and Republicans on environmental bills for ten states (of which none are southern states), for the years 1980–85;[20]

ii. U.S. Congress and Senate for Democrats and Republicans (excluding the South), for the years 1981–84.

Our theory suggests that there should be no differences in the support for environmental policy at different levels of policy making. Table III reveals no discernible differences in voting intentions at the Federal and State levels.

Second, the data for pollution levels reported by Rose-Ackerman [1995] are consistent with our theoretical expectations. She considers measures of environmental quality for the United States, which has centralized regulation, and for Germany, which has decentralized regulation. While acknowledging the obvious difficulties associated with mak-

19. In the latter case, the test statistic for the inclusion of all four capital control measures is $F(4, 23) = 0.35$.

20. The ten states and years are Alaska (1983–84), California (1980–84), Idaho (1980–85), Illinois (1981), Montana (1981, 83, 85), Oregon (1981, 1983), New York (1981–82), Washington (1981–84), Wisconsin (1981–84), and Wyoming (1981–83).

TABLE III
Mean Support Scores

Legislature	Democrats	Republicans
State House	73.5	34.5
State Senate	71.3	34.6
U.S. House	78.2	36.7
U.S. Senate	72.9	33.1

Source: Calvert [1989].

ing cross-country comparisons, she finds no evidence that one type of institutional design yields lower pollution levels than another.[21]

V. CONCLUSION

This article examined the implications of decentralized and centralized environmental policy making. We differentiated the two levels of environmental governance by the presence or absence of capital competition. Specifically, capital was mobile between jurisdictions of a federation, but immobile at higher or more centralized levels of governance. We assumed that environmental policies are politically determined, i.e., that policies are shaped by special interests or lobby groups. Organized lobby groups offer the government political contributions in return for more favored environmental policy outcomes. The government maximizes aggregate social welfare and political contributions.

In the case of decentralized environmental governance, we found that the emissions policy is efficient. However, the regulation is affected by capital competition because workers are adversely affected by capital flight and their lobbying influences the local policy maker to reduce the level of regulatory stringency.

Next, we discussed the policy outcomes for two scenarios under centralized environmental policy making. If capital owners do not lobby for political favors, the government sets a more stringent environmental standard than in the decentralized case. This result forms the foundation for the coordinated administration of environmental poli-

cies. For example, the large tax competition literature takes seriously the possibility of noncooperative equilibria with sub-optimally low levels of capital taxation. Similarly, minimum environmental standards or abatement requirements may exhibit "race to the bottom" tendencies when the standards and requirements are determined at local levels of government. These tendencies are thought to be mitigated if policies are harmonized at the highest level of government in a federal structure.

If the capital stock is immobile, however, the owners of capital also have an incentive to lobby the policy maker. We showed that the centralized regulatory outcome may degenerate to the decentralized regulatory outcome, i.e., the emission standard is independent of institutional design. This occurs because capital owner lobbying has an effect on environmental regulation similar to that induced by capital competition when policy is determined locally. While labor bears the costs of environmental regulation in the decentralized system, the burden is shared with capital in the centralized case. A possible implication of our article is that, given the independence of environmental policy and institution design, decentralized environmental governance may be preferable if there exists significant heterogeneity of the effects of pollution across jurisdictions.

APPENDIX

Proof of Proposition 1: Rearrange equation (11) as

$$(A1) \qquad 1/f_\alpha = (a + \delta^W)/[(a + \delta^E)\beta^E].$$

Since $f_\alpha = w_\alpha^*$, then multiplying both sides of (A1) by $\psi^* w^*$ gives part (i). Part (ii) of the Proposition follows immediately.

Proof of Proposition 2: (i) Substitution of equations (10), (12), and (13) into equation (8) gives equation (14). Now simply substitute $\psi^o = \alpha^o w_\alpha^o/w^o$, $\pi^o = kf_k = f - w^o$, and $\gamma^o = \alpha^o \pi_\alpha^o/\pi^o$, to obtain the required expression. (ii) If $\delta^E = \delta^W = \delta^K$, equation (14) is equivalent to equation (11).

21. Benchmarking at 1975 pollution levels, the 1988 levels for the United States (Germany) were: 103 (115) for nitrogen oxides, 65 (50) for suspended particulates, 77 (63) for carbon monoxide, 84 (93) for hydrocarbons, and 115 (103) for carbon dioxide.

REFERENCES

Antle, John M., and Gregg Heidebrink. "Environment and Development: Theory and International Evidence." *Economic Development and Cultural Change*, 43(3), 1995, 603–25.

Barrett, Scott A. "Self-Enforcing International Environmental Agreements." *Oxford Economic Papers*, 46(5), 1994, 878–94.

Bartik, Timothy J. "Small Business Start-Ups in the United States: Estimates of the Effects of Characteristics of States." *Southern Economic Journal*, 55(4), 1992, 1004–18.

Benedick, Richard E. "Protecting the Ozone Layer: New Directions in Diplomacy," in *Preserving the Global Environment: The Challenge of Shared Leadership*, edited by J. T. Mathews. New York and London: W. W. Norton & Company, 1991, 112–53.

Bosso, Christopher J. *Pesticides and Politics: The Life Cycle of a Public Issue*. Pittsburgh: University of Pittsburgh Press, 1987.

Calvert, Jerry W. "Party Politics and Environmental Policy," in *Environmental Politics and Policy*, edited by J. P. Lester. Durham, N.C.: Duke University Press, 1989.

Chao, Chi-Chur, and Eden S. H. Yu. "International Capital Competition and Environmental Standards." *Southern Economic Journal*, 64(2), 1997, 531–41.

Congleton, Roger D. "Political Institutions and Pollution Control." *Review of Economics and Statistics*, 74(3), 1992, 412–21.

Crandall, Robert W. *Controlling Industrial Pollution. The Economics and Politics of Clean Air*. Washington, D.C.: Brookings Institution, 1983.

Cropper, Maureen L., William L. Evans, Stephen J. Berardi, Maria M. Ducla-Soares, and Paul R. Portney. "The Determinants of Pesticide Regulation: A Statistical Analysis of EPA Decision Making." *Journal of Political Economy*, 100(1), 1992, 175–97.

Cumberland, John H. "Efficiency and Equity in Interregional Environmental Management." *Review of Regional Studies*, 10(2), 1981, 1–9.

Dasgupta, Susmita, Ashoka Mody, Subhendu Roy, and David Wheeler. "Environmental Regulation and Development. A Cross-Country Empirical Analysis." World Bank Policy Research Working Paper No. 1448, 1995.

Edwards, Jeremy, and Michael Keen. "Tax Competition and Leviathan." *European Economic Review*, 40(1), 1996, 113–34.

Ehrenberg, Ronald G. *Labor Markets and Integrating National Economies*. Washington, D.C.: Brookings Institution, 1994.

Esty, Daniel C. "Revitalizing Environmental Federalism." *Michigan Law Review*, 95(3), 1996, 570–652.

Esty, Daniel C., and Damien Geradin. "Environmental Protection and International Competitiveness: A Conceptual Framework." *Journal of World Trade*, 32(3), 1998, 5–46.

Feldstein, Martin S., and Charles Horioka. "Domestic Savings and International Capital Flows." *Economic Journal*, 90, 1980, 314–29.

Fredriksson, Per G. "The Siting of Hazardous Waste Facilities in Federal Systems: The Political Economy of NIMBY." *Environmental and Resource Economics*, 15, 2000, 75–87.

Fredriksson, Per G., and Noel Gaston. "The Ratification of the 1992 Climate Change Convention: What Determines Legislative Delay?" Forthcoming, *Public Choice*, 2000.

Freedom House. *Freedom in the World: Political Rights and Civil Liberties*. New York: Freedom House, 1993.

Friedman, Joseph, Daniel A. Gerlowski, and Jonathan Silberman. "What Attracts Foreign Multinational Corporations? Evidence from Branch Plant Location in the United States." *Journal of Regional Science*, 32(4), 1992, 403–18.

Golub, Jonathan. "State Power and Institutional Influence in European Integration: Lessons from the Packaging Waste Directive." *Journal of Common Market Studies*, 34(3), 1996, 313–39.

Gordon, Roger. H., and Lans Bovenberg. "Why is Capital So Immobile Internationally? Possible Explanations and Implications for Capital Income Taxation." *American Economic Review*, 86(5), 1996, 1057–76.

Grilli, Vittorio, and Gian Maria Milesi-Ferretti. "Economic Effects and Structural Determinants of Capital Controls." *IMF Staff Papers*, 42(3), 1995, 517–51.

Grossman, Gene M., and Elhanan Helpman. "Protection for Sale." *American Economic Review*, 84(4), 1994, 833–50.

Grossman, Gene M., and Alan B. Krueger. "Economic Growth and the Environment." *Quarterly Journal of Economics*, 112, 1995, 353–77.

Haas, Peter M. "Banning Chlorofluorocarbons: Epistemic Community Efforts to Protect Stratospheric Ozone." *International Organization*, 46(1), 1991, 187–224.

International Monetary Fund. *IMF Capital Controls Database*. Washington, D.C.: International Monetary Fund, 1998.

Jaffe, Adam B., Steven R. Peterson, Paul R. Portney, and Robert N. Stavins. "Environmental Regulation and the Competitiveness of U.S. Manufacturing: What Does the Evidence Tell Us?" *Journal of Economic Literature*, 33(1), 1995, 132–63.

Kimber, Cliona J. M. "Environmental Federalism: A Comparison of Environmental Federalism in the United States and the European Union." *Maryland Law Review*, 54, 1995, 1658–90.

Markusen, James R., Edward R. Morey, and Nancy D. Olewiler. "Environmental Policy when Market Structure and Plant Locations Are Endogenous." *Journal of Environmental Economics and Management*, 24(1), 1993, 69–86.

Murdoch, James C., and Todd Sandler. "The Voluntary Provision of a Pure Public Good: The Case of Reduced CFC Emissions and the Montreal Protocol." *Journal of Public Economics* 63(3), 1997, 331–49.

Oates, Wallace E. "Environment and Taxation: The Case of the United States," in *The Economics of Environmental Regulation*, edited by W. E. Oates, Brookfield, Vt.: Edward Elgar, 1996.

Oates, Wallace E., and Robert M. Schwab. "Economic Competition Among Jurisdictions: Efficiency Enhancing or Distortion Inducing?" *Journal of Public Economics*, 35(3), 1988, 333–54.

Pashigian, B. Peter. "Environmental Regulation: Whose Self-Interests Are Being Protected?" *Economic Inquiry*, 23(4), 1985, 551–84.

Paul, Joel R. "Free Trade, Regulatory Competition and the Autonomous Market Fallacy." *Columbia Journal of European Law*, 1, 1994/95, 29–62.

Persson, Torsten, and Guido Tabellini. "The Politics of 1992: Fiscal Policy and European Integration." *Review of Economic Studies*, 59(4), 1992, 689–701.

Rauscher, Michael. "On Ecological Dumping." *Oxford Economic Papers*, 46(5), 1994, 822–40.

Revesz, Richard L. "Rehabilitating Interstate Competition: Rethinking the "Race-to-the-Bottom" Rationale for Federal Environmental Regulation." *New York University Law Review*, 67, 1992, 1210–54.

Rose-Ackerman, Susan. *Controlling Environmental Policy. The Limits of Public Law in Germany and the United States.* New Haven, Conn.: Yale University Press, 1995.

Shafik, Nemat. "Economic Development and Environmental Quality: An Econometric Analysis." *Oxford Economic Papers* 46(5), 1994, 757–73.

Stewart, Richard B. "Madison's Nightmare." *University of Chicago Law Review*, 57, 1990, 335–55.

Ulph, Alistair. "International Environmental Regulation When National Governments Act Strategically." Discussion Paper in Economics and Econometrics, University of Southampton, No. 9518, 1995.

Ulph, Alistair. "Environmental Policy and International Trade When Governments and Producers Act Strategically." *Journal of Environmental Economics and Management*, 30(3), 1996, 265–81.

UNIDO. *Changing Patterns of Trade in World Industry: An Empirical Study on Revealed Comparative Advantage.* New York: United Nations, 1982.

United States Environmental Protection Agency. *Regulatory Impact Analysis: Protection of Stratospheric Ozone.* Washington, D.C.: U.S. EPA, 1988.

van Beers, Cees, and Jeroen C. J. M. van den Bergh. "An Empirical Multi-Country Analysis of the Impact of Environmental Policy on Foreign Trade Flows." *Kyklos*, 50(1), 1997, 29–46.

Wildasin, David E. "Nash Equilibrium in Models of Fiscal Competition." *Journal of Public Economics*, 35(2), 1988, 229–40.

Wilson, John D. "A Theory of Interregional Tax Competition." *Journal of Urban Economics*, 19(3), 1986, 296–315.

World Bank. *World Tables.* Washington, D.C.: World Bank, 1992.

World Bank. *World Development Indicators CD-ROM.* Washington, D.C.: World Bank, 1998.

[17]

JOURNAL OF REGIONAL SCIENCE, VOL. 40, NO. 3, 2000, pp. 453–471

REGULATORY FEDERALISM AND ENVIRONMENTAL PROTECTION IN THE UNITED STATES*

John A. List

Department of Agricultural and Resource Economics, University of Arizona, Tucson, AZ 85721 U.S.A.

Shelby Gerking

Department of Economics and Finance, University of Wyoming, Laramie, WY 82071 U.S.A. E-mail: sgerking@uwyo.edu

ABSTRACT. In this paper we address two aspects of regulatory federalism in U.S. environmental policy. First, we suggest that environmental quality in U.S. states responds positively to increases in income. Second, we provide evidence that environmental quality did not decline when President Reagan's policy of new federalism returned responsibility for many environmental regulations to the states. Thus, state environmental quality appears to reflect more than just the dictates of federal policy. Additionally, we find that a "race to the bottom" in environmental quality did not materialize in the 1980s.

1. INTRODUCTION

Should responsibility for setting environmental regulations and enforcement levels rest with national or state and local governments? The standard answer in the public finance literature is that if the economy is perfectly competitive and distortion free, and if available tax instruments are unconstrained, then both regional and national governments have incentives to establish economically efficient environmental policies. On the other hand, in a second-best world in which initial distortions are present, locally determined environmental regulations are likely to be suboptimal when jurisdictions compete with each other to attract capital. The former case is treated by Oates and Schwab (1988), whereas Wilson (1996) presents a comprehensive theoretical analysis of a number of situations where initial distortions are present and shows that local environmental regulations either may "race to the top" or "race to the bottom." Concern over a possible race to the bottom, predicted by Break

---

*We thank William Morgan, Charles Mason, Owen Phillips, Dale Menkhaus, Roger Bolton, David Plane, Gordon Mulligan, and three anonymous referees for helpful comments on previous versions of this manuscript. Also, we gratefully acknowledge the hospitality of CentER, Tilburg University, where portions of this paper were completed. Visiting grant B46-386 from the Netherlands Organization for Scientific Research (NWO) supported Gerking's stay at CentER during 1999–2000.

Received August 1998; revised July 1999; accepted November 1999.

© Blackwell Publishers 2000.
Blackwell Publishers, 350 Main Street, Malden, MA 02148, USA and 108 Cowley Road, Oxford, OX4 1JF, UK.

454 JOURNAL OF REGIONAL SCIENCE, VOL. 40, NO. 3, 2000

(1967) and Cumberland (1979, 1980) and reflected in Congressional testimony (House Report, 1979), was a factor that led the U.S. government to create the Environmental Protection Agency in 1968 and to pass subsequent legislation establishing national standards for air and water quality. The outcome was a dominating federal presence in environmental policy that has continued to the present day.

In this paper we address two questions concerning regulatory federalism in U.S. environmental policy. First, since the late 1960s tastes and technology have changed, information about consequences of environmental hazards has improved, and incomes have increased, suggesting that willingness to pay for environmental quality has increased as well. Thus, we ask whether aspects of environmental protection and environmental quality in U.S. states respond positively to increases in income. Although the evidence presented is not entirely clear-cut the results support the idea that this positive relationship exists. As a consequence, it appears that state environmental quality reflects more than just the dictates of federal policy. Second, we test whether environmental quality declined when President Reagan's policy of new federalism returned responsibility for many environmental regulations to the states (Nathan and Doolittle, 1983; Levinson, 1994). From this natural experiment we find that indicators of environmental quality at the state level either continued to improve or at least did not deteriorate through the 1980s. Thus, in this instance, the race to the bottom did not materialize. Moreover, this outcome may be of interest in other policy settings such as welfare reform in which a portion of the debate centers on predicted consequences of a decreased role for the federal government.

We divide the remainder of this paper into four sections. In Section 2 we outline the conceptual framework for the empirical analysis presented. In Section 3 we describe the data and econometric methods to be applied. In Section 4 we present the empirical results. Finally, in Section 5 implications and conclusions are drawn.

2. CONCEPTUAL FRAMEWORK

The empirical model to be estimated is a simple reduced form relationship

(1) $$P = f(Y, \mathbf{X}) + u$$

where P denotes pollution, Y denotes income, $\mathbf{X}$ denotes controls for additional factors that affect P, u denotes a disturbance term, and subscripts for industry, state, and time have been suppressed. Data sources, exact variable definitions, and econometric methods are discussed in the next section. Equation (1) is similar to regression models estimated in recent studies (i.e., Holtz-Eakin and Selden, 1995; Grossman and Krueger, 1995; Schmalensee, Stoker, and Judson, 1998) that test for a Kuznets relationship (inverted-U) between emissions or ambient pollution levels and a measure of income. These studies usually focus on countries at various stages of development and ask whether environmental quality (broadly defined) improves with income growth after a threshold level

© Blackwell Publishers 2000.

of income has been reached. If so, it suggests that further economic growth and improved environmental quality are compatible rather than competing objectives.

Several explanations have been offered for the hypothesized inverted-U shape of the P-Y relationship among countries. First, it may reflect a progression from relatively dirty technologies to cleaner technologies as countries industrialize (Stokey, 1998). Second, it may arise because less industrialized economies specialize in the production of the most polluting goods. Third, it may occur as consumers' tastes for environmental quality change as income grows (Jaeger, 1998). Fourth, it may be derived directly from the technological link between consumption of a desired good and abatement of its undesirable byproduct without reference to dynamics, institutions, or even externalities (Andreoni and Levinson, 1998).

Although this background is helpful in describing the genesis of our approach, our motivation for estimating Equation (1) differs from the studies cited above. We examine U.S. states rather than countries, and this paper is less concerned about the issue of whether economic growth is a panacea for environmental problems. Also, an inverted-U relationship between P and Y will not emerge if all states have income levels that exceed the threshold level (if indeed one can be demonstrated to exist). Instead, we may observe no statistical relationship between P and Y if minimum environmental standards imposed by the federal government were implemented simply "as is" by all states. On the other hand, if an inverse relationship between P and Y is identified, it means that state environmental quality improves with income growth and is not determined solely by one-size-fits-all federally prescribed standards. Therefore, higher incomes may lead to technology adoption by industry as well as interrelated actions taken by individuals, citizen groups, and lower levels of government to make environmental improvements. In other words, a negative association between income and pollution is good news in the sense that responsibility for providing this public good need not rest entirely with the federal government.

Two additional features of Equation (1) also warrant further discussion. First, Equation (1) is not derived from an explicit structural model. As noted above, it is interpreted as a reduced form that is consistent with many possible structural models. Also, possible explanatory variables that may be endogenously related to income growth are excluded to focus more directly on total effects of Y on P (see Holtz-Eakin and Selden, 1995 for a more fully developed discussion of this point in the context of the environmental Kuznets curve). Second, as discussed by Grossman and Krueger (1995), P and Y may be jointly determined. On the one hand, if environmental quality is a normal good then richer people demand more of it, *ceteris paribus*. Alternatively, under plausible assumptions tighter environmental regulations decrease income. Therefore, tests for simultaneity are conducted in all estimates of Equation (1) presented.

© Blackwell Publishers 2000.

456   JOURNAL OF REGIONAL SCIENCE, VOL. 40, NO. 3, 2000

3. DATA AND ECONOMETRIC METHODS

Equation (1) was estimated using three alternative measures of pollution or anti-pollution efforts P along with a measure of income Y, and other regressors X. These variables are described below followed by a discussion of econometric methods applied to Equation (1). Sources of data are listed in Appendix 1.

The first measure of P, which assists in addressing the question of whether state regulatory expenditures on environmental quality rise with income, uses data on air-quality-control expenditures by state governments over the period 1974–1980. Available data on expenditures for water quality and solid waste management were not used in the analysis because county or special district governments were more responsible for these functions than were state governments over this time period. Collection of these data was discontinued after 1980 because of budgetary cutbacks in the U.S. Department of Commerce.[1] In Equation (1), expenditures are expressed in real (1987 dollar) per capita terms in order to account (in a rough way) for the number of possible pollution sources to be regulated.

When regressed on Y the second measure of P suggests the extent to which private-sector pollution-control efforts in a state respond to regulatory pressure from state and local governments or public pressure from citizen groups that may increase with income. This measure uses data on operating expenditures (including depreciation, and costs of labor, materials, supplies, and equipment leasing, but excluding payments to government agencies) by manufacturing industries to abate air, water, and solid-waste pollution taken from the *Annual Survey of Manufactures* for the period 1973–1990.[2] Operating expenditures are expressed per 1,000 dollars of value-added to account for geographic and temporal variation in industry size. These data are analyzed for all manufacturing industries together as well as separately for four two-digit manufacturing classifications: (1) chemical and allied products, (2) paper and allied products, (3) food and kindred products, and (4) primary metals. These four industries were chosen because, among manufacturing sectors, they are relatively heavy spenders on pollution abatement.

To examine manufacturer's pollution control efforts, we could measure P in terms of quantity of pollution abated rather than in terms of abatement expenditures. However, such data do not exist. Abatement efforts also could be measured by expenditures for capital equipment. These data do exist but are not used in view of significant measurement problems. For example, the questionnaire used by the U.S. Department of Commerce asks corporate officials how

---

[1]Various other groups such as the State and Territorial Air Pollution Program Administrators, the National Association of State Budget Officers, and the Council of State Governments have attempted to fill in the gaps in this data series after 1980. However, these newer data sets were not collected on a regular basis and do not appear to be comparable with the 1974–1980 data used here.

[2]In estimates not reported here, payments to government agencies were included in the operating expenditures figures. Results do not appreciably differ from those reported in the next section.

© Blackwell Publishers 2000.

their capital expenditures would have been different in the absence of environmental regulations. Hence, these expenditure figures are hypothetical, not actual. Another possible shortcoming of the capital expenditures data is that they do not control for the mix of new versus existing plants in a state. New plants tend to face more stringent environmental regulations than existing plants so states with relatively newer plants may have higher compliance costs. Levinson (1994) argues that this problem may be more serious in the capital expenditure data than in the operating expenditure data.

The third measure of P, emissions by state of two criteria air pollutants, sulfur dioxide and nitrogen oxides, permit examination of how contributions to further environmental degradation change with income. Emissions data are obtained from the U.S. Environmental Protection Agency (*National Air Pollutant Emission Trends, 1900–1994*) for the period 1929–1994. Emissions data from 1929–1984 are calculated from a top-down approach in which a national emissions estimate based on economic activity, material flows, and consumption of various types of fuel is allocated to states based on state production activities. For the period 1985–1994 estimates are obtained using a bottom-up methodology that aggregates emissions from the plant or county level to the state level. An obvious problem with these data relates to splicing indirect estimates together with direct estimates; however, this appears to be the only way to generate a state-level emissions series that begins before President Reagan took office in 1981.

Several variables were tried as potential determinants of the three measures of P in Equation (1). Real per capita income (1987 dollar) Y was initially included in each regression model along with quadratic and cubic terms in Y. Additional controls **X** included state population density *DENSITY*, a measure of the importance of manufacturing in a state *%MFG*, and percent of population consisting of white residents *%WHITE*. *DENSITY* is measured as total state population divided by total state land area and can be computed annually from 1929–1994. The importance of manufacturing in a state *%MFG* is defined as state personal income derived from manufacturing divided by total state personal income. This ratio can be computed annually from 1929–1994. *%WHITE* is a proxy for the absence of minorities and is available on an annual basis for 1970–1994 only. We include only *DENSITY* and *%MFG* in **X** in our emission models whereas in the other two specifications we include all three regressors.[3]

Data to estimate Equation (1) always form a balanced panel and estimates are obtained for both random- and fixed-effects models. Both estimation approaches control for types of heterogeneity that would remain uncontrolled in a single cross-section for a particular year, in a single time series for a particular state, or if least squares was applied to the pooled data. One-way fixed and random-effects estimates control for unmeasured time-invariant (or slowly

---

[3]Note that we gathered data on median age and percent male from 1970–1990. Given that these variables were consistently insignificant we excluded them from each model.

© Blackwell Publishers 2000.

458   JOURNAL OF REGIONAL SCIENCE, VOL. 40, NO. 3, 2000

changing) state-specific effects including differences in industry mix, resource endowment, climate, and attitudes toward environmental protection (see Henderson, 1996). Two-way fixed and random-effects estimates control for both state-specific effects and time-specific effects that may arise from changes in national economic or environmental policy and temporal shifts in tastes for, or in costs of providing, environmental protection. Thus, application of these estimation methods to the panel data at hand automatically controls for numerous factors that otherwise would be difficult to enumerate and measure.

Generalized least squares (GLS) estimates (of the random-effects model) treat unmeasured characteristics as error components, economize on degrees of freedom, and yield coefficients that are not conditioned on unmeasured state and time effects. In contrast, least-squares-dummy-variable (LSDV) estimates treat unmeasured state and time effects as shifts in the constant term; hence, estimates of the marginal effects of Y on P are conditioned on the unmeasured characteristics. This distinction between conditional and unconditional estimates of Y on P is important in interpreting empirical results presented in Section 4. Also, if no other econometric problems are present, the GLS estimator is consistent under the null hypothesis of no correlation between state and time effects and Y, but it is biased and inconsistent otherwise. On the other hand, the LSDV estimator remains consistent whether or not this correlation exists, but it is inefficient because it ignores variation in income between states. However, the LSDV estimator has the advantage of yielding estimates of coefficients of time dummies that are useful in testing for consequences of President Reagan's new federalism policies toward the environment. Additionally, the LSDV estimates may be preferred because the sample consists of 50 states and is not a random draw from a larger population. Nevertheless, both sets of estimates turn out to be useful in interpreting relationships identified between P and Y.

As mentioned previously, a possible concern about the estimates reported is that P and Y could be jointly determined. This problem would arise in either the GLS or the LSDV estimates if Y is correlated with the disturbance term. Additionally, the GLS estimates appear to be particularly subject to simultaneity because, in this case, the error term includes the state- and time-specific effects. In any case, exogeneity tests were conducted using the average of incomes in adjacent states as an instrument for Y. This instrument is similar to one applied to GLS estimates in a related context by Holtz-Eakin (1994). Wald tests (see Davidson and MacKinnon, 1993, pp. 389–393) did not reject the null hypothesis of exogeneity of Y. In consequence, the matter of possible simultaneity is not pursued further here, although embedding Equation (1) in a more complete structural model of income determination and environmental quality may be a logical next step in future research.

Finally, a problem in estimating Equation (1) when P is measured using pollution-abatement operating expenditures in manufacturing is that complete data are not available for all states in all years for the four individual industries considered because of federal nondisclosure rules. Complete data are available for 34 states for the chemical and allied products sector, 37 states for the food

© Blackwell Publishers 2000.

and kindred products sector, 22 states for the paper and allied products sector, and 19 states for the primary metals sector. Because data are missing with greatest frequency for less populated states with comparatively little manufacturing employment, resulting sample truncation can cause biased and inconsistent estimates. This situation is handled by applying Heckman's (1979) two-step selection model, which treats truncation as an omitted variable problem. In the first step, the probit model shown in Equation (2) is estimated to explain whether P is observed

$$(2) \qquad D_{jkt} = h(MFG_{jkt}) + w_{jkt}$$

where D equals unity if P is observed and equals zero otherwise, MFG denotes number of persons employed in manufacturing, subscripts j, k, and t again denote industry, state, and time, respectively, and w is a normally distributed disturbance term. In the second step, the inverse Mills ratio is recovered from Equation (2) and used as a regressor in estimating Equation (1).

4. EMPIRICAL RESULTS

Table 1 presents one-way and two-way fixed- and random-effects estimates of Equation (1) using the previously described measure of state air-quality control efforts as the dependent variable. The log-linear functional form was selected over the linear functional form using a special case of the Box and Cox (1964) procedure outlined in Maddala (1992, pp. 221–222). In addition, given that income and higher-order terms to a cubic are significant they are included in our final specification. F and LM statistics indicate that in both fixed- and random-effects models the null hypothesis of homogeneity of unmeasured state- and time-specific effects is rejected at the 1 percent level. Hausman statistics imply that the null hypothesis of orthogonality between Y and the state and time effects should not be rejected at conventional significance levels in either model. Thus, the random-effects estimates are preferred because they are more efficient than their fixed-effect counterparts. However, in this case the inferences are similar.

Estimates for both random-effects models suggest that real per capita state air-quality expenditures respond positively to changes in real per capita state personal income in certain income ranges. Turning point (Up) estimates from the random-effects models in the bottom portion of Table 1 suggest that income and expenditures are positively related between income levels of approximately $10,000–$18,000. Given that the mean income in this subsample is $12,769, and the sampled income range is $8,396–$22,393, our results provide evidence that for most states the income-expenditure relationship is positive. A plausible interpretation of these results is that as a state's per capita income rises, people place greater pressure on government officials to improve air quality (and by implication other aspects of environmental quality as well). This pressure, which may operate through several channels including activities of environmental

© Blackwell Publishers 2000.

460   JOURNAL OF REGIONAL SCIENCE, VOL. 40, NO. 3, 2000

TABLE 1:   State Air Quality Control Expenditure Results [a, b]

Explanatory Variable	One-Way Fixed Effects	Two-Way Fixed Effects	One-Way Random Effects	Two-Way Random Effects
	\multicolumn{4}{c}{Estimation Method}			
Constant	—	4172.7	5753.4	5436.9
		(2.0)	(2.8)	(2.7)
$Ln(Y)^c$	−1258.9	−1306.2	−1818.1	−1712.5
	(−1.8)	(−2.0)	(−2.8)	(−2.7)
$[Ln(Y)]^2$	131.7	136.2	191.3	179.7
	(1.8)	(1.94)	(2.8)	(2.7)
$[Ln(Y)]^3$	−4.60	−4.74	−6.70	−6.28
	(−1.8)	(−1.92)	(−2.8)	(−2.7)
$Ln(DENSITY)$	0.40	−0.34	−0.17	−0.14
	(0.59)	(−0.49)	(−2.2)	(−1.5)
$Ln(\%MFG)$	0.99	0.34	0.51	0.38
	(3.11)	(0.79)	(2.9)	(1.7)
$Ln(\%WHITE)$	0.05	−0.16	0.01	−0.08
	(0.29)	(0.70)	(0.68)	(−0.38)
Summary Statistics[d]				
Homogeneity Test–State	28.4	27.9	—	—
	(49294)	(49294)		
Homogeneity Test–Time	—	6.4	—	—
		(6288)		
LM	—	—	653.1	653.3
			(1)	(2)
Hausman	—	—	6.4	9.0
			(6)	(6)
Turning Point (Up)	$11209	$11835	$9238	$10159
Turning Point (Down)	$17080	$16861	$18875	$17891
R^2	0.85	0.87	—	—

[a]Dependent variable is the natural logarithm of real ($1987) per capita air quality control expenditures by state governments.

[b]t-statistics in parentheses beneath coefficient estimates.

[c]Y is real ($1987) per capita personal income by state.

[d]degrees of freedom reported in parentheses beneath certain summary statistics.

public interest groups, causes the environmental policies of a state to reflect more than just a response to federal directives.

Coefficients estimated for the other regressors in the one-way random-effects model suggest that *DENSITY* and *%MFG* are important in determining air-quality control expenditures whereas *%WHITE* is insignificant.[4] However, this conclusion is weakened when the fixed-effects specifications and the two-way random-effects estimates are considered. In each of these three model types, only manufacturing presence is significant at conventional levels in the one-way

---

[4]Notice that the insignificant coefficient of *%WHITE* bears on the issue of environmental justice treated recently by Arora and Cason (1999).

© Blackwell Publishers 2000.

fixed-effects model. These results suggest that effects of these particular regressors may be difficult to distinguish from net effects of other variables that are constant across states but change over time. One possibility to consider in this regard is that general trends in population density and manufacturing importance are similar across states.

A related regulatory aspect to consider is whether firm-level expenditures for pollution abatement rise with increases in state income. This issue is addressed by estimating Equation (1) using pollution-abatement operating expenditures as the dependent variable after accounting for nondisclosed information using Equation (2). Estimates of Equation (1) specified in double-log form are presented in Table 2 for the four manufacturing industries identified in Section 2 as well as for all manufacturing. Again, the double-log functional form was selected over the linear functional form using the Box-Cox procedure described by Maddala (1992). Quadratic and higher-order polynomial terms were tried in preliminary regressions, but an order higher than quadratic was unnecessary as cubic terms (and above) had coefficients that generally were not significantly different from zero at conventional levels. For the chemical-and-allied-products regression we present only a linear specification in income because higher-order terms were insignificant. First-stage probit estimates of Equation (2), which show that disclosure of pollution abatement operating expenditures is more likely for states with higher levels of manufacturing employment, are reported in Appendix B.

Results are reported in Table 2 for two-way fixed-effects and random-effects models. F and LM statistics indicate that in both types of models and for all industry groupings considered, the null hypothesis of homogeneity of unmeasured state- and time-specific effects is rejected at the 5 percent level. Additionally, Hausman (1978) tests of the null hypothesis of zero correlation between Y and the state and time effects suggest that the orthogonality assumption underlying the random-effects estimates appears to be violated in each of the individual industry regressions but not in the pooled manufacturing regression. This outcome suggests that apart from the estimates for overall manufacturing, GLS yields inconsistent and biased coefficient estimates. Coefficients of the inverse Mills ratio (IMR) calculated from estimates of Equation (2) are significantly different from zero in five out of eight cases. Thus, incidental censoring appears to be a potential source of bias warranting treatment in the equations estimated. Control variables in each model appear to be largely insignificant. However, a closer examination of the parameter estimates suggests that more densely populated states and those with a large manufacturing presence tend to have lower pollution-abatement expenditures per $1,000 value-added, whereas abatement expenditures in overall manufacturing tend to be higher in states that have a disproportionately large white population. Finally, values of R^2 for the fixed-effects estimates range from about 0.50 to 0.81.

Estimates from the fixed-effects models presented in Table 2 suggest that state per capita income is a significant determinant of pollution-abatement operating expenditures in the four individual manufacturing industries considered, as

© Blackwell Publishers 2000.

462   JOURNAL OF REGIONAL SCIENCE, VOL. 40, NO. 3, 2000

TABLE 2: Two-Way Fixed- and Random-Effects Results
for Pollution-Abatement Expenditures[a,b]

Explanatory Variable	Chemical and Allieds FE (1)	RE (1)	Paper and Allieds FE (2)	RE (2)	Primary Metals FE (3)	RE (3)	Food and Kindred FE (4)	RE (4)	All Manufacturing FE (5)	RE (5)
Constant	−3.6	−3.8	−138	−144	118.2	−4.82	−58.5	−37.8	−171.1	−160.3
	(−0.8)	(−1.9)	(−3.2)	(−4.1)	(2.3)	(−0.2)	(−1.6)	(−1.3)	(−3.9)	(−3.9)
Ln(Y)[c]	0.76	0.76	34.3	36.1	−28.9	−0.5	13.9	8.50	35.7	33.6
	(1.5)	(3.3)	(3.2)	(4.1)	(−2.4)	(−0.5)	(1.6)	(1.3)	(4.0)	(3.9)
$[Ln(Y)]^2$	—	—	−1.75	−1.76	1.62	0.17	−0.78	−0.42	−1.84	−1.74
			(−3.2)	(−4.0)	(2.6)	(0.3)	(−1.6)	(−1.2)	(−3.9)	(−3.9)
Ln($DENSITY$)	0.25	−0.04	−0.07	−0.15	−0.51	−0.72	0.70	−0.40	−0.40	−0.09
	(0.6)	(−0.5)	(−0.2)	(−1.5)	(−1.1)	(−6.3)	(0.2)	(−0.6)	(−1.6)	(−1.1)
Ln($\%MFG$)	−0.43	−0.17	−1.14	−0.28	0.89	1.10	−0.60	−0.40	0.08	0.03
	(−1.1)	(−0.9)	(−2.3)	(−1.1)	(1.7)	(3.8)	(−1.6)	(−2.8)	(0.38)	(0.2)
Ln($\%WHITE$)	−0.36	0.14	−0.24	0.07	−0.55	0.64	0.22	0.27	0.51	0.60
	(−1.1)	(0.6)	(−0.7)	(0.3)	(−1.4)	(2.2)	(0.9)	(1.4)	(2.9)	(3.6)
IMR	−0.17	−0.17	0.21	0.85	0.24	0.36	1.92	0.48	—	—
	(−2.1)	(−2.1)	(0.4)	(3.0)	(0.6)	(1.5)	(3.1)	(2.2)		
D82	—[d]		—[d]		—[d]		—[d]		—[d]	
D83	0.06		0.07		0.08		−0.11		0.08	
	(0.4)		(0.7)		(0.7)		(−1.4)		(1.3)	
D84	0.17		0.08		0.07		−0.01		0.15	
	(1.2)		(0.8)		(0.6)		(−0.1)		(2.1)	
D85	0.25		0.10		0.16		0.04		0.18	
	(1.7)		(0.9)		(1.3)		(0.5)		(2.5)	
D86	0.33		−0.03		0.03		0.10		0.15	
	(2.2)		(−0.3)		(0.2)		(1.4)		(2.0)	
D88	0.20		−0.22		−0.37		0.10		0.15	
	(1.3)		(−1.6)		(−2.4)		(1.3)		(2.0)	
D89	0.21		−0.29		−0.23		0.16		0.12	
	(1.4)		(−1.9)		(−1.5)		(2.2)		(1.5)	
D90	0.30		−0.18		−0.17		0.15		0.15	
	(2.0)		(−1.2)		(−1.0)		(2.0)		(1.8)	
Summary Statistics[e]										
Homogeneity Test-State	22.1 (33539)	—	31.0 (21346)	—	17.6 (18298)	—	10.8 (36586)	—	38.6 (47763)	—
Homogeneity Test-Time	2.3 (16523)	—	2.0 (16330)	—	5.7 (16282)	—	1.6 (18568)	—	14.0 (16747)	—
LM Test	—	967 (2)	—	954 (2)	—	523 4 (2)	—	546 (2)	—	2776 (2)
Hausman	—	14.2 (5)	—	20.7 (6)	—	58.1 (6)	—	26.2 (6)	—	4.0 (5)
R^2	0.64	—	0.80	—	0.81	—	0.50	—	0.78	—
Turning Point	—	—	$18033	$28259	$7480	—	$20537	$24587	$16481	$15678

[a]Dependent variable is the natural logarithm of pollution-abatement operating expenditures per $1,000 of value-added by State.
[b]t-statistics in parentheses beneath coefficient estimates.
[c]Y is real ($1987) per capita personal income by State.
[d]denotes omitted dummy variable.
[e]degrees of freedom reported in parentheses.

© Blackwell Publishers 2000.

well as for all manufacturing industries combined. Although potentially unreliable, random-effects estimates of the coefficients of per capita income yield similar findings. Interesting insights can be gained within each model type. For example, the coefficient of income in the chemical-and-allied-products fixed-effects model, which is significant at the 10 percent level in a one-tailed t-test, suggests that the income elasticity of abatement expenditures is 0.76. Furthermore, in the other three industries we find that income and its square are at least jointly different from zero at the 1 percent level. Their coefficient estimates suggest that within relevant ranges of income firm-level pollution-abatement expenditures and income are directly related. In the overall manufacturing regression, we find that the relationship between income and abatement expenditures turns at approximately $16,000, a figure well above the subsample mean of $13,400. Therefore, per capita income does appear to play a powerful role in determining pollution-abatement operating expenditures in manufacturing at the state level.

Table 2 also reports selected coefficient estimates for the time dummies (denoted *D82* through *D90*) in the fixed-effects models. These estimates were constructed using 1982 as the base year and provide an indication of consequences from reduced emphasis on environmental concerns at the national level that occurred in the early years of the Reagan administration. As indicated in the introduction, the Reagan Administration "tried to get the states to assume greater responsibility for pollution control programs, both by delegating entire programs and by leaving to states particular functions which had been carried out by the federal government" (Davies, 1984, p. 151). By the end of 1982 state governments had been delegated enforcement responsibilities for over 95 percent of applicable national emissions standards for hazardous air pollutants and over 90 percent of applicable new source performance standards, up from 48 percent and 64 percent at the beginning of 1982 (Council on Environmental Quality, 1982). Additionally, between 1981 and 1983, the number of states authorized to administer air-quality deterioration prevention and hazardous-waste management rose from 16 to 26 and 18 to 34, respectively (Environmental Law Institute, 1983).

In other words, although each of these coefficients reflects the net impact of many potentially important state-invariant time effects, one of the effects captured would be shifts in national environmental policy. Thus, it is interesting that in two of the four industries considered, coefficients of the time dummies are generally positive. In fact, net of state income effects and other regressors, over the period 1982–1990 real pollution-abatement operating expenditures per $1000 of value-added rose by 30 percent in chemical and allied products, by 15 percent in food and kindred products, and by 15 percent in overall manufacturing. However, over this same period real pollution-abatement operating expenditures net of state income effects declined by 18 percent in the paper and allied products sector and first rose then fell in primary metals. Taken together, these results are mixed; but they do not present compelling evidence that states

© Blackwell Publishers 2000.

464   JOURNAL OF REGIONAL SCIENCE, VOL. 40, NO. 3, 2000

raced to the bottom in the early to late 1980s when given the opportunity to exert greater control over design and enforcement of environmental policies.

Whether increases in income lead to reduced emissions can be addressed more directly by examining the estimates reported in Tables 3 and 4. Table 3 regressions use the natural logarithm of sulfur dioxide emissions as the dependent variable and Table 4 presents results using the natural logarithm of oxides of nitrogen emissions as the environmental indicator. (The log-log functional form was again selected using the special case of the Box-Cox procedure outlined in Maddala, 1992). Both tables present two-way fixed- and random-effects estimates of equations in which the emissions variable is regressed on the natural logarithm of real per capita personal income, its square, and its cube. Both tables also present estimates for the 1929–1994 time period as well as estimates for the 1985–1994 time period (the 1985–1994 models only include expansions in income to a quadratic because cubed terms were unnecessary). Estimates from the longer time series are useful because the data span both the initiation of the environmental movement in the late 1960s and early 1970s as well as the Reagan presidency; whereas estimates from the 1985–1994 time period are based on only the bottom-up emissions data. Overall, our relatively parsimonious models perform well as coefficients of determination in the fixed-effects models are above 0.70; those for the 1985–1994 regressions are higher than those for the 1929–1994 regressions.

Homogeneity of state-specific effects is rejected at the 1 percent level in all equations, and homogeneity of time-specific effects is rejected at the same significance level. Also, Hausman (1978) tests indicate that the null hypothesis of zero correlation between per capita income and the state and time disturbances in the random-effects model is rejected at the 1 percent significance level in all equations reported. However, fixed-effects and random-effects estimates are quite similar numerically for both pollutants—an outcome that becomes more likely as the number of cross-sectional units and the length of the time series expand (see Hsiao, 1986, p. 54). Results from Tables 3 and 4 also suggest that population density and pollutant emissions are negatively correlated, a finding consistent with previous studies estimating income or pollution relationships in a cross-country setting (see for example, Selden and Song, 1994). In addition, for both sulfur dioxides and nitrogen oxides we find that a large manufacturing presence has a negative effect on emission rates from 1929–1994 but a positive effect from 1985–1994. This result may be a repercussion of the data-generation process or a fundamental difference in regulatory procedures across state and federal bodies. Given that each time period contains eras of both federal and state regulatory presence, disentangling the impacts is beyond the scope of the paper.

Over relevant income ranges, estimation results for the emissions-income equations presented in Tables 3 and 4 are broadly consistent with the Kuznets (inverted-U) relationship sometimes observed in prior studies (Selden and Song, 1994; Holtz-Eakin and Selden, 1995; Grossman and Krueger, 1995). In the 1929–1994 specifications for sulfur dioxide (both fixed and random effects)

© Blackwell Publishers 2000.

TABLE 3:   Two-Way Fixed- and Random-Effects Estimates
for SO$_2$ Emissions[a,b]

Explanatory Variable	Fixed 1929–1994	Fixed 1985–1994	Random 1929–1994	Random 1985–1994
Constant	317.8	−150.1	271.3	−127.9
	(11.8)	(−3.6)	(11.1)	(−3.2)
$Ln(Y)$[c]	−116.8	28.9	−101.4	25.5
	(−12.3)	(3.4)	(−11.7)	(3.1)
$[Ln(Y)]^2$	13.9	−1.42	12.4	−1.30
	(12.5)	(−3.1)	(12.3)	(−3.0)
$[Ln(Y)]^3$	−0.54	—	−0.50	—
	(−12.5)		(−12.9)	
$Ln(DENSITY)$	−0.72	−0.37	−1.46	−0.44
	(−1.7)	(−2.5)	(−4.3)	(−5.4)
$Ln(\%MFG)$	−0.48	0.30	−0.59	0.55
	(−9.1)	(2.7)	(−12.0)	(5.9)
D82	—	—	—	—
D83	−0.05	—	—	—
	(−0.63)			
D84	−0.04	—	—	—
	(−0.50)			
D85	−0.07	—	—	—
	(−0.88)			
D86	−0.11	—	—	—
	(−1.4)			
D87	−0.16	—	—	—
	(−2.0)			
D88	−0.11	—	—	—
	(−1.4)			
D89	−0.13	—	—	—
	(−1.6)			
D90	−0.17	—	—	—
	(−2.1)			
Summary Statistics[e]				
Homogeneity Test-State	143.4 (473115)	595.8 (47428)	—	—
Homogeneity Test-Time	7.1 (653050)	9.0 (9419)	—	—
LM	—	—	46019 (2)	1992 (2)
Hausman	—	—	237.4 (5)	60.1 (4)
R^2	0.77	0.99	—	—
Turning Point (Up)	$1637	—	$1611	—
Turning Point (Down)	$16040	$26080	$8935	$18141

[a]dependent variable is the natural logarithm of per capita SO$_2$.
[b]t-statistics in parentheses beneath coefficients.
[c]Y is real ($1987) per capita personal income by State.
[d]denotes omitted dummy variable.
[e]degrees of freedom reported in parentheses.

© Blackwell Publishers 2000.

466	JOURNAL OF REGIONAL SCIENCE, VOL. 40, NO. 3, 2000

TABLE 4: Two-way Fixed- and Random-Effects Estimates
for NO_x Emissions[a,b]

Explanatory Variable	Fixed 1929–1994	Fixed 1985–1994	Random 1929–1994	Random 1985–1994
Constant	110.3	−41.2	128.3	−114.8
	(7.7)	(−1.8)	(9.7)	(−2.7)
$Ln(Y)$[c]	−41.8	7.9	−47.6	23.1
	(−8.3)	(1.7)	(−10.3)	(2.6)
$[Ln(Y)]^2$	5.0	−0.41	5.7	−1.19
	(8.6)	(−1.7)	(10.5)	(−2.6)
$[Ln(Y)]^3$	−0.20	—	−0.22	—
	(−8.7)		(−10.6)	
$Ln(DENSITY)$	−2.8	−0.50	−2.55	−0.46
	(−12.2)	(−6.2)	(−14.6)	(−5.6)
$Ln(\%MFG)$	−0.02	0.33	−0.01	0.63
	(−0.63)	(5.3)	(−0.38)	(6.6)
$D82$	—	—	—	—
$D83$	−0.01	—	—	—
	(−0.2)			
$D84$	0.01	—	—	—
	(0.19)			
$D85$	−0.005	—	—	—
	(0.10)			
$D86$	−0.04	—	—	—
	(−1.0)			
$D87$	−0.03	—	—	—
	(−0.6)			
$D88$	0.03	—	—	—
	(0.6)			
$D89$	0.003	—	—	—
	(0.06)			
$D90$	−0.026	—	—	—
	(−0.52)			
Summary Statistics[e]				
Homogeneity Test-State	114.2	388.0	—	—
	(473115)	(47428)		
Homogeneity Test-Time	6.1	7.4	—	—
	(653050)	(9419)		
LM	—	—	36349	1914
			(2)	(2)
Hausman	—	—	114.7	19.3
			(5)	(4)
R^2	0.82	0.99	—	—
Turning Point (Up)	$1496	—	$1146	—
Turning Point (Down)	$12978	$15199	$26250	$16465

[a]dependent variable is the natural logarithm of per capita NO_x.
[b]t-statistics in parentheses beneath coefficients.
[c]Y is real ($1987) per capita personal income by State.
[d]denotes omitted dummy variable.
[e]degrees of freedom reported in parentheses.

© Blackwell Publishers 2000.

coefficients, that are different from zero at significance levels below 1 percent in all cases, of the linear terms are negative, coefficients of the quadratic terms are positive, and coefficients of the cubic terms are negative. Given that few states had incomes below $1,600 in our sample period, the estimates imply that sulfur dioxide emissions first rise and then fall with real per capita income, with a turning point at $16,040 (1987 dollars) for the fixed-effects estimates ($8,935 in the random-effects estimates). The estimated turning point in the random-effects model is roughly equal to those found in an international context for sulfur dioxide by Selden and Song (1994) who report their results in 1985 dollars. However, estimates based on the 1985–1994 time-period suggest turning points of $26,080 (fixed effects) and $18,141 (random effects). This result may imply that the environmental Kuznets curve shifts over time (an interpretation that is useful to evaluating similar estimates developed in an international context) or it may only reflect differences between emissions data constructed from top-down and bottom-up methodologies.

Table 4 suggests a similar pattern for oxides of nitrogen. As previously mentioned, estimates of coefficients for the income terms are significantly different from zero and imply that emissions first rise and then fall with increases in income over important ranges of income. Turning-point estimates obtained from the 1929–1994 models imply that oxides of nitrogen emissions are negatively related to income after a real per capita income of $12,978 ($26,250, random effects) has been reached. Estimates based on data from the 1985–1994 time period imply similar turning points; $15,199 and $16,465 for fixed- and random-effects models. Similar to the case of sulfur dioxide it appears that emissions of oxides of nitrogen are negatively related to income after a threshold level of income is obtained.

Period effects from Equation (1) are reported in Tables 3 and 4 based on fixed-effects estimates obtained from the 1929–1994 data. Again, these estimates provide a means to test whether environmental quality continued to improve during the 1980s and early 1990s. Results for sulfur dioxides indicate that emissions net of real per capita state income growth tended to decline after 1982. All of the coefficients of the time dummies presented are negative and those for $D87$ and $D90$ differ significantly from zero in a one-tailed t-test at the $p < 0.10$ level. Results for oxides of nitrogen suggest that emissions generally leveled off through the 1980s and early 1990s with insignificant increases occurring in 1988 and 1989. Although these results may reflect many factors that are constant across states but change over time, they do not appear to suggest that environmental quality was sacrificed as the federal government relinquished control in designing and implementing standards. This outcome reinforces the findings from the period effects presented in Table 2.

© Blackwell Publishers 2000.

468   JOURNAL OF REGIONAL SCIENCE, VOL. 40, NO. 3, 2000

5. SUMMARY AND CONCLUSION

In this paper three sets of panel data are used to empirically test the extent to which indicators of environmental quality respond to income changes at the state level and whether environmental quality was sacrificed as state and local governments acquired more latitude in implementing standards and in enforcing federal regulations. Indicators of environmental quality measured in this study include: (1) state expenditures for air-quality control, (2) pollution-abatement operating expenditures in manufacturing, and (3) emissions of sulfur dioxide and oxides of nitrogen. The results suggest that environmental quality at the state level improves as income grows and that environmental quality did not deteriorate in the early 1980s when President Reagan began to implement his new federalism policies. These results are good news in that they support the idea that responsibility for providing environmental quality need not rest entirely with the federal government. Locally-driven efforts by governmental or private organizations appear to be important as well. However, these conclusions should be interpreted cautiously because they are based on a reduced-form analysis that is consistent with a number of alternative structural models. In fact, embedding the relationship between pollution and income in a more complete model is a logical next step for future research.

REFERENCES

Andreoni, James and Arik Levinson. 1998. "The Simple Analytics of the Environmental Kuznets Curse," Department of Economics, University of Wisconsin (unpublished manuscript).

Arora, Seema and Timothy N. Cason. 1999. "Do Community Characteristics Influence Environmental Outcomes," *Southern Economic Journal*, 65, 691–716.

Box, George E.P. and D.R. Cox. 1964. "An Analysis of Transformations," *Journal of the Royal Statistical Society*, B, Part 2, 26, 221–243.

Break, George F. 1967. *Intergovernmental Fiscal Relations in the United States*. Washington, DC: The Brookings Institution.

Council on Environmental Quality. 1982. *Environmental Quality*, Washington, DC: Council on Environmental Quality.

Cumberland, John H. 1979. "Interregional Pollution Spillovers and Consistency of Environmental Policy," in H. Siebert, Ingo Walter, and Klaus Zimmerman (eds.), *Regional Environmental Policy: The Economic Issue*. New York: New York University Press, pp. 255–283.

———. 1980. "Efficiency and Equity in Interregional Environmental Management," *Review of Regional Studies*, 10, 1–9.

Davidson, Russell and James G. MacKinnon. 1993. *Estimation and Inference in Econometrics*. New York: Oxford University Press.

Davies, J. Clarence. 1984. "Environmental Institution and the Reagan Administration," in N. J. Vig and M. Kraft (eds.), *Environmental Policy in the 1980's*, Washington, DC: Congressional Quarterly Press.

Environmental Law Institute. 1983. *Environmental Forum*, 2, Washington DC: Environmental Law Institute.

Grossman, Gene M. and Alan B. Krueger. 1995. "Economic Growth and the Environment," *Quarterly Journal of Economics*, 110, 53–77.

Hausman, Jerry. 1978. "Specification Tests in Econometrics," *Econometrica*, 46, 1251–1271.

Heckman, James. 1979. "Sample Selection Bias as a Specification Error," *Econometrica*, 47, 153–161.

Henderson, J. Vernon. 1996. "Effects of Air Quality Regulation," *American Economic Review*, 86, 789–814.

© Blackwell Publishers 2000.

Holtz-Eakin, Douglas. 1994. "Public Sector Capital and the Productivity Puzzle," *Review of Economics and Statistics*, 76, 12–21.

Holtz-Eakin, Douglas and Thomas Selden. 1995. "Stoking the Fires? CO_2 Emissions and Economic Growth," *Journal of Public Economics*, 57, 85–101.

House Report 91-1146. 1979. *Legislative History of the Clean Air Act*. Washington, DC: U.S. Government Printing Office.

Hsiao, Cheng. 1986. *Analysis of Panel Data*. Cambridge: Cambridge University Press.

Jaeger, William. 1998. "A Theoretical Basis for the Environmental Inverted-U Curve and Implications for International Trade," Department of Economics, Williams College.

Levinson, Arik. 1994. "Environmental Regulations and Manufacturer's Location Choices: Evidence from the Census of Manufactures," Ph.D. dissertation, Department of Economics, Columbia University.

Maddala, G.S. 1992. *Introduction to Econometrics*, 2nd Ed. Englewood Cliffs, NJ: Prentice Hall.

Nathan, Richard and Fred C. Doolittle. 1983. *The Consequences of Cuts: The Effects of the Reagan Domestic Program on State and Local Governments*. Princeton: Princeton University Press.

Oates, Wallace E. and Robert M. Schwab. 1988. "Economic Competition Among Jurisdictions: Efficiency Enhancing or Distortion Inducing?" *Journal of Public Economics*, 35, 333–354.

Schmalensee, Richard, Thomas M. Stoker, and Ruth A. Judson. 1998. "World Carbon Dioxide Emissions: 1950–2050," *Review of Economics and Statistics*, 80, 15–27.

Selden, Thomas and Daqing Song. 1994. "Environmental Quality and Development: Is There a Kuznets Curve for Air Pollution Emissions?" *Journal of Environmental Economics and Management*, 27, 147–162.

Stokey, Nancy L. 1998. "Are There Limits to Growth?" *International Economics Review*, 39, 1–31.

Wilson, John D. 1996. "Capital Mobility and Environmental Standards: Is There a Theoretical Basis for a Race to the Bottom," in J. Bhagwati and R.P. Hudec (eds.), *Fair Trade and Harmonization: Prerequisites for Free Trade*, Vol. 1, Cambridge: MIT Press.

© Blackwell Publishers 2000.

470   JOURNAL OF REGIONAL SCIENCE, VOL. 40, NO. 3, 2000

APPENDIX A

DATA SOURCES

State Regulatory Expenditures: Real (1987) dollars spent by state governments for air quality control. Data include regulatory, administrative, operational, and other activities related to prevention, control and abatement of air pollution.

Source: U.S. Department of Commerce, Bureau of the Census, 1974–1980, *Environmental Quality Control*, State and Local Government Special Studies, Governmental Finances, Washington, DC.

Pollution Abatement Operating Expenditures: Firm-level pollution abatement operating expenditures to abate the media air, water, and solid/contained waste. These data include depreciation, labor, materials, supplies, and services and leasing (excluding payments to government agencies).

Source: U.S. Department of Commerce, Bureau of Census, 1973–1990 (excluding 1987), *Pollution Abatement Costs and Expenditures*, Current Industrial Report, Washington, DC.

Emissions: Emissions of two criteria air pollutants, sulfur dioxide and nitrogen oxides.

Source: U.S. Environmental Protection Agency, Office of Air Quality Planning and Standards, 1929–1994, *National Air Pollutant Emission Trends*, Washington, D.C.

Value-added: Real (1987) value-added by manufacturers.

Source: U.S. Department of Commerce, Bureau of Census, 1973–1990, *Annual Survey of Manufacturers*, Washington, DC.

Per Capita Income: Real (1987) per capita income from 1929–1994.

Source: Bureau of Economic Analysis, U.S. Department of Commerce.

Population Density: Population estimates from 1929–1994. Land area estimates are from 1994.

Source: Bureau of Economic Analysis, U.S. Department of Commerce (population) U.S. Bureau of the Census and TIGER/Geographic Information System (land area).

State Personal Income from Manufacturing/Total State Personal Income: Estimates from 1929–1994.

Source: Bureau of Economics Analysis, U.S. Department of Commerce. http://www.bea.doc.gov./bea/regional/data/htm.

Percent White: Estimated white population divided by total population from 1973–1990.

Source: Bureau of Economic Analysis, U.S. Department of Commerce (population).

© Blackwell Publishers 2000.

APPENDIX B

Probit Estimates—Chemical and Allied Products Sector, Paper and Allied Products Sector, Primary Metals Industry, and Food and Kindred Products Sector (Dependent variable = 1 if abatement expenditures observed; 0 otherwise)

Independent Variable	Estimated Coefficient[a]
CHEMICAL AND ALLIED PRODUCTS SECTOR	
Manufacturing Employment	0.0072
	(9.62)
Constant	−.23
	(−2.29)
Cragg-Uhler R^2	.44
PAPER AND ALLIED PRODUCTS SECTOR	
Manufacturing Employment	0.0040
	(13.9)
Constant	−.84
	(−10.1)
Cragg-Uhler R^2	.49
PRIMARY METALS INDUSTRY	
Manufacturing Employment	0.0035
	(12.6)
Constant	−.76
	(−9.30)
Cragg-Uhler R^2	.43
FOOD AND KINDRED PRODUCTS SECTOR	
Manufacturing Employment	0.0013
	(10.6)
Constant	−.84
	(−6.51)
Cragg-Uhler R^2	.60

[a]t-statistics in parentheses

© Blackwell Publishers 2000.

[18]

VOLUME 115   DECEMBER 2001   NUMBER 2

HARVARD LAW REVIEW

ARTICLE

FEDERALISM AND ENVIRONMENTAL REGULATION: A PUBLIC CHOICE ANALYSIS

Richard L. Revesz

TABLE OF CONTENTS

FEDERALISM AND ENVIRONMENTAL REGULATION:
A PUBLIC CHOICE ANALYSIS

Richard L. Revesz[*]

This Article challenges the influential claim that primary responsibility for environmental regulation should be assigned to the federal government because public choice pathologies cause systematic underrepresentation of environmental interests at the state level. The Article first disputes the theoretical argument by advocates of federal regulation who claim that environmental groups are less disadvantaged at the federal level because of economies of scale in organization. The relevant question, instead, concerns the relative effectiveness of environmental and industry groups at the federal and state levels. The Article casts doubt on the plausibility of the conditions under which federal regulation systematically benefits environmental groups. More generally, the public choice account on which supporters of federal intervention rely views environmental regulation as the product of a clash between environmental interests seeking more stringent standards and industrial interests seeking less stringent standards. This account, however, has little explanatory power. More compelling public choice theories do not point in the direction of federal intervention.

Professor Revesz then musters empirical data to challenge the view that states are ineffective environmental regulators. He shows that before the era of extensive federal involvement, which began in 1970, states had in fact made great strides with respect to those air pollution problems that were reasonably well understood. Moreover, at present, states are undertaking significant environmental protection measures that go well beyond what the federal government requires. The Article attempts to explain why some states have taken the lead with respect to protective environmental measures, while the efforts of other states have lagged. By comparing the regulatory actions of the states with the voting records of their members in the U.S. House of Representatives, it suggests that the differences stem from different levels of preference for environmental protection rather than from public choice pathologies.

INTRODUCTION

The dominant view in the legal academy on the allocation of responsibility for environmental regulation favors federal regulation on the ground that public choice pathologies cause environmental interests to be systematically underrepresented at the state level relative to

* Lawrence King Professor of Law, New York University School of Law. Eric Albert, Aaron Avila, Brian Cuthbertson, Shahzeb Lari, Jennifer Lyons, Daniele Oullette, Elizabeth Rohlfing, Albert Sturtevant, and Elena Zlatnick performed excellent research assistance. I am very grateful for the comments of Barry Friedman, Clayton Gillette, Lewis Kornhauser, and Richard Stewart. A prior version of this Article was presented at workshops at New York University and Stanford University; the comments were extremely helpful. The Filomen D'Agostino and Max E. Greenberg Research Fund at the New York University School of Law provided financial assistance.

business interests.[1] In the past, other arguments for federal regulation also were prominent in the public policy debate: that states would "race to the bottom" by offering industrial sources excessively lax standards[2] and that states would underregulate as a result of interstate ex-

---

[1] See Kirsten H. Engel & Scott R. Saleska, "Facts Are Stubborn Things": An Empirical Reality Check in the Theoretical Debate Over the Race-to-the-Bottom in State Environmental Standard-Setting, 8 CORNELL J.L. & PUB. POL'Y 55, 64 (1998) ("According to the economic theory of regulation, laws tend to respond to the wants of small, cohesive special interest groups, such as industry, at the expense of the wants of the larger, more diffuse public. The public, which is the intended beneficiary of stringent regulation, is often in a weaker political position than industry, which is the primary beneficiary of less regulation." (citation omitted)); Daniel C. Esty, Revitalizing Environmental Federalism, 95 MICH. L. REV. 570, 597–98 (1996) ("Notably, the costs of environmental regulation are generally more concentrated and tangible than the benefits. Costs are often borne by particular industries or enterprises, and are translated readily into monetary terms. Benefits, however, accrue to the general public in ways that are hard to discern and monetize . . . . [T]hese asymmetries may be more significant at the state and local levels . . . ." (footnotes omitted)); Joshua D. Sarnoff, The Continuing Imperative (But Only from a National Perspective) for Federal Environmental Protection, 7 DUKE ENVTL. L. & POL'Y F. 225, 285–86 (1997) ("As a descriptive matter, 'diffuse' environmental interests may be more successful than 'concentrated' compliance interests in affecting legislative and bureaucratic policy at the federal level than at the state level." (footnote omitted)); Richard B. Stewart, Pyramids of Sacrifice? Problems of Federalism in Mandating State Implementation of National Environmental Policy, 86 YALE L.J. 1196, 1213 (1977) ("Industrial firms, developers, unions and others with incentives to avoid environmental controls are typically well-organized economic units with a large stake in particular decisions. The countervailing interest in environmental quality is shared by individuals whose personal stake is small and who face formidable transaction costs in organizing for concerted action."); Peter P. Swire, The Race to Laxity and the Race to Undesirability: Explaining Failures in Competition Among Jurisdictions in Environmental Law, 14 YALE L. & POL'Y REV. & YALE J. ON REG. (SYMPOSIUM ISSUE), 67, 101 (1996) ("For many important environmental issues, regulations impose costs on cohesive industry groups, often led by a few firms facing large compliance costs if a rule is imposed. These industry groups would ordinarily be expected to succeed very well politically against the diffuse individuals who might benefit from environmental controls.").

[2] I challenge the validity of the race-to-the-bottom rationale as an across-the-board argument for federal intervention. See Richard L. Revesz, Rehabilitating Interstate Competition: Rethinking the "Race to the Bottom" Rationale for Federal Environmental Regulation, 67 N.Y.U. L. REV. 1210, 1233–44 (1992) [hereinafter Revesz, Race to the Bottom].

My article spawned a robust critical literature. See Kirsten H. Engel, State Environmental Standard-Setting: Is There a "Race" and Is It "to the Bottom"?, 48 HASTINGS L.J. 271 (1997); Esty, supra note 1; Sarnoff, supra note 1; Swire, supra note 1.

My response appears in Richard L. Revesz, The Race to the Bottom and Federal Environmental Regulation: A Response to Critics, 82 MINN. L. REV. 535 (1997) [hereinafter Revesz, Response to Critics]. For subsequent criticisms, see Engel & Saleska, supra note 1; Joshua D. Sarnoff, A Reply to Professor Revesz's Response in "The Race to the Bottom and Federal Environmental Legislation", 8 DUKE ENVTL. L. & POL'Y F. 295 (1998).

For commentary supporting my position, see, for example, Henry N. Butler & Jonathan R. Macey, Externalities and the Matching Principle: The Case for Reallocating Environmental Regulatory Authority, 14 YALE L. & POL'Y REV. & YALE J. ON REG. (SYMPOSIUM ISSUE) 23, 31 n.19, 42–45 (1996); James E. Krier, On the Topology of Uniform Environmental Standards in a Federal System — And Why It Matters, 54 MD. L. REV. 1226, 1236–37 (1995); Richard B. Stewart, Environmental Regulation and International Competitiveness, 102 YALE L.J. 2039, 2058–59 (1993) [hereinafter Stewart, Environmental Regulation]; Richard B. Stewart, International Trade and Environment: Lessons from the Federal Experience, 49 WASH. & LEE L. REV. 1329, 1343–44

ternalities.[3] In recent years, however, these arguments have somewhat receded from prominence, and proponents of federal environmental regulation have focused on the public choice justification.[4]

This Article refutes the orthodox view concerning the merits of centralized environmental regulation. It shows that the normative analysis underpinning this view is inadequate and presents extensive empirical evidence undercutting the orthodoxy's claims.

The analysis in this Article should interest the principal actors in the regulatory process. For example, to the extent that environmental groups come to understand that federal regulation is not a panacea, they will more effectively focus their energies at the state level. In addition, they will be able to mitigate two increasingly negative features of federal regulation: the threat of federal preemption of more stringent state standards[5] and the unsympathetic reception that their arguments tend to get in the D.C. Circuit, which has primary responsibility for the review of federal environmental policy.[6]

The current administration seems committed to pushing for significant decentralization of environmental regulation.[7] In addition, the

---

(1992) [hereinafter Stewart, *Lessons from the Federal Experience*];´ Stephen Williams, *Panel IV: Culpability, Restitution, and the Environment: The Vitality of Common Law Rules*, 21 ECOLOGY L.Q. 559, 560–61 (1994).

[3] I have analyzed the interstate externality justification for federal environmental regulation. *See* Richard L. Revesz, *Federalism and Interstate Environmental Externalities*, 144 U. PA. L. REV. 2341 (1996). The presence of interstate externalities is a compelling argument for federal regulation. For large-scale and complex environmental problems, such as air pollution covering a large area, Coasian bargaining is unlikely because uncertainty about pollution's geographic impact bars transactions. Moreover, depending on the source of pollution, the range of affected states will vary; this shifting composition of affected states makes cooperation even less likely.

The federal environmental statutes, however, have been generally ineffective at constraining interjurisdictional spillovers. They are overinclusive because they require states to reduce pollution that has only in-state consequences. *See id.* at 2350. They are also underinclusive because a state can meet the applicable ambient and emissions standards and still export a great deal of pollution to other jurisdictions. *Id.* In fact, the federal statutes have created incentives for states to do so: externalization gives them a competitive advantage by enabling them to attract more sources while ensuring that downwind states can attract fewer sources as a result of the federal regulatory constraint. *Id.* at 2352. A powerful illustration of the federal standards' perverse effect is that in the fifteen years following the enactment of the Clean Air Act the use of tall stacks — permitting greater externalization of the adverse effects of air pollution — expanded considerably. *Id.* at 2353. Whereas in 1970 only two stacks in the United States were higher than 500 feet, by 1985 more than 180 stacks were higher than 500 feet, and twenty-three were higher than 1000 feet. *Id.*

[4] *See* Revesz, *Response to Critics, supra* note 2, at 558–61.

[5] For recent literature on preemption, see Stephen A. Gardbaum, *The Nature of Preemption*, 79 CORNELL L. REV. 767 (1994); Caleb Nelson, *Preemption*, 86 VA. L. REV. 225 (2000).

[6] *See* Richard L. Revesz, *Environmental Regulation, Ideology, and the D.C. Circuit*, 83 VA. L. REV. 1717, 1717 n.1 (1997).

[7] *See* Mike Allen, *Bush Pushes Local Control of Conservation Matters*, WASH. POST, May 31, 2001, at A2; Mike Allen & Dan Balz, *Bush Unveils 'New Federalism'*, WASH. POST, Feb. 27, 2001, at A10; Douglas Jehl, *Whitman Promises Latitude to States on Pollution Rules*, N.Y.

Supreme Court's recent federalism jurisprudence is likely to constrain the federal government's regulatory authority.[8] This Article provides a metric by which to assess these emerging developments.

Part I addresses the arguments that environmental groups are relatively more disadvantaged at the state level. It contends that these arguments are not grounded in plausible accounts of public choice and lack empirical support. Most importantly, such accounts fail to explain why there is any environmental regulation at all, either at the state or the federal level. Moreover, even the more plausible public choice explanations do not establish that federal intervention is necessary to compensate for systematic underregulation at the state level.

Part II takes issue with the claim, used as evidence of public choice problems at the state level, that states were inadequate environmental regulators before the era of extensive federal intervention that began in 1970. Instead, during this period, states and municipalities took significant steps to combat those environmental problems that were reasonably well understood at the time.

Part III illustrates how the states have taken the lead, particularly in the 1990s, in attacking by various means a number of important environmental problems. Such state initiatives include automobile emissions standards, hazardous waste regulations, municipal solid waste regulations, requirements for the preparation of environmental impact statements contained in state environmental policy acts, and duty-to-warn measures.

Part IV evaluates this pattern of state environmental action. It shows that the federal government has implemented relatively few environmental initiatives. Instead, innovative approaches have come primarily from the state level, with a number of states taking actions that go well beyond federal requirements. The resulting pattern belies the claim that federal intervention is necessary to correct public choice pathologies at the state level. It suggests that differences in preferences for environmental improvements across the states more plausibly explain why certain states adopt more stringent regulations than do others.

This Article does not make a general claim against allocating responsibility for environmental regulation at the federal level. Quite to the contrary, as I explain elsewhere, there are compelling reasons for federal environmental regulation in certain contexts.[9] Instead, my aim

---

TIMES, Jan. 18, 2001, at A18; Robert Pear, *Shifting of Power from Washington Is Seen Under Bush*, N.Y. TIMES, Jan. 7, 2001, at 1; Eric Pianin, *Free-Market Environmentalists Gaining Stature*, WASH. POST, June 4, 2001, at A4; David M. Shribman, *Yes, It Matters*, BOSTON GLOBE, Mar. 18, 2001, at H1.

[8] *See, e.g.*, Solid Waste Agency v. U.S. Army Corps of Eng'rs, 121 S. Ct. 675 (2001).

[9] *See* Revesz, *Response to Critics*, *supra* note 2, at 543–45.

here is limited to questioning the dominant role of the public choice justification.

I. INTEREST GROUPS AND THE DEMAND FOR ENVIRONMENTAL REGULATION

This Part deals with the argument that underregulation at the state level results from the discrepancies in resources and organizational structures between the environmental groups seeking more stringent regulation and the industry groups seeking less stringent regulation. The discussion is thus demand-based. It considers the pressures that groups interested in the stringency of environmental regulation place on the suppliers of such regulation: legislatures and administrative agencies.[10]

Section A addresses the central argument of advocates of federal environmental regulation on public choice grounds: that, as a result of economies of scale in organization, environmental groups are less disadvantaged at the federal than at the state level. In turn, section B explains that these public choice arguments — under which regulation is the product of a clash between environmental and business interests — rely on implausible accounts of public choice. It then shows that even more plausible accounts do not support the claim of underregulation at the state level.

A. Assessing the Conventional Theory

1. Articulation of the Public Choice Claim. — The dominant claim among supporters of federal regulation on public choice grounds is that states adopt suboptimally lax environmental standards because industry groups that favor less stringent regulation are small and cohesive, whereas individuals who support more stringent regulation are a larger and more diffuse group.[11] Underregulation thus follows from a central tenet of public choice theory, generally traced to Mancur Olson's influential work.[12]

Some commentators do not explain, however, why these public choice problems would be any less serious at the federal level.[13] Oth-

---

[10] For a categorization of public choice accounts into demand and supply components, see Nathaniel O. Keohane, Richard L. Revesz & Robert N. Stavins, *The Choice of Regulatory Instruments in Environmental Policy*, 22 HARV. ENVTL. L. REV. 313 (1998).

[11] *See* sources cited *supra* note 1.

[12] *See* MANCUR OLSON, THE LOGIC OF COLLECTIVE ACTION: PUBLIC GOODS AND THE THEORY OF GROUPS 5–65 (1971) [hereinafter OLSON, THE LOGIC OF COLLECTIVE ACTION]; MANCUR OLSON, THE RISE AND DECLINE OF NATIONS: ECONOMIC GROWTH, STAGFLATION, AND SOCIAL RIGIDITIES 17–35 (1982) [hereinafter OLSON, THE RISE AND DECLINE OF NATIONS].

[13] *See* Engel & Saleska, *supra* note 1, at 64–65; Swire, *supra* note 1, at 101.

ers acknowledge that advocates of federal regulation on public choice grounds cannot simply say that state political processes undervalue the benefits of environmental regulation or overvalue the corresponding costs.[14] Instead, for the outcome at the federal level to be more socially desirable, either there must be less underregulation at the federal level, or any overregulation that occurs at the federal level must lead to smaller social welfare losses than underregulation at the state level.

A number of commentators assert that there would be less underregulation at the federal level. Daniel Esty states that "[a]t the centralized level, environmental groups find it easier to reach critical mass and thereby to compete on more equal footing with industrial interests."[15] He adds that "[t]he difficulty of mobilizing the public in many separate jurisdictions is well established."[16] Along similar lines, Richard Stewart states:

> In order to have effective influence with respect to state and local decisions, environmental interests would be required to organize on a multiple basis, incurring overwhelming transaction costs. Given such barriers, environmental interests can exert far more leverage by organizing into one or a few units at the national level.[17]

Stewart acknowledges that "[c]entralized decisionmaking may imply similar scale economies for industrial firms," although he says that "these are likely to be of lesser magnitude — particularly if such firms are already national in scope."[18] He adds that "effective representation may be less a function of comparative resources than of attainment of a critical mass of skills, resources, and experience. . . . [A] national forum for decision may greatly lessen the barriers to environmental interests' achievement of organizational critical mass, sharply reducing the disparity in effective representation."[19] Likewise, according to Joshua Sarnoff, "'diffuse' environmental interests may be more successful than 'concentrated' compliance interests in affecting legislative and bureaucratic policy at the federal level than at the state level. The relative degree of political success results from economies of scale and reduced transaction costs for organizing and lobbying."[20]

2. Mancur Olson and the Logic of Collective Action. — There are several reasons to be skeptical about the soundness of these general claims. Indeed, the starting point for Mancur Olson's analysis[21] — on which some advocates of the public choice justification for federal

---

[14] *See* Esty, *supra* note 1, at 649–51; Stewart, *supra* note 1, at 1213–14.

[15] Esty, *supra* note 1, at 650 n.302.

[16] *Id.* at 650–51.

[17] Stewart, *supra* note 1, at 1213.

[18] *Id.* at 1213–14.

[19] *Id.* at 1214. He adds that there may also be economies of scale in fundraising. *Id.*

[20] Sarnoff, *supra* note 1, at 285–86.

[21] *See* sources cited *supra* note 12.

regulation rely without much evaluation[22] — implies that acting at the federal level magnifies the free-rider problems that environmental groups face.

In fact, as an initial matter, Olson is skeptical of the feasibility of organizing any groups, regardless of size. He notes that "any group or organization, large or small, works for some collective benefit that by its very nature will benefit all of the members of the group in question."[23] An individual understands, however, that if the other members pay for the collective benefit, this benefit will be provided regardless whether he pays for it as well. But if the other members do not pay, the benefit will not be provided regardless whether the individual pays for it. Under either scenario, then, the individual is better off not paying for the collective benefit.[24] Thus, the logic of collective action establishes that a rational individual will not contribute to the formation of groups that provide collective benefits, at least not under a wide range of circumstances.

Olson underscores that this problem is common to both large and small groups:

> If this is a fundamental characteristic of all groups or organizations with an economic purpose, it would seem unlikely that large organizations would be much different from small ones, and unlikely that there is any more reason that a collective service would be provided for a small group than a large one.[25]

Although these problems are common to both small and large groups, Olson is more hopeful that a small group can provide a collective benefit. In small groups, Olson observes, it is more likely that one member can gain sufficient utility to justify the cost of paying for the benefit by himself.[26] Such an outcome is more likely when the potential members are unequally interested in the collective good.[27]

Olson also explains why other members of a small group might contribute to the provision of collective goods. He observes that collective goods are likely to have high initial or fixed costs: "Sometimes a group must set up a formal organization before it can obtain a collective good, and the cost of establishing an organization entails that the

---

[22] *See* Engel & Saleska, *supra* note 1, at 64; Sarnoff, *supra* note 1, at 286; Swire, *supra* note 1, at 101.

[23] OLSON, THE LOGIC OF COLLECTIVE ACTION, *supra* note 12, at 21.

[24] *See id.* As Olson explained in a later book: "Since any gain goes to everyone in the group, those who contribute nothing to the effort will get just as much as those who made a contribution. It pays to 'let George do it,' but George has little or no incentive to do anything in the group interest either . . . ." OLSON, THE RISE AND DECLINE OF NATIONS, *supra* note 12, at 18.

[25] OLSON, THE LOGIC OF COLLECTIVE ACTION, *supra* note 12, at 21.

[26] *Id.* at 22.

[27] *Id.*

first unit of a collective good obtained will be relatively expensive."[28] If a member with a large stake in the outcome is willing to pay for the fixed costs (in addition to some variable costs), members with smaller stakes might decide, given their interest in the collective benefit, to contribute to the additional variable costs.

Nonetheless, it is unlikely that even small groups would provide the optimal amount. At the point at which the optimal amount of the collective good is provided, the marginal cost of providing the good is equal to the marginal benefit obtained by the group's members. That is, the cost of an additional unit of a good must be equal to the benefit derived from that unit. For a group to provide the optimal amount of the good, however, the marginal cost and benefit must be equal not only for the group as a whole, but also for each of its members. Any member facing a marginal cost higher than his marginal benefit would not find it in his interest to contribute to the provision of the good. As Olson explains, "there is no conceivable cost-sharing arrangement in which *some* member does not have a marginal cost greater than his share of the marginal benefit, except the one in which every member of the group shares marginal costs in exactly the same proportion in which he shares incremental benefits."[29] Thus, Olson concludes that "groups with larger numbers of members will generally perform less efficiently than groups with smaller numbers of members,"[30] and "the larger the group, the farther it will fall short of providing an optimal amount of a collective good."[31]

Olson devotes some effort to explaining the existence of some large groups given the implication of his theory that "individuals in a large group have no incentive to organize a lobby to obtain a collective benefit."[32] He argues that large groups will be able to provide collective benefits only under two conditions: if they have the ability to coerce their members into paying dues, as do unions or certain professional associations; or if they provide noncollective benefits, such as magazine subscriptions or recreational activities, exclusively to group members.[33] But in providing these explanations, which themselves have been the subject of criticism,[34] Olson does not undercut his central claim that small groups are likely to perform better in the political process.

---

[28] *Id.*

[29] *Id.* at 31.

[30] *Id.* at 28.

[31] *Id.* at 35 (emphasis omitted); *see id.* at 31; Steven P. Croley, *Theories of Regulation: Incorporating the Administrative Process*, 98 COLUM. L. REV. 1, 13–15 (1998).

[32] OLSON, THE LOGIC OF COLLECTIVE ACTION, *supra* note 12, at 132.

[33] *See id.* at 132–34.

[34] *See infra* section I.A.3, pp. 563–65.

Therefore, contrary to the assertions of those who espouse the public choice rationale in support of federal environmental regulation, the theory of collective action does not predict greater success for environmental groups at the federal level. Much the opposite: it suggests that, given the necessarily larger size of groups acting at the federal level, groups will in fact be less effective there than at the state level.

Moreover, the national aggregation of environmental interests results in the loss of homogeneity of interests, thereby further complicating organizational problems.[35] For example, environmentalists in Massachusetts may care primarily about air quality, whereas environmentalists in Colorado may care more about limitations on logging on public lands. Other things being equal, state-based environmental groups seeking, respectively, better air quality in Massachusetts and more protection of public lands in Colorado are likely to be more effective than a national environmental group seeking both improvements at the federal level.

Olson sheds light on this question as well. He discusses the case of a "'federal' group," which he describes as "a group divided into a number of small groups, each of which has a reason to join with the others to form a federation representing the large group as a whole."[36] But such a federation would be effective only to the extent that the state groups had common interests. Olson explains that "socially heterogeneous groups ... are less likely to agree on the exact nature of whatever collective good is at issue or on how much of it is worth buying."[37] As a result, when such heterogeneity is present, "collective action can become still less likely."[38] For this reason, the geographic heterogeneity of environmental interests adversely affects the national aggregation of those interests.

   3. Beyond Olson's Theory. — Although academics advocating federal regulation on public choice grounds rely heavily on Olson's theory,[39] his work does not explain convincingly why large environmental groups exist at all. Unlike professional associations, environmental groups cannot coerce their members to pay dues.[40] They can, however, provide such noncollective benefits as magazine subscriptions

---

[35] *See* JACK L. WALKER, JR., MOBILIZING INTEREST GROUPS IN AMERICA 66 (1991) ("It is generally more difficult for potential groups with highly decentralized constituents to organize and speak with one voice in Washington, D.C."). A number of important environmental groups, such as the Sierra Club, the Natural Resources Defense Council, and Environmental Defense, work for disparate causes and thus may suffer because of the need to aggregate disparate interests.

[36] OLSON, THE LOGIC OF COLLECTIVE ACTION, *supra* note 12, at 63.

[37] OLSON, THE RISE AND DECLINE OF NATIONS, *supra* note 12, at 24.

[38] *Id.*

[39] *See* sources cited *supra* note 22.

[40] *See supra* p. 562.

and recreational activities. But this explanation has been the subject of strong criticism: for the noncollective benefit to fund the collective benefit, the price charged for the former must be excessively high. A firm that did not also attempt to provide the collective benefit could provide the noncollective benefit more cheaply: "To put the question in concrete terms, if members of Common Cause contribute to that group's lobbying activities simply because it buys them *Common Cause Magazine*, why would not some other, comparable magazine, not tied to any lobbying activities, be supplied to that group's membership at a lower price?"[41]

More recent works have focused on two other explanations for the existence of large groups.[42] One explanation takes issue with Olson's conclusion that members of large groups have a smaller incentive to contribute to the provision of the collective good because they get a smaller share of the benefit.[43] Olson's critics argue that this conclusion does not hold in the case of pure public goods — that is, goods that can be enjoyed by one member without reducing another member's enjoyment.[44] The technical literature shows that for pure public goods the amount of the good supplied may increase as the number of members in the group rises.[45] To achieve this result, however, there must be at least one member in the group willing to contribute to the collective good even if nobody else does. Because of that person's large stake in the outcome, it would not be in his interest to free-ride.[46] Russell Hardin, who has extended Olson's analysis, concludes that this condition is not met in the case of "virtually every large-scale political group that seeks a costly good whose value to each member of the group is a small fraction of its cost."[47]

---

[41] Croley, *supra* note 31, at 18 n.44. A study of major environmental organizations found that selective inducements do not play a large role in influencing the decisions of individuals to join such organizations. *See* Robert Cameron Mitchell, *National Environmental Lobbies and the Apparent Illogic of Collective Action, in* COLLECTIVE DECISION MAKING: APPLICATIONS FROM PUBLIC CHOICE THEORY 87, 105–12 (Clifford S. Russell ed., 1979).

[42] For this further extension of Olson's approach, see V. Kerry Smith, *A Theoretical Analysis of the "Green Lobby"*, 79 AM. POL. SCI. REV. 132 (1985).

[43] *See* OLSON, THE LOGIC OF COLLECTIVE ACTION, *supra* note 12, at 48.

[44] *See* GERALD MARWELL & PAMELA OLIVER, THE CRITICAL MASS IN COLLECTIVE ACTION: A MICRO-SOCIAL THEORY 41, 45–48 (1993); Croley, *supra* note 31, at 16.

[45] *See* John Chamberlin, *Provision of Collective Goods as a Function of Group Size*, 68 AM. POL. SCI. REV. 707, 712 (1974); Martin C. McGuire, *Group Size, Group Homogeneity, and the Aggregate Provision of a Pure Public Good Under Cournot Behavior*, PUB. CHOICE, Summer 1974, at 107, 109, 112; Lars Udéhn, *Twenty-Five Years with* The Logic of Collective Action, 36 ACTA SOCIOLOGICA 239, 241–42 (1993).

[46] *See* RUSSELL HARDIN, COLLECTIVE ACTION 127 (1982).

[47] *Id.* at 130.

A number of important environmental organizations, however, began with significant support from foundations.[48] These foundations may therefore have played the role of the group member willing to contribute to the provision of the collective benefit regardless of the actions of individual members.

A second explanation for the existence of large groups focuses on the moral motivations of group members.[49] Hardin maintains, for example, that "the bulk of the Sierra Club's political activity is supported by public-spirited donations that are not tied to reciprocal exclusive rewards to the donors," and that one cannot "sensibly construct rational arguments for individual contributions to Sierra Club political activities, at least not rational in the sense of narrowly self-interested."[50]

These extensions of Olson's work may explain the existence of environmental groups. They do not, however, suggest (much less establish) a public choice explanation for why environmental groups would do better at the federal level. Once one explains how environmental groups come into being at all, one needs to compare the effects of centralization on the relative strengths of environmental and industry groups — a question taken up in the following section.

4. Effects of Centralization on the Relative Effectiveness of Industry and Environmental Groups. — Advocates of federal environmental regulation who advance the public choice rationale must deal not only with the question whether environmental groups would be effective at the state or federal level, but also, and more importantly, with the question of how the effectiveness of environmental groups in these two fora compares to the effectiveness of the regulated community in re-

---

[48] *See* Paul B. Downing & Gordon L. Brady, *The Role of Citizen Interest Groups in Environmental Policy Formation, in* NONPROFIT FIRMS IN A THREE SECTOR ECONOMY 61, 72–73, 76 (Michelle J. White ed., 1981); R. Shep Melnick, *Strange Bedfellows Make Normal Politics: An Essay,* 9 DUKE ENVTL. L. & POL'Y F. 75, 81 (1998); Mitchell, *supra* note 41, at 99. For a discussion of foundations' influence on environmental groups, see generally Robert Charles Lowry, The Political Economy of Environmental Citizen Groups 89–166 (1993) (unpublished Ph.D. dissertation, Harvard University) (on file with the Harvard Law School Library).

A general survey of citizen groups found that 89% of them used aid from nonmembers, including foundations, to start their operations. WALKER, *supra* note 35, at 78. Even after a citizen group's formation, foundations continue to play an important financial role. *See id.* at 82. For example, in 1996, 71.27% of the revenues of Friends of the Earth came from foundations. *See* FRIENDS OF THE EARTH, 1996 ANNUAL REPORT 15 (1997).

[49] *See* HARDIN, *supra* note 46, at 104–06; Croley, *supra* note 31, at 20. For an extensive analysis of environmental groups consistent with this view, see Helen M. Ingram & Dean E. Mann, *Interest Groups and Environmental Policy, in* ENVIRONMENTAL POLITICS AND POLICY 135 (James P. Lester ed., 1989). For a supportive case study, see Steven M. Davis, *Environmental Politics and the Changing Context of Interest Group Organization,* 33 SOC. SCI. J. 343, 351–53 (1996).

[50] *See* HARDIN, *supra* note 46, at 105.

sisting their efforts. Public choice advocates largely ignore this question.[51]

For many environmental problems, firms with nationwide operations comprise an important portion of the regulated community.[52] For such firms, participation in the policymaking process at the federal level does not give rise to any additional free-rider problems or to any reduction in the homogeneity of the relevant interests. Moreover, many industries are sufficiently concentrated that either one or a small number of firms is able to dominate a national trade association, thereby solving the free-rider problem that normally exists when trade associations represent the interests of member firms.[53] As Olson himself notes, the national trade associations representing industrial interests are often dominated by a few large firms.[54] For example, Olson reports that in the lumber, furniture, and paper industries, 37.3% of the trade associations had a membership of fewer than twenty firms, and that the median membership ranged from twenty-five to fifty.[55]

Moreover, the decisionmaking authority in trade associations is not evenly distributed among its members. Typically, the extent to which a member controls an association's actions is linked to the member's contribution level.[56] Olson reports a study showing that in almost half the trade associations, "nearly 50 per cent of the cost is borne by a handful of members."[57] In the National Association of Manufacturers, for example, "[a]bout 5 per cent of the membership contribute about half the money."[58] As a result, "[a]bout eight tenths of one per cent of [its] members . . . have held 63 per cent of all directorships."[59]

In contrast, environmental groups face additional collective action problems at the federal level.[60] The relevant inquiry is whether these additional problems are outweighed by the benefits of unity and uniformity in the federal forum. Indeed, at the federal level the clash between interest groups takes place before a single legislature, before a single administrative agency, and, in part as a result of the exclusive venue of the D.C. Circuit over important environmental statutes, before a single court.[61]

---

[51] *See supra* pp. 559–60.

[52] The automobile industry is a prominent example. Large chemical and oil companies also have nationwide operations.

[53] *See* Keohane, Revesz & Stavins, *supra* note 10, at 332.

[54] *See* OLSON, THE LOGIC OF COLLECTIVE ACTION, *supra* note 12, at 143–46.

[55] *See id.* at 144.

[56] *See id.* at 145, 147.

[57] *Id.* at 145 (quoting V.O. KEY, POLITICS, PARTIES, AND PRESSURE GROUPS 96 (1958)) (internal quotation marks omitted).

[58] *Id.* at 147.

[59] *Id.*

[60] *See supra* p. 563.

[61] *See* Revesz, *supra* note 6, at 1717.

If one assumes that, beyond a certain threshold, additional resources do not increase a group's probability of success in the political
process, and that, at the federal level, this threshold is sufficiently
lower than the sum of the corresponding thresholds at the state levels,
environmental groups may not be disadvantaged at the federal level
even if they would be disadvantaged at the state level. In this case,
the economies of scale of operating at the federal level would outweigh
the increased collective action problems.

The assumptions behind such a model, however, are not particularly plausible. The threshold concept might hold for certain costs associated with effective participation in the regulatory process. For example, with respect to the regulation of a particular carcinogen, each
group might need to hire a scientist to review the regulator's risk assessment. A certain minimum expenditure may secure the services of
a competent scientist, and devoting additional resources to the problem
may be of little, if any, use. Thus, for costs of this type, the marginal
benefit of additional expenditures is zero, or close to zero, regardless of
the expenditures of the group seeking the opposite policy outcome.

However, additional resources also make it possible for concentrated industry interests to participate in more proceedings than do
dispersed consumer and environmental interests. A number of studies,
collected by Steven Croley, all point in this direction.[62] An extensive
report published in 1977 by the Senate Committee on Governmental
Affairs found that organizations purporting to represent the public interest participated in a far smaller number of regulatory proceedings
than did the regulated industries.[63] In the specific context of environmental regulation, a recent study conducted by Cary Coglianese found,
in rulemakings under the Resource Conservation and Recovery Act,[64]
that regulated businesses participated in 96% of the proceedings and
trade associations representing such firms participated in 80%. In
sharp contrast, environmental and citizen groups participated in only
12% of the proceedings.[65]

But even if the costs of effective participation in the regulatory
process were consistent with the threshold model, the structure of
other costs is likely to be quite different. For example, with respect to
success in the legislative process, a standard public choice account is

---

[62] *See* Croley, *supra* note 31, at 126–41.

[63] *See id.* at 126–27.

[64] 42 U.S.C. §§ 6901–6992k (1994 & Supp. IV 1998). The Act governs hazardous and solid
waste disposal.

[65] *See* Cary Coglianese, Challenging the Rules: Litigation and Bargaining in the Administrative Process 46–47 (1994) (unpublished Ph.D. dissertation, University of Michigan) (on file with
the Harvard Law School Library).

that the highest bidder prevails.[66] Thus, the benefit a party receives from its expenditures is a function of the other party's expenditures. Unless the costs of this type are quite small, the economies of scale of operating at the federal level are unlikely to outweigh the additional collective action problems that exist in the larger forum.

Even under more sophisticated models of the political process, the quantity of resources expended in securing favorable legislation matters. For example, Arthur Denzau and Michael Munger developed a model in which the price at which legislators will supply a policy depends in part on the distaste of voters for that policy.[67] Thus, the more distasteful the policy, the more resources legislators demand. But under this model, as under the simpler auction model, an interest group can increase its probability of success by expending additional resources. Thus, this account is inconsistent with the threshold model that underpins the public choice rationale for federal environmental regulation.

5. *A Path-Dependent Explanation for the Relative Strength of Environmental Groups at the Federal and State Levels.* — Warren Ratliff makes the path-dependent argument that, currently, national groups are strong and state groups are weak. He posits that, as a result, devolution of regulatory authority to the states would have the effect of weakening the environmental movement.[68] Ratliff recognizes that the start-up costs are smaller for local groups[69] and asks "if it is easier to found environmental groups at the local level, wouldn't devolution actually help environmental organizers?"[70] He then indicates that "[t]he answer to this question might have been 'yes' thirty years ago, when national environmental groups were virtually non-existent"[71] but suggests that the answer today should be "no" because of "the relative weakness of current state environmental groups compared to their national counterparts."[72] As a result, devolution would give rise to the need for state-level groups to expend large start-up costs.[73]

Ratliff's account that environmental organizations are primarily organized at the national level and that state-based organizations are

---

[66] *See* Sam Peltzman, *Toward a More General Theory of Regulation*, 19 J.L. & ECON. 211, 212 (1976); George J. Stigler, *The Theory of Economic Regulation*, 2 BELL J. ECON. & MGMT. SCI. 3, 12–13 (1971). For more discussion of this issue, see Keohane, Revesz & Stavins, *supra* note 10, at 320.

[67] *See* Arthur T. Denzau & Michael C. Munger, *Legislators and Interest Groups: How Unorganized Interests Get Represented*, 80 AM. POL. SCI. REV. 89, 99 (1986).

[68] *See* Warren L. Ratliff, *The De-Evolution of Environmental Organization*, 17 J. LAND RESOURCES & ENVTL. L. 45, 45–46 (1997).

[69] *See id.* at 62.

[70] *Id.* at 63.

[71] *Id.*

[72] *Id.* at 64.

[73] *See id.* at 71.

either nonexistent or largely ineffective bears little relationship to reality. Three observations are particularly relevant.

First, a survey of the ten major environmental organizations revealed that they tend to be federations of state chapters, as Olson's analysis suggests,[74] or have significant regional presences. For example, the Sierra Club is divided into sixty-eight chapters in the United States and Canada.[75] The Wilderness Society has eight regional offices.[76] Environmental Defense has six offices and two additional project offices.[77] The National Wildlife Federation has eleven regional field offices and forty-six state and territorial affiliates;[78] it describes itself as the "most 'local' national conservation group."[79] The National Audubon Society is made up of eighteen regional and state offices and 508 chapters in the United States, Canada, and Latin America.[80] The group plans to have offices in all fifty states; its annual report states that "[c]ommunity-based conservation has always been at the heart of the Audubon movement and . . . will be the prime mover of the conservation movement of the 21st Century."[81] Friends of the Earth has a field office in Seattle in addition to its national headquarters; it undertakes projects in conjunction with local environmental organizations.[82] The National Resources Defense Council has its headquarters in New York and field offices in Washington, D.C., San Francisco, and Los Angeles.[83] The National Parks and Conservation Association has eight regional offices.[84] The Nature Conservancy has nine regional offices and fifty-five field offices; it engages in land acquisition projects in each of the fifty states.[85] Ducks Unlimited has representatives in every state.[86]

Moreover, the local and regional offices of these national environmental groups enjoy increasing decisionmaking authority. For example, a recent study finds that "[t]he National Wildlife Federation, for

---

[74] *See* OLSON, THE LOGIC OF COLLECTIVE ACTION, *supra* note 12, at 63.

[75] *See* Sierra Club, *Sierra Club Chapters, at* http://www.sierraclub.org/chapters (last visited Nov. 6, 2001).

[76] *See* WILDERNESS SOC'Y, 1996 ANNUAL REPORT 25.

[77] *See* ENVTL. DEF. FUND, 2000 ANNUAL REPORT, at inside front cover (listing office locations), *available at* http://www.environmentaldefense.org/pubs/AnnualReport/2000.

[78] National Wildlife Federation, *How the National Wildlife Federation Works, at* http://www.nwf.org/about/how.html (last visited Nov. 6, 2001).

[79] *See* NAT'L WILDLIFE FED'N, 1997 ANNUAL REPORT 2.

[80] *See* NAT'L AUDUBON SOC'Y, 1997 ANNUAL REPORT 29–32.

[81] *Id.* at 15.

[82] *See* Friends of the Earth, *Friends of the Earth US — Northwest Office, at* http://www.foe.org/foenw (last visited Nov. 6, 2001).

[83] *See* NAT'L RES. DEF. COUNCIL, 1996 ANNUAL REPORT 34.

[84] NAT'L PARKS & CONSERVATION ASS'N, 1997 ANNUAL REPORT 5.

[85] *See* NATURE CONSERVANCY, 1997 ANNUAL REPORT 20-37, 56.

[86] *See* DUCKS UNLIMITED, 1997 ANNUAL REPORT ON OPERATIONS 39.

one, candidly acknowledges that with habitat conservation programs now dominant in endangered species policy, decision-making authority has already shifted from the center to localities."[87]   The study concludes that "[n]o longer able to influence the substantive rules directly, the national organizations must instead work to ensure a deeply participatory local process."[88]

Second, in addition to the national environmental organizations, active state and local organizations are taking the lead on a number of important environmental issues. In particular, the environmental justice movement is made up of a large number of advocacy groups concerned with issues such as the location and cleanup of hazardous waste sites.[89] A study by Robert Lowry found that these local groups have different outlooks than their national counterparts. For example, they are not comfortable with technocratic solutions and tend to view environmental problems in moral terms.[90]   More importantly, these groups strongly favor community-level action.   As Luke Cole, a prominent environmental justice advocate puts it: "The question of where — at what level of government — environmental decisions should be made is one which has been answered clearly and decisively by the Environmental Justice Movement: at the community level."[91] That such groups, which first emerged in the early 1980s,[92] now have considerable impact on public policy is strong evidence against Ratliff's thesis.

Third, over the last decade, the center of gravity of environmental organizations has shifted away from the national level. Trends in the allocation of foundation grants to environmental organizations reflect this shift. I compared foundation grants made for environmental purposes in 1996 with those made in 1989, the earliest year for which adequate data were available.[93] Table 1 shows how the 100 largest

---

[87] Charles Sabel, Archon Fung & Bradley Karkkainen, *Beyond Backyard Environmentalism: How Communities Are Quietly Refashioning Environmental Regulation*, BOSTON REV., Oct./Nov. 1999, at 4, 11; *see also id.* (referring to the "largely self-directed chapters of the Nature Conservancy").

[88] *Id.*

[89] *See* Robert C. Lowry, *All Hazardous Waste Politics Is Local: Grass-roots Advocacy and Public Participation in Siting and Cleanup Decisions*, 26 POL'Y STUD. J. 748, 751 (1998). For a discussion on the genesis of the environmental justice movement, see Lisa A. Binder, *Religion, Race, and Rights: A Rhetorical Overview of Environmental Justice Disputes*, 6 WIS. ENVTL. L.J. 1, 4–8 (1999).

[90] *See* Lowry, *supra* note 89, at 752.

[91] Luke W. Cole, *The Theory and Reality of Community-Based Environmental Decisionmaking: The Failure of California's Tanner Act and Its Implications for Environmental Justice*, 25 ECOLOGY L.Q. 733, 733–34 (1999).

[92] *See* Lowry, *supra* note 89, at 751.

[93] The research was conducted on the Foundation Grants Index, a Dialog database available through Westlaw.

grants given in each of these years were allocated between national organizations on the one hand and regional, state, and local organizations on the other.

TABLE 1. ALLOCATION OF THE 100 LARGEST ENVIRONMENTAL GRANTS MADE BY FOUNDATIONS (IN MILLIONS OF DOLLARS)

	National	Regional/ State/Local	Education/ Research	International
1996	25.018	77.358	22.571	11.207
1989	31.607	23.786	12.238	18.390

This table shows that whereas funds allocated to national organizations comprised 57.1% of total national, regional, state, and local grants in 1989, their share fell to 24.4% in 1996. The confidence shown in regional, state, and local organizations by the grant officers of major foundations suggests, contrary to Ratliff's claim, that such groups not only exist but also succeed.

B. Toward More Plausible Public Choice Accounts of Environmental Regulation

The public choice arguments advocating federal environmental regulation have a serious problem.[94] Indeed, the logic of collective action suggests that the small number of concentrated industrial interests, each having a large stake in the outcome of a particular standard-setting proceeding, will overwhelm the large number of environmentally conscious citizens, each having a relatively small stake in the outcome.[95] This disadvantage would exist at the federal as well as at the state level. In fact, the logic of collective action makes it difficult to explain why there is any environmental regulation at all.[96]

The more plausible public choice explanations for the existence of environmental regulation proceed along altogether different lines. The following five sections discuss the most compelling of these theories.

---

[94] *See supra* section I.A.1, pp. 559–60 (describing the public choice arguments for federal environmental regulation).

[95] Revesz, *Response to Critics, supra* note 2, at 542; *see also* JERRY L. MASHAW, GREED, CHAOS AND GOVERNANCE: USING PUBLIC CHOICE TO IMPROVE PUBLIC LAW 32–33 (1997); Daniel A. Farber, *Politics and Procedure in Environmental Law*, 8 J.L. ECON. & ORG. 59, 60 (1992); Melnick, *supra* note 48, at 75–76; Robert V. Percival, *Environmental Legislation and the Problem of Collective Action*, 9 DUKE ENVTL. L. & POL'Y F. 9, 9–10 (1998); Christopher H. Schroeder, *Rational Choice Versus Republican Moment — Explanations for Environmental Laws, 1969–73*, 9 DUKE ENVTL. L. & POL'Y F. 29, 29–30 (1998); Peter H. Schuck, *Against (and for) Madison: An Essay in Praise of Factions*, 15 YALE L. & POL'Y REV. 553, 566 (1997); Richard B. Stewart, *Environmental Quality as a National Good in a Federal State*, 1997 U. CHI. LEGAL F. 199, 199.

[96] Revesz, *Response to Critics, supra* note 2, at 542.

The final section argues that these theories do not support vesting responsibility for environmental regulation at the federal level.

1. Rents and Barriers to Entry. — The impetus for environmental regulation sometimes comes, implicitly or explicitly, from the regulated firms themselves, which can obtain rents and barriers to entry that give them an advantage over their competitors.[97] For example, a command-and-control standard that limits a firm's aggregate emissions might cause firms to reduce their output to meet the environmental requirement. This output restriction can push the price of a firm's product above its average cost. As a result, the firm earns a rent — the positive profit defined by the difference between the product's price and its average cost.[98]

If new firms can easily enter the market, this rent will dissipate through competition. Environmental regulation, however, also can result in the erection of barriers to entry. For example, new pollution sources are generally subject to far more stringent command-and-control standards than are existing sources.[99] Michael Maloney and Robert McCormick show that environmental regulation can generate rents even if firms do not respond to environmental regulation solely by restricting their output.[100] Environmental regulation can produce rents even if firms purchase new technology or change the mix of their inputs.[101] Maloney and McCormick also muster empirical support for the proposition that environmental regulation can raise an industry's profits.[102]

The Montreal Protocol on Substances that Deplete the Ozone Layer[103] provides a powerful example of environmental regulation creating rents and barriers to entry. Manufacturers of chlorofluorocarbon (CFC) products, which the international agreement would eventually ban,[104] came to support the regulatory program because in the interim they would capture large rents, estimated at between $1.8 and $7.2 billion.[105]

---

[97] Keohane, Revesz & Stavins, *supra* note 10, at 348–51; Todd J. Zywicki, *Environmental Externalities and Political Externalities: The Political Economy of Environmental Regulation and Reform,* 73 TUL. L. REV. 845, 860–64 (1999); *see also* Michael T. Maloney & Robert E. McCormick, *A Positive Theory of Environmental Quality Regulation,* 25 J.L. & ECON. 99, 100–06 (1982).

[98] Keohane, Revesz & Stavins, *supra* note 10, at 348–49. Absent the environmental regulation, firms in a competitive market would earn zero profits. *Id.* at 349.

[99] *See id.* at 350 & n.112.

[100] *See* Maloney & McCormick, *supra* note 97, at 100–06.

[101] *See id.*

[102] *See id.* at 108–21.

[103] Montreal Protocol on Substances That Deplete the Ozone Layer, Sept. 16, 1987, S. TREATY DOC. NO. 100-10, 1522 U.N.T.S. 3 (entered into force Jan. 1, 1989).

[104] *See id.* art. 2, 1522 U.N.T.S. at 31–32.

[105] Daniel F. McInnis, *Ozone Layers and Oligopoly Profits, in* ENVIRONMENTAL POLITICS: PUBLIC COSTS, PRIVATE REWARDS 129, 147 (Michael S. Greve & Fred L. Smith Jr. eds., 1992)

2. *Industries with Strong Economies of Scale.* — Some industries enjoy strong economies of scale. Firms in such industries tend to prefer uniform federal regulation to a patchwork of different state standards. Indeed, having to manufacture different products for sale in different states can destroy these economies of scale. If the economies of scale are sufficiently strong, regulated firms will prefer uniform federal standards even if the nonuniform state standards are less stringent, or if some states choose not to regulate at all.

An early public choice study of environmental regulation found that in the mid-1960s the automobile industry began to advocate federal emissions standards for automobiles.[106] At the time, California had adopted state standards, and a number of other states were considering similar legislation.[107] The automobile industry then decided to end its opposition to federal standards and became a supporter, provided that such standards preempted any more stringent state standards.[108]

3. *Differential Costs on Regulated Firms.* — Even if environmental regulation does not raise the profits of an entire industry, it can benefit certain firms within that industry.[109] Regulating an industry has the effect of raising the price of the industry's product. Such a price increase affects all polluters in a similar manner: each benefits in proportion to the number of goods sold. Firms within an industry, however, likely will incur different costs in meeting the regulatory requirements.[110] Some firms may be able to adjust their production processes more easily than others. These relative beneficiaries of government regulation are likely to oppose relaxing regulatory requirements and may even favor extending them.[111] For example, firms able to reduce the lead content of their gasoline at relatively low cost tended to support regulations that drastically reduced that content. In contrast,

---

[hereinafter ENVIRONMENTAL POLITICS]; Melnick, *supra* note 48, at 78; Zywicki, *supra* note 97, at 871.

[106] E. Donald Elliott, Bruce A. Ackerman & John C. Millian, *Toward a Theory of Statutory Evolution: The Federalization of Environmental Law*, 1 J.L. ECON. & ORG. 313, 330–31 (1985).

[107] *Id.* at 330.

[108] *Id.* at 330–31. For an acknowledgment of similar dynamics in connection with the regulation of pesticides, see Sherry Jo Wise & Todd Sandler, *Rent-Seeking and Pesticide Legislation*, 78 PUB. CHOICE 329, 331, 338 (1994).

[109] Keohane, Revesz & Stavins, *supra* note 10, at 351–53; Zywicki, *supra* note 97, at 864–66.

[110] ROBERT A. LEONE, WHO PROFITS: WINNERS, LOSERS, AND GOVERNMENT REGULATION 42–44 (1986).

[111] Jerry L. Mashaw & Susan Rose-Ackerman, *Federalism and Regulation, in* THE REAGAN REGULATORY STRATEGY 111, 136 (George C. Eads & Michael Fix eds., 1984); Melnick, *supra* note 48, at 89; Sharon Oster, *The Strategic Use of Regulatory Investment by Industry Sub-Groups*, 20 ECON. INQUIRY 604, 604 (1982).

firms with less efficient refineries "vehemently opposed" the regulatory program.[112]

   4. *Benefits to Producers of Pollution Control Equipment and Inputs to Production Processes.* — The impetus for regulation sometimes comes from manufacturers of pollution control equipment, environmentally friendly technologies, or inputs to production processes favored by the regulatory regime.[113] For example, firms specializing in the cleanup of hazardous waste sites emerged in response to the federal Superfund statute.[114] The hazardous-waste cleanup industry has become a powerful advocate of stringent Superfund cleanup standards.[115] Similarly, the ethanol industry has strongly supported stricter regulation of gasoline.[116] As a result of its efforts, the Clean Air Act's[117] clean fuels program provides strong incentives for the use of ethanol,[118] and the federal government has provided large subsidies to ethanol producers.[119]

   Bruce Ackerman and William Hassler provide a well-documented example of this phenomenon in *Clean Coal/Dirty Air*.[120] The book discusses the influence of the high-sulfur coal industry in the passage of the 1977 amendments to section 111 of the Clean Air Act[121] dealing with New Source Performance Standards (NSPS) for electric utilities.[122] The original NSPS provision requiring the Environmental Protection Agency (EPA) to set emission limitations for categories of new sources dated back to 1970. In 1971, EPA set a standard for electric utilities of 1.2 pounds of sulfur dioxide per million BTU of heat input.[123] Utilities could meet this standard by using low-sulfur coal, without employing any treatment technology, or by scrubbing high-

---

112 Keohane, Revesz & Stavins, *supra* note 10, at 351.

113 For a discussion of this phenomenon in the press, see Claudia H. Deutsch, *Scrubbing the Air, Buffing the Cleaners: Belated E.P.A. War on Pollutants May Infuse Value into Companies*, N.Y. TIMES, Oct. 17, 1997, at D1.

114 Comprehensive Environmental Response, Compensation, and Liability Act, 42 U.S.C. §§ 9601–9675 (1994 & Supp. V 1999).

115 Marc K. Landy & Mary Hague, *The Coalition for Waste: Private Interests and Superfund*, in ENVIRONMENTAL POLITICS, *supra* note 105, at 67, 77–79; Zywicki, *supra* note 97, at 858–59.

116 Jonathan H. Adler, *Clean Fuels, Dirty Air*, in ENVIRONMENTAL POLITICS, *supra* note 105, at 19, 28–30; Melnick, *supra* note 48, at 78.

117 42 U.S.C. §§ 7401–7671(q).

118 *Id.* §§ 7581–7589 (1994); *see* Zywicki, *supra* note 97, at 857.

119 Zywicki, *supra* note 97, at 857–58.

120 BRUCE A. ACKERMAN & WILLIAM T. HASSLER, CLEAN COAL/DIRTY AIR (1981).

121 Pub. L. No. 95-95, §§ 109(a)–(d)(1), (e), (f), 401(b), 91 Stat. 697–703, 791 (codified as amended at 42 U.S.C. § 7411).

122 ACKERMAN & HASSLER, *supra* note 120, at 31–54.

123 RICHARD L. REVESZ, FOUNDATIONS OF ENVIRONMENTAL LAW AND POLICY 216–17 (1997).

sulfur coal.[124] As a result, the standard discouraged the use of high-sulfur coal.[125]

The producers of high-sulfur coal, located primarily in West Virginia, lobbied vigorously for a statutory provision preventing the use of untreated low-sulfur coal. They prevailed in 1977. Congress required electric utilities to reduce emissions from the burning of untreated fuel by a given percentage, regardless of the fuel's characteristics. In this manner, the high-sulfur coal producers succeeded in imposing costs on the use of low-sulfur coal. Users of high-sulfur coal, however, did not bear any additional costs because they already were required to scrub their coal under the prior regulatory regime. The result was an expansion of the market for high-sulfur coal.[126]

5. Interregional Comparative Advantage. — Another explanation for environmental regulation relies on our government's federal structure. Environmental regulation often imposes disproportionate costs on some regions of the country. Regions that incur lower than average costs from regulation become comparatively more attractive to mobile capital, which brings economic benefits such as jobs and tax revenues. Such regions sometimes push for federal regulation that will impose disproportionate costs on other regions.

Peter Pashigian documented an example of this phenomenon in a 1985 article.[127] The piece explores Congress's adoption of the Prevention of Significant Deterioration (PSD) program in the 1977 amendments to the Clean Air Act.[128] Section 109 of the Clean Air Act required EPA to adopt uniform National Ambient Air Quality Standards (NAAQS) specifying the maximum permissible concentration of various pollutants nationwide.[129] Some regions had air quality better than the NAAQS. The statute did not explicitly address whether these regions could degrade their air quality to the level of the NAAQS or whether instead they would be subject to more stringent ambient standards.[130]

Congress answered this question in 1977 by adopting the PSD program, which allows only limited degradation in areas that have better air quality than the NAAQS require.[131] In contrast, the PSD program

---

[124] *Id.* at 217.

[125] *See id.*

[126] ACKERMAN & HASSLER, *supra* note 120, at 31–54.

[127] B. Peter Pashigian, *Environmental Regulation: Whose Self-Interests Are Being Protected?*, 23 ECON. INQUIRY 551 (1985).

[128] *See* 42 U.S.C. §§ 7470–7479 (1994).

[129] *Id.* § 7409(a)–(b).

[130] *See id.*

[131] *Id.* § 7473. Previously, a district court had interpreted the 1970 Clean Air Act to include a nondegradation requirement but had not specified the nature of this requirement. Sierra Club v. Ruckelshaus, 344 F. Supp. 253, 256 (D.D.C. 1972), *aff'd*, No. CIV. 1031-72, 1972 WL 2725 (D.C.

does not impose any regulatory requirements on states that violate the NAAQS. As a result, the PSD program negatively affects the ability of states that exceed the NAAQS to attract new firms.

Pashigian set out to determine whether support for the PSD program in the House of Representatives came from representatives of states with strong environmental records or from representatives of relatively dirty states, seeking to impose disproportionate costs on cleaner states. His results support the latter hypothesis.[132] Other empirical studies of congressional votes similarly found that legislators from industrialized regions supported environmental regulations that would limit growth in other regions.[133]

Conversely, states that have adopted strong environmental standards have an incentive to push for the federalization of those standards. Such federalization imposes no additional costs on those clean states, which must already meet the requirements, but does impose additional costs on other states. Federalization would therefore disadvantage the dirtier states in their competition for mobile capital.[134]

6. Implications for the Public Choice Argument in Favor of Federal Environmental Regulation. — The preceding discussion does not seek to establish that public choice explanations for environmental regulation are persuasive across the board. In fact, the diverse nature of the explanations underscores the extent to which they work better as post hoc interest group rationalizations than as ex ante predictions for future regulations.[135]

Each of the theories discussed above would justify the implementation of a different form of regulation. For example, if one were trying to predict the nature of some future regulatory program, should one postulate that states with stringent standards will prevail at getting these standards federalized? Will the winner be an industry trade association attempting to capture rents and protect them by using barriers to entry? Or will the form of the regulation be determined by the interests of a small group of firms able to meet the regulation's requirements more cheaply than their competitors? The public choice discipline is not sufficiently well developed to answer these questions.

The claim advanced here is more limited than a call for across-the-board adherence to public choice explanations for environmental regu-

---

Cir. Nov. 1, 1972), *aff'd by an equally divided Court sub nom.* Fri v. Sierra Club, 412 U.S. 541 (1973).

132 *See* Pashigian, *supra* note 127, at 580–81.

133 Bruce Yandle, *Public Choice at the Intersection of Environmental Law and Economics*, 8 EUR. J.L. & ECON. 5, 19–20 (1999).

134 *See* Susan Rose-Ackerman, *Does Federalism Matter?: Political Choice in a Federal Republic*, 89 J. POL. ECON. 152, 152–53 (1981).

135 *See* Melnick, *supra* note 48, at 79 ("It is doubtful that any simple, abstract model can either predict or explain the politics behind such massive, complex, detailed legislative products.").

lation. Instead, the argument is that the public choice explanations that have some currency are not those in which the relevant interest groups are environmentalists on one side and industry groups on the other. Olson's work has difficulty explaining even the existence of environmental groups. Even more sophisticated public choice theories cannot convincingly explain how the costs of political participation would make environmental groups more effective at the federal level.[136]

This discussion is not meant to suggest that environmental groups are irrelevant to the regulatory process. In fact, the literature contains examples of "Baptist-bootlegger" coalitions, in which the environmental groups, the "Baptists," have cooperated with polluters, the "bootleggers," to obtain environmental regulation through the political process.[137] Under Prohibition, those with "good" motives, who sought to ban drinking, allied themselves with those with "bad" motives, who sought higher prices for their liquor. Similarly, groups interested in environmental protection sometimes have interests coextensive with firms seeking to increase their profits. Ackerman and Hassler provide a classic example of this phenomenon: West Virginia coal producers interested in expanding the market for their products joined forces with Western environmental interests seeking, among other goals, protection of visibility across the Grand Canyon.[138]

But under this Baptist-bootlegger dynamic, as opposed to the Olsonian David-Goliath one, it is not clear whether environmental interests will systematically fare better at the federal or at the state level. In fact, the explanations discussed in the preceding sections point in opposing directions. When states invoke the federal regulatory apparatus to impose differential costs on other states, the result is more stringent environmental regulation than in the absence of federal legislation. In contrast, when industry seeks preemption of state standards, less stringent regulatory standards in the affected states generally result.[139] Finally, it is not clear from the current academic literature whether regulated firms or industries can obtain more stringent environmental regulations at the state or at the federal level.

To conclude, the claim advanced here does not depend on accepting public choice explanations for environmental regulation. Some

---

[136] *See supra* pp. 566–68, 571.

[137] Yandle, *supra* note 133, at 17.

[138] *See* ACKERMAN & HASSLER, *supra* note 120, at 29–41.

[139] Richard J. Lazarus, *Debunking Environmental Feudalism: Promoting the Individual Through the Collective Pursuit of Environmental Quality*, 77 IOWA L. REV. 1739, 1772 (1992) ("Recently, state and local governments frequently have imposed more stringent environmental protection controls, causing industry to seek the refuge of federal preemption to avoid their application."). In contrast, in states that had not previously entered the regulatory fray, the resulting standards will be more stringent under federal regulation.

commentators are skeptical of the explanatory power of such theories.[140] But a public choice call for federal environmental regulation must have as its premise some public choice theory; otherwise, one would simply assume that the states, like the federal government, seek to promote the public interest. The limited claim advanced here is that the more plausible public choice theories, as opposed to those relied upon by advocates of federal environmental regulation, establish neither that states would underregulate in the absence of interstate externalities nor that federal regulation would decrease the resulting social welfare losses.[141]

II. STATE ENVIRONMENTAL REGULATION BEFORE 1970

Public choice arguments for federal environmental regulation rest in part on the empirical claim that states largely disregarded environmental problems before 1970, the year Congress enacted the first major federal statutes.[142] Before evaluating the situation in 1970, it is important to stress that at that time the deck was stacked against state regulation. As noted below, the federal government is better suited than states to provide scientific information about the adverse health and environmental effects of various pollutants, because of the economies of scale in developing such information.[143] Before 1970, the federal government did comparatively little in this area,[144] and it probably continues to underinvest in such scientific information even today.[145] The states may not have regulated significantly because they lacked this information. Regardless, the view widely held in the legal literature that the states ignored environmental problems before 1970

---

140 *See* Farber, *supra* note 95.

141 One commentator has noted that public choice considerations do not clearly indicate the superiority of either centralization or decentralization because "the implications of the theory's application are both speculative and impossible to verify empirically." Rena I. Steinzor, *Unfunded Environmental Mandates and the "New (New) Federalism": Devolution, Revolution, or Reform?*, 81 MINN. L. REV. 97, 181 (1996); *see also* Lazarus, *supra* note 139, at 1772 ("[T]here is reason to be skeptical of the widely accepted notion that local government authorities are likely to be too favorably disposed to industry to engage in effective environmental protection.").

142 *See* Esty, *supra* note 1, at 600–01.

143 *See infra* p. 582.

144 *See infra* p. 582.

145 For example, in a recent comprehensive report, the National Research Council found:
> The United States has no national program addressing fundamental ecological research, to provide coordination and focus. One way of meeting that need could be to establish a program of focused fundamental research under the auspices of a federal lead agency. Properly structured, such a program could provide the direction and momentum that are missing in the nation's ecological research.

NAT'L RESEARCH COUNCIL, LINKING SCIENCE AND TECHNOLOGY TO SOCIETY'S ENVIRONMENTAL GOALS 43 (1996). For other critical perspectives, see MARK R. POWELL, SCIENCE AT EPA: INFORMATION IN THE REGULATORY PROCESS 111–17 (1999), and Stewart, *supra* note 95, at 216–17.

is simply not correct. The most extensive research, which focuses on air pollution, shows clearly that states and municipalities were making considerable strides before the federal regulatory era. In particular, the number of states, counties, and municipalities with regulatory programs to control air pollution was increasing rapidly, and the concentrations of important air pollutants were falling at significant rates.

Chicago and Cincinnati adopted the first municipal regulations of air pollution in 1881.[146] A comprehensive survey of state and local air pollution control found that the number of municipalities with effective controls on air pollution rose to 40 in 1920, 52 in 1940, 84 in 1960, and 107 in 1970, and that the number of counties with such controls rose from 2 in 1950 to 17 in 1960 and 81 in 1970.[147] Jurisdictions that had passed laws and ordinances but had failed to implement or enforce them are not included in these figures.[148] For instance, in 1940 there were about 200 municipalities with air pollution ordinances, but the survey included only the 52 with operating smoke abatement agencies.[149]

Pittsburgh provides an instructive example. At the turn of the century, probably no city in the United States was more closely associated with heavy smoke, poor visibility, and dark days.[150] The city passed a number of smoke control ordinances in the 1890s and early 1900s, but they were weakly enforced and generally unsuccessful.[151] In 1941, however, Pittsburgh passed an effective smoke control ordinance that triggered an important shift from bituminous coal to the use of smokeless fuels.[152] The effect was a dramatic increase in visibility.[153]

Like municipalities, states engaged in considerable pre-1970 regulation. In the 1910s, state efforts at regulation sought to control black smoke in metropolitan areas.[154] By the 1950s and 1960s, the smoke problem had been greatly ameliorated as a result of changes in fuel use, spurred in some cases by municipal programs such as Pittsburgh's. In 1951, Oregon became the first state to create a state air

---

[146] Arthur C. Stern, *History of Air Pollution Legislation in the United States*, 32 J. AIR POLLUTION CONTROL ASS'N 44, 44 (1982); *see* 1 ARNOLD W. REITZE, JR., ENVIRONMENTAL LAW 3–82 (2d ed. 1972).

[147] Stern, *supra* note 146, at 44.

[148] *See id.*

[149] *See id.*

[150] *See* Cliff I. Davidson, *Air Pollution in Pittsburgh: A Historical Perspective*, 29 J. AIR POLLUTION CONTROL ASS'N 1035, 1035–37 (1979).

[151] *See id.* at 1038.

[152] *See id.* at 1039. Implementation of this new ordinance was delayed for five years as a result of World War II. *See id.*

[153] *See id.* at 1040. By 1948, visibility had improved by 67%; by 1954, the city received 89% more sunshine; by 1958, smoke reduced visibility in only one out of sixty-five daylight hours, down from one out of every four daylight hours in 1946. *See id.*

[154] Stern, *supra* note 146, at 47.

pollution control agency with broad jurisdiction. California followed in 1957 with a regulatory program for automobile emissions.[155]

By 1960, eight states had general air pollution control laws; another nine had undertaken measures to control air pollution under their general public health laws; and eight others had authorized local air pollution control agencies to transcend municipal boundaries in their regulatory efforts.[156] By 1966, ten states had adopted at least some ambient air quality standards, which covered fourteen substances as well as deposited matter.[157] In addition, six states had emissions standards covering some stationary sources.[158]

State efforts to reduce air pollution received a boost from the passage of the Clean Air Act of 1963,[159] one of the predecessors of the modern federal regulatory regime. Though the Act did not impose regulatory requirements, it made grants-in-aid available to states that adopted air pollution control measures. Perhaps as a result of these incentives, the number of states with regulatory measures increased from eleven in 1963 to fifty by 1969.[160] One commentator has deemed these incentives, rather than the extensive federal regulatory involvement pursuant to the Clean Air Act of 1970, "the most significant result of federal air pollution control legislation."[161]

Three studies have attempted to quantify improvements in the ambient air quality levels for sulfur dioxide and particulates before 1970. The studies focused on these two contaminants because scientists understood their adverse health consequences before the 1970s.[162] Robert Crandall of the Brookings Institution conducted the first of the studies, using data compiled by the Conservation Foundation.[163] Crandall found that sulfur dioxide concentrations fell by 11.3% per year between 1964 and 1971 (before an active federal role in air pollution control), but fell by only 4.6% per year in the 1970s (in the era of federal regulation). Similarly, the average concentrations of total suspended particulates fell by 2.3% per year between 1960 and 1971, but fell by only 0.6% per year from 1972 to 1980.[164] Crandall concluded that "pollution reduction was more effective in the 1960s, before there

---

[155] *Id.* For a discussion of the California program, see section III.A.1, pp. 585–88, below.

[156] Stern, *supra* note 146, at 47.

[157] *Id.*

[158] *Id.* at 48.

[159] Pub. L. No. 88-206, 77 Stat. 392 (1963) (codified as amended at 42 U.S.C. §§ 7401–7671q (1994 & Supp. V 1999)).

[160] Stern, *supra* note 146, at 47–48.

[161] *Id.* at 48.

[162] *See infra* p. 582 (discussing the difficulties of state regulation without federal investments in scientific information).

[163] ROBERT W. CRANDALL, CONTROLLING INDUSTRIAL POLLUTION: THE ECONOMICS AND POLITICS OF CLEAN AIR 16–22 (1983).

[164] *Id.* at 19.

was a serious federal policy dealing with stationary sources, than since the 1970 Clean Air Act Amendments."[165] This conclusion is controversial because the first reduction in pollutant levels may have been easier to achieve than subsequent reductions, but Crandall's study nonetheless underscores the degree of improvement before the era of federal environmental regulation.

Paul Portney conducted the second study for Resources for the Future, based on data compiled by EPA.[166] Portney found that ambient levels of sulfur dioxide fell by an aggregate of 50% between 1966 and 1971 (8.5% per year) and that ambient levels of total suspended particulates fell by an aggregate of 22% between 1960 and 1970 (2.0% per year).[167] Portney concluded that "[t]hese data ... call into question one of the fundamental premises behind the [Clean Air Act] — that states and local governments would never impose the controls necessary to achieve healthful air."[168]

The final study appears in a book by Indur Goklany,[169] based on some of Goklany's prior work in this area.[170] Using data compiled by the Council on Environmental Quality (CEQ), Goklany found that ambient air quality levels for sulfur dioxide fell 38.8% between 1962 and 1969 (5.5% per year).[171] In contrast, using statistics compiled by EPA, Goklany found that these ambient concentrations declined at a slower rate after the beginning of extensive federal regulation. The total decline between 1974 and 1980 was 25.6% (4.3% per year). Subsequently, the rate of improvement went down substantially.[172] Goklany also reviewed different sources of CEQ data concerning suspended particles. He found that their concentration in urban areas decreased 15.7% between 1957 and 1970 (about 1% per year).[173]

It is not surprising that the pre-1970 improvements were particularly pronounced for sulfur dioxide and total suspended particulates.

---

[155] *Id.*

[166] Paul R. Portney, *Air Pollution Policy, in* PUBLIC POLICIES FOR ENVIRONMENTAL PROTECTION 27, 28–29, 50–51 (Paul R. Portney ed., 1990).

[167] *See id.* at 50.

[168] *Id.* at 51.

[169] INDUR M. GOKLANY, CLEARING THE AIR: THE REAL STORY OF THE WAR ON AIR POLLUTION (1999).

[170] *See* INDUR M. GOKLANY, DO WE NEED THE FEDERAL GOVERNMENT TO PROTECT AIR QUALITY? (Ctr. for the Study of Am. Bus. Policy, Policy Study No. 150, 1998), *available at* http://csab.wustl.edu/csab/CSAB pubs-pdf files/Policy Studies/PS150 Goklany.pdf; Indur M. Goklany, *Empirical Evidence Regarding the Role of Nationalization in Improving U.S. Air Quality, in* THE COMMON LAW AND THE ENVIRONMENT: RETHINKING THE STATUTORY BASIS FOR MODERN ENVIRONMENTAL LAW 27 (Roger E. Meiners & Andrew P. Morriss eds., 2000); Indur M. Goklany, *Did Federalization Halt a Race to the Bottom for Air Quality?*, EM, June 1998, at 12.

[171] GOKLANY, *supra* note 169, at 56.

[172] *See id.* at 56–57.

[173] *See id.* at 54–55.

Goklany has studied the timeline for the reduction of pollutants currently regulated by NAAQS under the Clean Air Act. For each pollutant, he determined a "period of perception," which he defined as "the period during which a substance in the air gains sufficient notoriety to be perceived as an air pollutant by the public and, perhaps more importantly, by policymakers."[174] Goklany also determined a "time of federalization" for each pollutant — the date when the federal government assumed principal regulatory authority over the pollutant.[175] Whether the states were dragging their feet on pollution control should be judged primarily by their efforts to control those pollutants for which there was sufficient time, between the period of perception and the time of federalization, to implement a state regulation. Of the pollutants Goklany studied, only particulate matter and sulfur dioxide were perceived as outdoor air pollutants before 1950.[176] For the other pollutants the period of perception was later, perhaps too close to federalization to give meaningful insight on a state's performance.[177] Perhaps the states should have tried to understand the adverse health effects of other pollutants earlier. But, as I have indicated elsewhere, there are strong economies of scale in developing and compiling scientific evidence on the adverse health effects of pollutants.[178] Moreover, free rider problems stand in the way of states' developing this evidence themselves. The federal government thus has a comparative advantage in determining the adverse consequences of pollutants.

These three studies, which suggest that states responded vigorously to those air pollution problems that were understood at the time, are consistent with the leading analysis of the genesis of federal environmental regulation.[179] That study maintains that the 1965 and 1967 predecessors to the Clean Air Act of 1970 were responses to industry pressure for federal intervention that would discourage states from setting *more stringent* (and nonuniform) standards.[180] As already indicated, the automobile industry became a supporter of federal standards as a way to avoid disparate and potentially more stringent state standards.[181] Similarly, the high-sulfur coal industry "acquiesce[d] in federal legislation in the hope that it might dampen local legislative initiatives"[182] — the very initiatives responsible for sulfur dioxide reduc-

---

[174] *Id.* at 3.

[175] *Id.*

[176] *See id.* at 40 tbl.1-1.

[177] *See id.*

[178] Revesz, *Response to Critics, supra* note 2, at 543.

[179] *See* Elliott, Ackerman & Millian, *supra* note 106.

[180] *See id.* at 330-33.

[181] *See supra* p. 573.

[182] Elliott, Ackerman & Millian, *supra* note 106, at 331.

tions in the 1960s, as identified in the Crandall, Portney, and Goklany studies.[183]

III. CURRENT STATE ENVIRONMENTAL REGULATORY EFFORTS

If state political processes exhibit public choice pathologies that undermine the effectiveness of environmental groups, state governments should exhibit less concern about environmental problems than does the federal government. This Part, however, shows that many states are implementing innovative protective measures that go well beyond what the federal government requires. Sections A through E deal, respectively, with state involvement in automobile emissions standards, hazardous waste regulation, municipal solid waste, state environmental protection acts, and duty-to-warn measures. Section F briefly assesses the improvements in state governments' competence over the last few decades.

Not every state is active in environmental regulation. The citizens of some states may prefer more lax environmental regulation than the federal government requires and may therefore have no reason to adopt additional environmental programs. But many states are adopting innovative forms of regulation and imposing costs on in-state firms. The discussion in these sections should be regarded as illustrative rather than encyclopedic; states are also innovating and undertaking measures that are not federally compelled in other areas, such as groundwater quality[184] and wetlands protection.[185]

---

[183] See supra pp. 580–81.

[184] There is no comprehensive federal program regulating groundwater quality. See Allyn G. Turner, Federal Groundwater Regulation and Policy: Improvements Under the Horizon?, 10 J. NAT. RESOURCES & ENVTL. L. 323, 326–34 (1994–1995) (noting that "[c]omprehensive federal groundwater protection laws have not come to pass" and describing the "[c]urrent [f]ederal [p]atchwork" of groundwater regulation, composed of "at least six major federal environmental statutes"); Benjamin R. Vance, Comment, Total Aquifer Management: A New Approach to Groundwater Protection, 30 U.S.F. L. REV. 803, 806 (1996). In particular, federal statutes do not require quality standards for groundwater, as they do for surface water, see 33 U.S.C. § 1313 (1994). In contrast, a number of states have implemented groundwater quality programs. See GROUND WATER PROTECTION COUNCIL, GROUND WATER REPORT TO CONGRESS: SUMMARY OF STATE GROUNDWATER CONDITIONS 20, 34, 36, 62 (1999) (Florida, Kansas, Kentucky, New Jersey).

[185] Although the federal memorandum of understanding between EPA and the Army Corps of Engineers sets "a goal of no overall net loss of values and functions" for wetlands, it does not require the replacement of wetlands in every case. Memorandums of Agreement (MOA), 55 Fed. Reg. 9210, 9211 (Mar. 12, 1990) ("[I]ndividual permit decisions . . . [may] not fully meet this goal because the mitigation measures necessary to meet this goal are not feasible, not practicable, or would accomplish only inconsequential reductions in impacts.").

A number of states, including Maryland, Minnesota, and Oregon, have adopted more stringent rules governing the replacement of wetlands that are drained or filled. See David C. Forsberg, The Minnesota Wetland Conservation Act of 1991: Balancing Public and Private Interests, 18 WM. MITCHELL L. REV. 1021, 1022–23 (1992); Stephen R. Rubin, Note, An Analysis of Non-

Before turning to the substantive programs, however, a few notes of caution are in order. First, the mere existence of state environmental statutes is not necessarily evidence of state environmental concern because the statutes may be merely symbolic and not enforced. But in the case studies presented below, the state programs in fact caused actual environmental improvements or, at the very least, imposed costs on in-state firms.

Second, state interventions that are federally compelled, such as the preparation of state implementation plans (SIPs) under the Clean Air Act,[186] are not good evidence of state environmental concern. Therefore, the state programs discussed below have all been implemented on a discretionary basis.

Third, state regulation that imposes costs on out-of-state actors to confer a competitive advantage on in-state industry — for instance, product regulation whose burden falls primarily on remote producers — is not inconsistent with the public choice arguments favoring federal regulation. Industry groups would welcome such state regulation as a way of obtaining a competitive advantage. The primary burden of the state programs discussed below, however, is borne by actors in the states enacting the regulatory controls.[187] Of course, even process regulation of in-state sources externalizes some costs to out-of-state consumers who buy products manufactured by these sources. But evidence of effective state regulation of in-state firms undercuts the ar-

---

tidal Wetland Regulation in Maryland, 16 VA. ENVTL. L.J. 459, 482 (1997); J. Brian Smith, Comment, *Western Wetlands: The Backwater of Wetlands Regulation,* 39 NAT. RESOURCES J. 357, 393–94 (1999). In some cases, each acre of lost wetland must be replaced by more than one acre elsewhere. *See* Rubin, *supra,* at 482.

For general discussions of federal and state programs governing wetlands replacement, see Ann Redmond, Terrie Bates, Frank Bernadino & Robert M. Rhodes, *State Mitigation Banking Programs: The Florida Experience,* in MITIGATION BANKING: THEORY AND PRACTICE 54, 54–56 (Lindell L. Marsh, Douglas R. Porter & David A. Salvesen eds., 1996), and John Studt & Robert D. Sokolove, *Federal Wetland Mitigation Policies,* in MITIGATION BANKING: THEORY AND PRACTICE, *supra,* at 37, 44.

For discussions of other significant state wetlands initiatives, see Thomas V. Grasso, *Wetlands Permitting Programs in the Chesapeake Bay Area,* in WETLANDS LAW AND REGULATIONS 139, 139 (A.L.I.-A.B.A. Course of Study, May 29–31, 1996), discussing the Chesapeake Bay Wetlands Policy, signed by Maryland, Virginia, Pennsylvania, and the District of Columbia in 1988, which calls for "a net resource gain in wetlands acreage and function over present conditions"; and Cymie Payne, *Local Regulation of Natural Resources: Efficiency, Effectiveness, and Fairness of Wetlands Permitting in Massachusetts,* 28 ENVTL. L. 519, 523, 526–27 (1998), showing that wetlands loss in Massachusetts has slowed considerably since the passage of the state's Wetlands Protection Act in 1991.

[186] 42 U.S.C. § 7410 (1994).

[187] *See infra* pp. 591–94 (air quality), pp. 622–23 (duty to warn). Hazardous waste, municipal solid waste, and the sorts of activities that require environmental impact statements tend to be matters of local concern, so there is little risk that states will use regulation in these areas to impose costs on out-of-state actors.

gument that states underregulate such firms because of public choice problems.

Fourth, the review of state environmental programs that follows does not purport to establish that all states — or even necessarily most states — have taken aggressive and innovative measures to address environmental problems. Only some states have taken the lead. Part IV explains that environmental leadership appears to have come from states with stronger preferences for environmental protection.

In summary, the fact that states are adopting environmental programs that are not federally compelled — particularly ones that impose costs on in-state actors — is evidence against the simplistic public choice argument for federal intervention. The robustness of the state programs analyzed in the following sections shows that at least some states are not at a disadvantage with respect to environmental regulation.

A. Automobile Emissions Standards

1. Federal and California Programs. — California pioneered the regulation of automobile emissions. Its regulatory regime dates back to 1960, when the state enacted its motor vehicle pollution control program.[188] The first emission control requirements on automobiles registered in California took effect in 1965.[189] The federal government, however, did not regulate automobile emissions until the passage of the federal Motor Vehicle Air Pollution Control Act of 1965.[190] The first set of federal controls became effective in the 1968 model year.[191]

The automobile industry feared that inconsistent state regulation would compromise the economies of scale in automobile manufacture.[192] Congress, prompted at least in part by automobile industry lobbying,[193] provided in the 1967 Air Quality Act that federal automobile emissions limitations would preempt not only any less stringent state standards, but also any more stringent state standards. There

---

[188] ROBERT V. PERCIVAL, ALAN S. MILLER, CHRISTOPHER H. SCHROEDER & JAMES P. LEAPE, ENVIRONMENTAL REGULATION: LAW, SCIENCE, AND POLICY 840 (2d ed. 1996) [hereinafter ENVIRONMENTAL REGULATION].

[189] *Id.* at 840–41. For an excellent case study of the genesis of the California and federal automobile standards, see JAMES E. KRIER & EDMUND URSIN, POLLUTION AND POLICY: A CASE ESSAY ON CALIFORNIA AND FEDERAL EXPERIENCE WITH MOTOR VEHICLE AIR POLLUTION 1940–1975 (1977).

[190] Motor Vehicle Air Pollution Control Act of 1965, Pub. L. No. 89-272, § 202(a), 79 Stat. 992.

[191] ENVIRONMENTAL REGULATION, *supra* note 188, at 841.

[192] *See* S. REP. NO. 90-403, at 33 (1967) ("The auto industry . . . was adamant that the nature of their manufacturing mechanism required a single national standard in order to eliminate undue economic strain on the industry."); *see also* Motor Vehicle Mfrs. Ass'n v. N.Y. State Dep't of Envtl. Conservation, 17 F.3d 521, 524–25 (2d Cir. 1994) (detailing concerns of the automobile industry).

[193] *See* Elliott, Ackerman & Millian, *supra* note 106, at 326, 331; *supra* p. 573.

was one exception, however: California was authorized to have more stringent standards.[194]

This basic structure of the federal regulatory program survived the enactment of the first comprehensive federal Clean Air Act in 1970 and the enactments of the Act's comprehensive amendments in 1977 and 1990. The federal automobile emissions standards continue to require uniformity,[195] a departure from the standard approach under the Clean Air Act and most federal environmental regulatory provisions, which is to preempt less stringent state standards but to allow states to impose more stringent standards.[196] Again, California is the only state allowed to have more stringent standards.[197]

Continuing an approach initially adopted in 1977,[198] the 1990 amendments authorize other states to choose between the federal standards and the more stringent California standards if they have non-attainment areas — areas that do not meet the NAAQS.[199] No state, however, may adopt any automobile emissions standards other than the California or federal ones. The resulting two-standard strategy reflects a compromise between two interests: the desire to protect the economies of scale in automobile production[200] and the desire to accelerate the process for attainment of the NAAQS.[201]

---

194 ENVIRONMENTAL REGULATION, *supra* note 188, at 841.

195 *See* 42 U.S.C. § 7543 (1994) ("No State or any political subdivision thereof shall adopt or attempt to enforce any standard relating to the control of emissions from new motor vehicles or new motor vehicle engines subject to this part."); *cf. id.* § 7545(c)(4) (fuels); *id.* § 7573 (aircraft emissions). *But cf. id.* § 7416 (preemption rules).

196 *See id.* § 7416; Revesz, *Response to Critics, supra* note 2, at 544.

197 *See* 42 U.S.C. § 7543(b)(1) (waiving preemption for "any State which has adopted standards . . . for the control of emissions from new motor vehicles or new motor vehicle engines prior to March 30, 1966"). While the provision is written in general terms, California is the only state that meets this requirement. *See* Danielle F. Fern, Comment, *The Crafting of the National Low-Emission Vehicle Program: A Private Contract Theory of Public Rulemaking*, 16 UCLA J. ENVTL. L. & POL'Y 227, 232 (1997/98). To be able to have its own standards, California must establish that its standards "will be, in the aggregate, at least as protective of public health and welfare as applicable Federal standards." 42 U.S.C. § 7543(b)(1). The EPA Administrator must also waive the application of the otherwise applicable preemption provision. *Id.*

198 Clean Air Act Amendments of 1977, Pub. L. No. 95-95, § 129(b), 91 Stat. 685, 745, 750 (codified at 42 U.S.C. § 7507); *see* Motor Vehicle Mfrs. Ass'n v. N.Y. State Dep't of Envtl. Conservation, 79 F.3d 1298, 1301 (2d Cir. 1996).

199 The authorization is not contained in the portion of the Clean Air Act that deals with emissions from moving sources. *See* 42 U.S.C. §§ 7521–7590. Instead, it is part of the Act's nonattainment provisions. These requirements apply to areas that fail to meet the NAAQS, which set forth maximum permissible concentrations of certain pollutants in the ambient air. *Id.* § 7507

200 *See supra* section I.B.2, p. 573.

201 The Clean Air Act explicitly provides that no state may "take any action of any kind to create, or have the effect of creating, a motor vehicle or motor vehicle engine different than a motor vehicle or engine certified in California under California standards (a 'third vehicle') or otherwise create such a 'third vehicle.'" 42 U.S.C. § 7507.

The 1990 amendments prescribe the emissions standards for four pollutants beginning with the 1994 model year[202] and specify that in each subsequent year a progressively increasing percentage of each manufacturer's sales must meet these standards.[203] The emission reductions resulting from this regulatory program are considerable. The permissible emissions of nitrogen oxides, for example, in some cases are 69% lower than under the prior regulatory requirements and 90% lower than the uncontrolled levels.[204]

But in 1988, before Congress even began to consider these limitations seriously,[205] California substantially strengthened its automobile emissions standards.[206] To implement these new standards, in September 1990 the California Air Resources Board (CARB) adopted a Low Emission Vehicle (LEV) program for automobiles sold in California.[207] Under the LEV program, automobile manufacturers must meet a fleet average requirement for emissions that becomes stricter each year.[208]

---

[202] *See id.* § 7521(g).

[203] *See id.* (mandating that 40%, 80%, and 100% of manufacturers' sales for model years 1994, 1995, and post-1995, respectively, meet the standards for NHMC, CO, and NOx (in the cases of both light-duty trucks and light-duty vehicles), and that 40%, 80%, and 100% of manufacturers' sales for model years 1995, 1996, and post-1996, respectively, meet the standards for PM (in the case of light-duty vehicles)).

[204] *See* Henry A. Waxman, Gregory S. Wetstone & Philip S. Barnett, *Cars, Fuels, and Clean Air: A Review of Title II of the Clean Air Act Amendments of 1990*, 21 ENVTL. L. 1947, 1957 (1991). *Compare* 42 U.S.C. § 7521(b)(1)(B) (1.0 grams per vehicle mile (gpm) beginning with the 1981 model year), *with id.* § 7521(g)(1) (0.4 gpm beginning with the 1994 model year for cars with a useful life of at least five years or 50,000 miles).

[205] *See* Waxman, Wetstone & Barnett, *supra* note 204, at 1953 (identifying May 1989 as the beginning of the debate over mobile source controls in the 101st Congress).

[206] CAL. HEALTH & SAFETY CODE § 43,018(a) (West 1996) (stating an intent "to achieve the maximum degree of emission reduction possible from vehicular and other mobile sources in order to accomplish the attainment of the state standards at the earliest practicable date").

[207] *See* CAL. CODE REGS. tit. 13, § 1960.1 (2000); Cal. Air Res. Bd., Staff Report: Low-Emission Vehicle and Zero-Emission Vehicle Program Review 1–3 (Nov. 1996) (unpublished manuscript, on file with the Harvard Law School Library) [hereinafter Staff Report]. The program contemplates four different types of vehicles: transitional low-emission vehicles (TLEVs), low-emission vehicles (LEVs), ultra-low-emission vehicles (ULEVs), and zero-emission vehicles (ZEVs). *See* S. William Becker & Nancy R. Kruger, *Wish They All Could Be California Cars*, ENVTL. F., May/June 1992, at 30; Leslie Harrison Reed, Jr., *California Low-Emission Vehicle Program: Forcing Technology and Dealing Effectively with the Uncertainties*, 24 B.C. ENVTL. AFF. L. REV. 695, 701 (1997).

[208] *See* CAL. CODE REGS. tit. 13, § 1960.1(g)(2); Staff Report, *supra* note 207, at 3. Beginning with model year 2003, a specified percentage of vehicles sold, however, must be ZEVs. Am. Auto. Mfrs. Ass'n v. Mass. Dep't of Envtl. Prot., 163 F.3d 74, 78 (1st Cir. 1998); Am. Auto. Mfrs. Ass'n v. Cahill, 152 F.3d 196, 198–99 (2d Cir. 1998); Control of Air Pollution from New Motor Vehicle Engines, 62 Fed. Reg. 31,192, 31,198 (June 6, 1997); Staff Report, *supra* note 207, at 1.

In January 1993, EPA granted the necessary waiver, *see supra* note 197, thereby enabling the California standards to go into effect. *See* California State Motor Vehicle Pollution Control Standards; Waiver of Federal Preemption, 58 Fed. Reg. 4166 (Jan. 13, 1993).

California's standards are considerably more stringent than the federal standards established in the Clean Air Act's 1990 amendments. EPA estimated that under the national LEV program discussed in the following section, which is not as stringent as California's, emissions would be approximately 70% lower than under statutory standards prescribed in the Clean Air Act.[209]

2. *Actions by Other States and the Emergence of a National LEV Program.* — After Congress enacted the 1990 Clean Air Act amendments and California adopted its LEV program, other states began to consider the choice between the California standards and the less stringent federal requirements.[210] These states included Texas, Michigan, Illinois, and Wisconsin, as well as the twelve northeastern states and the District of Columbia, which comprised the Ozone Transport Commission (OTC),[211] an organization established under the 1990 amendments to combat interstate ozone pollution.[212]

In October 1991, the OTC states signed a memorandum of understanding providing that each would take steps to adopt the California LEV standards.[213] Over the next two years, several states made efforts in this regard, but only Massachusetts and New York adopted the standards.[214] Some OTC states delayed action pending challenges to the legality of the Massachusetts and New York programs,[215] while

---

[209] *See* Final Rule on Ozone Transport Commission, 60 Fed. Reg. 4712, 4714 (Jan. 24, 1995) (codified at 40 C.F.R. pts. 51, 52, 85). In October 1999, CARB approved regulations governing the next, more stringent phase of the California LEV program, commonly referred to as "LEV II," which will become effective in model year 2004. *See* CAL. CODE REGS. tit. 13, § 1961 (2000). *See also id.* § 1962 (establishing a zero-emission vehicle program beginning with model year 2000). As indicated above, EPA has not yet promulgated more stringent federal emissions standards, which are due to become effective in model year 2004. *See* 42 U.S.C. § 7521(b)(1)(C).

[210] *See* Fern, *supra* note 197, at 227.

[211] *See id.*

[212] *See* 42 U.S.C. § 7511c. The OTC consists of Connecticut, Delaware, Maine, Maryland, Massachusetts, New Hampshire, New Jersey, New York, Pennsylvania, Rhode Island, Vermont, and the Consolidated Metropolitan Statistical Area, which includes the District of Columbia and a portion of Virginia. *See id.* § 7511c(a); *see also* Proposed Rulemaking on Ozone Transport Commission, 59 Fed. Reg. 21,720, 21,722 (Apr. 26, 1994) (describing the creation of the OTC).

[213] Proposed Rulemaking on Ozone Transport Commission, 59 Fed. Reg. at 21,723.

[214] *See id.*

[215] These challenges, brought by automobile manufacturers, ultimately failed. For details regarding the Massachusetts litigation, see *American Automobile Manufacturers Ass'n v. Massachusetts Department of Environmental Protection*, 31 F.3d 18, 21–22 (1st Cir. 1994), and John Hiski Ridge, Comment, *Deconstructing the Clean Air Act: Examining the Controversy Surrounding Massachusetts's Adoption of the California Low Emission Vehicle Program*, 22 B.C. ENVTL. AFF. L. REV. 163, 183–98 (1994). For details regarding the New York litigation, see *Motor Vehicle Manufacturers Ass'n v. New York State Department of Environmental Conservation*, 79 F.3d 1298, 1301–04 (2d Cir. 1996), and *Motor Vehicle Manufacturers Ass'n v. New York State Department of Environmental Conservation*, 17 F.3d 521, 523–31 (2d Cir. 1994). The Second Circuit, however, enjoined enforcement of New York's standards in the 1995 model year because manufacturers had not been given sufficient lead time to implement the changes. *See Motor Vehicle Mfrs. Ass'n*, 17 F.3d at 534–35.

others made their adoption of the California LEV standards contingent on the adoption of those standards by other states in the region.[216]

By a majority vote of the member states' governors, the OTC can recommend to EPA additional measures to control ozone pollution.[217] The Clean Air Act provides that if the EPA Administrator approves such a recommendation, she must require each OTC member (even members that opposed the recommendation) to adopt these additional controls.[218] In August 1993, three OTC members — Maine, Maryland, and Massachusetts — petitioned the OTC to recommend the application of California LEV standards to all states within the OTC.[219] The OTC approved this petition by a 9–4 vote.[220] In January 1995, EPA approved the OTC's recommendation, thereby requiring all OTC members to adopt California's LEV standards beginning in model year 1999.[221]

At the same time, however, EPA indicated that it would attempt to broker an agreement between the OTC states and automobile manufacturers to enable the adoption of a national LEV program.[222] The agency hoped to facilitate the creation of a mutually acceptable set of national automobile emissions standards.[223] EPA acknowledged that the Clean Air Act precluded it from requiring manufacturers to meet more stringent standards before model year 2004;[224] it therefore sought the voluntary agreement of automobile manufacturers.[225] Throughout

---

In addition to their LEV programs, Massachusetts and New York both required that ZEVs comprise a certain proportion of manufacturers' sales. The Second Circuit invalidated the New York ZEV requirement, *see* Am. Auto. Mfrs. Ass'n v. Cahill, 152 F.3d 196, 201 (2d Cir. 1998), and the First Circuit delayed its decision on the Massachusetts ZEV requirement to enable EPA to decide whether the Clean Air Act preempted the Massachusetts regulation, *see* Am. Auto. Mfrs. Ass'n v. Mass. Dep't of Envtl. Prot., 163 F.3d 74, 86–87 (1st Cir. 1998). For commentary on the ZEV requirement, see David Bennett, Note, *Zero Emission Vehicles: The Air Pollution Messiah? Northeastern States Mandate ZEVs Without Considering the Alternatives or Consequences*, 20 WM. & MARY ENVTL. L. & POL'Y REV. 333, 353–64 (1996).

[216] *See* Proposed Rulemaking on Ozone Transport Commission, 59 Fed. Reg. at 21,723; Fern, *supra* note 197, at 238 n.63.

[217] *See* 42 U.S.C. § 7511c(c)(1).

[218] *See id.* § 7511c(c)(5).

[219] *See* Proposed Rulemaking on Ozone Transport Commission, 59 Fed. Reg. at 21,723.

[220] *See id.* Delaware, New Hampshire, New Jersey, and Virginia opposed the recommendation. *Id.*

[221] *See* Final Rule on Ozone Transport Commission, 60 Fed. Reg. 4712, 4731 n.26 (Jan. 24, 1995) (codified at 40 C.F.R. pts. 51, 52, 85).

[222] *See id.* at 4713–15.

[223] *See id.* at 4713.

[224] *See* Control of Air Pollution from New Motor Vehicles and New Motor Vehicle Engines, 63 Fed. Reg. 11,374, 11,374–75 (Mar. 9, 1998); Final Rule on Ozone Transport Commission, 60 Fed. Reg. at 4713–14. *See generally* 42 U.S.C. § 7521(b)(1)(C) (1994).

[225] *See* Control of Air Pollution from New Motor Vehicles and New Motor Vehicle Engines, 63 Fed. Reg. at 11,374; Control of Air Pollution from New Motor Vehicles and New Motor Vehicle Engines, 62 Fed. Reg. 31,192, 31,192 (June 6, 1997) (codified at 40 C.F.R. pts. 85, 86).

the regulatory proceedings, however, EPA stressed that once a manufacturer opted in to the program, the agency could enforce the national standard against that manufacturer like any other binding automobile emissions standard.[226] In its approval of the OTC recommendation, EPA indicated that its order requiring the OTC states to adopt the California standards would become effective only if the national LEV program failed.[227]

This dual strategy suffered a significant setback in March 1997, when the D.C. Circuit held that EPA lacked authority to require OTC states to adopt California's LEV standards.[228] Despite losing this trump card, EPA succeeded in fashioning a national LEV program that shared important features with California's LEV program.[229] In two major respects, however, the national LEV program is less restrictive than its California counterpart. First, the fleet average emissions standard for one of the pollutants — nonmethane organic matter — is 19% higher in the national program: 0.075 grams per mile instead of 0.063 grams per mile.[230] Second, the national LEV program does not require Zero Emission Vehicles (ZEVs).[231]

In March 1998, EPA declared the national LEV program binding and effective, and announced that manufacturers must meet the program's emissions standards in the northeastern states in model year 1999 and nationally in model year 2001.[232] All twenty-three automobile manufacturers that sell cars in the United States entered into the agreement, as did nine OTC states.[233] The four remaining OTC states — Maine and Vermont in addition to Massachusetts and New York[234]

---

[226] See Control of Air Pollution from New Motor Vehicles and New Motor Vehicle Engines, 63 Fed. Reg. at 11,375; Control of Air Pollution from New Motor Vehicles and New Motor Vehicle Engines, 62 Fed. Reg. at 31,192.

[227] See Final Rule on Ozone Transport Commission, 60 Fed. Reg. at 4712.

[228] See Virginia v. EPA, 108 F.3d 1397, 1415, modified on other grounds, 116 F.3d 499, 501 (D.C. Cir. 1997). The court determined that the Clean Air Act prevents EPA from imposing more stringent automobile emissions standards before model year 2004. See id. at 1411 (citing 42 U.S.C. § 7521(b)(1)(C)). States, however, remained free to adopt the California standards. See 42 U.S.C. § 7507; see also supra p. 586 (discussing states' freedom to adopt the California standards).

[229] Compare EPA Exhaust Emission Standards for 1999 and Later Light-Utility Vehicles, 40 C.F.R. § 86.1708-99 tbl.R99-1 (2000) (national LEV program), with CAL. CODE REGS. tit. 13, § 1960.1(g)(1) (2000) (California LEV program).

[230] Compare 40 C.F.R. § 86.1708-99 tbl.R99-1 (national LEV program), with Staff Report, supra note 207, at 3.

[231] See Control of Air Pollution from New Motor Vehicles and New Motor Vehicle Engines, 63 Fed. Reg. 926, 933 (Jan. 7, 1998) (codified at 40 C.F.R. pts. 9, 85, 86 (2000)).

[232] See Control of Air Pollution from New Motor Vehicles and New Motor Vehicle Engines, 63 Fed. Reg. 11,374, 11,374–75 (Mar. 9, 1998).

[233] See id. at 11,375.

[234] See supra pp. 588–89.

— adopted the California standards instead.[235] EPA has estimated that for 2001 and subsequent model years, emission of volatile organic compounds and nitrogen oxides will be up to 66% and 73% lower, respectively, under the national LEV program than the federal standards would otherwise have required.[236]

More recently, thirteen states announced a joint plan in November 2000 to adopt emission limits for truck and bus engines that are far stricter than the current federal standards.[237] This group includes not only California and some northeastern states[238] — the leaders in automobile emissions standards — but also Georgia, Nevada, North Carolina, and Texas.[239] Because these states represent approximately 40% of the market for new trucks,[240] manufacturers may respond by adopting the more restrictive standard nationwide, as they eventually did in the case of automobiles. In this regard, the executive directors of both the State and Territorial Air Pollution Program Administrators and the Association of Local Air Pollution Control Officials stated: "Our hope is [that] with these states joining California, we will create the critical mass that will result in the engine manufacturers deciding to manufacture just one truck model, and it would be a much cleaner truck."[241]

3. Interpreting the Motivations of the States. — It can be difficult to determine whether states enact environmental regulations in response to actual environmental concerns or out of the desire to externalize costs or to comply with federal mandates.[242] The case of automobile emissions standards poses particular difficulties because of the prominent role of EPA in approving the OTC recommendation and brokering the national LEV program.[243] Nonetheless, a careful analysis of these regulatory developments indicates that several states were the primary catalysts for the establishment of stringent national LEV standards. Moreover, these states' actions do not fit the paradigm of jurisdictions' externalizing pollution costs outside their borders, and for the most part their actions did not result from federal requirements.

---

[235] *See* Taly L. Jolish, Note, *Negotiating the Smog Away,* 18 VA. ENVTL. L.J. 305, 345–48 (1999).

[236] *See* Final Rule on Ozone Transport Commission, 60 Fed. Reg. 4712, 4714 (Jan. 24, 1995) (codified at 40 C.F.R. pts. 51, 52, 85).

[237] Matthew L. Wald, *13 States To Unite To Cut Truck Emissions,* N.Y. TIMES, Nov. 20, 2000, at A20.

[238] The participating northeastern states were Connecticut, Maine, Massachusetts, New Hampshire, New Jersey, New York, Rhode Island, and Vermont. *See id.*

[239] *See id.*

[240] *Id.*

[241] *Id.*

[242] *See supra* p. 584.

[243] *See supra* section III.A.2, pp. 588–91.

First, several states took the lead at critical points in the regulatory process. Most importantly, California started the process in the 1960s by adopting its own controls and by providing a strong impetus for the first federal regulatory scheme.[244] It took the lead again in 1990 by adopting its LEV program, moving ahead of the federal government in terms of both the timing and the stringency of its standards.[245] This pattern continues today; for example, while California implemented more stringent controls through its LEV II program in October 1999,[246] the federal government missed a December 31, 1999, deadline for determining whether to strengthen the federal emissions standards.

Following California's lead, Massachusetts and New York were the primary catalysts for the OTC petition that ultimately led to the national LEV program.[247] Moreover, the threat that other states would also choose the California LEV standards, as Maine and Vermont ultimately did,[248] must have pressured the automobile industry to agree to the national LEV standards.

Second, federal nonattainment provisions did not compel these states to take the lead in automobile emissions standards. Indeed, California's interest in automobile emissions regulation predates not only the nonattainment provisions but also the federal Clean Air Act itself.[249] Similarly, it was the member states of the OTC, which owed its existence to the nonattainment status of its member states with respect to ozone,[250] that asked EPA to determine that more stringent emissions standards were necessary for the OTC region to move toward compliance.[251] Theoretically, these states might have adopted stringent limits on auto emissions to ease the regulatory pressure on stationary pollution sources, and thereby attract industrial firms. But as long as a region remains in nonattainment, any major new pollution source must obtain offsetting emission reductions from existing sources, so that once it begins operation the total emissions in the region decrease rather than increase.[252] New pollution sources must also meet strict emissions standards set by reference to the lowest achiev-

---

[244] *See supra* pp. 585–86.

[245] *See supra* pp. 587–88.

[246] *See supra* note 209.

[247] *See supra* pp. 588–89.

[248] *See supra* p. 591.

[249] *See supra* p. 585.

[250] *See* 42 U.S.C. § 7511c(c)(1) (1994) (providing that the OTC can make recommendations for additional measures only if "the commission determines such measures are necessary to bring any area . . . into attainment").

[251] *See* Final Rule on Ozone Transport Commission, 60 Fed. Reg. 4712, 4712 (Jan. 24, 1995) (codified at 40 C.F.R. pts. 51, 52, 85) ("At the request of the [OTC states], EPA is announcing today its final determination that reduction of new motor vehicle emissions . . . is necessary [in the OTC region].").

[252] *See* 42 U.S.C. § 7503(a)(1)(A).

able emission rate (LAER).[253]   These requirements apply to new stationary sources regardless of the stringency of the state automobile
emissions standards.

Third, automobile emissions standards are not the type of regulations that are imposed on out-of-state manufacturers to benefit in-state
industry. As discussed above,[254] such environmental regulations, however stringent, may result from protectionism rather than environmental concern.[255] Here, the states that took the lead in automobile
emissions standards did not benefit by protecting in-state manufacturers — as would be the case, for example, if a state that manufactured
paperboard cartons attempted to ban plastic containers.[256] Rather,
emissions regulations imposed costs on *in-state purchasers* of more expensive automobiles.[257] Consumers in other states bore part of the
costs only to the extent that more stringent regulations reduced the
economies of scale in automobile production. Out-of-state consumers
also sustained costs when auto manufacturers adopted more stringent
emissions standards nationwide, but neither California nor the OTC
states initially sought such uniformity.[258]

Moreover, California's standards covered not only automobiles, but
also trucks.[259] Thus, the regulations likely increased production costs
for in-state manufacturers of products requiring ground transportation
and placed them at a competitive disadvantage relative to firms in
states with less stringent regulations. The recent effort by several
states to adopt restrictive emissions standards for trucks is expected to
increase truck prices by $700 to $800 per vehicle.[260]

---

[253] *See id.* § 7503(a)(2).

[254] *See supra* p. 584.

[255] *See* Stewart, *Lessons from the Federal Experience, supra* note 2, at 1333.

[256] *See* Minnesota v. Clover Leaf Creamery Co., 449 U.S. 456, 471–74 (1981) (upholding a Minnesota recycling statute banning the sale of milk in plastic containers).

[257] In 1996, CARB estimated these increased costs, relative to the federal standards, to be $72
per vehicle for TLEVs, $120 per vehicle for LEVs, and $145 per vehicle for ULEVs. *See* Staff
Report, *supra* note 207, at 20.

        In 1997, EPA estimated that the additional cost per vehicle of the national LEV program
would be below the CARB estimates, due in part to economies of scale in production. *See* Control of Air Pollution from New Motor Vehicles and New Motor Vehicle Engines, 62 Fed. Reg.
31,192, 31,197 (June 6, 1997) (codified at 40 C.F.R. pts. 85, 86). Earlier estimates of the incremental cost per automobile under the California standards, however, were far higher, ranging up
to $2,000 per vehicle. *See* Virginia v. EPA, 108 F.3d 1397, 1403 n.5, *modified on other grounds*,
116 F.3d 499, 501 (D.C. Cir. 1997). In 1999, 2,041,143 new cars were sold in California. Telephone Interview by Elena Zlatnick with Bill Gengler, Media Relations, California Department of
Motor Vehicles (Feb. 14, 2000). Assuming an average additional cost per vehicle of $100, the
regulations impose on California consumers an additional annual cost of approximately
$200,000,000.

[258] *See supra* pp. 584–85, pp. 588–89.

[259] *See* CAL. CODE REGS. tit. 13, § 1956.8 (1999) (heavy-duty engines and vehicles); *id.*
§ 1961.1(g) (light-duty trucks).

[260] *See* Wald, *supra* note 237.

B. Hazardous Waste Regulation

This section reviews the actions of states with respect to three important programs: state Superfund provisions, voluntary cleanup and brownfield redevelopment programs, and land transfer statutes. It shows how many states have developed hazardous waste cleanup provisions that are stricter and more comprehensive than the federal Superfund statute.

1. State Superfund Provisions. — (a) Introduction: The Federal Program. — The Comprehensive Environmental Response, Compensation, and Liability Act (CERCLA)[261] — commonly known as the federal Superfund statute — is the most visible provision dealing with the cleanup of sites contaminated with hazardous substances. CERCLA imposes liability on an extensive set of so-called potentially responsible parties (PRPs): the current owner or operator of a site where hazardous substances are released into the environment, prior owners or operators who are connected to the release, certain transporters of hazardous substances to the site, and the generators of the hazardous substances.[262] CERCLA's liability regime weighs heavily against PRPs: the statute imposes strict liability; liability extends to actions that predate the statute; joint and several liability attaches if the harm at the site is indivisible; the causation requirements are highly attenuated; and the defenses are extremely limited.[263]

PRPs are responsible primarily for cleanup costs at the site.[264] Federal, state, and tribal governments may sue to recover such costs.[265] Private parties — generally PRPs that have paid some cleanup costs at the site and seek to recover a portion of these costs

---

[261] 42 U.S.C. §§ 9601–9675 (1994 & Supp. V 1999).

[262] *Id.* § 9607(a) (1994). For a general discussion of the Superfund liability regime, see Richard L. Revesz & Richard B. Stewart, *The Superfund Debate, in* ANALYZING SUPERFUND: ECONOMICS, SCIENCE, AND LAW 3 (Richard L. Revesz & Richard B. Stewart eds., 1995).

[263] 42 U.S.C. § 9607 (1994 & Supp. II 1996); *see also* Revesz & Stewart, *supra* note 262, at 6–7 (detailing CERCLA's liability regime). For discussions of the impact of joint and several liability, see Lewis A. Kornhauser & Richard L. Revesz, *Apportioning Damages Among Potentially Insolvent Actors,* 19 J. LEGAL STUD. 617 (1990); Lewis A. Kornhauser & Richard L. Revesz, *Evaluating the Effects of Alternative Superfund Liability Rules, in* ANALYZING SUPERFUND: ECONOMICS, SCIENCE, AND LAW, *supra* note 262, at 115; Lewis A. Kornhauser & Richard L. Revesz, *Joint and Several Liability, in* 2 THE NEW PALGRAVE DICTIONARY OF ECONOMICS AND THE LAW 371 (Peter Newman ed., 1998) [hereinafter Kornhauser & Revesz, *Joint and Several Liability*]; Lewis A. Kornhauser & Richard L. Revesz, *Multidefendant Settlements: The Impact of Joint and Several Liability,* 23 J. LEGAL STUD. 41 (1994); Lewis A. Kornhauser & Richard L. Revesz, *Multidefendant Settlements Under Joint and Several Liability: The Problem of Insolvency,* 23 J. LEGAL STUD. 517 (1994); Lewis A. Kornhauser & Richard L. Revesz, *Settlements Under Joint and Several Liability,* 68 N.Y.U. L. REV. 427 (1993); and Lewis A. Kornhauser & Richard L. Revesz, *Sharing Damages Among Multiple Tortfeasors,* 98 YALE L.J. 831 (1989).

[264] 42 U.S.C. §§ 9607(a)(4)(A), (B) (1994).

[265] *Id.* § 9607(a)(4)(A).

from other PRPs — can also bring suit.[266] In addition to these cleanup provisions, CERCLA authorizes federal, state, and tribal governments — but not private parties — to recover damages for harm to natural resources "belonging to, managed by, controlled by, or appertaining to" such governments.[267]

CERCLA also contains provisions to tax chemicals, petroleum products, and general corporate profits.[268] These taxes raise money for the Hazardous Substances Superfund, the source of the statute's popular name. The fund has two primary purposes: to pay for cleanups when the PRPs associated with a given site are either insolvent or unknown (or when some of them are insolvent or unknown and joint and several liability does not attach) and to advance money for EPA's activities at other sites pending recovery of cleanup costs from the PRPs.[269]

Under CERCLA, EPA is responsible for maintaining a National Priorities List (NPL) of the most hazardous sites in the country. Only NPL sites qualify for the expenditure by EPA of Superfund money for remedial actions — the long-term cleanups designed to remedy the contamination permanently.[270] At non-NPL sites — locations with contamination that is significant but insufficiently serious to warrant federal listing — the federal role is generally limited to removal actions, which are typically quicker and less extensive cleanups than remedial actions. Removal actions often are undertaken to address specific emergencies.[271]

Currently, approximately 1200 sites on the NPL await federally supervised cleanups.[272] In the twenty-year history of the Superfund program, only 197 cleanups have been completed at NPL sites.[273] In ad-

---

[266] *Id.* § 9607(a)(4)(B).

[267] *Id.* § 9607(f); *see id.* § 9607(a)(4)(C); *see also* Revesz & Stewart, *supra* note 262, at 20–21 (describing liability for damage to natural resources under CERCLA). PRPs are also responsible for health assessment or health effects studies. *See* 42 U.S.C. § 9607(a)(4)(D).

[268] Revesz & Stewart, *supra* note 262, at 7–8 (describing the CERCLA taxing regime). Although authority for Superfund taxes expired in December 1995, the Superfund is still receiving some taxes due to private sector arrears and adjustments by the Treasury Department. The fund is also still receiving interest revenue. Tax receipts into the fund in fiscal year 1998 were $79 million, down from $1.48 billion in fiscal year 1995. U.S. GEN. ACCOUNTING OFFICE, SUPERFUND: INFORMATION ON THE PROGRAM'S FUNDING AND STATUS 2–5 (1999).

[269] Revesz & Stewart, *supra* note 262, at 8.

[270] EPA Cooperative Agreements and Superfund State Contracts for Superfund Response Actions, 40 C.F.R. § 35.6015(27) (2000). For the definition of remedial actions, see 42 U.S.C. § 9601(24).

[271] *See* ENVTL. LAW INST., AN ANALYSIS OF STATE SUPERFUND PROGRAMS: 50-STATE STUDY, 1998 UPDATE 1 (1998). For the definition of removal actions, see 42 U.S.C. § 9601(23).

[272] *See* 40 C.F.R. pt. 300 app. B (2000).

[273] National Priorities List for Uncontrolled Hazardous Waste Sites, 65 Fed. Reg. 5468, 5470 (proposed Jan. 28, 2000) (to be codified at 40 C.F.R. pt. 300). The sites were subsequently delisted. *See id.*

dition, EPA has completed 595 removal actions at NPL sites and 2591 removal actions at other sites.[274]

(b) State Programs. — Despite the relatively small number of sites awaiting or benefiting from federal cleanup actions, a recent study reports that state environmental officials believe that approximately 24,000 sites require some type of cleanup and that the number of known and suspected contaminated sites — a category that includes sites that require investigation to determine whether cleanup is necessary — is approximately 69,000.[275] These numbers suggest that the federal Superfund program has not even chipped away at the tip of the iceberg.

State involvement in cleanups predates the enactment of CERCLA. New Jersey led the way with the enactment of the Spill Compensation and Control Act[276] in 1976, four years before the passage of CERCLA. In recent years, state attention has intensified to the point that every jurisdiction now has liability provisions for the cleanup of hazardous waste sites.[277]

These state provisions are modeled closely on CERCLA (which itself borrowed heavily from the New Jersey Spill Act).[278] The majority of state statutes define the same categories of PRPs as does CERCLA.[279] As with CERCLA, forty-three states have retroactive liability, and several of the states without such provisions have invoked CERCLA when retroactivity has been necessary to recover cleanup costs.[280] Similarly, as under CERCLA, forty-one states hold responsible parties strictly liable, and thirty-six states permit the imposition of joint and several liability.[281] Moreover, twenty-five states have more stringent provisions than CERCLA, providing punitive damages — treble damages in twenty-two states, double damages in one, and one-and-a-half damages in another — for noncompliance with enforcement orders.[282]

The vast majority of states have also established funds to pay for cleanups if PRPs cannot be found to do so.[283] By 1989, all but two

---

[274] *See* U.S. GEN. ACCOUNTING OFFICE, SUPERFUND: PROGRESS, PROBLEMS AND FUTURE OUTLOOK 5 (1999). As discussed below, CERCLA does not effectively encourage private parties to perform cleanups in the absence of governmental compulsion. *See infra* p. 600.

[275] *See* ENVTL. LAW INST., *supra* note 271, at 3.

[276] 1976 N.J. Laws 141 (codified as amended in scattered sections of N.J. STAT. ANN. tit. 58).

[277] *See* ENVTL. LAW INST., *supra* note 271, at 50–52 tbl.V-1, 103–04 tbl.V-15.

[278] *Id.* at 32.

[279] *Id.* at 31–32.

[280] *Id.* at 32, 102–04 tbl.V-15.

[281] *Id.* at 33–34, 102–04 tbl.V-15.

[282] *Id.* at 34–35, 105–07 tbl.V-16. Most state provisions, like CERCLA, also assess fines for noncompliance. 42 U.S.C. § 9606(b)(1) (1994) (CERCLA); ENVTL. LAW INST., *supra* note 271, at 35, 105–07 tbl.V-16.

[283] ENVTL. LAW INST., *supra* note 271, at 7.

states had such funds.[284] At the end of fiscal year 1997, the aggregate balance in these state funds totaled $1.41 billion.[285] The balance in the federal Superfund at the end of fiscal year 1999 was virtually identical: $1.4 billion.[286]

Another way to measure the size of state programs relative to the federal Superfund involves examining how much each spends on cleanup activities. Forty-four states reported spending a combined $565.1 million on cleanups in fiscal year 1997.[287] In contrast, expenditures from the federal Superfund during this period totaled $1.45 billion.[288] These figures indicate that the states play a significant role in financing cleanup activities. The magnitude of expenditures from these funds is not a perfect proxy for overall expenditures on cleanups, however, because PRPs are the primary source of cleanup financing as a result of their statutory liability.[289] Aggregate data on their expenditures are unfortunately not available.

Another means of comparison involves examining the number of staff working to remediate hazardous waste sites. If PRPs could be located to pay the full costs of cleanups (including the costs of governmental supervision of the cleanups), government entities would not need to spend anything. In such a case, a comparison of federal and state expenditures would obviously be meaningless. Nonetheless, the number of staff working on remediation matters might offer a rough measure of the relative scope of governmental effort. The forty-nine states that provided information on this matter reported a total of 3474 staff working in state cleanup programs.[290] Similarly, approximately 3000 federal employees worked on Superfund-related matters.[291]

Analyzing the numbers of state cleanups provides another perspective on the magnitude of state programs. During fiscal year 1997, the states completed 5552 cleanups.[292] In contrast, only about 200 sites

---

[284] *Id.* at 8, 71–75 tbl.V-7.

[285] *Id.* at 3, 16. These funds were not uniformly distributed across the states. Whereas ten states had less than $1 million, Pennsylvania and New Jersey had over $100 million each, and New York had over $600 million. *Id.* at 50–52 tbl.V-1, 71–75 tbl.V-7.

[286] *See* U.S. GEN. ACCOUNTING OFFICE, *supra* note 268, at 3.

[287] *See* ENVTL. LAW INST., *supra* note 271, at 3, 19–21, 72–75 tbl.V-7.

[288] U.S. GEN. ACCOUNTING OFFICE, *supra* note 268, at 20 app. 1.

[289] *See supra* p. 595.

[290] ENVTL. LAW INST., *supra* note 271, at 12–13, 64, 65–67 tbl.V-5. The report indicates that, in most cases, the number includes only state employees responsible for the remediation of hazardous substance contamination. In some cases, however, the number also includes employees dealing with related matters. *Id.* at 12–13.

[291] *See* Rena I. Steinzor, *The Reauthorization of Superfund: The Public Works Alternative*, 25 ENVTL. L. REP. 10,078, 10,079 (1995) (citing Benjamin F. Chavis, Jr., John W. Johnstone & Joseph W. Brown, *Perspective on the Superfund: Bring Fair Play to Toxic Cleanup*, L.A. TIMES, Feb. 9, 1994, at B7).

[292] ENVTL. LAW INST., *supra* note 271, at 9–11, 61, 62–63 tbl.V-4. An additional 13,713 cleanups were underway. *Id.* at 61, 62–63 tbl.V-4.

have been delisted from the NPL during the entire history of the Superfund program.[293] Although this comparison does not reflect the greater scope and complexity of the federal cleanups, it reveals a significant level of activity at the state level.[294]

The preceding comparisons give some sense of the relative magnitudes of the federal and state programs. They suggest that state programs fund over one quarter — and perhaps as much as one half — of efforts to remediate contamination. Unlike other environmental statutes, which compel state participation, CERCLA does not require states to enact their own Superfund programs.[295]

2. Voluntary Cleanup and Brownfield Redevelopment Programs. — (a) Voluntary Cleanups and CERCLA's Lost Opportunities. — A cleanup is typically labeled as voluntary if undertaken without enforcement action by a governmental entity.[296] As a result, many private party cleanups are not in fact voluntary. For example, under CERCLA, PRPs often perform cleanups pursuant to an administrative order issued by EPA or a judicially approved consent decree between the PRPs and EPA.[297]

From an environmental perspective, voluntary cleanups are highly advantageous. Governmental regulators face inevitable budgetary and personnel constraints and can therefore bring only a limited number of enforcement actions. As a result, voluntary cleanups can significantly increase the number of successfully remediated sites. Earlier intervention, made possible by not spending time in the litigation of enforcement actions, also reduces the time individuals are exposed to contamination.

Moreover, cleanup costs tend to rise sharply over time if the contamination is left unattended.[298] For example, the leakage of hazardous substances from damaged barrels may initially affect only the surrounding soil, which may be remediable through soil removal and incineration. Over time, however, the groundwater may become affected, significantly raising the costs and lowering the probability that the cleanup will be successful.[299]

---

[293] *See supra* p. 596.

[294] EPA estimates that the average cost of the cleanup of an NPL site is over $30 million. *See* National Priorities List for Uncontrolled Hazardous Waste Sites, 60 Fed. Reg. 20,330, 20,334 (Apr. 25, 1995).

[295] ENVTL. LAW INST., *supra* note 271, at 7.

[296] *Id.* at 39.

[297] Revesz & Stewart, *supra* note 262, at 12.

[298] Lewis A. Kornhauser & Richard L. Revesz, *Regulation of Hazardous Wastes, in* 3 NEW PALGRAVE DICTIONARY OF ECONOMICS AND THE LAW 238, 239 (Peter Newman ed., 1998).

[299] *See* Robert F. Copple, *The New Economic Efficiency in Natural Resource Damage Assessments,* 66 U. COLO. L. REV. 675, 698 n.79 (1995); Richard L. Revesz, *Environmental Regulation, Cost-Benefit Analysis, and the Discounting of Human Lives,* 99 COLUM. L. REV. 941, 990–91 (1999); *Right Angle Cuts Cleaning Costs,* WATER TECH. NEWS, June 1, 1998, 1998 WL 9857469.

Cleanups at brownfield sites are a subset of voluntary cleanups. The term "brownfields" generally refers to an industrial or commercial facility in an urban area that has been abandoned as a result, at least in part, of environmental contamination.[300] Redevelopment frequently follows brownfield cleanups, typically as part of a strategy to aid an economically or environmentally distressed area.[301] In recent years, the redevelopment of brownfield sites has found strong support among some environmental justice advocates who are concerned about the contamination of areas that are often disproportionately populated by racial minorities and the economically disadvantaged.[302] Brownfield redevelopments also have the broader environmental and land use advantages of preventing industrial activity from encroaching on greenfield sites in rural areas.[303]

In theory, CERCLA provides important incentives for voluntary cleanups. As discussed above, cleanup costs can rise rapidly if a contaminated site is left unattended. Thus, a PRP could reduce its liability by addressing a problem early, rather than waiting for years until an enforcement action is brought.[304] Moreover, CERCLA allows a PRP that has paid more than its apportioned share of the liability to bring a contribution action against other PRPs.[305] To the extent that other PRPs might have limited solvency, which they could dissipate over time, a PRP that expects to remain solvent over the long term has an incentive to incur cleanup costs so that it can bring a contribution action while such an action remains valuable.[306]

But in practice, CERCLA has not been effective in fostering incentives for voluntary cleanups. First, EPA has been slow in adding sites to the NPL; the number was relatively stable through the 1990s.[307] Second, removal actions (typically less extensive cleanups often undertaken in response to an emergency) have affected only a small propor-

---

[300] ENVTL. LAW INST., *supra* note 271, at 43.

[301] *Id.* at 44.

[302] *See* John S. Applegate, *Risk Assessment, Redevelopment, and Environmental Justice: Evaluating the Brownfields Bargain*, 13 J. NAT. RESOURCES & ENVTL. L. 243, 284–86 (1997–1998); Kirsten H. Engel, *Brownfield Initiatives and Environmental Justice: Second-Class Cleanups or Market-Based Equity?*, 13 J. NAT. RESOURCES & ENVTL. L. 317, 318 (1997–1998). Other environmental justice advocates, however, are concerned that brownfield cleanups might not be sufficiently extensive. *See* Applegate, *supra*, at 284–86; Engel, *supra*, at 319.

[303] *See* William W. Buzbee, *Remembering Repose: Voluntary Contamination Cleanup Approvals, Incentives, and the Costs of Interminable Liability*, 80 MINN. L. REV. 35, 39–40 (1995).

[304] Addressing the contamination early also increases the value of the contaminated site, thus offering an added incentive for the current owner to undertake a voluntary cleanup.

[305] 42 U.S.C. § 9613(f)(1) (1994).

[306] *Cf. In re* The Charter Co., 862 F.2d 1500, 1504 (11th Cir. 1989) (discussing CERCLA indemnity claims brought too late, when the PRPs had already filed for bankruptcy and were protected from contingent claims for contribution under the Bankruptcy Code).

[307] *See supra* pp. 595–596.

tion of sites.[308] Thus, in most cases the probability of a federal enforcement action is low.[309] As a result, the incentive to take action earlier, in order to avoid greater liability when the government brings an enforcement action, is substantially diluted.[310]

The other serious impediment to voluntary cleanups arises from concerns about residual liability following such cleanups. For non-NPL sites, there is no mechanism under CERCLA to determine what type of cleanup EPA would consider appropriate. Moreover, EPA does not have a procedure for certifying that a particular cleanup is sufficiently extensive.[311] As a result, a PRP undertaking a voluntary cleanup faces a risk that, at some point in the future, EPA will decide that the cleanup was inadequate and, consequently, bring the very enforcement action the PRP sought to avoid.[312]

(b) States' Initiatives in Voluntary Cleanups. — In contrast to the ineffectual role the federal government has played in promoting voluntary cleanups, the states have moved resolutely into this area.[313] A recent survey by the Environmental Law Institute found that, in 1997, forty-four states had voluntary cleanup programs, fifteen of which had been adopted between 1995 and 1997.[314] Moreover, of the seven remaining jurisdictions, several have taken significant steps toward establishing such programs.[315]

---

[308] *See supra* p. 596.

[309] Enforcement actions brought by the states, which implicate a broader set of sites, *see supra* pp. 597–598, therefore provide PRPs with stronger incentives to undertake voluntary cleanups.

[310] Moreover, even if EPA were more aggressive in supervising cleanups at NPL sites, the contamination at many brownfield sites would be unlikely to be sufficiently severe to merit listing. *See* Robert H. Abrams, *Superfund and the Evolution of Brownfields*, 21 WM. & MARY ENVTL. L. & POL'Y REV. 265, 274–75 (1997).

[311] *See* Buzbee, *supra* note 303, at 54–100.

[312] *See id.* at 50–53; Sarah W. Rubinstein, *CERCLA's Contribution to the Federal Brownfields Problem: A Proposal for Federal Reform*, 4 U. CHI. L. SCH. ROUNDTABLE 149, 151–63 (1997); Wendy E. Wagner, *Learning from Brownfields*, 13 J. NAT. RESOURCES & ENVTL. L. 217, 222–25 (1997–1998).

[313] *See* Anne Slaughter Andrew, *Brownfield Redevelopment: A State-Led Reform of Superfund Liability*, NAT. RESOURCES & ENV'T, Winter 1996, at 27, 27–30; William W. Buzbee, *Brownfields, Environmental Federalism, and Institutional Determinism*, 21 WM. & MARY ENVTL. L. & POL'Y REV. 1, 41 (1997).

[314] *See* ENVTL. LAW INST., *supra* note 271, at 39, 123, 124–25 tbl.V-22.

[315] *Id.* at 39. Approximately thirty-seven states limit participation in their voluntary cleanup programs, typically based on the characteristics of the site or the volunteer. *Id.* at 126, 127–30 tbl.V-23. In approximately twenty-five states, sites that are the subject of any federal or state enforcement action may not participate in such programs. *Id.* at 40. At least thirteen states impose some limitations on who may volunteer, barring firms responsible for the contamination at the site; firms that are the subject of enforcement actions, even with respect to other operations; or firms that are not in compliance with (or have been convicted of violating) provisions of the environmental laws. *Id.* Seven states that do not have categorical exclusions nonetheless retain the right to reject applications on a case-by-case basis. *Id.*

The same standards govern state voluntary cleanup programs as govern cleanups triggered by enforcement actions;[316] most states, however, provide other incentives to encourage participation in their voluntary cleanup programs.[317] Unlike the federal government,[318] most states have mechanisms for approving cleanups, and at least forty states limit the potential liability of PRPs that complete cleanups meeting state standards.[319]

A significant number of states rely extensively on voluntary cleanups. At least ten states have more than 100 voluntary cleanups underway; New Jersey leads this list with over 2300.[320] Similarly, a substantial number of voluntary cleanups have been completed. At least eight states reported completion of over 100 voluntary cleanups. Again, New Jersey leads the list, with over 4400 completed cleanups.[321]

Additionally, twenty-eight states had brownfield redevelopment programs in 1997, up from fifteen in 1995.[322] Despite the recent vintage of most of these programs, several states have made considerable progress in identifying brownfield sites as a first step toward redeveloping them. Six states have identified over 100 sites; Illinois is the leader with over 1000 sites. Five states have over 40 cleanups underway; Illinois has the most, with 439 cleanups in progress. Four states

---

[316] *Id.*

[317] *Id.* at 41.

[318] *See supra* p. 600.

[319] *See* ENVTL. LAW INST., *supra* note 271, at 42, 126, 127–30 tbl.V-23.

[320] *Id.* at 41.

[321] *Id.*

[322] *Id.* at 44, 131, 132–34 tbl.V-24. For other surveys, see BROWNFIELDS: A COMPREHENSIVE GUIDE TO REDEVELOPING CONTAMINATED PROPERTY (Todd S. Davis & Kevin D. Margolis eds., 1997); OFFICE OF TECH. ASSESSMENT, U.S. CONG., STATE OF THE STATES ON BROWNFIELDS: PROGRAMS FOR CLEANUP AND REUSE OF CONTAMINATED SITES (1995); and Joel B. Eisen, *"Brownfields of Dreams"?: Challenges and Limits of Voluntary Cleanup Programs and Incentives*, 1996 U. ILL. L. REV. 883, 914–79.

For discussion of the brownfield programs of particular states, see Phyllis E. Bross, Susan B. Boyle & Terri Smith, *The Greening of New Jersey's "Brownfields" — As Viewed by the Department of Environmental Protection*, 9 FORDHAM ENVTL. L.J. 541 (1998); Jane F. Clokey, *Wisconsin's Land Recycling Act: From Brownfield to Greenfield*, 2 WIS. ENVTL. L.J. 35 (1995); James W. Creenan & John Q. Lewis, *Pennsylvania's Land Recycling Program: Solving the Brownfields Problem with Remediation Standards and Limited Liability*, 34 DUQ. L. REV. 661 (1996); Michael B. Gerrard, *New York State's Brownfields Programs: More and Less than Meets the Eye*, 4 ALB. L. ENVTL. OUTLOOK 18 (1999); Tara Burns Koch, *Betting on Brownfields — Does Florida's Brownfields Redevelopment Act Transform Liability into Opportunity?*, 28 STETSON L. REV. 171 (1998); Eric D. Madden, *The Voluntary Cleanup and Property Redevelopment Act — The Limits of the Kansas Brownfields Law*, 46 U. KAN. L. REV. 593 (1998); Terry J. Tondro, *Reclaiming Brownfields To Save Greenfields: Shifting the Environmental Risks of Acquiring and Reusing Contaminated Land*, 27 CONN. L. REV. 789 (1995); and Alan D. Wasserman, *Michigan's Brownfields Redevelopment*, 1997 DETROIT C.L. MICH. ST. U. L. REV. 1217.

have more than ten commitments for redevelopment; Michigan leads with 144.[323]

State brownfield development programs, like state voluntary cleanup programs, offer liability protection.[324] Many states also offer program participants financial incentives, including low-interest loans, tax credits, and remedial cost reimbursements.[325]

In the last few years, EPA has taken limited steps to encourage state voluntary cleanup and brownfield redevelopment programs. The possibility of subsequent liability under the federal Superfund program remained a matter of concern to firms contemplating participation in these programs.[326] As a result, states pushed hard to get an agreement that EPA would not, in the future, bring enforcement actions against parties that had conducted voluntary cleanups or brownfield redevelopment projects and obtained protection against subsequent liability from the states. In 1995, EPA began entering into memorandums of agreement with some states, providing a certain degree of protection against subsequent federal enforcement actions;[327] sixteen states have now signed such agreements.[328]

These agreements provide that EPA will not bring actions to recover cleanup costs unless one of the following four conditions holds: EPA subsequently determines that conditions at the site pose "an im-

---

[323] See ENVTL. LAW INST., *supra* note 271, at 45–46, 135, 136–38 tbl.V-25.

[324] *Id.* at 46.

[325] *Id.* at 46–47. For a discussion about why nonenvironmental factors are also crucial for brownfield redevelopment, see Heidi Gorovitz Robertson, *One Piece of the Puzzle: Why State Brownfields Programs Can't Lure Businesses to the Urban Cores Without Finding the Missing Pieces*, 51 RUTGERS L. REV. 1075, 1091–95, 1108–21 (1999).

[326] In 1989, EPA issued a guidance document concerning agreements not to sue prospective purchasers of contaminated property. This policy could have provided the basis for relief for brownfield redevelopers. EPA, however, has rarely entered into such agreements. *See* Frona M. Powell, *Amending CERCLA To Encourage the Redevelopment of Brownfields*, 53 WASH. U. J. URB. & CONTEMP. L. 113, 126 (1998). For examples of other, isolated federal measures with respect to brownfields, see Steven B. Radel, *How the EPA Can Make Brownfield Redevelopment a Success and Not Just Another Overused Environmental Catch-Phrase*, 6 U. BALT. J. ENVTL. L. 45, 45–46 (1997). There also have been legislative proposals to encourage brownfield remediation, but none has passed. *See* Eisen, *supra* note 322, at 984–88; R. Michael Sweeney, *Brownfields Restoration and Voluntary Cleanup Legislation*, 2 ENVTL. LAW. 101, 119–21 (1995).

[327] *See* Notice of Availability of Final Draft Guidance for Developing Superfund Memoranda of Agreement (MOA) Language Concerning State Voluntary Cleanup Programs, 62 Fed. Reg. 47,495 (Sept. 9, 1997). As of August 1997, EPA had entered into memorandums of agreement with eleven states. *Id.* at 47,496. Subsequently, EPA withdrew this draft guidance but expressed interest in continuing to enter into memorandums of agreement on voluntary cleanups. *See* Memorandum from Timothy Fields, Jr., Acting Assistant Administrator, Office of Solid Waste and Emergency Response, and Steve A. Herman, Assistant Administrator, Office of Enforcement and Compliance Assurance, to Regional Administrators, Regions 1–10 (Nov. 26, 1997), http://www.epa.gov/swerosps/bf/html-doc/withdraw.htm.

[328] *See* EPA, *Memorandums of Agreement (MOAs) on State Voluntary Cleanup Programs (VCPs)*, *available at* http://www.epa.gov/swerosps/bf/pdf/statemoa.pdf (last visited Nov. 6, 2001).

minent and substantial endangerment to public health or welfare"; the state requests that EPA take action; subsequently discovered conditions at the site indicate that the voluntary cleanup does not protect human health or the environment; or the cleanup is no longer protective because of a change or proposed change in the use of the site.[329]

In addition, in 1994, EPA adopted a Brownfields Economic Redevelopment Initiative, under which it makes grants of up to $200,000 to cities, counties, towns, states, and tribes to help redevelop brownfields.[330]   EPA has also established a Brownfields Revolving Loan Fund, which lends up to $500,000 for brownfield redevelopment purposes. Congress did not fund this program until 1999, however, and so far only one such loan has been extended.[331]

In summary, the states have provided the bulk of the initiative with respect to voluntary cleanups and brownfield redevelopment. The federal role remains limited and largely reactive.[332]

3. Land Transfer Statutes. — This section focuses on the disclosure and cleanup obligations triggered by the sale or other transfer of real property. It first discusses the limited disclosure and lack of transfer-triggered requirements under federal law. Then it turns its attention to the extensive obligations imposed by New Jersey. It concludes with an assessment of how other states have responded to New Jersey's innovative legal regime.

(a) Federal Regime. — A provision of the Superfund statute that applies to federal property imposes the principal federal requirement concerning the transfer of contaminated land.[333] The provision, which Congress enacted in 1986,[334] covers "any real property owned by the United States on which any hazardous substance was stored for one year or more, known to have been released, or disposed of."[335] It requires that, before the date of any transfer, the government undertake "all remedial action necessary to protect human health and the envi-

---

[329] Notice of Availability of Final Draft Guidance for Developing Superfund Memoranda of Agreement (MOA) Language Concerning State Voluntary Cleanup Programs, 62 Fed. Reg. at 47,498.

[330] *See* Announcement of Competition for Final Five Brownfield Economic Redevelopment Initiative Pilots, 59 Fed. Reg. 60,012 (Nov. 21, 1994).

[331] *See Reps Ask Why Only One Loan from Brownfields Revolving Loan Fund*, HAZARDOUS WASTE NEWS, Nov. 8, 1999, 1999 WL 26079730.

[332] In recent years, there have been several legislative proposals to amend CERCLA to encourage the redevelopment of brownfields, but none has yet been enacted. *See* Powell, *supra* note 326, at 128–31.

[333] *See* 42 U.S.C. § 9620(h) (1994 & Supp. II 1996). For commentary, see Susan C. Borinsky, *The Use of Institutional Controls in Superfund and Similar State Laws*, 7 FORDHAM ENVTL. L.J. 1, 20–23 (1995).

[334] Superfund Amendments and Reauthorization Act of 1986, Pub. L. No. 99-499, § 120(h), 100 Stat. 1613, 1670–71 (codified as amended at 42 U.S.C. § 9620(h)).

[335] 42 U.S.C. § 9620(h)(3).

ronment with respect to any [hazardous] substance remaining on the property" and that, subsequent to the transfer, it undertake "any additional remedial action found to be necessary."[336] In addition, the statute requires that "to the extent such information is available on the basis of a complete search of agency files," the deed disclose "the type and quantity" of the hazardous substances, "the time at which such storage, release or disposal took place," and "a description of the remedial action taken, if any."[337] This provision primarily affects military bases and former nuclear weapons facilities managed by the U.S. Department of Energy.[338]

The federal Superfund statute does not apply any similarly broad disclosure or cleanup requirement to transfers of private land (or transfers of land owned by state or local governments). With respect to such transfers, the 1986 amendments to the statute impose liability on sellers with "actual knowledge of the release or threatened release of a hazardous substance" who transfer the property "without disclosing such knowledge."[339] Unlike transfers of federal property, with respect to which agencies have an obligation to search their files, transfers of private property trigger liability only when the transferor fails to disclose its "actual knowledge." Moreover, disclosure in the case of private transactions is necessary only if the knowledge is "of the release or threatened release of a hazardous substance." In contrast, for federal transfers, the requirement is triggered also by knowledge of the "storage" or "disposal" of such substances.[340] Finally, in the case of private land, lack of disclosure does not constitute a statutory violation; it exposes the nondisclosing party to adverse legal consequences only in the event of a subsequent cleanup.[341]

---

[336] *Id.* § 9620(h)(3)(A)(ii). The pretransfer cleanup obligation can be deferred under certain circumstances. *See id.* § 9620(h)(3)(C)(i).

[337] *Id.* § 9620(h)(3)(A)(i). The government also has disclosure obligations in connection with the contract for the sale of the property. *See id.* § 9620(h)(1).

[338] *See* Hercules Inc. v. EPA, 938 F.2d 276, 279 (D.C. Cir. 1991). *See generally* John S. Applegate & Stephen Dycus, *Institutional Controls or Emperor's Clothes? Long-Term Stewardship of the Nuclear Weapons Complex*, 28 ENVTL. L. REP. 10,631 (1998) (discussing cleanup efforts at nuclear facilities); Gregory F. Hurley, *Managing Construction Risks at Closing Military Bases*, PROCUREMENT LAW., Winter 1999, at 6 (discussing efforts at military bases). The disclosure requirement also applies when the federal government forecloses on property and subsequently sells it. *See Hercules*, 938 F.2d at 279.

[339] Superfund Amendments and Reauthorization Act § 101(35)(C), 42 U.S.C. § 9601(35)(C) (1994).

[340] Regulations promulgated pursuant to the Resource Conservation and Recovery Act of 1976, 42 U.S.C. §§ 6901–6987 (1994 & Supp. IV 1998), impose certain disclosure obligations upon sellers of property with active underground storage tanks. *See* EPA Technical Standards and Corrective Action Requirements for Owners and Operators of Underground Storage Tanks, 40 C.F.R. § 280.22 (2000); Eva M. Fromm, Edward C. Lewis & Heather M. Corken, *Allocating Environmental Liabilities in Acquisitions*, 22 J. CORP. L. 429, 433–37 (1997).

[341] 42 U.S.C. §§ 9601(35)(c), 9607(a) (1994).

Similarly, the transfer of private property does not trigger the need for a cleanup. The Superfund statute imposes liability both on the current owner of the property and on those who owned the property "at the time of disposal of any hazardous substance."[342] Moreover, the purchaser can raise a defense only by showing that at the time of the purchase it "did not know and had no reason to know" of the hazardous substances.[343] To satisfy the "no reason to know" requirement, the purchaser "must have undertaken, at the time of acquisition, all appropriate inquiry into the previous ownership and uses of the property consistent with good commercial or customary practice."[344] Although these incentives undoubtedly affect the pattern of property transfers as well as the price of property,[345] they neither require cleanups at the time of the transfer of ownership nor create strong incentives for cleanups to take place at that time. In cases in which cleanup costs would rise sharply in the absence of remedial action, private parties have an incentive to undertake a cleanup before the government requires one;[346] a transfer of ownership, however, does not influence this incentive.

(b) New Jersey's Approach. — In contrast to the narrow requirements of the federal Superfund statute, a number of states have implemented broad disclosure or cleanup requirements for the transfer of real property. New Jersey has been the pioneer in this area. In 1983, three years before Congress passed the limited disclosure obligations discussed above,[347] New Jersey adopted the Environmental Cleanup Responsibility Act (ECRA).[348] Ten years later, the state replaced ECRA with the Industrial Site Recovery Act (ISRA).[349]

ISRA is triggered by "transfer[al] [of] ownership or operations" at an "industrial establishment."[350] The seller must notify the New Jer-

---

[342] Id. § 9607(a)(2).

[343] Id. § 9601(35)(A)(i).

[344] Id. § 9601(35)(B).

[345] For discussion of the impact of Superfund on land transactions, see Kornhauser & Revesz, Joint and Several Liability, supra note 263.

[346] See supra pp. 599–600. The probability of subsequent detection by the government has a significant impact on this calculus. See supra pp. 599–600.

[347] See supra pp. 603–604.

[348] 1983 N.J. Laws 330 (codified at N.J. STAT. ANN. §§ 13:1K-6 to -14 (West 1991)) (amended 1993).

[349] 1993 N.J. Laws 139 (codified at N.J. STAT. ANN. §§ 13:1K-6 to -11.11, 58:10B-1 to -18, -20, 58:10-23.11g (West Supp. 2001)). For a discussion of the two laws, see Diana R. D'Alonzo, M. Kay Hennessy & Alysa B. Wakin, ECRA to ISRA: Is It More Than Just a Name Change?, 7 VILL. ENVTL. L.J. 51 (1996); Mark K. Dowd, New Jersey's Reform of Contaminated Site Remediation, 18 SETON HALL LEGIS. J. 207, 239–57 (1993); and I. Leo Motiuk, Sean T. Monaghan, Mark Benevenia & F. Michael Zachara, New Jersey's Hazardous Site Remediation Program: The Year of Reform, in AVOIDING ENVIRONMENTAL LIABILITY 585 (I. Leo Motiuk ed., 1993).

[350] N.J. STAT. ANN. § 13:1K-9(a) (West Supp. 2001). It is also triggered by "clos[ing] operations" at an "industrial establishment." Id.

sey Department of Environmental Protection (NJDEP) of the transaction "within five days after the execution of an agreement to transfer ownership or operations."[351] Before the transaction can proceed, the seller must obtain the NJDEP's approval of either a "negative declaration" that the land is not contaminated, or in the case of contaminated land, a "remedial action workplan" describing a proposed cleanup.[352] In the latter situation, the seller is obligated to remedy the contamination in a manner that meets the "health risk or environmental standards" set by the NJDEP.[353] The seller must also establish a "remediation funding source,"[354] such as a trust fund, insurance policy, line of credit, or self-guarantee, to pay for the cleanup.[355]

A seller may defer submitting or implementing a "remedial action workplan" under certain circumstances.[356] Most importantly, deferral is possible if the industrial establishment "would be subject to substantially the same use" following the transfer.[357] The purchaser (or transferee or mortgagee) must certify that it has the financial ability to pay for any necessary cleanup, but a cleanup does not need to be performed until the use changes or the operations at the site terminate. Deferral requires NJDEP's approval.[358]

Courts and administrative agencies have interpreted the scope of ISRA expansively. The New Jersey Supreme Court has upheld administrative regulations under which the sale of stock in a corporation owning or operating an industrial establishment triggers ISRA requirements when the sale effects a merger or consolidation or gives a party a controlling interest in the corporation.[359] As a result, the merger of large corporations can be delayed, pending NJDEP approval, if any party to the merger owns an industrial establishment in

---

[351] *Id.*

[352] *Id.* § 13:1K-9(c); *see also id.* § 13:1K-8 (defining "remedial action" and "negative declaration"). Under a statutory exception, a transaction can go forward before the approval of a negative declaration or a remedial action workplan if NJDEP approves a "remediation agreement" setting forth how the assessment of the site and any necessary cleanup would be conducted. In addition, the seller must make financial guarantees for the performance of a cleanup, if one is required. *Id.* § 13:1K-9(e). ISRA also provides a de minimis exception, which turns on the quantity of hazardous waste that the seller handled, *id.* § 13:1K-9.7, as well as a streamlined procedure for obtaining NJDEP approval when discharges at the industrial establishment are of "minimal environmental concern," *id.* § 13:1K-11.7.

[353] *Id.* § 13:1K-9(b)(1) (establishing the remediation requirement); *see id.* § 13:1K-8 (defining "remedial action").

[354] *Id.* § 13:1K-9(c).

[355] *Id.* § 58:10B-3(b).

[356] *Id.* § 13:1K-9(c) (referring to *id.* §§ 13:1K-11.2, -11.5, -11.6, -11.7).

[357] *Id.* § 13:1K-11(a)(1).

[358] *Id.* § 13:1K-11(b).

[359] *See In re* Adoption of N.J.A.C. 7:26B, 593 A.2d 1193, 1203-11 (N.J. Super. Ct. App. Div. 1991), *aff'd in part and rev'd in part on other grounds*, 608 A.2d 288 (N.J. 1992). These regulations remain in effect under ISRA as N.J. ADMIN. CODE tit. 7, § 26B-1.4 (2000).

New Jersey.[360] Likewise, the courts have upheld administrative regulations defining the term "industrial establishment" expansively, so that the sale of an uncontaminated parcel could give rise to an obligation to clean up contaminated adjoining parcels.[361]

ISRA subjects its violators to significant penalties. If the transferor does not obtain the necessary approval from the NJDEP, the transferee can void the transaction and recover damages.[362] Rescission of the transaction is an important remedy because it may enable the purchaser to avoid liability as a current owner under the federal Superfund statute.[363] The transferor also would be strictly liable for all remediation costs.[364] In addition, ISRA authorizes substantial fines: continuous noncompliance exposes the transferee to fines of up to $25,000 per day.[365]

ISRA has clearly promoted the cleanup of industrial sites in New Jersey. For example, in 1998 the NJDEP oversaw the completion of 59 ISRA cleanups; 255 additional ISRA cleanups were underway at the end of the state fiscal year. The NJDEP also issued 434 "no further action" letters based on the results of site investigations or remedial actions performed before a property transfer.[366] Expenditures by private parties on cleanups at ISRA sites totaled $16.4 million.[367] An additional $40.4 million was spent at voluntary cleanup sites.[368] Property owners may have undertaken some of these cleanups, in anticipation of a sale, as a means to obtain a "no further action" letter.

(c) *Actions by Other States.* — Many other states have followed New Jersey's lead by imposing requirements that, though more lenient than the provisions of ISRA, are nonetheless significant. A recent survey by the Environmental Law Institute indicates that from 1991 to 1997, the number of states with property transfer provisions applying to contaminated land increased from eighteen to thirty-one.[369] The

---

[360] For example, the General Electric takeover of RCA was delayed until General Electric posted a $36 million bond for NJDEP to approve the transfer of New Jersey properties. *See* Alexandra Biesada, *A Cautionary Tale: Overzealous Regulations in the Name of Environmental Protection Can Do More Harm than Good,* FIN. WORLD, Jan. 23, 1990, WL 1/23/90 FW 46.

[361] *See In re Adoption,* 608 A.2d at 296–98. These regulations remain in effect under ISRA as N.J. ADMIN. CODE tit. 7, § 26B-1.4 (2000).

[362] N.J. STAT. ANN. § 13:1K-13(a) (West Supp. 2001).

[363] *See* 42 U.S.C. § 9607(a)(1) (1994). For discussion of the rescission remedy, see *Dixon Venture v. Joseph Dixon Crucible Co.,* 584 A.2d 797, 798–800 (N.J. 1991).

[364] N.J. STAT. ANN. § 13:1K-13(a).

[365] *See id.* § 13:1K-13(b).

[366] N.J. DEP'T OF ENVTL. PROT., SITE REMEDIATION PROGRAM ANNUAL REPORT 25 (1998), *available at* http://www.state.nj.us/dep/srp/publications/annual_reports/1998/98annual.pdf.

[367] *Id.* at 9. For an earlier assessment of ECRA's impact, see David B. Farer, *ECRA Verdict: The Successes and Failures of the Premiere Transaction-Triggered Environmental Law,* 5 PACE ENVTL. L. REV. 113, 142–43 (1987).

[368] N.J. DEP'T OF ENVTL. PROT., *supra* note 366, at 9.

[369] ENVTL. LAW INST., *supra* note 271, at 36, 120–22.

survey found that twenty states required deed recordation of sites with hazardous substances, twenty states required that sellers disclose the presence of hazardous substances to purchasers of property, and three states — Connecticut and Hawaii as well as New Jersey — required cleanup as a condition of transfer.[370]

C. Municipal Solid Waste

The United States generates a staggering amount of municipal solid waste: 217.0 million tons in 1997, up from 88.1 million tons in 1960, 121.1 million tons in 1970, 151.6 million tons in 1980, and 205.2 million tons in 1990.[371] Each American generated an average of 4.44 pounds of solid waste per day in 1997, as compared with 2.68 pounds in 1960, 3.25 pounds in 1970, 3.66 pounds in 1980, and 4.50 pounds in 1990;[372] each American currently generates about three-quarters of a ton of municipal solid waste per year. Predictably, references to a solid waste "crisis" are commonplace.[373]

The environmental consequences of municipal solid waste are quite salient. There is great public awareness of municipal landfills that are too full to continue accepting waste;[374] of landfills that cause severe air and water pollution in surrounding areas;[375] of communities that must

---

[370] *Id.* at 36–37. *See generally* Tondro, *supra* note 322, at 792–94 (discussing Connecticut's statute).

[371] OFFICE OF SOLID WASTE, EPA, CHARACTERIZATION OF MUNICIPAL SOLID WASTE IN THE UNITED STATES: 1998 UPDATE 5 tbl.ES-1 (1999) [hereinafter MUNICIPAL SOLID WASTE]. The term "municipal solid waste" includes "durable goods, nondurable goods, containers and packaging, food wastes and yard trimmings, and miscellaneous inorganic wastes." *Id.* at 20. Such wastes can come from residential, commercial, institutional, or industrial sources. *Id.* at 20–21. For industrial sources, the definition excludes process wastes. *Id.* at 21.

[372] *Id.* at 5 tbl.ES-1. State recycling and source-reduction programs account for the decrease in per capita generation in the 1990s. *See infra* sections III.C.2, C.3, pp. 611–14.

[373] *See, e.g.,* Sidney M. Wolf, *The Solid Waste Crisis: Flow Control and the Commerce Clause,* 39 S.D. L. REV. 529, 529 (1994); Kristina Kelchner, Note, *State Options Are Wasting Away:* Oregon Waste Systems v. Department of Environmental Quality *and America's Solid Waste Crisis,* 74 OR. L. REV. 1395, 1395 (1995); Jonathan Phillip Meyers, Note, *Confronting the Garbage Crisis: Increased Federal Involvement as a Means of Addressing Municipal Solid Waste Disposal,* 79 GEO. L.J. 567, 567–68, 590 (1991) [hereinafter Meyers, *Confronting the Garbage Crisis*]; Catherine M. Myers, Note, *Minimum Recycled Content Requirements for Virginia: One Solution to the Solid Waste Crisis,* 13 VA. ENVTL. L.J. 271, 271–75 (1994) [hereinafter Myers, *Minimum Recycled Content Requirements*]; David Pomper, Comment, *Recycling* Philadelphia v. New Jersey: *The Dormant Commerce Clause, Postindustrial "Natural" Resources, and the Solid Waste Crisis,* 137 U. PA. L. REV. 1309, 1309–10 (1989).

[374] *See, e.g.,* Eric Lipton, *Efforts To Close Fresh Kills Are Taking Unforeseen Tolls,* N.Y. TIMES, Feb. 21, 2000, at A1.

[375] *See, e.g.,* Lorenza Munoz, *Base Says No Change in Plans for Landfills; Environment: State EPA, County Fear That Military's El Toro Cleanup Won't Block Ground Water Contamination,* L.A. TIMES, Jan. 29, 1998, at B7; Nancy Reckler, *New Yorkers Near World's Largest Landfill Say City Dumps on Them,* WASH. POST, Aug. 7, 1996, at A3; Jon Schmid, *EPA Fears Landslide at Big Dump,* CHI. SUN-TIMES, Mar. 14, 1999, at 18, WL 3/14/99 CHISUN 18.

transport their waste long distances;[376] and of communities that attempt to take steps, often unsuccessfully, to prevent being overrun by out-of-state waste.[377]

Over the last decade there have been extensive and at least partially successful regulatory efforts, primarily through recycling and source reduction, aimed at reducing the volume of municipal solid waste.[378] Very little of this activity has occurred at the federal level.

  1. Federal Inaction. — The federal Resource Conservation and Recovery Act of 1976 (RCRA)[379] governs all waste treatment but focuses on hazardous wastes.[380] With respect to municipal solid waste, RCRA establishes procedures for federal approval of state solid waste management plans designed to "conserve resources which contribute to the waste stream or to recover energy and materials from municipal waste."[381] The statute does not require states to prepare solid waste management plans, but makes federal financial and technical assistance contingent on the approval of such plans by EPA.[382] The statutory authorization for federal financial assistance, however, covered only the period from 1978 to 1988,[383] and by 1982, the Reagan Administration had effectively ended federal funding of waste management.[384] Moreover, even when such funds were available, only twenty-five states submitted solid waste plans to EPA for approval.[385]

---

[376] *See, e.g.,* Lipton, *supra* note 374.

[377] *E.g.,* Tom Campbell, *Judge Throws Out Trash Laws: Va. Will Appeal in Bid To Limit Imports,* RICHMOND TIMES-DISPATCH, Feb. 4, 2000, at A1; Douglas Martin & Dan Barry, *Giuliani Stirs up Border Tensions with Trash Plan,* N.Y. TIMES, Dec. 3, 1998, at A1; Patrick McGreevy, *L.A. Approves Landfill Expansion,* L.A. TIMES, Oct. 27, 1999, at B1; Andrew C. Revkin, *Senate Panel Weighs Curb on Shipment of Garbage,* N.Y. TIMES, June 18, 1999, at B5.

  For discussions of these phenomena in the academic literature, see W. Paul Robinson, *Waste Reduction, Solid Waste, and Public Policy,* 21 N.M. L. REV. 1, 1–3 (1990); Ann R. Mesnikoff, Note, *Disposing of the Dormant Commerce Clause Barrier: Keeping Waste at Home,* 76 MINN. L. REV. 1219, 1220–41 (1992); and Meyers, *Confronting the Garbage Crisis, supra* note 373, at 571–81.

[378] MUNICIPAL SOLID WASTE, *supra* note 371, at 91–102. EPA defines "source reduction" as "any change in the design, manufacturing, purchase, or use of materials or products (including packaging) to reduce the amount or toxicity before they become municipal solid waste." *Id.* at 91.

[379] 42 U.S.C. §§ 6901–6992k (1994 & Supp. IV 1998).

[380] *See id.* §§ 6921–6939e.

[381] *Id.* § 6943(c)(1)(A); *see id.* §§ 6943(c)(1)(B), (C), 6947.

[382] *See id.* § 6948(a)(1) (authorizing "financial assistance to States and local, regional, and interstate authorities for the development and implementation of plans approved by the Administrator").

[383] *Id.;* Mesnikoff, *supra* note 377, at 1224; Meyers, *Confronting the Garbage Crisis, supra* note 373, at 569.

[384] *See* OFFICE OF TECH. ASSESSMENT, U.S. CONG., FACING AMERICA'S TRASH: WHAT'S NEXT FOR MUNICIPAL SOLID WASTE? 305, 307–08 (1989). *See generally* Kirsten Engel, *Environmental Standards as Regulatory Common Law: Toward Consistency in Solid Waste Regulation,* 21 N.M. L. REV. 13, 17–18 (1990).

[385] Meyers, *Confronting the Garbage Crisis, supra* note 373, at 569.

RCRA also requires minimum performance standards for solid waste disposal facilities.[386] It prohibits disposal of waste at open dumps after a phase-out period[387] and requires EPA to promulgate regulations establishing health and environmental standards for sanitary landfills.[388] By increasing the costs of disposal, these regulations may encourage municipalities to reduce the volume of solid waste they send to landfills. Such incentives, however, are at best indirect, affecting municipalities rather than individuals. Moreover, the weak market demand for recycled products suggests that market incentives do not explain current recycling levels.[389]

Also, many state regulations governing municipal landfills are at least as stringent as their federal counterparts.[390] Thus, federal regulation of municipal solid waste landfills does not create added incentives for actors in these states.

One commentator has noted: "RCRA has not . . . been an effective means of achieving significant [municipal solid waste] reduction . . . for one fundamental reason: 'Congress did not grant [the] EPA authority to require state implementation of any Federal Standards relating to [municipal solid waste] management.'"[391] Indeed, unlike most federal pollution control statutes, particularly the Clean Air Act,[392] the Clean Water Act,[393] and the hazardous waste provisions of RCRA,[394] the municipal solid waste provisions of RCRA reflect a "basic philoso-

---

[386] *See* 42 U.S.C. §§ 6944, 6945 (1994).

[387] *Id.* §§ 6944(b), 6945(a).

[388] *Id.* § 6944. EPA promulgated its first set of regulations in 1979. *See* EPA Criteria for Classification of Solid Waste Disposal Facilities and Practices, 40 C.F.R. § 257.4 (2000). Pursuant to 1984 amendments to RCRA, EPA implemented, in 1991, a more stringent set of regulations, *see* EPA Criteria for Municipal Solid Waste Landfills, 40 C.F.R. pt. 258, that depending on the capacity or location of the facility, went into effect in 1993, 1994, or 1997, *see* 40 C.F.R. § 258.1(e). For discussion of the regulations, see John H. Turner, *Off to a Good Start: The RCRA Subtitle D Program for Municipal Solid Waste Landfills*, 15 TEMP. ENVTL. L. & TECH. J. 1 (1996).

[389] For a discussion of the weak demand for recycled plastic, see Anthony R. DePaolo, *Plastics Recycling Legislation: Not Just the Same Old Garbage*, 22 B.C. ENVTL. AFF. L. REV. 873, 881 (1995). The claim here is not that command-and-control mandates for recycling are desirable, but rather that they are programs environmentalists favor that cannot be attributed primarily to federal intervention. For a general discussion of the use of economic theories to gauge the value of recycling, see FRANK ACKERMAN, WHY DO WE RECYCLE?: MARKETS, VALUES, AND PUBLIC POLICY (1997).

[390] *See* Turner, *supra* note 388, at 1.

[391] Jonathan Schneeweiss, *Putting Packaging Waste in Its Place: The Case for Federal Legislation*, 15 VA. ENVTL. L.J. 443, 466 (1996) (second alteration in original) (quoting OFFICE OF TECH. ASSESSMENT, *supra* note 384, at 350); *see also id.* at 446–47 ("On the federal level . . . there has been a lack of legislation regarding source reduction, leaving the majority of such efforts to states and localities." (footnote omitted)).

[392] 42 U.S.C. §§ 7401–7671 (1994 & Supp. V 1999).

[393] 33 U.S.C. §§ 1251–1387 (1994 & Supp. V 1999).

[394] 42 U.S.C. §§ 6921–6939 (1994 & Supp. II 1996).

phy . . . that the federal government should play an advisory, and not a regulatory, role."[395]

2. *State Programs.* — In contrast to this federal passivity, states and municipalities have implemented numerous measures to encourage recycling and source reduction over the last decade.[396] These efforts have included residential curbside recycling programs, deposit-refund programs for beverage containers, and volume-based pricing of solid waste disposal services.

(a) *Recycling.* — In 1998, there were 9349 curbside recycling programs operating throughout the United States,[397] up from about 1000 in 1988 and 5000 in 1992.[398] These programs served 139.4 million people, about 54% of the population, and varied in availability throughout the country.[399] Whereas the Mid-Atlantic states' programs served 82% of their populations, the Rocky Mountain states' programs reached only 23% of theirs.[400] Among individual states, Connecticut, New York, and New Jersey served the greatest percentages of their populations — their programs reached 100%, 95%, and 90%, respectively.[401]

(b) *Bottle Bills.* — Nine states (Connecticut, Delaware, Iowa, Maine, Massachusetts, Michigan, New York, Oregon, and Vermont) have implemented traditional deposit-refund systems for beverage con-

---

[395] Roger W. Andersen, *The Resource Conservation and Recovery Act of 1976: Closing the Gap*, 1978 WIS. L. REV. 633, 642 (1978) (referring to the federal regulatory regime of the 1970s); *see also* OFFICE OF TECH. ASSESSMENT, *supra* note 384, at 5 (observing that the states are primarily responsible for disposal of municipal waste); Robinson, *supra* note 377, at 5 ("The EPA's emphasis on developing the regulatory system to implement other waste management areas with RCRA . . . ha[s] left solid waste authority in RCRA largely unimplemented."); Meyers, *Confronting the Garbage Crisis*, *supra* note 373, at 569 ("Unlike the disposal of hazardous waste, which is regulated extensively by the federal government, municipal solid waste disposal has generally been left to the states." (footnotes omitted)).

[396] *See* Robinson, *supra* note 377, at 9 ("Waste reduction is being accomplished largely within local communities."); Alice D. Keane, Recent Development, *Federal Regulation of Solid Waste Reduction and Recycling*, 29 HARV. J. ON LEGIS. 251, 276 (1992) ("The states have a considerable lead over the federal government in solid waste management.").

[397] Jim Glenn, *The State of Garbage in America*, BIOCYCLE, Apr. 1999, at 60, 63. In addition, in 1997 there were approximately 12,694 drop-off centers. MUNICIPAL SOLID WASTE, *supra* note 371, at 96.

[398] ROBIN R. JENKINS, SALVADOR A. MARTINEZ, KAREN PALMER & MICHAEL J. PODOLSKY, THE DETERMINANTS OF HOUSEHOLD RECYCLING: A MATERIAL SPECIFIC ANALYSIS OF UNIT PRICING AND RECYCLING PROGRAM ATTRIBUTES 1 (Res. for the Future, Discussion Paper 99-41-REV, 2000), *available at* http://www.rff.org/CFDOCS/disc_papers/PDF_files/9941rev.pdf.

[399] Glenn, *supra* note 397, at 64 tbl.3.

[400] *Id.* at 64.

[401] *Id.* In contrast, Delaware, Montana, and Hawaii each serviced 1% or less of their populations. *Id.* at 64 tbl.3.

tainers, primarily those used for beer and soft drinks.[402] Under these programs, consumers pay a deposit when they purchase a beverage and receive a refund when they return the empty container. In contrast, California operates a pure refund system: beverage distributors pay the deposit, but consumers receive a refund when they return their empty containers.[403] Apparently because of the success of curbside recycling, no state other than California has enacted new deposit-refund laws since the 1980s.[404]

EPA estimates that about 35% of recovered beverage containers come from the nine deposit-refund states, and that an additional 20% come from California.[405] In part as a result of these programs, the national recovery rate of beverage containers is quite high: 59.5% for aluminum containers and 37.3% for plastic soft drink containers.[406]

(c) Source Reduction. — State and municipal regulatory efforts have also extended to source reduction. In particular, a clear trend toward the adoption of volume-based pricing of solid waste disposal has emerged. Under such programs, households pay a fee for each container they discard. Whereas curbside recycling programs lower a household's cost of recycling (by eliminating the time and expense of taking recyclables to a dropoff center), volume-based pricing increases the cost of waste disposal.[407] As a result, it reduces the generation of waste.

---

[402] MUNICIPAL SOLID WASTE, *supra* note 371, at 98. *See generally* DePaolo, *supra* note 389, at 880–81 (discussing various states' beverage deposit laws).

[403] *See* MUNICIPAL SOLID WASTE, *supra* note 371, at 98; DePaolo, *supra* note 389, at 881. Presumably, however, the price of the product reflects the amount of the refund that the purchaser can obtain.

[404] MUNICIPAL SOLID WASTE, *supra* note 371, at 98.

[405] *Id.*

[406] *See id.* at 40, 44. However, market demand for plastic recovered in this manner has been weak. DePaolo, *supra* note 389, at 873, 878–79, 884–85. For a more general discussion of the problems in stimulating demand for recycled materials, see Myers, *Minimum Recycled Content Requirements, supra* note 373.

[407] Several works provide economic analyses of the policy issues involved in efforts to reduce municipal solid waste. *See, e.g.,* JENKINS, MARTINEZ, PALMER & PODOLSKY, *supra* note 398, at 1; KAREN PALMER, HILARY SIGMAN & MARGARET WALLS, THE COST OF REDUCING MUNICIPAL SOLID WASTE (Res. for the Future, Discussion Paper No. 96-35, 1996), *available at* http://www.rff.org/CFDOCS/disc_papers/PDF_files/9635.pdf (analyzing waste reduction policies by using supply and demand calculations); Don Fullerton & Thomas C. Kinnaman, *Household Responses to Pricing Garbage by the Bag,* 86 AM. ECON. REV. 971, 980–82 (1996) (analyzing policy justifications for volume-based pricing programs); Peter S. Menell, *Beyond the Throwaway Society: An Incentive Approach to Regulating Municipal Solid Waste,* 17 ECOLOGY L.Q. 655, 679–716 (1990) (discussing and comparing incentive effects of various waste disposal regulations and policies); Marie Lynn Miranda, Jess W. Everett, Daniel Blume & Barbeau A. Roy, Jr., *Market-Based Incentives and Residential Municipal Solid Waste,* 13 J. POL'Y ANALYSIS & MGMT. 681 (1994) (exploring market-based incentives of volume-based programs).

In the late 1980s, only a few dozen volume-based pricing (popularly known as "pay-as-you-throw") programs existed.[408] A 1999 report by EPA found that 4033 communities had such programs, and that they covered about 13% of the United States population.[409] Forty-three states had at least one community with a pay-as-you-throw scheme. Minnesota led the list with 1843 communities participating, about 45% of the total; Wisconsin and Washington followed with 466 and 249, respectively; California, Iowa, New York, Oregon, and Pennsylvania each had at least 100 communities with volume-based pricing.[410] A recent study by researchers at Duke University found that in communities with pay-as-you-throw systems, average waste reduction in the first year following adoption ranged between 14% and 27%, and recycling over that period increased between 32% and 59%.[411]

3. *An Assessment.* — The aggregate effects of state and municipal recycling efforts have been significant.[412] For example, the percentage of municipal solid waste recycled annually increased from 14.2% in

---

[408] *See* JENKINS, MARTINEZ, PALMER & PODOLSKY, *supra* note 398, at 1.

[409] *See* MARIE LYNN MIRANDA, SHARON LAPALME & DAVID Z. BYNUM, UNIT-BASED PRICING IN THE UNITED STATES: A TALLY OF COMMUNITIES (1999), *available at* http://www.epa.gov/epaoswer/non-hw/payt/pdf/jan99sum.xls (last visited Nov. 6, 2001). For highlights of an earlier study, see Janice Canterbury, *How to Succeed with Pay as You Throw*, BIOCYCLE, Dec. 1998, at 30, 30.

[410] *See* MIRANDA, LAPALME & BYNUM, *supra* note 409.

[411] Canterbury, *supra* note 409, at 30–32. Marie Lynn Miranda, a principal investigator in that study, has conducted extensive work on the performance of pay-as-you-throw programs under cooperative agreements with EPA. *See, e.g.*, SCOTT BAUER & MARIE LYNN MIRANDA, THE URBAN PERFORMANCE OF UNIT PRICING: AN ANALYSIS OF VARIABLE RATES FOR RESIDENTIAL GARBAGE COLLECTION IN URBAN AREAS (1996), *available at* http://www.epa.gov/epaoswer/non-hw/payt/pdf/upaperf1.pdf; MARIE LYNN MIRANDA, SCOTT D. BAUER & JOSEPH E. ALDY, UNIT PRICING PROGRAMS FOR RESIDENTIAL MUNICIPAL SOLID WASTE: AN ASSESSMENT OF THE LITERATURE 10–25 (1996), *available at* http://www.epa.gov/epaoswer/non-hw/payt/pdf/swlitrep.pdf; MARIE LYNN MIRANDA & SHARON LAPALME, UNIT PRICING OF RESIDENTIAL SOLID WASTE: A PRELIMINARY ANALYSIS OF 212 U.S. COMMUNITIES (1997), *available at* http://www.epa.gov/epaoswer/non-hw/payt/top17.htm; MIRANDA, LAPALME & BYNUM, *supra* note 409; Marie Lynn Miranda & Joseph E. Aldy, *Unit Pricing of Residential Municipal Solid Waste: Lessons from Nine Case Study Communities*, 52 J. ENVTL. MGMT. 79 (1998). One concern with pay-as-you-throw programs is that they might lead to an increase in illegal dumping. The Duke researchers, however, found no systematic relationship between pay-as-you-throw programs and illegal dumping; 48% of the communities surveyed experienced no change in illegal dumping, 6% experienced a decrease, 19% experienced an increase, and 27% had no information on the subject. *See* Canterbury, *supra* note 409, at 32.

[412] In addition to pay-as-you-throw programs, a number of states have created other incentives for recycling, such as tax credits for recycling operations, sales tax exemptions for the purchase of recycling equipment, and advance disposal fees for products that do not exceed specified rates of recycling with the state. DePaolo, *supra* note 389, at 885–88. Moreover, the majority of states have passed legislation requiring or encouraging state agencies to purchase products made of recycled materials where feasible. *Id.* at 887. Similarly, RCRA imposes on the federal government procurement requirements concerning recycled products. *See* 42 U.S.C. § 6962 (1994).

1990 to 22.4% in 1997.[413] Moreover, the percentage of materials eliminated from the waste stream rose from 16.2% in 1990 to 28.0% in 1997.[414] For certain kinds of materials, the proportion recovered through recycling is considerably higher: 42% for paper and paperboard, 41% for yard trimmings, and 39% for metals.[415]

In summary, virtually all innovation in waste volume reduction has come from states and municipalities. In fact, in the late 1980s, while states and local governments were acting aggressively on the recycling and source reduction fronts, the chair and ranking minority member of the Senate Committee on Environment and Public Works introduced a bipartisan bill that would have required greater federal attention to these issues.[416] The Bush administration, industry trade associations, and states and municipalities, however, opposed the bill, which ultimately failed.[417]

D. State Environmental Protection Acts

1. The Federal Program. — The National Environmental Policy Act of 1969 (NEPA)[418] was the first and most far reaching of the major federal environmental statutes. NEPA's ambitious preamble expresses Congress's intention "[t]o declare a national policy which will encourage productive and enjoyable harmony between man and his environment; to promote efforts which will prevent or eliminate damage to the environment and biosphere and stimulate the health and welfare of man."[419]

Section 101 of NEPA provides that "it is the continuing responsibility of the Federal Government to use all practicable means, consistent with other essential considerations of national policy, to improve and coordinate Federal plans, functions, programs, and resources" so that, among other related goals, "the Nation may . . . attain the widest range of beneficial uses of the environment without degradation, risk to health or safety, or other undesirable and unintended consequences."[420] The statute also provides that "the policies, regulations, and public laws of the United States shall be interpreted and administered in accordance with [NEPA's] policies."[421]

---

[413] MUNICIPAL SOLID WASTE, *supra* note 371, at 5 tbl.ES-1.

[414] *Id.*

[415] *Id.* at 80. These are 1997 figures. The corresponding figures in 1980 were 21%, 0%, and 5%, respectively. *Id.*

[416] *See* Keane, *supra* note 396, at 252–56.

[417] *See id.* at 251, 262–64.

[418] Pub. L. No. 91-190, 83 Stat. 852 (1970) (codified as amended at 42 U.S.C. §§ 4321–4370f (1994 & Supp. V 1999)).

[419] 42 U.S.C. § 4321 (1994).

[420] *Id.* § 4331(b).

[421] *Id.* § 4332(1).

In addition to these broad mandates, NEPA contains a specific procedural requirement concerning the preparation of environmental impact statements (EISs). It provides that "all agencies of the Federal Government" shall prepare EISs with respect to "every recommendation or report on proposals for legislation and other major Federal actions significantly affecting the quality of the human environment."[422]

However, the preparation of EISs relating to "proposals for legislation" has not been, in practice, an important component of NEPA.[423] The act's main impact, instead, has been on "other major federal actions." Such actions include not only activities that the federal government undertakes directly, such as the construction of highways or dams, but also private activities that require federal permits.[424]

During the 1970s, the lower courts interpreted NEPA quite expansively. In particular, the courts suggested that NEPA contains a substantive component pursuant to which they could strike down agency decisions that had not accorded sufficient weight to environmental concerns. For example, *Calvert Cliffs' Coordinating Committee, Inc. v. U.S. Atomic Energy Commission*[425] referred to section 101 as setting forth NEPA's "basic substantive policy" and indicated that Congress "desired a reordering of priorities, so that environmental costs and benefits will assume their proper place along with other considerations."[426] In its clearest statement on the nature of the substantive obligations NEPA imposed, the D.C. Circuit indicated:

> The reviewing courts probably cannot reverse a substantive decision on its merits, under Section 101, *unless it be shown that the actual balance of costs and benefits that was struck was arbitrary or clearly gave insufficient weight to environmental values*. But if the decision was reached procedurally without individualized consideration and balancing of environmental factors — conducted fully and in good faith — it is the responsibility of the courts to reverse.[427]

---

[422] *Id.* § 4332(2).

[423] ENVIRONMENTAL REGULATION, *supra* note 188, at 1119–20. A barrier to private enforcement of the EIS requirement for certain kinds of legislative proposals arose in *Public Citizen v. U.S. Trade Representative*, 5 F.3d 549, 551–53 (D.C. Cir. 1993). In *Public Citizen*, the court refused to hear a suit brought to force the U.S. Trade Representative to produce an EIS on the North American Free Trade Agreement before its submission to Congress. The court determined that the treaty was not "final agency action" and therefore was not ripe for judicial review. The concurring opinion questioned whether decisions involving "proposals for legislation" were judicially reviewable. *Id.* at 553–54 (Randolph, J., concurring).

[424] *See* Council on Environmental Quality Terminology and Index, 40 C.F.R. § 1508.18 (2000) (defining "major federal action").

[425] 449 F.2d 1109 (D.C. Cir. 1971).

[426] *Id.* at 1112.

[427] *Id.* at 1115 (emphasis added).

Other courts of appeals followed similar approaches.[428]

The Supreme Court, however, put an end to this substantive account of NEPA in *Strycker's Bay Neighborhood Council v. Karlen* — a short per curiam opinion filed in 1980.[429] Over a strong dissent by Justice Marshall,[430] the Court rejected the Second Circuit's decision below that "an agency, in selecting a course of action, must elevate environmental concerns over other appropriate considerations."[431] The Court concluded: "On the contrary, once an agency has made a decision subject to NEPA's procedural requirements, the only role for a court is to insure that the agency has considered the environmental consequences . . . ."[432] Thus, under the Supreme Court's interpretation, NEPA requires that an EIS identify a project's adverse environmental consequences, but does not require the mitigation of such consequences.[433]

After *Strycker's Bay*, many commentators described NEPA as little more than a disclosure requirement and lamented the opportunities lost by the Court's narrow interpretation.[434] Subsequent judicial ac-

---

[428] *See, e.g.*, Karlen v. Harris, 590 F.2d 39, 43 (2d Cir. 1978) (referring to NEPA as containing "the substantive standards necessary to review the merits of agency decisions"), *rev'd per curiam sub nom.* Strycker's Bay Neighborhood Council, Inc. v. Karlen, 444 U.S. 223 (1980); Envtl. Def. Fund, Inc. v. Corps of Eng'rs of the U.S. Army, 470 F.2d 289, 298 (8th Cir. 1972) ("Given an agency obligation to carry out the substantive requirements of [NEPA], we believe that courts have an obligation to review substantive agency decisions on the merits.").

[429] 444 U.S. 223 (1980) (per curiam).

[430] *Id.* at 228 (Marshall, J., dissenting).

[431] *Strycker's Bay*, 444 U.S. at 227.

[432] *Id.* The Supreme Court subsequently reaffirmed the *Strycker's Bay* approach:
[I]t is now well settled that NEPA itself does not mandate particular results, but simply prescribes the necessary process . . . . If the adverse environmental effects of the proposed action are adequately identified and evaluated, the agency is not constrained by NEPA from deciding that other values outweigh the environmental costs. . . . NEPA merely prohibits uninformed — rather than unwise — agency action.
Robertson v. Methow Valley Citizens Council, 490 U.S. 332, 350–51 (1989); Marsh v. Or. Natural Res. Council, 490 U.S. 360, 371 (1989) ("NEPA does not work by mandating that agencies achieve particular substantive environmental results.").

[433] This limitation on the scope of NEPA is particularly significant because under NEPA, an EIS is prepared by the same agency that is responsible for the project, *see* Council on Environmental Quality NEPA and Agency Planning, 40 C.F.R. § 1501.5 (2000), not by a different agency with an environmental mandate, which would likely be more sympathetic to environmental concerns. *See generally* Joseph L. Sax, *The (Unhappy) Truth About NEPA*, 26 OKLA. L. REV. 239 (1973) (discussing limitations of NEPA in its specific application to airport development).
Despite this limitation, NEPA may have contributed to environmental protection by creating a demand within government agencies for environmental professionals. For an excellent study showing how these professionals, though initially marginalized, eventually became influential within an agency with a previously abysmal environmental track record, see WENDY NELSON ESPELAND, THE STRUGGLE FOR WATER 135–81 (1998) (describing the experience of environmental professionals in the Bureau of Reclamation).

[434] *See, e.g.*, Lynton K. Caldwell, *Beyond NEPA: Future Significance of the National Environmental Policy Act*, 22 HARV. ENVTL. L. REV. 203, 205–06 (1998) (attributing NEPA's failure to "fulfill its potential" to executive agencies' refusal to follow NEPA's "goals and principles," and

tivity has been largely confined to the relatively arid inquiries concerning whether the government's involvement required the preparation of an EIS — that is, whether the involvement constituted "major federal action"[435] and whether such action "significantly" affected the environment[436] — and if so, whether the EIS prepared by the agency was adequate.[437]

2. *State Programs.* — A flurry of parallel activity on the part of states followed the passage of NEPA. By 1973, seventeen jurisdictions had adopted NEPA-like policies: ten states and Puerto Rico had adopted general statutes — referred to generically as State Environmental Protection Acts (SEPAs) — modeled at least in part on NEPA; two states had adopted statutes of limited applicability; and four states had administratively promulgated programs similar to NEPA.[438]

The number of states with such provisions has continued to grow over the years: recent surveys reveal that eighteen states, the District of Columbia, and Puerto Rico have SEPAs of general applicability in place, that another ten have statutes of limited applicability,[439] and that six have administratively promulgated NEPA-like programs.[440] Two of the states with administratively promulgated NEPA-like pro-

---

to "judicial misinterpretation"); Philip Michael Ferester, *Revitalizing the National Environmental Policy Act: Substantive Law Adaptations from NEPA's Progeny*, 16 HARV. ENVTL. L. REV. 207, 207, 255–56 (1992) (describing the Supreme Court as having reduced NEPA's "substantive policies and goals" to an "'essentially procedural' level"); Nicholas A. Robinson, *The "Ascent of Man": Legal Systems and the Discovery of an Environmental Ethic*, 15 PACE ENVTL. L. REV. 497, 510 (1998) ("[T]he U.S. Supreme Court over the past thirty years has declined to accept the substantive duty that NEPA was thought to have had . . . ."); Philip Weinberg, *It's Time To Put NEPA Back on Course*, 3 N.Y.U. ENVTL. L.J. 99, 104–08 (1994) (suggesting that by making NEPA "procedural only," the Supreme Court undermined "Congress's purpose").

[435] *See, e.g.,* Mayaguezanos por la Salud y el Ambiente v. United States, 198 F.3d 297, 301–02 (1st Cir. 1999) (holding that federal approval of a private activity does not constitute "major federal action," if approval is not a prerequisite for the activity); Citizens Awareness Network, Inc. v. U.S. Nuclear Regulatory Comm'n, 59 F.3d 284, 292–93 (1st Cir. 1995) (holding that the Commission's approval of financing and allowance of decommission, before the submission of a decommissioning plan, constituted "major federal action").

[436] The Council on Environmental Quality's regulation implementing NEPA provides a definition of the term "significantly." 40 C.F.R. § 1508.27.

[437] *See, e.g.,* Sierra Club v. Marita, 46 F.3d 606, 624 (7th Cir. 1995) (upholding a lower court finding that a Forest Service EIS was adequate); Sierra Club v. U.S. Army Corps of Eng'rs, 701 F.2d 1011, 1031 (2d Cir. 1983) (upholding a district court finding that an Army Corps EIS was inadequate).

[438] Nicholas C. Yost, *NEPA's Progeny: State Environmental Policy Acts*, 3 ENVTL. L. REP. 50,090, 50,090 (1973).

[439] Jeffrey L. Carmichael, Note, *The Indiana Environmental Policy Act: Casting a New Role for a Forgotten Statute*, 70 IND. L.J. 613, 622 & nn.81, 83 (1995).

[440] 4 FRANK GRAD, TREATISE ON ENVIRONMENTAL LAW § 9.08, at 9-294 & n.1 (1998 & Supp. 1999).

grams also have limited statutory provisions.[441] Thus, a total of thirty-two states, the District of Columbia, and Puerto Rico have at least some form of NEPA-related provision.

These state provisions broaden the protections of NEPA in two principal ways. First, they extend the requirements concerning the preparation of EISs beyond projects involving major federal action. In general, the obligation is triggered under the state provisions whenever there is state involvement. Thus, the state provisions reach large numbers of projects that are not covered by NEPA. In most regulating states, these provisions extend not only to projects directly undertaken by the state governments, but also to private projects for which the state issues permits.[442] Moreover, the statutes of a number of states, including California, Hawaii, Massachusetts, Minnesota, New York, and Washington cover local governments as well as state governments.[443] In these states, the EIS requirement applies to zoning and other local land use decisions, thereby greatly expanding the universe of decisions that require the preparation of an EIS.[444]

The structure of the state counterparts to NEPA thus differs from that of the state Superfund statutes discussed in a preceding section.[445] In the Superfund context, the state provisions are similar to their federal counterparts: what they add in terms of additional environmental protection is a state-led enforcement mechanism. In the case of NEPA, by contrast, the state provisions apply to large numbers of projects outside the purview of the federal statute.

A second extension of NEPA arises from the manner in which some states treat substantive claims. In contrast to the approach adopted by

---

[441] *See id.* at 9-294 n.1 (listing New Jersey and Nebraska as states with administratively promulgated NEPA-like programs); Carmichael, *supra* note 439, at 622 n.83 (listing those same states as having limited statutory provisions).

For other recent surveys of state provisions, see 5 ZONING AND LAND USE CONTROLS §§ 28.01, 28.02[1] (Patrick J. Rohan ed., Supp. 1997); David Sive & Mark A. Chertok, *"Little NEPA's" and Their Environmental Impact Assessment Processes,* in ENVIRONMENTAL LITIGATION 1233 (A.L.I.-A.B.A. Course of Study, June 23, 1997), WL SB91 ALI-ABA 1233.

[442] *See* Sive & Chertok, *supra* note 441, at 1242. Indiana is an exception. *See* Carmichael, *supra* note 439, at 640-41. In some states in which legislation does not address this issue, courts have required permit-granting agencies to prepare EISs. *Id.* at 640. Some state statutes also require the preparation of EISs even when the action in question does not have a "significant" effect on the environment. *See* ROBERT C. ELLICKSON & VICKI L. BEEN, LAND USE CONTROLS: CASES AND MATERIALS 432 (2d ed. 2000).

[443] *See* ELLICKSON & BEEN, *supra* note 442, at 431; Sive & Chertok, *supra* note 441, at 1240. In addition, some municipalities have their own NEPA-like ordinances. *See* 5 ZONING AND LAND USE CONTROLS, *supra* note 441, § 28.03[3]. For commentary on a prominent example, see J. Kevin Healy, *The Environmental Review Process in the City of New York: CEQR,* 5 PACE ENVTL. L. REV. 93 (1987).

[444] For discussion, see Sive & Chertok, *supra* note 441, at 1240.

[445] *See supra* section III.B.2.b, pp. 600-603.

Strycker's Bay, the statutes of California,[446] Massachusetts,[447] Minnesota,[448] New York,[449] and the District of Columbia[450] have a substantive component requiring the mitigation of adverse environmental effects. For example, in *Friends of Mammoth v. Board of Supervisors*,[451] the California Supreme Court stated: "Obviously if the adverse consequences to the environment can be mitigated, or if feasible alternatives are available, the proposed activity ... should not be approved."[452] Similarly, in *Jackson v. New York State Urban Development Corp.*,[453] the New York Court of Appeals noted that "unlike its Federal counterpart and model ... [the New York statute] is not merely a disclosure statute; it 'imposes far more "action-forcing" or "substantive" requirements on state and local decisionmakers than NEPA imposes on their federal counterparts.'"[454] An environmental project involving both federal and state action might thus survive a challenge under federal law and yet fail a challenge under state law.

In assessing whether the state schemes have substantive bite (as opposed to being largely symbolic gestures), two observations are rele-

---

[446] *See* CAL. PUB. RES. CODE § 21,002.1(b) (West 1996) ("Each public agency shall mitigate or avoid the significant effects on the environment of projects that it carries out or approves whenever it is feasible to do so.").

[447] *See* MASS. GEN. LAWS ch. 30, § 61 (2000) (requiring use of "all practicable means and measures to minimize damage to the environment").

[448] The Minnesota SEPA provides as follows:

No state action significantly affecting the quality of the environment shall be allowed, nor shall any permit for natural resources management and development be granted, where such action or permit has caused or is likely to cause pollution, impairment, or destruction of the air, water, land or other natural resources located within the state, so long as there is a feasible and prudent alternative consistent with the reasonable requirements of the public health, safety, and welfare and the state's paramount concern for the protection of its air, water, land and other natural resources from pollution, impairment, or destruction.

MINN. STAT. § 116D.04(6) (2000).

[449] *See* N.Y. ENVTL. CONSERV. LAW § 8-0109(1) (McKinney 1997) ("Agencies shall ... act and choose alternatives which, consistent with social, economic and other essential considerations, to the maximum extent practicable, minimize or avoid adverse environmental effects ...."). For commentary, see Philip H. Gitlen, *The Substantive Impact of the SEQRA*, 46 ALB. L. REV. 1241 (1982); and Kelly Munkwitz, Note, *Does the SEQRA Authorize Mitigation Fees?*, 61 ALB. L. REV. 595, 599–608 (1997).

[450] *See* D.C. CODE ANN. § 6-981 (2001) (requiring substitution of "an alternative action or mitigating measures for a proposed action, if the alternative action or mitigating measures will accomplish the same purposes as the proposed action with minimized or no adverse environmental effects").

[451] 502 P.2d 1049 (Cal. 1972).

[452] *Id.* at 1059 n.8. More recently, however, the California Supreme Court appears to have narrowed somewhat the substantive scope of the state statute. *See* Citizens v. Bd. of Supervisors, 801 P.2d 1161, 1168–71 (Cal. 1990) (en banc); Laurel Heights Improvement Ass'n v. Regents of the Univ. of Cal., 764 P.2d 278, 283 (Cal. 1988) (en banc). For commentary on the California cases, see Ferester, *supra* note 434, at 237–39.

[453] 494 N.E.2d 429 (N.Y. 1986).

[454] *Id.* at 434 (quoting Gitlen, *supra* note 449, at 1248).

vant. First, under provisions governing judicial review of administrative decisions, any individual — at least any individual with a sufficient injury — may challenge decisions made by state agencies under SEPAs.[455] Thus, public nonenforcement cannot render the state programs ineffectual. There is no suggestion in the literature that judicial review under these state programs is more restrictive than judicial review under NEPA; if anything, the opposite is true in some states.[456]

Second, in a number of states, particularly California and New York, but Massachusetts, Minnesota, and Washington as well, there are well-developed bodies of case law relating to EISs.[457] At least in those states, private litigants have vigorously challenged the actions of public agencies.[458] Thus, the state programs, in some instances, serve to extend NEPA significantly.

E. Duty-To-Warn Measures

This section first examines California's statutory provision creating a duty to warn of exposure to harmful substances. It then compares this provision to the most extensive comparable federal regime, the Emergency Planning and Community Right-To-Know Act (EPCRA).[459] Finally, it discusses the extent to which the California program has influenced other jurisdictions.

   1. California's Proposition 65. — In 1986, California voters overwhelmingly approved Proposition 65, titled the Safe Drinking Water and Toxic Enforcement Act,[460] which creates a broad warning requirement in situations involving the exposure of California residents to carcinogens and reproductive toxins. Proposition 65 provides that "[n]o person in the course of doing business shall knowingly and intentionally expose any individual to a chemical known to the state to cause cancer or reproductive toxicity without first giving a clear and reasonable warning to such individual."[461]

---

[455] *See* Jane Magee, *Environmental Impact Statements: Applications in Land Use Control*, 10 ZONING & PLAN. L. REP. 113, 117 (1987); Sive & Chertok, *supra* note 441, at 1249–51. For comparisons of some state provisions, see Ferester, *supra* note 434, at 235–37, 244, 251–54.

[456] *See* sources cited *supra* note 455.

[457] *See* ELLICKSON & BEEN, *supra* note 442, at 424; 5 ZONING AND LAND USE CONTROLS, *supra* note 441, § 28.04[3].

[458] The costs imposed on businesses by these court challenges can be considerable. *See* COUNCIL ON CAL. COMPETITIVENESS, CALIFORNIA'S JOBS AND FUTURE 37–39 (1992).

[459] 42 U.S.C. §§ 11,001–11,050 (1994).

[460] Initiative Measure, Proposition 65 (approved Nov. 4, 1986) (codified as amended at CAL. HEALTH & SAFETY CODE §§ 25,249.5–.13 (West 1999 & Supp. 2001)). The vote approving the measure was 63% to 37%. Marina Gatti, *Proposition 65: "Shoot First, Ask Questions Later" — Do the Bullets Really Work? Have We Shot the Wrong Party? Will They Call Out the Bazookas?*, 47 FOOD & DRUG L.J. 739, 740 (1992).

[461] CAL. HEALTH & SAFETY CODE § 25,249.6 (West 1999). In addition to imposing a duty to warn of carcinogenic or toxic chemicals, Proposition 65 also prohibits the discharge or release of

The warning requirement of Proposition 65 is subject to two exemptions. First, exposures "for which federal law governs warning in a manner that preempts state authority" are exempted.[462] This exemption, however, is narrowly tailored. It does not apply to all instances in which a warning is required by federal law, but only to instances in which the federal law displaces state authority.[463]

The second exemption applies if "the person responsible can show" that the risk of exposure is sufficiently low.[464] With respect to carcinogens, the warning requirements of Proposition 65 do not apply if "the exposure poses no significant risk assuming lifetime exposure at the level in question."[465] Regulations define the term "no significant risk" as "one excess case of cancer in an exposed population of 100,000, assuming lifetime exposure at the level in question."[466] In the case of reproductive toxins, the exemption requires that "the exposure will have no observable effect assuming exposure at one thousand . . . times the level in question."[467]

Proposition 65's warning requirements can be enforced not only by the California Attorney General and other public officials,[468] but also by means of a citizen suit provision, which authorizes any person to bring an action "in the public interest."[469] A "bounty-hunter's" provision rewards successful plaintiffs with 25% of the penalties.[470]

To evaluate the impact of Proposition 65, one must examine the enforcement patterns in some detail. The warning requirements apply both to products (many of which are manufactured outside California)

---

those chemicals "into water or onto or into land where such chemical passes or probably will pass into any source of drinking water." *Id.* § 25,249.5. For general commentary on Proposition 65 and its implementation, see Paulette L. Stenzel, *Right-to-Know Provisions of California's Proposition 65: The Naivete of the Delaney Clause Revisited,* 15 HARV. ENVTL. L. REV. 493 (1991); and Judith A. DeFranco, Note, *California's Toxics Initiative: Making It Work,* 39 HASTINGS L.J. 1195 (1988).

[462] CAL. HEALTH & SAFETY CODE § 25,249.10(a).

[463] As a result, this exemption does not appear to limit the warning requirement beyond those limits required by the Supremacy Clause of the U.S. Constitution, U.S. CONST. art. VI, cl. 2.

[464] CAL. HEALTH & SAFETY CODE § 25,249.10(c).

[465] *Id.*

[466] CAL. CODE REGS. tit. 22, § 12,703(b) (2000). There are three limited exceptions. *See id.* For criticism of this standard, see W. KIP VISCUSI, PRODUCT-RISK LABELING: A FEDERAL RESPONSIBILITY 24–26 (1993); and Michael Barsa, Note, *California's Proposition 65 and the Limits of Information Economics,* 49 STAN. L. REV. 1223, 1228–31 (1997).

[467] CAL. HEALTH & SAFETY CODE § 25,249.10(c).

[468] *See id.* § 25,249.7(c).

[469] *Id.* § 25,249.7(d) (West 1999 & Supp. 2001). For general commentary on citizen suits, see Julie Anne Ross, Comment, *Citizen Suits: California's Proposition 65 and the Lawyer's Ethical Duty to the Public Interest,* 29 U.S.F. L. REV. 809 (1995).

[470] *See* CAL. HEALTH & SAFETY CODE § 25,192(2) (West 1992 & Supp. 2001). For a discussion of the "bounty-hunter" provision and how it was received, see Kara Christenson, *Interpreting the Purposes of Initiatives: Proposition 65,* 40 HASTINGS L.J. 1031, 1059–60 (1989).

and to the production processes employed by in-state industrial plants.[471]

Critics may view the application of Proposition 65 to products manufactured out-of-state as a way for California to externalize the costs of environmental protection. If there are economies of scale in the manufacture of the products to which the Proposition 65 requirements apply, out-of-state actors bear a share of compliance costs.[472] Manufacturers could have a uniform nationwide response, reformulating their products, as many have done,[473] or providing the warnings regardless where the products are sold. Alternatively, they could comply with the dictates of Proposition 65 only for those products sold in California. Both approaches raise the costs to consumers everywhere: the former by imposing a more cumbersome requirement across the board and the latter by undercutting the economies of scale that otherwise exist. Actions brought against out-of-state manufacturers of products sold in California may be motivated, perhaps in large part, by their cost externalizing character.

The situation is different regarding Proposition 65's application to in-state industrial facilities that expose individuals to harmful substances as a result of their production processes. In this case, the costs are borne by in-state actors; the higher prices for in-state products result in smaller markets and lower profits.[474]

Those who advocate federal environmental regulation on public choice grounds fear that the concentrated interests of these in-state manufacturers will succeed against the more dispersed interests of the victims of pollution, and that enforcement related to these production processes will consequently be lax.[475] Therefore, vigorous enforcement with respect to the processes used by in-state manufacturers provides stronger evidence against the traditional public choice argument for federal regulation than does enforcement with respect to the products of out-of-state manufacturers.

Table 2 presents an analysis of duty-to-warn enforcement patterns under Proposition 65 that is based on brief descriptions, prepared by the California Attorney General, of Proposition 65 actions brought be-

---

[471] CAL. HEALTH & SAFETY CODE § 25,249.6 (West 1999).

[472] See supra pp. 584, 593.

[473] See Clifford Rechtschaffen, The Warning Game: Evaluating Warnings Under California's Proposition 65, 23 ECOLOGY L.Q. 303, 341–48 (1996). For example, manufacturers of products as diverse as flatware, food cans, brass faucets, submersible well water pumps, and crystal vases have significantly reduced or eliminated lead in their products. See id. at 341–43.

[474] To the extent that these manufacturers have out-of-state shareholders, however, even these measures give rise to cost externalization.

[475] See supra section I.A.1, pp. 559–60.

tween 1988 and 1996.[476]   The table divides actions by the type of plaintiff (public versus private) and by the type of defendant (in-state versus out-of-state). For the purpose of this analysis, actions concerning products (as opposed to processes) are assumed to involve out-of-state defendants. Thus, the analysis provides a lower bound on the proportion of overall actions that are brought against in-state firms. Table 2 reveals that nearly half the actions brought are against in-state firms and that this proportion does not vary significantly according to the identity of the plaintiff. Thus, both private suits and public enforcement actions impose substantial costs on in-state manufacturers, calling into question the public-choice arguments for federal environmental regulation.

TABLE 2. ANALYSIS OF PROPOSITION 65 LITIGATION 1988–1996

	Public Suits	Private Suits
In-state defendants	15	20
Out-of-state defendants	16	24

2. *Comparison with the Federal Regime.* — Proposition 65 is extremely broad with respect to the targets subject to its warnings requirement (any "person"), those to whom its protections extend ("any individual"), the substances it covers (any "chemical known to the state to cause cancer or reproductive toxicity"), and the nature of its enforcement provisions (both public and private enforcement).[477]   In contrast, EPCRA, the principal federal duty-to-warn scheme,[478] has a far narrower scope.

EPCRA imposes three principal notification requirements. Under section 312 of EPCRA, certain facilities regulated under the Occupational Safety and Health Act[479] must complete an annual "hazardous chemical inventory form."[480]   Under section 313, any facilities that have ten or more full-time employees and that fall within Standard Industrial Classification Codes 20 through 39 must complete an annual "toxic chemical release form" if they "manufactured, processed, or otherwise used a toxic chemical."[481]   Section 304, an emergency notifica-

---

[476] *See* Cal. Attorney General's Office, *Proposition 65 Litigation* (May 1, 1996), *at* http://www.calprop65.com/ag.html.

[477] CAL. HEALTH & SAFETY CODE § 25,249.6 (West 1999).

[478] *See* 42 U.S.C. §§ 11,001–11,050 (1994).

[479] 29 U.S.C. §§ 651–652 (1994 & Supp. IV 1998).

[480] 42 U.S.C. § 11,022(a)(1). For commentary, see Eric M. Falkenberry, *The Emergency Planning and Community Right-To-Know Act: A Tool for Toxic Release Reduction in the 90's,* 3 BUFF. ENVTL. L.J. 1, 8–10 (1995).

[481] 42 U.S.C. § 11,023(a)–(b)(1). Standard Industrial Classification Codes 20–39 cover manufacturing facilities of a variety of products, including "food, textiles, apparel, lumber, wood, furniture,

tion provision, requires disclosure, under certain circumstances, of "a release of an extremely hazardous substance ... from a facility at which a hazardous chemical is produced, used, or stored."[482]

Thus, the requirements of EPCRA apply principally to risks arising from industrial processes. Proposition 65, however, applies also to risks posed by consumer products; in fact, much of the litigation under this provision has involved commonplace products such as china, glassware, and faucets.[483] Moreover, EPCRA notification requirements pertain only to a subset of industrial facilities. The notification requirements of EPCRA do not necessarily apply when the release of a hazardous substance is the byproduct of an industrial process involving nonhazardous substances — for example, the burning of fossil fuel.[484]

The EPCRA release notification requirement also applies only if the amount of the chemical manufactured, processed, or otherwise used at the facility exceeds a given threshold.[485] For example, the thresholds set by the general notification provision of section 313 are not trivial: 10,000 pounds per year for chemicals used at a facility and 25,000 pounds per year for chemicals manufactured or processed at a facility.[486] Proposition 65 contains no comparable limitations.[487]

Moreover, the emergency notification requirements of EPCRA's section 304 exempt federally permitted releases.[488] Releases regulated

---

paper products, chemicals, petroleum products, rubber and plastics, leather goods, stone, glass, clay, metals, machinery, and other miscellaneous goods." Sidney M. Wolf, *Fear and Loathing About the Public Right To Know: The Surprising Success of the Emergency Planning and Community Right-To-Know Act*, 11 J. LAND USE & ENVTL. L. 217, 225 n.49 (1996).

[482] 42 U.S.C. § 11,004(a)(1)–(2). For general commentary on EPCRA, see Kevin J. Finto, *Regulation by Information Through EPCRA*, 4 NAT. RESOURCES & ENV'T 13 (1990); Rebecca S. Weeks, *The Bumpy Road to Community Preparedness: The Emergency Planning and Community Right-to-Know Act*, 4 ENVTL. LAW. 827 (1998); and Wolf, *supra* note 481.

[483] *See* Rechtschaffen, *supra* note 473, at 341–43; Cal. Attorney General's Office, *supra* note 476, pts. A.18, A.15, A.22.

[484] *See* John C. Dernbach, *The Unfocused Regulation of Toxic and Hazardous Pollutants*, 21 HARV. ENVTL. L. REV. 1, 41–42 (1997) (highlighting the absence of combustion byproducts from EPCRA lists).

[485] The threshold levels for the general notification provisions of section 313 are defined at 42 U.S.C. § 11,023(f)(1) (1994). The emergency notification provision of section 304 has parallel requirements, depending on whether notification is required under section 103(a) of CERCLA, 42 U.S.C. § 9603(a). *Compare* 42 U.S.C. § 11,004(a)(1) (governing releases requiring CERCLA notification), *with id.* § 11,004(a)(2) (governing releases not subject to CERCLA notification requirements). When CERCLA requires notification, its provisions also establish the threshold amount. *Id.* § 9602. Otherwise, the question is governed by EPCRA. *Id.* § 11,004(a)(2).

[486] 42 U.S.C. § 11,023(f)(1). Under section 312, the EPA Administrator may establish thresholds as well. *Id.* § 11,022(b).

[487] CAL. HEALTH & SAFETY CODE §§ 25,249.6, 25,249.10 (West 1999).

[488] *See* 42 U.S.C. § 11,004(a)(1) (referencing CERCLA's exemption of "federally permitted releases" at 42 U.S.C. § 9603(a)); *id.* § 11,004(a)(2)(A). For the definition of "federally permitted release," see 42 U.S.C. § 9601(10).

by federal statute and within the limits prescribed under the applicable statute need not be reported under section 304. Proposition 65 does not contain an analogous exemption for permitted releases.[489]

In addition, fewer people receive notices of release under EPCRA than under Proposition 65. Under regulations promulgated pursuant to Proposition 65, notice of environmental exposures (other than workplace or consumer-related exposures) must be (as appropriate) posted in the affected area, mailed once every three months to occupants in the affected area, or communicated once every three months through a public media announcement in the affected area.[490] By contrast, the general notification provisions of section 313 only require facilities to submit toxic chemical release forms to the EPA Administrator, who compiles the data into a publicly accessible computer database; and to officials of the states in which the facilities are located.[491] Information supplied under section 312 must be submitted to a local emergency planning committee, the state emergency response commission, and the local fire department.[492] Under the emergency notification provisions of section 304, facilities must provide notice to the community emergency coordinators and to state emergency committees for any jurisdictions likely to be affected by the release.[493] EPCRA prescribes that local emergency planning committees have broad membership, including various government officials as well as representatives of the print media and community groups.[494] Although information provided under EPCRA notice requirements may filter to the public through these committees, EPCRA, unlike Proposition 65, fails to provide immediate notice to a broad community audience.[495]

3. *Impact on Other Jurisdictions.* — Proposition 65 has served as a model for legislative proposals in other states as well as for several bills introduced in Congress. Legislative proposals similar to Proposi-

---

[489] *See* CAL. HEALTH & SAFETY CODE §§ 25,249.6, 25,249.10.

[490] CAL. CODE. REGS. tit. 22, § 12,601(d)(1) (1999). Workplace exposures require a product warning, posted signs in the workplace, or individual warnings to exposed employees, as appropriate. *Id.* § 12,601(c)(1). Consumer product exposures require product warning labels, store displays, or a public advertising campaign, as appropriate. *Id.* § 12,601(b)(1). The regulations impose stricter requirements on alcoholic products. *See id.* § 12,601(b)(1)(D).

[491] *See* 42 U.S.C. § 11,023(a). The database is called the Toxic Release Inventory (TRI). *See id.* § 11,023(j); Peter L. Gray, *Environmental Data on the Internet: A Wired Public Setting Environmental Policy*, 30 ENVTL. L. REP. 10,122, 10,122 (2000). News media sources have published data from the TRI since the database was created in 1988. Stenzel, *supra* note 461, at 542. 42 U.S.C. § 11,022(a). Some of this information is available to the public on request. *See id.* § 11,022(e)(3).

[492] *Id.* § 11,004(b).

[493] *Id.* § 11,001(c).

[495] *But see* Rechtschaffen, *supra* note 473, at 349–53 (arguing that the Proposition 65 warnings are insufficiently visible and informative to have the kind of positive impact that EPCRA has had).

tion 65 have been introduced in Hawaii, Illinois, Massachusetts, Missouri, Ohio, Oregon, and New York.[496]

At the federal level, Representative Frank Pallone introduced a bill in 1996 requiring that facilities report chemical use and authorizing citizen suits against the EPA Administrator for failure to perform the actions the bill required.[497] In 1997, Representative Henry A. Waxman introduced a bill that also required chemical reporting and authorized citizen suits against the Consumer Product Safety Commission.[498] Most recently, in 1999, Representative Waxman introduced an identical bill, which gathered 121 cosponsors.[499]

Although none of these measures has been adopted to date, the recent sustained legislative activity suggests that the issue is very much alive on the public policy agenda. Moreover, as a result of California's adoption of Proposition 65, more than 11% of the U.S. population will remain covered by an extensive duty-to-warn regime even if no other state or the federal government should follow suit in the near future.[500]

F. Improvements in the Competence of State Governments

In presenting parts of my prior work on federalism and environmental regulation to the EPA General Counsel's Office a few years ago, I was asked a question along these lines: "How can you trust the states, which have been responsible for evils such as racial segregation, to take care responsibly of something as important as the environment?" Though most individuals advocating federal intervention on public choice grounds are not so blunt, they too probably doubt that state environmental regulators are up to the task, despite the strong state initiatives discussed in the preceding sections.

A comprehensive survey by the Advisory Commission on Intergovernmental Relations (ACIR) found the following:

> States in the middle of the 20th century had failed to modernize their governments and to change with the times. Their legislatures were malapportioned, their constitutions archaic, and their governmental structures and process in need of remodeling. They often neglected to deal with the pressing public problems facing them, especially as these related to urban

---

[496] However, none of these proposals was enacted. *See* Gatti, *supra* note 460, at 744 & n.29; James T. O'Reilly, *Stop the World, We Want Our Own Labels: Treaties, State Voter Initiative Laws, and Federal Pre-Emption*, 18 U. PA. J. INT'L ECON. L. 617, 630 (1997).

[497] *See* Public Right-To-Know and Children's Environmental Health Protection Act, H.R. 4234, 104th Cong. §§ 203, 208 (1996).

[498] *See* Children's Environmental Protection and Right To Know Act, H.R. 1636, 105th Cong. §§ 112, 114 (1997).

[499] *See* Children's Environmental Protection and Right To Know Act of 1999, H.R. 1657, 106th Cong. (1999).

[500] The populations of California and the United States are approximately 33 million and 285 million, respectively.

areas. In many instances, particularly in the south, they were often more concerned with promoting states' rights than with protecting the rights of citizens and assuring them equal access to governmental institutions and services.[501]

It is unfair, however, to indict current state governments on the basis of actions taken when significant segments of the population were excluded from the franchise.[502] By many accounts, state governments have improved substantially since that period.[503] The ACIR study found a significant improvement in the competence of state governments:

> One by one and little by little, states undertook to reform their institutions and processes, particularly in the ... 1960s and 1970s. ... Reformed and revitalized in the past quarter century, [states] undergird American federalism. Their increased capacities and responsibilities enable them to play an even greater role in national and local activities as well as to perform their own functions with increased efficiency, effectiveness, responsiveness, openness and accountability.[504]

State governments now serve as important sources of policymaking innovation.[505] Indeed, some surveys suggest that state and local gov-

---

[501] ADVISORY COMM'N ON INTERGOVERNMENTAL RELATIONS, THE QUESTION OF STATE GOVERNMENT CAPABILITY 364 (1985); *see also* PETER H. SCHUCK, *Some Reflections on the Federalism Debate, in* THE LIMITS OF LAW: ESSAYS ON DEMOCRATIC GOVERNANCE 93, 94 (2000). Schuck argues:

> Federalism had nourished some of America's most repellent and repressive political regimes, most notably in the deep South: lynchings tolerated if not abetted by state officials, governors barring black children from entering public schools, Bull Connor's dogs attacking civil rights demonstrators in Alabama, widespread poverty and disease in the Mississippi Delta, corrupt and insular Bourbon courthouse machines.

Id.; see also Barry Friedman, *Valuing Federalism*, 82 MINN. L. REV. 317, 367–68 (1997) (discussing widespread lack of faith in states to solve critical social problems).

[502] *See* ADVISORY COMM'N ON INTERGOVERNMENTAL RELATIONS, *supra* note 501, at 2.

[503] *See, e.g.,* DEWITT JOHN, CIVIC ENVIRONMENTALISM: ALTERNATIVES TO REGULATION IN STATES AND COMMUNITIES 274 (1994) ("[T]he institutional capacity of state governments ... is much greater today than ever before."); SCHUCK, *supra* note 501, at 94 ("Neither the federal government nor the states are even remotely what they were during the civil rights era, when many of our strongest impressions of the federal system were first formed."). For a general assessment, see ADVISORY COMM'N ON INTERGOVERNMENTAL RELATIONS, *supra* note 501, at 1–25. For a discussion of the improvement in the capacity of local governments, see Paul S. Weiland, *Environmental Regulations and Local Government Institutional Capacity*, 22 PUB. ADMIN. Q. 176, 196–97 (1998).

[504] ADVISORY COMM'N ON INTERGOVERNMENTAL RELATIONS, *supra* note 501, at 2. For a summary of the study's findings and recommendations, see *id.* at 363–406.

[505] For detailed studies of state political processes, see DANIEL J. ELAZAR, AMERICAN FEDERALISM: A VIEW FROM THE STATES (3d ed. 1984); and Margeret E. Goertz, *State Education Policy in the 1990s, in* THE STATE OF THE STATES 179, 187–203 (Carl E. Van Horn ed., 3d ed. 1996), describing state reform efforts in education.

ernments command more respect from the public than does the federal government.[506]

One way to evaluate the claim that state environmental agencies lack EPA's competence is to compare the backgrounds of top officials at the federal and state agencies. Evidence that a significant number of individuals with policymaking responsibilities at EPA had previously held leading positions in state environmental agencies, or vice versa, would at least partly undercut the claim of differential competence.

A review of environmental officials' biographies reveals that a noteworthy proportion of high-level EPA officials — both present and past — previously served in important positions in environmental protection (or related areas) at the state level.[507] Carol Browner, who served as Administrator from 1993 to 2001, had previously been the Secretary of the Florida Department of Environmental Regulation. Among the other former Administrators, Douglas Costle (1977–1981) had served as Commissioner of the Connecticut Department of Environmental Protection,[508] and Lee Thomas (1985–1989) had served as the Director of the South Carolina Division of Public Safety Programs, responsible for comprehensive emergency management.[509] This review reveals that former state environmental officials have led EPA for twelve of its thirty-one years, and former state officials with at least some environmental responsibilities have led it for more than half its history.

Of the EPA Deputy Administrators, Fred Hansen (1994–1998) had served as Director of the Oregon Department of Environmental Quality.[510] Richard Farrell, who served as Associate Administrator for Reinvention from 1999 to 2001, a position that has since been renamed Associate Administrator for Policy, Economics, and Innovation, had served as Secretary of the Florida Department of Business and Professional Regulation, the state's largest regulatory and consumer protection agency. J. Charles Fox, the Associate Administrator for Reinvention in 1997, had served as Assistant Secretary and Chief Operating Officer of the Maryland Department of the Environment.[511]

The backgrounds of EPA's four Assistant Administrators, who bear responsibility for the various pollution media, follow a similar pattern.

---

[506] See Andrew E. Busch, Political Science and the 1994 Elections: An Exploratory Essay, 28 PS: POL. SCI. & POL. 708, 709 (1995). For an earlier survey, see ADVISORY COMM'N ON INTERGOVERNMENTAL RELATIONS, supra note 501, at 365–66.

[507] See History Office, EPA, Administrators, at http://www.epa.gov/history/admin/index.htm (last visited Nov. 6, 2001).

[508] See id.

[509] See id.

[510] See id.

[511] See id.

In the Office of Air and Radiation, Robert Perciasepe, who held the position from 1998 to 2001, had been Maryland's Secretary of Environment.[512] His predecessor, Mary Nichols (1993–1997), had chaired the California Air Resources Board, the agency responsible for the automobile emissions standards discussed above.[513] In the Office of Water, J. Charles Fox (1998–2001) and Robert Perciasepe (1993–1998) had held high-level positions in Maryland, as indicated above. Another predecessor, Eckardt Beck (1979–1981), had served as Deputy Commissioner of Connecticut's Department of Environmental Protection.[514] In the Office of Prevention, Pesticides, and Toxic Substances, Lynn Goldman (1993–1998) had served as head of the Division of Environmental and Occupational Disease Control at the California Department of Health Services.[515] In the Office of Solid Waste and Emergency Response, Lee Thomas (1983–1985), who later became Administrator, had served in a high-level position in South Carolina.

Many heads of state environmental agencies have likewise had prior federal experience.[516] Michele Brown, Commissioner of the Alaska Department of Environmental Conservation, served as Senior Environmental Advisor with the U.S. Agency for International Development.[517] Jacqueline Schafer, Director of the Arizona Department of Environmental Quality, was Assistant Secretary of the Navy for Installations and the Environment, a member of the President's Council on Environmental Quality, and Regional Director of EPA Region II (headquartered in New York).[518] Jane Norton, formerly Executive Director of the Colorado Department of Public Health and the Environment, had been Regional Director for Region VIII of the U.S. Department of Health and Human Services.[519] David Struhs, Secretary of the Florida Department of Environmental Protection, served as Chief of Staff to the U.S. Council on Environmental Quality.[520] Martha Kirkpatrick, Commissioner of the Maine Department of Environmental Protection, served as Branch Chief in the EPA Office of Water.[521] Robert Varney, Commissioner of the New Hampshire Depart-

---

[512] See id.

[513] For a discussion of California's automobile emissions standards, see section III.A.1, pp. 585–88, above.

[514] See History Office, supra note 507. In addition, Andrew Breidenbach (1976–1977) had served as Director of Research for the Solid Waste Management Division of the City of Cincinnati. See id.

[515] See id.

[516] For biographies of state environmental officials, see ENVTL. COUNCIL OF THE STATES, ANNUAL REPORT AND ALMANAC (2000).

[517] See id. at 22.

[518] See id. at 23.

[519] See id. at 24.

[520] See id. at 26.

[521] See id. at 31.

ment of Environmental Services, is currently Chairman of the Governmental Advisory Committee on issues relating to the Environmental Side Agreement to the North American Free Trade Agreement.[522] James Seif, Secretary of the Pennsylvania Department of Environmental Protection, served as Regional Administrator of EPA Region III.[523] Thus, eight of the fifty state agency heads have backgrounds that include significant environmental experience (or in one case, health policy experience) at the federal level.

The establishment in 1993 of the Environmental Council of the States (ECOS), a national, nonprofit, nonpartisan association that represents the state and territorial environmental commissioners, attests to the increasing visibility of state environmental regulators.[524] ECOS has played a significant role in the Ozone Transport Assessment Group (OTAG), which seeks to remedy one of the most difficult environmental problems in the eastern United States. OTAG, a partnership between EPA, ECOS, and various industry and environmental groups, worked between 1995 and 1997 to craft a consensus agreement for reducing the transport of ground-level ozone across states.[525] ECOS is currently beginning work on a major study of state enforcement actions, which was requested by Congress and the National Academy of Public Administration.[526]

One cannot draw broad conclusions from this partial and impressionistic study of career patterns. Nonetheless, the patterns observed suggest that, at least at their top levels, state and federal regulatory agencies draw talent from similar pools.

IV. EVALUATING THE PATTERN OF STATE ENVIRONMENTAL MEASURES

Part III shows that a substantial number of states have adopted innovative environmental policies extending beyond the requirements imposed by federal regulation, even when doing so has imposed nontrivial costs on in-state firms. Yet this pattern is far from universal. Indeed, most states have not adopted such policies. This Part suggests an explanation for why some states have taken environmentally protective measures while others have not.

Section A shows that in the 1990s, when most innovative state measures were adopted, the federal government enacted few significant pieces of environmental legislation. Section B explores why some

---

[522] See id. at 36.
[523] See id. at 41.
[524] See id. at 1.
[525] See EPA, What Is OTAG?, at http://www.epa.gov/ttn/rto/otag/aboutotg.html (last updated Apr. 17, 2001).
[526] See ENVTL. COUNCIL OF THE STATES, supra note 516, at 3.

states have expanded their environmental programs into new areas when the federal government has chosen not to do so. The willingness of some states to extend environmental programs at a time of federal inaction undercuts the claim that state legislative processes have more serious public choice pathologies than the federal legislative process.

A. Federal Pollution Control Measures in the 1990s

The bulk of the state regulatory efforts discussed in Part III took place in the 1990s. The only significant exceptions were state environmental policy acts, for which most of the activity took place in the 1970s.[527] By contrast, the federal government has passed little significant legislation since 1990 in the five areas analyzed in Part III or in other areas of environmental protection.

The last flurry of significant federal legislative activity in environmental protection occurred in 1990,[528] during the Bush Administration, when Congress enacted comprehensive amendments to the Clean Air Act,[529] the Oil Pollution Act,[530] and the Pollution Prevention Act.[531] In particular, the first of these statutes was significant in establishing a scheme of marketable permits to control acid deposition,[532] amending the regulatory regime governing nonattainment areas,[533] and creating a permitting program for new plants.[534]

Since 1990, Congress has enacted only two significant pieces of federal environmental legislation: the Safe Drinking Water Act (SDWA) Amendments of 1996[535] and the Food Quality Protection Act of 1996 (FQPA),[536] which amended provisions of both the Federal Food, Drug, and Cosmetic Act (FFDCA) and the Federal Insecticide, Fungicide, and Rodenticide Act (FIFRA). Neither of these enactments clearly extended the preexisting environmental protections. Indeed, provisions of the SDWA amendments have arguably weakened, rather than strengthened, regulatory control. For example, the amendments relax

---

[527] *See supra* section III.D.2, pp. 617–20.

[528] *See* Michael B. Gerrard, *Trends in the Supply and Demand for Environmental Lawyers*, 25 COLUM. J. ENVTL. L. 1, 3 (2000).

[529] Clean Air Act Amendments of 1990, Pub. L. No. 101-549, 104 Stat. 2399 (codified as amended at 42 U.S.C. §§ 7401–7671q (1994 & Supp. II 1996)).

[530] Pub. L. No. 101-380, 104 Stat. 484 (codified as amended at 33 U.S.C. §§ 2701–2761 (1994 & Supp. IV 1998)).

[531] Pub. L. No. 101-508, §§ 6601–6610, 104 Stat. 1388, 1388-321 to 1388-327 (codified at 42 U.S.C. §§ 13,101–13,109 (1994)).

[532] 42 U.S.C. §§ 7651–76510 (1994).

[533] *Id.* §§ 7511–7515 (1994 & Supp. II 1996).

[534] *Id.* §§ 7661–7661f (1994).

[535] Pub. L. No. 104-182, 110 Stat. 1613 (codified as amended at 42 U.S.C. §§ 300f–300j and in scattered sections of 16 U.S.C., 21 U.S.C., 33 U.S.C., and 40 U.S.C.).

[536] Pub. L. No. 104-170, 110 Stat. 1489 (codified as amended in scattered sections of 7 U.S.C. and 21 U.S.C.).

the previous requirement that EPA publish regulations for no fewer than twenty-five contaminants every three years.[537] EPA must now publish these regulations for no fewer than five contaminants every five years.[538] The amendments also require the Administrator to apply cost-benefit analysis in establishing drinking water regulations.[539] Previously, the SDWA required Administrators to promulgate a maximum contaminant level goal (MCLG) for a particular pollutant "at the level at which no known or anticipated adverse effects on the health of persons occur and which allows an adequate margin of safety."[540] The Administrator would then set the enforceable limit — the maximum contaminant level (MCL) — "as close to the maximum contaminant level goal as is feasible."[541] The Administrator had no discretion to weaken an MCL whose cost outweighed its benefits. Pursuant to the amendments, however, the Administrator now must determine "whether the benefits of the maximum contaminant level justify, or do not justify, the costs."[542] If the benefits do not justify the costs, the Administrator "may" set a less stringent standard.[543]

Nevertheless, certain provisions of the SDWA amendments strengthen environmental protection. For example, in selecting contaminants to regulate, EPA must consider the interests of groups that are at greater risk of adverse health effects, such as children, the elderly, and individuals with serious illnesses.[544] The amendments also require each community water system to inform its customers annually of contaminant levels in the system's drinking water.[545]

The FQPA, which modified the regulatory regimes governing the treatment of pesticides,[546] also weakened regulatory controls in certain

---

[537] 42 U.S.C. § 300g-1(b)(3)(C) (amended 1996).

[538] See id. § 300g-1(b)(1)(B) (Supp. II 1996). For a discussion of the 1996 amendments' effects on the regulation of water contaminants, see William E. Cox, Evolution of the Safe Drinking Water Act: A Search for Effective Quality Assurance Strategies and Workable Concepts of Federalism, 21 WM. & MARY ENVTL. L. & POL'Y REV. 69, 91 (1997) ("[T]he pace of regulation promulgation was substantially slowed . . . ."); and Wendy P. Feiner, Note, Just When You Thought It Was Safe To Go Back in the Water: A Guide to Complying with the 1996 Amendments to the Safe Drinking Water Act, 4 ENVTL. LAW. 193, 196–200 (1997).

[539] See 42 U.S.C. § 300g-1(b)(3)–(4) (Supp. II 1996).

[540] Id. § 300g-1(b)(4) (1994) (amended 1996).

[541] Id.

[542] Id. § 300g-1(b)(4)(C) (Supp. II 1996).

[543] See id. § 300g-1(b)(6)(A).

[544] See id. § 300g-1(b)(1)(C).

[545] See id. § 300g(c)(4).

[546] James Smart provides a comprehensive analysis of the events leading to the passage of the FQPA. See James Smart, All the Stars in the Heavens Were in the Right Places: The Passage of the Food Quality Protection Act of 1996, 17 STAN. ENVTL. L.J. 273 (1998); see also James Handley, The Food Quality Protection Act + EPA's Adverse Effects Reporting Rule = New Data and Better Pesticide Risk Decisions, 28 ENVTL. L. REP. 10, 241 (1998) (discussing enforcement and compliance issues relating to EPA's adverse effects rule); Alison D. Carpenter, Note, Impact of the

ways. Most important, the FQPA limited the scope of the Delaney Clause,[547] which had prohibited the use of potentially carcinogenic additives in processed food, by restricting the categorical meaning of "food additives."[548] For instance, although the FQPA did not amend the Delaney Clause, it excluded chemical pesticide residues from the definition of food additives.[549] Consequently, the regulatory regime now permits the presence of pesticide residues even if they pose some risk of cancer. The FQPA also extended the scope of preemption of state regulations. Specifically, the FQPA preempts more stringent state regulation of pesticide residues in food.[550] Industry groups thereby succeeded in their decade-long quest for protection from more stringent state regulations.[551]

Like the SDWA amendments, however, the FQPA was not a total defeat for environmentalists. Most important, it mandates that EPA pay particular attention to the effects of pesticide residues on infants and children.[552] In assessing threshold risks, for instance, EPA must incorporate an additional tenfold margin of safety.[553]

Environmentalists also secured a victory in the requirement of special screening for estrogenic and other endocrine effects.[554] In setting permissible levels of pesticide residues in food, EPA must consider whether "the pesticide chemical may have an effect in humans that is similar to an effect produced by a naturally occurring estrogen or other endocrine effects."[555]

Since 1990, no other federal legislation has extended the scope of environmental protection in significant ways. I reviewed all the amendments enacted since 1990 (from the 102nd through 106th Congresses) to the major federal environmental statutes: the Clean Air Act, the Clean Water Act, CERCLA, RCRA, NEPA, and the Endangered Species Act.[556] Congress did not amend the latter three statutes at all.

Food Quality Protection Act of 1996, 3 ENVTL. LAW. 479 (1997) (describing the FQPA's changes to the existing scheme of pesticide regulation).

[547] *See* 21 U.S.C. § 348(c)(3)(A) (1994).

[548] EPA, which is responsible under the FFDCA for setting permissible levels of pesticide residues, had employed a variety of tactics to avoid invoking the Delaney Clause. *See* Smart, *supra* note 546, at 283–86, 293–95. In 1992, however, the Ninth Circuit mandated strict application of the Delaney Clause, finding that "Congress intended the EPA to prohibit all additives that are carcinogens, regardless of the degree of risk involved." Les v. Reilly, 968 F.2d 985, 986 (9th Cir. 1992), *cert. denied sub nom.* Nat'l Agric. Chems. Ass'n v. Les, 507 U.S. 950 (1993).

[549] *See* 21 U.S.C. § 321(s) (1994 & Supp. II 1996).

[550] *Id.* § 346a(n)(4).

[551] *See* Smart, *supra* note 546, at 275.

[552] *See* 21 U.S.C. § 346a(b)(2)(C)(ii) (Supp. II 1996).

[553] *See id.*

[554] Smart, *supra* note 546, at 340.

[555] 21 U.S.C. § 346a(b)(2)(D)(viii).

[556] 16 U.S.C. §§ 1531–1544 (1994).

The amendments to the Clean Air Act,[557] the Clean Water Act,[558] and CERCLA[559] deal almost exclusively with narrow technical issues.

---

[557] Chemical Safety Information, Site Security and Fuels Regulatory Relief Act, Pub. L. No. 106-40, §§ 2, 3, 113 Stat. 207, 208 (1999) (amending 42 U.S.C. § 7412(r)(4), (7)); Federal Reports Elimination Act of 1998, Pub. L. No. 105-362, §§ 402(b), 1501(b), 112 Stat. 3280, 3283, 3294 (repealing 42 U.S.C. §§ 7408(f)(3)–(4) and 7412(n)(2)(C)); Border Smog Reduction Act of 1998, Pub. L. No. 105-286, § 2, 112 Stat. 2773 (amending 42 U.S.C. § 7511(b) by adding subsection (h)); Omnibus Consolidated and Emergency Supplemental Appropriations Act of 1999, Pub. L. No. 105-277, § 764, 112 Stat. 2681, 2681-36 to 2681-37 (1998) (amending 42 U.S.C. § 7671c by adding subsections (d)(5), (d)(6), (e)(3), and (h)); General Accounting Office Act of 1996, Pub. L. No. 104-316, § 122(r), 110 Stat. 3826, 3838 (repealing section 812(b) of the Clean Air Act Amendments of 1990); Federal Aviation Reauthorization Act of 1996, Pub. L. No. 104-264, § 406(b), 110 Stat. 3213, 3257 (amending 42 U.S.C. § 7571(a)(2) by adding subsection (B)); Act of Oct. 9, 1996, Pub. L. No. 104-260, § 1, 110 Stat. 3175 (adding subsection (D) to the end of 42 U.S.C. 7506(c)(4)); Act of Dec. 23, 1995, Pub. L. No. 104-70, § 1, 109 Stat. 773 (amending 42 U.S.C. § 7511a(d)(1)(B)); National Highway System Designation Act of 1995, Pub. L. No. 104-59, § 305(b), 109 Stat. 568, 580 (amending 42 U.S.C. § 7506(c)); Act of Nov. 2, 1994, Pub. L. No. 103-437, § 15(s), 108 Stat. 4581, 4594 (amending 42 U.S.C. § 7625-1(a)(2)); Act of Dec. 4, 1991, Pub. L. No. 102-187, 105 Stat. 1285 (amending 42 U.S.C. § 7412(b)(1)).

[558] Coast Guard Authorization Act of 1998, Pub. L. No. 105-383, § 411, 112 Stat. 3411, 3432 (amending 33 U.S.C. § 1321(a)(8), (c)(4)(A), and adding subsection (a)(25)); Higher Education Amendments of 1998, Pub. L. No. 105-244, § 102(a)(11), 112 Stat. 1581, 1620 (amending 33 U.S.C. § 1262(a)(1)); Coast Guard Authorization Act of 1996, Pub. L. No. 104-324, §§ 1143–1144, 110 Stat. 3901, 3992 (amending 33 U.S.C. § 1321(c)(3)(B), (j)(2)(A), (j)(4)(C)(v)); Water Resources Development Act of 1996, Pub. L. No. 104-303, § 583, 110 Stat. 3658, 3791 (amending 33 U.S.C. § 1269(e)); National Defense Authorization Act for Fiscal Year 1996, Pub. L. No. 104-106, § 325(b)–(c), 110 Stat. 186, 254, 259 (1996) (amending 33 U.S.C. § 1322 by adding subsection (n) and amending 33 U.S.C. § 1362); Federal Reports Elimination and Sunset Act of 1995, Pub. L. No. 104-66, § 2021(a)–(d), 109 Stat. 707, 726–27 (repealing 33 U.S.C. §§ 1252(d) and 1375(d), and amending 33 U.S.C. §§ 1311(n)(8) and 1324(d)(3)); Ocean Pollution Reduction Act, Pub. L. No. 103-431, § 2, 108 Stat. 4396 (1994) (amending 33 U.S.C. § 1311(j) by adding subsection (5)); Federal Acquisition Streamlining Act of 1994, Pub. L. No. 103-355, § 8301(a), 108 Stat. 3243, 3396 (amending 33 U.S.C. § 1368 by adding subsection (f)); Water Resources Development Act of 1992, Pub. L. No. 102-580, § 364, 106 Stat. 4797, 4862 (amending 33 U.S.C. § 1342(p)(1), (6)); Department of Transportation and Related Agencies Appropriations Act, 1993, Pub. L. No. 102-388, § 349, 106 Stat. 1520, 1554 (amending 33 U.S.C. § 1321(b) by adding subsection (12)).

[559] Departments of Veterans Affairs and Housing and Urban Development, and Independent Agencies Appropriations Act, 1999, Pub. L. No. 105-276, tit. III, 112 Stat. 2461, 2497 (1998) (amending 42 U.S.C. § 9619(e)(2)(C), (g)(5)); Act of Oct. 11, 1996, Pub. L. No. 104-287, § 6(j), 110 Stat. 3388, 3399 (amending 42 U.S.C. §§ 9601(26) and 9607(c)(1)(C)); Omnibus Consolidated Appropriations Act, 1997, Pub. L. No. 104-208, § 2502, 110 Stat. 3009, 3009-462 (1996) (amending 42 U.S.C. § 9601(20) by adding subsection (E) and amending 42 U.S.C. § 9607 by adding subsection (n)); National Defense Authorization Act for Fiscal Year 1997, Pub. L. No. 104-201, §§ 330-331, 334, 110 Stat. 2422, 2484, 2486 (1996) (amending 42 U.S.C. § 9620(d), (h)(3), (h)(4)(A)); National Defense Authorization Act for Fiscal Year 1996, Pub. L. No. 104-106, § 2834, 110 Stat. 186, 559 (amending 42 U.S.C. § 9620(h)(3)); Act of Oct. 31, 1994, Pub. L. No. 103-429, § 7(e), 108 Stat. 4377, 4390 (amending 42 U.S.C. §§ 9601(26) and 9607(c)(1)(C)); National Defense Authorization Act for Fiscal Year 1993, Pub. L. No. 102-484, § 331(a), 106 Stat. 2315, 2373 (1992) (amending 42 U.S.C. § 9619); Preventive Health Amendments of 1992, Pub. L. No. 102-531, § 312(h), 106 Stat. 3469, 3506 (amending 42 U.S.C. § 9604); Community Environmental Response Facilitation Act, Pub. L. No. 102-426, § 3, 106 Stat. 2174, 2175–77 (1992) (amending 42 U.S.C. § 9620(h) by adding subsection (4)).

The lack of important federal legislative activity since 1990 is not surprising, given the decade's political dynamics. The 102nd Congress (1991–1992) followed the ambitious environmental enactments of the 101st Congress in 1990.[560] It is understandable that other issues occupied congressional attention.[561]   Congress considered reauthorizing three important environmental statutes — RCRA, the Clean Water Act, and the Endangered Species Act — but ultimately reauthorized none of them.[562] In fact, this Congress accomplished little in the domestic sphere as it focused most of its efforts in the foreign policy arena.[563]

The 103rd Congress (1993–1994) sat during the first two years of the Clinton Administration, when the Administration's other domestic priorities, notably its failed attempt at health care reform, took center stage.[564] The Administration had a broad environmental agenda, but received criticism for not identifying its top priorities in a timely manner or lobbying sufficiently for the bills that it backed.[565]

Both the House and the Senate shifted to Republican control in the 104th Congress (1995–1996), which devoted its energy to consideration of the antiregulatory planks of the "Contract with America." In particular, the Contract with America contained three elements designed to make the enactment of environmental regulation more cumbersome: a limitation on unfunded environmental mandates imposed upon state and local governments; a regulatory reform initiative requiring the use of cost-benefit analysis, which included a petition process for the retrospective challenge of existing regulations; and a takings provision significantly expanding compensation requirements.[566] The Congress en-

---

[560] *See* David Wallenberg, *Great Expectations: Reviewing the 101st Congress,* 21 ENVTL. L. REP. 10,008, 10,008 (1991) ("The 101st Congress in 1989 and 1990 was one of the most environmentally active congresses in two decades."); *supra* p. 631.

[561] *Cf.* James E. Satterfield, *High Hopes and Failed Expectations: The Environmental Record of the 103d Congress,* 25 ENVTL. L. REP. 10,089, 10,090 (1995) ("During the 103d Congress, efforts to reform health care, reduce the deficit, combat crime, and approve trade acts such as [NAFTA] consumed enormous amounts of congressional time.").

[562] *See* James E. Satterfield, *A Tale of Sound and Fury: The Environmental Record of the 102d Congress,* 23 ENVTL. L. REP. 10,015, 10,020–25 (1993).

[563] *See* Adam Clymer, *The Gridlock Congress: The 102d Will Be Remembered as Much for Its Embarrassments as Its Legislation,* N.Y. TIMES, Oct. 11, 1992, at A1. This lack of accomplishment is not surprising given that following the election of this Congress, the White House Chief of Staff announced: "There's not a single piece of legislation that needs to be passed in the two years for this President. In fact, if Congress wants to come together, adjourn and leave, it's all right with us. We don't need them." *Id.* (internal quotation marks omitted).

[564] *See* Satterfield, *supra* note 561, at 10,090.

[565] *Id.* at 10,102.

[566] *See* James E. Satterfield, *A Funny Thing Happened on the Way to the Revolution: The Environmental Record of the 104th Congress,* 27 ENVTL. L. REP. 10,019, 10,020 (1997). For a journalist's account of the magnitude of the proposals, see Cindy Skrzycki, *Hill Republicans Promise*

acted only the unfunded mandates provision, though the regulatory reform provision passed in the House.[567]

Despite President Clinton's reelection in 1996, Republicans retained control of the House and the Senate for the 105th and 106th Congresses (1997–1998 and 1999–2000). As a result, the promise of any viable proposals for important pro-environmental legislation rested with the Clinton Administration. Partisanship, however, inhibited the passage of any significant environmental legislative reform.[568]

As this section has illustrated,[569] the states, not the federal government, produced the most innovation in pollution control legislation in the 1990s.[570]

B. Explaining the Differences in the Stringency of State Programs

The discussion in Part III reveals that some states took a clear lead in various environmental areas; of course, other states lagged in their efforts. These different responses might be explained in several ways. For instance, public choice pathologies may preclude at least some states from enacting the types of environmental regulation that reflect

---

a Regulatory Revolution: Lawmakers Target Rules and Rulemakers, WASH. POST, Jan. 4, 1995, at A1.

[567] Satterfield, *supra* note 566, at 10,026–28. Congress instead enacted a more narrow regulatory proposal: the Small Business Regulatory Enforcement Fairness Act of 1996, Pub. L. No. 104-121, § 251, 110 Stat. 868, 868–74 (codified at 5 U.S.C. §§ 801–808 (Supp. II 1996)). The Act gives Congress sixty days to review "major" federal rules before they become final.

[568] *See* Michael J. O'Grady, *Going Nowhere Fast: The Environmental Record of the 105th Congress*, 29 ENVTL. L. REP. 10,085, 10,087 (1999) ("Legislators began the 105th Congress with a list of environmental legislation that required reform. Partisan politics and the general legislative malaise doomed most efforts to pass any of the 105th Congress' environmental priorities.").

[569] This summary has not dealt with the Clinton Administration's actions with respect to federal lands.

[570] A number of commentators have reached similar conclusions based on earlier assessments. *See* JOHN, *supra* note 503, at 80 ("Virtually all states have taken some steps to go beyond federally imposed requirements, and some have taken the lead in several areas."); EVAN J. RINGQUIST, ENVIRONMENTAL PROTECTION AT THE STATE LEVEL: POLITICS AND PROGRESS IN CONTROLLING POLLUTION, at xiii (1993) ("[I]n many instances state governments, not 'the feds,' are at the forefront in efforts to protect the environment."); David L. Markell, *States as Innovators: It's Time for a New Look to Our "Laboratories of Democracy" in the Effort To Improve Our Approach to Environmental Regulation*, 58 ALB. L. REV. 347, 355 (1994) ("[I]nnovations at the state level are likely to hold a great deal of promise as potential strategies for addressing concerns about federal approaches to environmental regulation."); Portney, *supra* note 166, at 283 ("Over the past decade or so some of the most interesting environmental initiatives have arisen at the state level.").

While Congress failed to enact any innovative pollution control measures, federal agencies undertook a number of important regulatory initiatives during the 1990s. For example, in 1997, EPA strengthened the National Ambient Air Quality Standards for Particulate Matter and Ozone. 40 C.F.R. § 50.7 (1999). The D.C. Circuit struck down these standards on nondelegation grounds. *See* Am. Trucking Ass'ns v. EPA, 175 F.3d 1027, 1034, *modified*, 195 F.3d 4 (D.C. Cir. 1999). The Supreme Court reversed. Whitman v. Am. Trucking Ass'ns, 121 S. Ct. 903 (2001).

the preferences of their citizens.[571] Alternatively, it may be that preferences for environmental protection are not distributed homogeneously throughout the country, and that citizens of states with less stringent environmental standards value environmental protection less than they value competing goals. Under this account, the pattern of regulation observed across the states would not be the product of public choice pathologies but instead would mirror differing preferences for environmental protection.

Comparing the environmental efforts of various state legislatures with the voting records of their members of the U.S. House of Representatives may suggest which account is more plausible. If those who support federal regulation on public choice grounds are right about the pathologies of state regulatory processes, one would expect that state regulation would reflect those public choice pathologies. Moreover, if they are right that federal regulation corrects these pathologies,[572] the voting records of members of Congress, which determine the scope of federal regulation, should be aligned more closely with citizen preferences for environmental protection.

Table 3 ranks states based on the voting records of their members of Congress. The information compiled in Table 3 is derived from ratings computed by the League of Conservation Voters for 1999 surveying the first session of the past Congress.[573] These ratings are based on each representative's votes on sixteen environmental issues selected by the organization: a pro-environmental vote (either an affirmative vote on a pro-environmental matter or a negative vote on an anti-environmental matter) receives a score of one; an anti-environmental vote receives a score of zero. Each representative's rating is calculated by averaging her scores.

For each state's congressional delegation, Table 3 shows the median ratings for Democratic representatives and Republican representatives,

---

[571] A number of recent studies, however, cast doubt on this view. For example, Evan Ringquist notes that with respect to air pollution, "[s]tates with strong polluting industries appear to be able to resist industry pressure and pass tougher air pollution control regulations, though the same fortitude is not displayed when it comes to resisting the demands of electric utilities." RINGQUIST, *supra* note 570, at 193. With respect to water pollution, "[s]tates are able to resist pressures for lax regulations from heavily polluting industries, but this political backbone is lacking when it comes to resisting pressures from mining industries." *Id.; see also id.* at 117–20, 161–65 (discussing and analyzing various causal models of group policy influence); Barton H. Thompson, Jr., *Environmental Policy and State Constitutions: The Potential Role of Substantive Guidance*, 27 RUTGERS L.J. 863, 893 (1996) (suggesting that "industry groups generally do not enjoy undue influence in resisting stronger environmental laws" at the state level).

[572] *See supra* section I.A.1, pp. 559–60.

[573] LEAGUE OF CONSERVATION VOTERS, 1999 NATIONAL ENVIRONMENTAL SCORE-CARD (Feb. 2000), *available at* http://www.lcv.org/pdfs/scorecard99.pdf.

as well as the median ratings for the delegation as a whole.[574] Table 3 also provides a ranking of states from most environmentally protective to least environmentally protective based on those voting records.

TABLE 3. ANALYSIS OF LEAGUE OF CONSERVATION VOTER RECORDS BY CONGRESSIONAL DELEGATIONS (NUMBER OF REPRESENTATIVES IN PARENTHESES)

State	Median Democrat	Median Republican	Median Overall	Rank
Alabama	0.00 (2)	0.00 (5)	0.00 (7)	48
Alaska	NA (0)	0.06 (1)	0.06 (1)	43
Arizona	0.80 (1)	0.07 (6)	0.07 (7)	39
Arkansas	0.53 (2)	0.03 (2)	0.17 (4)	31
California	0.93 (28)	0.07 (24)	0.57 (52)	17
Colorado	1.00 (2)	0.13 (4)	0.13 (6)	33
Connecticut	0.90 (4)	0.83 (2)	0.90 (6)	6
Delaware	NA (0)	0.75 (1)	0.75 (1)	10
Florida	0.83 (8)	0.13 (15)	0.27 (23)	24
Georgia	0.93 (3)	0.12 (8)	0.13 (11)	33
Hawaii	0.93 (2)	NA (0)	0.93 (2)	3
Idaho	NA (0)	0.06 (1)	0.06 (1)	43
Illinois	0.93 (10)	0.13 (9)	0.67 (19)	15
Indiana	0.73 (4)	0.07 (6)	0.17 (10)	31
Iowa	0.47 (1)	0.10 (4)	0.20 (5)	27
Kansas	0.80 (1)	0.00 (3)	0.07 (4)	39
Kentucky	0.20 (1)	0.07 (5)	0.07 (6)	39
Louisiana	0.33 (2)	0.00 (6)	0.00 (8)	48
Maine	0.83 (2)	NA (0)	0.83 (2)	8
Maryland	0.83 (4)	0.37 (4)	0.73 (8)	11
Massachusetts	0.97 (10)	NA (0)	0.97 (10)	2
Michigan	0.87 (10)	0.13 (6)	0.70 (16)	14
Minnesota	0.80 (6)	0.40 (2)	0.73 (8)	11
Mississippi	0.40 (3)	0.03 (2)	0.33 (5)	22
Missouri	0.80 (5)	0.10 (4)	0.33 (9)	22
Montana	NA (0)	0.06 (1)	0.06 (1)	43
Nebraska	NA (0)	0.13 (3)	0.13 (3)	33
Nevada	0.73 (1)	0.07 (1)	0.40 (2)	21
New Hampshire	NA (0)	0.27 (2)	0.27 (2)	24

continued overleaf

---

[574] The pattern that emerges from using means rather than medians is quite similar. Using medians, however, limits the influence of outliers on the ratings.

TABLE 3 (continued)

State	Median Democrat	Median Republican	Median Overall	Rank
New Jersey	1.00 (7)	0.63 (6)	0.93 (13)	3
New Mexico	0.87 (1)	0.03 (2)	0.07 (3)	39
New York	0.93 (19)	0.37 (12)	0.80 (31)	9
North Carolina	0.80 (5)	0.07 (7)	0.20 (12)	27
North Dakota	0.56 (1)	NA (0)	0.56 (1)	18
Ohio	0.87 (8)	0.00 (11)	0.20 (19)	27
Oklahoma	NA (0)	0.00 (6)	0.00 (6)	48
Oregon	0.87 (4)	0.07 (1)	0.87 (5)	7
Pennsylvania	0.80 (11)	0.07 (10)	0.47 (21)	19
Rhode Island	0.93 (2)	NA (0)	0.93 (2)	3
South Carolina	0.77 (2)	0.10 (4)	0.27 (6)	24
South Dakota	NA (0)	0.06 (1)	0.06 (1)	43
Tennessee	0.47 (4)	0.13 (5)	0.13 (9)	33
Texas	0.60 (17)	0.00 (13)	0.10 (30)	38
Utah	NA (0)	0.13 (3)	0.13 (3)	33
Vermont	1.00 (1)*	NA (0)	1.00 (1)	1
Virginia	0.47 (6)	0.07 (5)	0.20 (11)	27
Washington	0.87 (5)	0.10 (4)	0.60 (9)	16
West Virginia	0.47 (3)	NA (0)	0.47 (3)	19
Wisconsin	0.93 (5)	0.20 (4)	0.73 (9)	11
Wyoming	NA (0)	0.06 (1)	0.06 (1)	43
Full House	0.87 (213)	0.07 (222)	0.40 (435)	NA

*Independent

The rankings of the states can now be compared to the lists of states that provided leadership with respect to the programs discussed in Part III (the rankings from Table 3 are provided in parentheses):

Automobile standards: California (17), Maine (8), Massachusetts (2), New York (9), and Vermont (1);
State Superfunds: New Jersey (3);
Voluntary cleanups and brownfields redevelopment: Illinois (15), Michigan (14), New Jersey (3);
Land transfer provisions: Connecticut (6), Hawaii (3), New Jersey (3);
Curbside recycling: Connecticut (6), New Jersey (3), New York (9);
Pay as you throw: Minnesota (11), Washington (16), Wisconsin (11);
Bottle bills: Connecticut (6), Delaware (10), Iowa (27), Maine (8), Massachusetts (2), Michigan (14), New York (9), Oregon (7), Vermont (1);

State environmental protection acts: California (17), Massachusetts (2), Minnesota (11), New York (9), Washington (16);
Duty to warn measures: California (17).

These lists include a total of sixteen states. Of these, fifteen were ranked in the top seventeen, or the top third of all the states. Only Maryland and Rhode Island had rankings in the top third but did not adopt any of the listed measures. Moreover, these lists include only one state not in the top third (Iowa).

This close correspondence between state environmental initiative and congressional voting records does not result from my choice of the programs reviewed in Part III. For example, a study undertaken in the early 1990s ranked states on the basis of their adoption of "green" policies.[575] Of the sixteen states categorized as having undertaken innovative measures on the basis of the review in Part III, fifteen ranked in the top seventeen positions.[576]

Table 3 also reveals that the median rating for the House as a whole, 0.40, is below the median ratings of the congressional delegations from fifteen of the sixteen states that adopted innovative state environmental protection measures. Indeed, at 0.57, California had the lowest median rating among these states. The federal median, meanwhile, was equal to that of the state ranked twenty-first, Nevada.

In summary, congressional voting records are closely aligned with state leadership roles in environmental regulation.[577] Moreover, the members of Congress from the states that undertook innovative environmental protection measures in the 1990s all have more pro-environmental records than the House as a whole.

The parallel between state-level environmental innovation and pro-environmental voting at the federal level undermines the public choice argument for federal regulation. Either both congressional voting records and state programs reflect preferences for environmental protec-

---

[575] *See* BOB HALL & MARY LEE KERR, 1991–92 GREEN INDEX 3 (1991). For other environmental rankings, see RINGQUIST, *supra* note 570, at 106, 158; David M. Hedge & Michael J. Scicchitano, *The States and Environmental Regulation in the 1980s: A Test of the New Federalism, in* STATE POLICY PROBLEMS 129, 139 (Fred A. Meyer, Jr. & Ralph Baker eds., 1993); and James P. Lester, James L. Franke, Ann O'M. Bowman & Kenneth W. Kramer, *Hazardous Wastes, Politics, and Public Policy: A Comparative State Analysis,* 36 W. POL. Q. 257, 268 (1983).

[576] Delaware and Hawaii were the only exceptions. *See* HALL & KERR, *supra* note 575. For a discussion of the rankings of states by environmental policy, see Hedge & Scicchitano, *supra* note 575, at 134–41.

[577] For more general discussion of differences in public opinion across the states, see ROBERT S. ERIKSON, NORMAN R. LUTTBEG & KENT L. TEDIN, AMERICAN PUBLIC OPINION: ITS ORIGINS, CONTENT, AND IMPACT 195–99 (3d ed. 1988); and ROBERT S. ERIKSON, GERALD C. WRIGHT & JOHN P. MCIVER, STATEHOUSE DEMOCRACY: PUBLIC OPINION AND POLICY IN THE AMERICAN STATES 47–72 (1993). For discussion of the relationship between these differences and the adoption of public policies, see *id.* at 73–95.

tion within a given state, or they both reflect similar public choice pathologies. But if the federal legislative process had less serious pathologies than state processes had, one would not expect to see the close correspondence between above-median congressional voting records and state environmental regulatory policies beyond federal requirements. To the contrary, one would expect a consistent pattern in which even states with voting records above the median would do no more than satisfy federal requirements.

CONCLUSION

This Article rejects, on the basis of both theoretical and empirical analyses, the general argument that public choice problems at the state level lead to systematic underregulation absent federal intervention. This negative conclusion, however, should not be read to imply any of three other conclusions: that states enact socially optimal environmental regulation, that state environmental regulation is more likely to be welfare maximizing than federal environmental regulation, or that state governments exhibit less serious public choice pathologies than the federal government. The political processes that produce environmental regulation are sufficiently complex that any general conclusion of this sort is almost certain to be wrong. The Article's major contribution, rather, is to debunk an oft-repeated and influential general argument in favor of federal intervention.

[19]

Journal of Urban Economics **51**, 101–122 (2002)

doi:10.1006/juec.2001.2239, available online at http://www.idealibrary.com on **IDEAL**®

Strategic Interaction and the Determination of Environmental Policy across U.S. States

Per G. Fredriksson and Daniel L. Millimet

Department of Economics, Southern Methodist University,
Box 750496, Dallas, Texas 75275-0496
E-mail: pfredrik@mail.smu.edu; millimet@mail.smu.edu

Received November 8, 2000; revised April 30, 2001; published online July 20, 2001

We examine whether U.S. states are engaged in strategic environmental policymaking. In particular, do states incorporate the stringency of environmental policies in neighboring states into their own decision calculus? Our analysis suggests that states are influenced by their neighbors—both contiguous and regional neighbors—and the effect operates within a five year window. Moreover, the response is *asymmetric*. States are "pulled" to higher levels of abatement costs by improvements in neighbors with regulations that are already relatively stringent. Improvements by states with relatively lax regulations have no effect on their neighbors' environmental policymaking. © 2001 Elsevier Science

1. INTRODUCTION

What determines environmental quality and policy in federal systems? Some authors argue that decentralized environmental policymaking induces a "race to the bottom" with suboptimally lax environmental standards (see, e.g., [1, 29, 30, 37, 41]).[1] Two common reasons for why decentralized authority is thought to result in inefficiently weak environmental policies are transboundary pollution problems and interjurisdictional capital competition [46].[2] Much of the

We thank Arik Levinson and John List for making the data available and Randy Becker, Thiess Buettner, Ted Crone, Ami Glazer, Douglas Holtz-Eakin, Bob Inman, Angeliki Kourelis, James Murdoch, Thomas Selden, Olaf Unteroberdoerster, and workshop participants at the University of Texas at Dallas (UTD) and ZEW (Mannheim) for helpful comments and suggestions. The editor, Jan Brueckner, and two anonymous referees provided constructive suggestions, greatly improving the paper. A portion of the paper was written while the first author visited the Department of Economics at the University of Lund and he is grateful for the department's hospitality. The usual caveats apply.

[1] If environmental regulations are set below the optimal level, the marginal cost of pollution damage is greater than the marginal cost of pollution abatement. Wilson [51] provides a useful survey of the literature on strategic environmental policymaking.

[2] Others analyze the political economy of environmental policy choice in federations. Oates and Schwab [39] study decentralized environmental policymaking and capital taxation under majority rule voting, but without strategic interaction. Assuming homogenous workers, jurisdictions are found to set optimal environmental regulations. However, with a positive (negative) capital tax,

0094-1190/01 $35.00
© 2001 Elsevier Science
All rights reserved.

policy-oriented literature argues that decentralized environmental policy will result in a race to the bottom (see, e.g., [15, 19, 20]). Such predictions lie behind some of the most significant developments of environmental policymaking in the U.S. Fears of a race to the bottom were a significant factor leading to the formation of the EPA in 1968 [28], and Revesz [42] argues that such considerations explain why the U.S. Clean Air Act is implemented at the federal level. These fears have also motivated calls for regulatory harmonization across the European Union (EU) and NAFTA [20]. Given the importance of the belief in the race to the bottom, free riding, and interjurisdictional competition between the U.S. states, it appears imperative to test the empirical validity of this hypothesis.

Pollution control in the U.S. is essentially a combination of centralized standard setting and state-level implementation and enforcement. Consequently, U.S. states retain considerable flexibility in their environmental policymaking despite the presence of federal legislation, as shown in various studies utilizing variation in regulatory intensity across states (see, e.g., [33, 35]). For pollutants such as acid rain and ground-level ozone, states employ a combination of federally prescribed control measures and methods of their own choice [14]. The Clean Air Act grants states considerable latitude in selecting methods of pollution control, particularly in nonattainment areas [14, 27]. Similar flexibility is permitted under the Clean Water Act as well. In a recent study of free riding behavior in state river pollution abatement, Sigman [44] finds that the Clean Water Act, by allowing the federal EPA to authorize state issuance and enforcement of discharge permits, facilitates such free riding behavior.[3] Helland [23, 24] also shows that enforcement and monitoring of U.S. environmental laws vary across locations. Wetstone and Rosencranz [47] report some anecdotal evidence for SO_2 pollution abatement. In 1982, for example, the EPA did not intervene when the state of Kentucky charged that a large power plant located in Indiana near their common border contributed significantly to pollution problems in the nearby city of Louisville, KY. Wetstone and Rosencranz [47, p. 102] conclude that the EPA was "a major obstacle to state efforts to combat interstate pollution." Thus, it appears that transboundary pollution and the nature of current federal regulation leave states considerable incentive and latitude to act strategically.

Unfortunately, empirical evidence on the race to the bottom issue is lacking, and the policy debate remains severely uninformed. Moreover, the theoretical

---

jurisdictions have an incentive to set environmental regulations which are inefficiently weak (strong) in order to stimulate (discourage) capital inflows and gain capital tax revenues. Fredriksson and Gaston [22] argue that the regulatory choice is independent of institutional design because the lower degree of capital competition in a centralized system is neutralized by greater capital owner lobbying.

[3] Sigman [44] reports that rivers contained entirely within one state exhibit 24% lower pollution levels than rivers crossing state borders. Free riding is observed only at upstream locations, and pollution declines as the distance from the state border increases.

literature, which presumes the existence of strategic environmental policymaking, has thus far received little empirical validation. In this paper, we aim to fill this gap in the literature. In particular, our goal is to begin addressing the question of whether a race to the bottom has taken place between the U.S. states. Specifically, are states' regulatory abatement costs affected by the choices made in neighboring states?

To analyze this issue, we begin by presenting a simple theoretical model of two representative states with populations affected by transboundary pollution. Since the states ignore the external benefits of their abatement choices, pollution control measures are inefficiently weak. When the states' abatement levels are selected strategically, the reaction function has a nonzero slope. If, on the other hand, there is no strategic interaction, the slope of the reaction function is zero. Similar to some previous models of strategic interaction in other policy arenas, we find that the states' abatement reaction functions can slope either up or down, depending on the relative size of terms (see, e.g., [4, 7]). The empirical question that emerges is consequently whether the slope estimate differs significantly from zero. This would indicate the presence of spillovers, which tend to generate inefficient outcomes.

Using panel data on two measures of environmental stringency—(i) Levinson's [33] industry-adjusted index of relative state environmental abatement costs and (ii) unadjusted pollution abatement and control expenditures (PACE) per dollar of manufacturing output by state—we find strong evidence that states do take their neighboring states' regulatory choices into account.[4] There is a positive association between the environmental abatement costs incurred by manufacturing industries in neighboring states, even after controlling for the nonuniform distribution of industries within the U.S. This finding verifies the assumptions made in the theoretical literature on strategic interaction in environmental policymaking. One must be cautious, however, in drawing any conclusions regarding the existence of a race to the bottom (or to the top). For a race to the bottom to occur, environmental policies must be inefficiently weak *and* remain equally weak (or become weaker) compared to the efficient level of regulation. Since the efficient level of pollution abatement is unobserved, our results at this stage cannot be used to answer this question.

Our analysis yields three additional insights. First, the data suggest that interaction across states in the determination of regulatory abatement costs operates within a five-year window. Second, not all regions of the U.S. engage in such strategic behavior in environmental policy. We find stronger evidence of strategic environmental policymaking in the Northeast and West regions of the U.S. Third, we find that states respond asymmetrically to environmental changes in neighboring states. Specifically, states are responsive to abatement cost changes

---

[4]Thus, even if federal legislation acts as a floor for environmental standards, we find significant interaction across states in the determination of environmental policy within the permissible range.

in neighboring states with initially more stringent environmental policy, but we detect no significant impact of changes in neighbors with lower abatement costs. Given the overall trend in the U.S. toward higher abatement costs, this implies that states are being "pulled" toward higher abatement costs by improvements in neighbors with already higher abatement costs.

To our knowledge, the existing evidence on the effects of decentralized environmental policymaking in the U.S. is mostly indirect and does not address the merits of the theoretical arguments discussed above. Levinson's [31] study of hazardous waste taxes in the U.S. focuses on both locally produced and imported waste (see also [32]). The author provides a theoretical model which predicts that taxes on waste imports will be excessively high. Empirically, Levinson [31] finds that such NIMBY (not in my backyard) taxes have had a significant negative effect on interstate waste shipments. In addition, List and Gerking [36] use U.S. state level data to show that environmental quality did not deteriorate after President Reagan's decentralization of environmental policymaking in the 1980s. The authors conclude that no race to the bottom materialized. These papers, however, do not explicitly analyze the strategic nature of government policymaking and do not discuss environmental abatement costs. The analyses of Sigman [44], Murdoch, Sandler and Sargent [38], and Eliste and Fredriksson [18] are exceptions. Murdoch *et al.* [38] document evidence of strategic free-riding behavior by 25 European countries in voluntary reductions of sulfur and nitrogen oxide emissions. Eliste and Fredriksson [18] find some cross-sectional evidence of strategic interaction across countries in the determination of environmental policy in the agricultural sector. The degree of regulatory interaction is found to depend on geographical distance and the degree of openness to trade between trade partners.

The present paper is also closely related to the theoretical and empirical public finance literature on interjurisdictional tax and welfare benefit competition (for some theoretical papers, see [5, 8, 17, 48–50, 52]). In an important empirical investigation of interstate fiscal competition, Case, Hines, and Rosen [12] estimate a model of strategic interaction among U.S. state governments, using expenditures as the strategic variable. Brueckner [4] estimates a model of strategic interaction among California cities in the choice of growth control measures, whereas Heyndels and Vuchelen [26] and Brueckner and Saavedra [7] investigate strategic behavior by local governments in property taxation. Figlio, Kolpin, and Reid [21], Brueckner [6], and Saavedra [43] discuss strategic competition in welfare benefit provision among states. In addition, yardstick competition, where voters reelect incumbents depending on their performance relative to neighboring jurisdictions, may play an important role also in environmental policymaking, as it does for income taxes [3].

The remainder of the paper is organized as follows. In Section 2 we set up a simple theoretical model which shows that states choose inefficiently low abatement levels. In Section 3 we present the basic empirical model, the data, and the two regional classifications used, as well as a few extensions to the basic model. In Section 4 we present and discuss our findings. Section 5 concludes.

2. A SIMPLE MODEL

Consider two identical states, i and $j, i \neq j$, with one polluting sector. Pollution, P, is perfectly transboundary and depends on the total pollution abatement in the two states, a_i and a_j. Thus, $P(a_i + a_j)$ gives the pollution level in the two states as a function of the individual abatement levels, where $P' < 0$ and $P'' > 0$. Let c denote the cost of abatement and y the income level in each state. Consumption net of abatement cost in state i is given by $x = y - ca_i$, and aggregate utility in state i is given by $U(y - ca_i, P(a_i + a_j))$, which is increasing and concave in x and decreasing and convex in P. We make no assumptions about the cross-partials.

The first-order condition of this function with respect to a_i is given by

$$\frac{U_P}{U_x} = \frac{c}{P'}. \tag{1}$$

The same condition holds for state j, so that each state selects the same inefficiently low abatement level a^* given that the negative externality suffered by the neighbor is not internalized. Recognizing symmetry, the jointly efficient abatement level maximizes total utility $2 * U(y - ca, P(2a))$, which gives the first order condition

$$\frac{U_P}{U_x} = \frac{c}{2P'}. \tag{2}$$

Since the factor 2 appears on the right-hand side of (2), it follows that the tradeoff between pollution and consumption has changed compared to that given in (1). The new abatement level a^{**} must be greater than a^* since for the LHS of (2) to fall in absolute value compared to the LHS of (1) the marginal disutility of pollution (the absolute value of U_P) must fall relative to the marginal utility of consumption (U_x). It follows that in a decentralized system the two states will undertake inefficiently low abatement efforts, reflecting a "race to the bottom." Rauscher [41] denotes this situation "ecological dumping," where environmentally harmful activities are priced lower than the marginal cost of environmental degradation.

The first order condition (1) generates state i's abatement reaction function, which gives a_i as a function of a_j. Treating a_j as exogenous, differentiation of (1) yields

$$\frac{da_i}{da_j} = \frac{U_{xP}P'c - U_{PP}P'^2 - U_PP''}{|D|} \tag{3}$$

where $|D| < 0$ is the second order condition of (1) with respect to a_i and is required to be negative for a maximum. The sign of the expression in (3) is ambiguous (since U_{xP} is ambiguous), and thus the slope of the reaction function may take either sign. Since it is nonzero except for knife-edge cases, state j's abatement decision will affect state i's abatement choice, and vice versa. This indicates that spillovers occur, which in general may lead to inefficient outcomes. In the empirical work below, we test whether the abatement reaction function of U.S. states exhibits a nonzero slope. If the empirical findings indicate a slope significantly different from zero, the results are consistent with strategic policymaking. An insignificant result would suggest that the reaction function has a zero slope and no strategic behavior occurs in state environmental policymaking.

3. EMPIRICAL ANALYSIS

3.1. *Basic Model of Strategic Interaction*

The econometric model used to test for strategic interaction between states in the determination of environmental policy draws on the literature on the determination of state welfare benefits. The regression equation estimated takes the general form

$$E_{it} = \alpha_i + \gamma_t + \delta \sum_{j=1}^{48} \omega_{ijt} E_{jt} + x_{it}\beta + \epsilon_{it}, \quad i = 1, \ldots, 48, \ j \neq i, \quad (4)$$

where E_{it} is a measure of environmental policy stringency in state i at time t; α_i are state fixed effects; γ_t are time fixed effects; ω_{ijt} is the weight assigned to state j by state i at time t ($j \neq i$), where some of the weights may be zero; E_{jt} is the measure of environmental policy in state j at time t; δ is the parameter of interest; x_{it} is a vector of state characteristics; and ϵ_{it} represents idiosyncratic shocks uncorrelated across states and over time.[5] The test for strategic interaction among states requires testing for the significance of δ; a nonzero coefficient implies that one state's environmental policy depends on the status of the environment in other states. The measures of environmental policy (discussed below) include: (i) Levinson's [33] industry-adjusted measure of relative state environmental abatement costs and (ii) unadjusted pollution abatement and control expenditures (PACE) per dollar of state manufacturing output.

There are two issues to be addressed when estimating an equation such as (4). The first issue is the choice of weights, ω. The simplest weighting scheme is to assign a weight of zero to noncontiguous states and equal weights to all contiguous states. In other words, $\sum_j \omega_{ijt} E_{jt}$ simplifies to the mean of the environmental stringency in neighboring states. In this case, the weights for each state are time invariant. An alternative weighting scheme also assigns a weight of zero to noncontiguous states, but weights each contiguous state by its

---

[5]Only 48 states are used in the emperical analysis; Alaska and Hawaii are excluded (discussed below).

population. Specifically, $\omega_{ijt} = \mathrm{pop}_{jt} / \sum_{j \in J_i} \mathrm{pop}_{jt}$, where J_i is the set of states neighboring state i. This scheme assigns a weight to each state equal to its share of the total population of all neighboring states. Unlike the previous weighting scheme that simply averages over neighboring states, the weights assigned by this scheme will vary by year. Similarly, we also use time-varying weights based on per capita income shares rather than population shares.[6]

To ensure that the results obtained are not sensitive to the admittedly ad hoc choice of weights, six other weighting schemes are also reported based on regional averages (as opposed to averaging only over contiguous neighbors). Interactions at the regional level have been shown to be important in other contexts; for example, Pashigian [40] found that regional voting was an important factor in the determination of federal air regulations. In the empirical work, we adopt two regional breakdowns for the 48 mainland U.S. states (see Appendix). For each regional breakdown, we then compute the regional mean of environmental policy (excluding the state in question), giving each state a weight based on either its share of total regional (i) population or (ii) income (again, excluding the state in question). We also present results weighting states equally within regions.

The two regional classifications come from the U.S. Bureau of Economic Analysis (BEA) and Crone [13]. The BEA regional classification system was introduced in the 1950s and has never been amended. While this classification system is widely used by economists in studying regional economic activity (see, e.g., [9–11]), Crone [13] devised an alternative regional breakdown for U.S. states using cluster analysis to group states according to similarities in economic activity.[7]

The second issue of concern in the estimation of (4) pertains to the potential endogeneity of the environmental policy of other states. If there is strategic interaction among the states, then states are choosing their environmental

---

[6] Implicit in the choice of weights is the assumption that states may be more responsive to environmental policy in neighboring states responsible for greater generation of transboundary pollution. To the extent that population and per capita income indicate a higher level of pollution-generating activity, states may assign relative importance based on these attributes. For example, over the period 1929–1994, aggregate state sulfur dioxide emissions (obtained from the EPA's *National Air Pollutant Emission Trends, 1900–1994*) and per capita state income (population) have a correlation of 0.10 (0.55); for nitrogen oxide emissions the correlation is 0.36 (0.80).

[7] As with the choice of weights, the choice of neighboring states is motivated by the nature of the transboundary pollution problem highlighted in the theoretical model in Section 2. To the extent that the hazards of transboundary pollution are more local in nature (e.g., river pollution), strategic policymaking should involve primarily contiguous or neighboring regional states. However, if a state emits a particular pollutant that exacerbates global environmental problems (e.g., ozone or carbon dioxide), then states that contain similar industries—regardless of where they are located—may be the relevant subset of states over which one should expect to find evidence of strategic behavior. Furthermore, if states enage in strategic behavior with states with similar industrial composition, then this will be captured under the Crone regional weighting schemes.

policies simultaneously and incorporating their expectations about the decisions of other states into their own decision-making process. This may give rise to concerns about the direction of causation. In addition, there may be unobservable regional or national shocks that are correlated with the decisions of multiple states. To address these concerns, we include state and time fixed effects (α_i and γ_t, respectively) in (4). The state fixed effects capture time invariant state-specific attributes. The time fixed effects will control for national events that occur in a given period and may impact all states through a reshaping of attitudes. Well known environmental disasters such as the Exxon Valdez shipwreck or the nuclear disaster at Chernobyl are prime examples. The time fixed effects will also capture changes in federal environmental regulations such as the Clean Air Act Amendments.

However, the inclusion of state and time fixed effects alone will not circumvent the reverse causation story alluded to earlier or control for unobservable shocks that have differential effects across regions. We employ three solutions to these potential problems. First, we devise instrumental variables for neighboring environmental policy stringency.[8] IV estimation also has the benefit of providing consistent estimates of the parameters even in the presence of spatially correlated error terms [43]. In testing for the existence of strategic policymaking, this is crucial; otherwise, the presence of spatially correlated unobservables could lead one to incorrectly conclude that strategic behavior is evident. We shall refer to the estimates obtained via IV estimation including fixed effects as IV-FE.

The instruments used are some of the attributes included in x_{it} in (4) for neighboring states, employing the same weighting scheme for the instruments as we do for neighboring environmental stringency.[9] State characteristics such as population, population density, and the degree of urbanization are valid instruments if they affect the state's own environmental policy, but not the environmental decisions in neighboring states conditional on the environmental stringency in neighboring states. In other words, if a state's environmental policies are independent of the attributes of neighboring states' conditional on neighboring environmental policy, these attributes serve as appropriate instruments (see Figlio *et al.* [21] for a similar argument with respect to state welfare policy). We present the results of Lagrange multiplier tests verifying the validity of our instrument set in many cases [16, p. 236].

Because policy responses may not be implemented instantaneously, our second solution replaces the weighted averages of neighboring states' environmen-

---

[8]Alternative maximum likelihood methods are also available. See, e.g., Saavedra [43], Brueckner [4], and Murdoch *et al.* [38].

[9]For example, if the variable included on the right-hand side of the estimating equation is the income-weighted average of environmental stringency in contiguous neighbors, then the instruments are the income-weighted averages of the appropriate *x*'s from one's contiguous neighbors.

tal stringency in (4) with two-year or five-year lagged values (see Smith [45] for a similar model in the welfare literature). The benefit of this specification is twofold. First, if there is a lag in the response of own state environmental policy to policies in neighboring states, ignoring lagged effects may miss much of the strategic interaction effect. Second, using lagged values will circumvent the problem with reverse causation since current own environmental stringency cannot impact the past environmental policies of neighboring states. The use of lagged variables will also control the bias that may arise due to spatially correlated, time-specific unobservables. As a result, in the models using neighbors' lagged environmental policy, we present estimates based on ordinary least squares with fixed effects (OLS-FE).

Finally, we also estimate the various models after splitting the sample into four regions (see Figlio *et al.* [21] for a similar model in the welfare literature). Unfortunately, splitting the sample does not provide sufficient variation to identify separate year effects within each region. However, estimation by region does allow each region to have its own linear time trend as well as allow the degree of strategic interaction to vary by region.

3.2. Asymmetric Responses

As an extension to the basic model, we allow for asymmetric strategic interaction. Specifically, we estimate the model

$$E_{it} = \alpha_i + \gamma_t + \delta_0 I_{it} \sum_{j=1}^{48} \omega_{ijt} E_{jt} + \delta_1 (1 - I_{it}) \sum_{j=1}^{48} \omega_{ijt} E_{jt}$$

$$+ x_{it} \beta + \epsilon_{it}, \qquad i = 1, \ldots, 48, \; j \neq i, \tag{5}$$

where

$$I_{it} = \begin{cases} 1 & \text{if } E_{it} > \sum_{j=1}^{48} \omega_{ijt} E_{jt}, \; j \neq i, \\ 0 & \text{otherwise.} \end{cases}$$

This specification allows for a differential effect of changes in the environmental policies of neighboring states depending on whether the weighted average of environmental stringency in neighboring states is above or below the own state's current environmental stringency. If the weighted average of environmental stringency of one's neighbors is currently below the own state's environmental stringency, the strategic interaction effect is given by δ_0; otherwise, the effect is given by δ_1.

3.3. Data

To test for the presence of strategic environmental policymaking, we require an adequate measure of state environmental regulations. Unfortunately, it is questionable whether such a measure exists. Previous research has typically used pollution abatement and control expenditures per unit of manufacturing output to proxy for environmental stringency. However, such a measure has been shown to offer a poor approximation of environmental stringency due to the nonuniform distribution of industries across the U.S. This problem is potentially even more serious in the present analysis since industry composition is highly correlated within regions. Other potential measures of environmental stringency are varying Green Indices offered by conservation groups, typically based on voting records of policymakers. Such measures are also of suspect quality given the subjective nature of ranking states. In addition, such measures may not capture the end result of environmental policies since implementation may not translate into higher industry abatement costs if the policies are not adequately enforced. Finally, recent work has used county-level attainment status under the Clean Air Act to proxy for regulatory stringency (see, e.g., Becker and Henderson [2]). However, attainment status focuses on a highly detailed area of environmental policymaking. Thus, while interesting, attainment status is not broad enough for the questions we seek to address.

As a result, we use two measures of environmental abatement costs: PACE per unit of manufacturing and a recently developed index aimed at capturing the stringency of environmental regulation within each state. The index is developed in Levinson [33] and spans the years 1977–1994, except 1987. The measure accounts for differences in state industrial composition (at the two-digit SIC level) and is defined as

$$S_{it}^* = \frac{S_{it}}{\widehat{S}_{it}}, \tag{6}$$

where $S_{it} = PACE_{it}/Y_{it}$ is the actual pollution abatement cost, $PACE_{it}$, per dollar of output, Y_{it}, produced in state i at time t. $\widehat{S}_{it}$ is the predicted pollution abatement cost per dollar of output and is calculated as

$$\widehat{S}_{it} = \frac{1}{Y_{it}} \sum_{m=20}^{39} \left(\frac{Y_{imt}}{Y_{mt}}\right) PACE_{mt}, \tag{7}$$

where $m = 20, \ldots, 39$ indexes the two-digit SIC manufacturing sectors, Y_{imt} is the total output in state i at time t from sector m, Y_{mt} is the total national output (GDP) from sector m, and $PACE_{mt}$ is the total national pollution abatement costs spent by industries in sector m.

Equation (7) gives the average pollution abatement costs per dollar of state output in state i at time t if each firm in the state conformed to the national average for its industry. Consequently, the index (6) expresses the ratio of *actual* pollution costs per dollar of output to *predicted* pollution costs per dollar of output. A value greater than one indicates that industries in the state spent relatively more per dollar of output on pollution abatement than did identical industries located in other states. If S_{it}^* is less than one, industries in the state

TABLE 1
Summary Statistics

Variable	Years	Mean	Std Dev	Minimum	Maximum
Levinson index of environmental abatement costs	1977–1994 (except 1987)	0.99	0.29	0.23	2.59
Per capita pollution abatement and control expenditure (PACE) ($1000s)	1977–1994 (except 1987)	0.01	0.01	0.00	0.22
Per capita state income ($1000s)	1977–1994	15.16	2.31	9.25	22.46
Population (1,000,000s)	1977–1994	10.30	7.85	0.43	31.40
Population density (per sq. km.)	1977–1994	81.73	83.41	1.70	411.72
Urban population, percent	1977–1994	0.74	0.13	0.31	0.93

Note. Values are population-weighted averages across all states.

spent relatively less on pollution abatement.[10] The reader is referred to Levinson [33] for further details.

State-level data on income as well as other attributes are obtained from the U.S. Bureau of Economic Analysis (http://www.bea.doc.gov). Summary statistics are given in Table 1. In addition, Fig. 1 plots the values (weighted by state population) for the two abatement cost measures over time. Since the early 1980s, PACE per unit of manufacturing output has increased approximately 200%. Because the Levinson index is a relative measure, it does not have a trend.

4. RESULTS

Basic Results. Table 2 contains the first set of results. The estimates of the parameter of interest (i.e., δ from Eq. (4)) are presented after taking the

---

[10]To make the connection between PACE per unit of manufacturing and the Levinson index more straightforward, we can perform some simple algebraic manipulation. Given that $PACE_{it} = \sum_m PACE_{imt}$, one can rewrite $S_{it} = (1/Y_{it}) \sum_m PACE_{imt}$ and $\widehat{S}_{it} = (1/Y_{it}) \sum_m \pi_{imt} PACE_{mt}$, where π_{imt} is the share of total manufacturing in sector m occurring in state i in year t. Consequently, the Levinson index is given by $S^*_{it} = \sum_m PACE_{imt} / \sum_m \pi_{imt} PACE_{mt}$. Thus, the index is the ratio between *actual* aggregate state PACE and *expected* aggregate state PACE given the national abatement expenditures by sector and the share of each manufacturing sector located in the state. Alternatively, one could view the Levinson index as $S^*_{it} = S_{it}/E[S_{it}|\{\pi_{imt}, PACE_{mt}\}^{39}_{m=20}]$. Thus, the Levinson index is PACE per unit of manufacturing scaled appropriately to remove differences across states due to differences in manufacturing size and composition. Unlike using PACE per unit of manufacturing to measure environmental stringency, simply knowing that two states have an identical manufacturing sector provides no information a priori on how they will compare in terms of the Levinson index.

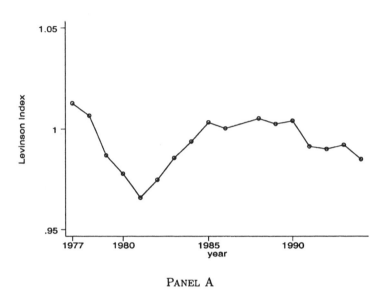

PANEL A

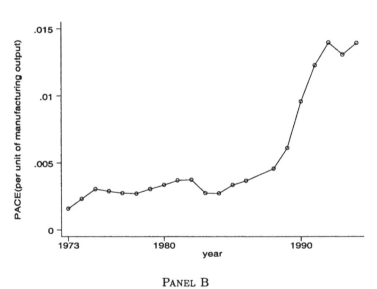

PANEL B

FIG. 1. Environmental abatement costs by year. Values are population-weighted averages across all states.

TABLE 2
Strategic Interaction over Environmental Policy across States (Elasticities)

Dependent variable	Lag length	Weighting scheme								
		Contiguous			BEA region			Crone region		
		Eq. weight	Inc. weight	Pop. weight	Eq. weight	Inc. weight	Pop. weight	Eq. weight	Inc. weight	Pop. weight
Levinson index	0	1.95 (3.40) [p = 0.32]	1.87 (2.96) [p = 0.24]	-6.29 (-1.50) [p = 0.78]	1.15 (3.23) [p = 0.01]	1.05 (3.41) [p = 0.00]	-0.17 (-0.27) [p = 0.00]	1.05 (2.03) [p = 0.24]	1.04 (1.66) [p = 0.20]	-0.30 (-0.56) [p = 0.44]
	2	0.25 (3.04)	0.24 (2.96)	0.32 (3.58)	0.09 (1.07)	0.08 (0.99)	-0.00 (-0.05)	-0.20 (-1.65)	-0.20 (-1.52)	-0.44 (-3.21)
	5	-0.05 (-0.45)	-0.05 (-0.47)	-0.16 (-1.40)	0.26 (2.45)	0.24 (2.31)	0.29 (2.43)	0.35 (2.09)	0.32 (1.80)	0.07 (0.40)
PACE	0	-0.22 (-0.42) [p = 0.01]	0.27 (0.35) [p = 0.00]	-0.73 (-2.09) [p = 0.00]	1.16 (4.14) [p = 0.14]	1.33 (3.85) [p = 0.06]	0.81 (2.89) [p = 0.00]	0.63 (2.38) [p = 0.26]	0.97 (2.25) [p = 0.36]	-0.16 (-0.57) [p = 0.22]
	2	-0.11 (-1.49)	-0.12 (-1.55)	-0.08 (-1.03)	-0.01 (-0.06)	-0.12 (-1.24)	0.08 (0.81)	-0.02 (-0.21)	-0.02 (-0.21)	-0.12 (-1.03)
	5	0.07 (0.80)	0.06 (0.74)	-0.10 (-1.07)	0.10 (0.94)	0.11 (1.05)	-0.02 (-0.16)	0.06 (0.44)	0.04 (0.32)	-0.03 (-0.15)

Notes. t-Statistics are given in parentheses. Brackets contain p-values associated with the null hypothesis of instrument exogeneity. Each regression also includes state and time fixed effects, per capita state income (along with higher order terms), population, population density, and urbanization. Lag 0 models are estimated by IV-FE estimation; Lag 2 and 5 models are estimated via OLS-FE. Instrument set includes population, population density, and urbanization from neighboring states, using the same weighting scheme as the independent variable.

log transformation of own and neighboring environmental stringency. Thus, the parameters are interpretable as elasticities. The coefficients are obtained by instrumental variable estimation with state and time fixed effects (IV-FE) in the Lag 0 models and OLS-FE in the Lag 2 and Lag 5 models. In all the regressions, controls for per capita income (and higher order terms), population, population density, and the share of the population living in urban areas are included in addition to the fixed effects (results are not presented here but are available from the authors upon request).

For the Levinson index, the elasticity of own state environmental stringency with respect to current neighboring environmental abatement costs is positive and significant at at least the 10% level of significance under the equal or income weighting schemes and all three definitions of "neighbor." However, using the BEA regions to define one's neighbors, we reject the null hypothesis that our instruments are exogenous. Using contiguous neighbors or Crone regional neighbors, we do not reject the null of instrument exogeneity. Finally, we fail to find any significant level of strategic interaction using the three population weighted averages. In terms of the magnitude of the findings, a 10% increase in relative abatement costs in one's contiguous (Crone regional) neighbors—weighted by income—implies an increase in own state relative environmental abatement costs by roughly 19% (10%). For example, Pennsylvania had a Levinson index value of 0.86 in 1994; the (income-weighted) mean Levinson index for the contiguous neighbors of Pennsylvania was 0.93. Consequently, had Pennsylvania's contiguous neighbors strengthened their average environmental stringency to 1.02, Pennsylvania would have raised its value of the Levinson Index to 1.02, thereby equalizing its relative abatement costs with its neighbors.

The fact that at least some of the strategic interaction coefficients are greater than one may be surprising. In many cases, this implies that states may alter their own environmental stringency at a greater than one-to-one rate in response to changes in neighboring states. In the example above, Pennsylvania exactly caught up to its neighbors. In other examples, a state that is initially more lax may overtake ("leapfrog") past its neighbors. This finding may indicate that policy responses are lumpy. Rather than make constant, marginal changes to state abatement costs, states may alter their environmental policy less often, but undertake larger one-time changes.

Next, we estimate the same model using PACE per unit of state manufacturing output as the dependent variable. Although we may expect current PACE to be positively correlated across neighboring states even in the absence of strategic interaction, the results provide a useful comparison.[11] Despite this caveat,

---

[11]To the extent that the industrial composition of states changes slowly over time and largely reflects historical patterns (see, e.g., Henderson *et al.* [25]), most of this spurious correlation, however, may be captured by the state fixed effects.

the IV-FE estimates are positive and significant (at the 95% level of significance) using either the BEA or Crone regional assignments and equal or income-based weights. Moreover, we also fail to reject the null hypothesis of instrument exogeneity under these four weighting schemes (at the 95% level of significance). The estimates from the remaining models are insignificant and/or we reject the validity of the exclusion restrictions. The fact that the positive effect of neighboring states' PACE levels only holds using the regional weighting schemes provides some indication that the results are not driven entirely by the distribution of industries. In sum, then, the results based on both the Levinson index and PACE per unit of state manufacturing are consistent with the state reaction functions having a nonzero slope.

Lagged Results. The next set of estimates in Table 2 replaces neighboring relative environmental abatement costs with their lagged values, using lags of two and five years. Estimation is via OLS-FE. For the Levinson index, an interesting pattern emerges. Using two-year lags, we still find a statistically significant and positive effect of neighboring relative abatement costs on own state environmental policy, but only under the three contiguous neighbor weighting schemes. Under the two regional weighting schemes, neighboring environmental stringency has either no effect (BEA region) or a negative effect (Crone region). Moreover, the elasticities under the contiguous weighting schemes are smaller in magnitude relative to the elasticities obtained using neighbors' current relative abatement costs.

Moving to five-year lags, however, the results reverse. Now, own state environmental stringency is positively related to the relative abatement costs in one's regional neighbors (either BEA or Crone regions), but not in one's contiguous neighbors. The elasticities are comparable in magnitude to those obtained under the contiguous weighting schemes using two-year lags. Combining these results, it appears that states adjust their own relative abatement costs to changes in their contiguous neighbors within a two-year window, but adjustments with respect to more distant regional neighbors take approximately five years.

For PACE per unit of manufacturing output, the coefficients are never statistically significant in the lagged specifications. This finding may actually provide some indication that the significant, positive estimates found using current PACE in neighboring states are not driven solely by spatial correlation in manufacturing size and composition.

Regional Results. Table 3 contains the next set of results. The results are analogous to those from Table 2, except the sample is subdivided into four regions, with the models estimated separately for each region. The four regions are Northeast (composed of BEA Regions 1 and 2; see Appendix A), Midwest (BEA Regions 3 and 4), South (BEA Regions 5 and 6), and West (BEA Regions 7 and 8). In the interest of brevity, we only present results from the weighting scheme based on contiguous neighbors weighted by income.

FREDRIKSSON AND MILLIMET

TABLE 3
Strategic Interaction over Environmental Policy across States, by Region (Elasticities)

	Dependent variable					
	Levinson index			PACE		
Region	Lag 0	Lag 2	Lag 5	Lag 0	Lag 2	Lag 5
Northeast	3.06	0.37	0.54	1.18	−0.02	−0.04
only	(2.62)	(2.66)	(2.73)	(1.28)	(−0.18)	(−0.28)
	[$p = 0.58$]			[$p = 0.47$]		
South only	2.06	−0.06	−0.25	0.53	0.12	0.09
	(0.50)	(−0.51)	(−1.53)	(0.88)	(0.92)	(0.52)
	[$p = 0.03$]			[$p = 0.06$]		
Midwest	−2.37	−0.23	0.10	0.17	0.04	0.25
only	(−1.34)	(−1.48)	(0.45)	(0.55)	(0.27)	(1.39)
	[$p = 0.50$]			[$p = 0.06$]		
West only	−0.39	0.55	−0.54	2.21	0.12	0.23
	(−0.55)	(2.47)	(−1.88)	(3.09)	(0.55)	(0.86)
	[$p = 0.00$]			[$p = 0.09$]		

Notes. Weighting scheme is contiguous neighbors weighted by income. Regressions include a linear time trend instead of time fixed effects. Northeast region includes BEA regions 1 and 2; midwest region includes BEA regions 3 and 4; south region includes BEA regions 5 and 6; west region includes BEA regions 7 and 8. See Table 2 for other details.

Examining the elasticities shows that the results presented in Table 2 are driven primarily by two regions, the Northeast and the West. In the Northeast, a 10% increase in (income-weighted) neighboring relative abatement costs increases own state environmental stringency by over 30%. Thus, returning to our example pertaining to Pennsylvania, we see now that if Pennsylvania's neighbors had increased their (income-weighted) average Levinson index from 0.93 to 1.02 in 1994, Pennsylvania would have more than surpassed its neighbors by increasing its relative abatement costs from 0.86 to 1.12. Furthermore, the elasticities with respect to lagged neighboring environmental policy are also statistically significant and positive in the Northeast (two- and five-year lags) and West regions (two-year lag only). None of the coefficients are significant for the Midwest and South regions.

For PACE, the significant coefficients given in Table 2 using neighbors' current PACE are driven solely by the West region. For this region, a 10% increase in (income-weighted) average PACE per unit of manufacturing in one's contiguous neighbors increases own state PACE by over 22%. None of the other PACE coefficients—using current or lagged values for the independent variable—are significant. The fact that no other coefficients are significant again suggests that the significant result for the West region is not simply due to spatially correlated manufacturing sectors.

Asymmetric Responses. Table 4 presents the results from the model in (5), allowing for asymmetric responses by states depending on whether environmental stringency in neighboring states is initially stricter or more lax than their own environmental stringency. In addition to the estimates, we also report the results of F-tests for the equality of the two responses. In the interest of brevity, we report the results using contiguous, BEA regional, and Crone regional neighbors weighted by income only.

While we obtain little insight by allowing for asymmetric responses using PACE as the dependent variable, the differential effects using the Levinson index are noteworthy. First, we note that the coefficient on neighboring relative abatement costs is larger in magnitude when neighboring states are initially more stringent than the own state in eight of nine cases. For example, under the contiguous weighting scheme, a 10% increase in current relative abatement costs in neighboring states leads to a 24% increase in own state relative abatement costs if relative abatement costs are already higher in neighboring states. If relative abatement costs are initially more lax in neighboring states, then changes in neighboring states have no statistically significant effect.[12] However, the coefficients are not statistically different at conventional levels. Similar differences are also found using the BEA and Crone region specifications. Second, consistent with the results in Table 2, the effect of improvements in relatively stringent contiguous neighbors fades over time, disappearing somewhere between two and five years. Moreover, the differential effects are statistically different using two-year lags. Changes in the relative abatement costs at the regional level are found to still influence own state abatement costs five years later, consistent with the results in Table 2.

The fact that increases in relative abatement costs have larger effects on the own state if neighbors initially have relatively stricter environmental standards implies that states are "pulled" to stricter levels by improvements in relatively clean states (where marginal abatement costs may be the greatest). Furthermore, since many of the elasticities are greater than unity, the results do not suggest that states simply increase their environmental stringency while still remaining more lax than their neighbors. As the Pennsylvania examples above illustrate, increases in neighboring states may cause the own state to leapfrog ahead of its neighbors. NIMBY behavior or yardstick competition may lie behind this result; however, further investigation is required to explain these forces.

---

[12]One possible explanation for this result may be that states' environmental policy reaction curves exhibit large discontinuities, as discussed by Markusen, Morey, and Olewiler [37].

TABLE 4
Strategic Interaction over Environmental Policy across States, Differential Effects (Elasticities)

		Weighting scheme								
		Contiguous states income weight			BEA region income weight			Crone region income weight		
Dependent variable	Lag length	Coefficient (below) (δ_0)	Coefficient (above) (δ_1)	F-test for equality	Coefficient (below) (δ_0)	Coefficient (above) (δ_1)	F-test for equality	Coefficient (below) (δ_0)	Coefficient (above) (δ_1)	F-test for equality
Levinson index	0	0.82 (0.87) [$p = 0.89$]	2.39 (3.24)	$F(1,744) = 2.40$ [$p = 0.12$]	0.16 (0.18) [$p = 0.00$]	1.68 (2.49)	$F(1,744) = 1.15$ [$p = 0.28$]	−0.78 (−0.45) [$p = 0.27$]	2.56 (1.70)	$F(1,744) = 1.29$ [$p = 0.26$]
	2	0.11 (1.07)	0.32 (3.62)	$F(1,603) = 4.95$ [$p = 0.03$]	0.05 (0.43)	0.10 (1.12)	$F(1,603) = 0.28$ [$p = 0.60$]	−0.40 (−2.16)	−0.04 (−0.25)	$F(1,603) = 2.36$ [$p = 0.13$]
	5	−0.18 (−1.49)	0.05 (0.45)	$F(1,455) = 0.06$ [$p = 0.80$]	0.16 (1.23)	0.30 (2.53)	$F(1,462) = 1.07$ [$p = 0.30$]	0.45 (1.89)	0.21 (0.99)	$F(1,462) = 0.70$ [$p = 0.40$]
PACE	0	−3.20 (−0.54) [$p = 0.69$]	−2.31 (−0.47)	$F(1,744) = 0.48$ [$p = 0.49$]	2.15 (1.64) [$p = 0.65$]	1.63 (1.77)	$F(1,744) = 0.66$ [$p = 0.42$]	0.51 (0.97) [$p = 0.20$]	0.63 (1.40)	$F(1,744) = 1.41$ [$p = 0.24$]
	2	−0.10 (−1.31)	−0.09 (−1.18)	$F(1,603) = 0.57$ [$p = 0.45$]	−0.05 (−0.51)	−0.03 (−0.27)	$F(1,603) = 4.98$ [$p = 0.03$]	−0.02 (−0.22)	−0.03 (−0.22)	$F(1,603) = 0.01$ [$p = 0.93$]
	5	0.02 (0.21)	−0.00 (−0.04)	$F(1,462) = 4.02$ [$p = 0.04$]	−0.01 (−0.08)	−0.05 (−0.42)	$F(1,462) = 11.16$ [$p = 0.00$]	−0.03 (−0.23)	−0.06 (−0.40)	$F(1,462) = 3.80$ [$p = 0.05$]

Notes. *t*-Statistics are given in parentheses. Brackets underneath the *t*-statistics contain the *p*-values associated with the null hypothesis of instrument exogeneity. See Table 2 for other details.

5. CONCLUSION

In this paper we address the question of whether U.S. states engage in strategic environmental policymaking. The theoretical literature pertaining to the optimal institutional design of environmental policy presumes that strategic environmental policymaking does occur. However, the empirical relationship between neighboring states' environmental policy choices is not well established. To fill this notable gap, we present a simple model indicating that transboundary pollution may lead to state reaction functions with nonzero slopes. We then test empirically for such strategic behavior using state-level panel data on two measures of environmental abatement costs over the period 1977–1994. The analysis suggests that there is a positive association between states' environmental policies. This lends support to the modeling approach used in the theoretical literature on strategic environmental policymaking.

Besides indicating the presence of strategic behavior on the part of U.S. states, the results yield three additional insights. First, the interaction across *contiguous* neighboring states in the determination of regulatory abatement costs operates within a two- to five-year window. However, states are responsive to changes in abatement costs in *regional* neighbors over at least a five-year period. Second, we find that not all regions of the U.S. engage in such strategic behavior in the environmental arena. Specifically, we find much stronger evidence of strategic environmental policymaking in the Northeast and West regions of the U.S. Finally, we find that states respond *asymmetrically* to environmental changes in neighboring states. States are "pulled" toward higher abatement costs by improvements in neighbors with already higher relative abatement costs and are much less responsive (if they respond at all) to changes in states with initially lower abatement costs. Future research into the source of such asymmetry is clearly warranted.

APPENDIX: DATA

The BEA regional classifications are as follows:

1. New England	Maine, New Hampshire, Vermont, Massachusetts, Rhode Island, and Connecticut
2. Mideast	New York, New Jersey, Pennsylvania, Delaware, and Maryland
3. Great Lakes	Ohio, Indiana, Illinois, Michigan, and Wisconsin
4. Plains	Minnesota, Iowa, Missouri, North Dakota, South Dakota, Nebraska, and Kansas
5. Southeast	Georgia, Florida, Virginia, West Virginia, North Carolina, South Carolina, Kentucky, Tennessee, Alabama, Mississippi, Arkansas, and Louisiana
6. Southwest	Oklahoma, Texas, Arizona, and New Mexico

120   FREDRIKSSON AND MILLIMET

7. Rocky Mountain Montana, Idaho, Wyoming, Colorado, and Utah
8. Far West   Washington, Oregon, California, and Nevada

The Crone [13] regions—based on a cluster analysis of similar economic activity—are as follows:

1. Maine, New Hampshire, Massachusetts, Arizona, Utah, and Montana
2. Ohio, Indiana, Illinois, Michigan, Iowa, and Delaware
3. Georgia, Florida, Virginia, North Carolina, South Carolina, Missouri, Kentucky, Tennessee, Alabama, Mississippi, Arkansas, Oklahoma, and Rhode Island
4. New York, New Jersey, Pennsylvania, Maryland, Connecticut, West Virginia, and Vermont
5. Washington, Oregon, California, Nevada, Idaho, Nebraska, Texas, Wyoming, Minnesota, Louisiana, and Kansas
6. North Dakota, South Dakota, Colorado, New Mexico, and Wisconsin

REFERENCES

1. S. Barrett, Strategic environmental policy and international trade, *Journal of Public Economics*, **54**, 325–338 (1994).
2. R. A. Becker and J. V. Henderson, Effects of air quality regulations on polluting industries, *Journal of Political Economy*, **108**, 379–421 (2000).
3. T. Besley and A. Case, Incumbent behavior: Vote-seeking, tax setting, and yardstick competition, *American Economic Review*, **85**, 25–45 (1995).
4. J. K. Brueckner, Testing for strategic interaction among local governments: The case of growth controls, *Journal of Urban Economics*, **44**, 438–467 (1998).
5. J. K. Brueckner, A Tiebout/tax-competition model, *Journal of Public Economics*, **77**, 285–306 (2000).
6. J. K. Brueckner, Welfare reform and the race to the bottom: Theory and evidence, *Southern Economic Journal*, **66**, 505–525 (2000).
7. J. K. Brueckner and L. A. Saavedra, Do local governments engage in strategic property-tax competition?, *National Tax Journal* (May 2001).
8. S. Bucovetsky and J. D. Wilson, Tax competition with two instruments, *Regional Science and Urban Economics*, **21**, 333–350 (1991).
9. G. A. Carlino and R. H. DeFina, Regional income dynamics, *Journal of Urban Economics*, **37**, 88–106 (1995).
10. G. A. Carlino and L. O. Mills, Are regional incomes converging? A time series analysis, *Journal of Monetary Economics*, **32**, 335–346 (1993).
11. G. A. Carlino and L. O. Mills, Testing neoclassical convergence in regional incomes and earnings, *Regional Science and Urban Economics*, **26**, 565–590 (1996).
12. A. Case, J. Hines, and H. Rosen, Budget spillovers and fiscal policy interdependence: Evidence from the states, *Journal of Public Economics*, **52**, 285–307 (1993).
13. T. M. Crone, Using state indexes to define economic regions in the U.S., *The Journal of Economic and Social Measurement*, **25**, 259–278 (1998/1999).
14. Congressional Budget Office, "Federalism and Environmental Protection: Case Studies for Drinking Water and Ground-Level Ozone," U.S. Congress, Washington, DC (1997).
15. J. H. Cumberland, Interregional pollution spillovers and consistency of environmental policy, in "Regional Environmental Policy: The Economic Issue" (H. Siebert *et al.*, Eds.), NYU Press, New York (1979).

16. R. Davidson and J. MacKinnon, "Estimation and Inference in Econometrics," Oxford University Press, New York (1993).

17. J. Edwards and M. Keen, Tax competition and leviathan, *European Economic Review*, **40**, 113–134 (1996).

18. P. Eliste and P. G. Fredriksson, Does trade liberalization cause a race-to-the-bottom in environmental policies? A spatial econometric analysis, in "New Advances in Spatial Econometrics" (L. Anselin and R. Florax, Eds.), Springer-Verlag, Berlin (forthcoming).

19. D. C. Esty, Revitalizing environmental federalism, *Michigan Law Review*, **95**, 570–652 (1996).

20. D. C. Esty and D. Geradin, Environmental protection and international competitiveness: A conceptual framework, *Journal of World Trade*, **32**, 5–46 (1998).

21. D. N. Figlio, V. W. Kolpin, and W. E. Reid, Do states play welfare games?, *Journal of Urban Economics*, **46**, 437–454 (1999).

22. P. G. Fredriksson and N. Gaston, Environmental governance in federal systems: The effects of capital competition and lobby groups, *Economic Inquiry*, **38**, 501–514 (2000).

23. E. Helland, The revealed preferences of state EPAs: Stringency, enforcement, and substitution, *Journal of Environmental Economics and Management*, **35**, 242–261 (1998).

24. E. Helland, The enforcement of pollution control laws: Inspections, violations, and self-reporting, *Review of Economics and Statistics*, **80**, 141–153 (1998b).

25. J. V. Henderson, A. Kuncoro, and M. Turner, Industrial development in cities, *Journal of Political Economy*, **103**, 1067–1090 (1995).

26. B. Heyndels and J. Vuchelen, Tax mimicking among Belgian municipalities, *National Tax Journal*, **51**, 89–101 (1998).

27. G. Holmes, B. R. Singh, and L. Theodore, "Handbook of Environmental Management and Technology," Wiley, New York (1993).

28. U.S. House of Representatives, Legislative history of the Clean Air Act, House Report 91-1146, U.S. Government Printing Office, Washington, DC (1979).

29. P. W. Kennedy, Equilibrium pollution taxes in open economies with imperfect competition, *Journal of Environmental Economics and Management*, **27**, 49–63 (1994).

30. A. Levinson, A note on environmental federalism: Interpreting some contradictory results, *Journal of Environmental Economics and Management*, **33**, 359–366 (1997).

31. A. Levinson, NIMBY taxes matter: The case of state hazardous waste disposal taxes, *Journal of Public Economics*, **74**, 31–51 (1999).

32. A. Levinson, State taxes and hazardous waste shipments, *American Economic Review*, **89**, 666–677 (1999).

33. A. Levinson, An industry-adjusted index of state environmental compliance costs, in "Behavioral and Distributional Effects of Environmental Policy" (C. Carraro and G. E. Metcalf, Eds.), University of Chicago Press, Chicago, IL (2001).

34. J. A. List, Have air pollutant emissions converged among U.S. regions? Evidence from unit root tests, *Southern Economic Journal*, **66**, 144–155 (1999).

35. J. A. List and C. Y. Co, The effects of environmental regulations on foreign direct investment, *Journal of Environmental Economics and Management*, **40**, 1–20 (2000).

36. J. A. List and S. Gerking, Regulatory federalism and environmental protection in the United States, *Journal of Regional Science*, **40**, 453–471 (2000).

37. J. Markusen, E. Morey, and N. Olewiler, Competition in regional environmental policies when plant locations are endogenous, *Journal of Public Economics*, **56**, 55–77 (1995).

38. J. C. Murdoch, T. Sandler, and K. Sargent, A tale of two collectives: Sulphur versus nitrogen oxides emission reduction in Europe, *Economica*, **64**, 281–301 (1997).

39. W. E. Oates and R. M. Schwab, Economic competition among jurisdictions: Efficiency enhancing or distortion inducing?, *Journal of Public Economics*, **35**, 333–354 (1988).

40. B. P. Pashigian, Environmental regulation: Whose self-interests are being protected?, *Economic Inquiry*, **23**, 551–584 (1985).

41. M. Rauscher, On ecological dumping, *Oxford Economic Papers*, **46**, 822–840 (1994).

42. R. L. Revesz, Rehabilitating interstate competition: Rethinking the "race-to-the-bottom" rationale for federal environmental regulation, *New York University Law Review*, **67**, 1210–1254 (1992).

43. L. A. Saavedra, A model of welfare competition with evidence from AFDC, *Journal of Urban Economics*, **47**, 248–279 (2000).

44. H. Sigman, Federalism and interstate pollution in U. S. rivers, unpublished manuscript, School of Forestry and Environmental Studies, Yale University (2001).

45. M. W. Smith, State welfare benefits: The political economy of spatial spillovers, unpublished manuscript, Department of Economics, Yale University (1997).

46. A. Ulph, Harmonization and optimal environmental policy in a federal system with asymmetric information, *Journal of Environmental Economics and Management*, **39**, 224–241 (2000).

47. G. S. Wetstone and A. Rosencranz, "Acid Rain in Europe and North America," The Environmental Law Institute, Washington, D.C. (1983).

48. D. E. Wildasin, Nash equilibrium in models of fiscal competition, *Journal of Public Economics*, **35**, 229–240 (1988).

49. J. D. Wilson, A theory of interregional tax competition, *Journal of Urban Economics*, **19**, 296–315 (1986).

50. J. D. Wilson, Trade in a Tiebout economy, *American Economic Review*, **77**, 431–441 (1987).

51. J. D. Wilson, Capital mobility and environmental standards: Is there a theoretical basis for a race to the bottom, in "Fair Trade and Harmonization: Prerequisites for Free Trade," Vol. 1 (J. Bhagwati and R. P. Hudec, Eds.), MIT Press, Cambridge/London (1996).

52. G. R. Zodrow and P. Mieszkowski, Pigou, Tiebout, property taxation, and the underprovision of local public goods, *Journal of Urban Economics*, **19**, 356–370 (1986).

Part IV
Assessing the Use of Economic Analysis in Environmental Policy

[20]

Journal of Environmental Economics and Management **39**, 375–399 (2000)

doi:10.1006/jeem.1999.1119, available online at http://www.idealibrary.com on **IDE∧L**®

The Impact of Economics on Environmental Policy

Robert W. Hahn[1]

American Enterprise Institute–Brookings Joint Center for Regulatory Studies,
1150 17th Street, NW, Suite 1100, Washington, DC 20036

Received December 12, 1999

Environmental economists have seen their ideas translated into the rough-and-tumble policy world for over two decades. They have witnessed the application of economic instruments to several environmental issues, including preserving wetlands, lowering lead levels, and curbing acid rain. This essay examines the impact of the rise of economics in the policy world on the making of environmental policy. I focus on two related, but distinct phenomena—the increasing interest in the use of incentive-based mechanisms, such as tradable permits, to achieve environmental goals; and the increasing interest in the use of analytical tools such as benefit–cost analysis in regulatory decision making.

I argue that economists and economic instruments have had a modest impact on shaping environmental, health, and safety regulation, but that economists will play an increasingly important role in the future. Although the role of economics is becoming more prominent, it does not follow that environmental policy will become more efficient. This apparent inconsistency can be explained by the political economy of environmental policy. © 2000 Academic Press

1. INTRODUCTION

Many scholars dream about having their ideas put into practice. Yet, when the dream becomes a reality, it frequently feels different—in large part because of the gulf between the ivory tower and the real world. Environmental economists have seen their ideas translated into the rough-and-tumble policy world for over two decades. They have played an important role in shaping some key aspects of policy. They have, for example, witnessed the application of economic instruments to several environmental issues, including preserving wetlands, lowering lead levels, and curbing acid rain. Despite a few notable successes, the influence of economists on environmental policy to date has been modest.

I will focus on two related, but distinct phenomena—the increasing interest in using incentive-based mechanisms, such as tradable permits, to achieve environmental goals, and the increasing interest in using analytical tools such as

[1] The author is Director of the AEI–Brookings Joint Center for Regulatory Studies, a Resident Scholar at AEI, and a Research Associate at Harvard University. The views in this paper reflect those of the author and do not necessarily represent the views of the institutions with which he is affiliated. The helpful comments of Dallas Burtraw, Maureen Cropper, Henry Lee, Anne Sholtz, and Robert Stavins are gratefully acknowledged. Petrea Moyle and Fumie Yokota provided valuable research assistance.

375

0095-0696/00 $35.00
Copyright © 2000 by Academic Press
All rights of reproduction in any form reserved.

benefit–cost analysis in regulatory decision making.[2] For purposes of this essay, an economic instrument is defined as any instrument that is expected to increase economic efficiency relative to the status quo. This broad definition includes traditional incentive-based mechanisms, process reforms, and economic analysis that is used as a basis for designing more efficient policies.[3]

Economists can influence environmental policy in several ways. One is by advocating the use of particular tools for achieving better environmental outcomes through research, teaching, and outreach to policy makers. Another is by analyzing the benefits and costs of regulations and standards, which may demonstrate the inefficiencies of the goals themselves. A third way is by analyzing how decisions are made—by examining the political economy of environmental regulation.[4] Each of these approaches can eventually have an impact on the different branches of government.

My thesis is that economists and economic instruments are playing an increasingly important role in shaping environmental, health and safety regulation. Although the role of economics is becoming more prominent, it does not follow that environmental policy will become more efficient. This apparent inconsistency can be explained by the political economy of environmental policy. I argue that economists need to do more than simply develop good ideas to influence policy. They need to understand how the political process affects outcomes, and actively market the use of appropriate and feasible economic instruments for promoting more efficient environmental policy.

Section 2 provides background on U.S. laws and regulations. Section 3 highlights the use of economic instruments in environmental policy.[5] Section 4 examines critical factors leading to the increased prominence of economics in environmental policy and also explains why economic efficiency is rarely central in environmental decision making. Section 5 summarizes the main arguments and suggests ways to enhance the impact of economists on environmental policy.

---

[2] Other tools include cost-effectiveness analysis and risk–risk analysis. By risk–risk analysis, I mean an evaluation of potential increases in health risks that may arise from efforts to combat a targeted health risk. Such an evaluation can help decision makers compare policies [50]. Farmers, for example, may increase the use of an equally toxic alternative pesticide if use of the original pesticide is restricted or banned to prevent drinking water contamination. For a more detailed description of risk–risk analysis, see Graham and Wiener [34].

[3] The narrow definition of economic instruments is typically restricted to incentive-based mechanisms, such as emission taxes, deposit-refund schemes, tradable permits, subsidies, and removal of subsidies. Such mechanisms have the potential to achieve environmental outcomes at a lower cost than direct regulation. For a broader perspective on economic instruments that highlights the importance of transaction costs, see Richards [73]. Note that the definition used here explicitly allows for command-and-control regulation to be an economic instrument in situations where it would lead to improvements in economic efficiency.

[4] See, for example, Metrick and Weitzman [55] for an analysis of choices related to biodiversity preservation.

[5] I focus on the United States because that is the country with which I am most familiar; however, I believe the theses advanced in the paper are generally applicable to a wide range of developed countries as well as some developing countries.

2. LAWS, REGULATIONS, AND THE NEED FOR ECONOMIC INSTRUMENTS

Most environmental laws cover specific media, such as air, water, and land, and specific problems such as the control of toxic substances and the prevention of oil spills. They give rise to a staggering array of regulations requiring firms to obtain permits and meet specific requirements and guidelines. In some cases, firms must gain permission from federal or state authorities before making changes to production processes that have little or no impact on environmental quality.

There are now at least 10 major U.S. federal laws that address environmental quality.[6] The largest in terms of estimated costs are the Clean Air Act (CAA), the Resource Conservation and Recovery Act (RCRA), and the Safe Drinking Water Act (SDWA).[7] According to the first comprehensive government report on the benefits and cost of federal regulation produced by the Office of Management and Budget, the direct cost of federally mandated environmental quality regulations in 1997 is approximately $147 billion (OMB, 1997).[8, 9] This is more than half of total federal government spending on all domestic discretionary programs.[10] Estimates of direct and indirect costs using general equilibrium approaches suggest that the costs are substantially higher [40, 44].[11] The benefits from these laws are less certain than the costs. Some estimates suggest that aggregate benefits are in the neighborhood of costs [29, 63]; others suggest that they substantially exceed costs [91].[12]

The aggregate analysis of benefits and costs masks some important information on individual regulations, such as evidence that many environmental regulations would not pass a standard benefit–cost test. For example, more than two-thirds of

---

[6] Consider the following laws that primarily the EPA administers: the Federal Insecticide, Fungicide, and Rodenticide Act, Clean Water Act, Clean Air Act, Resource Conservation and Recovery Act, Ocean Dumping Act, Safe Drinking Water Act, Toxic Substance Control Act, Comprehensive Environmental Response, Compensation, and Liability Act (Superfund), Emergency Planning and Community Right-To-Know Act, and Pollution Prevention Act. The list would be longer if it included laws not primarily under EPA's jurisdiction, such as the Endangered Species Act.

[7] According to the present value of compliance costs for final regulations published between 1982 and 1996, the CAA is the most burdensome with $192 billion, second is RCRA with $121.6 billion, and third is SDWA with $43.6 billion in 1995 dollars [35].

[8] Direct costs include the costs of capital equipment and labor needed to comply with a standard or regulation. Most of the cost estimates of individual regulations used by the OMB to calculate the aggregate costs only include direct costs, although a few also include indirect net changes in consumer and producer surplus. The OMB derives the aggregate cost estimate by using the EPA's estimate of the federally mandated compliance cost [89] as the baseline estimate for 1988 and adding the incremental costs from EPA's major regulations finalized between 1987 and 1996 [62].

[9] Unless otherwise stated, all dollar figures have been converted to 1997 dollars using the GDP implicit price deflator [19].

[10] The total outlays in 1997 for domestic discretionary programs were $258 billion [6]. This figure does not include expenditures related to national defense or international affairs.

[11] Hazilla and Kopp [40] find that although social costs were below EPA's compliance cost estimates in 1975, they exceeded compliance costs in the 1980's. This result is partially explained by people's substitution of leisure for direct consumption as a result of pollution control regulation, thereby decreasing output over time.

[12] The EPA estimates that the total benefits from the Clean Air Act between 1970 and 1990 are in the range of $5.6 to $49.4 trillion in 1990 dollars, while the direct compliance costs for the same period are $0.5 trillion in 1990 dollars [91]. For an insightful critique of the EPA's estimate, see Lutter [53].

the federal government's environmental quality regulations from 1982 to 1996 fail a strict benefit–cost test using the government's own numbers.[13] Indeed, if the government did not implement all major social regulations that failed a benefit–cost test during this period, net benefits would have increased by about $280 billion [35]. Moreover, there is ample room to reallocate expenditures to save more lives at lower cost [31, 57]. A reallocation of mandated expenditures toward the regulations with the highest payoff to society could save as many as 60,000 more lives a year at no additional cost [83].

For over two decades, economists have highlighted two significant problems with the current legal framework in U.S. environmental policy. The first is that the laws are overly prescriptive. Both laws and regulations frequently specify a preferred technology or set of technologies for achieving an outcome. For example, scrubbers were required for some power plants as part of a compromise reached under the 1977 Clean Air Act Amendments [1]. Economists have argued that a more flexible approach, such as an emissions tax, could achieve the same or similar environmental results at much lower cost (see, e.g., [12, 86]). A second problem is that, while some statutes now require agencies to at least consider, if not balance, the benefits and costs of regulations, many laws prohibit such balancing [20, 70]. According to the courts interpretation of Section 109 of the Clean Air Act, for example, the Environmental Protection Agency cannot consider the costs of determining national ambient air quality standards for designated pollutants. The result has been that many environmental programs and regulations have been put in place that would not pass a strict benefit–cost test. Both observations suggest that economic instruments could play a critical role in designing more efficient policies.

3. AN OVERVIEW OF ECONOMIC INSTRUMENTS

As noted above, an economic instrument is one that is expected to increase economic efficiency. That definition of economic instruments has the advantage that it includes a wide array of instruments. One drawback is that, unlike the conventional definition, an instrument is not necessarily an economic instrument just because it is incentive-based. For example, an emission fee need not be an economic instrument using my definition if it leads to a reduction in economic efficiency. The definition used here requires the ability to specify a counterfactual —what would have happened in the absence of the application of a particular economic instrument—to determine how the policy would affect efficiency. I offer this definition because it seems natural that we should want economic instruments to improve economic efficiency.

Economists rarely frame the instrument choice problem in such general terms. Instead, they tend to focus on particular mechanisms, such as fees and permits, which are known to have efficiency-enhancing properties in theory. Below I examine these instruments, but I also consider other instruments, including the increasing role of economic analysis in the formulation of environmental policy.

It is useful to consider two categories of economic instruments for framing policy choices: incentive based mechanisms and process reforms. The two categories are related in the sense that process reforms could help policy makers determine

---

[13] Of the 70 final EPA regulations analyzed, monetized benefits exceeded the costs for only 31% [35].

whether to use different types of incentive-based mechanisms. Incentive-based mechanisms include emission fees, tradable permits, deposit-refund schemes, direct subsidies, removal of subsidies with negative environmental impacts, reductions in market barriers, and performance standards.[14] The idea behind such instruments is that they create incentives for achieving particular goals that are welfare enhancing. Generally not included in this category are highly prescriptive technology-based standards. Process reforms include accountability mechanisms and analytical requirements. Accountability mechanisms include peer review, judicial review, sunset provisions, regulatory budgets, and requirements to provide better information to Congress. Analytical requirements include mandates to balance costs and benefits, consider risk–risk tradeoffs, and evaluate the cost-effectiveness of different regulatory alternatives.

The Increasing Use of Incentive-Based Mechanisms

A broad array of incentive-based mechanisms have been used in U.S. federal environmental policy. Table I highlights some of the more important federal applications of fees, subsidies, tradable permits, and the provision of information. These mechanisms have been used for all media in a variety of applications.[15] Perhaps best known in terms of their potential for achieving cost savings are tradable permits. As can be seen from the table, their use has steadily increased over time at the federal level. Moreover, there has been increasing interest in the potential application of economic instruments as well [90].

The table shows that the ideas of economists regarding economic instruments are being taken seriously. President Clinton's 1993 Executive Order 12866 for Regulatory Planning and Review provides a good example. The order directs agencies to identify and assess incentive-based mechanisms, such as user fees and tradable permits, as an alternative to traditional command-and-control regulation, which provides less flexibility in achieving environmental goals.

The use of incentive-based mechanisms at the state level is also growing. Table II shows that many states are exploring a diverse array of incentive-based approaches. There are also many programs at the regional level, such as Southern California's Regional Emissions Clean Air Incentives Market (RECLAIM), that allow polluters to trade emission allowances to achieve air pollution goals.

The interest in using incentive-based mechanisms is also growing in other countries. A survey by the Organization for Co-operation and Development (OECD) showed that, in 1992, 21 OECD countries had various fees and charges for emissions, 20 had fees and charges for specific high pollution products, 16 countries had deposit-refund programs, and 5 countries had a tradable permit program [65]. Although the United States has predominantly used the tradable permits scheme at the federal level, European countries have more often used fees to help achieve their environmental goals. These fees typically have not had a

---

[14] See Stavins [80] for a good overview of instrument types and their application. Kneese and Schultze [48] provide an early treatment of some of the practical issues to consider in shifting to effluent taxes.

[15] This section focuses on efforts to improve environmental quality through pollution control measures, and does not review incentive-based mechanisms used in natural resource management. There are, however, notable initiatives at the state and federal level such as wetlands mitigation banking programs.

TABLE I

Examples of Federal Incentive-Based Programs

Fees/charges/taxes		
Air	1978–	Gas Guzzler Tax
	1990–	Air Emission Permit Fees
	1990–	Ozone Depleting Chemicals Fees
	2005–	Ozone Nonattainment Area Fees
Land	1980–1995	Crude Oil and Chemical Taxes (Superfund)
	NA	Public Land Grazing Fees
Water	NA	National Pollution Discharge Elimination Permit System Fees
Subsidies		
Air	NA	Clean Fuel and Low-Emission Vehicle Subsidies
	NA	Renewable Energy and Energy Conservation Subsidies
Land	1995–	Brownfield Pilot Project Grants
Water	1956–	Municipal Sewage Treatment Construction
Cross media	early 1980's–	Supplemental Environmental Projects for Non-Compliance Penalty Reduction
Tradeable permits		
Air	1974–	Emissions Trading Program
	1978–	Corporate Average Fuel Economy Standards
	1982–1987	Lead Credit Trading
	1988–	Ozone Depleting Chemicals Allowance Trading
	1990–	Heavy-Duty Truck Manufacturers Emissions Averaging
	1992–	Reformulated Gasoline Credit Trading Program
	1992–	Hazardous Air Pollutant Early Reduction Program
	1992–	Greenhouse Gas Emission Reduction Joint Implementation Program
	1994–	Synthetic Organic Chemical Manufacturing Emissions Averaging (NESHAPS)
	1995–	Acid Rain Allowance Trading for SO_2 and NO_x
	1995–	Petroleum Refining Emissions Averaging (NESHAPS)
	1995–	Marine Tank Vessel Loading Operations Emissions Averaging (NESHAPS)
	1998–	Open Market Trading Ozone
	pending	El Paso Region Cross Border Air Emission Trading
	NA	Clean Fuel Vehicle Credit Trading Program
Water	1983	Iron and Steel Industry Effluent "Bubble" Trading System
Other		
Cross media	1986	Emergency Planning and Community Right-To-Know Act

Note. NESHAPS = National Emissions Standards for Hazardous Air Pollutants.
Sources. Anderson and Lohof [3]; Stavins [80].

direct effect on pollution because they have not been set at a level that directly affects behavior.[16]

In principle, the use of these mechanisms has the potential to achieve environmental objectives at the lowest cost. Many economic studies have projected cost savings from replacing the traditional command-and-control regulations with more flexible incentive-based regulations. A review of *ex ante* empirical studies on cost savings from achieving least-cost air pollution control pattern shows significant potential gains from incentive-based policies [87]. The ratio of costs from a

---

[16] Revenues from these fees, however, are often used to invest in improvements in environmental quality.

TABLE II

Examples of State/Regional Incentive-Based Programs

Deposit-refund schemes		
Land	1972–	Beverage Container Deposit Systems
	1985–	Maine Pesticide Container Deposit System
	1988–	Rhode Island Tire Deposit
	NA	Lead–Acid Battery Deposit Systems
	NA	Performance Bonds
Fees/charges/taxes		
Air	1989–	Texas Clean Fuel Incentive Charge
	1995–	Congestion Pricing Schemes
	NA	California "Hot Spots" Fees
Land	1993–1995	Advance Product Disposal Fees
	1995–	Minnesota Contaminated Property Tax
	NA	Variable Cost Pricing for Household Waste
	NA	Landfill Operator Taxes
	NA	Hazardous Waste Generation and Management Taxes
	NA	Tire Charges
	NA	Rhode Island "Hard-to-Dispose Materials" Tax
	NA	Fertilizer Charges
	NA	"Pay-as-you-throw" Garbage Disposal Fees
	NA	Wetlands Compensation Fees
	NA	Public Land Grazing Fees
	NA	Wetlands Mitigation Banking
Water	NA	California Bay Protection and Toxic Cleanup Fees
	NA	Stormwater Runoff Fees
Subsidies		
Air	NA	Polluting Vehicle Scrappage Programs
	NA	Clean Fuel and Low-Emission Vehicle Subsidies
Land	1990–	New Jersey Illegal Dumping Information Awards Program
	NA	Recycling Loans and Grants
	NA	Recycling Tax Incentives
	NA	Brownfield Tax Incentives and Loans
Cross media	1990–1992	Louisiana Environmental Scorecard
	NA	Tax Benefits for Pollution Control Equipment
	NA	Loans and Tax-exempt Bonds for Pollution Control Projects
Tradeable permits		
Air	1987–	Colorado Wood Stove and Fireplace Permit Trading
	1990–	Spokane Grass Burning Permit Trading
	1993–	Texas Emission Credit Reduction Bank and Trading Program
	1994–	Los Angeles Regional Clean Air Incentives Market
	1995–	Massachusetts Emissions Trading for VOC, NO_x, and CO
	1996–	Delaware Emissions Trading for VOCs and NO_x
	1996–	Michigan Emissions Trading for VOCs and Criteria Pollutants
	1996–	Wisconsin Emissions Trading for VOCs and NO_x
	1997–	Illinois Clean Air Market for VOCs
	1999–	OTC/OTAG Regional NO_x Reduction Program
	pending	New Jersey Emissions Trading
Water	1981–	Wisconsin Fox River Point-to-Point Source Effluent Trading
	1984–	Point-to-Nonpoint Source Effluent Trading

Note. If a state is not specified, multiple states have implemented similar programs.

Source. Anderson and Lohof [3].

traditional command-and-control approach to the least-cost policy for the 11 studies reviewed ranged from 1.07 to 22.00, with an average of 6.13. These studies generally assume that a market-based approach will operate with maximum efficiency to achieve the same level of environmental quality at lower cost. In the real world, the counterfactual is less clear. It would be more realistic to compare actual command-and-control policies with actual market-based approaches [37].

An aggregate savings estimate from all current incentive-based mechanisms for air, water, and land pollution control in the United States was developed by Anderson and Lohof [3] using published estimates of potential savings and rough estimates where no studies were available. The authors estimate that in 1992, existing incentive-based programs saved $11 billion over command-and-control approaches, and that they will save over $16 billion by the year 2000. This estimate includes significant state programs in addition to federal initiatives.

Although such an estimate provides a rough picture of the magnitude of potential cost savings, it does not provide an assessment of the actual cost savings. Many of the studies used to compile the estimate are based on *ex ante* simulations that assume incentive-based mechanisms achieve the optimal result. This is rarely the case in practice. Political obstacles frequently lead to markets that have high transaction costs and institutional barriers that reduce the potential for cost savings. Another problem with the estimation of savings is that it is difficult to assess what would have happened in the absence of a particular program. Even where cost savings are measured based on actual market data, it is not always clear if the program in question can be solely credited with the savings.[17]

There are three general categories of cost savings estimates for incentive-based mechanisms. The first is *ex ante* savings estimates that generally rely on simulations that assume the least cost abatement pattern is achieved. The second is *ex post* savings estimates that rely on market simulations similar to the *ex ante* estimates. The third is *ex post* savings estimates that use actual data from trades. Although there are a number of *ex ante* simulation studies of potential cost savings from achieving the least-cost pollution abatement scheme for various pollutants, there are relatively few *ex post* assessments of actual incentive-based programs and even fewer *ex post* assessments of actual cost savings. Table III highlights some of the problems with current knowledge of cost savings. The table shows *ex ante* and/or *ex post* estimates of cost savings for five tradable permit programs for air pollution control. I chose these programs since they represent programs where the most information is available; however, as the table shows, there are relatively few assessments of the actual impact of programs.

I was not able to find any *ex ante* assessments of the potential savings from the various parts of the Emissions Trading Program designed to reduce the cost of meeting air pollution regulation.[18] Hahn and Hester [36] produced the only comprehensive study of cost savings based on actual trades. They estimated that the program achieved savings on the order of $1.4 to $19 billion over the first 14 years. These savings, however, do not represent the full extent of potential cost

---

[17] For example, railroad deregulation led to lower than expected prices for sulfur dioxide allowances by reducing the premium for low-sulfur coal [16].

[18] For examples of early assessments of cost savings from using market-based approaches to achieve particular air pollution goals, see General Accounting Office [30] and Tietenberg [85].

ECONOMICS AND ENVIRONMENTAL POLICY 383

TABLE III

Estimates of Cost Savings over Command-and-Control Approach

Emission Trading Program (1974–)		
ex ante	No comprehensive studies on compliance cost savings.	
ex post	Total cost savings between 1974 and 1989 were between $960 million and $13 billion. "Netting" portion of the program was estimated to have saved $25 million to $300 million in permitting costs and $500 million to $12 billion in emission control costs. "Bubbles" provision of the program was estimated to have saved $300 million from federally approved trades and $135 million from state approved trades (1984 dollars).	Hahn and Hester [36]
Lead Credit Trading (1982–1987)		
ex ante	Refiners were expected to save approximately $200 million over the period 1985 to 1987 (1983 dollars).	EPA [88]
ex post	None as of 1998.	
Ozone Depleting Chemicals Allowance Trading (1988–)		
ex ante	The total compliance cost would be $77 million, or roughly 40% less than a command and control approach, between 1980 and 1990 (1980 dollars).	Palmer *et al.* as reported in GAO [30]
ex post	None as of 1998.	
Sulfur Dioxide Allowance Trading (1995–)		
ex ante	$689 million to $973 million per year between 1993 and 2010 or 39 to 44% less than the costs without allowance cost trading (1990 dollars).	ICF [42]
	Annual savings in 2002 is $1.9 billion with internal trading, $3.1 billion with interutility trading or 42 and 68% less than the cost absent trading (1992 dollars).	GAO [31]
ex post	Total annual compliance cost savings in 2010 under the least cost approach is $600 million or 35% less than the command and control approach (1995 dollars).	Carlson *et al.* [17]
	$225 to $375 million dollars or 25 to 35% of compliance costs absent trading (1995 dollars).	Schmalensee *et al.* [75]
RECLAIM (1994–)		
ex ante	The RECLAIM program is expected to reduce compliance costs by $38.2 million in 1994, $97.8 million in 1995, $46.6 million in 1996, $32.9 million in 1997, $67.7 million in 1998, and $64.0 million in 1999 (1987 dollars). In the early years, the compliance costs are approximately 80% less than under a command and control approach, and close to 30% less in the later years.	Johnson and Pekelney [43]
ex post	None as of 1998.	

savings. The program generally failed to create an active market for emission reduction credits, but it did allow for the environmental goals to be met at a lower cost [36].

Lead trading, on the other hand, comes much closer to the economist's ideal for a smoothly functioning market. The EPA originally projected cost savings of $310 million to refiners from the banking provision of the program between 1985 and 1987 [88]. The actual cost savings may be much higher than anticipated since the level of banking was higher than EPA's expectations. There are no *ex post* estimates of cost savings based on actual trading.

There was at least one *ex ante* study of cost savings using an incentive-based approach to curb the use of ozone-depleting chemicals. Palmer *et al.* estimated that between 1980 and 1990, a price-based incentive policy would save a total of $143 million over a command-and-control approach [30]. The EPA implemented an allowance trading program, and a tax on the ozone depleting chemicals was later added. Although the primary intent of the tax was to raise revenue, it may have been set high enough to have a significant incentive effect. The actual cost savings from the two approaches are unclear since there are no comprehensive *ex post* studies.

There have been some *ex ante* and *ex post* studies of the sulfur dioxide allowance trading program to reduce acid rain. *Ex ante* studies projected savings on the order of $1 billion per year [42]. The magnitude of actual cost savings achieved is estimated to be significantly less.[19]

The pattern of prices provides one indicator of cost savings, assuming that the marginal cost of abatement equals the price and total costs increase as marginal costs increase. In 1990, predictions of SO_2 permit prices were $400 to $1,000 per ton. The estimates from the beginning of the current phase of the program were significantly lower—between $250 and $400 per ton. Today actual SO_2 permit prices are about $90 to $110 per ton.[20] The discrepancy arises for a couple of reasons. First, early analyses did not include all provisions of the final bill such as the distribution of 3.5 million extra bonus allowances. The one estimate that included the extra allowances predicted prices of $170 to $200 per ton. Second, much of the remaining difference between predicted and actual permit prices is due to railroad deregulation, the resulting fall in the price of low-sulfur coal, and the decision to scrub [18, 75].

Although the absolute savings that were projected have not materialized, relative savings are in the range predicted by *ex ante* studies—approximately 25 to 35% of costs absent trading [17]. Interestingly, Burtraw [16] has found that the primary source of cost savings was not directly from trading across utilities, but rather from the flexibility in choosing abatement strategies within utilities, which is consistent with earlier predictions. Therefore, improving the trading program may allow utilities to achieve further cost savings.[21]

The RECLAIM program in Southern California has received much attention over the past few years. The program was expected to produce significant cost savings. The South Coast Air Quality Management District (SCAQMD) had estimated that the program would yield cost savings of $52 million in 1994 [43]. Although the potential savings are sizable and a review of the trading activity to date suggests significant cost savings have been achieved, there are no comprehensive studies that have assessed the actual savings.

---

[19] This discussion draws from Stavins [81].

[20] Actual incremental SO_2 abatement costs may be on the order of $200 per ton. Permit prices are lower than abatement costs for three reasons. First, in the 1990 CAA Amendments, allowances are "not property rights," which means that the allowance would have a lower value than if they were a secure property right. Second, public utility commissions place restrictions on some utilities' ability to purchase permits, thus raising their abatement costs. Third, utilities may have believed early high price predictions, and so over invested in scrubbers.

[21] However, these savings are likely to be less than the savings that accrue from intrautility trading [41].

As these examples show, the use of these mechanisms has increased and the potential savings are substantial; however, a more detailed review of these applications suggests that their performance has varied widely [36]. The variation in performance of these programs can be explained, in part, by differences in the underlying politics governing the choice and design of these programs. These political forces have led to policies that deviate from the economist's ideal.

Although the tradable permit schemes reviewed here did not exhaust cost savings, the programs generally improved environmental quality at a lower cost than alternatives under consideration. In contrast, the purpose of many environmental taxes and fees in the U.S. has been to raise revenue rather than reduce pollution. For example, the Superfund tax levied on crude oil, chemicals, and gross business profits is used to help finance cleanup. When fees have been levied directly on pollution, they have not been large enough to have significant impacts on behavior. Absent adequate incentives from fees, regulators have relied on command-and-control approaches to achieve desired levels of environmental protection. Thus, most environmental fees in the U.S. would not be economic instruments using the definition in this paper.[22]

The incentive based mechanisms considered above are primarily concerned with issues of cost effectiveness—that is, achieving a given goal at low cost. In contrast, the regulatory analysis considered below addresses the choice of goals.

Moves Toward Analyzing the Benefits and Costs of Environmental Regulation

To address the dramatic increase in regulatory activity beginning in the late 1960s, the past five Presidents have introduced mechanisms for overseeing regulations with varying degrees of success. A central component of later oversight mechanisms was formal economic analysis, which included benefit–cost analysis and cost-effectiveness analysis.

As a result of concerns that some environmental regulations were ineffective or too costly, President Nixon established a "Quality of Life" review of selected regulations in 1971. The review process, administered by OMB, required agencies issuing regulations affecting the environment, health, and safety to coordinate their activities. In 1974, President Ford formalized and broadened this review process in Executive Order 11281. Agencies were required to prepare inflationary impact statements of major rules. President Carter further strengthened regulatory oversight in 1978 by issuing Executive Order 12044, which required detailed regulatory analyses of proposed rules and centralized review by the Regulatory Analysis Review Group. This group consisted of representatives from the Executive Office of the President, including the Council of Economic Advisers, and regulatory agencies. A major focus of this review group was on environmental regulations such as the ozone standard, diesel particulate emissions, and heavy-duty truck emissions [92].

Since 1981, Presidents have required agencies to complete a regulatory impact analysis (RIA) for every major regulation. President Reagan's Executive Order 12291 required an RIA for each "major" rule whose annual impact on the

---

[22] Some fees in Europe, such as Sweden's charge on nitrogen oxides from stationary sources, would be economic instruments [78].

economy was estimated to exceed $100 million [77].[23] The aim of this Executive Order was to develop more effective and less costly regulation. President Bush used the same Executive Order. President Clinton issued Executive Order 12866, which is similar to Reagan's order in terms of its analytical requirements but adds and changes some requirements. Generally, Clinton's Executive Order directs agencies to choose the most cost-effective design of a regulation to achieve the regulatory objective, and to adopt a regulation only after balancing the costs and benefits. Clinton's order requires agencies to promulgate regulations if the benefits "justify" the costs. This language is generally perceived as more flexible than Reagan's order, which required the benefits to "outweigh" the costs. Clinton's order also places greater emphasis on distributional concerns.[24] Clinton's order requires a benefit–cost analysis for major regulations as well as an assessment of reasonably feasible alternatives to the planned regulation and a statement of why the planned regulation was chosen instead of the alternatives. Most of the major federal environmental, health, and safety regulations that have been reviewed to date are promulgated by the EPA because those regulations tend to be the most expensive.

The Congress has been slower to support efforts to require the balancing of benefits and costs of major environmental regulations. In 1982 the Senate unanimously passed such a law, but it was defeated in the House of Representatives. The two primary environmental statutes that allowed the balancing of benefits and costs prior to the mid-1990s are the Toxic Substances Control Act and the Federal Insecticide, Fungicide, and Rodenticide Act [27]. Recently, Congress has shown greater interest in emphasizing the balancing of benefits and costs. Table IV reviews recent regulatory reform initiatives, which could help improve environmental regulation and legislation. The table suggests that Congress now shares the concern of the Executive Branch that the regulatory system is in need of repair and could benefit from economic analysis [20]. All reforms highlighted in the table emphasize a trend towards considering the benefits and costs of regulation, although the effectiveness of the provisions is as of yet unclear. Perhaps owing to the politicized nature of the debate over regulatory reform, these reform efforts have come about in a piecemeal fashion, and there is some overlap in the requirements for analysis.[25] These incremental efforts fall into the two categories of process reforms described earlier in the paper: accountability mechanisms and analytical requirements.

Examples of accountability mechanisms include the provision in the Small Business Regulatory Enforcement Fairness Act of 1996 that requires agencies to

---

[23] While the definition of "major" has changed somewhat over time, it is currently defined as a regulation that has "an annual effect on the economy of $100 million or more, or adversely affects, in a material way, a sector of the economy, productivity, competition, jobs, the environment, public health or safety, or state, local, or tribal government or communities" (3(f)(1)(EO 12866)).

[24] For instance, Clinton's Principles of Regulation instructs that "...each agency shall consider...distributive impacts, and equity. On the other hand, Reagan's Executive order instructs agencies merely to identify the parties most likely to receive benefits and pay costs.

[25] There has been some recent interest in Congress in reducing this overlap by establishing a single congressional agency that would have the responsibility for assessing the government regulation. This agency would be similar to the Congressional Budget Office but have responsibility for regulation. It could help stimulate better analysis and review of agency rules by providing an additional source of information.

TABLE IV

Recent Regulatory Reform Regulation

Legislation	Description
Unfunded Mandates Reform Act of 1995	Requires the Congressional Budget Office to estimate the direct costs of unfunded federal mandates with significant economic impacts. Directs agencies to describe the costs and benefits of the majority of such mandates. Requires agencies to identify alternatives to the proposed mandate and select the "least costly, most cost-effective, or least burdensome alternative" that achieves the desired social objective.
Small Business Regulatory Enforcement Fairness Act of 1996	Requires agencies to submit each final regulation with supporting analyses to Congress. Congress has sixty days to review major regulations, and can enact a joint resolution of disapproval to void the regulation if the resolution is passed and signed by the President. Strengthens judicial review provisions to hold agencies more accountable for the impacts of regulation on small entities.
Food Quality Protection Act of 1996	Eliminates the Delancy Clause of the Food, Drug, and Cosmetic Act, which set a zero-tolerance standard for pesticide residues on processed food. Establishes a "safe" tolerance level, defined as "a reasonable certainty of no harm." Allows the Administrator of the Environmental Protection Agency to modify the tolerance level if use of the pesticide protects consumers from health risks greater than the dietary risk from the residue, or if use is necessary to avoid a "significant disruption" of the food supply. Amends the Federal Insecticide, Fungicide, and Rodenticide Act by requiring a reevaluation of the safe tolerance level after the Administrator determines during the reregistration process whether a pesticide will present an "unreasonable risk to man or the environment, taking into account the economic, social, and environmental costs and benefits of the use of any pesticide."
Safe Drinking Water Act Amendments of 1996	Amends the procedure to set maximum contaminant levels for contaminants in public water supplies. Adds requirement to determine whether the benefits of the level justify the costs. Maintains feasibility standard for contaminant levels, unless feasible level would result in an increase in the concentration of other contaminants, or would interfere with the efficacy of treatment techniques used to comply with other national drinking water regulations. Requires the Administrator to set contaminant levels to minimize the overall risk of adverse health effects by balancing the risk from the contaminant and the risk from other contaminants in such cases.
Regulatory Accountability Provision of 1996, 1997, and 1998	In separate appropriations legislation in 1996, 1997, and 1998, Congress required the Office of Management and Budget to submit an assessment of the annual benefits and costs of all existing federal regulatory programs to Congress for 1997, 1998, and 2000, respectively. The Office of Management and Budget already must review and approve analyses submitted by agencies estimating the costs and benefits of major proposed rules. The annual report provisions build on this review process.

Source. Hahn [35].

submit final regulations to Congress for review. The Telecommunications Act of 1996 requires the Federal Communications Commission to conduct a biennial review of all regulations promulgated under the Act. Congress added regulatory accountability provisions to senate appropriations legislation in 1996, 1997, and 1998 that require the Office of Management and Budget to assess the benefits and costs of existing federal regulatory programs and present the results in a public report. The OMB must also recommend programs or specific regulations to reform or eliminate. The reports represent the most significant recent step towards strengthening the use of economic analysis in the regulatory process.[26]

The addition of analytical requirements has generally received more attention than the addition of accountability mechanisms, partly because of their prominence in the Reagan and Clinton executive orders and partly because of controversy regarding their impact. The variation of the language and the choice of analytical requirement for each of the statutes listed in Table IV reflect the results of the ongoing controversy regarding analytical requirements, which takes place every time Congress debates using them. Some statutes require only cost-effectiveness analysis, some require full-fledged benefit–cost analysis, and some combine some form of benefit–cost analysis with risk–risk analysis.

The Unfunded Mandates Reform Act of 1995 requires agencies to choose the "most cost-effective" alternative and to describe the costs and benefits of any unfunded mandate, but does not require the benefits of the mandate to justify the costs. The Safe Drinking Water Amendments of 1996 require the Administrator of the Environmental Protection Agency to determine whether the benefits justify the costs of a drinking water standard, but the Administrator does not have to set a new standard if the benefits do not justify the costs.[27] Amendments in 1996 to the process through which the Secretary of Transportation sets gas pipeline safety standards, on the other hand, require the Secretary to propose a standard for pipeline safety *only* if the benefits justify the costs. Other statutes simply require the agency to only consider costs and benefits. The Food Quality Protection Act of 1996 is even more vague. The Act eliminates the Delaney Clause in the Food, Drug, and Cosmetic Act, the zero-tolerance standard for carcinogenic pesticide residues on processed food. Instead, the Administrator of the Environmental Protection Agency must set a tolerance level that is "safe," defined as "reasonable certainty of no harm." While the Food Quality Protection Act does not explicitly require the Administrator to consider benefits and costs when determining safe tolerance levels, the new language suggests increased balancing of costs and benefits relative to the original requirement. While the addition of such language to statutes represents an improvement over the status quo, it is clear that the major aims of the efforts to date have been to require more information on the benefits and costs of regulations and to increase oversight of regulatory activities and agency performance. Ensuring that regulations pass some form of a benefit–cost test has not been a priority.

There is evidence that states are also moving toward the systematic analysis of significant regulatory actions. According to a survey by the National Association on

---

[26] Other examples in the policy category include the Paperwork Reduction Act, which sets measurable goals to reduce the regulatory burden, and the Government Performance and Results Act, which establishes requirements for agencies to develop mission statements, performance goals, and measures of performance.

[27] The Amendments also require some form of risk–risk analysis. They require the Administrator of the Environmental Protection Agency to set maximum levels for contaminants in drinking water at a "feasible" level, defined as feasible with the use of the best technology and treatment techniques available, while "taking cost into consideration." The Administrator must ignore the feasibility constraint if the feasible level would result in an increase in the concentration of other contaminants in drinking water or would interfere with the efficacy of treatment techniques used to comply with other national primary drinking water regulations. If the feasibility constraint does not apply, the Administrator must set the maximum level to minimize "the overall risk of adverse health effects by balancing the risk from the contaminant and the risk from other contaminants."

Administrative Rules Review (NAARR) in 1996, administrative law review officials in 27 states noted that their state statutes require an economic impact analysis for all proposed rules, and 10 states require benefit–cost analysis for all proposed rules.[28] Table V highlights efforts in six states. The first section describes efforts to review existing rules and procedures including any measures of success, and the second section describes the analysis requirements for new activities. While the efforts vary in their authority, coverage of activities, and amount of resources, they all place greater emphasis on economic analysis and the review of existing regulations and procedures. In addition, some states have begun to document the success of their efforts; however, the measures have generally been limited to the number of rules reviewed or eliminated. No estimates of actual welfare gains are available.

The use of economic analysis is also increasing in other countries. Although the requirements for analysis and the structure of oversight vary from country to country, there are 18 OECD countries, including the United States, that require some assessment of the impacts of their regulations [66]. Although there is some anecdotal evidence of significant impacts RIAs have had on policy, the OECD study concluded that RIAs generally only have a "marginal influence" on decision making. Just as the review of U.S. federal experience with RIAs in Hahn [35] showed inconsistencies in the quality of the analysis, the same pattern appears to exist in other countries.

The preceding discussion suggests that both incentive-based mechanisms and process reforms are playing a more important role in environmental policy. One key challenge is to better understand the ways in which economics can influence the environmental policy debate.

4. UNDERSTANDING THE ROLE OF ECONOMICS AND ECONOMISTS IN SHAPING THE REFORMS

This section addresses the avenues through which economists have affected environmental policy, the limited influence of economics on policy, and the likely impact economists will have on future policy.

Avenues of Impact

There are three ways in which economists have influenced the debate over environmental policy—through research, teaching, and outreach.

The literature on economic instruments is voluminous and growing. There are three key ideas in the literature that have had an important impact on environmental policymaking: first, incentive-based instruments can help achieve goals at a lower cost than other instruments; second, benefit–cost analysis can provide a useful framework for decision making; and third, all policies and regulations have opportunity costs. Those ideas may seem obvious to economists, but they have not always been heeded in policy debates.

Economists have provided a normative framework for evaluating environmental policy and public goods (see, e.g., [9, 74]).[29] The literature on using incentive-based

---

[28] All 50 states, except for Rhode Island, responded to a questionnaire sent by the NAARR [58]. Unfortunately, little is known about the level of compliance with these requirements, the quality of the analysis, and the influence it has on decision making.

[29] An excellent survey of the academic literature is provided by Cropper and Oates [22].

TABLE V

State Efforts to Assess the Economic Impacts of Regulation

	Review of existing rules			Analysis of new rules		
	Initiated	Coverage	Examples of results	Key revisions[a]	Required analysis	Requirement that benefits exceed costs
Arizona	1986	Continuous (S)	49% of 1,392 rules reviewed in FY 1996 were identified for modification.	1993	Economic impact (S)	All rules (S)
California	1995	One-time (E)	3,900 regulations were identified for repeal; 1,700 were recommended for modification.	1991–1993, 1997	Economic impact (S, E)	Selected rules (S, E)
Massachusetts	1996	One-time (E)	Of the 1,595 regulations reviewed, 19% were identified for repeal and 44% were identified for modification.	1996	Economic impact (E)	All rules (E)
New York	1995	One-time (E)	In progress.	1995	Economic impact (S, E); Benefit–cost for selected rules (E)	All rules (E)
Pennsylvania	1996	One-time (E)	The Department of Environmental Protection identified 1,716 sections of regulations to be eliminated.	1996	Economic impact for selected rules (S); Benefit–cost for selected rules (E)	All rules (E)
Virginia	1994	Continuous (E)	Of the rules reviewed, 27% were identified for repeal and 40% for modification.	1994	Economic impact (S, E)	None

Note. Authority: E = Executive Order, S = Statute.

Source. Hahn [35].

[a] Many of these states previously had some very limited requirements for analysis of new rules. Important revisions were made through new executive orders and statutory changes to clarify and expand requirements and establish oversight.

instruments to internalize externalities dates back to Pigou [69], and for tradable permits to Crocker [21] and Dales [24]. The application of benefit–cost analysis to public projects begins with Eckstein [25]. Economists have also been helpful in comparing benefit-cost analysis with other frameworks for assessing the impacts of policies (see, e.g., [50, 67]).

Studies of incentive-based instruments have revealed that there are large potential cost savings from applying those instruments [86]. Moreover, economists have now marshaled some evidence of the potential cost savings of such systems in practice, as shown in Table III.

The second way in which economists have translated their ideas into policy is by educating students who subsequently enter the world of policy and business. Many of those students embrace aspects of the economist's paradigm, in this case, as it applies to environmental policy. Thus, for example, as more students in policy schools, business schools, and law schools are exposed to the idea of pollution taxes and tradable permits, it is more likely that they will consider applying economic ideas to particular problems, such as curbing acid rain and limiting greenhouse gas emissions.

Formal education is part of the process of diffusion from the ivory tower to the policy world. Most major environmental groups, businesses, and agencies involved in environmental policy now have staff members with at least some graduate training in economics. Environmental advocates are more likely to support policies that embrace incentive-based mechanisms, and their advocacy is more likely to be couched in the language of economics. A comparison of today's debate over policy instruments for climate change with earlier debates on emission fees is revealing. In the seventies, emission fees and tradable permits were more likely to be viewed as "licenses to pollute." Today, most policy discussions on climate change identify the need for using incentive-based instruments to achieve goals in a cost-effective manner. The sea change in attitude toward the use of incentive-based instruments represents one of the major accomplishments of environmental economics over the last three decades.

A third, more direct way that economists have translated their ideas into policy is through policy outreach and advocacy. They have become increasingly effective "lobbyists for efficiency" [47].[30] For example, my colleague, Robert Stavins, developed a very influential policy document that helped affect the course of the debate on acid rain by highlighting the potential for using incentive-based mechanisms [79]. Another example is the letter on climate change policy signed by over 2,500 economists [6]. I have personally been involved in several efforts that developed a consensus among academics to help inform the broader policy community [5, 20]. The impact of such consensus documents, while difficult to measure, should not be underestimated.

To increase their influence on policy, economists may wish to think carefully about how they allocate their time among the activities discussed above. In terms of getting policies implemented effectively, it is generally not sufficient simply to develop a good idea. Some kind of marketing is necessary before the seedling can grow into a tree.

---

[30] There are also a growing number of economic consultants and part-time consultants that may serve to impede the cause of efficiency [59].

Limitations of Impact: *Economics in the Broader Policy Process*

Economists, of course, are only one part of the environmental policy making puzzle. Politics affects the process in many ways that can block outcomes that would result in higher levels of economic welfare. Indeed, one of the primary lessons of the political economy of regulation is that economic efficiency is not likely to be a key objective in the design of policy [10, 59].

Policy ideas can affect interest group positions directly, which can then affect the positions of key decision makers (such as elected officials and civil servants), who then structure policies through the passage of laws and regulations that meet their political objectives. Alternatively, ideas may influence decision makers directly.[31]

Policy proposals can help shape outcomes by expanding the production possibility frontier; however, the precise position on the frontier is determined by several factors. Take, for example, the design of incentive-based instruments for environmental protection (see, e.g., [18, 28, 38]). Several scholars have argued that the actual design of economic instruments typically departs dramatically for political reasons from the "efficient" design of such instruments (see, e.g., [7, 15, 36, 46, 54]). Frequently, taxes have been used to raise revenues rather than to reflect optimal damages [7]. Standards have been made more stringent on new sources than old sources as a way of inhibiting growth in selected regions [1]; and agricultural interests have fought hard against the idea of transferable water rights because of concerns over losing a valuable entitlement. In some cases, the government has argued for a command-and-control approach when affected parties were ready to endorse a more flexible market-oriented approach. This was the case, for example, in the debate over restoring the Everglades [68]. In short, rent-seeking and interest group politics have been shown to have a very important impact on the design of actual policy [93].[32]

Political concerns affect not only the design of incentive-based instruments, but also the use and abuse of economic analysis in the political process. Notwithstanding such concerns, some scholars have argued that economic analysis has had a constructive impact on the policy process [27, 56, 71]. In certain instances, research suggests that such optimism is justified; however, one must be careful about generalizing from a small sample. In many situations, analysis tends to get ignored or manipulated to achieve political ends. This is particularly true for environmental issues that have political saliency.[33] At the same time, by exposing such analysis to sunshine and serious reanalysis, there is a hope that politicians may be encouraged to pursue more efficient policies in some instances. My own experience suggests that analysis can help shape the debate in selected instances by making trade-offs clearer to decision makers.[34]

---

[31] In this discussion, the institutional environment (e.g., the three branches of government and the rules governing each branch) is taken as a given. Obviously, other ideas can affect the structure of those institutions.

[32] In addition, examination of particular rule-making proceedings has shown the relative influence of particular factors in shaping environmental decisions (see, e.g., [23, 53a]).

[33] See, for example, the optimistic account of the cost to the U.S. of reducing greenhouse gases provided by the Council of Economic Advisers [95].

[34] The impact of analysis on policy outcomes is not well understood; however, participants in the process can usually point to special cases where analysis was important. For example, in the clean air debate over alternative fuels, analysis of the cost and benefits of imposing of requiring companies to sell a large fraction of methanol-powered vehicles made this option look very unattractive.

The key point is that environmental economists should not be too optimistic about implementing some of their most fervently held professional beliefs in the real world. By improving their understanding of the constraints imposed by the political system, economists can help design more efficient policies that have a higher probability of being implemented.[35]

Likely Impact in the Future

To understand the likely impact of economics on environmental policy in the future, it is helpful to understand the reasons for its importance in the past. A simple story is that federal environmental policy was initially designed without much regard to cost in the wake of Earth Day in 1970, which marked the beginning of an acute national awareness of environmental issues. As the costs increased and became more visible, and the goals became more ambitious, the constituencies opposing such regulation on economic grounds grew. Currently, the political (as opposed to economic) demands for environmental quality are high, but the costs are also high in many instances. This is an obvious situation in which economists can help by building more cost-effective mechanisms for achieving goals.

So far, environmental economists have enjoyed limited success in seeing their ideas translated into practice. That success is likely to continue in the future. In particular, there are likely to be more incentive-based mechanisms, greater use of benefit–cost analysis, and more careful consideration of the opportunity costs of such policies. But that does not mean that the overall net benefits of environmental policy will necessarily increase because the political forces that lead to less efficient environmental policy will still be strong.[36]

For those who believe benefit–cost analysis should play a more prominent role in decision making—in particular, the setting of goals—it will be a long, uphill struggle. The recent fight over the Regulatory Improvement Act of 1998 sponsored by Senators Levin and Thompson provides a good example. This bill essentially codifies the Executive Orders calling for benefit–cost analysis of major rules; yet many within the environmental community are strongly opposed, arguing that it could lead to an analytical quagmire [39, 76]. There are at least three reasons such opponents would take this stand: first, because making such claims is good for mobilizing financial support;[37] second, because of concerns that such legislation could help lead to more serious consideration of economics in environmental decision making; third, because opponents are concerned that agencies will misuse cost–benefit analysis and related analytical tools. In particular, there is concern with what will happen if politicians decide that cost is no longer a "four-letter"

---

[35] For example, in the debate over acid rain, it was clear there would be some implicit or explicit compensation to high sulfur coal interests. The challenge was to develop approaches that would maximize cost savings subject to that constraint.

[36] Environmentalists have been successful in framing the debate as being either "for" or "against" the environment, making it difficult to introduce the notion of explicit trade-offs. Their success is likely to continue for the foreseeable future.

[37] The 1994 Republican plan to repeal regulations, for example, breathed new life into the green movement. The highly publicized plan resulted in a dramatic increase in memberships to environmental groups and an increase in donations by active members [85]. To the extent that benefit–costs analysis is perceived as a means to repeal regulations, opposing the use of such tools may have a similar revenue-enhancing effect.

word—so that benefits and costs can be compared explicitly! Given the limited scope of this bill and the level of resistance encountered thus far, it is clear that the potential for change in the short term is limited.

The problem facing economists who want benefit–cost analysis to play a greater role in decision making is that it is difficult for politicians to oppose environmental laws and regulations simply because they may fail a benefit–cost test. After all, who could be against an environmental policy if it has some demonstrable benefits for some worthy constituency? It is hard to make arguments opposing such regulation in a ten-second soundbite on television.

But economists will continue to make slow progress in the area of balancing benefits and costs. In the short term, they will do so by making arguments about the potential for reallocating regulatory expenditures in ways that can save more lives or trees. Over the longer term, they will build a better information base that clearly shows that many environmental policies will pass a benefit–cost test if they are designed judiciously, but many also will not.

5. CONCLUDING THOUGHTS

This paper has made a preliminary attempt to assess the impact of economics on environmental policy. There are at least three key points to be made about the nature of this impact. First, the impact often occurs with considerable time lags. Second, the introduction of economic instruments occurs in a political environment, which frequently has dramatic effects on the form and content of policy. Third, economists are not very close to a public policy heaven in which benefit–cost analysis plays a major role in shaping environmental policy decisions that governments view within their domain.

The latter topic concerning the appropriate domain for environmental policy may be one on which the profession contributes a great deal in the future. In particular, it is difficult to determine when it is "appropriate" for a particular level of government to intervene in the development of environmental policy [61, 72]. This is a subject on which there is a great deal of legitimate intellectual and political ferment. At one extreme, free market environmentalists wish to leave most, if not all, choices about such policy to the market [2, 49]. At the other extreme, some analysts believe there is a need for many levels of government intervention, including the design of a global environmental institution (see, e.g., [26]). Achieving some degree of consensus on that issue is likely to be difficult, but not impossible. For example, most economists agree that for global environmental problems, it is difficult to address them effectively without having some kind of international agency or agreement. At the same time, many economists recognize that the arguments suggesting competitive jurisdictions will under-provide environmental amenities is somewhat weaker than was suggested two decades ago (see, e.g., [82]).

Environmental economists will have many opportunities to shape the policy debate in new areas. Examples include international trade and the environment and the development of new taxation systems [11, 33, 45, 84]. One of the critical factors that will affect the rate of diffusion of ideas from environmental economists to the policy world is the *perception* of their success. If, for example, markets for environmental quality are viewed as a successful mechanism for achieving goals by both business and environmentalists, their future in the policymakers' tool chest looks brighter. The same can be said of benefit–cost analysis.

There are many challenges that lie ahead for the environmental economics community. The most important one is becoming more policy-relevant.[38] To achieve that end, economists need to become more problem-driven rather than tool-driven. There seems to be a move in this direction, but there are also incentives in the profession that still push it in the opposite direction—most notably publish or perish.

Another challenge for the economics community is to determine how far it is willing to push the paradigm. Some would like government regulations, including environmental regulations, to at least pass a broadly defined benefit–cost test [20]. Others more skeptical about the tool and less skeptical about the outcomes of certain kinds of government intervention think economists and policy makers should not ask benefit–cost analysis to bear too much weight (see, e.g., [14, 50]).

Finally, economists need to get more comfortable with the idea of being lobbyists for efficiency or advocates for policies in which they believe. This comfort level is increasing slowly. Moreover, economists are finding ways to institutionalize their power in certain policy settings. A good example is the Environmental Economics Advisory Committee within the Science Advisory Board at the Environmental Protection Agency. The primary function of that group is to help provide economic guidance to the agency on important regulatory issues. Now economists have a voice.

In sum, the impact of economists on environmental policy to date has been modest. Economists can claim credit for having helped changed the terms of the debate to include economic instruments—no small feat. They can also claim some credit for legislation that promotes greater balancing of costs and benefits. But specific victories of consequence are few and far between. Most of the day-to-day policy that real folks must address involves the activities associated with complying with standards, permits, guidelines and regulations. While economists have said a few intelligent things about such matters, their attention has largely been focused on those parts of environmental policy that they enjoy talking about—areas where theoretical economics can offer relatively clean insights. Perhaps if we expand our domain of inquiry judiciously and continue to teach tomorrow's decisionmakers, we can also expand our influence. Hope springs eternal.

REFERENCES

1. B. A. Ackerman and W. T. Hassler, "Clean Coal/Dirty Air: Or How the Clean Air Act Became a Multibillion-Dollar Bail-Out for High-Sulfur Coal Producers and What Should Be Done About It," Yale Univ. Press, New Haven, CT (1981).

[38] It is possible that the influence of economics on environmental policy in developing countries may be greater because these countries have fewer resources to waste. That is, governments in developing countries may more likely use the tools advocated by economists to develop policies. While there are certainly many applications of economics in environmental policy in developing countries, the general thesis has yet to be demonstrated (see, e.g., [94]). Moreover, judging by the levels of inefficiency of other policies in developing countries, it is unclear why environmental policies may be designed more efficiently (see e.g., [87]).

2. T. L. Anderson and D. R. Leal, "Free Market Environmentalism," Pacific Research Institute for Public Policy, San Francisco, (1991).

3. R. C. Anderson and A. Q. Lohof, "United States Experience with Economic Incentives in Environmental Pollution Control Policy," Environmental Law Institute, Washington, DC (1997).

4. R. C. Anderson, A. Carlin, A. McGartland, and J. Weinberger, Cost savings from the use of market incentives for pollution control, *in* "Market-Based Approaches to Environmental Policy" (R. Kosobud and J. Zimmerman, Eds.), Van Nostrand Reinhold, New York, (1997).

5. K. J. Arrow, M. L. Cropper, G. C. Eads, R. W. Hahn, L. B. Lave, R. G. Noll, P. R. Portney, M. Russell, R. Schmalensee, V. K. Smith, and R. N. Stavins, "Benefit-Cost Analysis in Environmental, Health, and Safety Regulation: A Statement of Principles," AEI Press, Washington, DC (1996).

6. K. J. Arrow, D. Jorgenson, P. Krugman, W. Nordhaus, and R. Solow, "The Economists' Statement on Climate Change," Redefining Progress, San Francisco, CA (1997).

7. T. A. Barthold, Issues in the design of environmental excise taxes, *J. Econom. Perspect.* **8**, 133–151 (1994).

8. R. H. Bates, "Markets and States in Tropical Africa: The Political Basis of Agricultural Policies," Univ. of California Press, Berkeley, CA (1981).

9. W. Baumol and W. Oates, "The Theory of Environmental Policy," 2nd ed., Prentice–Hall, Englewood Cliffs, NJ (1988).

10. G. Becker, A theory of competition among pressure groups for political influence, *Quart. J. Econom.* **97**, 371–400 (1983).

11. J. Bhagwati and T. N. Srinivasan, Trade and the environment: Does environmental diversity detract from the case for free trade?, *in* "Fair Trade and Harmonization: Prerequisites for Free Trade?" (J. Bhagwati and R. Hudec, Eds.), MIT Press, Cambridge, MA (1996).

12. P. Bohm and R. S. Clifford, Comparative analysis of alternative policy instruments, *in* "Handbook of Natural Resource and Energy Economics, Volume I" (A. V. Kneese and J. L. Sweeney, Eds.), pp. 395–460, North-Holland, Amsterdam (1985).

13. A. Bovenberg and L. H. Goulder, Optimal environmental taxation in the presence of other taxes: general equilibrium analyses, *Amer. Econom. Rev.* **86**, 985–1000 (1996).

14. D. W. Bromley, The ideology of efficiency: Searching for a theory of policy analysis, *J. Environ. Econom. Management* **19**, 86–107 (1990).

15. J. M. Buchanan and G. Tullock, Polluters' profits and political response: Direct controls versus taxes, *Amer. Econom. Rev.* **65**, 139–147 (1975).

16. D. Burtraw, "Cost Savings Sans Allowance Trades? Evaluating the SO$_2$ Emission Trading Program to Date," Discussion Paper 95-30-REV, Resources for the Future, Washington, DC (1996).

17. C. Carlson, D. Burtraw, M. Cropper, and K. L. Palmer, "SO$_2$ Control by Electric Utilities: What Are the Gains from Trade?" Discussion Paper, Resources for the Future, Washington, DC, forthcoming (1998).

18. T. N. Cason, Seller incentive properties of EPA's emission trading auction, *J. Environ. Econom. Management* **25**, 177–195 (1993).

19. Council of Economic Advisers, "Economic Report of the President," U.S. Government Printing Office, Washington, DC (1998).

20. R. W. Crandall, C. DeMuth, R. W. Hahn, R. E. Litan, P. S. Nivola, and P. R. Portney, "An Agenda for Reforming Federal Regulation," AEI Press and Brookings Institution Press, Washington, DC (1997).

21. T. Crocker, The structuring of atmospheric pollution control systems, *in* "The Economics of Air Pollution" (H. Wolozin, Ed.), pp. 61–86, Norton, New York, (1966).

22. M. L. Cropper and W. E. Oates, Environmental economics: A survey, *J. Econom. Lit.* **30**, 675–740 (1992).

23. M. L. Cropper *et al.*, The determinants of pesticide regulation: A statistical analysis of EPA decision making, *J. Pol. Econom.* **100**, 175–197 (1992).

24. J. H. Dales, "Pollution, Property and Prices," University Press, Toronto, (1968).

25. O. Eckstein, "Water-Resource Development: The Economics of Project Evaluation," Harvard Univ. Press, Cambridge, MA (1958).

26. D. C. Esty, "Greening the GATT: Trade, Environment, and the Future," Institute for International Economics, Washington, DC (1994).

27. A. G. Fraas, The role of economic analysis in shaping environmental policy, *Law Contemp. Problems* **54**, 113–125 (1991).

28. R. Franciosi, R. M. Isaac, D. E. Pingry, and S. S. Reynolds, An experimental investigation of the Hahn–Noll revenue neutral auction for emissions licenses, *J. Environ. Econom. Management* **24**, 1–24 (1993).

29. A. M. Freeman, Water Pollution Policy, *in* "Public Policies for Environmental Protection" (P. R. Portney, Ed.), Resources for the Future, Washington, DC (1990).

30. General Accounting Office, "A Market Approach to Air Pollution Control Could Reduce Compliance Costs without Jeopardizing Clean Air Goals," PAD-82-15, General Accounting Office, Washington, DC, (1982).

31. General Accounting Office, "Air Pollution: Allowance Trading Offers an Opportunity to Reduce Emissions at Less Costs," GAO/RCED-95-30, Resources, Community, and Economic Development Division, General Accounting Office, Washington, DC (1994).

32. I. Goklany, Rationing health care while writing blank checks for environmental hazards, *Regulation*, 14–15, (1992).

33. L. Goulder, Environmental taxation and the "double dividend:" A reader's guide. *Int. Tax Public Finance* **2**(2), 157–184 (1995).

34. J. D. Graham and J. B. Wiener (Eds.), "Risk vs. Risk: Tradeoffs in Protecting Health and the Environment," Harvard Univ. Press, Cambridge, MA (1995).

35. R. W. Hahn, "Reviving Regulatory Reform: A Global Perspective," AEI Press and Brookings Institution, New York, NY, forthcoming (2000).

36. R. W. Hahn and G. L. Hester, Marketable permits: Lessons for theory and practice, *Ecology Law Quart.* **16**, 361–406 (1989).

37. R. W. Hahn and R. N. Stavins, Economic incentives for environmental protection: Integrating theory and practice, *Amer. Econom. Rev.* **82**, 464–468 (1992).

38. K. Hausker, The politics and economics of auction design in the market for sulfur dioxide pollution, *J. Policy Anal. Management* **11**, 553–572 (1992).

39. D. Hawkins and G. Wetstone, Regulatory obstacle course, *Washington Post*, A18, March 9 (1998).

40. M. Hazilla and R. J. Kopp, The social cost of environmental quality regulations: A General equilibrium analysis, *J. Polit. Econom.* **98**, 853–873 (1990).

41. ICF Resources, Inc., "Economic, Environmental, and Coal Market Impacts of SO_2 Emissions Trading under Alternative Acid Rain Control Proposals," prepared for the U.S. Environmental Protection Agency, OPPE, Fairfax, VA (1989).

42. ICF Resources, Inc., "Regulatory Impact Analysis of the Final Acid Rain Implementation Regulations," prepared for the Office of Atmospheric and Indoor Air Programs, Acid Rain Division, U.S. Environmental Protection Agency, Washington, DC, October 19 (1992).

43. S. L. Johnson and D. M. Pekelney, Economic assessment of the regional clean air incentives market: A new emissions trading program for Los Angeles, *Land Econom.* **72**, 277–297 (1996).

44. D. W. Jorgenson and P. J. Wilcoxen, Environmental regulation and U.S. economic growth, *Rand J. Econom.* **21**, 314–340 (1990).

45. J. P. Kalt, Exhaustible resource price policy, international trade, and intertemporal welfare, *J. Environ. Econom. Management*, **17**, (1989).

46. N. Keohane, R. Revesz, and R. N. Stavins, The positive political economy of instrument choice in environmental policy, *in* "Environmental Economics and Public Policy: Essays in Honor of Wallace Oates" (Arvind Panagariya, P. Portney and R. Schwab, Eds.), Edward Elgar, London, 1999, p. 89–125.

47. S. Kelman, "What Price Incentives? Economists and the Environment," Auburn House, Boston (1981).

48. A. V. Kneese and C. L. Schultze, "Pollution, Prices, and Public Policy," Brookings Institution, Washington, DC (1975).

49. J. E. Krier, The tragedy of the commons, part two, *Harvard J. Law Pub. Policy* **15**, 325–347 (1992).

50. L. B. Lave, "The Strategy of Social Regulation," Brookings Institution, Washington, DC (1981).

51. L. B. Lave, Benefit–cost analysis: Do the benefits exceed the costs? *in* "Risks, Costs, and Lives Saved: Getting Better Results from Regulation" (R. W. Hahn, Ed.), Oxford Univ. Press/AEI Press, New York (1996).

52. R. E. Litan and W. D. Nordhaus, "Reforming Federal Regulation," Yale Univ. Press, New Haven, CT (1983).

53. R. Lutter, "An Analysis of the Use of EPA's Clean Air Benefit Estimates in OMB's Draft Report on the Costs and Benefits of Regulation," Regulatory Analysis 98-2, AEI–Brookings Joint Center for Regulatory Studies, Washington, DC (1998).

53a. W. Magat, A. Krupnick, and W. Harrington, "Rules in the Making: A Statistical Analysis of Regulatory Agency Behavior," Resources for the Future, Washington, DC (1986).

54. M. Maloney and R. E. McCormick, A positive theory of environmental quality regulation, *J. Law Econom.* **25**, 99–123 (1982).

55. A. Metrick and M. L. Weitzman, Conflicts and choices in biodiversity preservation, *J. Econom. Perspectives* **12**(3), 21–34 (1998).

56. R. D. Morgenstern (Ed.), "Economic Analysis at EPA: Assessing Regulatory Impact," Resources for the Future, Washington, DC (1997).

57. J. F. Morrall, A review of the record, *Regulation* **10**, 25–34, (1986).

58. National Association on Administrative Rules Review, "The National Association on Administrative Rules Review 1996–97 Administrative Rules Review Directory and Survey," The Council of State Governments, Midwest Office, Lexington, KY (1996).

59. R. G. Noll, The economics and politics of the slowdown in regulatory reform, *in* "Reviving Regulatory Reform: A Global Perspective" (R. W. Hahn, Ed.), Cambridge Univ. Press/AEI Press, New York, forthcoming (1998).

60. R. G. Noll, Economic perspectives on the politics of regulation, *in* "Handbook of Industrial Organization" (R. Schmalensee and R. Willig, Eds.), North-Holland, Amsterdam (1989).

61. W. E. Oates and R. M. Schwab, Economic competition among jurisdictions: Efficiency enhancing or distortion inducing? *J. Public Econom.* **35**, 333–354 (1988).

62. Office of Management and Budget, "More Benefits, Fewer Burdens: Creating A Regulatory System that Works for the American People," a Report to the President on the Third Anniversary of Executive Order 12866, Office of Management and Budget, Office of Information and Regulatory Affairs, Washington, DC (1996).

63. Office of Management and Budget, "Report to Congress on the Costs and Benefits of Federal Regulations," Office of Management and Budget, Office of Information and Regulatory Affairs, Washington, DC (1997).

64. Office of Management and Budget, "Budget of the United States Government, Fiscal Year 1999: Historical Tables," Executive Office of the President, Office of Management and Budget, Washington, DC (1998).

65. J. B. Opschoor, A. F. de Savornin Lohman, and H. B. Vos, "Managing the Environment: Role of Economic Instruments," Organisation for Economic Co-operation and Development, Paris, France (1994).

66. Organisation for Economic Co-operation and Development, "Regulatory Impact Analysis: Best Practices in OECD Countries," Organisation for Economic Co-operation and Development, Paris, France (1997).

67. T. Page, "Conservation and Economic Efficiency: An Approach to Materials Policy," published for Resources for the Future, Johns Hopkins University Press, Baltimore, MD (1977).

68. P. Passell, A free-enterprise plan for an Everglades cleanup, *New York Times*, May 1 (1992).

69. A. C. Pigou, "The Economics of Welfare," Macmillan & Co., London, (1932); 4th ed. (1952).

70. P. R. Portney (Ed.), "Public Policies for Environmental Protection," Resources for the Future, Washington, DC (1990).

71. P. R. Portney, Counting the cost: The growing role of economics in environmental decisionmaking, *Environment* **40**, 14–21 (1998).

72. R. L. Revesz, Rehabilitating interstate competition: Rethinking the 'race-to-the-bottom' rationale for federal environmental regulation, *New York Univ. Law Rev.* **67**, 1210–1254 (1992).

73. K. R. Richards, "Framing Environmental Policy Instrument Choice, Working Paper, School of Public and Environmental Affairs, Indiana University, Bloomington, Indiana (1998).

74. P. A. Samuelson, The pure theory of public expenditure, *Rev. Econom. Stat.* **36**, 387–389 (1954).

75. R. Schmalensee, P. L. Joskow, A. D. Ellerman, J. P. Montero, and E. M. Bailey, An interim evaluation of sulfur dioxide emissions trading, *J. Econom. Perspect.*, **12**(3) 53–68 (1998).

76. C. Skrzycki, A bipartisan bill runs into a Lott of opposition, *Washington Post*, F01, March 20 (1998).

77. V. K. Smith (Ed.), "Environmental Policy under Reagan's Executive Order: The Role of Cost-Benefit Analysis," Univ. North Carolina Press, Chapel Hill, NC (1984).

78. S. Smith and H. B. Vos, "Evaluating Economic Instruments for Environmental Policy," Organisation for Economic Co-operation and Development, Paris, France (1997).

79. R. N. Stavins (Ed.), "Project 88: Harnessing Market Forces to Protect Our Environment—Initiatives for the New President," Public Policy Study sponsored by Senator Timothy E. Wirth and Senator John Heinz, Washington, DC (1988).

80. R. N. Stavins, "Market Based Environmental Policies," Discussion Paper 98-26, Resources for the Future, Washington, DC (1998).

81. R. N. Stavins, What can we learn from the grand policy experiment: Positive and normative lessons from the SO_2 allowance trading, *J. Econom. Perspect.* **12**(3), 69–88 (1998).

82. R. B. Stewart, Pyramids of sacrifice? Problems of federalism in mandating state implementation of national environmental policy, *Yale Law J.* **86**, 1196–1272 (1977).

83. T. O. Tengs and J. Graham, The opportunity cost of haphazard social regulation, *in* "Risks, Costs and Lives Saved: Getting Better Results from Regulation" (R. W. Hahn, Ed.), Oxford Univ. Press/AEI Press, Washington, DC (1996).

84. D. Terkla, The efficiency value of effluent tax revenues, *J. Environ. Econom. Management* **11**, 107–123 (1984).

85. The *Economist*, The defense of nature (2): Sprouting again, The Economist Newspaper Limited, April 12, 1997.

86. T. Tietenberg, "Emissions Trading: An Exercise in Reforming Pollution Policy," Resources for the Future, Washington, DC (1985).

87. T. Tietenberg, Economic instruments for environmental regulation, *Oxford Rev. Econom. Policy* **6**, 17–33 (1990).

88. U.S. Environmental Protection Agency, "Costs and Benefits of Reducing Lead in Gasoline," Final Regulatory Impact Analysis III-2, U. S. Environmental Protection Agency, Office of Policy Analysis, Washington, DC (1985).

89. U.S. Environmental Protection Agency, "Environmental Investments: The Cost of a Clean Environment," U. S. Environmental Protection Agency, Office of Policy, Planning and Evaluation, Washington, DC (1990).

90. U.S. Environmental Protection Agency, "Economic Incentives: Options for Environmental Protection," U. S. Environmental Protection Agency, Policy, Planning and Evaluation, Washington, DC (1991).

91. U.S. Environmental Protection Agency, "The Benefits and Costs of the Clean Air Act: 1970 to 1990," U. S. Environmental Protection Agency, Office of Air and Radiation, Washington, DC (1997).

92. L. J. White, "Reforming Regulation: Processes and Problems," Prentice–Hall, Englewood Cliffs, NJ (1981).

93. B. Yandle, Bootleggers and Baptists in the market for regulation, *in* "The Political Economy of Government Regulation" (J. F. Shogren, Ed.), Topics in Regulatory Economics and Policy Series, Kluwer, Dordrecht/London, Norwell, MA (1989).

94. D. Wheeler, "Pollution Charge Systems in Developing Countries," World Bank, mimeo, Washington, DC (1998).

95. J. Yellen, statement of Janet Yellen, Chair, White House Council of Economic Advisers, before the U.S. Senate Committee on Agriculture, Nutrition, and Forestry on the Economics of the Kyoto Protocol, Washington, DC March 5 (1998).

[21]

FROM RESEARCH TO POLICY: THE CASE OF ENVIRONMENTAL ECONOMICS

Wallace E. Oates[*]

In his contribution to this symposium issue, Professor Oates examines the impact of economic analysis on environmental policy over the last thirty years. He begins by describing the exclusive reliance on a command-and-control approach in the early years of environmental regulation and explains why economics and economists had so little impact at that stage of policymaking. Next, drawing on examples from the history of environmental regulation, Professor Oates details the evolution of environmental policy instruments and the methods used to set environmental standards, tracing the emergence of tradable emission permit systems as the dominant form of incentive-based policy instruments in the United States (in contrast to Europe). He then describes the virtues and limits of benefit-cost analysis in the environmental policy arena and concludes with some reflections on the importance of economic research and theory to sound environmental policymaking.

I. INTRODUCTION

Over the past thirty years, a striking evolution of regulatory mentality has manifested itself in environmental policy. The Clean Air Act Amendments of 1970[1] and the Clean Water Act Amendments of 1972,[2] the cornerstones of the new federal legislation emerging from the environmental revolution of the 1960s, were firmly grounded in the traditional command-and-control approach to regulatory management. Under these measures, the environmental authorities were to set standards with little regard to their economic implications and were then to promulgate directions to polluting sources instructing them on reductions in their levels of waste emissions.

---

* *Professor of Economics, University of Maryland; University Fellow, Resources for the Future.*
1. Pub. L. No. 91-604, 84 Stat. 1676.
2. Pub. L. No. 92-500, 86 Stat. 816.

But there have been dramatic changes. In the 1990 Clean Air Act Amendments,[3] for example, Congress established a national market for sulfur emissions to address the troubling acid rain problem.[4] Under these provisions, sources across the nation are now buying and selling entitlements to a limited quantity of sulfur discharges into the atmosphere, leaving sources themselves with the discretion to determine both their own levels of emissions and their abatement technology.[5] Under this regime, sulfur emissions in this country have been cut in half over the decade.[6] There is, moreover, serious ongoing consideration— on an international scale—of a system of tradable carbon allowances for the containment of global climate change.[7] But more generally, it is now simply inconceivable that a major piece of environmental legislation could come under serious consideration without a systematic study of its prospective benefits and costs and without some attention to the potential use of economic incentives in the regulatory mechanism.

This evolution away from a system exclusively of direct controls that pays little attention to the economic implications of environmental measures to one where more market-oriented approaches to regulatory management hold sway represents a remarkable transformation. How has this change occurred? And, in particular, what role (if any) have economists and their research played in this process? This article will explore these questions. Following some description and reflections on the course of this regulatory evolution, I will offer some thoughts on the more general insights this experience provides into the nature of effective policy research. But first it will be helpful for purposes of reference to review briefly the state of environmental economics during the early phases of the environmental movement and to recall the reception that the economic approach to environmental problems received in the policy arena during the formulation of the first major pieces of environmental legislation.

II. THE ECONOMIC PERSPECTIVE ON ENVIRONMENTAL REGULATION AND ITS INITIAL RECEPTION IN THE POLICY ARENA

Economists were, in one sense, well prepared for the arrival of the environmental revolution in the 1960s. They had a systematic view of environmental degradation, a view that both explained the nature of the "market failure" that caused excessive pollution and contained, as a corollary, a direct prescription for policy measures to correct the malfunc-

---

3. Pub. L. No. 101-549, 104 Stat. 2399 (codified as amended at 42 U.S.C. §§ 7401–7700 (1994)).
4. See id. § 401, 104 Stat. 2399, 2585.
5. For an excellent description and assessment of the workings of this market, see generally Paul L. Joskow et al., *The Market for Sulfur Dioxide Emissions*, 88 AM. ECON. REV. 669 (1998).
6. See id. at 669.
7. See generally Jonathan Baert Wiener, *Global Trade in Greenhouse Gas Control*, 129 RESOURCES 13 (1997).

tion.[8] In brief, economists saw the source of our major environmental problems in terms of the "external costs" that polluters imposed on society. These costs, associated with such activities as the emission of pollutants into the atmosphere or waterways, arise because polluting sources bear no pecuniary responsibility for the costs (or damages) resulting from their emissions.[9] Although they must pay for the labor, materials, and other resources they consume in their production activities, polluting firms need not pay for their use of various scarce environmental resources such as clean air and water. Since these scarce resources are available free of charge, they are quite naturally used to excess. The straightforward prescription for this form of market failure is for an appropriate public authority to introduce the correct "price" into the system in the form of a tax or effluent fee on polluting emissions.[10] Such a tax or fee would represent the surrogate price required to induce polluters to reduce their polluting activities to socially appropriate levels.[11] It would internalize the external costs of polluters and force polluters to take cognizance of society's environmental concerns.

This perspective on environmental regulation, developed in the first half of this century by A.C. Pigou and others,[12] was, by the 1960s, well embedded in the literature.[13] This was true not only at the more formal level; the basic microeconomic texts also contained descriptions of the smoky factory spewing its fumes over residential neighborhoods and called for taxes on emissions of the offending pollutants as a corrective measure.

The economics profession was thus well positioned to take an active and influential role in the design and implementation of the early rounds of environmental legislation. Yet, as mentioned in the introduction, such was not the case. The economic perspective on environmental management played essentially no role in the determination of the major legislation of the early 1970s; it was, in fact, ignored. The Amendments to the Clean Air Act in 1970[14] and to the Clean Water Act in 1972[15] made no pretense of weighing benefits against costs in the setting of environmental standards. The former instructed the Environmental Protection Agency (EPA) to set maximum limitations on pollutant concentrations

---

8. *See generally, e.g.,* ALLEN V. KNEESE & BLAIR T. BOWER, MANAGING WATER QUALITY: ECONOMICS, TECHNOLOGY, INSTITUTIONS (1968).

9. *See generally id.* For a more formal analysis, see WILLIAM J. BAUMOL & WALLACE E. OATES, THE THEORY OF ENVIRONMENTAL POLICY 14–56 (1988).

10. *See* KNEESE & BOWER, *supra* note 8, at 312–18.

11. *See id.*

12. *See, e.g.,* A.C. PIGOU, THE ECONOMICS OF WELFARE (1932).

13. For example, see KNEESE & BOWER, *supra* note 8, at 75–129.

14. Clean Air Amendments of 1970, Pub. L. No. 91-604, 84 Stat. 1676 (codified as amended at 42 U.S.C. § 7401 (1994)).

15. Federal Water Pollution Control Act Amendments of 1972, Pub. L. No. 92-500, 86 Stat. 816 (codified as amended at 33 U.S.C. § 1251 (1994)).

in the atmosphere "to protect the public health."[16] The latter stated as its basic objective the "elimination of the discharge of *all* pollutants into the navigable waters by 1985."[17] These objectives were to be achieved through a set of directives to polluters that instructed them on limits to their emissions and/or the control technologies they were to employ.[18]

Why was the economic approach to environmental management so uninfluential in this early legislation? My answer to this question comes in three parts. First, there was no constituency or interest group for whom the economists' policy prescription had much appeal. Environmentalists were decidedly suspicious of, if not outrightly hostile to, reliance on a system of "environmental prices."[19] For many, the market system was the culprit: it was the source of environmental damage.[20] The implication to many environmentalists was that polluting activities needed to be prohibited or, at least, strictly controlled.[21] Some saw the economic approach to environmental management as basically immoral because it involved placing a price on invaluable environmental assets.[22] Moreover, most environmentalists distrusted the pricing approach; their response to the economist was that polluters would simply pay the fee or tax and continue polluting.[23] Prices, in short, simply could not be depended upon to induce the needed abatement efforts.[24]

Likewise, polluting industry was generally unsupportive of such measures.[25] New taxes on firms are rarely viewed with much enthusiasm in the business community. One might have thought that managers would prefer a system of taxes — which would allow some flexibility in the firm's response — to a set of direct controls that prescribed technologies for pollution abatement. But this did not seem to be the case.[26] In

---

16. 42 U.S.C. § 7409(b).

17. 33 U.S.C. § 1251(a) (emphasis added). Although the 1970 Amendments to the Clean Air Act stated that standards were to be determined solely on the basis of health criteria, this legislation did include "economic feasibility" among the guidelines for determining source-specific standards. Roger Noll has suggested to me that the later 1977 Amendments to the Clean Air Act were, in fact, more "anti-economic" than any that preceded them. For a systematic analysis of this legislation, see Matthew D. McCubbins et al., *Structure and Process, Politics and Policy: Administrative Arrangements and the Political Control of Agencies*, 75 VA. L. REV. 431, 431–82 (1989).

18. *See* A. Myrick Freeman III, *Water Pollution Policy*, *in* PUBLIC POLICIES FOR ENVIRONMENTAL PROTECTION 97, 103–10 (Paul R. Portney ed., 1990).

19. For a careful treatment of the opposition to a system of pollution taxes, see STEVEN J. KELMAN, WHAT PRICE INCENTIVES? ECONOMISTS AND THE ENVIRONMENT 110–11 (1981).

20. *See id.* at 115.

21. *See id.* at 115–16.

22. *See id.* at 109–11.

23. *See id.*

24. This often pervasive distrust of the efficacy of prices is quite striking to an economist. In spite of all the evidence to the contrary, the public response to pricing measures is often that they will not work. People seem to believe that the demand for nearly everything is almost perfectly price inelastic!

25. *See* KELMAN, *supra* note 19, at 120.

26. It is quite possible, incidentally, for a program of effluent fees to impose higher costs on polluting firms than a program of direct controls that achieves similar outcomes. The relatively high abatement costs under a regime of direct controls may still be less than the control costs *plus* the taxes on any remaining emissions under a fee program. For an interesting empirical analysis of the costs of

fact, the command-and-control approach, in many instances, worked to the advantage of *existing* firms. Environmental legislation often imposed much more extensive and costly controls on *new* firms than on existing ones,[27] a phenomenon known as "new source bias." In this way, such measures typically erected new barriers to entry that protected established firms from the competition of entrants.[28] The proposal for environmental taxes or fees, in short, did not find broad-based support in the business community.

Finally, the fraternity of regulators was not favorably disposed to incentive-based policy instruments.[29] Regulators were more familiar with the traditional approaches that make use of source-specific permits, which either specify limits on emissions or prescribe abatement practices. The idea of discarding this approach in favor of an unfamiliar system of fees did not sit well in the regulatory community, as polluters' responses to the fees would be uncertain.[30] In sum, no interest groups existed to champion the case of economic incentives for environmental protection.

The second part to my answer involves the state of environmental economics itself in the late 1960s and early 1970s. Although, as I have suggested,[31] there existed a coherent economic view of the environmental problem and its resolution, it was just that: a view with little concrete work addressing the complex issues of program design and implementation. Economic theory calls for a fee or tax on polluting activities equal to marginal social damage.[32] But as soon as one tries to build an actual regulatory program on this principle, all sorts of complications arise.

For example, because the damages caused by various emissions into the atmosphere or a body of water frequently depend on the location of the discharger, the Pigouvian prescription would, in principle, call for a set of taxes tailored to these damages; the effluent fee (or tax) would be source-specific to reflect the damage caused by emissions at the source's particular location.[33] In addition, the damages resulting from waste discharges may vary with the time of the emission, for the state of winds in the atmosphere or river flow typically varies with the season or even the

alternative programs for pollution control that produces such a finding, see Eugene Seskin et al., *An Empirical Analysis of Economic Strategies for Controlling Air Pollution*, 10 J. ENVTL. & ECON. MGMT. 112, 112–24 (1983).

27. *See* Paul R. Portney, *Air Pollution Policy*, *in* PUBLIC POLICIES FOR ENVIRONMENTAL PROTECTION, *supra* note 18, at 27, 79.

28. *See* James M. Buchanan & Gordon Tullock, *Polluters' Profits and Political Response: Direct Controls Versus Taxes*, 65 AM. ECON. REV. 139, 139–47 (1975).

29. *See* FREDERICK ANDERSON ET AL., ENVIRONMENTAL IMPROVEMENT THROUGH ECONOMIC INCENTIVES 155–57 (1977).

30. *See id.* at 155.

31. *See supra* text accompanying notes 8–13.

32. *See* BAUMOL & OATES, *supra* note 9, at 45.

33. Because the damages from waste emissions may depend on the precise location at which they are discharged into the environment, the effluent fee (or tax) would, in principle, need to be adjusted by location to reflect the differentials in damages. *See id.* at 169.

time of day. This would suggest that an ideal set of fees would vary not only spatially but temporally with environmental conditions.

Moreover, to determine the source's tax bill requires reasonably accurate measurements of emissions, since the tax liability is equal to the fee multiplied by the quantity of waste discharges. This can be difficult and expensive in some cases. It is true that certain forms of command-and-control regulatory practices also require regular monitoring of emissions, but some do not. A regulation. for example, that requires the use of a particular abatement technique, like a scrubber, may involve only a periodic check to see that the relevant equipment is functioning properly. I will not belabor the point further, but there are many matters, some quite challenging, to be addressed in the design of a *real* system of effluent charges. And (as we have seen in the drafts of some actual bills) if these matters are not dealt with properly, it is easy to emasculate a fee system by blunting the very incentives that embody its rationale.

In sum, these formidable issues of the actual design and implementation of incentive-based policy instruments received little attention. There simply were not many economists working on such matters. There was not yet an established field of "environmental and natural resource economics" with course offerings in graduate programs leading to a specialization in the field. Likewise, there was not an organized community of environmental economists working in concert on economic incentives for environmental management; the Association for Environmental and Resource Economics, now a large and energetic organization with close to a thousand members, was not founded until 1979.

Instead, there was only a small group of dedicated and able economists working on these issues. A few of them were beginning to address the tough issues of policy design and implementation. Allen Kneese and Blair Bower at Resources for the Future, for example, published a path-breaking study of the economics of water quality management that explored the relevant scientific dimensions of the problem, looked at real institutions, and then treated the design of systems of fees for the control of water pollution.[34] But such work was not widespread. The second part to my answer, then, is that although economists could offer a general approach to environmental policy, they were not yet ready to come to grips very effectively with the actual design and implementation of systems of effluent charges.

The third part to my answer is, in a way, related to the second. It concerns the general lack of understanding outside the economics profession itself of the economic approach to environmental management. To the economist, the logic of this approach seems straightforward and compelling. But to the uninitiated, it is much less clear. Most members of the policy-making community in the early years of the major environ-

---

34. *See* KNEESE & BOWER, *supra* note 8.

mental legislation simply did not understand the logic or the potential of incentive-based policy approaches.[35] In fact, even a decade later, Steven Kelman published the very sobering results of a study in Washington of the environmental policy-making community in which he was able to find virtually no one who could express a clear understanding of the basic rationale for incentive-based policy measures.[36] There was, in short, little understanding or appreciation of the economic approach; there was a great need for educational efforts and not many environmental economists around to take up the task.

With such hindsight, it is not so difficult to see why early environmental legislative efforts ignored economics. There was little in the way of experience, detailed policy design, or general understanding in the policy-making community to marshal.

III. THE CHOICE OF POLICY INSTRUMENTS

How did we get from this nearly total disregard of the economics of environmental management to the recently created markets in emissions rights? And what role has the community of environmental economists and its research played in all this? To address these two questions, it is useful (if not strictly legitimate at rigorous levels of analysis) to separate the problem of environmental regulation into two elements: (1) the setting of standards (or targets) for environmental quality; and (2) the design and implementation of a set of regulatory rules to attain these standards.[37] This distinction does, in fact, correspond in many instances to the way in which the policy process is structured. Under the 1970 Clean Air Act, for example, the EPA was directed, first, to establish a set of standards for ambient air quality and, second, to institute a regulatory system to attain these standards.[38] As I will suggest, the extent of the appeal and the degree of support for the economic approach has differed somewhat between these two parts of the environmental policy problem.

I turn first to the latter issue, the choice of policy instruments. This is in itself a fascinating story with some surprising twists. To this point, my discussion of the economic approach to environmental management has run exclusively in terms of price instruments: effluent fees or taxes for the regulation of waste discharges. In fact, there has been only very modest use of such price instruments in the United States for environmental purposes.[39] In contrast to Europe where "green taxes" have re-

---

35. *See* KELMAN, *supra* note 19, at 32.

36. *See id.* at 96.

37. The two are clearly interrelated in certain ways. The choice of a policy instrument will, for example, influence the costs of pollution control, which in turn will have some effect on the level of environmental quality for which marginal benefits equal marginal control costs.

38. *See* Portney, *supra* note 27, at 31.

39. For a survey of the ways in which various taxes at the federal, state, and local levels in the United States affect the environment, see Wallace E. Oates, *Environment and Taxation: The Case of*

ceived much bigger play,[40] the tax approach simply has not enjoyed much appeal or success in this country. Interestingly, environmental policy-makers in the United States have turned to an alternative market-based instrument: tradable emissions permits.[41]

How did this happen? Environmental economists were certainly not unaware of this alternative to effluent fees. But my recollection is that they focused most of their attention, in discussions with policymakers at least, on the fee instrument. During the 1960s, a political scientist at the University of Toronto, J.H. Dales, published a slim volume advocating a market approach to environmental management making use of a "quantity" rather than a "price" instrument.[42] Dales's proposal was to establish explicit property rights in environmental assets and make these rights marketable.[43] It is quite straightforward to show that with full information, the desired level of environmental quality can be achieved at the least cost *either* by setting the appropriate price on waste emissions (the correct effluent fee) or by determining the quantity directly through the issuance of the requisite number of permits and allowing trading activity to establish the market-clearing price. The outcome is, in principle, identical under both approaches.[44]

My first reaction to the appearance of Dales's book was one of skepticism. I had found myself subjected to harsh criticism in various forums for proposing a pricing approach to environmental regulation. As I mentioned earlier, some critics regarded the whole idea as basically immoral. And here comes Dales pushing the point yet harder — he was advocating that we effectively put the environment up for sale! But I was proved wrong.

On reflection, I believe that my mistake in underestimating the potential of the tradable permit approach was the result of two quite different things: one, a largely fortuitous event following the 1970 Clean Air Act Amendments; and the other, my failure to appreciate fully the "political economy" of quantity instruments. Under the 1970 Clean Air Act Amendments, the EPA established a set of standards for ambient air quality consisting of maximum allowable concentrations in the atmosphere for a group of "criteria" air pollutants.[45] The EPA then directed

the United States, in ENVIRONMENT AND TAXATION: THE CASES OF THE NETHERLANDS, SWEDEN, AND THE UNITED STATES 103, 113–20 (Organisation for Econ. Co-Operation & Dev. ed., 1994).

40.   *See generally* ORGANISATION FOR ECON. CO-OPERATION & DEV., ENVIRONMENTAL TAXES IN OECD COUNTRIES (1995). For a description and assessment of the limited use of environmental taxes in the United States, see Oates, *supra* note 39, at 107.

41.   *See* Maureen L. Cropper & Wallace E. Oates, *Environmental Economics: A Survey*, 30 J. ECON. LITERATURE 675, 687 (1992).

42.   *See* J.H. DALES, POLLUTION, PROPERTY, AND PRICES 107–08 (1968).

43.   *See id.*

44.   *See* BAUMOL & OATES, *supra* note 9, at 58. However, as Martin Weitzman showed in his seminal paper, the outcomes under the price and quantity approaches can be quite different in a setting of imperfect information. *See* Martin L. Weitzman, *Price vs. Quantities*, 41 REV. ECON. STUD. 477, 477–78 (1974).

45.   *See* THOMAS H. TIETENBERG, EMISSIONS TRADING: AN EXERCISE IN REFORMING

the states to attain these standards by 1975.[46] Each state was to design a state implementation plan that would provide for the attainment of the prescribed air quality standards on schedule.[47] As the decade progressed, however, it became increasingly evident that many cities would be unable to meet the standards for all the criteria air pollutants by the mandated deadline.[48] An unpleasant confrontation loomed on the horizon, for the prospective penalty for "nonattainment areas" was severe— a ban on new sources of emissions or significant expansion of existing sources,[49] implying a virtual cessation of economic growth.

Congress and the EPA avoided this confrontation by introducing an innovative provision into the 1977 Amendments to the Clean Air Act, a provision creating a system of "emission offsets."[50] Under the offset provision, new sources could enter a nonattainment area under two conditions: (1) that the new source adopt the most effective abatement technology available;[51] and (2) that existing sources reduce emissions sufficiently such that a net improvement in air quality would result (that is, the increment to aggregate emissions from new sources would be more than offset by reduced emissions from existing polluters).[52] This provision effectively authorized the transfer of emissions entitlements from one source to another. And there were a number of highly publicized transactions under which such transfers of entitlements took place across the country.[53] The new legislation had effectively (and, I suspect, somewhat unwittingly) laid the foundation for what would become a more extended system of tradable emissions rights. New elements were later added to the system leading to the emissions trading program[54] that includes bubbles[55] and, in some areas, a provision allowing polluters to "bank" credits from emissions reductions for future use. Interestingly, the legislation and the EPA set out only a general rubric for the program; it was left to the states to define in more detail and to implement individ-

---

POLLUTION POLICY 2 (1985). For a listing of these pollutants and the specific standards applied to each of them, see Portney, *supra* note 27, at 34.

46. *See* RICHARD A. LIROFF, REFORMING AIR POLLUTION REGULATION: THE TOIL AND TROUBLE OF EPA'S BUBBLE 21 (1986).

47. *See* 42 U.S.C. § 7410 (1994); *see also* TIETENBERG, *supra* note 45, at 3 (recommending specific improvements to the emissions trading program).

48. *See* TIETENBERG, *supra* note 45, at 5.

49. *See id.*

50. *See* LIROFF, *supra* note 46, at 25; TIETENBERG, *supra* note 45, at 7.

51. *See* LIROFF, *supra* note 46, at 25.

52. *See id.*

53. *See id.* at 37–38.

54. The term "emissions trading program" came to describe a collection of measures including "offsets," "bubbles," "banking," and "netting" that introduced greater flexibility in meeting emissions standards. *See* TIETENBERG, *supra* note 45, at 7–11 (providing a detailed treatment of each of these emissions trading program measures).

55. The EPA's bubble policy allows polluters to substitute reductions at one site (or plant) for required reductions at another site (or plant) as though the entire operation were under a huge plastic bubble, and only emissions emerging from the bubble counted.

ual measures for their own jurisdictions.[56] And many states have done just this.[57] But, somewhat serendipitously, it was a prospective confrontation over nonattainment that gave birth to this new policy instrument.

Once in place, it became clear that the quantity instrument had some very important advantages in a policy setting over the fee systems proposed earlier. From the perspective of the regulator, a system of tradable permits offers more direct control over the levels of emissions. The setting of fees, in contrast, places the regulating agency in the less comfortable position of influencing the aggregate level of emissions only indirectly through price. If the fee is set too low, the resulting emissions will be excessive, and the mandated level of environmental quality will not be achieved. In a policy setting in which the regulator must ensure that specified levels of pollutant concentrations are not exceeded (as under the Clean Air Act[58] in the United States), a preference for control of quantity over control of price is easily understandable. Much of the appeal, it seems to me, of the new tradable permit program for sulfur emissions is the direct path it offers to cutting national emissions by fifty percent simply by limiting the available emissions allowances to the requisite quantity.

Closely related to this point are the complications that result from economic growth and price inflation. Under a system of effluent fees, continuing inflation will erode the real value of the fee; similarly, expanding production from existing and new firms will increase levels of waste emissions if fee levels are held constant. Both these forces will require the fee to be raised periodically if environmental standards are to be maintained. In short, the burden of initiating action under a fee system is on environmental officials; the choice will be between unpopular increases in fees or nonattainment of standards. Under a system of tradable permits, market forces automatically accommodate inflation and economic growth with no increase in pollution. The rise in the demand for emissions translates directly into a higher market price for permits.[59]

Finally, regulators likely found the permit instrument a somewhat more familiar and comfortable one. The introduction of a fee system involves a wholly new form of environmental management with uncertain consequences from the perspective of the administering agency. Permits already exist. It would seem a much less radical move to make permits transferable than to supplant permits altogether with a new form of price regulation. For all these various reasons, the quantity approach had more appeal to the community of regulators than the use of a fee system.

---

56. *See* LIROFF, *supra* note 46, at 27.
57. *See id.*
58. 42 U.S.C. § 7409(a)(1)(A) (1994).
59. *See* BAUMOL & OATES, *supra* note 9, at 181–89 (offering an analytical treatment of systems of transferable emissions permits).

The tradable permit approach likewise offers some compelling advantages to polluters. As I mentioned earlier, the business community is never happy with a new form of taxation of firms.[60] A system of tradable permits will, like fees, impose new costs on polluters if the permits are issued through an auction.[61] But this need not be the case. Instead of auctioning off the permits, the environmental authority can set the system in motion with an initial distribution of permits to sources. Trading can then proceed from this initial allocation. This is, in fact, the way in which such systems have typically operated in the United States. Permits have been distributed to existing sources through some sort of grandfathering procedure based on historical levels of emissions.[62] In this way, *existing* sources are not subjected to new taxes or the costs of purchasing permits in an auction. On the contrary, they are the recipients of a new and valuable asset: a permit that entitles them to a certain level of waste discharges used either to validate their own emissions or sold for a profit to another source. Not surprisingly, such a system has much more appeal to the sources of pollution than does a system of effluent charges.

It is thus clear in retrospect that systems of tradable permits were immune to some of the more formidable opposition that confronted the introduction of fee systems that I described earlier. However, I frankly doubt if such systems would ever have made it off the drawing board without the initial opening the offset provision in the 1977 Amendments to the Clean Air Act provided.[63] The potentially divisive political confrontation over nonattainment gave rise to a seemingly modest compromise that has engendered a much expanded application of tradable permit systems. The experience with offsets demonstrated that an apparently new and esoteric approach to environmental management was both promising and feasible.[64]

In contrast, as Robert Hahn describes in his excellent survey of the experience with incentive-based instruments for environmental protection, European regulators have never really latched on to the tradable permit instrument.[65] Although Europeans have expressed some interest in the study of the U.S. experience,[66] policymakers in Europe seem to regard it as something of a curiosity. Where they have chosen to depart from command-and-control techniques, European regulators have opted instead for green taxes, to some extent, I think, because of their appreciation of the revenue potential of such measures.

---

60. *See supra* notes 25–28 and accompanying text.

61. *See* BAUMOL & OATES, *supra* note 9, at 178.

62. *See* TIETENBERG, *supra* note 45, at 113.

63. *See* Air Quality Standards, Interpretative Ruling, 41 Fed. Reg. 55,524, 55,525 (1976) (codified at 40 C.F.R. pt. 51).

64. *See* TIETENBERG, *supra* note 45, at 188–89.

65. *See* Robert W. Hahn, *Economic Prescriptions for Environmental Problems: How the Patient Followed the Doctor's Orders*, J. ECON. PERSP., Spring 1989, at 104–06.

66. *See, e.g.,* GERT T. SVENDSEN, PUBLIC CHOICE AND ENVIRONMENTAL REGULATION: TRADABLE PERMIT SYSTEMS IN THE UNITED STATES AND CO$_2$ TAXATION IN EUROPE (1998).

But this surely is not the whole story. Over the 1970s and 1980s, the community of environmental economists grew. Fields of specialization in "environmental and natural resource economics" appeared in numerous graduate programs around the country. Students completed dissertations in the field and moved into positions in government agencies as well as in academia. Their numbers supplemented those of various existing economists who shifted their research efforts to environmental issues. As Paul Portney has suggested to me, perhaps at least as important was the growing role of economists in schools of law and of public policy. This was a time when training in economics was becoming an important part of the basic education of students in American law schools and in public policy programs. In this forum, many future policymakers received direct exposure to the economic approach to environmental decisionmaking.

The emerging body of new research was of some importance. At a theoretical level, it both clarified the properties of various incentive-based policy instruments and provided some new insights. The seminal paper by Martin Weitzman,[67] for example, provided a new way of thinking about the choice between price and quantity instruments in a setting of uncertainty, and this insight is now widely appreciated in the policy-making community.[68] Equally important was a growing list of empirical studies that quantified the potential cost savings from using market-based instruments instead of the current command-and-control regulatory techniques; these studies suggested that the potential savings were enormous.[69] Although the methodology used in these studies likely resulted in some exaggeration of the extent of these savings,[70] studies provided an important empirical base to support regulatory reform in environmental policy.

All this study coincided with what John Kay has described as a new "faith in market forces."[71] The coming of reaganomics and of Mrs. Thatcher signaled a basic change in the intellectual setting for social and economic policy, one characterized by a shift "from concern with the failure of markets to concern about the failure of regulation."[72] There has developed a new interest in the use of market incentives for solving social problems.[73] From this perspective, the adoption of new incentive-based techniques for environmental regulation can be seen as part of a

---

67. *See* Weitzman, *supra* note 44.

68. For an explication and brief discussion of the Weitzman theorem, see BAUMOL & OATES, *supra* note 9, at 57–78, and Cropper & Oates, *supra* note 41, at 682–83.

69. For a useful survey of the early studies making such cost comparisons, see TIETENBERG, *supra* note 45, at 56–58.

70. *See* Wallace E. Oates et al., *The Net Benefits of Incentive-Based Regulation: A Case Study of Environmental Standard Setting*, 79 AM. ECON. REV. 1233, 1237 (1989).

71. John Kay, *Faith in Market Forces, in* TAX POLICY IN THE TWENTY-FIRST CENTURY 203, 203–20 (Herbert Stein ed., 1988).

72. *Id.* at 207.

73. *See generally, e.g.,* ANDREI SHLEIFER & ROBERT W. VISHNY, THE GRABBING HAND: GOVERNMENT PATHOLOGIES AND THEIR CURES (1998).

larger movement for fundamental changes in our approach to regulatory policies. I will develop this particular point further in the next section, for it is important to recognize this new receptivity to market-based approaches to regulation.

In the summer of 1992, I attended a large conference on the environmental aspects of energy policy. The conference, with perhaps a hundred participants, brought together a diverse group: politicians; federal, state, and local regulators; representatives of major environmental groups; and heads of private energy companies. The conference began with two keynote speeches. In the first, a U.S. senator made an impassioned and well-informed plea for a reorientation of U.S. environmental policies to place a heavier reliance on green taxes; in the second, the head of a major environmental group, the Environmental Defense Fund, made a strong and sophisticated case for the use of a system of tradable emission permits on an international scale to contain global warming. These speeches were followed by three days of continuous sessions. In these sessions, I heard time and again the various arguments in support of a shift to incentive-based policy instruments to replace existing regulatory structures. There was not a single instance of dissent. What a contrast to discussions twenty years earlier!

On the other hand, when we turned to the matter of setting environmental standards, things became much more contentious. The economic approach to determining targets for environmental quality, making use of benefit-cost analysis, was (and is) much less widely accepted. And this is not surprising.

IV. THE SETTING OF STANDARDS FOR ENVIRONMENTAL QUALITY

As already noted, the major early legislation eschewed any balancing of benefits and costs in the determination of environmental standards.[74] Under the Clean Air Act, for example, ambient standards for the amount of air pollutants are to be set such that they protect the health of the most sensitive persons in the population without regard to cost.[75]

Cost considerations surely entered the calculus, at least in a de facto way, when it came to setting source-specific standards for emissions. But a major milestone in formally introducing benefit-cost analyses was Executive Order 12,291, introduced under the Reagan administration in 1981.[76] This order required that benefit-cost analyses be carried out for

---

74. *See supra* text accompanying notes 13–18.
75. *See supra* notes 14, 16 and accompanying text.
76. *See* Exec. Order No. 12,291, 46 Fed. Reg. 13,193 (1981) (superseded by Exec. Order No. 12,866, 58 Fed. Reg. 51,735 (1993)); *see also* Richard A. Liroff, *Federal Experience: Cost-Benefit Analysis in Federal Environmental Programs*, in COST-BENEFIT ANALYSIS AND ENVIRONMENTAL REGULATIONS 35, 35 (Daniel Swartzman et al. eds., 1982); Richard D. Morgenstern, *The Legal and Institutional Setting for Economic Analysis at EPA*, in ECONOMIC ANALYSIS AT EPA: ASSESSING REGULATORY IMPACT 5, 10 (Richard D. Morgenstern ed., 1997).

all major regulations (defined as those having annual costs in excess of $100 million).[77] In addition, the order specified that, to the extent permitted by law, regulations be undertaken only if the benefits exceeded the costs.[78]

Executive Order 12,291 thus called for benefit-cost analyses of all major environmental regulations.[79] As we have seen, however, the extent to which such analyses can be considered in setting environmental standards is limited by the enabling statutes.[80] Of the major environmental statutes, only two, the Toxic Substances Control Act[81] and the Federal Insecticide, Fungicide, and Rodenticide Act,[82] explicitly require that benefits and costs be weighed in the setting of standards.[83] Some standards—specifically those pertaining to new sources under the Clean Air Act and to the setting of effluent limitations under the Clean Water Act—allow costs to be taken into account but do not suggest that benefits and costs be equalized at the margin.[84] In contrast, the National Ambient Air Quality Standards and regulations for the disposal of hazardous waste under the Resource Conservation and Recovery Act[85] and the Comprehensive Environmental Response, Compensation, and Liability Act[86]—more commonly known as Superfund—are to be determined without regard to compliance costs.[87]

In spite of these limitations, the EPA has been undertaking benefit-cost analyses of environmental regulation since the Carter administration.[88] But the EPA was permitted to weigh benefits against costs in the actual setting of standards for only five of the eighteen major regulations it issued between 1981 and 1986.[89]

The resistance to the use of benefit-cost analysis for the setting of environmental standards is understandable. There is, first of all, a matter of principle here. The approach assumes that the value of environmental

---

77. *See* Liroff, *supra* note 76, at 38–39.

78. *See id.* at 39. During the 1970s, Presidents Nixon, Ford, and Carter all issued executive orders calling for limited economic analyses of regulatory measures. *See* Morgenstern, *supra* note 76, at 10. But President Reagan's order went further and received far more attention than its predecessors. *See* Liroff, *supra* note 76, at 38.

79. For a more detailed description of the use of benefit-cost analyses for environmental programs, see OFFICE OF POLICY ANALYSIS, EPA, EPA'S USE OF BENEFIT-COST ANALYSIS: 1981–1986 (1987), and Cropper & Oates, *supra* note 41, at 722–28.

80. *See supra* notes 14–17 and accompanying text; *see also* Morgenstern, *supra* note 76, at 6–12 (describing EPA administrator implementation of major laws and minor statutes).

81. 15 U.S.C. §§ 2601–2629 (1994).

82. 7 U.S.C. §§ 136–1364 (1994).

83. *See* Morgenstern, *supra* note 76, at 8.

84. *See* Cropper & Oates, *supra* note 41, at 723.

85. 42 U.S.C. §§ 6901–6992 (1994).

86. *Id.* §§ 9601–9675.

87. *See* Cropper & Oates, *supra* note 41, at 723.

88. *See* Richard D. Morgenstern, *Conducting an Economic Analysis: Rationale, Issues, and Requirements, in* ECONOMIC ANALYSIS AT EPA: ASSESSING REGULATORY IMPACT, *supra* note 76, at 25, 25.

89. *See* Cropper & Oates, *supra* note 41, at 723.

improvements is equal to what people are willing to pay for such improvements.[90] Environmental values are thus treated by economists like the value of goods and services provided in the marketplace. This is simply unacceptable in certain quarters on philosophical grounds; some would argue that animal species, for example, have a value in their own right apart from any value that humanity places upon them.

But even aside from matters of principle, there are formidable problems of implementation inherent in the benefit-cost technique. Benefits and costs necessarily must be measured in monetary terms. This is no easy matter. The benefits of programs that reduce air pollution, for example, are largely in the form of improved health and extended longevity. Determining the monetary magnitude of such benefits presents real challenges.[91] Responding to these challenges, environmental economists (and others) have developed an imaginative array of analytical techniques for estimating such benefits. People, for example, reveal what they are willing to pay for cleaner air (all other things being equal) in the premiums they pay for houses located in areas with relatively low levels of air pollution.[92] In a similar vein, we can observe the value that people place on reduced risk in terms of the premiums that must be paid to people in dangerous occupations or the expenditures they make for safer vehicles.[93] Economists have, in fact, developed a whole range of techniques that exploit the links between observed market behavior and the implicit valuation of environmental amenities.[94] And these can be used to place monetary values on the expected improvements from proposed programs (or, for that matter, to value programs ex post as Congress has required the EPA to do in the case of the Clean Air Act[95]).

What has proven even more difficult is the recognition that there exist benefits and costs of environmental programs (or events like oil spills) that extend beyond the directly affected population.[96] People may well be willing to pay substantial amounts to protect natural systems like the Grand Canyon, even though they have no intention of ever going there. Such nonuse values cannot be registered in the marketplace (or inferred from any related market behavior). Here again, economists (and others, including psychologists) have developed a variety of survey techniques to ascertain what people are willing to pay for the preservation of

---

90. *See* A. MYRICK FREEMAN III, THE MEASUREMENT OF ENVIRONMENTAL AND RESOURCE VALUES: THEORY AND METHODS 8 (1993).
91. *See id.* at 27–33.
92. *See id.* at 368–69.
93. *See id.* at 421–23.
94. For a discussion and assessment of these techniques, see Cropper & Oates, *supra* note 41, at 93. The basic source for a comprehensive and rigorous treatment of the methods for valuation of environmental amenities is FREEMAN, *supra* note 90, at 430–38.
95. *See* OFFICE OF AIR & RADIATION, EPA, PUB. NO. 410-R-97-002, FINAL REPORT TO CONGRESS ON BENEFITS AND COSTS OF THE CLEAN AIR ACT, 1970 TO 1990, at 1 (1997).
96. *See* FREEMAN, *supra* note 90, at 141–64.

such things as natural environments or endangered species.[97] The general approach, known as the contingent valuation method, entails asking people to value specific environmental changes.[98] Whether or not the responses to such questions can be regarded as valid measures of real willingness to pay is still a hotly debated issue,[99] but researchers have made great progress in learning how to elicit more reliable responses in such surveys.[100]

Although we have made great strides in the improvement of benefit-cost analyses, there remain solid reasons for rejecting a benefit-cost test as the *sole* criterion for the enactment of environmental programs. Aside from philosophical objections, there are fundamental conceptual issues (such as the choice of an appropriate rate of discount) and ranges of imprecision in measurement that render any benefit-cost calculation a very rough approximation at best.[101] In addition, we may have real concerns about the distribution of the benefits and costs among various segments of the population. Were we to rely solely on a benefit-cost test, we would be required to accept only programs for which our best estimates of aggregate willingness to pay (that is, willingness to pay summed over all individuals) exceeded our estimates of costs. This, I (and many economists[102] — let alone others) believe is too rigid and narrow a criterion for making environmental decisions.[103]

Nonetheless, benefit-cost analyses are extremely valuable. Where we find, for example, that the prospective costs of a program significantly outweigh the estimated benefits, it should give us serious pause and suggest that we look again with care at the proposed program. Often times, such analyses can focus our attention on the crucial element in the calculation. In the analysis of recent programs for further reductions of ground-level ozone concentrations, for example, a positive "bottom line" is found to be heavily dependent upon the estimated impact of the pro-

---

97. *See id.* at 165–98.

98. *See id.* at 169–76; *see also* THE CONTINGENT VALUATION OF ENVIRONMENTAL RESOURCES (David J. Bjornstad & James R. Kahn eds., 1996) (collecting papers on the contingent valuation method).

99. *See, e.g.,* Peter A. Diamond & Jerry A. Hausman, *Contingent Valuation: Is Some Number Better than No Number?,* J. ECON. PERSP., Fall 1994, at 45.

100. *See* NOAA Natural Resource Damage Assessments Under the Oil Pollution Act of 1990, 15 C.F.R. ch. IX (1993).

101. *See, e.g.,* Alan Randall, *Taking Benefits and Costs Seriously, in* THE INTERNATIONAL YEARBOOK OF ENVIRONMENTAL AND RESOURCE ECONOMICS 1999/2000, at 250 (Henk Folmer & Tom Tietenberg eds., 1999).

102. *See, e.g.,* Lester B. Lave, *Benefit-Cost Analysis: Do the Benefits Exceed the Costs, in* RISKS, COSTS, AND LIVES SAVED 104 (Robert W. Hahn ed., 1996).

103. It is interesting in this regard that President Clinton superceded President Reagan's famous Executive Order 12,291 that required that "the potential benefits outweigh the costs" for new regulations. *See* Exec. Order No. 12,866, 58 Fed. Reg. 51,735 (1993). With his Executive Order 12,866 in September 1993, Clinton replaced the Reagan condition with the stipulation that there exist "a reasoned determination that the benefits of the intended regulation justify its costs." *Id.; see also* Morgenstern, *supra* note 76, at 10–11.

gram on mortality rates.[104] And there is much scientific uncertainty here.[105] This result focuses our attention on the importance of determining the impact of ground-level ozone concentrations on longevity.

Benefit-cost analyses can thus serve the important purpose of raising a red flag where programs promise only modest gains relative to their expected cost or, alternatively, can provide valuable support for programs where large net gains to social welfare appear to exist. Such information is clearly very valuable in setting standards for environmental quality. In reflecting upon a set of careful reviews of economic analyses of environmental programs within the EPA, Richard Morgenstern, who directed the EPA Office of Policy Analysis for over a decade, concluded: "In all the cases examined, the economic analyses did, in fact, contribute to improving the rules: the value of such improvements likely dwarfs the one-time cost of conducting the analyses."[106]

The current setting, because of the differing requirements of various environmental programs for the setting of standards, is a confusing and sometimes inconsistent one. As Morgenstern wrote, "Various statutes forbid, inhibit, tolerate, allow, invite, or require the use of economic analysis in environmental decisionmaking."[107] Nevertheless, current sentiment represents a major and quite dramatic contrast to the state of affairs three decades ago, when the tendency was to prohibit (or at least play down) *any* role for economic analyses in environmental management.[108]

V. RESEARCH AND POLICY DESIGN

The striking evolution of environmental policymaking is fairly straightforward to document. A much harder matter is the assessment of the precise role that research in environmental economics has played in this evolution. The tale is certainly not a simple one in which environmental economists presented a superior policy alternative, persuaded policymakers to adopt the alternative, and then helped guide the process of design and implementation. Actual history suggests a much more complicated, even torturous, evolution involving political confrontations and some quite serendipitous events.

Nevertheless, it is clear that ideas with a compelling underlying rationale are important in the determination of public policy, even if the

---

104. *See* OFFICE OF AIR QUALITY PLANNING & STANDARDS, EPA, REGULATORY IMPACT ANALYSES FOR THE PARTICULATE MATTER AND OZONE NATIONAL AMBIENT AIR QUALITY STANDARDS AND PROPOSED REGIONAL HAZE RULE 12–43 (1997).

105. *See id.*

106. Richard D. Morgenstern & Marc K. Landy, *Economic Analysis: Benefits, Costs, Implications, in* ECONOMIC ANALYSES AT EPA: ASSESSING REGULATORY IMPACT, *supra* note 76, at 455, 456. Morgenstern's work also contains a valuable collection of case studies that examine the role of economic analyses in a wide range of EPA programs.

107. Morgenstern, *supra* note 76, at 20.

108. *See supra* notes 14–18 and accompanying text.

exact timing and course of events exhibit a less predictable course. Let me return to one important and fascinating example: systems of tradable emissions allowances. As I read it, the matter began with the earlier-discussed political confrontation in the 1970s that led to a compromise in the form of pollution offsets.[109] But once this mechanism was in place, an emerging body of theory and empirical work existed to give it some legitimacy and to suggest important ways in which the program could be extended and improved.[110] This led to a process of interaction between research and experience in the policy arena that over time produced the emissions trading program.[111]

It is interesting in this regard that although the enabling rubric for emissions trading was laid out by the federal government, it was the states (via their local governments) that actually designed and put in place the various emissions trading programs across the country.[112] The states were "laboratories for experiments" in a real sense, and we learned much from both the successes and shortcomings of these programs in the various states. When it came time to consider a national trading program for sulfur allowances, the experience with emissions trading proved invaluable. In fact, I seriously doubt that we could ever have enacted such a radical idea as a market for buying and selling sulfur allowances on a national scale without the historical precedent of emissions trading. Emissions trading, if nothing else, showed that systems of tradable emissions permits were feasible. They could, in fact, work.

Moreover, the experience with emissions trading taught us a number of important lessons that have vastly improved the system for trading sulfur allowances.[113] As a kind of add-on to the existing command-and-control system, emissions trading programs were often unclear as to just what was being traded and on what terms.[114] In consequence, trading typically involved a fairly complicated procedure among buyers, sellers, and regulating agents.[115] This resulted in high transaction costs that seriously impeded the trading process.[116] In contrast, in the design of the new sulfur allowance program, the commodity to be traded is clearly understood (that is, tons of sulfur emitted), and the trading rules are simple: a ton of emissions in one place trades directly for a ton of emissions in an-

---

109. *See supra* notes 50–59 and accompanying text.
110. *See* TIETENBERG, *supra* note 45, at 7–8.
111. *See id.* at 7.
112. *See* LIROFF, *supra* note 46, at 27.
113. Robert Hahn and Gordon Hester provide valuable treatments of some of the problems encountered with emissions trading—problems from which we learned much for the design of sulfur allowance trading. *See generally* Robert W. Hahn & Gordon Hester, *Marketable Permits: Lessons for Theory and Practice*, 16 ECOLOGY L.Q. 361 (1989); Robert W. Hahn & Gordon Hester, *Where Did All the Markets Go? An Analysis of EPA's Emissions Trading Program*, 6 YALE J. ON REG. 109 (1989) [hereinafter Hahn & Hester, *Where Did All the Markets Go?*].
114. *See* Hahn & Hester, *Where Did All the Markets Go?*, *supra* note 113, at 116, 140.
115. *See id.* at 140.
116. *See id.*

other location. This has led to the emergence of a highly active market in which there are few obstacles to trading.[117] In fact, sulfur allowance trading is now handled by well-established securities dealers in a highly routine way with quite small commission charges.[118]

The recognized success of allowance trading in realizing environmental targets in ways that greatly reduce costs is leading to consideration of its employment elsewhere. In the United States, for example, there are proposals in the works for the trading of other pollutants.[119] Even more dramatic and challenging are the proposals to address global climate change through an international system of trading of carbon allowances.[120]

My remarks in this concluding section have focused on the emergence of trading systems. Indeed, this is a fascinating story. But as I mentioned earlier, research in environmental economics has fed in important ways into other facets of environmental policymaking. The extensive work in developing techniques for estimating the benefits from environmental programs and their costs has greatly improved our capacity for systematic analyses of environmental programs.[121]

In sum, it is difficult to lay out neatly the ways in which economic research has influenced environmental policy. I can find no well-defined process of diffusion here, but there surely has been an important impact. Both the conceptual work involving properties of regulatory techniques and the associated empirical work measuring the relative magnitudes of policy impacts have influenced the process of policy determination. Such analyses are now a regular part of the assessment of new policy proposals.[122] This is an area in which economists can take some real satisfaction in the contribution that they have made in the policy arena.

---

117. For some valuable studies of the workings of the new sulfur allowance trading program, see Joskow et al., *supra* note 5; Richard Schmalensee et al., *An Interim Evaluation of Sulfur Dioxide Emissions Trading*, J. ECON. PERSP., Summer 1998, at 53; Robert N. Stavins, *What Can We Learn from the Grand Policy Experiment? Lessons from SO₂ Allowance Trading*, J. ECON. PERSP., Summer 1998, at 69.

118. *See* sources cited *supra* note 117.

119. For example, there are currently efforts to introduce a system of tradable nitrous-oxide allowances to address ozone problems in the northeastern states. *See* Final Rule: Finding of Significant Contribution and Rulemaking for Certain States in the Ozone Transport Assessment Group Region for Purposes of Reducing Regional Transport of Ozone, 40 C.F.R. pts. 51, 72, 75, 96 (1998).

120. *See generally* Wiener, *supra* note 7.

121. For a recent assessment of the capacities of benefit-cost analysis, see Robert W. Hahn, *Regulatory Reform: What Do the Government's Numbers Tell Us?, in* RISKS, COSTS, AND LIVES SAVED, *supra* note 102, at 208.

122. *See supra* note 79 and accompanying text.

[22]

ENVIRONMENTAL REGULATION IN THE 1990S: A RETROSPECTIVE ANALYSIS

Robert W. Hahn*
Sheila M. Olmstead**
Robert N. Stavins***

I. INTRODUCTION

This Article addresses the influence of economics on environmental and resource policy-making during the 1990s. We focus on the Clinton administration and highlight important trends and changes in the impacts of economic concepts such as efficiency, cost-effectiveness and distributional equity.[1] The continuing controversy over the appropriate role for economics in environmental policy design makes this a particularly good time to analyze environmental policy during the 1990s from an economic perspective.

We note that the role of efficiency as a criterion for assessing environmental and natural resource rules and regulations was very controver-

---

* Director, AEI-Brookings Joint Center for Regulatory Studies, and Resident Scholar, American Enterprise Institute.

** Assistant Professor of Environmental Economics, School of Forestry and Environmental Studies, Yale University.

*** Albert Pratt Professor of Business and Government, John F. Kennedy School of Government, Harvard University, and University Fellow of Resources for the Future. Helpful comments on a previous version of this Article were provided by: Arthur Fraas, George Frampton, Myrick Freeman, José Gómez-Ibáñez, Alan Krupnick, Randall Lutter, Albert McGartland, Richard Morgenstern, Paul Portney, Richard Schmalensee, Jason Shogren, and Murray Weidenbaum. Research assistance was provided by Simone Berkowitz, and financial support was provided by the Savitz Family Fund for Environment and Natural Resource Policy and the Ford Fund at Harvard University. The authors alone are responsible for any remaining errors. A longer, related paper by Sheila M. Cavanagh et al. includes comprehensive tables describing specific environmental and resource statutes and regulations. *See* SHEILA M. CAVANAGH (OLMSTEAD) ET AL. NATIONAL ENVIRONMENTAL POLICY DURING THE CLINTON YEARS (John F. Kennedy School of Government, Center for Business and Government, Regulatory Policy Program Working Paper RPP-2001-10, 2001). For surveys of environmental and resource policy in the 1980s, see PAUL R. PORTNEY, NATURAL RESOURCES AND THE ENVIRONMENT: THE REAGAN APPROACH (1984) and W. Kip Viscusi, *Health and Safety Regulation, in* AMERICAN ECONOMIC POLICY IN THE 1980s 453 (Martin Feldstein ed., 1994).

[1] We follow the standard definition of an "efficient" environmental policy as being one which involves a target—such as a fifty percent reduction in sulfur dioxide ("SO_2") emissions—that maximizes the difference between social benefits and social costs (i.e., a target level at which marginal benefits and marginal costs are equated). By "cost-effective" policies, we refer to those which take (possibly inefficient) targets as given by the political process, but achieve those targets with policy instruments—such as a tradeable permit system in the SO_2 case—that minimize aggregate costs. Assessments of the "distributional" implications of environmental policies include analyses of the distributions of costs and benefits.

sial in the Clinton administration, while efficiency emerged as a central goal of the regulatory reform movement in Congress. Cost-effectiveness was embraced by both the Administration and Congress in the 1990s as a criterion for adopting specific policy instruments. In addition, the decade witnessed an increasing role for equity concerns as a consideration in environmental policy-making.

The attention given to environmental and natural resource issues in the United States has grown over the past several decades, a period during which greater consideration has been given to economic analysis of laws and regulations intended to protect the environment or improve natural resource management. Although several of the major environmental statutes are ambivalent about the role of economic analysis, in some cases prescribing it, in others proscribing it, a series of Presidential executive orders has called for a larger role for economic analysis.

Administrations can have substantial influence over the application of economics to environmental policy through a variety of mechanisms. The conventional wisdom in the United States is that Democratic administrations are predisposed toward more active environmental regulation, and less inclined toward economic analysis of environmental policy than their Republican counterparts. The Clinton administration, for example, is widely perceived to have been predisposed to environmental quality and resource preservation, and less supportive of economic analysis of such issues, in comparison with its Republican predecessor and successor (the administrations of George H. W. Bush and George W. Bush, respectively).

In fact, environmental and natural resource policy in the 1990s was characterized by continuity and by change. Two important trends that began in the 1970s continued through the 1990s—environmental quality improved, and environmental targets were made more stringent. In some cases, these improvements can be linked directly to federal policies and regulations; in others, such linkage has yet to be established.[2]

Trends in emissions of Clean Air Act criteria air pollutants are described in Table 1 (see Appendix). Emissions of some of these pollutants decreased significantly during the decade.[3] Although a number of studies show continued improvements in water quality during the 1990s,[4] following

---

[2] In order to attribute environmental quality improvements to specific policies, we must compare actual emissions to what they would have been in the absence of policies.

[3] *See* U.S. EPA Pub. No. 454/R-00-002, National Air Pollutant Emission Trends 1900-1998 (2000) [hereinafter EPA, 1900-1998 Trends Report]; U.S. EPA Pub. No. 454/R-00-003, National Air Quality and Emission Trends Report, 1998 (2000). Real improvements in environmental quality would be measured by changes in exposure and resulting changes in human morbidity and mortality, ecosystem health, etc. Improvements in emissions are not, themselves, measures of environmental quality improvements, although they may be highly correlated with such improvements.

[4] *See* Tayler H. Bingham et al., A Benefits Assessment of Water Pollution Control Programs Since 1972 (U.S. EPA, revised draft report, 1998); Myrick A. Freeman, *Water Pollution Policy*, *in* Public Policies for Environmental Protection 169 (Paul R. Portney and Robert N. Stavins eds., 2000); Myrick A. Freeman, *Environmental Policy*

the pattern of thirty-year trends, improvements in water quality during the 1990s were both less dramatic and more difficult to measure than improvements in air quality.[5]

Emissions of many air and water pollutants declined dramatically from 1970 to 1990, when the "low-hanging fruit" among air and water quality problems were being addressed.[6] For example, air emissions of lead, which declined significantly due to the shift to unleaded gasoline (completed in 1987), saw little further improvement during the 1990s.[7] Pollutant emissions to water declined dramatically during the 1970s and 1980s due to expanded municipal sewage treatment, a shift that was largely completed before 1990.[8]

In addition to environmental quality, the stringency of environmental targets continued to increase during the 1990s. An important example was the Clinton administration's 1997 National Ambient Air Quality Standards ("NAAQS") for ambient ozone and particulate matter. The new NAAQS were far stricter than previous standards, carrying substantial potential benefits and costs.

Public policy affecting natural resource management during the Clinton years was heavily weighted toward environmental protection. The Administration proposed initiatives to reduce subsidies for private resource extraction on public lands, but Congress was not receptive. The Administration did, however, shift U.S. Forest Service ("USFS") priorities away from timber production to resource protection, placing some sixty million acres of federal forests off limits to road building. President Clinton also designated more than twenty new national monuments, thereby restricting the use of six million additional acres of federal lands.[9]

Our ability to offer sound judgments about the influence of Clinton-era policies on environmental quality improvements is restricted by two problems. First, the fact that quality improvements occurred contempora-

---

Since Earth Day I—What Have We Gained?, 16 J. ECON. PERSP., Winter 2002, at 125.

[5] Improvements in water quality have been achieved largely through point source regulation. James Boyd, The New Face of the Clean Water Act: A Critical Review of the EPA's Proposed TMDL Rules 4 (Resources for the Future, Discussion Paper 00-12, Mar. 2000). Non-point source pollution in the form of runoff from cities and agricultural areas may actually have increased during the 1990s. Freeman, *supra* note 4, at 137.

[6] Important exceptions are emissions of toxic substances to air and water. Unlike conventional pollutants, decreases in air and water toxics emissions during the 1990s were likely greater than decreases in previous decades. The Toxics Release Inventory ("TRI") data show a decrease in toxic discharges to air of forty percent, and a decrease in toxic discharges to surface water of sixty-seven percent, between 1990 and 1994. Environmental Defense, *Toxics Release Inventory Data Summary*, at http://www.scorecard.org/env-releases/us.tcl#data_summary (last visited Apr. 25, 2003) (on file with the Harvard Environmental Law Review).

[7] *See* EPA, 1900–1998 TRENDS REPORT, *supra* note 3.

[8] Boyd, *supra* note 5, at 3. The percentage of the U.S. population connected to wastewater treatment systems increased from forty-two percent to seventy-four percent between 1970 and 1985.

[9] Reed McManus, *Six Million Sweet Acres*, SIERRA, Sept.-Oct. 2001.

neously with the term of a particular administration or legislature is not proof that policies promulgated during this term actually caused those quality improvements. With the exception of reduced emissions of criteria air pollutants in the 1990s, we find no studies that establish such a causal relationship between 1990s policies and environmental quality changes.[10]

Second, a fundamental issue that would confront any assessment of policy initiatives associated with a particular administration is the choice of an appropriate basis of comparison for evaluating policy initiatives—a counterfactual. It might appear reasonable to contrast first-term Clinton administration initiatives with what might have been anticipated from a hypothetical second-term administration of George H. W. Bush. But what would be the appropriate counterfactual for the second Clinton term?

For these reasons, establishing a causal relationship between improvements in environmental quality or resource management and the policies of any particular administration or Congress is difficult, if not impossible, and is not attempted here. Instead, we apply economic criteria for policy assessment—principally efficiency, cost-effectiveness and distributional equity.

The combined trends of more stringent standards for air and water quality, and increased private land-use restrictions and protections for public lands, have brought both increased benefits and an increasing price tag. As a result, economic concepts like benefit-cost analysis and the selection of least-cost environmental and natural resource regulations have received more attention since the late 1980s than they did in the early years of U.S. federal environmental regulation.

We note in this Article that, rather than a simple split along party lines, politicians in the 1990s endorsed the use of the efficiency criterion where its results were likely to coincide with their own ideological agendas. For example, Congress during the 1990s supported improvements in the efficiency of pollution control standards, which would have lightened regulatory burdens on some industries, and did not support increased efficiency in natural resource management, where subsidy reduction would have hurt communities dependent on resource extraction in the conservative West. The Administration, likewise, promoted the reduction of natural resource extraction subsidies, but was unsupportive of benefit-cost analysis of pollution control regulations; both viewpoints were consistent with those of supporters in the environmental community. We analyze these issues in light of the increased focus on the distribution of benefits and costs of environmental and natural resource regulation.

---

[10] Based on EPA modeling of trends in emissions within and without the Clean Air Act, the observed decreases in emissions of criteria air pollutants between 1990 and 2000 can be attributed to the Clean Air Act and its amendments. Freeman, *supra* note 4, at 127–28.

Our analysis is primarily qualitative, although in cases in which quantitative economic analyses of environmental policies have been produced, we discuss those results. The analysis is not exhaustive, but we do our best to consider the most important and most prominent intersections of economics and environmental regulation over the decade.

In Part II, we highlight the ways in which the role of efficiency as a criterion for assessing environmental and natural resource rules and regulations was very controversial in the Clinton administration, while economic efficiency emerged as a central goal of the regulatory reform movement in Congress. In Part III, we examine how cost-effectiveness was embraced by both the Administration and Congress in the 1990s as a criterion for adopting specific policy instruments. In Part IV, we examine how and why the decade witnessed an increasing role for equity concerns as a consideration in environmental policy-making. In Part V, we conclude.

II. EFFICIENCY AS A CRITERION FOR ASSESSING RULES AND REGULATIONS

The primary economic criterion for the analysis of environmental and natural resource regulation is efficiency. An efficient policy enacts a level of pollution control or rate of resource extraction that maximizes the difference between social benefits and social costs.[11] Assessing the efficiency of policies requires benefit-cost analysis.

The Clinton administration established a framework for benefit-cost analysis of major regulations that was very similar to those of previous administrations, but the influence of economic thinking in analyzing environmental rules and regulations within EPA declined significantly during the 1990s. While economists in other parts of the Administration strongly pressed for efficiency in natural resource management, a negligible portion of their initiatives became policy. Congress did not support the Administration's proposals for efficiency in natural resource management, but did embrace efficiency as a criterion for environmental policy as part of its overarching regulatory reform agenda, and succeeded in making substantive, efficiency-related changes to a handful of existing environmental statutes.

---

[11] In a dynamic context, the efficient rate of resource extraction or pollution control maximizes the present value of net social benefits.

A. Role and Acceptance of the Efficiency Criterion in the Clinton Administration

1. Executive Order on Regulatory Impact Analysis

The Clinton administration, like its two immediate predecessors, is-sued an Executive Order ("EO") requiring benefit-cost analysis of all federal regulations with expected annual costs greater than $100 million.[12] Through-out the Reagan and Bush administrations, these Regulatory Impact Analyses ("RIAs") were required under Reagan EOs 12,291 and 12,498.[13] President George H. W. Bush created a Council on Competitiveness, chaired by Vice President Dan Quayle, which reviewed the impact on industry of selected regulations.

Shortly after taking office in 1993, Clinton abolished the Council on Competitiveness and revoked both of the Reagan orders, replacing them with EO 12,866, "Regulatory Planning and Review."[14] The Clinton EO was substantively and administratively similar to the Reagan orders. It was quali-tatively different in tone, however, signaling a less strict efficiency test. While the Reagan orders required that benefits *outweigh* costs, the Clinton order required only that benefits *justify* costs. The Clinton EO allowed that: (1) not all regulatory benefits and costs can be monetized; and (2) non-monetary consequences should be influential in regulatory analysis.[15]

The requirements for RIA, however, have not necessarily improved the efficiency of individual federal environmental rules. In the first fifteen years of the review process, under both Republican and Democratic ad-ministrations, about two-thirds of the federal government's approved en-vironmental quality regulations failed benefit-cost analyses using the gov-

---

[12] Exec. Order No. 12,866, 58 Fed. Reg. 51,735 (Sept. 30, 1993). The threshold is not indexed for inflation and has not been modified over time. Elsewhere in this Article, we refer to year 2000 dollars, unless we indicate otherwise.

[13] Exec. Order No. 12,291, 46 Fed. Reg. 13,193 (Feb. 17, 1981) required agencies to conduct a RIA for all proposed and final rules that were anticipated to have an effect on the national economy in excess of $100 million. EO 12,291 has been called the "foremost development in administrative law of the 1980s." *See* Richard D. Morgenstern, *The Legal and Institutional Setting for Economic Analysis at EPA, in* ECONOMIC ANALYSES AT EPA: ASSESSING REGULATORY IMPACT 5–23 (Richard D. Morgenstern ed., 1997). But, the Reagan EOs were not the first presidential effort at regulatory efficiency. Nixon required a "Quality of Life" review of selected regulations in 1971. Robert W. Hahn, *The Impact of Economics on Environmental Policy*, 39 J. ENVTL. ECON. & MGMT. 375, 385 (2000). Ford formalized this process in 1974 with Exec. Order 11,821, 39 Fed. Reg. 41,501 (November 29, 1974). Carter's EO 12,044 required analysis of proposed rules and centralized review by the Regulatory Analysis Review Group. Hahn, *supra*. The Administration of President George W. Bush has continued to enforce the RIA requirements of Clinton's EO 12,866 rather than issuing a new EO. *See* John D. Graham, *Presidential Review of Agency Rule-making by OIRA*, Memorandum for the President's Management Council (2001), available at www.whitehouse.gov/omb/inforeg/oira_review-process.html, (last visited Apr. 25, 2003) (on file with the Harvard Environmental Law Review).

[14] Exec. Order 12,866, *supra* note 12.

[15] W. Kip Viscusi, *Regulating the Regulators*, 63 U. CHI. L. REV. 1423, 1430 (1996).

ernment's own numbers.[16] A good example during the Clinton years is the 1997 NAAQS for ozone, for which EPA submitted a RIA that listed $2.0 to $11.2 billion in monetized benefits and $12.7 billion in costs through 2010, assuming full attainment.[17]

Regulatory impact analysis is required only for major rules,[18] a small fraction of all rules issued by EPA and other agencies. Rules that do not meet this threshold pass under the efficiency radar, as do EOs such as those Clinton used to designate twenty new national monuments comprising six million additional acres, restricting natural resource extraction and other commercial activities therein.

2. Diminished Role of Economic Analysis at EPA[19]

Given the increase in requirements for and attention to benefit-cost analysis by Congress during the 1990s, discussed below, EPA probably was required to do more applied economic analysis during the 1990s than at any other time in its thirty year history. Perhaps in response to this workload, the share of EPA employees with graduate degrees in Economics grew during the 1990s.[20] However, the influence of economists and the acceptance of economic analysis at EPA were almost certainly lowered during the Clinton years.[21]

The mixed record of political and administrative integration of economic analysis within EPA during the Clinton years reflects the ambiva-

---

[16] Hahn, *supra* note 13.

[17] U.S. Off. of Mgmt. & Budget, Report to Congress on the Costs and Benefits of Federal Regulations 55 (1998). In other cases, issuing agencies do not provide enough information to assess the benefits and costs of rules. During the Clinton Administration, a good example is the RIA for the U.S. Forest Service's Roadless Areas proposal, which discusses benefits and costs in general and qualitative terms but does not offer the information necessary to make a direct, quantitative comparison of costs and benefits. *See* U.S. Forest Service, Regulatory Impact Analysis for the Roadless Area Conservation Rule (2001).

[18] Exec. Order 12,866, *supra* note 12.

[19] We discuss at length the use and acceptance of economics at the EPA, since rules promulgated by EPA comprise a substantial majority of total costs and benefits of all federal environmental regulation. Fifty-four percent of total annual regulatory benefits and fifty percent of total annual regulatory costs identified by the Office of Management and the Budget ("OMB") in 1997 were attributed to environmental regulations. Susan Dudley and Angela Antonelli, *Shining a Bright Light on Regulators: Tracking the Costs and Benefits of Federal Regulation*, in The Heritage Foundation Backgrounder (1997); Off. of Mgmt. & Budget, *supra* note 17. Discussion of similar issues at the Departments of Energy, Agriculture, the Interior and other agencies is beyond the scope of this study.

[20] Between 1996 and 2000, the percentage of EPA employees with graduate degrees who held either masters or doctoral degrees in economics increased by fifteen percent, compared to a 7.7% overall increase in EPA employees with graduate degrees. Richard D. Morgenstern, *Decision making at EPA: Economics, Incentives and Efficiency*, Draft conference paper, "EPA at Thirty: Evaluating and Improving the Environmental Protection Agency," Duke University, 36–38 (2000).

[21] *See id.*

lence of the major environmental statutes with respect to the role of economic analysis.[22] EPA is not an economic agency. It has a mandate to protect human health and the environment through the Administration of the major statutes.[23] Many of those statutes constrain economic analysis, and the representation of economists within most EPA offices is relatively thin, particularly at the level of the Senior Executive Service.[24] However, there is a good deal of flexibility in the extent to which economic analysis influences EPA processes and decisions. As a result, the use and role of economic analysis at EPA has varied substantially from one administration to another.

a. Organizational Location of Core Economics Staff

During the Clinton administration, economics staff at the agency were marginalized. When Clinton took office in 1992, the core economics staff at EPA were located within the Office of Policy, Planning and Evaluation (OPPE), as they had been since before 1980. OPPE reviewed all draft regulations and provided the Administrator with an independent economic perspective, which could be quite different from program office analyses. Within weeks of the Clinton inauguration, however, this role was eliminated.

The substantive role of economic analysis in the development and review of EPA regulations was abandoned by EPA in 1995, when the program offices, rather than the Administrator, became the official recipients of these analyses.[25] In 1999, OPPE was eliminated, shifting the core economics staff to a new Office of Policy and Reinvention. The shifts in organizational location of the core economics staff at EPA are documented in Table 2.

Administrator Browner was openly dismissive of economics as an appropriate framework for environmental decisions. In her remarks in honor of the thirtieth anniversary of the first Earth Day, she commented on the establishment of EPA, and recalled that "the nation committed itself to the task of eliminating pollution, to restoring our lands and waters to their uses, and to protecting public health without regard to cost. Let me repeat

---

[22] U.S. environmental laws alternately "forbid, inhibit, tolerate, allow, invite, or require the use of economic analysis in environmental decision making." *Id.* at 20.

[23] The term "major environmental statutes" in this Article refers to the following federal laws (and all amendments thereto): the Clean Air Act ("CAA"); Federal Water Pollution Control Act (Clean Water Act, "CWA"); Toxic Substances Control Act ("TSCA"); Federal Insecticide, Fungicide and Rodenticide Act ("FIFRA"); Comprehensive Environmental Response, Compensation and Liability Act ("CERCLA"); Resource Conservation and Recovery Act ("RCRA"); and Safe Drinking Water Act ("SDWA").

[24] *See* Morgenstern, *supra* note 13, at 16. Of the 193 EPA Senior Executive Service members with graduate degrees in 1996, only four (two percent) held graduate Economics degrees; in contrast, almost one-third held law degrees, and one-fifth held graduate science degrees. Despite their minority status relative to lawyers, scientists and engineers, EPA probably employs more economists working on environmental issues than any other single institution. *Id.* at 14.

[25] Morgenstern, *supra* note 20, at 39.

those last four words—without regard to cost."[26] The Administrator referred to the introduction of benefit-cost analysis into EPA regulations intended to protect public health as "poison[ing] the well."[27] The reduction in acceptance of economic analysis at EPA was likely influenced by Vice President Al Gore, who was known to be skeptical about the application of benefit-cost analysis to environmental policy.[28]

b. Role of the Environmental Economics Advisory Committee

Despite the reduced role of economists within EPA, policy advising by government economists outside of EPA occurred throughout the 1990s. Deputy Administrator Fred Hansen worked closely with the Environmental Economics Advisory Committee ("EEAC") within EPA's Science Advisory Board to develop an aggressive mission statement for EEAC that focused on giving expert advice on broad issues of importance to the Agency, rather than simply carrying out end-of-pipe reviews of agency RIAs.[29] During the 1990s, the EEAC conducted the first comprehensive review and revision in fifteen years of EPA's Economic Analysis Guidelines.[30] They also thoroughly reviewed EPA's methodology for valuing reductions in cancer-induced mortality.[31] External economists also served on the Advisory Council on Clean Air Act Compliance, required under the 1990 CAA Amendments to provide technical and economic input on EPA's benefit-cost analyses of CAA impacts.[32] The Council had a major impact on the identification of key research issues and the treatment of uncertainty in these analyses.[33]

---

[26] Carol M. Browner, Speech marking the 30th anniversary of Earth Day, John F. Kennedy School of Government, Harvard University (Apr. 17, 2000) (transcript available at http://www.epa.gov/history/topics/epa/30a.htm) (last visited Apr. 25, 2003) (on file with Harvard Environmental Law Review).

[27] *Id.* Although she referred to benefit-cost analysis, what Administrator Browner described was more like a strict benefit-cost test that would disallow rules unless quantified benefits outweighed costs.

[28] *See generally* AL GORE, EARTH IN THE BALANCE: ECOLOGY AND THE HUMAN SPIRIT (1992).

[29] The EEAC was established by the Science Advisory Board in 1990.

[30] *See* U.S. EPA, GUIDELINES FOR PREPARING ECONOMIC ANALYSES, 240-R-00-003 (Sept. 2000); SCIENCE ADVISORY BOARD, U.S. EPA, AN SAB REPORT ON THE EPA GUIDELINES FOR PREPARING ECONOMIC ANALYSES, EPA-SAB-EEAC-99-020 (Sept. 1999).

[31] SCIENCE ADVISORY BOARD, U.S. EPA, AN SAB REPORT ON EPA'S WHITE PAPER "VALUING THE BENEFITS OF FATAL CANCER RISK REDUCTION," EPA-SAB-EEAC-00-013 (July 2000).

[32] 42 U.S.C. § 7612 (2000).

[33] *See* Morgenstern, *supra* note 20.

3. Role of Other Executive Branch Economists in Natural Resource Policy

Having noted the diminished role of economics at EPA during the Clinton years, it is also important to recognize economists external to EPA. In particular within the Council of Economic Advisors ("CEA"), OMB, and the Treasury Department, economists did have some influence over the Administration's policy proposals regarding efficiency in natural resource management.[34]

The most important artifact of the White House economic agencies' influence in emphasizing efficiency in environmental and natural resource policy is the Clinton administration's 1993 economic stimulus and deficit reduction proposal.[35] The Administration proposed a variety of policies related to natural resource subsidy reduction. First, it proposed increasing the baseline federal grazing fee on public lands by almost 200%. The baseline federal grazing fee had been calculated at only fifty-six to eighty-three percent of federal costs per animal unit month in 1990 and was a much smaller percentage (perhaps eighteen to forty percent) of private market rates.[36] In theory, below-market fees for grazing livestock on public lands cause (economic) over-grazing. In practice, low fees have been criticized from a budgetary perspective, since current fees do not cover the costs of federal public range management.[37]

Similarly, below-cost timber sales from federal lands theoretically lead to logging at faster-than-efficient rates, and where revenues do not cover costs, they also contribute to budget deficits. The Administration's 1993 budget proposal sought to phase out below-cost timber sales. By USFS estimates, 77 of the 120 national forests showed net losses from timber sales over the period FY 1989-FY 1993, and sixty reported losses in every year over this period.[38]

---

[34] *See* Jonathan Orszag et al., *The Process of Economic Policy-Making During the Clinton Administration, in* AMERICAN ECONOMIC POLICY IN THE 1990s 983, 994 (Jeffrey A. Frankel & Peter R. Orszag eds., 2002).

[35] Richard L. Berke, *Clinton Backs Off From Policy Shift on Federal Lands*, N.Y. TIMES, Mar. 31, 1993, at A1; *Last Round Up for the Old West*, ECONOMIST, Mar. 6, 1993, at 23.

[36] Betsy A. Cody, *Grazing Fees: An Overview* (Congressional Research Service Report for Congress 96–450 ENR, 1996), *available at* http://www.ncseonline.org/NLE/ CRSreports/ Agriculture/ag-5.cfm (on file with the Harvard Environmental Law Review).

[37] *Id.* The baseline grazing fee for federal lands in 1990 was $1.81 per animal unit month (AUM), while the various livestock grazing programs' cost to government ranged from $2.18 to $3.24 per AUM. The fair market value of grazing on federal land was last updated in 1986 and ranged from $4.68 to $10.26 per AUM for cattle and horses, varying by region. (These figures have not been converted to constant dollars.) The Administration continued to lobby for fee increases, and the 104th Congress established a new fee formula that resulted in a small increase in the baseline fee, still many times lower than the average private market rate.

[38] *See* Ross W. Gorte, Below-Cost Timber Sales: Overview (Congressional Research Service Report for Congress 95-15 ENR, 1994).

Neither subsidy reduction proposal—the grazing fee increase nor the below-cost timber sales phase-out—became law, however. The grazing fee proposal led to a Senate filibuster on FY 1994 Interior Appropriations during the 103d Congress, and was taken up again in the 104th Congress, resulting in a negligible price increase, leaving rates still many times lower than the average private market rate. The plan to reduce below-cost timber sales was eliminated from Clinton's final budget proposal, and a USFS draft plan to phase out below-cost sales on one-half of forest service lands over four years was not adopted by the Administration.[39]

The Administration's attempt to reduce natural resource subsidies in the 1993 budget proposal also included introduction of royalties for hardrock mining on public lands governed under the 1872 General Mining Law,[40] increased fees for recreational use of federal public lands, and a British Thermal Unit ("BTU") tax, which would have taxed essentially all fuels. The BTU tax proposal faced stiff opposition in the first session of the 103d Congress, narrowly passing the House of Representatives. Recognizing that the proposal did not have enough votes in the Senate, the Administration removed the BTU tax from its budget proposal.[41]

During the 1990s, economists at the U.S. Department of Commerce ("DOC") began work on the issue of "green accounting." Incorporating natural resource depletion and other non-market activity within the National Income and Product Accounts ("NIPA") has been a longstanding recommendation of economists.[42] In 1993 the Clinton administration ordered the Bureau of Economic Analysis ("BEA") at the DOC to begin working on this process.[43] The BEA produced the first official U.S. Integrated Environmental and Economic Satellite Accounts in 1994, accounting only for selected subsoil minerals. Shortly afterward, Congress suspended BEA's work on environmental accounting, pending external review by a blue-ribbon panel convened by the National Research Council's Committee on National Statistics. Though the panel's review, released in 1999, strongly supported BEA's efforts and endorsed further efforts to

---

[39] *Id.*

[40] 30 U.S.C §§ 22–54 (2000).

[41] The Senate later passed a much more modest Transportation Fuels Tax in 1993, with revenues flowing to the General Fund. This was a retail tax on commercial gasoline sales of less than five cents per gallon. The BTU tax would have been imposed on coal, natural gas, liquid petroleum gases, nuclear electricity, hydroelectricity, and all imported electricity ($0.0257/million BTU); a higher tax ($0.0599/million BTU) would have been imposed on refined petroleum products. *See* FEDERAL BUDGET ISSUE: DO WE NEED AN ENERGY TAX?, National Center for Policy Analysis Policy Backgrounder No. 127 (June 4, 1993).

[42] *See, e.g.,* ARTHUR C. PIGOU, THE ECONOMICS OF WELFARE (1920); Martin L. Weitzman, *On the Welfare Significance of National Product in a Dynamic Economy,* 90 Q. J. ECON. 156 (1976); Robert Solow, "An Almost Practical Step Toward Sustainability," Invited Lecture on the Occasion of the Fortieth Anniversary of Resources for the Future (October 1992); NATURE'S NUMBERS: EXPANDING THE NATIONAL ECONOMIC ACCOUNTS TO INCLUDE THE ENVIRONMENT (William D. Nordhaus & Edward C. Kokkelenberg eds., 1999).

[43] Nordhaus & Kokkelenberg, *supra* note 42, at 154.

extend the NIPA,[44] Congress did not fund additional work on green accounting.

B. Role and Acceptance of the Efficiency Criterion in Congress

While Congress was unsupportive of efficiency as a criterion for natural resource management, benefit-cost analysis of environmental regulation emerged as a major goal of Congressional regulatory reform efforts of the 1990s. We examine general and specific regulatory reform proposals considered by the 103d through 106th Congresses, as well as changes to individual environmental statutes.[45]

1. Cross-cutting Regulatory Reform Proposals

The 103d Congress (1993–1995), the Clinton administration's first legislative "partner," actively debated benefit-cost analysis and risk analysis as methods for informing environmental protection decisions.[46] Three of the lightning rods for regulatory relief interests were "takings" issues or private property rights, unfunded mandates, and risk analysis. With Democratic majorities in both houses, none of the Republican minority's initiatives were enacted into law during the 103d Congress, or even offered for Presidential signature.

The regulatory reform movement gained momentum when members of the 104th Congress (1995–1997) took their seats after the 1994 midterm election, in which Republicans gained control of both the Senate and the House of Representatives. Reform-oriented bills in 1995-1996 included mandates for benefit-cost analysis, maximum likelihood risk assessments (rather than upper bounds), and regulatory process reforms.[47]

a. General Regulatory Reform: The Contract with America

Most of the 104th Congress' general regulatory reform proposals either failed to pass both Houses or were vetoed by President Clinton. Item 8 of the 1994 Contract with America, the "Job Creation and Wage

---

[44] *Id.* at 155.

[45] A comprehensive summary of successful and unsuccessful regulatory reform initiatives of the Congresses of the 1990s that would have influenced the application of efficiency, risk analysis, or cost-effectiveness criteria to environmental regulation is found in Table 2 of SHEILA M. CAVANAGH (OLMSTEAD) ET AL., NATIONAL ENVIRONMENTAL POLICY DURING THE CLINTON YEARS (Regulatory Policy Program Working Paper RPP-2001-10, Center for Business and Government, John F. Kennedy School of Government, 2001).

[46] *See* John E. Blodgett, Environmental Policy and the Economy: Conflicts and Concordances (Congressional Research Service Report for Congress 95-147 ENR, 1995), *available at* http://www.ncseonline.org/NLE/CRS.../econ-1.cfm; Martin R. Lee, Environmental Protection: From the 103rd to the 104th Congress (Congressional Research Service Report for Congress 95-58 ENR, 1995).

[47] *See* Viscusi, *supra* note 15.

Enhancement Act of 1995,"[48] did not reach the President's desk. It would have made Reagan's EO 12,291 statutory, superseding the Clinton EO—as well as the language in several other important statutes—and would have required that the benefits of regulations outweigh their costs.[49] Although this component of the Contract with America did not become law, it did lead to a prominent public debate over regulatory reform, in which benefit-cost analysis was a central issue.

b. Specific Regulatory Reform Proposals

The Small Business Regulatory Enforcement Fairness Act[50] ("SBREFA") amended the 1980 Regulatory Flexibility Act. As one of the affected agencies, EPA must prepare a regulatory flexibility analysis of all rules with "significant economic impact" on a "substantial number" of small entities (businesses, non-profits, and small government organizations).[51] Embedded within SBREFA, but for the most part unrelated to its other provisions, was the Congressional Review Act (CRA),[52] which established a process of Congressional review and possible rejection of agency rules on efficiency grounds.[53]

In late 1996, in another attempt to emphasize efficiency in regulation, the 104th Congress attached a benefit-cost requirement to Section 645(a) of the Treasury, Postal Services and General Government Appropriations Act of 1997.[54] To meet this requirement, the OMB is required to

---

[48] H.R. 9, 104th Cong. (1995).

[49] Item 8 also focused on the reduction of so-called "unfunded mandates," and on strengthening the Regulatory Flexibility Act of 1980, 5 U.S.C. §§ 601–612 (2000), resulting in the Small Business Regulatory Enforcement Fairness Act of 1996 (SBREFA), 5 U.S.C. §§ 801–808 (2000) and the Unfunded Mandates Reform Act of 1995, 2 U.S.C. §§ 658, 1501–1571 (2000). There were many other unsuccessful attempts at regulatory reform legislation during the 104th Congress, including: "Risk Assessment and Cost-Benefit Act of 1995," H.R. 1022, 104th Cong. (1995); H.R.J. Res. 27 & 54, 104th Cong. (1995), proposing a Constitutional amendment to ban unfunded mandates; "Regulatory Relief and Reform Act," H.R. 47, 104th Cong. (1995); and H.R. 122, 104th Cong. (1995) to establish a Regulatory Sunset Commission. Detailed discussion of these is beyond the scope of this study. We mention them only to emphasize the scope and depth of the 104th Congress' focus on regulatory reform.

[50] 5 U.S.C. §§ 801–808.

[51] *Id.* These analyses, which are reviewed by Congress, examine the type and number of small entities potentially subject to the rule, record-keeping and compliance requirements, and significant regulatory alternatives. The statute does not require formal benefit-cost analysis beyond that already required by environmental regulations and EO; rather, it requires that EPA submit to Congress "a complete copy of the benefit-cost analysis of the rule, if any," along with the regulatory flexibility analysis. *Id.* From an economic efficiency perspective, the focus on small entities makes little, if any sense.

[52] *Id.* at §§ 801–802.

[53] The CRA was the basis for the George W. Bush Administration's overturning of the Occupational Safety and Health Administration's ergonomics rule in March 2001. Pub. L. 107-5, 115 Stat. 7 (2001). The CRA has not been used to overturn any environmental regulations.

[54] Pub. L. No. 104-208, 110 Stat. 3009 (1997). This provision was typically referred to

390   *Harvard Environmental Law Review*   [Vol. 27

submit to Congress a report estimating the "total annual costs and benefits of federal regulatory programs, including quantitative and non-quantitative measures."[55] The legislation also requires OMB to estimate individually the benefits and costs of rules with annual costs to the economy of $100 million or more. Importantly, OMB also is required to recommend the reform or elimination of any regulation that appears to be inefficient. Under this requirement, reports were submitted yearly, 1997 through 2000.[56] The requirement has further centralized regulatory oversight in the hands of OMB, which already had been charged with reviewing the RIAs required by EOs since 1981.

Congressional regulatory reform efforts continued through the end of the Clinton administration. The 105th and 106th Congresses considered establishing further checks on agency regulation. The Regulatory Improvement Act of 1999 (also known as the Thompson-Levin bill) would have allowed courts to remand or invalidate rules formulated by an agency that fails to perform sufficient benefit-cost analyses.[57] While this bill never became law, the 106th Congress did pass a major piece of regulatory reform legislation, the Truth in Regulating Act ("TIRA")[58], which was signed into law by President Clinton in October 2000. The TIRA established a three-year pilot project beginning in early 2001, which required the Government Accounting Office ("GAO") to review RIAs to evaluate agencies' benefit estimates, cost estimates, and analysis of alternative approaches, upon request by Congress. Because funding was never provided, TIRA was not implemented. If TIRA had been implemented, it likely would have increased the importance of economic analysis in regulatory decision making.

2. Successful Changes to Individual Statutes

In addition to these attempts at cross-cutting regulatory reform, the Congresses of the Clinton years pursued efficiency within environmental statutes themselves.[59] In general, Congress was more successful during

---

as "regulatory accounting."

[55] *See* U.S. OMB, *supra* note 17.

[56] The continuation of this provision was proposed by the Regulatory Right-to-Know Act of 1999, S. 59, 106th Cong. (1999). Introduced as H.R. 1074, 106th Cong. (1999) in the House, the bill would have required much more stringent analysis by OMB: an annual accounting statement of total costs and benefits of federal regulations, including direct and indirect impacts on federal, state, local and tribal government; the private sector; small business; wages; and economic growth.

[57] The Regulatory Improvement Act was first proposed as S. 981, 105th Cong. (1997) in 1997 and continued with the same title into 1998. It was introduced in various versions in both Houses of Congress throughout 1997–1999, and took on the Thompson-Levin moniker in May 1999.

[58] Pub. L. No. 106-312, 114 Stat. 1248 (2000).

[59] During the 1990s, Congress also pursued reforms of non-environmental statutes that affected environmental regulation. For example, the Accountable Pipeline Safety and Part-

the 1990s at passing cross-cutting regulatory reform bills than it was at reforming individual environmental statutes, although important exceptions were the 1996 SDWA amendments[60] and the partial reform of pesticide permitting under the Federal Food, Drug and Cosmetic Act ("FFDCA").

a. SDWA Amendments of 1996

The 1996 SDWA amendments[61] include the most far-reaching requirement for benefit-cost analysis in any environmental statute. The amendments focus EPA regulatory efforts on contaminants that pose the greatest health risks by: (1) requiring benefit-cost analysis of new rules; (2) removing the mandate that EPA regulate twenty-five new contaminants every three years; (3) allowing EPA to use cost information to adjust its "feasibility standards" for water system reduction of contaminants; and (4) requiring the Administrator to balance risks among contaminants to minimize the overall risk of adverse health effects.[62] While the Amendments require EPA to determine whether the benefits of each new drinking water maximum contaminant level ("MCL") regulation justify the costs, they also allow the Agency to adopt more stringent standards than those that maximize net benefits, explaining the reasons for not selecting the efficient standard.[63]

b. Food Quality Protection Act of 1996

The Food Quality Protection Act of 1996 ("FQPA")[64] amends both FIFRA[65] and FFDCA,[66] removing pesticide residues on processed food from the group of Delaney "zero-risk standard" substances. The Delaney standard has long been a target of economic criticism on the grounds that it specifies an often unachievable regulatory standard for the benefits of regulation, and hence leads to associated costs that may greatly exceed benefits. While the standard continues to apply to non-pesticide food ad-

nership Act of 1996, 49 U.S.C. § 60102(b)(5) (2000), requires the Secretary of Transportation to issue pipeline safety regulations only upon justification that benefits exceed costs. *See* John E. Blodgett, *Environmental Reauthorizations and Regulatory Reform: From the 104th Congress to the 105th* (Congressional Research Service Report for Congress 96-949 ENR, 1998), *available at* http://www.ncseonline.org/NLE/CRSreports/legislative/leg-22.cfm (last visited Apr. 25 2003).

[60] 42 U.S.C. § 300 (2000), *amended by* Pub. L. No. 104-182, 110 Stat. 1613 (1996).

[61] 110 Stat. 1613.

[62] Mary Tiemann, *Safe Drinking Water Act Amendments of 1996: Overview of P.L. 104-182* (Congressional Research Service Report for Congress 96-722, 1999), *available at* http://www.ncseonline.org/nle/CRSreports/water/h2o-17.cfm (last visited Apr. 25 2003).

[63] *See* 42 U.S.C. § 300g-1(a). The amendments do not allow standards published before the SDWA to be subjected to an *ex-post* benefit-cost analysis.

[64] Pub. L. No. 104-170, 110 Stat. 1489 (1996).

[65] 7 U.S.C. § 136 (2000).

[66] 21 U.S.C. §§ 301–397 (2000).

ditives, the FQPA eliminated the distinction between pesticide residues on raw foods (which had been regulated under FFDCA section 408[67]) and processed foods (which had been regulated under FFDCA section 409— the Delaney Clause).[68]

c. Failed Attempts at Changes to Individual Statutes

Two of the environmental statutes most frequently criticized on efficiency grounds—CERCLA (Superfund)[69] and the CWA[70]—remained relatively untouched by Congress in the 1990s, despite its focus on regulatory reform. Superfund's critics have focused on the low benefits and high costs of achieving the statute's standards.[71] Reauthorization and reform were considered during the 105th Congress, but no legislation was passed. Rather than efficiency, liability issues and questions of how to finance Superfund were the major foci of legislative discussions. The taxes that support the Superfund trust fund (primarily excise taxes on petroleum and specified chemical feedstocks and a corporate environmental income tax) expired in 1995 and have not been reinstated.[72]

The 104th Congress also pursued efficiency-oriented reform of the CWA through the reauthorization process, but the effort failed in the Senate. During the 104th Congress, the House passed a comprehensive CWA reauthorization[73] that would have been more flexible and less prescriptive than the current statute, but the Senate did not take up the bill.[74] No reauthorization legislation was considered in the 105th or 106th Congress.

---

[67] 21 U.S.C. § 346a (1994).

[68] *Id.* at § 348. The FQPA also mandates that EPA coordinate pesticide regulation under FIFRA and FFDCA. For example, once a pesticide registration is canceled under FIFRA, the food-use tolerance under FFDCA must be revoked within 180 days, rather than the average six year time frame noted in a 1994 GAO report. *See* Linda Jo Schierow, *Pesticide Legislation: Food Quality Protection Act of 1996* (Congressional Research Service Report for Congress 96-759 ENR, 1996), *available at* http://www.ncseonline.org/nle/crsreports/pesticides/pest-8.cfm; U.S. GEN. ACCOUNTING OFFICE, PESTICIDES: REDUCING EXPOSURE TO RESIDUES OF CANCELED PESTICIDES, GAO/RCED-95-23 (1994).

[69] 42 U.S.C. §§ 9601–9675 (2000).

[70] 33 U.S.C. §§ 1251–1387 (2000).

[71] *See, e.g.*, W. KIP VISCUSI, FATAL TRADEOFFS: PUBLIC AND PRIVATE RESPONSIBILITIES FOR RISK (1992); STEPHEN BREYER, BREAKING THE VICIOUS CIRCLE: TOWARD EFFECTIVE RISK REGULATION (1993); James T. Hamilton & Kip W. Viscusi, *How Costly is Clean?: An Analysis of the Benefits and Costs of Superfund Site Remediations*, 18 J. POL'Y ANAL. & MGMT. 2 (1999).

[72] The revenue now flowing into the trust fund comes from so-called "potentially responsible parties," interest on the fund's investments, fines, and penalties. Then-Chairman of the House Ways and Means Committee, Bill Archer (R-Tex.), made it known that no reinstatement of the Superfund taxes would be considered without major reform of the statute's liability provisions and other features. Mark Reisch, Superfund Reauthorization Issues in the 106th Congress (Congressional Research Service Issue Brief for Congress IB10011, 2000).

[73] H.R. 961, 104th Cong. (1995).

[74] The 103d Congress had considered similar legislation H.R. 3948, S. 2093, 103d Cong. (1994). However, no floor action on CWA reauthorization was taken in either house.

C. Limited Effect of Regulatory Reform Legislation and Changes to Statutes

The cross-cutting legislative regulatory reform measures passed in the 1990s and the efficiency-related changes to specific environmental statutes had limited effects on regulation during the decade. This is in part due to differences between the Administration and Congress in the acceptance of efficiency as an appropriate criterion for managing the environment and natural resources. An additional explanation is the existing statutory bias against benefit-cost analysis in some cases, particularly under the CAA. In such cases, substantial movement toward efficiency in regulation cannot be expected without substantial changes in the authorizing legislation.

The SDWA Amendments of 1996 incorporated a strong benefit-cost criterion, in comparison to other environmental statutes. However, the decisions made on MCLs since the SDWA Amendments have not placed great weight on the results of required benefit-cost analyses. Two major rules proposed since the 1996 Amendments were those regulating allowable levels of arsenic and radon in drinking water.[75] EPA's benefit-cost analyses for the radon and arsenic MCLs can be interpreted as indicating that monetized costs exceed monetized benefits for both rules (by more than $50 million annually for radon, and $30 million annually for arsenic). The Agency maintained, however, that benefits of both rules justify their costs when unquantified benefits are included.[76]

Importantly, the regulatory reform initiatives passed by Congress in the 1990s apparently did not influence EPA's issuance of NAAQS for ozone and particulate matter in July 1997. Due to their high potential compliance costs, the revised standards were immediately controversial; both the decision to tighten the standards and the quality of the research used

---

[75] The arsenic rule was finalized on January 22, 2001, but implementation was delayed while the rule was taken under review by the George W. Bush Administration, citing concerns about the rule's costs and benefits. After an expedited review by the National Academy of Sciences, in October, 2001, EPA Administrator Christine Whitman announced the Agency's intention to enforce the Clinton arsenic standard. *See* Press Release, EPA, EPA Announces Arsenic Standard For Drinking Water of 10 Parts Per Billion (Oct. 31, 2001) (on file with Harvard Environmental Law Review). No final action has been taken on radon.

[76] *See* U.S. EPA, PROPOSED ARSENIC IN DRINKING WATER RULE: REGULATORY IMPACT ANALYSIS (2000), U.S. EPA, HEALTH RISK REDUCTION AND COST ANALYSIS FOR RADON IN DRINKING WATER (2000). EPA's cost and benefit figures for these rules were presented as annualized 1999 dollar values using a seven percent discount rate. The AEI-Brookings Joint Center for Regulatory Analysis performed its own benefit-cost analysis of the arsenic rule, and concluded that in all likely scenarios the cost per life saved by the rule would never be less than $6.6 million, and that in its "most likely" scenario, cost per life saved was approximately $67 million. *See* Jason K. Burnett & Robert W. Hahn, EPA's Arsenic Rule: The Benefits of the Standard Do Not Justify the Costs (AEI-Brookings Joint Center for Regulatory Studies, Regulatory Analysis 01-02, Jan. 2001). For a critical review of the EPA analysis and Burnett & Hahn, see Cass Sunstein, *The Arithmetic of Arsenic*, 90 GEO. L.J. 2255 (2002).

to support the new standards came under fire. EPA's cost estimates for the ozone standard were singled out for criticism; some analysts found them to be too low by a considerable margin.[77] On the other hand, the particulate standard exhibited expected benefits that could well exceed costs by a considerable margin. Table 3 provides EPA's estimated benefits and costs for both standards.

The regulated community challenged the new NAAQS in court, and the case reached the U.S. Supreme Court in October, 2000.[78] Under the CAA, EPA is required to set health-based standards for specified pollutants without consideration of costs. In February 2001, the Supreme Court ruled unanimously that the CAA does not allow EPA to consider costs in setting NAAQS for the criteria air pollutants, and that the statute's mandate that the NAAQS protect the public health with "an adequate margin of safety" allows an acceptable scope of discretion to EPA.[79]

Given that the ozone standard's estimated costs appear to outweigh its benefits by a significant margin, EPA has been under considerable pressure to revise the standard, despite the Supreme Court's decision.[80] The situation is very different, of course, for particulate matter, for which estimated benefits appear to outweigh estimated costs. If the courts continue to uphold the standards and if the statutes preventing cost considerations remain unchanged, the stricter NAAQS for ozone and particulate matter may be one of the Clinton administration's most enduring environmental legacies, in terms of both potential benefits and potential costs.[81]

The differences in opinion between Congress and the executive branch (especially EPA) on the usefulness of efficiency analysis resulted

---

[77] *See* Jason F. Shogren, *A Political Economy in an Ecological Web*, 11 ENVTL. & RESOURCE ECON. 557; Randall Lutter, *Is EPA's Ozone Standard Feasible?*, (REGULATORY ANALYSIS 99-6, AEI-Brookings Joint Center for Regulatory Studies) (1999).

[78] *See* Whitman v. Am. Trucking Ass'ns, Inc., 531 U.S. 457 (2001). A group of forty economists filed a brief *amici curiae* in the Supreme Court, suggesting that benefit-cost analysis should be considered in the setting of ambient air quality standards. *See* AEI-Brookings Joint Center *et al.* Brief Amici Curiae in the Supreme Court of the United States, American Trucking Ass'ns v. Browner, 530 U.S. 1202 (2000) (No. 99-1426).

[79] *See Am. Trucking Ass'ns*, 531 U.S. at 457. The Supreme Court decision was greeted positively by EPA Administrator Whitman: " . . . Congress delegated to EPA the standard-setting function, and EPA carried it out appropriately." *See* Press Release, EPA, Supreme Court Upholds EPA Position on Smog, Particulate Rules (Feb. 27, 2001) (on file with Harvard Environmental Law Review). The Court acknowledged that EPA and the states could continue to take costs into account in implementing the standards, which may serve as an impetus for the adoption of cost-effective policy instruments.

[80] EPA has agreed to reconsider its analysis of ozone NAAQS benefits in at least one respect. The agency's initial analysis did not consider the possible damages associated with *decreases* in ground-level ozone, which leads to increases in some ultraviolet radiation ("UV-B") exposure. *See* Randall Lutter & Christopher Wolz, *UV-B Screening by Tropospheric Ozone: Implications for the National Ambient Air Quality Standard*, 31 ENVTL. SCI. & TECH. 142A (1997).

[81] It remains to be seen whether some urban areas will be able to comply with the new ozone standards. One analyst estimates the costs to Los Angeles of meeting the ozone standard in 2010 will be about $15 billion in constant 2000 dollars, assuming a five percent decrease in current abatement costs due to technological change. Lutter, *supra* note 77, at 7.

in an effective stalemate. Even where statutes were explicitly altered to require benefit-cost analysis, as was the case for the setting of MCLs under the SDWA, rules promulgated during the 1990s do not appear to be any more or less efficient than rules promulgated during earlier decades.

III. Cost-Effectiveness as a Criterion for Assessing Public Policies

Many or most environmental laws and regulations are not cost-effective, typically specifying technologies or uniform emissions limits, despite tremendous variation in abatement costs among sources.[82] While uniform standards may effectively limit emissions of pollutants, they typically exact relatively high costs in the process, by forcing some firms to resort to unduly expensive means of controlling pollution. For example, under current regulations, the marginal cost of abating lead emissions ranges from $13 per ton in the non-metal products sector to $56,000 per ton in the food sector.[83]

Market-based approaches to environmental protection can be used to achieve the least-cost allocation of pollution reduction, even if the aggregate target is not efficient. Thus, cost-effectiveness is a criterion quite separate and distinct from efficiency.[84] A cost-effective regulatory policy takes environmental quality or natural resource extraction targets as given by the political process, but achieves those targets at minimum aggregate cost. Since the 1970s, the advantages of market-based (or economic-incentive) approaches in reducing the costs of environmental regulation have received serious political attention, and there have been increasing numbers of applications in the United States and other countries.[85] Both the Clinton Administration and Congress embraced cost-effectiveness as a criterion for adopting environmental and natural resource policies during the 1990s.

A. Support for the Cost-Effectiveness Criterion Within the Clinton Administration

The Clinton administration's support for the use of a cost-effectiveness criterion in choosing environmental policies was demonstrated in a

[82] See Richard G. Newell & Robert N. Stavins (2003), Cost Heterogeneity and the Potential Savings from Market-Based Policies, 23 J. Reg. Econ. 43 (2003); T.H. Tietenberg, Economic Instruments for Environmental Regulation, 6 Oxford Rev. Econ. Pol'y 17 (1990).

[83] See Raymond S. Hartman et al., The Cost of Air Pollution Abatement (World Bank Policy Research Working Paper #1398, Dec. 1994); Morgenstern, supra note 20, at 17–18.

[84] William J. Baumol & Wallace E. Oates, The Use of Standards and Prices for Protection of the Environment, 73 Swed. J. Econ. 42 (1971).

[85] Robert N. Stavins, Experience with Market-Based Environmental Policy Instruments, in The Handbook of Environmental Economics (Karl-Göran Mäler & Jeffrey Vincent eds., forthcoming 2003).

The Political Economy of Environmental Regulation

variety of contexts. The Administration included selection of cost-effective regulatory alternatives within Clinton EO 12,866, requiring regulatory impact analysis. And in the same Earth Day speech that was so critical of benefit-cost analysis, EPA Administrator Browner highlighted EPA's cost-effective regulatory measures and flexible approaches to pollution reduction.[86] During the Clinton years, EPA continued to emphasize cost-effective approaches to pollution control, including the use of information disclosure and voluntary programs, and the Administration aggressively promoted international market-based policy instruments for greenhouse gas emissions control (specifically, emissions trading).

1. Reinventing EPA

Administrator Browner announced the creation of EPA's Office of Reinvention in 1997, although it is fair to say that reform efforts at EPA had been underway since the mid-1980s. Vice President Gore's National Performance Review Report and the Government Performance and Results Act of 1993[87] brought increased attention to such efforts at EPA, and the Agency launched the centerpiece of its "reinvention" program, the Common Sense Initiative ("CSI") in 1994.[88]

Although the CSI can be considered within the umbrella of policies intended to foster greater cost-effectiveness, it is unclear whether the CSI improved the cost-effectiveness of environmental regulation in the 1990s. The CSI engaged six major industries in dialogue with EPA with the purpose of reducing compliance costs, introducing flexibility by moving toward regulation by industry rather than by pollutant, and reducing costly litigation through stakeholder participation.[89] But in 1997, two GAO reports found that too many CSI resources had been spent on process, and too few on substance and results. In addition, progress had been limited by the lack of consensus among industry workgroups on the most important issues, and the effort lacked results-oriented measures to assess progress.[90]

---

[86] Browner, *supra* note 26.

[87] Pub. L 103-62, 107 Stat. 285 (1993).

[88] Other organizations and institutions may also have played a role in EPA's focus on reinvention. A 1995 National Academy of Public Administration report suggested reforms at EPA, including better use of risk and cost information to rank priorities. In 1996, the Center for Strategic and International Studies launched "Enterprise for the Environment," an effort to build consensus for systematic environmental management reform. And the regulatory reform focus of the 104th Congress may also have prompted EPA to attempt to carry out reform efforts, in part to forestall Congressionally mandated changes. *See* Claudia Copeland, *Reinventing the Environmental Protection Agency and EPA's Water Programs* (Congressional Research Service Report to Congress 96-283 ENR, Mar. 1996), *available at* http://www.nsceonline.org/NLE/CRSreports/water/h2o-20.cfm.

[89] The participating industries were auto manufacturing, computers and electronics, iron and steel, metal finishing, petroleum refining, and printing.

[90] *See* U.S. Gen. Accounting Office, GAO/RCED-97-155, Environmental Protection: Challenges Facing EPA's Efforts to Reinvent Environmental Regulation (1997); U.S. Gen. Accounting Office, GAO/RCED-97-164, Regulatory Reinven-

In 1995, Vice President Gore and Administrator Browner announced a set of twenty-five specific reinvention reforms at EPA, in addition to the CSI. One of these new programs was Project XL ("Excellence and Leadership"), which set a goal of fifty pilot projects allowing regulated firms to propose alternatives to existing command-and-control regulations that would attain higher levels of pollution control at lower cost.[91] The National Environmental Performance Partnership System sought to give states greater flexibility in achieving environmental goals by allowing them to convert some types of categorical federal grants into more flexible block grants.

In its assessment of EPA's reinvention program, GAO noted that EPA's efforts could have only limited success in introducing cost-effective changes, because significant progress would require reform of the legislative framework for environmental protection, rather than process reforms within EPA.[92]

2. *Information Disclosure and Voluntary Programs*

In addition to its reinvention efforts, EPA significantly increased use of information disclosure regulations during the 1990s. TRI was initiated in 1988 under the Emergency Planning and Community Right-to-Know Act Section 313[93] and requires firms to report on use, storage and release of hazardous chemicals. A 1993 Clinton EO required TRI reporting by federal facilities.[94] In 1994, EPA added 286 new chemicals to the list requiring TRI reporting, an eighty percent increase in the number of listed chemicals.[95] Further, EPA lowered reporting thresholds in 1999 for many persistent bioaccumulative toxic chemicals and added more of these chemicals to the TRI list.[96] The Clinton administration announced another expansion of TRI on January 17, 2001, considerably lowering the threshold for reporting lead emissions.[97]

TION: EPA's COMMON SENSE INITIATIVE NEEDS AN IMPROVED OPERATING FRAMEWORK AND PROGRESS MEASURES (1997).

[91] Lisa C. Lund, *Project XL: Good for the Environment, Good for Business, Good for Communities*, 30 Envtl. L. Rep. (Envtl. L. Inst.) 10,140 (2000).

[92] U.S. GAO, GAO/RCED-97-155, *supra* note 90.

[93] P.L. 99-499, Title III, § 313, 100 Stat. 1741 (1986) (codified as amended at 42 U.S.C. § 11023 (2000)).

[94] Exec. Order 12,856, 58 Fed. Reg. 41981 (August 6, 1993).

[95] Linda Jo Schierow, Toxics Release Inventory: Do Communities Have a Right to Know More?, (Congressional Research Service Report for Congress 97-970 ENR, 1997).

[96] The EPA under Clinton also continued the 33/50 program, started under the Bush Administration, which engaged TRI-reporting industries in achieving voluntary accelerated emissions reduction targets in exchange for public "certification."

[97] 40 C.F.R. § 372.28 (2000). The previous standard required reporting by facilities that manufacture or process more than 25,000 pounds of lead annually, or that use more than 10,000 pounds annually. The newer standard required reporting by any facility that manufactures, processes, or uses more than 100 pounds annually. The Bush Administration announced its intention to uphold the new threshold on April 17, 2001.

398   Harvard Environmental Law Review   [Vol. 27

Releases reported under TRI declined by forty-five percent from 1988 to 1998, but no analysis has yet been able to attribute that reduction to the policy itself. Limited evidence exists that publicly available information about firms' TRI emissions (either in absolute terms or relative to some benchmarks) negatively affects stock prices.[98] Other possible avenues through which the TRI may influence emissions are green consumerism, redirection of firms' attention toward measures that increase environmental performance while saving costs, and community pressure, but there is little solid evidence that any of these forces are at work.[99]

In addition to the TRI, EPA established new and expanded existing information programs during the 1990s. In 1997, EPA expanded the existing Energy Star Buildings program, consolidating it with the Green Lights program, both of which are information disclosure programs related to energy efficiency. In 1998, the Agency began requiring public water systems to issue annual Drinking Water Consumer Confidence Reports.[100] In 2000, it posted automobile "pollution rankings" on the EPA Web site, ranking vehicles based on hydrocarbon and NO_x tailpipe emissions. While these programs could, in theory, provide cost-effective ways of reaching environmental objectives, there is no solid evidence of their actual effects.

3. Cost-Effectiveness and Climate Change Policy

In October 1993, the Administration released its Climate Change Action Plan, which recommended fifty-two voluntary measures to meet greenhouse-gas emissions goals.[101] The nature of the initiatives in the plan is not unlike those that might have been expected from a second-term Bush administration, with their emphasis on voluntary programs, government-industry cooperation, cost-effectiveness, use of market incentives, and minimal mandatory government intervention.[102] But, even if not different

---

[98] See James T. Hamilton, *Pollution as News: Media and Stock Market Reactions to the Toxics Release Inventory Data*, 28 J. ENVTL. ECON. & MGMT. 98 (1995); Shameek Konar & Mark A. Cohen, *Information as Regulation: The Effect of Community Right to Know Laws on Toxic Emissions*, 32 J. ENVTL. ECON. & MGMT. 109 (1997); Madhu Khanna et al., *Toxics Release Information: A Policy Tool for Environmental Protection*, 36 J. ENVTL. ECON. & MGMT. 243 (1998).

[99] See Lori D. Snyder, Regulating Pollution Through Information Disclosure: Modeling Firm Response to the Toxics Release Inventory (Kennedy School of Government, Draft Working Paper, May 2001).

[100] U.S. EPA, Pub. No. 240/R-01-001, THE UNITED STATES EXPERIENCE WITH ECONOMIC INCENTIVES FOR PROTECTING THE ENVIRONMENT 161 (2001).

[101] Climate Change Action Policy, *available at* http://gcrio.gcrio.org/USCCAP/toc.html (Oct. 1993) (last visited Apr. 25, 2003) (on file with the Harvard Environmental Law Review).

[102] In 1993, the Administration also established the U.S. Initiative on Joint Implementation under the Climate Change Action Plan. Joint implementation arrangements allow firms or other entities in one country to meet part of their greenhouse gas reduction commitments by financing mitigation in another country. The U.S. Initiative through 1997 had approved twenty-two arrangements whereby U.S. firms agreed to finance projects in eleven

in substance, the Clinton administration's Climate Action Plan differed greatly in tone from what had been Bush administration policy. Whereas the Bush administration was moderate in its characterization of the climate change problem, the Clinton administration characterized the challenge in much more dramatic terms. Not surprisingly, this complex set of voluntary initiatives had relatively little effect. By 1995, the U.S. acknowledged that it would fall short of its goals by at least fifty percent.

A key component of the Clinton administration's climate change policy was its strong and unwavering support for cost-effective approaches, including market-based instruments, and in particular, tradeable permit mechanisms.[103] The Administration's formal proposal released in preparation for the Third Conference of the Parties of the Framework Convention on Climate Change, held in Kyoto, Japan in November 1997, called for domestic and international emissions trading.[104] In fact, it was largely because of the efforts of the U.S. negotiating team that the Kyoto Protocol included significant provisions for international emissions trading among industrialized nations, as well as what came to be known as the Clean Development Mechanism for offsets in developing countries.

Subsequently the United States proposed rules for international emissions trading in 1998, at preparatory talks for the Fourth Conference of the Parties. The U.S. proposal faced substantial opposition, most significantly from the European Union. No agreement was reached on emissions trading at the Fourth (1998), Fifth (1999), or Sixth (2000) Conferences of the Parties. Indeed, at the Sixth Conference of the Parties, which met in The Hague in November 2000, disagreements between the United States and the European Union over the role of carbon sequestration and emissions trading led to the ultimate breakdown of the talks.[105]

Economic considerations appear to have played a much more substantial role in the development of the Administration's international negotiating position on climate change than they did in the development of domestic regulatory policies with substantial economic costs, such as the NAAQS for ozone and particulate matter. Within the White House, weekly (and even more frequent) meetings on climate change leading up to the Kyoto conference were chaired by the National Economic Council ("NEC"),

---

other countries. WORLD BANK, ENVIRONMENTALLY SUSTAINABLE DEVELOPMENT STUDIES AND MONOGRAPHS SERIES NO. 18, FIVE YEARS AFTER RIO: INNOVATIONS IN ENVIRONMENTAL POLICY 40 (1997).

[103] The prior Bush Administration had taken a similar though less aggressive position. See, e.g., Richard B. Stewart & Jonathan B. Wiener, The Comprehensive Approach to Global Climate Policy: Issues of Design and Practicality, 9 ARIZ. J. INT'L. & COMP. L. 83 (1992).

[104] See Press Release, White House Office of the Press Secretary, President Clinton to Participate in White House Conference on Climate Change (Oct. 2, 1997) (on file with the Harvard Environmental Law Review).

[105] Andrew C. Revkin, Odd Culprits in Collapse of Climate Talks, N.Y. TIMES, Nov. 28, 2000, at F1.

the coordinating body for economic policy during the Clinton years.[106] In contrast, EPA was relatively disengaged on this issue.

The NEC was created by Clinton to coordinate the development and implementation of the Administration's major domestic and international economic policies. During the Clinton years, the Council of Economic Advisers ("CEA") continued to provide economic analysis, forecasting, and advice on the topics of regulatory reform and the environment, as well its traditional areas of expertise. The NEC acted for the White House as a coordinating filter and organizer of information from agencies engaging in economic policy throughout the administration, including the CEA.[107]

CEA testimony on this and many other occasions emphasized the enormous cost savings that could be achieved through emissions trading and through participation by developing countries, possibly contributing to the passage of Senate Resolution 98.[108] In addition, in its 1998 report on the costs of complying with the Kyoto Protocol, the CEA resisted pressure to adopt overly optimistic assumptions about technological change and energy efficiency advanced by the so-called "DOE Five Lab study" and by the Interagency Analytical Team study on the economic effects of global climate change policies.

B. Support for the Cost-Effectiveness Criterion from Congress

In 1995, the 104th Congress enacted the Unfunded Mandates Reform Act.[109] The main purpose of the Act was to require quantitative assessment of benefits, and comparison of benefits with costs for proposed and final rules with expected costs of $100 million or more to state, local, and tribal governments or to the private sector. The Act also mandated that agencies choose the least-cost regulatory alternative, or explain why they have not done so.[110]

C. Mixed Results on Cost-Effectiveness of Specific Policies

Integration of the cost-effectiveness criterion into environmental policy-making made more progress than the efficiency criterion in the 1990s.

---

[106] The major role of the economic agencies in developing U.S. climate change policy began at least as early as July 1997, when then-Chair of the CEA, Janet Yellen, testified before the House Commerce Committee, Subcommittee on Energy and Power. Statement Before the Senate Committee on Environment and Public Works (July 17, 1997), *available at* www.senate.gov/~epw/105th/yell7-17.htm (last visited Apr. 25, 2003) (on file with the Harvard Environmental Law Review).

[107] Orszag et al., *supra* note 34, at 995.

[108] S. Res. 98, 105th Cong. (1997). The "Byrd-Hagel resolution" stated that the United States should not approve any agreement at the Third Conference of the Parties in Kyoto, that did not impose binding emission reduction targets on major developing countries as well as industrialized nations.

[109] Pub. L. No. 104-4, 109 Stat. 48 (codified in scattered sections of 2 U.S.C.).

[110] 2 U.S.C. § 1535 (2000).

We consider implementation of the 1990 CAA Amendments during the decade as a case study.

1. Implementation of the 1990 CAA Amendments

While the judiciary in the 1990s upheld CAA provisions preventing EPA from taking costs into account when setting the NAAQS, the 1990 Amendments provided the basis for implementation of cost-effective regulation. Under Title IV of the amendments, Congress directed EPA not to mandate specific pollution control technologies for sulfur dioxide ("SO_2") emissions from power plants, but set up instead a permit trading system.[111] Not all regulations promulgated under the 1990 CAA Amendments were equally as cost-effective, however. The Amendments explicitly required EPA to issue technology standards for 188 toxic air pollutants, perhaps one of the most expensive and least cost-effective components of the statute.[112]

a. Market-Based Instruments in CAA Amendment Implementation

EPA provided averaging, banking, and trading opportunities for most of the new standards promulgated under the 1990 CAA Amendments, including those aimed at mobile sources. EPA's implementation of the reformulated gasoline provisions of Title II of the Amendments allowed refinery-level trading of oxygen, aromatics, and benzene content.[113] Title II also authorized EPA to regulate particulate matter, NO_x, and other emissions from heavy-duty trucks. The resulting regulations were promulgated at the vehicle engine-manufacturing level, and allow averaging, banking, and trading.[114] The Tier 2 emissions standards for cars and light-duty trucks, issued in February 2000, allow vehicle manufacturers to average NO_x emissions throughout their fleets to meet the new national tailpipe standards. They also allow refiners and gasoline importers to average, bank, and trade gasoline sulfur content to meet new Tier 2 standards.[115]

With respect to stationary sources, the regional NO_x cap-and-trade program in the Northeast is another significant market-based policy in-

---

[111] Paul R. Portney, *Air Pollution Policy*, in PUBLIC POLICIES FOR ENVIRONMENTAL PROTECTION 77, 89 (Paul R. Portney & Robert N. Stavins eds., 2000).

[112] Paul R. Portney, *Policy Watch: Economics and the Clean Air Act*, J. ECON. PERSP., Fall 1990, at 173, 178.

[113] U.S. EPA, *supra* note 100, at 88. The initial guidance for the reformulated gasoline trading programs was issued in October 1992, during the Bush Administration. Trading at the refinery level has been very active.

[114] *Id.* at 89. While a great deal of averaging and banking has taken place, only one trade was completed through 2000.

[115] *Id.* The average sulfur content cap drops annually between 2004 and 2006, and credits produced within that time frame have a limited life, while credits produced after the introduction of the strictest standard (2006) have unlimited life.

strument developed and implemented under the 1990 CAA Amendments. Although the SO_2 allowance trading program was created under the Bush administration, implementation of Phase I and Phase II occurred during the 1990s. These two programs are described below, as are two significant rulemakings that have been more heavily criticized from an economic perspective: the revised NAAQS for ozone and particulate matter; and new regulations on toxic air pollutants.

b. SO_2 Allowance Trading

The tradeable permit system that regulates SO_2 emissions, the primary precursor of acid rain, was established under Title IV of the CAA Amendments of 1990. The statute is intended to reduce SO_2 and NO_x emissions from 1980 levels by ten million tons and two million tons, respectively.[116] The first phase of SO_2 emissions reductions was started in 1995, with a second phase of reduction initiated in the year 2000.[117]

A robust market of bilateral SO_2 permit trading emerged in the 1990s, resulting in cost savings on the order of $1 billion annually, compared with the costs under some command-and-control regulatory alternatives.[118] Although the program had low levels of trading in its early years,[119] trading levels increased significantly over time.[120]

c. Regional NO_x Budget Program

Under EPA guidance, twelve northeastern states and the District of Columbia implemented a regional NO_x cap-and-trade system in 1999 to reduce compliance costs associated with the Ozone Transport Commission ("OTC") regulations of the 1990 CAA Amendments.[121] Required reductions

---

[116] *See* Brian L. Ferrall, *The Clean Air Act Amendments of 1990 and the Use of Market Forces to Control Sulfur Dioxide Emissions*, 28 HARV. J. ON LEGIS. 235, 241 (1991).

[117] In Phase I, individual emissions limits were assigned to 110 plants, located largely at coal-fired power plants east of the Mississippi River. Under Phase II of the program, beginning January 1, 2000, all electric power generating units greater than 25 MW burning fossil fuels were brought within the system. Dallas Burtraw, *The SO₂ Emissions Trading Program: Cost Savings Without Allowance Trades*, 14 CONTEMP. ECON. POL'Y, at 79, 82 (1996).

[118] Curtis Carlson et al., *Sulfur Dioxide Control by Electric Utilities: What Are the Gains from Trade?*, 108 J. POL. ECON. 1292 (2000).

[119] *See* Burtraw, *supra* note 117, at 82.

[120] *See* R. Schmalensee et al., *An Interim Evaluation of Sulfur Dioxide Emissions Trading*, J. ECON. PERSP., Summer 1998, at 53; Robert N. Stavins, *What Can We Learn from the Grand Policy Experiment? Lessons from SO₂ Allowance Trading*, J. ECON. PERSP., Summer 1998, at 69; Dallas Burtraw & Erin Mansur, *Environmental Effects of SO₂ Trading and Banking*, 33 ENVTL. SCI. & TECH. 3489 (1999).

[121] 42 U.S.C. §§ 7401–7671 (1970), *amended by* Pub. L. No. 101-549 (1990). Seven OTC states have also implemented state-level NO_x trading programs: New Jersey, Connecticut, Delaware, New York, Massachusetts, New Hampshire, and Maine. *See* Barry D. Solomon, *New Directions in Emissions Trading: The Potential Contribution of New Insti-*

are based on targets established by the OTC and include emissions reductions by large stationary sources. The program is known as the Northeast Ozone Transport Region.[122]

EPA distributes NO_x allowances to each state, and states then allocate allowances to sources in their jurisdictions. Each source receives allowances equal to its restricted percentage of 1990 emissions, and sources must turn in one allowance for each ton of NO_x emitted over the ozone season. Sources may buy, sell, and bank allowances. Potential compliance cost savings of 40% to 47% have been estimated for the period 1999–2003, compared with a base case of continued command-and-control regulation without trading or banking.[123]

d. Maximum Available Control Technology for Air Toxics

The air toxics regulations necessitated by the 1990 CAA Amendments could be among the least cost-effective components of the CAA, depending on how they are implemented. The Amendments mandated that EPA issue standards for 188 toxic air pollutants, substances that are less common than the criteria pollutants for which NAAQS are promulgated, but may pose threats to human health.

Unlike in the case of the NAAQS, however, the Administrator of EPA is directed to require the maximum degree of emissions reduction achievable, taking costs into consideration. Despite the fact that EPA is allowed to take costs into account when determining standards for hazardous air pollutants, the type of regulation required by the CAA Amendments is a technology standard—Maximum Achievable Control Technology—not a market-based approach. From 1992 through August 2000, EPA issued technology standards for 45 of these substances, covering 82 categories of industrial sources.

While there are no estimates of the total monetized costs and benefits of this new set of technology standards for hazardous air pollutants, one analyst in 1990 estimated that when fully implemented, compliance costs would range from $7.9 to $13.2 billion per year, and benefits would range from $0 to $5.3 billion per year.[124] The lower bound of zero on potential benefits is indicative of the considerable uncertainty over risks posed by these pollutants to human health. Some analysts have been particularly

---

tutional Economics, 30 ECOLOGICAL ECON. 371 (1999).

[122] *See* Alex Farrell et al., *The NO_x Budget: Market-Based Control of Tropospheric Ozone in the Northeastern United States*, 21 RESOURCE & ENERGY ECON. 103 (1999).

[123] *Id.* at 117.

[124] *See* Portney, *supra* note 112, at 178–79. These figures were Portney's "educated guess" in 1990, based on the George H. W. Bush Administration estimates and those of a 1990 consulting firm study. We have converted them to 2000 dollars, assuming that they were originally stated in 1990 dollars.

critical of EPA's very conservative estimates of risks to human health from air toxics in its promulgation of standards.[125]

The mix of market-based and command-and-control regulations within the 1990 CAA Amendments demonstrates that while cost-effective-ness was increasingly accepted by the Administration and Congress, application to actual policies was inconsistent. In reality, market-based policy instruments are used to implement only a very small fraction of environmental regulation in the United States.

2. *Cost-Effectiveness of Selected EPA Regulations*

Most of the "stock" of regulations currently on the books were created without regard to choosing least-cost compliance alternatives, and the cost-effectiveness criterion influences only a small portion of the "flow" of regulations. To keep this fact firmly in mind, we provide the cost per statistical life saved of selected EPA rules from the 1980s and the 1990s in Table 4.

IV. INCREASING ROLE OF DISTRIBUTIONAL EQUITY

The increase in attention to efficiency and cost-effectiveness in environmental regulation is correlated with the substantial increase in the cost of such regulations to the U.S. economy from the 1970s through the 1990s.[126] There has also been an increase in the benefits of environmental regulation over the same period. The third theme in our analysis suggests that as both costs and benefits of environmental and natural resource regulation have increased, attention to the *distribution* of these costs and benefits has increased as well.

A. *Environmental Justice and the Distribution of Environmental Benefits*

In addition to requiring RIAs, Clinton's EO 12,866 instructed agencies to select regulatory approaches that would maximize net benefits, *including distributive impacts and equity*, unless a statute required otherwise.[127] This was the first time that distributional concerns had been included within the series of Presidential EOs dealing with regulatory analysis.

---

[125] *See* Richard L. Stroup, *Air Toxics Policy: Liabilities from Thin Air*, in CUTTING GREEN TAPE: TOXIC POLLUTANTS, ENVIRONMENTAL REGULATION AND THE LAW 59 (Richard L. Stroup & Roger E. Meiners eds., 2000); George M. Gray & John D. Graham, *Risk Assessment and Clean Air Policy*, 10 J. POL'Y ANAL. & MGMT. 286 (1991).

[126] *See* Paul R. Portney, *Counting the Cost: The Growing Role of Economics in Environmental Decisionmaking*, ENV'T, Mar. 1998 at 14; Adam B. Jaffe et al., *Environmental Regulation and the Competitiveness of U.S. Manufacturing: What Does the Evidence Tell Us?*, 33 J. ECON. LITERATURE 132 (1995).

[127] Exec. Order No. 12,866, 58 Fed. Reg. 51,735 (Sept. 30, 1993).

Increased attention to equity concerns during the 1990s was frequently characterized under the rubric of "environmental justice." In 1994, EO 12,898 instructed federal agencies to identify and address "disproportionately high and adverse human health or environmental effects of its programs, policies, and activities on minority populations and low-income populations."[128]

In practice, agencies have responded to the two EOs by including a separate distributional impact analysis within RIAs. Subsequent to EO 12,898, environmental justice was mentioned in RIAs for rules in which agencies were required to address the issue, but only infrequently was quantitative analysis included.[129] In no case did the Administration's explicit concern for equity clearly alter proposed policies.

B. *Property Rights Movement and the Distribution of Regulatory Costs*

Increased attention to the distribution of the costs of environmental and natural resource regulation in the 1990s was exemplified by the rise of the "property rights" movement, concerned with costs to private landowners, especially in Western states, of laws such as the Endangered Species Act ("ESA")[130] and wetlands regulations under Section 404 of the CWA.[131] In addition, concern about the distribution of costs may partly underlie continued inefficient subsidization of natural resource extraction during the 1990s.

1. *Endangered Species Act*

The distributional implications of the ESA were the focus of much debate during the 1990s. Private landowners objected to restrictions they claimed amounted to *de facto* seizures of private property ("takings") under the Fifth Amendment to the U.S. Constitution. Such interpretation of regulatory restrictions on private land use under the ESA as "takings" has generally not been upheld by the courts, but from an economic perspective, the concern of private property owners that they bear the costs of public goods provision is a distributional issue.

Attempts to reauthorize the ESA in the 1990s failed, but the Clinton administration made substantive administrative changes, aimed at rationalizing the incentives for private landowners under the Act.

The Administration implemented four provisions that had been included within many of the unsuccessful Congressional reauthorization attempts and had broad bipartisan support. First, the Administration em-

---

[128] Exec. Order No. 12,898, 59 Fed. Reg. 7,629 (Feb. 11, 1994).
[129] In some cases, RIAs mention that distributional impact analysis was conducted, but the analysis is not presented.
[130] 16 U.S.C. §§ 1531–1543 (2000).
[131] 33 U.S.C. § 1344 (2000).

phasized habitat conservation plans ("HCPs") as a tool to manage endangered and threatened species on non-federal lands. Under Section 10 of the ESA, private landowners applying for an "incidental take" permit must submit a HCP, in which they agree to restrict some uses in the interest of species and habitat protection in exchange for the permit.[132] More than 250 HCPs were completed between 1992 and 2000, compared to 14 between 1982 and 1992.[133] HCPs are considerably more flexible than direct enforcement of the Act. Second, voluntary "safe harbor" agreements guarantee that increases in species populations on private lands will not restrict future land use decisions.[134] Third, the "no surprises" rule guarantees that a landowner properly carrying out a habitat conservation plan will not experience further restrictions or costs without mutual consent. Fourth, "candidate conservation agreements" allow landowners to protect declining species that are not yet listed, in exchange for assurance that no additional measures will be required if species are listed.[135] The changes had broad bipartisan support in Congress.

2. Wetlands Regulation

The debate over land-use restrictions governed by wetlands regulation under Section 404 of the CWA in the 1990s was similar in nature to the ESA "takings" debate. Congress did not pass any major changes to federal wetlands regulation, although a series of actions by the Clinton administration during the decade exemplify conflicts over distributional concerns within the regulatory framework. In 1998, the Army Corps of Engineers greatly reduced the scope of nationwide permit 26, which authorizes discharges into non-tidal headwaters and isolated waters, a change that resulted in lawsuits by the development and commercial communities.[136] In addition, the Clinton administration endorsed the concept of wetlands mitigation banking in 1993. Mitigation banking would likely reduce the costs of wetlands regulation to private land owners and developers, but it has been opposed by environmental advocacy groups on the grounds that it does not adequately protect these ecologically valuable areas.

---

[132] 16 U.S.C. § 1539(a) (2000).

[133] Timothy Beatley, *Habitat Conservation Plans: A New Tool to Resolve Land Use Conflicts*, LAND LINES (Lincoln Inst. of Land Policy) Sept. 1995.

[134] *See* EUGENE H. BUCK ET AL., ENDANGERED SPECIES: DIFFICULT CHOICES 13 (CRS Issue Brief for Congress IB10072, 2003).

[135] *Id.*

[136] *See* COPELAND, *supra* note 88. The so-called "nationwide permits" authorize landowners to proceed with specified categories of activities without obtaining individual permits, reducing regulatory burdens.

3. Natural Resource Extraction Subsidies

Within its first budget proposal to Congress, the Clinton administration proposed reducing a variety of natural resource extraction subsidies, including those for logging, mining, and grazing livestock on public lands. These efforts were opposed vigorously by advocates of the "property rights" movement. Congress opposed all of the natural resource initiatives in the Clinton proposal, with one exception: the 104th Congress established a framework for user fee demonstration projects within the National Park Service.[137]

C. Efficiency and Equity as Issues of Political Convenience

The Clinton administration's focus on environmental justice in the 1990s could be seen as the desire of a Democratic administration to reach out to minority and low-income communities. The Administration's many attempts to introduce greater efficiency in natural resource management through subsidy reduction could be seen as an attempt to support efficiency where efficient policies were in close alignment with the preferences of the environmental community, a strong base of Democratic support.[138]

Similarly, Congressional opposition to natural resource subsidy reduction, when compared with its strong support for efficiency in environmental pollution control regulation, could be seen as the desire of a Republican legislature to forward the interests of supporters in the regulated community, typically conservative voters. Congressional support for extensive subsidies to grazing, timber extraction, mining, and other activities expanded the message of regulatory reform from the traditional industry association community to working-class, resource-based com-

---

[137] Omnibus Consolidated Rescissions and Appropriation Act of 1996, Pub. L. No. 104-134, 110 Stat. 1321 (1996). Congress also opposed, in one important case, the application of the cost-effectiveness criterion to natural resource management. The Sustainable Fisheries Act of 1996, 18 U.S.C. § 1853(d)(1) (2000), amended the Magnuson-Stevens Fishery Conservation and Management Act, 16 U.S.C. § 1881d(e) (2000), imposing a four-year moratorium on new individual transferrable quota programs among the nation's eight regional fishery management councils and repealing one such program that had been created in 1995. *See* Eugene H. Buck, *Magnuson Fishery Conservation and Management Act Reauthorization*, (Congressional Research Service Issue Brief for Congress IB95036, 1996), *available at* http://www.ncseonline.org/nle/crsreports/marine/mar-3.cfm (last visited Apr. 25, 2003). The Act did not, however, repeal the five other existing ITQ programs.

[138] The views of economists on natural resource extraction and pricing are closely aligned with those of strict conservationists, while economists' views on pollution control often contradict those of strict conservationists. That is, current rates of natural resource extraction in many countries are likely greater than the efficient rates, due to substantial subsidies and unregulated negative externalities. Thus, the economist's call for efficiency in resource management often supports higher prices and slower extraction. In contrast, the economist's call for efficiency in environmental regulation may often support a decrease in existing pollution control standards, as most industrialized countries have experienced a period of increasing stringency of environmental pollution control regulation over the past thirty years, and some of this regulation may have costs that exceed associated benefits.

munities, particularly in the Western United States. Congress in the 1990s appears to have supported efficiency when efficient policies were in close alignment with the preferences of its conservative base.

The notion of using benefit-cost analysis as a guide to regulation for environmental protection and natural resource management does not appeal to most interest groups or policy partisans, except where it is seen as a tool to achieve pre-determined goals. Politicians may thus endorse the use of the efficiency criterion only where its results are likely to be compatible with their own ideological agendas. The inconsistent application of efficiency analysis to environmental and natural resource regulation in the 1990s is part of a wider pattern of focus on the distribution of the costs and benefits of environmental and natural resource regulation in the United States.

D. Distribution Becomes More Salient as the Economic Impacts of Policies Increase

The tremendous increase in the aggregate costs and benefits of environmental and natural resource regulation over the past thirty years has focused substantial attention on the efficiency and cost-effectiveness of regulation. In addition, the presence of large costs and benefits from regulation has focused the attention of lawmakers and other participants in the policy process on the distribution of these costs and benefits.

Where pollution damages are highly localized, regulations that set aggregate standards for pollution emissions or concentrations can have differential distributional impacts that may be unappealing on equity grounds.[139] Policies that restrict natural resource management alternatives have inherently differential distributional impacts in the United States, where economic dependence upon resource extraction is highly localized. Even where it may be efficient to proscribe specific commercial activities or other resource uses from a national perspective, some local communities will experience substantial net losses from such policies.

An example may be the USFS Roadless Areas Initiative ("Roadless Rule"). The USFS regulatory impact analysis for the rule did not quantify benefits and costs. Hence, no definitive efficiency conclusions can be drawn. But inventoried roadless areas comprise about two percent of the U.S. landmass, and thirty-one percent of the USFS's property. These areas are characterized by rugged terrain and low-value timber, and they may be ecologically sensitive. These characteristics may suggest relatively low costs to leaving them in their current state, and relatively high

---

[139] Uneven distributional impacts can have implications for the efficiency of a regulation, as well, if damages are nonlinear. If marginal damages increase at an increasing rate, total damages (hence total benefits of regulation) may increase when damages are concentrated in certain areas.

environmental benefits of preservation.[140] Nonetheless, any reduction in commercial timber harvest associated with the Roadless Rule negatively affects some communities.[141]

Given that natural resource management regulations will necessarily have uneven distributional impacts, Congressional opposition to increasing efficiency and cost-effectiveness in natural resource management during the 1990s is not surprising. When the "winners" from a natural resource management policy are American citizens as a whole and the "losers" are identifiable members of particular Congressional districts, members of Congress are reluctant to impose those losses on their own district or a colleague's district. Similarly, as the substantial gains from thirty years of environmental pollution control regulation have been seen to accrue disproportionately to some communities over others, the debate has shifted somewhat from efficiency to distributional equity.

The implications of the increased focus on distribution in environmental and natural resource policy are twofold from the perspective of economics. First, while economists can analyze the distribution of costs and benefits from a regulation, they have little to contribute to the debate over how costs and benefits *should* be distributed. Second, in some cases, attempts to meet distributional goals (whether they succeed or not) may interfere with attempts to satisfy criteria of efficiency and cost-effectiveness.

V. Conclusions

Three conclusions emerge from our review of the role of economic analysis in environmental and natural resource policy during the 1990s. First, the use of efficiency as a criterion for assessing environmental and natural resource rules and regulations was controversial in the Clinton administration, while economic efficiency emerged as a central goal of the regulatory reform movement in Congress. Second, cost-effectiveness as a criterion for adopting specific policy instruments was embraced by

---

[140] Clinton Forest Service Chief Mike Dombeck pointed out that these areas were the 58.5 million acres of Forest Reserves created between 1891 and 2000, many of which had remained roadless through twenty presidencies. In addition, by USFS calculations, less than 0.3% of the U.S. timber harvest and less than 0.4% of U.S. oil and natural gas reserves will be affected by the Roadless Rule. Mike Dombeck, *Roadless Area Conservation: An Investment For Future Generations, at* http://roadless.fs.fed.us/documents/rule/dombeck_stmt.htm (last visited Apr. 25, 2003) (Jan. 5, 2001) (on file with the Harvard Environmental Law Review). Any benefit-cost calculation would also have to account for the costs of maintaining forest system roads. In 2000, USFS maintained a road system of more than 386,000 miles, with a maintenance backlog in excess of $8 billion. *Id.*

[141] The state of Idaho, the Kootenai Indian tribe, and logging groups challenged the Roadless Rule in federal court. In May 2001, a U.S. District Court judge in Idaho issued a preliminary injunction blocking the rule. Kootenai Tribe of Idaho v. Veneman, 142 F.Supp.2d 1231 (D. Idaho 2001). The Bush administration declined to appeal the ruling. In December 2002, the U.S. Court of Appeals for the Ninth Circuit overturned the District Court ruling, reinstating the Roadless Rule. Kootenai Tribe of Idaho v. Veneman, 313 F.3d 1094 (9th Cir. 2002).

both the Administration and Congress in the 1990s. Most interest groups in the environmental community and the regulated community could support cost-effectiveness because it reduced the burden of compliance on industry and made stringent environmental targets more affordable. But benefit-cost analysis raised the issue of goals or standards, as well as costs, and the process of setting goals was, and is, inherently more controversial than minimizing the costs of achieving them.

Third, during the 1990s, equity concerns played increasing roles in environmental and natural resource policy debates. Both the efficiency and the cost-effectiveness criteria may be hard to swallow when the distributional impacts of regulation are highly skewed. Examples continue to surface regularly in debates over the fairness of policies such as individual transferable quota systems for fisheries management, differential exposure to environmental hazards, and impacts on western farming communities of reduced availability of irrigation water to protect endangered species. The focus on equity in environmental policy debates is likely to intensify as the costs and benefits of regulation continue to rise.

APPENDIX

TABLE 1. U.S. EMISSIONS OF SEVEN MAJOR POLLUTANTS, 1970–1998

Year	SO2	NOx	VOCs	CO	Lead	PM10	PM2.5
1970	100	100	100	100	100	N/A	N/A
1980	83	117	85	91	34	N/A	N/A
1989	75	114	73	82	3	100	N/A
1990	76	115	68	76	2	54	100
1991	74	116	68	78	2	53	97
1992	73	118	67	75	2	53	96
1993	72	119	67	76	2	50	92
1994	70	121	70	79	2	56	100
1995	62	119	67	72	2	48	90
1996	61	118	60	74	2	61	103
1997	63	119	61	73	2	63	107
1998	63	117	58	69	2	64	105

Notes: Figures are indexed from EPA data, with 1970 aggregate U.S. emissions equal to 100 for all pollutants except PM10 (1989=100) and PM2.5 (1990=100). Data for 1970 and 1980 drawn from U.S. EPA, Pub. No. 454/R-00-002, NATIONAL AIR POLLUTANT EMISSION TRENDS 1900-1998 (2000). Data for 1989, 1991–1995, and 1997 drawn from U.S. EPA, Pub. No. 454/R-00-003, NATIONAL AIR QUALITY AND EMISSIONS TRENDS REPORT, 1998 (2000). Data for 1990, 1996, and 1998 appear in both reports. (Data for PM10 differ between the two reports—for this pollutant, the 1998 Report data were used exclusively.) Data for particulate matter ("PM") include only directly emitted PM. No figures are shown for PM10 and PM2.5 in 1970 or 1980; while estimates exist, they do not include natural sources, agriculture, forestry, fugitive dust and other sources which together comprise almost ninety percent of directly emitted PM10 and almost seventy percent of directly emitted PM2.5 in 1990.

TABLE 2. SHIFTS IN ORGANIZATIONAL LOCATION OF ECONOMIC
ANALYSIS AT EPA

Years	Location of Core Economics Staff at EPA
1980–1983	Benefits Staff, Office of Policy Evaluation, Office of Policy and Resource Management
1983–1987	Benefits Branch, Office of Policy Analysis, Office of Policy, Plan-ning and Evaluation
1987–1990	Economic Analysis Branch, Office of Policy Analysis, Office of Policy, Planning and Evaluation
1990–1996	Economic Analysis and Research Branch, Office of Policy Analysis, Office of Policy, Planning and Evaluation
1996–1999	Economy and Environment Division, Office of Economy and Environment, Office of Policy, Planning and Evaluation
1999–2000	Economic and Policy Analysis Division and Economy and Environment Division, Office of Economy and Environment, Office of Policy and Reinvention
2000–2001	National Center for Environmental Economics, Office of Policy, Economics and Innovation

Source: U.S. EPA, National Center for Environmental Economics World Wide Web site, *available at* http://www.yosemite.epa.gov/ee/epa/eed.nsf/ pages/aboutncee#OrganizationalStructureandHistory (last visited Mar. 16, 2003) (on file with the Harvard Environmental Law Review).

TABLE 3. BENEFITS AND COSTS, REVISED NAAQS FOR OZONE AND
PARTICULATE MATTER

NAAQS (1997)	Annual Monetized Benefits	Annual Monetized Costs
Ozone	$2.0 to $11.2 billion	$12.7 billion
Particulate Matter	$26.4 to $145 billion	$48.8 billion

Source: U.S. OMB, REPORT TO CONGRESS ON THE COSTS AND BENEFITS OF FEDERAL REGULATIONS (1998). EPA estimates were in constant 1990 dollars; those reported here are 2000 dollars. Cost and benefit estimates assume full attainment.

TABLE 4. COST OF SELECTED EPA REGULATIONS PER STATISTICAL
LIFE SAVED

Environmental Protection Agency Regulation	Year	Cost per Statistical Life Saved (millions of 2000 $)
Benzene fugitive emissions	1984	5
Radionuclides at uranium mines	1984	11
Asbestos prohibitions: manufacture, importation, processing and distribution in commerce (total)	1989	21
National primary and secondary water regulations—Phase II: MCLs for 38 contaminants	1991	28
Hazardous waste management system—wood preservatives	1990	57
Sewage sludge use and disposal regulations, 40 CFR Part 503	1993	215
Land disposal restrictions for third scheduled waste	1990	215
Hazardous waste management system: final solvents and dioxins land disposal restrictions rule	1986	226
Prohibition on land disposal of first third of scheduled wastes ("second sixth" proposal)	1988	452
Land disposal restrictions, Phase II: universal treatment standards and treatment standards for organic toxicity, characteristic wastes, and newly listed wastes	1994	1,030
Drinking water regulations, synthetic organic chemicals, phase V	1992	10,800
Solid waste disposal facility criteria, 40 CFR Parts 257 and 258	1991	40,700

Source: ROBERT W. HAHN ET AL., DO FEDERAL REGULATIONS REDUCE MORTALITY? 16–17 (AEI-Brookings Joint Center for Regulatory Studies, Washington, D.C., 2000). "Cost per statistical life saved" refers to net costs (costs minus cost savings, but not taking into account benefits in terms of reduced mortality risk) of discounted lives saved. The estimates for the first two rules in the table (both 1984) are from W. Kip Viscusi, *Regulating the Regulators*, 63 U. CHI. L. REV. 1423 (1996), noting that all values are millions of 2000 dollars annually. These final rules are ranked in order of decreasing cost-effectiveness.

Name Index

The International Library of Critical Writings in Economics